Sharīʿa

In recent years, Islamic law, or Sharīʿa, has increasingly occupied center stage in the languages and practices of politics in the Muslim world as well as in the West. Popular narratives and quasi-scholarly accounts have distorted Sharīʿa's principles and practices of the past, conflating them with distinctly modern, negative and highly politicized reincarnations. Wael Hallaq's magisterial overview sets the record straight by examining the doctrines and practices of the Sharīʿa within the context of its history, and by showing how it functioned within pre-modern Islamic societies as a moral imperative. In so doing, Hallaq takes the reader on an epic journey, tracing the history of Islamic law from its beginnings in seventh-century Arabia through its development and transformation in the following centuries under the Ottomans, and across lands as diverse as India, Africa and South-East Asia, to the present. In a remarkably fluent narrative, the author unravels the complexities of his subject to reveal a love and deep knowledge of the law which will engage and challenge the reader.

Wael B. Hallaq is James McGill Professor in Islamic Law in the Institute of Islamic Studies at McGill University. He is a world-renowned scholar whose publications include *The Origins and Evolution of Islamic Law* (Cambridge, 2005), *Authority, Continuity and Change in Islamic Law* (Cambridge, 2001) and *A History of Islamic Legal Theories* (Cambridge, 1997).

Sharīʿa

Theory, Practice, Transformations

Wael B. Hallaq

CAMBRIDGE
UNIVERSITY PRESS

CAMBRIDGE
UNIVERSITY PRESS

University Printing House, Cambridge CB2 8BS, United Kingdom

Published in the United States of America by Cambridge University Press, New York

Cambridge University Press is part of the University of Cambridge.

It furthers the University's mission by disseminating knowledge in the pursuit of education, learning and research at the highest international levels of excellence.

www.cambridge.org
Information on this title: www.cambridge.org/9780521678742

First published 2009
3rd printing 2012

A catalogue record for this publication is available from the British Library

Library of Congress Cataloguing in Publication data
Hallaq, Wael B., 1955–
Shari'a between past and present : theory, practice and modern transformations / Wael B. Hallaq.
p. cm.
Includes bibliographical references and index.
ISBN 978-0-521-86147-2
1. Islamic law – History. I. Title.
KBP144.H356 2009
340.5'909–dc22

2009005860

ISBN 978-0-521-86147-2 Hardback
ISBN 978-0-521-67874-2 Paperback

Contents

Preface and acknowledgments

Following the collapse of the Soviet Union, Islam has come to fill a pivotal conceptual role of an antithesis to the West, the self-described abode of liberal democracies and the rule of law. With the widespread rise of the Islamist movements during the last three or four decades, so-called Islamic law, or Sharīʿa, has increasingly occupied center stage in the languages and practices of politics – mainly in the Islamist camp itself, but also in the Western world. Popular narratives and a staggering array of quasi-scholarly accounts have distorted Sharīʿa beyond recognition, conflating its principles and practices in the past with its modern, highly politicized, reincarnations. This book is about distinctions; about what Sharīʿa – as doctrine and practice – represented in history; how it functioned within society and the moral community; how it coexisted with the body-politic; and how it was transformed and indeed appropriated as a tool of modernity, wielded above all by the nation-state.

Although this book has, in many ways, been in the making for over two decades, it was written between 2004 and 2008, during which period much in my thinking on the subject continued to change and develop. Over time, this thinking and the resultant book became increasingly grounded in frameworks of enquiry beyond the field of law in general and Islamic law in particular. And like many other books, its several chapters and sections were written under variable conditions. In part owing to these variations, and in part because of the inherently diverse nature of its subject-matter, the book deals with issues at various levels of description and analysis, and can therefore be read on more than one plane. Students beginning their exploration of the Sharīʿa and its history as well as readers peripherally interested in theoretical moorings may ignore the theoretical parts of the book, especially the second section of the Introduction and perhaps chapter 13 – a license that neither the specialist nor the advanced student might want to take.

I am fully aware that some readers might find the second section of the Introduction difficult to negotiate, even misconstruing its relevance to the work as a whole. This latter impulse should be resisted, since that theoretical section is vital to positioning the work in the larger context of scholarship and the manner in which academic discourse has shaped modern politics and, importantly, our conceptions of law. This positioning is normative practice in such fields as anthropology, but has yet to be attempted in Islamic legal studies. Its value resides in depriving scholarly work of a claim to authoritative knowledge, in creating a dialectic between authorial intention and readership, and – more crucially – in positioning scholarship in a specific and highly localized context from which an attempt is made to understand the Other, the Subject. This positioning, which relativizes scholarly discourse, tends to reduce the risk of reconstituting the Other, which has thus far been a problematic enterprise in modern academia. This section, heavily Foucauldian, is therefore *not* about my ways of analyzing the subject-matter of Islamic law throughout the book (although I am no doubt indebted to Foucault, among many others, for certain analyses in Part III), but rather about the *book itself* and its place in the knowledge that has been generated in the field.

In the Introduction, I also point to the Bibliography at the end of this book as a register of the extensive debt I have incurred to others, be they legal historians, legal anthropologists, philosophers or thinkers from other disciplines. I learned a great deal from them even in those cases where I vehemently disagreed with much of what they had to say. Not to be excluded from this register of debt are my "*aṣḥāb*," the traditional Muslim jurists whose brilliant intellects and erudition continue to instruct in the exquisite art of methodical reasoning and systematic thinking. More personally, I have also incurred numerous debts to various individuals at McGill University, the most notable being Robert Wisnovsky, Laila Parsons, and Rula and Malek Abisaab – all of whom challenged my thinking and imagination on various issues of scholarship, and offered their friendship and care. With these colleagues, good dinners invariably turned into intellectual feasts.

My students deserve a special note of thanks for assisting me in the preparation of this book. Walter Young has been a magnificent assistant and a joy to work with. He checked the manuscript for consistency of footnotes and other technical errors, and supplied the great majority of references to three English translations of *fiqh* works in Part II (cited in square brackets). Fachrizal Halim, Ratno Lukito, Gregory Mack, Junaid Quadri, Aida Setrakian and Mida Zantout have all been very helpful in providing me with research materials. Emily Zitter-Smith, a finely trained lawyer and scholar, made valuable cautionary remarks that drew my attention to the various ways a Western lawyer might misinterpret what I have to say.

To Steve Millier I record here my continuing debt for his editing of my writings. Marigold Acland (of Cambridge University Press) has been a model of generosity, efficiency and perspicacity, to whom I have accumulated a large debt over the years. An anonymous reader of the Press made a host of constructive and thoughtful comments, from which the book benefited. To her/him, I am deeply grateful. As Dean of Arts at McGill, the magnanimous John Hall has created an academic environment from which I have reaped great benefit. His successor, Chris Manfredi, admirably continues his unwavering support to a scholarly tradition otherwise increasingly under attack in North American academia. To both of them, I am immensely grateful. Last but not least, I record my profound debt to Charry Karamanoukian for her patience, immense kindness and moral support, as well as, no less, for her habit of engaging me in the larger theoretical issues that underlie this book.

Introduction

1. The prisons of language and modernity

To write the history of Sharīʿa is to represent the Other.[1] Yet, such a representation brings with it an insoluble problem that ensues from our distinctly modern conceptions and modern "legislation" of language.[2] As our language (in this case, obviously, twenty-first-century English) is the common repository of ever-changing modern conceptions, modern categories and, primarily, the nominal representation of the modern condition,[3] we stand nearly helpless before the wide expanse of what we take to be "Islamic law" and its history. Our language fails us in our endeavor to produce a representation of that history which not only spoke different languages (none of them English, not even in British India), but also articulated itself conceptually, socially, institutionally and culturally in manners and ways vastly different from those material and non-material cultures that produced modernity and its Western linguistic traditions.

Take for instance the most central concept underlying this study, the very term "law." Arguably, cultural and conceptual ambiguities related to this term (never to my knowledge identified, let alone problematized, by legal Orientalism) are responsible for a thorough and systematic

[1] If not the Double-Other who is the Other in history. It is taken for granted here that history, both Islamic and European, is the modern's Other, and since in the case of Islam this history is preceded by another Other – namely contemporary Islam – then it would arguably qualify for the status of Double-Other or, if you will, a Once-More-Otherized-Other.

[2] F. Nietzsche saw this "legislation" as constituting a fundamental quandary where a "word becomes a concept" having "to fit countless more or less similar cases … which are never equal and thus altogether unequal" ("On Truth and Lies," 81, 83). Creating truths of its own, this legislation establishes concepts that become commonly accepted as "fixed, canonical, and binding," when in fact truths themselves "are metaphors" that represent "the duty to lie according to a fixed convention" (*ibid.*, 84). The quandary then resides in the originary fact that "*Every word is a prejudice.*" Nietzsche, *Human, All Too Human*, 323 (emphasis mine).

[3] On the modern condition, see Bauman, *Society under Siege*; Bauman, *Liquid Modernity*; Giddens, *Consequences of Modernity*; Toulmin, *Cosmopolis*.

misunderstanding of the most significant features of the so-called Islamic law. Subjected to critical scrutiny in Europe for over a century, Islamic law could only disappoint. It could never match up to any version of European law. It was seen as ineffective, inefficient, even incompetent. It mostly applied to the "private" sphere of personal status, having early on "divorced" itself from "state and society."[4] Its penal law was regarded as little more than burlesque; it "never had much practical importance" and was in fact downright "deficient."[5] Of course much of this was colonialist discourse and doctrine (though no less potent for all that) cumulatively but programmatically designed to decimate the Sharīʿa and replace it with Western codes and institutions. But linguistics played a part here too, for if concepts are defined by language, then language is not only the framework that delimits concepts (no mean achievement) but also that which controls them. Prime evidence of this is the routine and widespread pronouncement, usually used to introduce Islamic law to the uninitiated, namely, that the Sharīʿa does not distinguish between law and morality. The absence of distinction becomes a clear and undoubtable liability, for when we speak of any law, our paradigmatic and normative stance would be to expect that that law must measure up against what *we* consider to be "our" supreme model. The moral dimension of Islamic law, in language and in its conceptual derivation, is thus dismissed as one of the causes which rendered that law inefficient and paralyzed. The morality that is so enshrined in it introduces an ideal element distancing it from messy and disorderly social and political realities. Morality is therefore fated to be dismissed as rhetoric, nothing more. Its adverse effects in the law are cause for lament, but not usually for analysis, although when attempted in very recent studies,[6] analysis has yielded some enlightening results.

It turns out that Islamic law's presumed "failure" to distinguish between law and morality equipped it with efficient, communally based, socially embedded, bottom–top methods of control that rendered it remarkably efficient in commanding willing obedience and – as one consequence – less coercive than any imperial law Europe had known since the fall of the Roman Empire. Thus the very use of the word law is *a priori* problematic; to use it is to project, if not superimpose, on the legal culture of Islam notions saturated with the conceptual specificity of nation-state law, a punitive law that, when compared to Islam's jural forms, *lacks* (note

[4] These stereotypes remain tenacious even in recent scholarship. See, for example, the descriptions of Collins, "Islamization of Pakistani Law," 511–22.

[5] The words of one of the foremost scholars on the penal law of Islam. Heyd, *Studies*, 1.

[6] E.g., Peirce, *Morality Tales*; Würth, "Sanaʿa Court," 320–40.

the reversal)[7] the same determinant moral imperative. (It is in light of these reservations that the use of the expression "Islamic law" in this work must be understood.) In order for this expression to reflect what the Sharīʿa stood for and meant, we would be required to effect so many additions, omissions and qualifications that would render the term itself largely, if not entirely, useless. (Yet, such conceptual alterations, if carried out systematically – as they ideally should – for every technical term, would ultimately paralyze expression and writing altogether; hence my earlier insistence that the problem is insoluble.)

Closely related to the issue of state coercion, and its homogenizing effects, is the attribution of failure in the applicability of "Islamic law" to the realia of social, political and other practice, a failure to assert the integrity of the law's order and its sovereign will. Yet this alleged failure represents in fact another modern misreading of history, i.e., of the hands-off approach adopted by the Sharīʿa as a way of life and as a matter of course. The notorious and extraordinary diversity of *fiqh*, or legal doctrine, is ample attestation to this approach, although *juristic* diversity was only one of many other forms of pluralism, all of which, even in their extreme forms, were recognized by the so-called "law" of *fiqh*. These conceptual conflations lie at the root of Western misjudgment of the relationship between legal doctrine and real practice, a problem that continues to plague the field today.

Incriminated in this terminological and linguistic distortion is also a vast array of concepts that, charged with latent meanings, seem to be supremely ideological. Witness, for instance, the standard term describing the legal transmutations that were effected in the Muslim world through direct and indirect European domination. The term of choice is "reform,"[8] articulating various political and ideological positions that inherently assume the Sharīʿa to be deficient and in need of correction and modernizing revision.[9] "Reform" thus insinuates a transition, on the one level, from the pre-modern to the modern, and on the other, from uncivilized to civilized. It is framed by a notion of universalist historicism in which the history of the Other merges into the major and

7 Reversal, that is, of the widely used critical pronouncements to the effect that, for instance, "Islamic law does not have a general theory of contract," or "does not distinguish between law and morality," and that it is therefore altogether representative of a history of absences.

8 Forcefully attesting to the confining effects of the prison of language is the fact that I was, despite all efforts, unable to avoid the use of the term in Part III of this book, where issues of "reform" are discussed in detail. This failure bespeaks not as much of inconsistency (at least not an unconscious one), but rather of the inherently systemic connectedness between perceived "historical facts" and their conceptualization in language.

9 More on this term, see chapter 16, section 1, below.

defining currents of the European (read: universal) civilizational march. Universalism, a conceptual translation of what was once called "ontological imperialism,"[10] represents a tool of encompassing the Other into the Self through a range of modifications that always aim at altering the Other's essence.

Thus, the very term "reform" epistemologically signifies an unappealable verdict on an entire history and a legal culture standing in need of displacement, even eradication from both memory and the material world. If the study of "reform" is thus engulfed by these ideological associations, then the scholarly trajectory and agenda can safely be said to have been predetermined. All that needs to be done is to show how Western-inspired "reform" was parachuted in to rescue Sharīʿa's subjects from the despotisms of the jural (if not also political) tyranny of the past and to escort them along the path of modernity and democracy. Closely intertwined with this project, and stemming from the same set of ideological assumptions, is another goal: that of saving "brown women from brown men."[11] If "reform" is viewed as the most recent stage in Sharīʿa's history, then that history has been organically and structurally ordered in a narrative that had no choice but to produce a particular closure, a particular ending, so to speak, to a drama that is seen as having been predetermined from the very beginning of its own history. So much then for a dispassionate study of pre-modern Sharīʿa, except as a relic of a dead past that has neither a true genealogy nor a spatiotemporal continuity. The epistemic ordering of historicity from the vantage point of "reform" constitutes an integral, though not the most important, part of a larger field of discourse which continues to deny, and thus fails to integrate, its epistemic and cultural relationship to colonialism.

From another perspective, the ideology of "reform" has also meshed with scholarly discourse, affecting it in fundamental ways, in both Western and Islamic academia. Justifications of "reform" – ranging from corruption and abuse to an endless variety of systemic maladies – are reenacted as historiographical premises and as historical facts.[12] The fundamental ideological assumptions of the reforms, suffused by the political need to centralize, bureaucratize and homogenize (all of which are harnessed in the interest of building and strengthening a modern, controlling state) become paradigmatic scholarly truths. For instance, the logic of modern state taxation

[10] The expression is that of Emmanuel Lévinas. See Young, *White Mythologies*, 44–45.

[11] For a theoretical context, see Spivak, "Can the Subaltern Speak?" esp. 91–104. Adverse effects of this project are discussed in chapter 16, below.

[12] Representative of this discourse is Ṭāriq al-Bishrī (*al-Waḍʿ al-Qānūnī*, 6–7, 78–80) who echoes such notions as those discussed in chapter 17, below.

becomes an unquestionable, nay axiomatic, truth of polity, whereas decentralized salarization – a practice thousands of years old – now translates into "corruption," "abuse," "inefficiency" and "disorder." In all of this, *modern* scholarship proceeds with extraordinary innocence, unaware of the culpable dependency of its project on the ideology of the state.[13]

No less incriminated in the "legislation of language" is the perduring adjective "religious," which seems not only inseparable from the epithet "Islamic Law" but also apodictically and semantically present in its very linguistic structure. "Islamic law" for long did not signify a geography, a living sociology or a materially engaged culture but a religion, a religious culture, a religious law, a religious civilization, or an irrationality (hence the presumed "irrational nature" of this law).[14] By the rules of linguistic entailment, therefore, the "religious" functioned in opposition to such concepts as "rationalism" and, more starkly, "secularism." In other words, the very utterance of the word "religious" spoke of the absence of the secular and the antonymic rational. With this essentialist, yet language-driven, conception of "Islamic law," the emphasis continued to be more on the religious, irrational and un-secular "nature" of the discipline, and less on how it functioned in social/economic/political sites, and what its "religiosity" meant practically to the actors involved in its production, application and reception.

Furthermore, repugnance toward religion, especially when seen to be intertwined with law, undercuts a proper apprehension of the role of morality as a jural form, to name only one effect. Such a predetermined stand *vis-à-vis* religion and its morality renders inexplicable what is otherwise obvious. The cultural logic of capitalism tends to chip away at the centrality of the moral in the pre-modern universe. Historical evidence must thus be fitted to measure what makes sense to us, not what made sense to a "non-rational" pre-capitalist, low-level material culture. For an entrenched repugnance to the religious – at least in this case to the "Islamic" in Muslim societies – amounts, in legal terms, to a foreclosure of the force of the moral within the realm of the jural. Theistic teleology, eschatology, socially grounded moral gain, status, and much else of a similar type, are all reduced in importance, if not totally set aside, in favor of other explanations that "fit better" within our preferred, but distinctly modern, counter-moral systems of value. History is brought to

13 It is disappointing, but hardly surprising, that this innocence continues to infect scholarship up to this day. See, for one example among countless others, the otherwise commendable work of J. Akiba, especially "From Kadı to Naib," 44–46, and *passim*. Further on this problem, see Bourdieu, "Rethinking the State," 53 ff.

14 See, e.g., Schacht, *Introduction*, 202–04.

us, according to our terms, when in theory no one denies that it is our (historiographical) set of terms that should be subordinated to the imperatives of historical writing.

2. On being self-conscious

"Knowledge," Foucault wrote,

> must struggle against a world without order, without connectedness, without form, without beauty, without wisdom, without harmony, and without law. That is the world that knowledge deals with. There is nothing in knowledge that enables it, by any right whatever, to know this world. It is not natural for knowledge to be known. Thus, between the instincts and knowledge, one finds not a continuity but, rather, a relation of struggle, domination, servitude, settlement. In the same way, there can be no relation of natural continuity between knowledge and the things that knowledge must know. There can only be a relation of violence, domination, power, and force, a relation of violation. Knowledge can only be a violation of the things to be known, and not a perception, a recognition, an identification of or with those things.
>
> It is for that reason that in Nietzsche we find the constantly recurring idea that knowledge ... simplifies, passes over differences, lumps things together, without any justification in regard to truth.[15]

The most central and determinative fact about the academic field within which this book situates itself is that it was born – like many other fields dominating today's academia – out of the violent, yet powerfully homogenizing ventures of nineteenth-century Europe. It was born within, and out of, a global project of domination whose web-like matrix of power structures would generate the unprecedented analytical prognoses of Friedrich Nietzsche and Michel Foucault. The passage quoted above, however insightful, merely alludes to the epistemic structures of political, economic and cultural power within which "Islamic law" as a field of enquiry was conceived, raised and nurtured. Stated contrapuntally, there would have been no such construction as "Islamic legal history" – and, as a consequence, no such book as the one offered here – outside of, and external to, the discursive parameters of nineteenth-century Europe. Out of "a world without order, without connectedness" and "without form," Europe invented the knowledge that is Islamic law.

The discourses of power that shaped this invented field never presented themselves as a uniform body, but were considerably varied and often internally oppositional. These discourses argued for particular, at times unique, colonialist interests, and simultaneously conceptualized Islamic

[15] Foucault, "Truth and Juridical Forms," 9, 14.

cultures and societies in dramatically different ways. They produced histories of science and geographies, and as many approaches to the study of the Muslim world as the humanities and the social sciences could muster. But these discourses of power, despite their variegated orientations, were at once eminently unidirectional and launched on a trajectory that vigorously labored in the service of a group of mutually integrated and coherent goals. It was precisely these goals that predetermined their linear trajectory.

This is not to say, however, that power's discourses – even when they emanate from a common source and share a single teleology – are inherently, intrinsically or essentially linear, for they often (if not consistently) take into account and embrace those discourses that are produced, *inter alia*, by power's own subjects, the very site of its unfolding effects as well as its temporal and cerebral manifestations. To this extent, Foucault was right when he argued that "[w]e must make allowance for the complex and unstable process whereby discourse can be both an instrument and an effect of power, but also a hindrance, a stumbling block, a point of resistance and a starting point for an opposing strategy."[16] Such allowances may be neither ignored nor underrated because the actor's will-to-power – whether it unfolds in primeval or systemic and structured ways – is inherently entangled with its subject's negation of both the processes and the effects of that power. The subject not only harnesses these processes and mechanisms to resist that power, but also – and equally, by force of entailment – militates to reverse these processes. It is in the nature of power, therefore, to be not only self-contradictory but, due to this inherent self-contradiction, productive of internally opposing and resisting elements. Power is inherently productive of discourses that both expose and obscure its schemes, as well as discourses that construct and augment – and simultaneously undermine – its own ambitions. It is precisely because of this internal contradiction that power has in every way and consistently been engaged in eternal processes of generation and corruption.

Foucault had thus come to revise an earlier position on this theme[17] and posit, as we see here, the non-linearity of power discourses. It is argued that in his *Orientalism*, Edward Said failed to take note of this non-linearity in Foucault's thought and thus commensurately neglected to account for the subject's agency in the formation of Occidental knowledge about the

[16] Foucault, *History of Sexuality*, 101. For a useful commentary on theorizing resistance, see Hirsch, "Khadi's Courts," 208–11.
[17] Young, "Foucault on Race and Colonialism," 57–58.

Orient.[18] This is certainly possible. But it is also equally possible, and perhaps more probable, that Said was interested not so much in dissecting the mechanisms of colonial power and its oppositional discourses at home and in the colonies, as in analyzing the *effects* of power, not only as the latter stem from a particular body of knowledge but also as they generate and foster a particular set of representations which in turn *constitute* their subjects. These effects – most especially in the colonial context – do not seem to have concerned Foucault.[19]

Yet, when speaking of the programmatic modalities of power, especially as exercised in the colonial context, it is the effects that count most, for they demonstrate – though *ex post facto* – the results of the interplay between actor and subject. These results, the final accounting, adjudge at the end of the day who influences whom (and whose *will* dominates another's). In as much as power is "a field of force relations," and in as much as it inherently encompasses opposing discourses in this field, there must be, in the very name of power, a dominating discourse or set of discourses that not only outdo competing and oppositional discourses but, more importantly, outlive them; hence the centrality of power-effects as a discrete analytical unit. For if power were not productive of a particular hegemony – that is, a hegemony of particular relations – it could no longer be called power; thus, power must continue to embody subversive oppositional discourses that operate against it, both as process and as effect. While the limits of subversive discourse may place restrictions on the dominant relations of power, these relations must ultimately win the day. It bears repeating that this asymmetry must ineluctably obtain in order for us to identify power as power.

The theoretical construct of this asymmetry appears less to have been ignored than to have been tacitly assumed by Said in his *Orientalism*. On the other hand, the "unscrupulously Eurocentric"[20] work of Foucault may explain his emphasis on the process of power relations rather than on their effect, for his justifiable preoccupation with the European complexity of what he called "discursive formations" and "epistemes"[21] diverted his attention from the quite different logic of power relations in

[18] *Ibid.* See also Slemon, "Scramble for Post-colonialism," 50–52.

[19] For Foucault's disinterest in power as "a general system of domination exerted by one group over another," see his *History of Sexuality*, 92, as well as 93–94, 97.

[20] Young, "Foucault on Race and Colonialism," 57 and 61 where Young observes that Foucault's "apparent endorsement of an ethnology which would analyse not the forms of knowledge developed by other societies for themselves but how they conformed to a general theoretical model of how societies function, developed out of western structural linguistics, seems today startlingly ethnocentric."

[21] Foucault, *Les mots*, 14–15 and *passim*; Foucault, *Archaeology of Knowledge*, 34–78.

the colonialist project. This was a logic of asymmetry that refused entry to the oppositional and resistant relations that existed in the wholly internal European scene.

I do not wish to engage in a total negation of such relations in the laboratory of colonialism, but I would argue that this laboratory poses a different set of conditions that cannot successfully be subjected to Foucault's theoretical and critical apparatus. For one,[22] Foucault's field of power relations and discourses did not have to account for sudden and colossal ruptures in epistemologies, cultures, institutions, psychologies, and theologies. His field was applicable to a span of about four centuries that witnessed the *systemic* evolution (however rapid) of surveillance, discipline and punishment, but less so the all-too-quick downfall of the systems from which these new forms emerged. In other words, in the systemic structures he called "episteme," there were – *comparatively speaking* – no genuinely foreign or violently crude impositions, and no qualitatively different and culturally and systemically alien will-to-power.[23] In fact, and again with the benefit of comparative perspective, these new European forms – inextricably connected with the rise of nation-states in particular and modernity in general – *gradually and internally metamorphosed* into their present incarnations. Europe, in other words, emerged out of itself. It is precisely this background that allows, nay drives, Foucault to declare that these discourses of power, in their oppositional trajectories, are inseparable, for discourses "are tactical elements or blocks operating in a field of force relations; there can exist different and even contradictory discourses within the same strategy; they can, on the contrary, circulate without changing their form from one strategy to another, opposing strategy."[24] In the colonialist context, hegemonic strategies cannot turn into their opposite, for if they did, there would emerge the absurdity, if not aporia, of the perfect interchangeability of actor and subject.

Thus, for power to deserve the name it bears, its processes and strategies – in their confluence and opposition – must yield particular effects that both directly and obliquely flow from these processes and strategies. That power can neither exercise total control, nor precisely predict its own effects, is evident both in Foucault's Europe and in the colonial laboratory. But this is not to say, as Foucault does, that the same strategy, as

22 See n. 19, above.
23 This colonial "sovereignty" over epistemic and other transformations is powerfully documented and analyzed in Massad, *Colonial Effects*. See also Chatterjee, *Nation and its Fragments*; Merry, "Legal Pluralism," 872–74.
24 Foucault, *History of Sexuality*, 101–02.

opposed to the effect, can itself turn into an "opposing strategy." For to argue this position amounts not merely to vitiating the substance of power, but to depriving it fully of its *own* agency, let alone potency.

With these caveats in mind as to the lack of predictability in the field of power-effects, and duly acknowledging the non-linearity of power discourses, it is still possible to argue, as this book does, that one of the strategies of colonialist power was the production, in the midst of undeniable diversity, of a considerably linear body of knowledge that invented two interrelated realities: one, thus far, with predictable effects and the other lacking (then as now) any form of predictability. The former consisted of a scholarly narrative of Islamic legal history, a narrative that brought into existence the field of "Islamic legal studies," if not the very constructed entity we now call "Islamic law." For it can easily be maintained that, at the very least, there existed no sociology of knowledge about Islamic law as the law of the Other before the rise of the colonialist project. It remains true, however, that the narrative was a slowly emerging phenomenon, wavering between opposing strategies within power discourses until the end of the eighteenth century, and was not to be streamlined into a more linear strategy until the second half of the nineteenth century, the zenith of the development of the colonialist laboratory. By that time, the foundations of the power discourses on "Islamic legal culture" were established, thereby ushering in the invention of the new tradition we have come to call "Islamic legal studies."

This tradition, to be sure, was not constructed for its own sake, nor was it merely an appurtenance of intellectual curiosity in European academe; for it would be naive of us to think that the fields nowadays subsumed under the humanities and the social sciences were created in isolation from the colonialist project, itself subordinate to the larger project of modernity.[25] Thus, due to sheer relevance – quite evident when compared, say, to psychoanalysis – the tradition came to serve (in the most systemic, though not always systematic, of ways) the imperatives of the colonialist project. The invented narrative of "Islamic legal studies" aided not only in fashioning colonialist policies that transformed the native legal cultures, but also in shaping the culture of empire itself.[26] Yet this culture was not the site where this invented reality proved most unpredictable or where it stood beyond the control of the processes and strategies of power

[25] See N. Dirks' introduction to Cohn's *Colonialism and its Forms of Knowledge*. For a useful critique of knowledge generated in the social sciences, see Wallerstein, *Uncertainties of Knowledge*.

[26] On this theme, see Said, *Culture and Imperialism*; Cohn, *Colonialism and its Forms of Knowledge*; and Dirks, *Scandal*.

itself, although it was no doubt a preeminent instance of this unpredictability. The latter, instead, lay in the effects of power-processes as they unfolded in the native legal cultures of the colonies. And it is here, in the formation and unfolding of these two invented realities, that the concerns of this book lie.

Thus, if every discourse must partake in the field of force relations (here taken for granted), then every discourse inevitably enters into a relationship with the processes of power. Of necessity, this entrance, the ticket to participation, is granted equally to every discourse, whether or not it is subversive and oppositional to the very structures and processes of power. This inclusivism is an essential attribute of power, for power by virtue of its constitution must absorb any oppositional discourse in order to maintain and, when need be, transform itself into new forms. But it does not follow that the field of force relations admits all discourses as equally effectual or equally legitimate. Within that field, total legitimization is the prerogative of those discourses that accommodate the dominant practices of power and validate these practices as a system of knowledge. Oppositional discourses, on the other hand, are often absorbed through silencing, a process that, by allowing these discourses an entry into the field of force relations, guarantees managing them into marginalization instead of permitting their exclusion to develop into an independent field of force relations. Unless, that is, these oppositional discourses gather so powerful a momentum as to displace the otherwise paradigmatic discourses, in which case we will be witness to no less than a Kuhnian revolution that operates on the level of power-systems.[27]

An all too obvious consequence of the foregoing is the contention that there exists no discourse that locates itself in complete isolation from power-systems, entirely outside their structures and interests. Every discourse, to be meaningful and relevant, must take a stance in the field of force relations, a stance that ranges from the ontologically and epistemically affirmative to the contradictory and invalidating. If this much is accepted, then it cannot be claimed that only colonialist and Orientalist discourses are allowed entry into the field of force relations, exclusive of the discourses that oppose them. Yet, if we admit the proposition that every discourse about the "Orient" carves for itself a place in the field of discursive force relations, and that Euro-American Orientalism does not hold a monopoly over that field, then what is the meaning of power in relation to oppositional, even invalidating, discourses? Conversely stated, how would the latter hold up against the hegemonic force relations and the

[27] Kuhn, *Structure of Scientific Revolutions.*

systemic jury that reserve for themselves the right of dismissal or acceptance, legitimation or delegitimation?

If both the jury and advocates – namely, the oppositional discourses competing for a favorable verdict – are necessarily bounded by the system in which they operate, then it would apodictically follow that they themselves are subject to the laws dictating how the power-system runs. That is to say, oppositional discourses within the field of force relations, including those that provide "a starting point for" a subversive and "opposing strategy," stand entirely subordinated to the laws and rules of power-systems. The Kuhnian and post-Kuhnian commentary on shifting paradigms may provide, at least in part, several insights into the workings of subversive discourses, but the point which must be unequivocally stated is that whatever conflictual relations oppositional discourses may develop in their bids to control the arenas of power (power being the only site of their existence) they can only pretend to the ownership of an otherwise nonexistent truth.

It goes without saying then that there exists no necessary relation between truth and the systemic rules of power, for power posits its own parameters of truth. The subjecting of these rules to subversive discourses, in which the latter invoke and appropriate the former, constitutes the first act of resistance. Subversive discourses are at their most effective when they feed on the decaying organs of the entrenched power-discourses, those which partook in the very definition of the systemic rules. The post-modern post-colonial critique is such a predator, born out of modernity's deliquescence, out of its weaknesses and the decline of its absolutist claims. It has not been (and is not likely to be) able to free itself of the system or its rules,[28] but, as a subversive strategy, it has effected a metamorphosis in the truth of power. It has provided and (more accurately) is in the process of providing a glimpse into a *transmuted* truth, but a truth of power nonetheless. It is only within these constrictive and inescapable parameters that one can write, and it is squarely within these parameters that any discourse can emerge.

But this is not to say that the transmutation, however modest, is anything less than an improvement, not in the sense of modernity's myth of progress, but in the amoral sense that such a transmutation opens, ever so slightly wider, the door to the articulation of subversive strategies. Some might call this a new knowledge, a state-of-the-art, an epistemic and a scientific progress, and in this they might be right. Some others might call it no more than a pawn in the complex game of power, and in this they might

[28] Spivak, "Can the Subaltern Speak?" 87 ff.

be equally correct. The present book constitutes, in a deliberate and conscious way, a protracted footnote on the dialectic between these two visions.

3. The scope and organization of this book

It is obvious that the present book navigates a vast expanse of territory, both geographically and historically. It sets out from seventh-century Arabia, with all the attendant – though only presumed – backgrounds that find their beginnings in as early an epoch (and legal culture) as ancient Babylonia. For it is one of the central assumptions of this book that Islamic law is a creature of the legal culture of the Near East, especially those forms of it that the Arabs of the south and the north lived and experienced between the fifth and seventh centuries AD. The book ends its narrative with the present, a temporally wide expanse that matches its vast geographical coverage. While a systematic, spatiotemporal account is impossible to achieve, a deliberate effort has been made to break the conventional mold that assigns to the Arab Middle East a privileged status. Although this approach entails maintaining a proper coverage of the Middle East while permitting other areas to be more or less represented, no claim can be made here to the effect that all important Islamic legal cultures in time and place have been accounted for (Sub-Saharan Africa, for instance, readily comes to mind). Such a comprehensive project – where Islamic law past and present will be discussed – presupposes the existence of decades of research and scholarly writing that, in this field, have barely begun.

Nonetheless, a non-exhaustive but still wide spatiotemporal coverage has its own epistemic and methodological problems, especially if attempted within the realistic constraints of page economy (scholarly publication being increasingly subject to the harsh rules of profit and loss). For instance, how, when we posit a theory of universals that insists on the uniqueness of all individuals in the world,[29] do we justify generalizing about any feature of Islamic law? How can we, for example, trust any proposition proclaiming that the law college, the *madrasa*, conducted its affairs in a particular fashion when legal education differed so much between, say, East Java and Egypt? Or, how can any portrayal of the workings of the Islamic law court be trustworthy when courts in one and the same region have been shown to practice and apply law differently? How can we offer any account of the courts, law colleges and every other subject within our purview, without making allowances for spatiotemporal variations?

[29] For a frame of reference, see Aaron, *Theory of Universals*.

It must be asserted once and for all that definitive, water-tight solutions or answers to these perennial questions – about Islamic law or any subject – entail either one of two responses: silence (which *ipso facto* contradicts the very act of scholarly writing, clearly not an option), or the production of strictly micro-accounts that can hardly traverse their atomic realities (for if they were to claim transcendence into the general, they would fall into the same epistemic predicament that forced them into their micro-existence in the first place). The passage from the micro to the macro, furthermore, has been a common practice, often entangled in the same epistemic and historiographical dilemmas plaguing grand narratives. So how can one write any macro-history – without which, arguably, scholarship would remain both atomized and fragmentary – in a manner that avoids the pitfalls associated with generalization?

One possible answer relevant to our context is that such pitfalls, strictly speaking, are inevitable, that they come with the territory, arising whenever a proposition purports to describe more than a single, atomic particular. At a certain level, therefore, this epistemic predicament is also the lot of micro-history, since even here the historian routinely deals with a plurality of particulars, all of which are uniquely individual, but some of which will be, perforce, discursively marginalized in relation to those which stand at the center of the historian's gaze. In principle, this deprivileging of data represents the same predicament we are associating with macro-history. Micro-history's "thick description," it is readily admitted, "succeeds in using microscopic analysis of the most minute events as a means of arriving at the most far-reaching conclusions."[30] It might be said that the intended purpose of this history is to reveal the workings of the larger structures. Yet such leaps from the seemingly insignificant particulars, the subject-matter of the micro-historian, to the general has, in strictly epistemological terms, escaped historiographical scrutiny, whereas macro-history has been an obvious and easy target. And this epistemological bias is hardly the result of qualitative differences in the historiographical practices of the two types of history-writing, despite the obvious external differences in their approaches. It is the undisguised plurality in the heart of macro-history that exposes the latter to criticism. To speak about Cairo, Damascus, Shiraz and Fez in one stroke seems far more objectionable than speaking of a staggering multiplicity of professions, institutions, networks, classes, practices, and a broad variety of cultural and other features of a Cairo, a Damascus or a Kayseri. What makes such micro-accounts more palatable is not particularly a more

[30] Levi, "On Microhistory," 102.

convincing rationale or epistemic, "scientific" justification, but a perception of the historian's successful management of data, a perception (if not the illusion) that the constitutive elements of the subject studied are manageable and therefore can be accounted for, calculated, checked and, ultimately, controlled. That control is the micro-historian's assurance that her conclusions result directly from the evidence she has used and adduced. But what, in the end, makes this so different from the writing of macro-histories?

An answer to this question provides the justification for the scope of this volume. A generalization purporting to describe a class is obviously falsifiable, or deemed problematic, if one or more instances presumed to belong to members of the class turn out to be at variance with, or to contradict, that generalization. An accurate historical narrative is therefore one which can account for exceptions and show that, in all its propositions, it is anchored in a set of valid lines of reasoning that derive from the evidence deployed. Without engaging in Foucault's "evidence as illustration,"[31] I think it is useful to borrow his notion of "episteme," a notion referring to systems of knowledge and practice that share in common a particular structure of concepts which qualitatively distinguish them from other systems of the same species. Foucault's interest lay of course in the distinction between modern systems and their respective predecessors (or corresponding antecedents), as well as in the "epistemic breaks" that occurred in these systems.[32] But the concept of episteme can be usefully applied to map out the system of knowledge and practice that is Islamic law. The local and regional differences of this practice are infinitely varied, having been influenced by a multiplicity of cultural, economic, customary, geographical, historical and myriad other factors, from Morocco to the Indonesian Archipelago. Given this endless variety, how can one, without being reductive, speak of Islamic law?

It is crucial for a proper understanding of this book to distinguish between the systemic components of the Sharīʿa – those referred to as an episteme – and other contingent features that vary from one place or time to another. In other words, until the dawn of modernity, there always existed within the Sharīʿa structures of authority and discursive and cultural practices that did not change over time and space – that is, until they met their structural death[33] in the nineteenth and early twentieth

31 Gutting, "Foucault and the History of Madness," 47–67.
32 Foucault, *Archaeology of Knowledge*, 34–78; Flynn, "Foucault's Mapping," 31–33.
33 "Structural death" refers to the collapse of the organic features that made the Sharīʿa system, in the first place possible, and, in the second, reproductive. The veneer of the Sharīʿa that survives today in the civil codes of Sunnite Muslim countries and in the

centuries. For instance, the function and modalities of legal education, despite the shades of difference in educational practices across time and space, were constants, defining in part what it is to be a Sharīʿa-trained scholar or Sharīʿa-trained student. The same applies to the functions of the jurisconsult (*muftī*), the judge (*qāḍī*), the author-jurist (*muṣannif*), the law professor (*shaykh*), the notary (*shurūṭī*), the court scribe (*kātib*), and several other "functionaries" who were constants insofar as their *structural* performances were concerned.[34] For these performances were not dictated only by the forces driving the system, by sheer necessity or by a logic of forward motion. Indeed, they were also dictated by a deeply rooted ethic, the realization of which constituted an integral part of the fulfillment of these "functions" and the highest achievement in practicing, performing and living the Sharīʿa.

This is not to say that, like education, court practices did not differ from one place or time to another. They did, at times considerably, depending upon the society in which the courts operated, and upon the polity that ruled. In fact, it is eminently arguable that court practices differed from court to court within the same city or town, with the changing of *qāḍī*s in the same court, or even the changing of the scribe. As much as villages adjacent to each other differed relatively in cultural practices, so did their notions of justice and the ways in which their judges, deputy-judges, witnesses and scribes carried these notions through. But the structural mechanisms, procedures, substantive laws, values and ethic of adjudication followed a unified notion of justice, whether adjudication took place in eleventh-century Fez or fifteenth-century Samarqand. This paradigmatic notion of justice was constituted, shaped and defined by a synthesis whose elements ranged from a particular, grounding religious ethic that was overwhelmingly Quranic, to a social ethic that placed primary emphasis on the integrity of community and social harmony; to a fairly unified body of adjectival law; to an undisputable and cohesive body of legal doctrine; to a particular set of assumptions about the moral community as a participant in the law court and legal process; to a particular relationship between legal knowledge and political power; etc. There was, it is true, a great jural variety effected by, among other factors, differences in customs and social norms, but the variety existed within *a structural and systemic unity*. It is this unity that the present work attempts to delineate,

politicized education of "traditional law" has been severed from its juridical, juristic and legal ability to reproduce, precisely due to the absence – or death – of those structural and systemic features that allow us to inspect and speak of the Sharīʿa's episteme.

34 Including the important *waqf* and its educational and legal functions. On this institution as functioning across "chronological, geographical and ethnic boundaries," see Deguilhem, "Government Centralization of Waqf," 223.

but not without accounting – to the extent permitted within the bounds of a single volume – for a number of jural varieties that existed in certain places and times throughout the lands of Islam.

Another point of central importance is that this book is about Islamic law, not about law in Islam – two considerably different subjects of enquiry. Islamic societies, like almost all societies before they were subjected to the imperatives of modernity, were extremely pluralistic in "legal" constitution, permitting several levels of jural and moral governance, legal mechanisms, and mediation-based and arbitrative resolution. Legal norms were generated, among others, by the family, the clan, the tribe, the village, the neighborhood, the socio-religious community and the dynast. To study the Sharīʿa can never amount to the study of the entirety of these forms, for the latter, like the Sharīʿa, stand on their own as subjects of enquiry. Subordinating them to the Sharīʿa amounts to denying their importance, if not existence. And this is precisely what this volume does not intend to do, although there is an urgent need to begin exploring these corollary norms, not only for intrinsic reasons – on their own an abundantly sufficient motive – but also because without such an exploration we cannot hope to understand the Sharīʿa in a better and fuller manner. It is essential for this attempt at understanding to account, in both practice *and* theory, for these corollary systems and norms that the Sharīʿa inevitably meshed with, promoted, resisted or suppressed.

As the subject of this book, the Sharīʿa is taken to be the total sum of its synchronic and diachronic history. In other words, understanding the Sharīʿa of a particular time and place is untenable without coming to terms with its cumulative tradition, for its own history continued to be, at every turn in its life, an integral part of its living experience. History not only provided continuity, a recurring experience on a linear progression, but also augmented its totalistic experiences in every moment the Sharīʿa came to be substantiated in a particular place and time. Its sources, its theoretical and legal principles, and its textual narratives were constantly reproduced and recreated, providing the substrate and subject-matter for its practices and discourses at every turn. To argue that the Sharīʿa is what it is at a particular moment of its subjects' experiences, that its history obfuscates and distorts its spatiotemporal manifestation, is analogous to setting aside considerations of past and childhood experiences in the psychoanalysis of an individual. For every stage in the Sharīʿa, both in fact and in doctrine, has contributed to creating, defining and shaping the next.

Accordingly, in the first chapter, I begin by offering a synopsis of the epoch in which the Sharīʿa came into existence, of the background against which it grew, and of the socio-legal formations within the first centuries.

The demographic, cultural, linguistic and economic ties that existed between the Southern and Northern Arabs constituted a crucial element in the formation of an early Islamic legal culture. The main argument here is that the sources of the Sharīʿa's formation were not foreign intrusions such as those which modern legal systems adopt or are forced to adopt from other hegemonic systems. This dominant mode of legal transplantation seems to discolor modern scholarship's perception of the imperceptible ways most pre-modern systems interacted with one another. In the seventh and eighth centuries, when the body of the law – at least as substantive doctrine – came into being, the sources that supplied the raw materials had already permeated the practices of the Near East for centuries. It was not an identifiable source of a Jewish or Roman law book that made contribution, but the aggregate and synthetic practices already existing in the region, in their Iraqian, Syrian, Peninsular and North African variations. In short, it is a vain effort to try to identify discrete sources that Muslims encountered, and from which they derived such materials as could have conceivably been integrated on a wide scale within the expansive geography of legal culture. Nor can one, with any reasonable assurance, determine the exact origins of a legal concept or juridical institution, for such a determination would then be engulfed in arbitrary historiographical exercises, nationalist anachronism, and the remarkable ability to ignore the pliability and mutations of such concepts and institutions in the course of their less-than-neat development.

The first chapter, then, offers an account of the emergence of the Sharīʿa out of a synthetic legal tradition that pervaded the Near East for millennia, an evolution whose determinants were many and the foremost of which was a new sociological formation represented in the nascent Muslim community and its private, highly individualistic legal experts. These experts, the jurists (*fuqahāʾ*), defined the contours of the *sharʿī* system that emerged, not only in its law and legal institutions, but also in its uniquely private, independent, and socially and morally grounded nature. The jurist-as-a-private-individual, as a politically independent, socially responsible figure, was signally an Islamic invention that determined the course of legal history for the next twelve centuries. But this type of jurist was in turn determined and shaped by a new concept of community that the new religion brought into existence.

The remainder of the first chapter follows the evolution of an Islamic judiciary as well as the formation of the legal schools (*madhāhib*; sing. *madhhab*), both of which constituted the first two of four major developments that gave the Sharīʿa its final shape. The third of these developments was the rise of a fully formed legal theory and interpretive methodology (*uṣūl al-fiqh*), the concern of chapter 2. Since the fourth development, i.e., substantive legal doctrine, requires more expansive attention – even if presented in outline – its discussion in the book is deferred to form the entirety of Part II.

In chapter 3, I turn to legal education, the means by which the juristic class was reproduced. Hence, this chapter offers a brief account of the workings of the educational circle (*ḥalaqa*) as well as of the law college (*madrasa*) that oftentimes enveloped the circle's activities. The *madrasa*, an important but by no means the exclusive educational forum, provided not only a point of contact between law and politics, but also an effective corridor through which the ruling class attempted to create and augment political and religious legitimacy. Topics covered in this chapter are no doubt intrinsically important, but they are also fundamental for understanding nineteenth- and twentieth-century developments where the appropriation of the Sharīʿa by the modern state was made possible through dynastic control of traditional legal education.

With chapter 3, and with the doctrinal background provided in Part II, the essential and structural features of the law will have been covered. Chapter 4, "Law and society," assumes this coverage in taking into account the interaction of law with society and its moral props. Customary practices of mediation and arbitration are shown to intersect with judicial practice and complement it as well – a dialectic latent in the prescriptions of legal doctrine. The *qāḍī*'s assembly, the equivalent of the Western court of law, is discussed as an arena of social and moral contestation, where society, notions of honor and the ruling regime compete and strategize for a share in justice. The dependency of the court on the all-important *muftī* (jurisconsult) betrays the latter's centrality to the judicial functioning of the system and to the structural capability of the Sharīʿa in accommodating change through the *fatwā*, a change to which the author-jurist (the *muṣannif*) also contributed significantly. Finally, in the last section, this chapter provides a brief discussion of the place of women in the legal system.

It will be noted that most of our data on the operation of the court in chapter 4 come from the Ottoman period, it being assumed (largely on the basis of pre-sixteenth-century literary sources) that, aside from limited changes the Ottomans implemented, the court practices were continuous until the beginning of the nineteenth century.

Closing Part I is chapter 5, which introduces the role of government that was epitomized in the metaphoric usage "Circle of Justice," a long-standing Near Eastern culture of political management that engaged the Sharīʿa as a means not only toward garnering legitimacy but also toward maximizing administrative capabilities. It is summed up in the following logic of sequence: for good government to achieve its *raison d'état* there must be justice, and for justice to be realized there must be good government. The Circle worked well for both the ruling elite and the jurists – the former, in their capacity as utilizers of the civil population; the latter, in their capacity as the population's representatives and its defenders. As the jurists saw it, sustaining just rule was the ultimate means of realizing God's law. As the ruling elite saw it, the law was a means to an end: the welfare of rule and ruler. Be that as it may, it was clear that both the Sharīʿa and the ruling elite stood in a mutually beneficial relationship. This chapter then goes on to deal with the legal balance that was achieved through the symbiotic relationship that existed over the centuries between the Sharīʿa and executive power, from Iran to North Africa. But the legal balance described here was also the discursive practice that needed to be integrated into the "Circle," and this necessarily reflected the interaction of various elements of a pluralistic legal culture, where within the ambit of the Sharīʿa, and constantly interacting with it, there existed customary law, professional regulations, neighborhood by-laws, and royal edicts and proclamations.

With the same spirit of economy practiced throughout the book, Part II provides a synopsis of some important aspects of legal doctrine (cf. Appendix A). One or two caveats must be noted, however. First and foremost, note should be taken of the simplified presentation in Part II. Many works of legal doctrine, notwithstanding their technical efficiency of expression and virtuoso style of exposition, filled multiple thick volumes, at times reaching two or three dozen.[35] Part II, in contrast, purports to give no more than an outline of select topics. Each of these is material rich enough for several analytical and descriptive tomes, in which one could adopt a legal, anthropological, moral-philosophical, economic or other approach, depending on the nature of the subject-matter. Furthermore, although the coverage attempts to account for the four Sunnite schools as well as that of the Twelver-Shīʿites, I cannot claim to have been successful in providing sufficient coverage for each school on every point of law I discuss. On some points, the schools were not equal in coverage, and in some cases one or two of them may have been silent. In most cases, only the school's authoritative doctrine was noted, but no school had a standard, unified body of laws, and so there might be worthy opinions, at variance with the authoritative doctrine of the school, that were not noted. Thus, what I have attempted to do is to present those opinions and substantive principles that show the structure and framework of legal doctrine, for any full, all-school analysis of even a single point of law would

[35] See, for instance, the Bibliography, for the works of Sarakhsī, Māwardī, Ibn Māza, ʿAynī and Majlisī.

require many pages of writing. Finally, the absence from this Part of an account of the all-important law of *waqf* may be noted, but a succinct exposé of it will be necessary for, and is therefore found in, the narrative of chapter 4.

With Part III, the book moves to the modern period, not a chronological measure of time so much as a dramatic transformation in the episteme and structure of the law. Hence, the "modern" takes off where and when such transformations occur, in India, for example, at least half a century earlier than in the Ottoman Empire and North Africa. One of the major themes here is the constellation of effects brought about by the introduction into the Muslim legal landscape of the modern project of the state, perhaps – together with capitalism – the most powerful institution and feature of modernity.[36] The identification of the bureaucratic, corporate and technological state as the major player in modernity requires an analytical dissection – however brief – of its ramifying effects on the Sharīʿa, its institutions, epistemologies and paradigmatic, discursive practices. This dissection, conceptual in nature, is the concern of chapter 13. The next chapter begins a historical narrative of legal colonialism in India, Indonesia and the Malayas, three regions that experienced direct military occupation. Chapter 15 turns to the Ottoman Empire, where the absence of such an occupation did not significantly alter the extent of legal transformations or of Sharīʿa's dismantling. Similar accounts are given for Egypt, Algeria, Morocco and Iran. The list of countries covered is obviously far from exhaustive, it being the case again that a full discussion and analysis of even a single country would warrant an independent volume, if not many more. But in keeping with our approach to the "episteme" (discussed above), the intention is to draw out through various examples systemic and structural changes that are deemed central to the modern transformation – what Hodgson aptly called "The Great Western Transmutation."[37] In this analysis, Indonesia, India (and in chapter 16, Pakistan), Iran, the Ottoman Empire, Egypt and Algeria are deemed central case-studies illustrating varieties in the transformation of (or break in) the episteme.

Chapter 16 continues the discussion of the transformation after World War I, focusing, first, on the methods through which changes in the law were effected. Second, as the Sharīʿa was reduced to little more than altered provisions pertaining to family law, the coverage of this sphere becomes a central concern – a sphere wholly determined by the state's will-to-power. Precisely because family law preserved the semblance of

[36] Hodgson, *Rethinking World History*, 44–71. [37] *Ibid.*

Sharīʿa's substantive law, it is of particular interest to examine how a new patriarchy, engineered by the state, came to replace its predecessor. This fundamental change in *legal episteme* is but one register of the drastically different conditions that modernity came to impose on family life and matrimonial relationships, on legal institutions, and on society at large. These changes, coupled with the emergence of oppressive modern states and a deep sense of moral loss, have all combined (together with much else) to produce a massive movement that is dominantly political but also legal and cultural in orientation. This is the Islamist movement which has been influencing much of what is happening in the Muslim world today. The remaining parts of chapter 16 therefore address the intricate relationship between the state, Islamists and the ulama in a number of key countries – key, as developments in them have deeply affected most other regions in the Muslim world.

The place of the Sharīʿa in the modern world is no better exemplified than in the debates occurring in today's Muslim world over legal theory, what had been termed in Sharīʿa history as *uṣūl al-fiqh*. These debates illustrate the crises that engulfed the Sharīʿa, both as a legal tradition and as a marker of cultural – even political – identity. The discourses of several prominent thinkers are discussed in chapter 17, with a view to showing how these discourses articulate the Muslims' self-perception of where they stand in the modern world, in its complex forms of secularity, its counter-morality and its staunch materialist bent.

In writing this book, I have incurred a profound intellectual debt to at least two groups of scholars and thinkers. Although the academic study of "Islamic law" has yet to expand commensurately with its staggering current importance, recent scholarship, particularly since the turn of the millennium, has produced much of scholarly value and use to this book. Standing foremost on the list are, on the one hand, legal anthropologists whose work has helped reinvent Islamic legal studies, and, on the other, social and socio-legal historians of the Ottoman period, the best-covered area in the historical study of the Muslim world. Of no less importance for the theoretical grounding of this book are the works of post-colonial writers, as well as of historians of the formation of modern Europe. The Bibliography represents a register not only of the works I have used, but also of that debt.

Needless to say, the wide scope of this volume makes it necessary that I deal with questions and themes that I myself have previously studied and written about, with the inevitable consequence that some parts of the book have come to draw on my earlier work. Therefore, chapter 1 and section 2 of chapter 3 sum up much of my *Origins and Evolution of Islamic Law*; and apart from the first, second and last sections of chapter 2 and sections 1, 4, 5, 6 and 10 of chapter 17, the material in those chapters generally derives from my *History of Islamic Legal Theories*, although important abridgment, revision and added analytical commentary have taken place in every case.

It should be noted that a number of footnote citations in Part II are placed in square brackets. These citations, referring to three recent English translations of *fiqh* works,[38] are supplied for the benefit of those who cannot read the original Arabic texts and who wish to delve further into the study of legal doctrine. While most of these references have been added subsequent to the completion of Part II, a few, based on the original texts, had already been relied upon in writing this Part. Therefore, any reference to these works outside square brackets will refer to the original Arabic source, not to its translation.

Finally, a word about calendars. In Parts I and II, this book uses a dual system of dating (e.g., 505/1111). The first date refers to the Hijri calendar, the other to the Gregorian. The Hijri dating is abandoned in Part III, since the sources, many of which are European or Europeanized, generally use the Gregorian dates.

[38] They are: Miṣrī, *The Reliance of the Traveller*; Marghīnānī, *Al-Hidāya*, I (vol. II yet unpublished); and Ibn Rushd, *The Distinguished Jurist's Primer*.

Part I

The pre-modern tradition

1 The formative period

1. The Near Eastern background

By the time of his death in 11/632, the founder of Islam had left behind a small state in Medina (previously Yathrib) whose ideological props were fiercely uncompromising moral principles fitted into a larger context of tribal justice. With the rapid conquests of lands lying between western China and the Iberian Peninsula, the new religion generated a full-fledged, sophisticated law and legal system in the relatively short span of the three and a half centuries that followed its inception. Our concern in the present chapter and partly the next is to sketch the outlines of this formative development.

Long before Islam appeared on the scene, Mecca and Medina had a long history of settlement and formed part of the cultural continuum that had dominated the Near East for millennia. The two towns were not at the center of imperial culture, but they were tied to it in countless ways. Prior to the Arab expansion in the name of Islam, Arabian society throughout the region had developed the same types of institutions and forms of culture already long established in the lands to the south and north, a development that would later facilitate the Arab conquest of the entirety of that region, including its two major Empires.[1]

In the century or so before the rise of Islam, there existed three centers of empire, the Byzantine (around the eastern Mediterranean coast), the Sasanid (today's eastern Iraq and Persia) and the Yemenite (in the south-east of the Arabian Peninsula itself). The Yemen was subsidiary to the former two by virtue of being, at different times, either a vassal state of the Ethiopian kingdom – which in turn was a constant ally of the Eastern Roman Empire – or under the direct occupation of the Sasanids. But early on the Yemen had experienced a long history of independent kingdoms that attained a high level of civilization, both material and cultural. It possessed a strategic commercial position, lying on the ancient trade

[1] Lapidus, "Arab Conquests," 50.

route from the Indonesian Archipelago and India to Syria. Spices, incense, leather, silk, ivory, gold, silver, glue and precious stones were among the many items that made their way through the Yemen to Pharaonic Egypt and later to the Greek, Roman and Byzantine Empires. The Maʿīnite, Sabaʾite and Ḥimyarite kingdoms that flourished there developed a sedentary style of life and governance, complex forms of religion, and an elaborate urban existence complete with markets, palaces and imposing houses, supported by sophisticated agrarian and commercial networks. During the last decades of the sixth century, the Sasanids took over the Yemen, having much earlier set up an autonomous state headed by the Lakhmid kings to rule Ḥīra, a major city on the west side of the Euphrates. Facing the Sasanids on the other side of the Fertile Crescent stood the Roman and, later, Byzantine Empires which relied on the Ghassānids to protect their interests in the region against the Sasanids.

The Ghassānids and the Lakhmids served the purposes of their imperial overlords well. Originally southern tribal confederations, they had long experience with citied life, high civilization and the forms of rule typical of such cultures. Both had their roots in the eastern parts of the Yemen which, since the second or third century BC, if not earlier, had enjoyed a high level of spiritual and religious culture, complex forms of political life, and knowledge of agriculture, trade and commerce. Ḥīra, the Lakhmid capital, was a center of the fine arts, sciences (particularly medicine), architecture and literature. It possessed a rich agricultural and commercial economy, exclusively controlled by the Lakhmid tribal confederation. It manufactured leather and steel armor, and produced all sorts of cotton, wool and linen textiles. It had been the recipient of massive Arab migration since the first century AD, when the Azd, a constituent group of the Tanūkh confederation, settled its surrounding area. The Ghassānids of Syria, on the other hand, had developed a sophisticated agriculturalist economy and an active trade network, and engaged in the manufacture of a variety of products. Their religious beliefs and mythologies had ancient pedigrees, having been significantly influenced by Mesopotamian spirituality, and in turn affecting (in this as well as in material ways) the Roman Empire, of which Syria was a province.[2]

To the south of the Lakhmid and Ghassānid vassal kingdoms lay a vast area inhabited by Bedouin tribes, and dotted with oases where agriculturalists could produce wheat, grapes, dates and other foodstuffs sufficient to sustain their sedentary existence and to provide for the passing caravans.

[2] Ball, *Rome in the East.*

The Bedouin tribes, as part of their normal activities, engaged in an extensive system of trade and commerce, a system that prevailed in the lands between the lower eastern Mediterranean and the Arabian Sea and between this latter and north-eastern Arabia. They also provided passing caravans with camels, afforded them protective escorts, and themselves engaged in trade on a relatively significant scale. The agriculturalists in turn depended to some extent on the resources afforded by camel-nomadism and by commercial and trading activities based on the camel industry.[3] Thus, the Bedouin played an important role in the life of the three polities that surrounded them. In the south, the large tribe of Kinda controlled the trade routes from the Yemen through Ḥadramawt and its ports, as well as many routes that connected the Yemen and Ḥadramawt with the Najd.[4] When Islam appeared on the scene, these latter regions were predominantly Arabic-speaking; and in the north-east, the Arab migrations had already begun to displace Aramaic-speaking populations as early as the first century AD. Likewise, by the same time, the entire area that lay between northern Arabia and Edessa, including Palmyra, was mainly Arabic-speaking. The spread of Arabic and the displacement of Aramaic were in good part due to the energetic work of the Bedouin Arabs as traders, caravanists and soldiers.[5]

Through trade and nomadic migration, the Bedouin were thus in close contact with each other throughout the Near East, from Syria to Najd, and from Iraq to the Yemen. Large markets and international fairs provided the tribes with the opportunity to collect taxes, and opened the eastern parts of the Peninsula to contacts with merchants from India and China.[6] The markets had a religious function as well, in that they apparently housed idols and hosted religious festivals and ritual performances. In this network of trade and worship, the most significant commercial center of western and central Arabia was Mecca. Strategically located at the juncture of two intersecting trade routes, it was in contact with the Syrian and Iraqi north, the Yemenite south, central and eastern Najd, and, through the Red Sea coastal area, Abyssinia and eastern Africa. The city's involvement in trade certainly started before the first century AD, when it became a cultural satellite of the Nabatean Arabs, as evidenced by the fact that the people of the region adopted Nabatean Arabic for writing and worshiped major Nabatean deities, such as Hubal, Manāt and al-Lāt – all of whom came to

[3] Donner, "Role of Nomads," 73–88.
[4] Piotrovsky, "Late Ancient and Early Medieval Yemen," 213–20, esp. at 217.
[5] Potts, *Arabian Gulf*, I, 227; Dussaud, *Pénétration*.
[6] Potts, *Arabian Gulf*, II, 251, 332, 339–40; During Caspers, "Further Evidence," 33–53; Levenson, *European Expansion*, 11.

play a significant role in the religious life of Mecca and Yathrib. The Hejaz was also a commercial satellite of the Nabateans and a focus of their trade; in fact, various pecuniary and commercial contracts they used were to continue as part and parcel of the Sharīʿa.[7] In more ways than one, Mecca was connected not only with every major tribe and locale in the Peninsula, but also with the Near East at large.

Thus, Peninsular society led a dynamic existence, with direct and indirect ties to an international market of material goods and cultural and institutional products. Although its geographical and material conditions did not allow the full absorption of southern and northern imperial institutions, the region nonetheless developed a level of culture and all sorts of material products that played a part in Arabian social, economic and legal life.[8] Moreover, from a legal standpoint, Arabian society was in possession of two sets of laws, one serving sedentary, agriculturalist and commercial needs, the other supporting nomadic tribal conditions, heavily dependent on customary laws. This dichotomy clearly was not collateral with social structure, but rather with the type of activity engaged in by particular groups. In criminal matters, for instance, both the Bedouin nomads and the sedentary populations followed, more or less, the same set of customary Bedouin laws. The murder of a man, Bedouin or not, required either commensurate revenge or payment of blood-money, an ancient Near Eastern law that was as much present in the pre-Islamic Peninsula (documented in the Quran) as in ancient Mesopotamia.[9] In commercial dealings, on the other hand, even the nomads entered into pecuniary and mercantile transactions and contracts that had commonly been practiced in the Near East for centuries, probably as long ago as Babylonian and Assyrian times. In ancient Thamūdite and Liḥyānite inscriptions (dating from several centuries before Islam in north-west Arabia), many texts deal with property rights, both movable and immovable (wells, land), as well as with penal cases and pecuniary transactions.[10] As early as the first century BC, the Yemen had already produced a sophisticated system of law. The Qaṭabānian kingdom was in possession of a commercial "code," including a Law Merchant, which, among other things, applied to foreign traders in their dwelling places outside the city gates.[11]

All in all, the Peninsular Arabs maintained extensive relations with their neighbors to the south and north, with whom they shared ethnic, linguistic

[7] See, e.g., Ibn Qudāma, *Mughnī*, IV, 312. See also, more generally, Edens and Bawden, "History of Taymāʾ," 48–97.
[8] For a detailed account of economic and material life in pre-Islamic Arabia, see ʿAlī, *Mufaṣṣal*, VII.
[9] VerSteeg, *Early Mesopotamian Law*, 107 ff. [10] ʿAlī, *Mufaṣṣal*, V, 475.
[11] Piotrovsky, "Late Ancient and Early Medieval Yemen," 214. See also ʿAlī, *Mufaṣṣal*, V, 476.

and cultural grounds. The Meccan traders, as well as the Prophet and his Companions, were thoroughly familiar with the cultures of the Fertile Crescent and Yemen, and developed a sophisticated knowledge of legal practices which, through various channels, came to inform the law that was to develop in time into the Sharīʿa.

2. Quranic legality

Muhammad's mission in Mecca was religious and ethical, calling for humility, generosity and belief in a God who has neither a son nor a father, being categorically dissociated from the idols worshiped by the Arabian tribes. His call was largely concerned with faith, morality and the purity of mundane existence. During this early phase, the message was articulated in terms of continuity with monotheism, but representing a purer form of the otherwise corrupted versions of Christianity and Judaism. Muhammad himself was a member of the monotheistic Ḥanīfiyya, a Meccan religion formed around the figure of Abraham and the worship at the Kaʿba, which the latter reportedly built.[12] Insofar as we know about its beliefs and practices, the Ḥanīfiyya appears to have been an agnate of Judaism, providing the spiritual background and precedent for the new religion.

Upon migrating to Medina, Muhammad began to face new realities, as he now was no longer fighting for recognition but rather stood in the role of leader. He also had to deal with the Medinan Jews who, like the Meccan tribes, opposed him and viewed his novel message with suspicion. Deeply disappointed by their position, he began to veer away from certain practices that the new religion had thus far shared with Judaism. Jerusalem was replaced by the Kaʿba as the sacred shrine of nascent Islam. Quranic revelation soon began to reflect further independence in the identity of a new Islamic community, the Umma, which had now become entitled to its own Law that paralleled, but was distinct from, other monotheistic laws. New verses were revealed, ushering in a list of commands, admonitions and explicit prohibitions concerning a great variety of issues, from eating swine to theft. Throughout, we find references to the Jews and Christians and their respective scriptures. But the message becomes ever clearer: if the Jews and Christians were favored with legally binding revelations, so too are the Muslims. Each community of believers must thus have its own law.[13] The Quran repeatedly stresses that the believers must judge by what was revealed to them, for "who is better than God in judgment."[14]

[12] Rubin, "Ḥanīfiyya and Kaʿba." [13] Goitein, "Birth-Hour of Muslim Law," 24–25.
[14] Quran, 5:49–50. See also 2:213; 3:23; 4:58, 105; 5:44–45, 47; 7:87; 10:109; 24:48.

The formation of a new identity was further reflected in the increasing rate of substantive legislation, above and beyond matters of ritual. Wine drinking, gambling and several other practices were subjected to limitations or outright prohibition. The ancient tax of the *zakāt*, known in South Arabia two centuries before Islam emerged,[15] was rehabilitated in order to provide for the weak and dispossessed, and to assist in the common cause of the new religion. Similarly, a ban on feuding was imposed, and criminal penalties were made commensurate with the injury caused. The fixing of penalties and the establishment of a centrally distributed alms-tax permitted the creation of a unified community, an Umma, whose members began to regard themselves as individuals independent of tribal affiliation.[16]

The limitations placed on tribal solidarity are also evidenced in the Quranic legislation on inheritance, according to which the family, including the deceased's male agnates, are declared the sole heirs. And while the male retained much of the powerful status that he had enjoyed in pre-Islamic Arabia, Islam granted wives and daughters substantial rights, including the recognition that females are full legal persons. Meccan practice, nearly identical to Mesopotamian law prevalent since Assyrian times,[17] required the bride's family (normally her father) to give her the dowry that the husband had paid to them. This practice of enhancing the financial security of women was confirmed by the Quran, and further augmented by allotting a daughter a share of inheritance equal to one half of the share of her brother.[18] This allotment appears to have been unprecedented in Arabia. Rights to the dowry and inheritance were connected to another principle that was to become central in later Islamic law, namely, the financial independence of wives: all property acquired by the woman during marriage, or property that she brought into the marriage (including her dower and trousseau),[19] remained exclusively hers, and the husband had no claim to any part of it.[20]

Another novel rule was the introduction of the principle of *ʿidda*, a waiting period imposed on divorced women. Whereas before Islam divorce was complete and final upon its declaration by the husband, the Quran now prescribed postponement of the irrevocable dissolution of the marriage until three menstrual cycles had been completed or, if the woman were pregnant, until the birth of the child. During this period, which allowed for reconciliation between the spouses, the husband was

[15] Beeston, "Religions," 259–69, esp. at 264. [16] Hodgson, *Venture*, I, 181.
[17] See Stol, "Women," 126; VerSteeg, *Early Mesopotamian Law*, *passim*.
[18] See chapter 8, section 6, below.
[19] On the trousseau, see chapter 4, section 5, below. [20] Quran, 4:19 ff.

obliged to provide both domicile and financial support for the wife. Furthermore, a divorced woman with a child was to suckle it for a period of two years, and the father was required to provide for mother and child during this same period. If she chose to do so, she could remarry her husband only after she had been married to (and divorced by) another.[21] Then as now, the intention was to force men to think hard before they rushed into divorcing their wives.

The Quran provided more or less detailed coverage of other areas of family law, as well as of ritual, commercial and pecuniary rules. Yet, although these rules surely did not constitute a system, their fairly wide coverage and the rapidity with which they appeared suggest a conscious effort toward building a new legal system. This new conception does not mean that there occurred a clean break with the legal traditions and customary laws of Arabia. Despite his critical attitude toward the local social and moral environment, Muhammad was very much part of this environment which was deeply rooted in the traditions of Arabia and other parts of the Near East. Furthermore, as a prominent arbitrating judge (*ḥakam*), he could not have abandoned entirely, or even largely, the legal principles and rules by which he performed this prestigious (but now prohibited) function. Yet, while maintaining continuity with past traditions and laws, the new religion exhibited a tendency to articulate a distinct law for the Umma – a tendency that marked the beginning of a new process whereby all events befalling the nascent Muslim community henceforth were to be adjudicated according to God's law, whose agent was none other than the Prophet. This was clearly attested in both the Quran and the Constitution of Medina, and became a cardinal tenet of jurists for centuries to come.[22]

Although many new rules and principles were introduced, the old institutions and ancient customs remained largely unchallenged. Indeed, as we shall see later, much of Arabian law continued to occupy a place in Sharīʿa, but not without modification. Examples include, among many others, prayer (*ṣalāt*), fasting, alms-tax,[23] mercantile transactions, contracts,[24] forms of sale, barter, retaliation and *qasāma*.[25] The

[21] *Ibid.*, 2:237; 65:1–6; 2:233; 2:230.

[22] Serjeant, "Constitution," 3. For the later jurists, see the opening pages of Shāfiʿī's *Risāla*.

[23] See Goitein, *Studies*, 73–89, 92–94.

[24] VerSteeg, *Early Mesopotamian Law*, 178; Schacht, "From Babylonian to Islamic Law"; Schacht, *Introduction*, 218.

[25] If the body of a murdered person was found on lands occupied by a tribe, or in a residential quarter in a city, town or village, fifty of the inhabitants had each to take an oath to the effect that they neither had caused the person's death nor had any knowledge of who did. If fewer than fifty persons were available, those present had to swear more than

adoption of these ancient laws by the mature Sharīʿa was justified by the jurists on the grounds that the Prophet did not repeal them and, in fact, sanctioned them implicitly, if not explicitly, by adopting them in his own practice and dealings.[26]

3. Conquests and emerging communtities

Within a decade or so after the Prophet's death in 11/631, extensive military campaigns, accompanied by an effective administration, were under way. Although not systematic, the campaigns were geared toward major centers. The Muslim army consisted primarily of tribal nomads and semi-nomads who, rather than take up residence in the newly won cities of the Fertile Crescent, Egypt and Iran, for the most part inhabited garrison towns as a separate class of conquerors. These garrisons usually consisted of a mosque surrounded by markets and an army camp. The tribal fighters were accompanied by their wives, children and slaves, all of whom were accustomed to living in open spaces. The camp was typically divided in such a way as to maintain each tribe or clan separately from each other, with spaces in between. However, as the camp was gradually transformed into a permanent settlement and the population of the conquerors expanded, these spaces were filled, and a commingling of clans was inevitable. The product was a compact town having a permanent sedentary society,[27] the context in which Islamic law and its juristic community were to flourish.

In addition to Old Cairo (Fusṭāṭ), Kūfa and Baṣra in southern Iraq constituted the chief settlements during the early stages of conquest. Damascus in Syria was exceptional in that the new arrivals chose to dwell in an already established city – one that was already inhabited by Arabs and was thus intimately familiar to them from before the rise of the new religion.

Despite its tribal and other differences, the new Muslim leadership saw itself as the promulgator of a religion whose lynchpin and cornerstone was the command of God, a command embedded in, and given expression by, the Quran. It did not escape the chief leaders in Medina, the capital, or their military representatives in the garrison towns, that their warriors needed to learn the principles of the new order, its new ethic and worldview. Tribal Bedouins to the core, the soldiers must have found alien the

once until fifty oaths had been obtained. By doing so, they freed themselves of criminal liability, but nonetheless remained bound to pay blood-money to the agnates of the person slain. Nawawī, *Rawḍa*, VII, 235 ff.; Maqdisī, *ʿUdda*, 529–31.

26 E.g., Ibn Ḥazm, *Muʿjam*, II, 838–39.

27 For a description of settlement in Fusṭāṭ, see Abu-Lughod, *Cairo*, 13.

new ideas of Islam, its mode of operation and its generally non-tribal conception, not to mention its organization. ʿUmar I and his advisors (many of whom had also been Companions of the Prophet) quickly realized that they could not count for long upon appeasing the Bedouin contingents through allocations of booty, and that they must – in order to transform their tribal character – induct these men and their children into the ideas of the new religion. This explains why, in each garrison town and in every locale where there happened to be a Muslim population, a mosque was erected.[28] This place of worship was to serve several functions for the emerging Muslim community, but at the outset it was limited mainly to bringing together the Muslims residing in the garrison town for the Friday prayer and sermon, both intended, among other things, to imbue the audience with religious values.

In keeping with the policy of the Prophet, Caliph ʿUmar I's aim was to promote Quranic values as the basis of communal life, for these values not only were the distinctive features of the new enterprise but also were essential to its continued success. To this end, he deployed to the garrison towns Quran teachers who enhanced the religious values propagated by the commanders and their assistants.[29] The Quran represented the rallying doctrine that shaped the identity of the conquerors, thereby distinguishing and separating them from the surrounding communities.

The propagation of this new religious ethic was as much needed in Arabia as anywhere else. The great majority of the tribes inhabiting Mecca, Medina, Ṭāʾif and the various agricultural oases, not to mention the nomads of the desert, were still little accustomed to the new political order and even less so to its unworldly and uniquely monotheistic ideas and principles. In the spirit of the Quran, and in accordance with what he deemed to have been the intended mission of the Prophet (to which he himself had contributed significantly), ʿUmar I promulgated a number of ordinances and regulations pertaining to state administration, family, crime and ritual. As a leading Companion, Caliph and charismatic leader, he regulated, among other things, punishment for adultery and theft, declared temporary marriage (*mutʿa*) illegal, and granted rights to concubines who bore the children of their masters. Similarly, he upheld Abū Bakr's promulgations, such as enforcing the prohibition on alcohol and fixing the penalty for its consumption.[30] He is also reported to have insisted forcefully on adherence to the Quran in matters of ritual and worship – a policy that culminated in a set of practices and beliefs that

[28] Hoyland, *Seeing Islam*, 561 ff., 567–73, 639.
[29] Shīrāzī, *Ṭabaqāt*, 44, 51; Ibn Ḥibbān, *Thiqāt*, 149, 157.
[30] Jammāʿīlī, *ʿUmda*, 463.

were instrumental in shaping the new Muslim identity and that later became integral to the law.

While Abū Bakr's and ʿUmar I's enforcement of Quranic laws points to the centrality of the Quran in the emerging state and society, it is also clear that the new order had to navigate an uncharted path for which the Quran provided little guidance. A large portion of pre-Islamic Arabian laws and customs remained applicable and, as we saw earlier, survived in somewhat modified form into the legal culture that was being constructed. But the new Quranic laws created their own juristic problems that rendered many of the old customary laws irrelevant. For instance, the Quran prohibited the consumption of alcohol, but did not specify a penalty. This penalty, thought to have been fixed arbitrarily, was soon altered by ʿUmar I to eighty lashes, apparently on the ground that inebriation was analogous to falsely accusing a person of committing adultery (*qadhf*), for which offense the Quran fixed the penalty at eighty lashes. The connection between fornication and inebriation is at best tenuous, but the analogy shows us how, from the beginning, the Quran provided the framework for legal thinking, bringing its contents to bear upon as many situations as nominally could be justified. Generally speaking, any matter that could be conceived of as falling within its juristic purview, even through expansive reasoning, was dealt with in Quranic terms or an extension thereof. And it was within this larger framework of the permeating effect of the Quran that pre-Islamic customary laws underwent modification and change.

4. The early judges and the evolution of Prophetic authority

Appointed during the first decade of the Hijra, the earliest *qāḍī*s were men who had been proficient tribal arbitrators (*ḥakam*s) and who possessed experience, wisdom and charisma. Although their verdicts were not binding in a modern legal sense, disputants normally conformed to their findings. Many of the proto-*qāḍī*s were recruited from the ranks of these pre-Islamic arbitrators, although other appointees did not have the benefit of such experience.

The first judges enjoyed hardly any general jurisdiction, having been confined to the garrison towns where the conquering Arab armies resided with their families and other members of their tribes.[31] The policy of the central power at Medina was clear on this matter from the outset: the conquered communities were to regulate their own affairs exactly as they had been doing prior to the advent of Islam. Abū Bakr's letter to his

[31] Dimashqī, *Tārīkh*, I, 202.

generals is typical, and represents the standard Muslim policy adopted during the entire period of the conquests. The new Arab masters were to "establish a covenant with every city and people who receive[d]" them, to give these people "assurances and to let them live according to their laws."[32] This attitude was to become standard policy and law throughout the rest of Islam's history.

The proto-*qāḍī* was directly responsible to the chief commander of the garrison town, who appointed, supervised and dismissed him. He was regarded as the commander's assistant as well as his deputy, acting in his stead whenever the commander left the town on a campaign. Thus, many early judges were assigned policing responsibilities, while others were charged with finance and administration.[33] In matters of law, roughly defined, the judgeships were limited in jurisdiction, not only to the newly formed Muslim communities but also to adjudging disputes and conflicts that arose among tribal groups whose main occupation was soldiering. During the first decades, when military activities were at their peak, the Arab tribes had not yet formed into communities of the sort that existed among the conquered populations, with their complex forms of social and economic life. It was only with the passage of time, when this occupying population had finally settled permanently in these towns, that their lives acquired this same complexity, constituting a full-fledged society whose daily, mundane problems spanned the entire range of law. This was the state of affairs nearly a century after the Prophet's death, as reflected in the changing character of the *qāḍī*'s office.

The early *qāḍī*s also engaged in the cultural practice of story-telling, as many of them were appointed with this double function. This additional duty usually entailed recounting stories of a generally edifying nature, related to the Quranic narratives of ancient peoples and their fates, biblical characters and, more importantly, the exemplary life of the Prophet. The first official judicial appointment appears to have been made by the Caliph Muʿāwiya in or around 41/661,[34] who enjoined them with the specific duty of "cursing the enemies of Islam" after the morning prayer and of explaining the Quran to worshipers after the Friday prayer. This last performance may have ranged from a popular ceremony to a more serious discussion of the Prophet's biography and interpretation of the Quran. It was activities of this sort that promoted (a) the cultivation of the Quranic and Prophetic narratives among the new Muslims, making these narratives the cultural, ideological and spiritual base of the emerging community; (b) the redefinition of the *qāḍī*'s jural scope of activities in religious

[32] Brock, "Syriac Views," 204–05. [33] Wakīʿ, *Akhbār*, III, 223.
[34] Dimashqī, *Tārīkh*, I, 200.

terms; and (c) initiating the study circle, an educational and intellectual institution that was to emerge two centuries later as the centerpiece of Islamic legal education and training in legal practice.

By the last quarter of the first Islamic century, a new generation had lived almost entirely under the acculturating effects of the new religion, having grown up under the influence of Quranic teachings and various kinds of religious preaching and instruction. Unlike their parents, who had become Muslims at a later stage in their lives, at times under coercion (by virtue of the apostasy wars), they, together with the children of non-Arab converts, had imbibed from infancy the rudimentary religious morality and values of the new faith. By the time they reached majority, they were frequent mosque-goers (i.e., regular consumers of religious preaching and religious acculturation) and were involved in various activities relating to the expansion and building of a religious empire. It was therefore the learned elite of this generation – which flourished roughly between 60/680 and 90/708 – who embarked upon promoting a religious ethos that permeated, indeed impregnated, so much of Muslim life and society. Many *qāḍīs* began to show serious interest in religious narratives, including stories and biographical anecdotes about the Prophet. The story-tellers were among those who promoted this narrative, which was to become paradigmatic. Already in the 60s/680s, some *qāḍīs* had started propounding Prophetic traditions, the precise nature of which is still unclear to us.[35]

The early sources appear to support the view that legal authority during the better part of the first Islamic century was in no way exclusively Prophetic. It must be remembered that by the time Muhammad died, his authority as a Prophet was anchored in the Quranic event and in the fact that he was God's spokesman – the one through whom this event materialized. To his followers, he was and remained nothing more than a human being, devoid of any divine attributes (unlike Christ for his community, for instance). But by the time of his death, when his mission had already met with great success, he was the most important living figure the Arabs knew. Nonetheless, these Arabs also knew the central role that ʿUmar I, Abū Bakr and a number of others had played in helping the Prophet, contributing to the success of the new religion. Like him, they were charismatic men who commanded the respect of the faithful. Inasmuch as Muhammad's authority derived from the fact that he upheld the Quranic Truth and never swerved from it, these men – some of whom later became caliphs – derived their own authority as privileged

[35] Ibn Ḥibbān, *Mashāhīr*, 122; Wakīʿ, *Akhbār*, I, 120, 125, 130.

Companions and caliphs from the same fact, namely, upholding the Quranic Truth. Thus, caliphal authority would not have been seen as derivative of that of the Prophet; in fact, it ran parallel to it. Muhammad was the messenger through whom the Quranic Truth was revealed – the caliphs were the defenders of this Truth and the ones assigned to implement its decrees. Thus, the early caliphs (even until the middle of the second/eighth century) tended to see themselves, and were seen, as God's direct agents in the mission to enforce His statutes, commands and laws. The titles they bore speak for themselves: "God's Deputy on Earth" and "The Commander of the Faithful." They held their own courts and personally acted as *qāḍīs*.[36] They also adjudicated – during the first century – issues that required authority-statement solutions, without invoking Prophetic authority.

Caliphal legislation, however, did not always derive authority from the office itself, as has been argued by some scholars.[37] Much of caliphal legal authority rested on precedent, consisting mainly of generally accepted custom and the practice of earlier caliphs, of the Prophet's close Companions and, naturally, of the Prophet himself. In fact, any good model was to be emulated. ʿUmar I reportedly advised the judge Shurayḥ to ensure that his rulings conformed with Quranic stipulations, the decisions (*qaḍāʾ*) of the Messenger of God and those of the "just leaders."[38] There is no reason to believe that the caliphs themselves did not abide by the same sources for legal guidance. When ʿIyāḍ al-Azdī, Egypt's *qāḍī* in 98/716, asked ʿUmar II about a case apparently involving the criminal liability of a boy who had violated a girl with his finger, the caliph answered: "Nothing has come down to me in this regard from past authorities." He delegated to the *qāḍī* full authority to deal with the case "in accordance with your discretionary opinion (*raʾy*)."[39] Had the caliphs been legislators in their own right, they would have deployed their own codes of law, and ʿUmar II would not have hesitated to rule in this matter. The caliphs and their office, in other words, were not independent agents of legislation, but integrally dependent upon prior exemplary conduct and precedent, only one source of which happened to be the decisions of previous caliphs (who themselves acted on the same sources of religious authority).

Thus, throughout most of the first century, the scheme of authoritative sources was: the Quran, the *sunan* (including a thin layer of caliphal law) and considered opinion (*raʾy*).[40] Sunna (pl. *sunan*) is an ancient Arab

[36] Crone and Hinds, *God's Caliph*, 43. [37] *Ibid.* [38] Wakīʿ, *Akhbār*, II, 189.
[39] Kindī, *Akhbār*, 334. The judge ruled for the girl, granting her fifty *dīnārs* in damages.
[40] Wakīʿ, *Akhbār*, I, 77, 113, 135 ff., 139, 325–26, 312–74.

concept, meaning an exemplary mode of conduct, and the verb *sanna* has the connotation of "setting or fashioning a mode of conduct as an example that others would follow." In pre-Islamic Arabia, as in many tribally structured societies, any person renowned for his rectitude, charisma and distinguished stature was, within his family and clan, deemed to provide a *sunna*, a normative practice to be emulated.[41] Some caliphal practices came to constitute *sunan* since they were viewed as commendable.[42] The concept of *sunna* thus existed before Islam and was clearly associated with the conduct of individuals, and not only with the collective behavior of nations, as is abundantly attested in the Quran.

When the caliphs and proto-*qāḍīs* referred to *sunan*, they were speaking of actions and norms that were regarded as ethically binding but which may have referred to various types of conduct. Such *sunan* may have indicated a specific way of dealing with a case, but they could also have constituted, collectively, a general manner of good conduct, such as when it was said that "so-and-so governed with justice and followed the good *sunna*." The earlier Prophets, as well as Muhammad, represented a prime source of *sunan*. In a general sense, therefore, *sunan* were not legally binding narratives, but rather subjective notions of justice that were put to various uses and discursive strategies.

Within three or four decades after the Prophet's death, it became customary to refer to his biography and the events in which he was involved as his *sīra*. While this term indicates a manner of proceeding or a course of action concerning a particular matter, a *sunna* describes the manner and course of action as something established, and thus worthy of being imitated.[43] Yet, the Prophet's *sīra*, from the earliest period, constituted a normative, exemplary model, overlapping with notions of Sunna.[44] At the time of his election as caliph, for instance, ʿUthmān promised to follow "the *sīra* of the Prophet." This phrase in ʿUthmān's oath refers to the personal and specific practice of the Prophet, a practice that is exemplary and thus worth following. It was his violation of this practice that allegedly led to ʿUthmān's assassination. An early poem accuses him of having strayed from the established *sunna* (*sunnat man maḍā*), especially the Prophet's *sīra*, which he had promised to uphold.[45]

By the time of ʿUthmān's caliphate (23/644–35/656), the Prophet's *sīra* and Sunna no doubt carried significant weight as exemplary conduct. In fact, evidence suggests that the Sunna of the Prophet emerged immediately after his death, which was to be expected given that many far less

41 Bravmann, *Spiritual Background*, 139 ff. See also Ansari, "Islamic Juristic Terminology," 259 ff.
42 Ibn Aʿtham, *Futūḥ*, I, 252. 43 Bravmann, *Spiritual Background*, 138–39, 169.
44 *Ibid.*, 167; also at 130, 154–55. 45 *Ibid.*, 126–29, 160.

significant figures were seen by the Arabs as having laid down *sunan*. It would be difficult to argue that Muhammad, the most influential person in the nascent Muslim community, was not regarded as a source of normative practice. In fact, the Quran itself explicitly and repeatedly enjoins believers to obey the Prophet and to emulate his actions. The implications of Q. 4:80 – "He who obeys the Messenger obeys God" – need hardly be explained. So too Q. 59:7: "Whatsoever the Messenger ordains, you should accept, and whatsoever he forbids, you should abstain from." Many similar verses bid Muslims to obey the Prophet and not to dissent from his ranks.[46] Moreover, Q. 33:21 explicitly states that "in the Messenger of God you [i.e., believers] have a good example." All this indicates that to obey the Prophet, by definition, was to obey God. In establishing his *modus operandi* as exemplary, the Prophet could hardly have received better support than that given to him by the society in which he lived and by the Deity that he was sent to serve.

That the Prophet's Sunna constituted an authoritative source of action cannot be doubted, but its status as an exclusive *sunna*-based authority was not to emerge until much later. Thus, the process that ultimately led to the emergence of Prophetic Sunna as a substitute to *sunan* went through a number of stages before its final culmination as the second formal source of the law after the Quran. In the first stage, his Sunna was one among many, however important it was increasingly coming to be. For example, in the hundreds of biographical notices written about the early *qāḍī*s by Muslim historians, it is striking that Prophetic Sunna surfaces relatively infrequently – certainly no more frequently than those of Abū Bakr and ʿUmar I. The second stage of development appears to have begun sometime in the 60s/680s, when a number of *qāḍī*s, among others, began to transmit Prophetic material, technically referred to by the later sources as *ḥadīth*. This activity of transmission is significant because it marks the beginning of a trend in which special attention was paid to the Sunna of the Prophet. It is also significant because it was the only *sunna* to have been sifted out of other *sunan*, and to have been increasingly given an independent status. No religious scholar or *qāḍī* is reported to have exclusively studied, collected or narrated the Sunna of Abū Bakr, for instance; nor that of the more distinguished ʿUmar I. The fact that the Prophet's Sunna acquired an independent and special status is emblematic of the rise of the Prophet's model as embodying not just spiritual but legal authority.

The distinction drawn between Prophetic Sunna and other *sunan* constituted an unprecedented and fundamental transformation, albeit one

[46] See, e.g., Quran 3:32, 132; 4:59 (twice), 64, 69, 80; 5:92; 24:54, 56; 33:21; 59:7.

gradual in nature. It was both the result of a marked growth in the Prophet's authority and the cause of further epistemic and pedagogical developments. Epistemic, because the need to know what the Prophet said or did became increasingly crucial for determining what the law was. In addition to the fact that Prophetic Sunna – like other *sunan* – was already central to the Muslims' perception of model behavior and good conduct, it was gradually realized that this Sunna had an added advantage in that it constituted part of Quranic hermeneutics; i.e., to know how the Quran was relevant to a particular case. To know how it was to be interpreted, Prophetic verbal and practical discourse, often emulated by the Companions, was needed. And pedagogical, because, in order to maintain a record of what the Prophet said or did, approved or disapproved, certain sources had to be mined, and this information, once collected, needed in turn to be imparted to others as part of the age-old oral tradition of the Arabs, now imbued with a religious element.

Along with the Prophet's Companions, the story-tellers contributed to the crystallization of the first stage of Prophetic dicta. Both of these groups constituted the sources from which the Prophetic biography, in both its real and legendary forms, was derived. At this early stage, however, all Prophetic information was practice-based, oral, fluid and mixed with non-Prophetic material. On the other hand, the men and women who had been close to the Prophet, especially those who had interacted with him on a daily basis, could speak in real and credible terms of details of the Prophet's life. They knew him intimately and they knew the Quran equally well. These persons – together with the story-tellers – kept the memory of the Prophet alive, and it was these people and the information they stored in their minds and imaginations that became important for another group of Muslims: the legists (who were often story-tellers themselves).

The early Muslim leadership – caliphs, Companions, military commanders and men of social standing and charisma – acted within a social fabric inherited from tribal Arab society, in which forging social consensus before reaching a decision or taking an action was normative practice. This is one of the most significant facts about the early Muslim polity and society. In the spirit of this social consensus, people sought to conform to the group, and to avoid swerving from its will or normative practice, as embodied in a cumulative history of action and specific manners of conduct. What their fathers were perceived to have done or said was as important as, if not more important than, what their living peers might say or do. When an important decision was to be taken, be it by a caliph or a *qāḍī*, a precedent, a *sunna*, was nearly always sought. It should not then be surprising that the Prophet's own actions were largely rooted in certain practices, mostly those deemed to have fallen within the province of *sunan*.

Thus, when the Quran lacked relevant or obvious provisions, the natural thing to do was to look for leading models of behavior or a collective conduct perceived to have been a good course of action. It is not unexpected therefore that the Prophet's *sīra* should have been the focus of such a search, for he was the most central figure of the Muslim community, the Umma. It was this constant pursuit of a model combined with available Prophetic dicta (accumulated during the first few decades after Muhammad's death) that explains the emergence by the 60s/680s of a specialized interest in his Sunna. This is not to say, however, that the Prophetic Sunna replaced, except in a slow and gradual fashion, other sources of authority, or that it was committed to writing at an early date. By this time, Prophetic Sunna was, among the available *sunan*, no more than a *primus inter pares*, used by *qāḍīs* along with the *sunan* of Abū Bakr, ʿUmar I, ʿUthmān, ʿAlī and other Companions. In fact, reference to non-Prophetic *sunan* continued to be made for long thereafter.

Apart from this repertoire of *sunan* and the superior Quran, the *qāḍīs* and caliphs also relied heavily on considered opinion, which was, during the entire first Islamic century and part of the next, a major source of legal reasoning and thus of judicial rulings. But considered opinion was not always restricted to personal, individual reasoning. Around 65/684, Shurayḥ was reportedly asked by another judge about the value of criminal damages for causing the loss of any of the hand's five fingers, and in particular whether or not they are of equal value. Shurayḥ answered: "I have not heard from any one of the people of *raʾy* that any of the fingers is better than the other."[47] Here, "the people of *raʾy*" are persons whose judgment and wisdom is to be trusted and, more importantly, emulated. In Shurayḥ's usage, *raʾy*, or considered opinion, comes very close to the notion of *sunna* from which, in this case, *raʾy* cannot in fact be separated. Considered opinion was also associated with the notion of consensus, especially when the former emanated from a group or from a collective tribal agreement. Consensual opinion of a group (*ijtamaʿa raʾyuhum ʿalā* ...) provided an authoritative basis not only for action but also for the creation of *sunna*. A new *sunna* might thus be introduced by a caliph on the basis of a unanimous resolution of a (usually influential) group of people. Other forms of consensus might reflect the common, unanimous practice of a community, originally of a tribe and later of a garrison town or a city.

If there was a consensus to be reckoned with, it was that of the learned men who lived in the cities, both the established centers and those that had begun as garrison towns. These men, flourishing between 80 and 120 H

[47] Wakīʿ, *Akhbār*, I, 299.

(c. 700 and 740 AD), were private individuals whose motive for engaging in the study of law was largely a matter of piety. While it is true that a number of these did serve as judges, their study of the law was not necessarily associated with this office or with the benefits or patronage accruing therefrom. Instead, they were driven above all by a profoundly religious commitment to study, and this, among other things, meant the articulation of a law that would in time come to deal with all aspects of social reality. (That they were men of piety did not make them idealists, for their *sunan*, considered opinions and interpretations of the Quran were not only practice-based but largely positivist commodities placed in the service of the very society that gave rise to these products.)

Intense personal study of religious narratives was largely a private endeavor, but it overlapped and mutually complemented the scholarly activity in the specialized circles of learning (*ḥalaqa*s), usually held in the mosques. Some circles were exclusively concerned with Quranic interpretation, while others were occupied with Prophetic narrative (to emerge later as Prophetic Sunna). Yet, a number of circles were of an exclusively juristic nature, led by and attracting the most distinguished legal specialists in the lands of Islam. The scholars of the legal circles were acknowledged as having excelled in law, then termed *fiqh* or *ʿilm*. Some of these scholars possessed a special mastery of Quranic law, especially inheritance, while others were known for their outstanding competence in ritual law or in *sunan*.

During the period in question, the eminent legal specialists conducted their activities in the major centers of the new empire, namely, Medina, Mecca, Kūfa, Baṣra, Damascus, Fusṭāṭ, the Yemen and, marginally, Khurāsān. The Hejaz and Iraq claimed the lion's share of these activities, generating close to 70 percent of the entire body of legal scholarship.[48] Early legal scholarship was thus conducted where the Arabs, together with their Arabicized clients, constituted a significant proportion of the population.[49]

The activities of the legal specialists initiated what was to become a fundamental principle of Islamic law, namely, that legal knowledge as an *epistemic* quality was to be the final arbiter in law-making. They made piety itself an integral part of this knowledge, for piety dictated behavior in keeping with the Quran and the good example of the predecessors' *sunan*. Those who made it their concern to articulate and impart legal knowledge acquired both a special social status and a position of privileged epistemic authority. In other words, those men in possession of a greater store of

[48] Hallaq, *Origins*, 65.
[49] For more on this, see Motzki, "Role of Non-Arab Converts," 293–317.

knowledge grew more influential than others less learned, gaining in the process – by the sheer virtuousness of their knowledge – exclusive authority as legists. Irrespective of their economic or ethnic background, the legal scholars emerged as distinguished leaders, men of integrity and rectitude, by virtue of their knowledge and personal conduct. This epistemic and moral authority became a defining feature of Islamic law.

The emergence of legal specialists was one development that got under way once Muslims began engaging in religious discussions, story-telling and instruction in the circles. Another, concomitant development, starting during the 60s/680s and continuing long thereafter, was the emergence of Prophetic authority as a legal source independent of other narratives and model practices. The Prophetic model may have, *in terms of authority*, challenged and competed with other *sunan* as well as with *ra'y* but it was more often the case that the *sunan* and the *ra'y* constituted the subject-matter from which the content of Prophetic narrative was itself derived. Prophetic *ḥadīth* was a logical substitution for these sources, since the latter – by virtue of the Companions' intimate knowledge of the Prophet – represented for Muslims an immediate extension of the former.

The dramatic increase in Prophetic authority at the turn of the second/eighth century involved projecting on Muhammad post-Prophetic *sunan* as well. Legal practices and doctrines originating in various towns and cities in the conquered lands, and largely based on the Companions' model, began to find a representational voice in Prophetic Sunna. The projection of the Companions' model back onto the Prophet was accomplished by a long and complex process of creating the narrative of *ḥadīth*. Part of this narrative consisted in the Companions' recollection of what the Prophet had said or done, but another part of it involved extending the chain of authority back to the Prophet when it in fact had previously ended with a Companion. The creation of massive quantities of *ḥadīth* – including fabrications that had little to do with the acknowledged, continuous tradition of legal practice – began to compete not only with Arabian, caliphal and Companion *sunan*, but also with those of the Prophet that had become the basis of legal practice.

Until recently, Western scholarship subscribed to the view that the rise of this genre signified the emergence of Islamic law out of secular beginnings, or what has been termed the "administrative" and "popular" practices of the Umayyads.[50] In other words, law could become Islamicized only upon the creation of a link between secular legal doctrine and the verbal

[50] Schacht, *Origins*, 190–213; Schacht, *Introduction*, 23–27.

expression of Prophetic Sunna, namely, the *ḥadīth*. This view can be validated only if it is assumed that the *sunan* that appeared prior to Prophetic *ḥadīth* were not conceived by the new Muslims as being religious in nature, that they were disconnected from any religious element that may be defined as Islamic, however rudimentary. But this would be to assume wrongly, since the *sunan*, which preeminently included Prophetic *sīra* and Sunna, were indeed religious and furthermore were inspired by the early Muslims' interpretation of what Islam meant to them. They also included the *sunan* of the Companions and early caliphs and these must be seen, *on their own*, as representations of Islam's religious experience. The very process by which these *sunan* were projected back onto, and subsumed under, the Prophetic authority in itself attests to the significant level of their Islamic content.

While Prophetic *sunan* and *sīra* had existed from the very beginning, it is undeniable that much of the *ḥadīth* was inauthentic, representing accretions and significant additions to this Prophetic history that the early Muslims knew. Masses of *ḥadīth*s, all of them equipped with their own chains of transmission, were put into circulation throughout Muslim lands, but they often contradicted the memory and practice of Muslim communities in some regions. Nowhere was this more obvious than in the case of the Hejaz, especially Medina, where the legal scholars believed that their memory of the Prophet's actions – performed there as part of his Sunna – still survived amongst them. For these scholars, the Prophetic Sunna and their own practice were identical, and reference to one was nearly always a reference to the other, although it was often the case that the Prophetic example was both implied and even taken for granted rather than explicitly mentioned.

With the rapid proliferation of *ḥadīth* narratives during the course of the second/eighth century, significant differences between *ḥadīth* and Prophetic Sunna began to manifest themselves – especially to those living in the Prophet's homeland. For the Hejazis, these *ḥadīth* had little to do with what they viewed as the "true" and "authentic" Sunna preserved by the actual practice of their own community. For Medinan scholars then, the true Sunna of the Prophet was attested by their own practice, and not by a literary narrative that had nothing to commend it except its own self-affirmation. The continuous practice of the Medinans, as reflected in the cumulative, common opinion of the scholars, became the final arbiter in determining the content of the Prophet's Sunna. The literary narrative of *ḥadīth* acquired validity only to the extent that it was supported by this local usage.[51] The Medinese scholars' conception was that *their own* practice represented the

[51] Mālik, *Muwaṭṭa'*, 664, 665, 690, 698, and *passim*.

logical and historical (and therefore legitimate) continuation of what the Prophet lived, said and did, and that the newly circulating *ḥadīth*s were at best redundant when they confirmed this practice and, at worst, false when they did not accord with the Prophetic past as continuously documented by their own living experience of the law.

Nor was the Iraqian concept of Prophetic Sunna always expressed in *ḥadīth* from the Prophet. Their *sunna* was embedded in the legal realia of practice and, like that of Medina, it did not always need to be identified as Prophetic. It was nearly always understood to have emanated from the Prophetic past, although the scope of this past often exceeded that of the Prophet himself to include the experience of some of his Companions. The Iraqians, in other words, also saw themselves as connected through their own practice, or "living tradition," with the Prophetic past via an appeal to the Companions, many of whom had left the Hejaz to settle in the garrison towns of southern Iraq and elsewhere.

This picture of legal practice as Prophetic Sunna is representative of developments at least until the end of the second century (c. 815 AD). Each locale, from Syria to Iraq to the Hejaz, established its own legal practices on the basis of what was regarded as the *sunna* of the forefathers, be they the Companions or the Prophet, although the Prophet more often than not merely sanctioned the ancient Arabian *sunan*. The pre-Islamic *sunan* adopted by the Prophet, like those *sunan* sanctioned by the post-Prophetic generations, became lodged within the realm of Prophetic authority. The Prophet, in time, was to emerge as the single axis of this authority.

The central phenomenon associated with the rise of an exclusive Prophetic authority was the proliferation of formal *ḥadīth* which came to compete with the practice-based *sunan* – what we call here *sunna*ic practice. The competition was thus between a formal and nearly universal conception of the Prophetic model and those local practices that had their own view of the nature of Prophetic Sunna. With the emergence of a mobile class of traditionists, whose main occupation was the collection and reproduction of Prophetic narrative, the formal, literary transmission of *ḥadīth* quickly gained the upper hand over *sunna*ic practice. The traditionists were not necessarily jurists or judges, and their impulse was derived more from a religious ethic than from the demands and realities of legal practice. Nevertheless, at the end of the day, their *ḥadīth* project proved victorious, leaving behind as distant second the local conceptions of Prophetic Sunna – a Sunna that did not have the overwhelmingly personal connection to the Prophet claimed by the traditionist version. That many local jurists participated in the traditionist project to the detriment of their own *sunna*ic practice is eloquent testimony to the power of the newly emerging *ḥadīth*.

By the end of the second/eighth century, it had become clear that the traditionist movement was in a position to achieve significant victory over *sunna*ic practice, a victory that would be complete about half a century – or more – later. For Shāfiʿī (d. 204/820), who was one of the most vocal *ḥadīth* protagonists of his day, Prophetic Sunna could be determined only through formal *ḥadīth*. He attacked the *sunna*ic practice as a mass of inconsistencies, decidedly inferior to what he saw as the authentic *ḥadīth* of the Prophet. The most distinctive feature of his theory was the paramount importance of *ḥadīth*, which he took to override the authority of Iraqian, Medinese and Syrian *sunna*ic practices. Yet, his insistence on the supremacy of Prophetic *ḥadīth* (and the Quran) as the paramount sources of the law did not gain immediate acceptance, contrary to what some modern scholars have argued.[52] It took until more than half a century after his death for the *ḥadīth* to become (with the Quran, of course) the exclusive material source of the law, thereby once and for all trumping *sunna*ic practice.[53]

During the first two centuries of Islam, the concept of *sunna*ic practice could hardly be distinguished from consensus, since the sanctioning authority of the former resided in the overwhelming agreement of the legal specialists who collectively upheld this practice. As an expression of *sunna*ic practice, consensus was seen not only as binding but also as determinative of *ḥadīth*. It was not conceived merely as "the agreement of recognized jurists during a particular age," a definition that became standard in later legal theory. Rather, consensus during this early period strongly implied the agreement of scholars based on continuous practice which was, in turn, based on the consensus of the Companions. It should be stressed here that the latter was viewed as essential to the process of grounding later doctrine in Prophetic authority, since the consensus of the Companions, *ipso facto*, was an attestation of Prophetic practice and intent. The Companions, after all, could not have unanimously approved a matter that the Prophet had rejected or prohibited. Nor, in the conception of early jurists, could they have pronounced impermissible what the Prophet had declared lawful.

Throughout the second/eighth century (and for decades thereafter), the legally minded employed *raʾy* in their reasoning. Whether based on knowledge of *sunna*ic practice or not, *raʾy* encompassed a variety of

[52] Spectorsky, "*Sunnah*," 51–74.

[53] But not among the Mālikites who continued to uphold a revised form of Medinese *sunna*ic-consensual practice; Bājī, *Iḥkām*, 480–85.

inferential methods that ranged from loose reasoning to arguments of a strictly logical type, such as analogy or the *argumentum a fortiori*. The Medinese, the Iraqians and the Syrians made extensive use of it during the second/eighth century, subsuming under it nearly all forms of argument. By the beginning of the second/eighth century, more sophisticated techniques of reasoning began to surface, although many of the old, and somewhat archaic, juristic formulations were not phased out completely. *Ra'y*, therefore, became the umbrella term for a wide variety of legal arguments, and it remained for nearly a century thereafter the standard term designating legal inferences.

During the second half of the second/eighth century, a new generation of scholars was reared in an environment permeated by Prophetic *ḥadīth*, which had come to assert, more than at any time before, the personal authority of the Prophet. The more pronounced this authority became, the less freedom the jurists had in expounding discretionary opinion. For after all, the *raison d'être* of Prophetic authority was its ability to induce conformity of conduct to the Prophetic model. Insofar as it included discretionary and personal opinion, *ra'y* frequently – though not always – stood as antithetical to this notion of authority.

Because it included what later came to be considered loose methods of reasoning, *ra'y* inevitably acquired negative connotations and as a result suffered a significant decline in reputation toward the end of the second/eighth century. It was not fortuitous that this decline coincided with the rise of *ḥadīth* as an incontestable expression of Prophetic Sunna. The latter, in other words, could leave no room for reasoning not based on textual evidence, demanding that a choice be made between human and Prophetic/Divine authority. Non-textual *ra'y* obviously was no match for the Sunna.

By the middle of the second century (c. 770 AD), and long before *ḥadīth* asserted itself as an unrivaled entity, *ra'y* had already incorporated systematic and logical arguments of the first order, arguments that were in turn far from devoid of Sunnaic support. These types of argument were too valuable to be jettisoned, and so had to be protected as valid forms of reasoning. In a gradual process of terminological change that began immediately after the middle of the second/eighth century and which reached its zenith sometime before the middle of the next century, *ra'y* appears to have been broken down into three categories of argument, all of which had originally been offshoots of the core notion.

The most general of these categories was *ijtihād*, which term, during the first/seventh and most of the second/eighth century, appeared frequently in conjunction with *ra'y*, namely, as *ijtihād al-ra'y*, which meant the exertion of mental energy for the sake of arriving, through reasoning, at a considered opinion. Later, when the term *ra'y* was dropped from the combination, *ijtihād* came to stand alone for this same meaning, though this terminological transformation was short-lived.

The second category of arguments to emerge out of *ra'y* was *qiyās*, signifying disciplined and systematic reasoning on the basis of the revealed texts, the Quran and *ḥadīth*. In addition to analogy, its archetypal form, *qiyās* encompassed the *a fortiori* argument in both of its forms – the *a maiore ad minus* and the *a minore ad maius*. For example, if uttering an impolite word before one's parents is prohibited by the Quran, then striking them would obviously be equally prohibited. The same is the case with selling wine: if drinking it is unlawful, then selling it, though less offensive, would be equally impermissible.[54]

Another argument under the heading of *ra'y* was *istiḥsān*, commonly translated as "juristic preference." We have no adequate definition of this reasoning method from the period before Shāfiʿī, most of our knowledge of it being derived either from Shāfiʿī's polemics against it (hardly trustworthy) or from late Ḥanafite theoretical reconstructions of it (which involved an ideological remapping of legal history). It seems, however, safe to characterize the second/eighth-century meaning of *istiḥsān* as a mode of reasoning that yields reasonable results, unlike strictly logical inference such as *qiyās* which may lead to an undue hardship. But it was also employed as a method of achieving equity, driven by reasonableness, fairness or/and common sense. For example, according to strict reasoning, punishment for thievery (cutting off the hand) is to be inflicted on the person who moved the stolen goods from the "place of custody" (*ḥirz*), irrespective of whether or not he had accomplices.[55] According to *istiḥsān*, if several people have committed theft, even though only one person moved the stolen object from its *ḥirz*, they must all face the same penalty.[56] This latter mode of reasoning was deemed preferable, for since the rationale of punishment in Islamic law is deterrence, all participating thieves should be held accountable. However, like *ra'y*, which acquired a bad name because it included personal opinions that lacked formal grounding in the revealed texts, *istiḥsān* too was rejected. But unlike *ra'y*, it survived in the later Ḥanafite and Ḥanbalite schools as a secondary method of reasoning, though not without ingenious ways of theoretical rehabilitation.[57]

One jurist whose writings exemplify the transition from what we may call the pre-*ḥadīth* to the *ḥadīth* period was Shāfiʿī, a champion of

[54] Mālik, *Muwaṭṭa'*, 737–39. [55] For later doctrine, see chapter 10, section 2, below.
[56] Cited in Ansari, "Islamic Juristic Terminology," 294.
[57] Hallaq, *History*, 107–13. See also Makdisi, "Ibn Taymīya's Autograph," 446–79.

Prophetic narrative as an exclusive substitute for *sunna*ic practice. His writings manifest a stage of development in which *ra'y* met with the first major attack in an offensive that ultimately led to its ouster (terminologically and to a certain extent substantively) from Islamic jurisprudence. Categorically labeling *ra'y* as arbitrary, he excluded it, along with *istiḥsān*, from the domain of reasoning altogether. *Ḥadīth* on the other hand reflected, for him, divine authority, leaving no room for human judgment except as a method of inference, which he interchangeably called *qiyās*/*ijtihād*.

Shāfiʿī appears to have been the first jurist consciously to articulate the notion that Islamic revelation provides a full and comprehensive evaluation of human acts. The admittance of *qiyās* (*ijtihād*) into his jurisprudence was due to his recognition of the fact that divine intent is not completely fulfilled by the revealed texts themselves, since these latter do not afford a *direct* answer to every eventuality. But to Shāfiʿī, acknowledging the permissibility of *qiyās* does not bestow on it a status independent of revelation. If anything, without revelation's sanction of the use of this method it would not be allowed, and when it is permitted to operate, it is because *qiyās* is the only method that can bring out the meaning and intention of revelation regarding a particular eventuality. *Qiyās* does not itself generate rules or legal norms; it merely discovers them from, or brings them out of, the language of revealed texts. This theory was to become the basis of all later legal theories, elaborated under the rubric of *uṣūl al-fiqh*.

5. Evolution of the judiciary

By the close of the second century H, the *qāḍī*'s court had taken its final shape. All the basic personnel and logistical features had been introduced by this point, so that the size of each court was a function of the business arising before the court. A *qāḍī* might have one, two or more scribes depending on the size of his court and the demands placed on it, but the scribe's function itself was by then integral to the proceedings, whatever their magnitude. The same went for all other court officials and functions.

As early as the 130s/750s, witness examiners became a fully established institution.[58] Its beginnings appear several decades earlier, when the proto-*qāḍī*s needed to enquire into the rectitude of witnesses who either testified to the claims of litigants or attested to the legal records, contracts, and nearly all transactions passing through the court. Once the examiners

[58] Wakīʿ, *Akhbār*, III, 106, 138.

were satisfied, the judge appointed these witnesses to the court.[59] Thus, by this time, witnesses had become not only a fixture of the court but also paid employees of the *qāḍī*, who always controlled the budget of the court.

The court's prestige and authority were enhanced by the presence in it of men learned in the law. These, we have seen, were the legal specialists (*fuqahā'*, *muftī*s) who, mostly out of piety, made the study and understanding (lit. *fiqh*) of religious law their primary private concern, and it was this knowledge that lent them authority.[60] The sources are frequently unclear as to whether or not these specialists were always physically present in the court, but we know that from the beginning of the second century (c. 720 AD) judges were encouraged to seek the counsel of these learned men and that, by the 120s/740s, they often did.[61] It is fairly certain that the legal specialists were regularly consulted on difficult cases and points of law, although evidence of their *permanent* physical presence in the court is meager. The practice of consulting trained jurists was therefore normative, although it was not necessarily required by any official political authority. In Andalusia, on the other hand, soliciting the opinions of legal specialists was mandatory, insisted upon by both the legal profession and the political sovereign. There, a judge's decision was considered invalid without the prior approval of the learned jurists.

The court's personnel also included a number of assistants (*a'wān*) who performed a variety of tasks. One of these was the *jilwāz*, the court chamberlain, whose function it was to maintain order in the court, including supervising the queue of litigants and calling upon various persons to appear before the judge. Some courts whose jurisdiction included regions inhabited by various ethnic and linguistic groups were also staffed by an interpreter or dragoman.

In addition to witnesses, chamberlains, and often legal specialists, the courts also used the services of other functionaries, generally known as the *qāḍī*'s assistants. Among these were men whose function it was to search out and apprehend persons charged with a felony or to bring in defendants against whom a plaintiff had presented the court with a claim. They were also sent out by the judge to look for witnesses who might have seen, for example, an illegal act being committed. It is possible that at times these functions were discharged in part by the court examiner himself, although we have reason to believe that, in larger courts dealing with a considerable volume of cases, there would have been other officials assigned specifically to perform such tasks. Some of these assistants specialized in "public calling," thus acquiring the technical title *munādī*s. These *munādī*s usually

[59] *Ibid.*, III, 422, 494. [60] Hallaq, *Authority*, ix, 166–235.
[61] Wakī', *Akhbār*, II, 423; III, 86. See also chapter 4, section 3, below.

appeared in markets and public spaces, communicating the *qāḍī*'s messages to the public on court-related matters. They also summoned to court certain individuals, sought either as witnesses or as defendants.

The judge's assistants also included a number of *umanāʾ al-ḥukm* (lit. trustees of the court) whose tasks involved the safekeeping of confidential information, property and even cash. One such official was responsible for the court's treasury, known as the *tābūt al-quḍāt* (the judge's security chest). Its location was in the state Treasury but the key to it remained with the judge and/or his trustee. All sorts of monies were kept in it, especially those belonging to heirless deceased persons, to orphans and to absentees.[62]

Another trustee, the *qassām*, was responsible for dividing cash and property among heirs or disputed objects among litigants. This official was usually hired for his technical skills and knowledge of arithmetic. Last, but by no means least, a major official of the court was the judge's scribe (*kātib*), who usually sat immediately to the right or left of the judge, recorded the statements, rebuttals and depositions of the litigants, and, moreover, drew up legal documents on the basis of court records for those who needed the attestation of the judge to one matter or another. His appointment to the court appears to have been the first to be made when a new judge assumed office, and he was required to be of just character, to know the law and to be skilled in the art of writing.[63]

The scribe's function was closely linked with the rise of the institution of the *dīwān*, which represented the totality of the records written by the scribe, kept by the judge and normally filed in a bookcase.[64] The *dīwān* usually contained records of actions and claims made by two parties in the presence of the judge, who typically signed them before witnesses. It also contained: (a) records of statements made by witnesses to the effect that a certain action, such as a sale or a pledge, had taken place; (b) a list of court witnesses whose just character was confirmed; (c) a register of trustees over *waqf* properties, orphans' affairs and divorcees' alimonies; (d) a register of bequests;[65] (e) copies of contracts, pledges, acknowledgments, gifts, donations and written obligations as well as other written instruments;[66] (f) copies of letters sent to, and received from, other judges, including any relevant legal documents attached to such letters;[67] and (g) several other types of registers, such as a record of prisoners' names

62 Kindī, *Akhbār*, 405. 63 Hallaq, "*Qāḍī*'s *Dīwān*," 423.
64 Wakīʿ, *Akhbār*, II, 159; Ibn al-Najjār, *Muntahā*, II, 582.
65 Kindī, *Akhbār*, 379; Qalqashandī, *Ṣubḥ*, X, 284.
66 Wakīʿ, *Akhbār*, II, 136; Kindī, *Akhbār*, 319, 379; al-Ḥusām al-Shahīd, *Sharḥ*, 57–62; on written obligations, see Thung, "Written Obligations," 1–12.
67 Kindī, *Akhbār*, 410; Samarqandī, *Rusūm*, 46.

and the terms of their imprisonment, a list of guarantors (*kufalāʾ*), and a list of those possessing powers of attorney.[68]

The *dīwān* was acknowledged to be the backbone of legal transactions and the means by which the judge could review his decisions as well as all cases and transactions passing through his court. It therefore embodied the complete record of the judge's work in the court, and represented the chief tool by which judicial practice preserved its continuity. By the middle of the second/eighth century, it had become the established practice of outgoing judges to deliver their *dīwān*s over to the newly appointed *qāḍī*s succeeding them, a practice that was to undergo gradual change thereafter when, beginning with the last decade of the second century (805–815 AD) or thereabouts, the new judge began his duties by having his scribe copy the *dīwān* of his predecessor. This transfer or copying was normally the second step taken by the judge upon receiving investiture, the first being his appointment of a scribe.

Whatever the means of transferring the *dīwān*, access to predecessors' records was essential not only for continuing the new judge's work in protracted cases but also for reviewing the work of earlier judges, especially the immediate predecessor. Such a review was usually prompted either by complaints against the outgoing judge or by credible suspicion on the part of the new judge of abuse, corruption or one form or another of miscarriage of justice that might be associated with his predecessor. It was access to the *dīwān*s that allowed judicial review in Islam to take on a meaningful role, a role that was, to some limited extent, equivalent to the practice of appeal in Western judicial systems.[69]

In addition to arbitrating disputes and deciding cases,[70] the *qāḍī* supervised the performance of all his assistants and deputies, and engaged in the following extra-judicial activities: (a) supervision of charitable trusts (*awqāf*), their material condition, their maintenance and the performance of those who managed them; (b) acting as guardian for orphans, administering their financial affairs and caring for their general well-being; (c) attending to the property of absentees, as well as that of anyone who died heirless; (d) hearing petitions for conversion from other religions to Islam, and signing witnessed documents to this effect for the benefit of new Muslims; (e) attending to public works; and (f) leading Friday prayers and prayers at funerals, as well as announcing the rising of the moon, which signaled the end of the Ramadan fast.[71]

[68] Hallaq, "*Qāḍī*'s *Dīwān*," 421, 428–29; Qalqashandī, *Ṣubḥ*, X, 274, 291–92; Samarqandī, *Rusūm*, 34, 39 ff.

[69] On non-formal venues of appeal within the Sharīʿa, see Gradeva, "On Judicial Hierarchy."

[70] Wakīʿ, *Akhbār*, II, 415; III, 89, 135.

[71] Wakīʿ, *Akhbār*, II, 58, 65; Kindī, *Akhbār*, 383, 424, 444, 450.

Sometime after the middle of the second/eighth century, there appeared a new set of tribunals that stood at the margins of the Sharīʿa courts. These were the *maẓālim* (lit. "courts of grievances"), generally instated by governors and viziers, theoretically on behalf of the caliph, and presumably for the purpose of correcting wrongs committed by state officials. Theoretically, too, they were sanctioned by the powers assigned to a ruler to establish justice and equity according to the religious law (*siyāsa sharʿiyya*).[72] At times, however, they represented absolutist governance and interference in the Sharīʿa, however marginal this may have been given that the jurisdiction of these tribunals was both limited and sporadic.

The *maẓālim* tended to apply a wide range of procedural laws – wider, at any rate, than those adopted by the Sharīʿa court judges.[73] They seem also to have been far less stringent about testimonial evidence, admitting, for instance, coerced statements and issuing summary judgments. Their penalties, furthermore, exceeded the prescribed laws of the Sharīʿa. They thus applied penal sanctions in civil cases, or combined civil and criminal punishments in one and the same case. Yet, the *maẓālim* tribunals functioned less as an encroachment on the Sharīʿa courts than as a supplement to their jurisdiction. Characterized as courts of equity, where the sovereign showed himself to be conducting justice, the *maẓālim* tribunals operated within four main spheres: (a) they dealt with claims against government employees who transgressed the boundaries of their duties and who committed wrongs against the public, such as unlawful appropriation of private property; (b) they prosecuted injustices committed in the performance of public services, such as unfair or oppressive collection of taxes, or non-payment of salaries by government agencies; (c) they heard complaints against Sharīʿa judges that dealt mainly with questions of conduct, including abuses of office and corruption; and (d) they enforced Sharīʿa court decisions that the *qāḍī* was unable to carry out. It is noteworthy that *maẓālim* tribunals did not arrogate to themselves the power to hear appeals against Sharīʿa court decisions which, as we have seen, were to all intents and purposes final.[74]

6. The great rationalist–traditionalist synthesis

Thus far we have seen that by the beginning of the third/ninth century, the judiciary had reached a mature stage of development, with all its essential features having taken final shape. By this time, substantive law had also

[72] More on *siyāsa sharʿiyya*, see chapter 5, section 3, below. [73] Māwardī, *Aḥkām*, 74–75.
[74] For a discussion of successor review, see Powers, "Judicial Review," 315–41; and, briefly, in chapter 12, section 1, below. Further on the *maẓālim* tribunals, see chapter 5, section 2, below.

become more comprehensive and highly detailed in coverage.[75] Yet, the dawn of the third/ninth century marked the beginning of a second phase of evolution that was nearly as long as the first. Put differently, while legal developments during the first two centuries of Islam were no mean feat, they were only the foundation of what was to be erected later. For there remained two absolutely essential and fundamental features of the law that had yet to emerge, or at least had not done so in a mature form. And it was not until much later that these two features took final hold and shape. These features were, first, the emergence – out of the Great Synthesis – of an integral theory of law and, second, the formation of the doctrinal schools (to be discussed in the next section). We first turn to the arrival of the Great Synthesis, without which no legal theory (indeed no Sunnism) could have emerged.

We may recall that the traditionalist movement (*ahl al-ḥadīth*) gained momentum toward the end of the second/eighth century, thereby pushing further aside the school of *ra'y* which, not long before, had enjoyed a strong position in the articulation of the law. By the middle of the third/ninth century, *ḥadīth* achieved further victories against *ra'y*, leaving it trailing behind. Long before this century ended, there emerged six "canonical" *ḥadīth* collections, designed – in their contents and arrangement – to service the law. Furthermore, a clear pattern of scholarly affiliation with these two movements began to manifest itself. Whereas a few jurists of the second/eighth century were seen as traditionalists (and many of these acquired such descriptions posthumously, decades after the century came to a close), the third/ninth century produced more traditionalists and traditionists than rationalists, and they were clearly identified as such. It is also significant that, during this century, migration (or conversion) from the rationalist to the traditionalist camp was frequent, whereas movement in the opposite direction was rare to non-existent. While we are unable to unearth examples of conversion to the rationalist camp from this century, the sources tell of such movement for the preceding century.[76]

After the close of the second/eighth century, exclusive affiliation to one or the other camp became the general rule, clearly marking the gap between the two approaches. By the end of the third/ninth century, on the other hand, most jurists are reported to have combined the two in some way, and Muslim historians and biographers make it a point to mention this Synthesis in the biographies of jurists flourishing during that period. A century later, only a few are described as exclusively

[75] See Part II, below. [76] Ibn Khallikān, *Wafayāt*, I, 342.

belonging to one camp or the other. Indeed, few jurists who lived before and after this period are described as having "combined" the methods of the two camps. In other words, this designation was most relevant during the period in question, and for good reason.

The intellectual and legal history of Islam between 150 and 350 H (c. 770 and 960 AD) represents a dynamic competition among several forces that crystallized in the opposing movements of traditionalism and rationalism, movements out of which emerged the Great Synthesis. During most of the third/ninth century, the traditionalist movement opposed rationalism, including its method of *qiyās*. The Inquisition (Miḥna), pursued by the caliphs and rationalist scholars between 218/833 and 234/848, was about whether or not the Quran was created, but perhaps even more about the role of human reason in interpreting the divine texts. The final defeat of the rationalists implied (and in effect consisted of) an acknowledgment that human reason could not stand on its own as a central, much less exclusive, method of interpretation but had rather to operate solely, in the final analysis, in the service of revelation. The defeat, therefore, was relative, with the Miḥna marking the climax of a struggle between two opposing movements, namely, the traditionalists, whose cause Ibn Ḥanbal was seen to champion, and the rationalists, headed by the caliphs and the Muʿtazilites, among whom there were many Ḥanafites. The forms that these two movements took by the end of the Miḥna represented the most extreme positions in the religious/hermeneutical spectrum, and if conflict between them was about anything fundamental, it was, at the end of the day, about interpretation.

Most jurists subscribed to neither of the two positions as they emerged at the end of the Miḥna or even later. The traditionalism of Ibn Ḥanbal was seen as too austere and rigid, and the rationalism of the Muʿtazila and their supporters among the *ahl al-raʾy* as too libertarian. When Ibn Ḥanbal and the traditionalists won the Miḥna, moreover, they did not prevail on account of their interpretive stand, nor by virtue of their doctrinal and intellectual strength (although their tenacious piety no doubt won them popular admiration). Rather, their victory was due in part to the weakening of pronounced rationalism and in part to the withdrawal of political support from a stance that was becoming unpopular. Hence, the limited success of the traditionalists was largely a function of the weakness of the rationalists. Indeed, the conflict represented by the Miḥna meant that extreme forms of traditionalism and rationalism did not appeal to the majority of Muslims. It was the mid-point between the two movements that constituted the normative position of the majority; and it was from this centrist position that Sunnism, the religious and legal ideology of the majority of Muslims, was to emerge. The middle point between rationalism and traditionalism was thus the happy synthesis that emerged and continued, for centuries thereafter, to represent the normative Sunnite position. The end of the Miḥna was the take-off point of this Synthesis. By the middle of the fourth/tenth century, the Synthesis was fully in place. Therefore, it was not the defeat of rationalism or the absolute victory of traditionalism that underpinned the emergence of *uṣūl al-fiqh*, but rather a redefinition and methodical disciplining of the former and the rise and dramatic increase of the latter.

The Synthesis, we have said, was a process that began toward the very end of the second/eighth century and the beginning of the next, when Prophetic *ḥadīth* asserted itself as a competitor to *ra'y* and even to regional legal practice. The internationalization of legal scholarship – i.e., the intense geographical mobility of legal scholars within the wide expanse of Muslim territory, from Andalusia in the west to Transoxiana in the east – began early on, but became a truly normative practice by the end of the second/eighth century. And with this crucial phenomenon in place, loyalty to the *sunna*ic practice diminished. A scholar who traveled far and wide found the variations in regional *sunna*ic practice difficult, if not impossible, to transpose. The Islamicization of such regions as Khurāsān or Transoxiana could not depend on the *sunna*ic practices of the Kūfans, Baṣrans or Medinese. A universally transmitted *ḥadīth* from the Prophet proved more appealing as a material and textual source of the law than the living, *sunna*ic practice as defined by a specific city or legal community, since the latter had developed their own judicial and juristic peculiarities in keeping with their own particular environment. Prophetic *ḥadīth* was free of these peculiarities, and was, as a *textual entity*, more amenable to use in new environments. Medina, Mecca, Kūfa, Baṣra and Damascus ceased to be the only major centers of the Muslim empire, and were rivaled, after the first century of Islam came to a close, by major new centers, such as those in Khurāsān, Transoxiana, Egypt and North Africa. Even the garrison towns finally succumbed to *ḥadīth*, acknowledging that their doctrines could not continue to withstand the mounting pressure from this genre. Their legal doctrine may not have undergone significant change due to the influx of *ḥadīth*, but it needed to be anchored afresh in the rock of this imposing material. The Ḥanafites had to accommodate this new genre no later than in the third/ninth century, and the radical traditionalists had to moderate their ways of thinking as well. Movements ignored the *ḥadīth* and the emergent Synthesis at the peril of extinction. Rationalism, too, had to be met half-way. Ibn Ḥanbal's jurisprudence – restrictive in its ways of reasoning – was soon abandoned by his immediate and later followers. The later Ḥanbalite school adopted not only *qiyās*, abhorrent to Ibn Ḥanbal, but also, in the long run, *istiḥsān*, originally a

Ḥanafite principle that Shāfiʿī had severely attacked as amounting to "human legislation."[77] In other words, for the Ḥanbalite school to survive, it had to move from conservative traditionalism to a mainstream position, one that accepted a synthesis between traditionalism and rationalism. The Ẓāhirite school, by contrast, gradually disappeared from the scene, largely due to its uncompromising insistence on the literalist/traditionalist approach.

By the beginning of the fourth/tenth century, the majority had come to embrace the Synthesis between rationalism and traditionalism. It was with this development that *uṣūl al-fiqh* (legal theory) was at last defined. Expressed differently, though somewhat tautologically, legal theory emerged as a result of this Synthesis, which itself embodied, and was reflected by, this theory. One of the first groups to begin propounding legal theory in its organic and comprehensive form was a circle of Baghdadian Shāfiʿites, headed by the distinguished jurist Ibn Surayj (d. 306/918). He and his disciples were traditionalists, jurists and speculative theologians, a combination that was uncommon in the preceding era, but had by his time become largely normative. This group was to conceptualize legal theory as a synthesis between rationality and the textual tradition, that is, between reason and revelation. Thus, Ibn Surayj must be credited with paving the way for his students, who would discourse on this Synthesis and elaborate it in greater detail. This explains why the first and foremost Shāfiʿite authors to write works on *uṣūl al-fiqh* (as a full-fledged methodology) were his students, such as Abū Bakr al-Fārisī (fl. c. 350/960), Ibn al-Qāṣṣ (d. 335/946), Abū Bakr al-Ṣayrafī (d. 330/942) and al-Qaffāl al-Shāshī (d. 336/947). However, it must be emphasized that the legal theory produced by this circle of scholars was not the product of an ongoing process of elaboration based on an established tradition, as later theory came to be. Instead, it was largely the product of the specific historical process that had begun a century or so earlier, and that had culminated under the influence of the Synthesis formed at the close of the third/ninth century and the first half of the fourth/tenth. Their theory can thus be characterized as the child of its environment, and it owed little more to Shāfiʿī than partial and nominal affiliation. The Ḥanafites, for instance, did not lag far behind in elaborating their own theory of law.

In due course, I will address the process by which the authority of Shāfiʿī as founder of the Shāfiʿite school was both constructed and augmented, but for now it suffices to assert that the achievements of Ibn Surayj, of his

[77] On *istiḥsān*, see next chapter, section 7.

generation and of the generation to follow, were projected back onto Shāfiʿī as the first synthesizer, namely, as the architect of the all-important *uṣūl al-fiqh*. In fact, Shāfiʿī had little to do with the elaboration of *uṣūl al-fiqh*, since he advocated the Synthesis in a rudimentary and incomplete form.[78] And there were others, during the decades after his death, who discoursed on certain aspects of legal methodology and reasoning, usually advocating or refuting one specific position or another. Thus Shāfiʿī's theory was not accepted as a standard[79] by the community of third/ninth-century jurists, while his followers, until Ibn Surayj's time, remained few. It is likely, however, that it was his thesis, however modest, that made it possible for Ibn Surayj and his students to attribute the achievement of *uṣūl al-fiqh* to him.[80] By the middle of the fourth/tenth century, therefore, an elaborate and comprehensive theory of *uṣūl* had emerged. The next century and a half witnessed a phase in the history of this theory that produced the standard works on which later expositions so heavily depended, but the essential developments had already occurred by 350/960 or thereabouts.

7. The formation of legal schools

Concurrently with the emergence of the Great Synthesis, and not entirely dissociated from it, a fourth and final development had taken place, bringing Islamic law to full maturity, or, to put it differently, to the end of the formative period. This development was represented by the full emergence of the doctrinal legal schools, the *madhhab*s, a cardinal evolution that in turn presupposed the rise of various systemic, juristic, educational and judicial elements.[81]

Two stages of development preceded and paved the way for the rise of the doctrinal schools: the first was the stage of study circles and the second the stage of the personal schools. In order to understand this process of evolution, it is perhaps best to begin with a survey of the meanings that are associated with the Arabic term *madhhab*, customarily translated into the English language as "school."

[78] For the order of legal sources (*uṣūl*) in Shāfiʿī, see the important work of Lowry, "Does Shāfiʿī Have a Theory of Four Sources of Law?"; Lowry, "Legal-Theoretical Content of the *Risāla*."

[79] Which *uṣūl al-fiqh* works became after the fourth/tenth century. To appreciate the significance of this assertion, it is important to realize that while later legal genres were consistently defined along school lines (*madhhab*s), *uṣūl al-fiqh* was the only important discourse that was not amenable to *madhhab*ic affiliation. See Hallaq, "*Uṣūl al-Fiqh*: Beyond Tradition," 191–97.

[80] For a detailed discussion of these issues, see Hallaq, "Was al-Shafiʿi the Master Architect?"

[81] On the many aspects of the *madhhab* in Islamic legal history, see the various valuable contributions in the recent work of Bearman *et al.*, eds., *Islamic School of Law*.

Generally, the term *madhhab* means that which is followed and, more specifically, the opinion or idea that one chooses to adopt; hence, a particular opinion of a jurist. Historically, it is of early provenance, probably dating back to the end of the first/seventh century, but certainly to the middle of the second/eighth. By the early third/ninth century, its use had become frequent, although the doctrinal schools – for which the term was later reserved – had not yet emerged.

The term *madhhab* is associated with four meanings that have emerged out of, and subsequent to, this basic usage, and which contributed to, or reflected, the formation of schools. The first of these was the technical meaning of the term as a principle underlying a set of cases subsumed under such a principle. For example, a posited assumption of the Ḥanafites is that misappropriation (*ghaṣb*), in order to obtain, must involve the unlawful removal of property from its original place, where it had been in the possession of the owner.[82] The Ḥanbalites, on the other hand, define misappropriation as mere seizure of property, whether or not it is removed from its original place of ownership. Thus, taking possession of a rug by sitting on it (without removing it) is considered *ghaṣb* by the Ḥanbalites, but not by the Ḥanafites. In terms of recovery of damages, this basic difference in definition contributed to generating significant differences between the two *madhhab*s. Whereas the Ḥanbalites make the wrongdoer (*ghāṣib*) liable to the original owner for all growth of, and proceeds from, the misappropriated object, the Ḥanafites place severe restrictions on the ability of the owner to recover his accruing rights. The reasoning is that the growth or proceeds of the misappropriated property were not yet in existence when the property was "removed" from the hands of the rightful owner, and since they were not in existence, no liability on the part of the *ghāṣib* is deemed to arise. This example illustrates a central meaning of the term *madhhab* as a legal doctrine concerning a group of cases, in this instance cases pertaining to the recovery of damages, which are subsumed under a larger principle. And it is in this sense that it can be said that one school's *madhhab* differs, sometimes significantly, from another's.

The second meaning of *madhhab* represents a combination of the basic meaning outlined above and the first technical meaning, namely, a principle underlying a group of derivative cases, as exemplified in the case of damages. Once jurists consciously developed such principles, it was possible to use the singular term *madhhab* to refer to the collective doctrine of a school or of a *mujtahid*, first with reference to a segment of the

[82] For a treatment of misappropriation (*ghaṣb*), see chapter 9, section 3, below.

law (e.g., the law of misappropriation) and second, by implication, the entirety of a school's, or a *mujtahid*'s, substantive law. Historically, it must be stressed, the reference to a *mujtahid*'s collective doctrine preceded reference to a school, since schools developed out of these *mujtahids*' doctrines.

The third sense of *madhhab* referred to the *mujtahid*'s individual opinion when this enjoys the highest authority in the collective doctrinal corpus of the school, irrespective of whether or not this *mujtahid* was the school's so-called founder. The most fundamental feature of what we will call here "*madhhab*-opinion" was its general and widespread acceptance in practice, as reflected in the courts and *fatwā*s. Thus, when an opinion is characterized as "*al-madhhab*" (with the definite article added), it signifies that that opinion is the standard, normative doctrine of the school, determined as such by the fact that practice is decided in accordance with it. The emergence and use of this term entailed a unanimity of doctrine and practice, which in turn entailed the existence of a school that, by definition, shared a common doctrinal ground.

Finally, the term *madhhab* refers to a group of jurists and legists who are loyal to a distinct, integral and, most importantly, *collective* legal doctrine attributed to an eponym, a master-jurist, so to speak, from whom the school is known to have acquired particular, distinctive characteristics. Thus, after the formation of the schools, jurists began to be characterized as Ḥanafite, Mālikite, Shāfiʿite or Ḥanbalite, as determined by their *doctrinal* (not personal) loyalty to one school or another. This doctrinal loyalty, it must be emphasized, is to a cumulative and accretive body of doctrine constructed by generations of leading jurists, which is to say, conversely, that loyalty is not extended to the individual doctrine of a single jurist-*mujtahid*. This, fourth, meaning of *madhhab* must thus be distinguished from its rudimentary predecessor, namely, a group of jurists who followed (but who, as we shall see, were not necessarily loyal to the doctrine of) a single, leading jurist. The latter's doctrine, furthermore, was not only non-accretive and non-collective (in the sense that it was the product of the labor of a single jurist), but also merely represented a collection of the individual opinions held by that jurist. By the middle of the fourth/tenth century, or shortly thereafter, these meanings were all present, and were used variably in different contexts.

How and when did the concept of *madhhab* evolve from its basic meaning into its highly developed sense of a doctrinal school? As we have already seen,[83] the early interest in law and legal studies evolved within the environment of the study circles, where men learned in the Quran and

[83] In section 4, above, but see also chapter 3, below.

the general principles of Islam began to discuss, among other things, various quasi-legal and often strictly legal issues. By the early part of the second century (c. 720–40 AD), such learned men had already assumed the role of teachers whose circles often encompassed numerous students interested specifically in *fiqh*, the discipline of law. However, by that time, no obvious methodology of law and legal reasoning had yet evolved, so that one teacher's lecture might not have been entirely distinguishable, methodologically and as a body of principles, from another's. Even the body of legal doctrine they taught was not yet complete, as can be attested from each teacher's particular interests. Some taught rules of inheritance, while others emphasized the law of ritual. More importantly, we have little reason to believe that the legal topics covered later were all present at this early stage.

By the middle of the second/eighth century, with substantive law having become more systematic, the jurists had begun to develop their own legal assumptions and methodology. Teaching and intense scholarly debates within study circles must have sharpened methodological awareness, which in turn led jurists to defend their own, individual conceptions of the law. Each jurist, on adopting a particular method, gathered around him a certain following who learned their jurisprudence and method from him.

Yet, it was rare that a student or a young jurist would restrict himself to one circle or one teacher; indeed, it was not uncommon for aspiring jurists to attend several circles in the same city. During the second half of the century, aspiring jurists did not confine themselves to circles within one city, but traveled near and far in search of reputable teachers. Each prominent teacher attracted students who "took *fiqh*" from him. A judge who had studied law under a teacher was likely to apply the teacher's doctrine in his court, although, again, loyalty was not exclusive to a single doctrine. If he proved to be a sufficiently promising and qualified jurist, he might "sit" (*jalasa*) as a professor in his own turn, transmitting to his students the legal knowledge he gained from his teachers, but seldom without his own reconstruction of this knowledge. The legal doctrines that Abū Ḥanīfa, Mālik and Shāfiʿī, among many others, taught to their students were largely a transmission from their own teachers. None of these, however, despite the fact that they were held up as school founders, constructed his own doctrine in its entirety, as later Islamic theoretical discourse would have us believe. Rather, all of them were in fact as much indebted to their teachers as these latter were indebted to their own.

During the second/eighth century, therefore, the term *madhhab* meant a group of students, legists, judges and jurists who had adopted the doctrine of a particular leading jurist, such as Abū Ḥanīfa or Thawrī (d. 161/777) – a phenomenon that I will call here a "personal school." Those who adopted or followed a jurist's doctrine were known as *aṣḥāb*, or associates, namely, those who studied with or were scholarly companions of a jurist. Most leading jurists had *aṣḥāb*, a term that often also meant "followers." Thus, Abū Ḥanīfa, Awzāʿī, Abū Yūsuf and Thawrī, to name only a few, each had *aṣḥāb*, and each was associated with having a *madhhab*, namely, a personal school revolving around both his circle (*ḥalaqa*) and personal doctrine (*fiqh*). This was true even in the cases of Abū Ḥanīfa and his student Abū Yūsuf, each of whom initially had independent followings, even personal *madhhab*s, although these personal *madhhab*s were later brought together under one doctrinal (not personal) *madhhab* – that of the Ḥanafites.[84] (Incidentally, the cases of Abu Ḥanīfa and Abū Yūsuf illustrate and document the development from personal to doctrinal schools.)

Nonetheless, doctrinal loyalty was not yet in order. It was not unusual for a legist to shift from one doctrine to another or simultaneously adopt a combination of doctrines belonging to two or more leading jurists.[85] Around 185/801, for instance, the Egyptian judge Isḥāq b. al-Furāt is said to have combined the doctrines of several jurists, foremost among whom were the Medinese jurist Mālik, whose disciple he was, and the Kūfan Abū Yūsuf.[86] Even after the middle of the third/ninth century, some jurists were not yet sure of their affiliation, a fact that became inconceivable once the doctrinal schools emerged. Muḥammad b. Naṣr al-Marwazī (d. 294/906) was said to have long been unable to decide which doctrine he should follow: that of Shāfiʿī, that of Abū Ḥanīfa or that of Mālik.[87] The fact that he finally adopted Shāfiʿī's doctrine, without combining it with others, is significant, since by his time it had become normative practice to adopt a single doctrine, and the combination of parts of various doctrines had ceased to be acceptable conduct.

Personal schools were not, strictly speaking, either normative or exclusively dominating. Only when a leading jurist attracted a loyal following of jurists who applied nothing other than his doctrine in courts of law or in study circles, or issued *fatwā*s in accordance with it, can we say that a personal school of his existed. This was indeed the case with a number of prominent jurists, including Abū Ḥanīfa, Ibn Abī Laylā, Abū Yūsuf, Shaybānī, Mālik, Awzāʿī, Thawrī and Shāfiʿī. All these had loyal followers, but they also had many more students who did not adhere exclusively to their respective doctrines.

[84] On the spread of the Ḥanafite school, see Tsafrir, *History of an Islamic School.*
[85] See Kindī, *Akhbār*, 383; Schacht, *Origins*, 7.
[86] Kindī, *Akhbār*, 393, and 477 for another case; also Subkī, *Ṭabaqāt*, II, 213–14.
[87] Subkī, *Ṭabaqāt*, II, 23.

Indeed, the standard reference of the technical term *madhhab* was to the doctrinal school that possessed several characteristics lacking in its personal counterpart. First, the latter, when fulfilling the condition of exclusive loyalty, comprised the substantive legal doctrine of a single leading jurist, and, at times, his doctrine as transmitted by one of his students. The doctrinal school, on the other hand, possessed a cumulative doctrine of substantive law in which the legal opinions of the leading jurist, now the supposed "founder" of the school, were, at best, *primi inter pares* and, at least, equal to the rest of the opinions and doctrines held by various other jurists, also considered leaders *within* the school. In other words, the doctrinal school was a collective, authoritative and authorized entity, whereas the personal school remained limited to the individual doctrine of a single jurist. For example, in the Ḥanafite doctrinal school, three categories of doctrine were recognized. The first, the so-called *ẓāhir al-riwāya*, was attributed to Abū Ḥanīfa and his two students, Abū Yūsuf and Shaybānī. In theory, this possessed the highest level of authority, since it was transmitted, and surely elaborated, by jurists considered to have been among the most qualified in the school. The second category, known as *al-nawādir*, also consisted of doctrine belonging to these three masters, but without the sanctioning authority of the later, distinguished jurists. Finally, the third, termed *al-nawāzil*, represented the doctrinal constructions of the later, prominent jurists.[88] In contrast with the personal school of Abū Ḥanīfa, where his own doctrine constituted the basis of his following, the later doctrinal school of the Ḥanafites was a composite one, in which Abū Ḥanīfa's personal doctrine was one among many.

The second characteristic was that the doctrinal school constituted as much a methodological entity as a substantive, doctrinal one. In other words, what distinguished a particular doctrinal school from another was largely its legal methodology and the substantive principles it adopted – as a composite school – in dealing with its own law. Methodological awareness on this level had not yet existed in the personal schools, although it was on the increase beginning with the middle of the second/eighth century.

Third, a doctrinal school was defined by its substantive boundaries, namely, by a certain body of law and methodological principles that clearly identified the outer limits of the school as a collective entity. The personal schools, on the other hand, had no such well-defined boundaries, and departure from these boundaries in favor of other legal doctrines and principles was a common practice.

[88] For a detailed discussion of these doctrines, see Hallaq, *Authority*, 47–48, 181 f.

The fourth characteristic, issuing from the third, was loyalty, for departure from legal doctrine and methodological principles amounted to abandoning the school, a major event in the life (and the biography) of a jurist. Doctrinal loyalty, in other words, was barely present in the personal schools, whereas in the later doctrinal schools it was a defining feature of both the school itself and the careers of its members.

How, then, did the doctrinal schools emerge? A central feature of the doctrinal school – yet a fifth characteristic distinguishing it from the personal school – was the creation of an axis of authority around which an entire methodology of law was constructed. This axis was the figure of the one who came to be known as the founder, the leading jurist, in whose name the cumulative, collective principles of the school were propounded. Of all the leaders of the personal schools – and they were many – only four were raised to the level of "founder" of a doctrinal school: Abū Ḥanīfa, Mālik, Shāfiʿī and Ibn Ḥanbal, to list them in chronological order. The other schools, perhaps with the possible exception of the Ẓāhirite school, did not advance to this stage, with the result that, as personal schools, they did not survive beyond a relatively short duration.

The so-called founder, the eponym of the school, thus became the axis of authority construction.[89] As bearer of this authority, he was called the imam, and characterized as the absolute *mujtahid*, presumably responsible for having created the school's methodology on the basis of which its substantive legal principles and legal doctrine were constructed. The absolute *mujtahid*'s knowledge of the law was presumed to be all-encompassing and thus wholly creative. The school was named after him, and he was purported to have been its originator. His knowledge included mastery of legal theory (*uṣūl al-fiqh*) in all its attendant disciplines: Quranic exegesis, *ḥadīth* and its criticism, legal language, the theory of abrogation, *fiqh*, arithmetic, and the all-important science of juristic disagreement (*ikhtilāf*).

All these disciplines were necessary for the imam because he was the only one in the school who could engage directly with the revealed texts, from which, presumably, he derived the foundational structure of the school's legal doctrine. The imam's doctrine therefore constituted the only purely juristic manifestation of the legal potentiality of revealed language. Without it, in other words, revelation would have remained just that, revelation, lacking any articulation as law. Furthermore, his doctrine laid claim to originality not only because it derived directly from the revealed texts, but also, and equally importantly, because it

[89] For a detailed analysis, see *ibid.*, 24–56.

was gleaned systematically from the texts by means of clearly identifiable hermeneutical and substantive legal principles. Its systematic character was seen as the product of a unified and cohesive methodology that only the founding imam could have forged; but a methodology itself inspired and dictated by revelation. To explain all of this epistemic competence, the imam was viewed as having been endowed with exceptional personal character and virtuosity. The embodiment of pure virtue, piety, modesty, mild asceticism and the best of ethical values, he represented the ultimate sources of epistemic and moral authority.

This conception of the founding imams cannot be considered historically accurate, at least not entirely, for although they were highly knowledgeable jurists, they were certainly not as singularly accomplished as they were made out to be in the Muslim tradition. Yet, this conception of them as absolute *mujtahid*s amounted to nothing less than what we might call a process of authority-construction that served, in turn, an important function, and can hardly be dismissed as either misrepresentation of history or historical myth. In order to elevate the founding imams to this sublime rank of absolute *mujtahid*s, each of whom could be made responsible for founding a school, a number of things had to happen. Two of these deserve special attention. First, as we saw earlier, no leading jurist around whom a personal school evolved constructed his own doctrine in its entirety. Indeed, a substantial part of any doctrine was transmitted from teachers and other mentors. Yet, the doctrinal school founder is made – in the discourse of each school – solely responsible for forging his own doctrine directly out of the revealed texts and, furthermore, through his own methodologies and principles. This process was accomplished by dissociating the doctrines of the imams from those of their predecessors, to whom in fact they were very much in debt.[90] Much of legal doctrine adopted by the imam from his teachers was claimed by his immediate and later followers to originate with the imam himself, thus severing the link – and with it abolishing the debt – to his predecessors.[91]

The second is a complementary process of authority construction whereby the imams were made to appropriate the juristic accomplishments of their successors. Aḥmad Ibn Ḥanbal provides a pronounced instance of this form of authority construction. Whereas Abū Ḥanīfa, Mālik and Shāfiʿī were, to varying extents, jurists of high caliber, Ibn Ḥanbal could hardly be said to have approached their rank, as many of his own followers in fact admitted. For instance, the distinguished Ḥanbalite jurist, Ṭūfī (d. 716/1316), openly acknowledged that Ibn

[90] For a detailed treatment of this process, see *ibid.*
[91] Mālik, *Muwaṭṭa'*, 748; cf. Saḥnūn, *Mudawwana*, IV, 563.

Ḥanbal "did not transmit legal doctrine, for his entire concern was with *ḥadīth* and its collection."[92] Yet, within less than a century after his death, Ibn Ḥanbal emerged as the founding imam of a legal school of some renown. We may suppose, despite Ṭūfī's statement, that Ibn Ḥanbal did address some legal problems as part of his preoccupation with *ḥadīth*. This is probably the nucleus with which his followers worked, and which they later expanded and elaborated.[93] It is therefore reasonable to assume that the bare beginnings of legal Ḥanbalism, which had already established itself as a theological school, are to be located in the activities of jurists belonging to a generation or two after Ibn Ḥanbal's death. Of particular importance to the construction of legal Ḥanbalism was Abū Bakr al-Khallāl (d. 311/923) and ʿUmar b. Ḥusayn al-Khiraqī (d. 334/945), whose extensive juristic efforts essentially transformed Ibn Ḥanbal into the author of a methodologically coherent legal doctrine that sustained all later doctrinal developments. To say that Khallāl, Khiraqī and their associates (*aṣḥāb*) were the real founders of the Ḥanbalite school is to state the obvious.[94]

Yet, Khallāl and Khiraqī would never have claimed for themselves anything more than credit for having elaborated the law in a Ḥanbalite fashion – whatever that may have meant to them – and they themselves possessed none of the prestige that was conveniently bestowed on Ibn Ḥanbal and that they efficiently used to construct a school in the master's name. That Khallāl and Khiraqī long escaped notice as the real founders of a doctrinal Ḥanbalite school illustrates the second process of authority construction we alluded to earlier, namely, that the doctrines of the reputed founders were not only dissociated from those of their predecessors, but *also expanded to include the juristic achievements of their followers*.

The generation of Khallāl, as well as the two that followed, produced jurists who, by later standards, were known as the *mukharrijūn* (sing. *mukharrij*), a rank of legal scholars whose juristic competence was first rate but who, nonetheless, contributed to the construction of a doctrinal school under the name of a reputed founder. The activity in which the *mukharrij* engaged was known as *takhrīj* (lit. finding solutions), said to be exercised either on the basis of a particular opinion that had been derived by the founding imam or, in the absence of such an opinion, on that of the revealed texts, whence the *mukharrij* would derive a legal norm according to the principles and methodology of his imam. In both direct and indirect *takhrīj*, then, conformity with the imam's constructed legal theory and his general and particular principles regarding the law was deemed theoretically an essential feature.

[92] Ṭūfī, *Sharḥ*, III, 626–27. [93] Hurvitz, "*Mukhaṭṣar* of al-Khiraqī," 4–16.
[94] Hallaq, *Authority*, 40–43, 49; Hurvitz, "*Mukhaṭṣar* of al-Khiraqī," 4–16.

However, a close examination of this juristic activity during the formation of the doctrinal schools reveals that the imam's legal doctrine and methodology were by no means the exclusive bases of reasoning. For example, the early Shāfiʿite jurist Ibn al-Qāṣṣ reports dozens, perhaps hundreds, of cases in which *takhrīj* was practiced both within and without the boundaries of the imam's legal principles and *corpus juris*. In fact, he acknowledges, despite his clearly Shāfiʿite affiliation, that his work is based on both Shāfiʿī's and Abū Ḥanīfa's doctrines.[95] For example, in the case of a person whose speaking faculty is impaired, Shāfiʿī and Abū Ḥanīfa apparently disagreed over whether or not his testimony might be accepted if he knows sign language. Ibn Surayj (who was the Shāfiʿite equivalent of the Ḥanbalite Khallāl, and Ibn al-Qāṣṣ's professor) conducted *takhrīj* on the basis of these two doctrines, with the result that two contradictory opinions were accepted for this case: one that such testimony is valid, the other that it is void. What is significant about Ibn al-Qāṣṣ's report is that Ibn Surayj's *takhrīj* activity in deriving these two solutions was deemed to fall within the hermeneutical contours of the Shāfiʿite school. The two opinions, Ibn al-Qāṣṣ says, were reached "according to Shāfiʿī's way."[96] At times, however, Ibn Surayj's *takhrīj* became Shāfiʿī's own opinion. As to how the judge should deal with the plaintiff and defendant in the courtroom, Ibn al-Qāṣṣ reports that "*Shāfiʿī's opinion* is that the judge should not allow one of the two parties to state his arguments before the court without the other being present. *Ibn Surayj produced this opinion by way of takhrīj*."[97]

The *madhhab* thus meant not only the doctrine of the reputed founding imam but also the cumulative substantive doctrine propounded by his successors, a doctrine that was at times claimed by these successors, but at others attributed by them to the imam himself. The eponym (whose knowledge was presumed to have been all-encompassing, and to have been utilized by him to confront revelation directly) thus becomes the absolute and independent *mujtahid*, and all subsequent *mujtahid*s and jurists, however great their contributions, remain attached by their loyalty to the tradition of the *madhhab* that is symbolized by the figure of the founder. What made a *madhhab* (as a doctrinal school) a *madhhab* is therefore this feature of authoritative doctrine whose ultimate font is presumed to have been the absolute *mujtahid*-founder, not the mere congregation of jurists under the name of a titular eponym. This congregation would have been meaningless without the centripetal effect of an authoritative, substantive and methodological doctrine constructed in the name of a founder.

[95] Ibn al-Qāṣṣ, *Adab*, I, 68. [96] *Ibid.*, I, 306. [97] *Ibid.*, I, 214 (emphasis added).

But why did the doctrinal schools come into being in the first place? Wholly native to Islamic soil, the *madhhab*s' gestation was entirely occasioned by internal needs. The embryonic formation of the schools started sometime during the eighth decade after the Hijra (c. 690 AD), taking the form of study circles in which pious scholars debated religious issues and taught interested students. The knowledge and production of legal doctrine began in these circles – nowhere else. Legal authority, therefore, became epistemic rather than political, social or even religious. That epistemic authority is *the* defining feature of Islamic law need not be doubted, although piety, morality and religiosity played supporting roles.[98] A masterly knowledge of the law was the sole criterion in deciding where legal authority resided; and it resided with the scholars, not with the political rulers or any other source. This was as much true of the last third of the first/seventh century as it was of the second/eighth century and thereafter. If a caliph actively participated in legal life – as ʿUmar II did – it was by virtue of his recognized personal knowledge of the law, not so much by virtue of his political office. Thus, legal authority in Islam was personal and private; it was in the persons of the individual jurists (be they laymen or, on occasion, caliphs) that authority resided, and it was this epistemic competence that was later to be known as *ijtihād* – a cornerstone of Islamic law.

Devolving as it did upon the individual jurists who were active in study circles, legal authority did not reside in the government or ruler, and this was a prime factor in the rise of the *madhhab*. Whereas law – as a legislated system – was often "state"-based in other imperial and complex civilizations, in Islam the ruling powers had, until the dawn of modernity, almost nothing to do with the production and promulgation of legal knowledge. Therefore, in Islam, the need arose to anchor law in a system of authority that was not political, especially since the ruling political institutions were, as we shall see, deemed highly suspect. The study circles, which consisted of no more than groups of legal scholars and interested students, lacked the ability to produce a unified legal doctrine that would provide an axis of legal authority. For while every region, from Kūfa to Medina and from Fusṭāṭ to Khurāsān, possessed its own distinct, practice-based legal system, there was nevertheless a multiplicity of study circles in each, and within each circle scholars disagreed on a wide variety of opinions.

The personal schools afforded the first step toward providing an axis of legal authority, since the application (in courts and *fatwā*s) and teaching of a single, unified doctrine – that is, the doctrine of a leading jurist around

[98] On epistemic authority as the defining feature of Islamic law, see Hallaq, *Authority*.

whom a personal school had formed – permitted a measure of doctrinal unity.[99] Yet, the large number of personal schools was only slightly more effective than the multiplicity of study circles, so an axis of authority was still needed. The personal schools, forming around all the major scholars, were doctrinally divergent and still very numerous, numbering perhaps as many as two dozen. Furthermore, the leader's doctrine (which was little more than a body of legal opinions) was not always applied integrally, being subjected, as it were, to the discretion or even reformulation of the judge or jurisconsult applying it. Doctrinal and juristic loyalty was also still needed.

The second/eighth-century community of jurists not only formulated law but also administered it in the name of the ruling dynasty. In other words, this community was – juristically speaking – largely independent, having the competence to steer a course that would fulfill its mission as it saw fit. Yet, while maintaining juristic (and largely judicial) independence, this community did serve as the ruler's link to the masses, aiding him in his bid for legitimacy. As long as the ruler benefited from this legitimizing agency, the legal community profited from financial support and an easily acquired independence.[100] Rallying around a single juristic doctrine was probably the only means for a personal school to gain loyal followers and thus attract political/financial support. Such support was not limited to direct financial favors bestowed by the ruling elite, but extended to prestigious judicial appointments that guaranteed not only handsome pay but also political and social influence. These considerations alone – not to mention others – can explain the importance of such rallying around outstanding figures whose legal authority as absolute *mujtahid*-imams had to be constructed in order to raise their personal schools to doctrinal entities. This construction, involving – among other things – the backward and forward attribution of doctrines to the imam, was a way to anchor law in a source of authority that constituted an alternative to the authority of the body-politic; or, to put it more accurately, it came to fill a gap left untouched by Muslim rulers. Thus, whereas in other cultures the ruling dynasty promulgated the law, enforced it, and constituted the locus of legal authority (or legal power), in Islam it was the doctrinal *madhhab* that produced law and afforded its axis of authority. In other words, legal authority resided in the collective, juristic doctrinal enterprise of the school, not in the ruler or in the doctrine of a single jurist.

[99] On the importance of teaching and students in the formation of legal schools, see Melchert, *Formation of the Sunni Schools of Law*.

[100] As will be discussed in detail in chapters 3 and 5, below.

2 Legal theory: epistemology, language and legal reasoning

In the foregoing chapter, I took up two out of four developments that contributed to the formation of the Sharīʿa, namely, the judiciary and the legal schools. Part II of this book will present a conspectus of *fiqh*, the third development. In this chapter, the aim is to sketch the fourth and last component of the Sharīʿa, namely, legal theory, properly known as *uṣūl al-fiqh*.

In the previous chapter, I also discussed the Great Synthesis, which gave rise to a foundational definition of the conflated roles of reason and revelation in Sunnite Islam. Legal theory was perhaps the most determinative manifestation of this Synthesis which, in its final stages, emerged around the middle of the fourth/tenth century. This, needless to say, is precisely the period that witnessed the elaboration of the first *complete* system of legal theory. It is not easy, however, to reconstruct this system from the fragmentary sources that have survived from that period. Thus, to offer an informative and – for the later period – representative account of this theory, I utilize mainly the prolific and magnificently elaborated sources from the fifth/eleventh century, but not without occasional references to earlier and later works. The choice of that century has to recommend it the added fact that its theoreticians produced some of the most influential treatises for the course of theoretical developments in the centuries to come. In the case of Twelver-Shīʿite jurisprudence, I shall present an outline of the significant theoretical controversies that emerged after the ninth/fifteenth century, since these controversies have come not only to define the character of that jurisprudence but also to effect significant legal and political changes in Iran and consequently the rest of the Muslim world.

1. The function of legal theory

Before proceeding with our account of the subject-matter of legal theory, it is pertinent to enquire into the use and function of this theory. Until the 1960s, little work was done on *uṣūl al-fiqh*, due in part to the extraordinary difficulty of this field. Since the 1970s, by contrast, the field has benefited from several important contributions, but the population of scholars working on this specialized domain has unfortunately remained very small, and by all current indications, it is shrinking progressively. The expansion of this field during the 1980s and 1990s has done little to ensure either further growth or even a steady continuity.

Be that as it may, and despite a number of excellent contributions, there remains a serious problem that continues to be – perhaps unnecessarily – a subject of great controversy. Many scholars have viewed legal theory as an exclusively theological discourse, studying it as though it were an extension of that genre. In doing so, they have in effect reduced it to a discourse that has little to do with *fiqh*, much less with the realia of judicial practice. (Although it must be at once said that the flipside of this misplaced valuation was a positive result, namely, bringing our attention to the intellectual complexity and exquisite theorization of *uṣūl al-fiqh*, intrinsically important in themselves.)

There is little doubt that the abstract nature of legal theory – not to mention the frequent theological and linguistic questions in which it found itself implicated – was conducive to nurturing this approach. But these cannot alone be held responsible. For it is readily conceivable that, despite these highly intellectual preoccupations, the approach of modern scholars might have been otherwise. The more responsible culprit is the dominating but erroneous perception that Islamic law, even in its practice-oriented law (*fiqh*), was dissociated from social and political reality: an old scholarly doctrine developed in the wake of colonialism.[1] If the substantive legal doctrine of *fiqh* was viewed thus, then little wonder that abstract legal theory was relegated to a theorized entity where juristic output remained insulated from the society that produced it.

The next few chapters will show this perception to be entirely flawed. For now, and given the thrust of the arguments to follow, we do well to ask: In what ways did legal theory function in the Islamic legal system? Was its role descriptive or prescriptive? And, if one or the other, to what purposes?

To begin with, the relevant historical data are obvious and subject to no disagreement. Most important in this context is that legal doctrine represented by *fiqh* historically preceded the conscious, deliberate and discursive elaboration of *uṣūl al-fiqh* theory. The much later emergence of this theory thus precludes it from being prescriptive of foundational law, which acquired a full-fledged form as early as the end of the second/eighth

[1] On the background that gave rise to such notions, see chapters 14 and 15, below. See also Motzki, *Origins*, 295.

century. Legal doctrine grew out of varied juristic approaches and included methods of reasoning that were rejected by the later theory. Nonetheless, very little of *fiqh* law was changed or revised in light of the systematic and strict methodology insisted upon by *uṣūl al-fiqh* theory. For example, the juristic opinions of the second/eighth-century Ḥanafites largely remained intact throughout the centuries, despite the modifications that legal theory introduced to the *ra'y* forms of reasoning, said by Shāfiʿī and his like to be arbitrary in nature. The substantive effects of these modifications were instead limited to the accommodation into a textual environment, not of the opinions (or conclusions) themselves, but rather of the lines of reasoning sustaining these opinions. The juristic efforts of Abū Shujāʿ al-Thaljī are a case in point.[2] As significant as this accommodation to traditionalist jurisprudence may have been, it remains true that the juristic *fiqhī* conclusions of the second/eighth century persisted, thereby limiting the effects on this law of the legal theory that was to emerge later. To this extent, therefore, *uṣūl al-fiqh* cannot readily qualify as a descriptive theory.

If legal theory neither prescribed nor (in any historiographical sense) described the foundational law of the second/eighth century, then what was its function? Which is also to ask, on a larger scale: Why did it come about in the first place? Before providing an answer, it is necessary to refine the premise implied in the first question. While it is true that legal theory was least interested in articulating an "objective" historical description of a juristic reality, it was not devoid of an intense concern to present an idealistic reading of history, a reading that sought to articulate norms, not the historical facts of discursive practice. Yet, this reading, as exemplary as it sought to be, was connected in fundamental ways to that discursive practice. In other words, it was not a figment of the jurists' intellectual imagination, but the culmination of an effort to spell out, in concrete terms, the best way of "doing" law. And this way was the best that reality could offer, however eclectic the theoreticians might have been in appropriating this reality. In sum, and insofar as the first two centuries of legal doctrine were concerned, legal theory was not prescriptive, but *normatively* and thus *eclectically* descriptive.

Inasmuch as *fiqh* itself represented the normative construction of law for societies that articulated their world – and lived customary practices – in a variety of ways, so did *uṣūl al-fiqh* seek to capture the normatively preferable methods of interpretation and reasoning employed in the world of *fiqh* law and its interaction with the social and judicial world. Thus, by

[2] Hallaq, *Origins*, 126–27.

the very act of its coming into existence, legal theory was announcing the jurists' intention of "doing" law in a particular way, whose details are the aggregate elements making up that theory. From around the middle of the fourth/tenth century, therefore, legal theory took up the role of a prescriptive system while simultaneously maintaining its normative, descriptive function.

As of this time, the descriptive function was fulfilled by the successive productions of theoretical works that both reflected and articulated the developments within legal practice, legal doctrine and, ultimately, legal theory itself. In other words, the legal theoreticians, by virtue of their constant and intense interpretive engagement with their own tradition, managed to inventory accretions and developments within their own field. But this inventory was not so much for its own sake as it was a part of the internal dialogical needs of the theory itself, where synchronic developments are recorded as part of the argument in favor of continuity. If the synchronic (read: continuous) practice of the past is X, then X is not only legitimate but should also be upheld as a model for future action. This typical argumentative stand represents the transition from the descriptive to the prescriptive modes of legal theory. In other words, the descriptive meshes into, and finally becomes, the prescriptive. An example of this descriptive/prescriptive role is the discourse that evolved over the changing qualifications of the *muftī*, where early theory associated him with the master-jurist (*mujtahid*) while later formulations relegated his credentials to the level of *taqlīd* (i.e., a jurist who is not qualified to practice *ijtihād*). This reduction in qualifications was of course descriptive, but it played a rationalizing role in rendering normatively acceptable the dissociation of the *muftī* from the ranks of *mujtahids*.[3]

The prescriptive function, however, was often far more complex than we have thus far allowed for, and, juristically speaking, it had far-reaching consequences. Legal theory's formally declared purpose is to provide a juristic methodology and a hermeneutic that can be utilized in the formulation of rules on the basis of the "four sources" (*uṣūl*), the first pair of which are the material sources, the Quran and the Sunna. The other two were juristic consensus (*ijmāʿ*) and a set of inferential tools labeled together as *qiyās*. This stated purpose thus smacks of notions of fresh interpretive confrontations with the material sources, as if for the first time. The jurist-*mujtahid* is assumed to embark on finding the law concerning a particular case for the first time ever, or at least, *his* first time. There is little in the discourse of legal theory to forewarn the

[3] See Hallaq, "*Ifta*ʾ and *Ijtihad* in Sunni Legal Theory," 33–43.

jurist-*mujtahid* of the hermeneutical need to reckon with a formidable, preexisting body of *fiqh* law (although knowledge of this law was deemed a requirement).[4] On first impression, therefore, legal theory appears to prescribe a methodology that was used, or should be used, by the so-called absolute *mujtahid* whose knowledge is assumed to be all-encompassing and whose juristic and interpretive capabilities permit him to construct a system of legal doctrine out of the raw textual materials available to him. Yet, there was no doubt in anyone's mind that this era of the "great *mujtahid*s" was completely over by the time legal theory managed to formulate this discourse. Nor was there, after this era, any perceived need to have a new system of *fiqh* constructed. Yet, the high standard of juristic-interpretive expectations was maintained until the early nineteenth century, when law and its celebrated legal theory were largely decimated.

That this standard was consistently maintained should in no way be surprising, since legal theory was designed for the purpose of showing how *fiqh* can be constructed from beginning to end. In other words, the legists might just as well have said, the theory was intended to afford jurists all the interpretive tools needed to address any eventuality, from those novel, unprecedented cases to those preexisting ones that require a minor or not-so-minor hermeneutical tweak to accommodate them within a social context. In actual historical reality, however, cases of the novel type were highly infrequent, and the major thrust of theory was in fact directed toward servicing the preexisting type.

After the fourth/tenth century, legal doctrine had reached an exquisite level of detail and sophistication, and one would be at pains to find a case entirely without precedent. Yet, the jurists needed legal theory after this time no less than they had before. Just as many elements of it were employed to construct early law, it was summoned in later periods to adjudicate between the many legal opinions that it had itself produced over time. It is well known that Islamic jurisprudence was highly individualistic, giving rise to an extreme version of "jurists' law." Each case may engender two, three or even a dozen opinions, each espoused by a different jurist and each located along a spectrum ranging from the norm of permission to that of prohibition, with several grades of each in between. While this staggering plurality is a cardinal feature of Islamic legal doctrine, the *uṣūl* system managed to develop juristic mechanisms and strategies that could effectively deal with this multiplicity. Different opinions on a single issue were to be pitted against each other in an effort to

4 *Ibid.*, 35; Shawkānī, *Irshād*, 252.

determine which of them was epistemologically the soundest or the weightiest, with the understanding that epistemology did not operate for its own sake but functioned as both the mechanism and the yardstick of rationalizing mundane and other contingencies. Pitting opinions against each other through systematic comparison was a process known as *tarjīḥ*, namely, weighing conflicting or incongruent evidence.[5] What was at stake therefore was that body of evidence made up of textual raw materials and lines of legal reasoning that support and justify an opinion about a particular case. The scope of this evidence was vast, ranging from the Quranic, Sunnaic and consensus-based materials to numerous types of linguistic inferences and ways of legal reasoning. Legal theory provided for the entire spectrum of these activities, laying down the guidelines and principles as to what kind of evidence was superior and which inferior. For example, legal theory defines what univocal language means, and declares this category of texts to be superior to other textual sources which are also defined. In the same vein, the theory details how legal reasoning is to be conducted, and on the basis of what type of textual evidence the jurist should or can argue.[6]

Now, the operation of rendering one opinion preponderant over another was closely identified with the juristic activity of *taṣḥīḥ*,[7] literally meaning "making something correct," but technically used to refer to a hermeneutical process by which an opinion is established, among all the competing opinions, as the most authoritative in the school. Depending on the nature of the case being "authorized," the activity of *taṣḥīḥ* could draw on any aspect of legal theory.[8] What needs to be asserted is that this activity was as important to the history of the Sharīʿa as the development of the legal schools themselves, for if we appreciate the role these schools (*madhhab*s) played in taking over the legislative functions (and thus legal power) of the ruler, then we also must appreciate the importance of reducing the multiplicity of opinions into a single juristic voice that represents the single stance of a school on any particular case of law. The efficiency of the schools would have been greatly (if not totally) diminished had they been unable to develop this "strategy" for coping with multiplicity of opinion (*ikhtilāf*), and their success and the success of this strategy of *taṣḥīḥ* were heavily dependent on the tools of legal theory. The latter's prescriptive functions were necessary hermeneutical, juristic and even political assets. That legal theory had hermeneutical and juristic

[5] Weiss, *Search*, 729–38; Hallaq, *Authority*, 126–32. [6] Rāzī, *Maḥṣūl*, II, 434–88.
[7] On the relationship between *tarjīḥ* and *taṣḥīḥ*, see Hallaq, *Authority*, 133–35.
[8] For an array of widely different examples, see *ibid.*, 139–46.

functions is now hardly a novel position,[9] although there remains much room for further appreciation of its intimate connections with the practical rulings of *fiqh*.[10] That it was implicated in political functions is also clear, although this oblique but real involvement remains farthest from current scholarly thinking on the subject. On the evidence of our foregoing analysis, there should remain no doubt that legal theory afforded the tools that enabled the schools to act as a substitute for the absent legal power of the sovereign.

2. Theological and epistemological foundations

It is one of the fundamental premises of this book that a dialectical relationship existed between any juristic discourse and the site in which this discourse was designed and intended to function. The dialectic itself should be seen as a distinct discursive type, different from both the source and the site. It is also different in the sense that it constitutes the effect of this admixture, or the result of the two coming together or confronting each other. We shall see that these abstract and theoretical principles will apply to Islamic legal culture from beginning to end, a delineated sphere that is not necessarily diachronic but rather, and above all, conceptual and real. In other words, both structurally and conceptually, Islamic legal culture moved from one layer of discourse to the next through a dialectic that injected itself in between; a dialectic that, when absent, bars any transition to the second layer. We will see these principles in operation throughout the pages that follow, as we discuss legal doctrine, its application, and the juristic discourse that was prompted as a result of the encounter between the written juristic word and the social world. They will also become evident in our account of legal theory, which conceptually affords the widest range that law can carve out for itself in the socio-political universe. Yet, this theory, having exhausted its philosophical-legal claims on this universe, goes on to build on this layer of discourse yet another. The result is a multi-layered theory that altogether constitutes and affords a "complete" set of discourses that can interact with and act upon other sets, producing at every stage of interaction a dialectical effect. We shall see this to be also the case in other aspects of Islamic legal culture, but to make a first attempt at clarification, we should point to the juristic-interpretive role of legal theory in enabling the schools to assume the legal/legislative role that sovereigns

[9] Hallaq, *History*, *passim*; Hallaq, *Authority*, *passim*.
[10] See, e.g., my review of Weiss, *Search*, and "Alta Discussion" in Weiss, *Studies*, 399 ff. A marked advance in recent scholarship is Ahmad, *Structural Interrelations of Theory and Practice*.

usually play. The points of interaction, first between the interpretive rules of legal theory and the competing opinions of legal doctrine, and second between these two and the judicial demands of social reality, represent together a point of conflation that produces a dialectical relationship (one that was, as we will see in due course, highly particularized and localized). In other words, legal theory, legal doctrine and the social sphere (the latter defined to include economic and other spheres within society) were three fields of practice operating each on its own, yet influencing each other in a nearly infinite number of ways.

What might be considered the first layer of discourse in Islamic jurisprudence is one that anchors law in the web of divine creation, undoubtedly the single most important narrative about this law. Ultimately, law[11] was the systemic hallmark of submission to the Lord of the World, *Rabb al-ʿĀlamīn*, who literally owns everything – everything being, after all, created by Him.[12] Technically, therefore, law becomes subservient to, and dependent on, the mother science of theology which established not only the existence, unity and attributes of God, but also the "proof" of prophecies, revelation and all the fundaments of religion. Taking these theological conclusions (the domain of theological science itself) for granted, law goes on to build upon them. The Quran was shown by theology to be the Word of God, while the Prophetic Sunna was established as a religious foundation by virtue of the demonstrative proofs of Muhammad's Prophecy. These two sources were therefore shown to be demonstrably true by means of theological and thus strictly rational argument – a process with which legal theory had no direct concern. Thus established, the two primary sources constituted in principle the final authority on all matters legal.

Consensus, on the other hand, was a purely juristic tool, requiring, from within the law, conclusive authorization as a legal source. Since the Quran and the Sunna logically constituted the only demonstrative, certain sources, it was from these two veins that arguments for the authority of consensus were mined. As it turned out, and after several initial attempts to support consensus with Quranic provisions, the jurists realized that the Quran did not possess the arguments necessary to accomplish the task. It was probably no earlier than the end of the third/ninth century that Prophetic *ḥadīth* was adduced to support the premise that the Islamic community as a whole could never err. Only then did consensus find the

[11] In this context, as in any other in which I refer to the Sharīʿa, my use of the term "law" is predicated on qualifications I made in the Introduction, section 1, above.

[12] For a lucid discussion of these and related theological themes, see Weiss, *Spirit*, 24–37.

textual support to qualify it as a certain source of law,[13] although it must be added that the very epistemological theory that demanded this proof of certitude had itself not long since achieved a degree of maturity.

Similar to this was the case of *qiyās*, the fourth formal source of the law. While the Quran proved somewhat more useful here, it was again the Sunna and the practices of the Companions (as an extension of Prophetic authority) that permitted the jurists to formulate an authoritative, probative basis for this source.

If man is the most sublime of God's creatures, then his intellectual faculty is distinguished by the highest degree of sophistication. Unlike the eternal and indescribable knowledge of God, human knowledge is both definable and quantifiable, being, in other words, liable to classification, division and assessment. It is classifiable into the necessary and the acquired, two epistemological pegs on which the entire theoretical and *fiqhī* discourse of the law was hung. It was the chief intellectual tool that allowed the jurists and the community of Muslims to make sense of the legal fragments encountered on a daily basis, whether in the noble books of jurisprudence, in the courts of law, or in the family or marketplace.

Necessary knowledge is that which is imposed on the mind and which can by no means be rejected or subjected to doubt. By definition, it does not arrive there by inference, since it is either *a priori* or engendered by sense perception. The knowledge that one exists and the principle that a particular thing cannot be present in two different places at the same time are necessary forms of apprehension that need no reflection or inference. Some jurists labeled this knowledge as innate, while others called it intellective, assuming it to exist in the mind *ab initio*. Sensory knowledge likewise engenders necessary knowledge, such as, for example, when I burn my tongue drinking hot tea. I no more need inference to know that I scalded my taste buds than I am able to dissociate this knowledge from my mind. I immediately feel it even as the sensation of burning grips my mind. On the other hand, acquired knowledge is by definition attained through inference and reasoning, and as such remains subject to falsification. Acquired knowledge is, therefore, no more than probable, whereas necessary knowledge engenders nothing short of certitude.

The epistemic dichotomy of probability/certainty occupied the heart of Islamic theoretical discourse and was to shape the intellectual world of both Sunnite and Shīʿite jurists for over a millennium. Several grades of knowledge below certainty were distinguished, ranging from strong

[13] For a detailed discussion of juristic developments on this issue, see Hallaq, "On the Authoritativeness of Sunni Consensus," 427–54.

probability to weak. Receding below probability there were degrees of doubt (*shakk*) and ignorance (*jahl*), and when the latter was exacerbated, it was identified as complex ignorance (*jahl murakkab*).

For sound knowledge to obtain, concepts must be predicated upon each other, and these in turn must be predicated upon a definition whose delimitation, tautologically speaking, is essential for determining the meaning of concepts and the reality of knowable things. "Definition" is thus defined (*ḥadd al-ḥadd*) as a statement that includes those attributes belonging to a concept and that simultaneously excludes those that do not belong to that concept. It must be coextensive and coexclusive with the *definiendum*; namely, the definition must exist whenever and wherever the *definiendum* exists; similarly, whenever and wherever the *definiendum* does not exist, the definition must not exist. It must, in other words, be true in all instances that those qualities belonging to the thing defined be existent in that thing, whereas those that are not necessary parts of that thing be left out.

During the fifth/eleventh century, elements of Greek logic were introduced into the theory of definition, tying it to the theory of universals, Porphyry's five predicables, syllogistics and a host of other subjects. On this theory, definition can be attained by means of genus and differentia, which Ghazālī accepted but which Ibn Taymiyya refuted as arbitrary and subjective.[14] This split over Greek logical elements in legal theory was to characterize the Islamic legal tradition until the dawn of modernity. But it must be stressed that even in the case of those who incorporated Greek logical categories into their discourse on definition and select other topics, the legal theories they elaborated remained largely preoccupied with the epistemic dichotomy of certitude and probability. It was this dichotomy, as well as the traditional non-Aristotelian definition, that had an effect on the *fiqh* construction of rulings.

Be that as it may, certainty was a juristic desideratum, at least insofar as the legal sources (rather than the individual opinions of *fiqh*) were concerned. On this both Sunnite and Shīʿite jurists agreed. Knowledge of God, for instance, must be certain for one to be a true Muslim; in other words, one cannot claim membership in the community of believers if one is not sure whether God exists or whether or not He created the world or sent Muhammad as a Messenger. Nor can one claim such membership if one entertains doubts about the Quran as the Word of God, or the Sunna of Muhammad as that of a Prophet. By the same token, there is no place for doubt about consensus or *qiyās*, whose overall certainty must be

[14] See Hallaq, *Ibn Taymiyya*, 4–6n.

accepted without any qualification (for the Twelver-Shīʿite perspective, see below). Doubts raised about any of these sources would mean that the entire edifice of the law, the foundation of the community, is subject to uncertainty; and any such doubt would therefore give rise to the possibility that there is a disjunction between God and his creation and that his followers instead constitute a community of pretenders.

Yet, while the sources themselves, as sources, had to be known with certainty, the particular legal conclusions or opinions drawn from them did not need to be more than probable, i.e., more likely true than not. Outside of the four sources, therefore, probability dominated. As a set of rules applied to society, *fiqh* was mostly an exercise in probability, since a jurist could only conjecture what the law might be in any particular case. For God did not reveal a law but only texts containing what the jurists characterize as indications (or indicants: *dalīl*s). These indicants guide the jurist and allow him to *infer* what he thinks to be a particular rule for a particular case at hand. And since each qualified jurist (*mujtahid*) employs his own tools of interpretation in undertaking the search for God's law, his conclusions may well differ from those of another. One jurist's inference is therefore as good as that of the next, hence the cardinal maxim: "All qualified jurists (*mujtahid*s) are correct." All jurists are assumed to be "doing the right thing" in exerting their juristic effort (*ijtihād*) in reaching a rule or an opinion. This individual *ijtihād* – that is, the *ijtihād* of the individual *mujtahid* – explains the plurality of opinion in Islamic law, known as *khilāf* or *ikhtilāf*. Each case may elicit two, three, sometimes up to eight or more opinions (*aqwāl*), all of which remain "opinions" that are equally valid, although one of them – for the purposes of practice and application – must be viewed as superior to the others (considered weak or less sound) and is thus chosen by a jurist or his school to be the authoritative opinion to be applied in law courts and issued in *fatwā*s. The so-called "weak" opinions, on the other hand, are subject to verification or revision, although for other jurists or schools, these very opinions may be deemed to possess the highest authority. Thus weakness or soundness is a relative matter; the less sound opinion is deemed so in relation to another, "stronger" opinion. In theory and logic, however, a given problem can have only one correct solution, irrespective of whether or not the community of jurists knows which one it is. Obviously, in all cases outside the purview of consensus, the jurists cannot decide which is the correct solution, for the matter remains inherently subjective. Hence the other cardinal maxim: "The *mujtahid* whose opinion is correct is rewarded twice [i.e., both for exercising his effort and for getting it right], while the *mujtahid* whose opinion is incorrect, is rewarded only once [for his effort]."

To sum up, the theological-epistemological premises of legal theory set the stage for a legal project that is thoroughly religious in nature: thoroughly, in the sense that there is implied a continuous link between the Lord and human beings – a link sustained and nourished by the guiding spirit of the Quran and the Prophethood (which ended with Muhammad). This is not a Hobbesian conception where God created man and endowed him with a disposition that allows him to live by a certain, all-knowing rationality. Nor is it a Greek conception, where the gods created the world according to an intellectual plan and left it to run by eternally functioning organizing rules. Instead, God is ever-present, and is acutely conscious of the details of human life.[15] That "God does not know particulars," as the Hellenized philosophers claimed, was for Muslim jurists and thinkers not only unthinkable but also a form of complex ignorance, for such a scenario would have left man to his own devices, where no law or deterrence, moral or otherwise, may be possible. This Greek formula was regarded as a successful recipe for anarchy in this world and eternal punishment in the hereafter, despite the widespread recognition that the all-wise philosopher-king ruled the here and now. The Hobbesian formula, on the other hand, would have fared even worse in Muslim juristic thinking, for this scenario is devoid of any source of epistemic authority other than the rational faculty of man. The bottom line here is that no man, however wise, rational or "philosophically predisposed," can rule the lives of his fellow men or dictate to them the terms of a good life. This capacity to rule was God's and God's alone. His, not man's, is the only rule that counts.

Yet none of this contradicts the fundamental belief that man is the most sublime of God's creatures, and as such is endowed with a magnificent intellect, unrivaled by that of any other created being. For while Muslim thinking duly recognizes that man's intellect is superior, it is only a relative attribute. Man is knowing but obviously not omniscient, capable of accomplishment but hardly omnipotent. Comparatively, man's knowledge and rationality are deficient and unable to unravel the secrets of the universe. Thus, if the Grand Plan of Existence is a mystery, then what is it that makes our ways of living good or bad, sound or unsound, destructive or healthy? To know all of this is to listen to a higher voice, but to listen and understand is to interpret, and to interpret is to be engaged with God and his Speech. Knowledge of the law in Islam is what was seen as a happy synthesis between human reason and the divine word.

[15] The Quran is replete with assertions to this effect. See, among many others, 9:15, 11:5, 29:62, 35:38 and 57:3.

3. The legal norms

If divine guidance is needed, it is for the purpose of setting human life in good order. The purpose is not to control or discipline, the two most salient missions of modern law and the modern state that commands it. Rather, in Muslim thinking, it is to live in peace: first, with oneself; second, with and in society; and third, with and in the world. It is to do the right thing, whoever or wherever one is. The state permits and forbids, and when it does the latter, it punishes severely upon infraction. It is not in the least interested in what individuals do outside of its spheres of influence and concern. Islamic law, on the other hand, has an all-encompassing interest in human acts. It organizes them into various categories ranging from the moral to the legal, without however making such distinctions. In fact, there are no words in Arabic, the lingua franca of the law, for the contrastive notions of moral/legal. Thus, subsumed under five norms, acts are regarded as *sharʿī* (i.e., subject to the regulation of the Sharīʿa *and therefore pronounced as law*). Accordingly, each human act must fall under one norm or another. The category of the forbidden (*ḥarām*) entails punishment upon commission of an act deemed prohibited, whilst that of the obligatory (*wājib*) demands punishment upon omission of an act whose performance is decreed as legally necessary. Breach of contract or committing adultery/fornication (*zinā*),[16] not to mention uprooting trees or hunting within the Meccan sanctuary, are just some of the infractions falling within the *ḥarām* category, while prayer and payment of pecuniary debts are instances of the *wājib*. Both categories require punishment upon non-compliance, while the diametrical, ungraded opposition punishable/non-punishable deprives the individual of any freedom of action or choice. The distinctly punitive outlook embedded in these two categories led many scholars to the notion, now a century old, that the Sharīʿa qualifies and acts as "law" only when rules belonging to these two categories are involved ("law" here is, of course, essentially assumed to be that which prevails as a *positive* system of rules). The three remaining categories – the recommended (*mandūb*), neutral (*mubāḥ*) and disapproved (*makrūh*) – do not, in the view of this scholarship, constitute law proper, as they do not possess any *truly* coercive or punitive content. In other words, they are said to be unenforceable, since commission of the disapproved and non-commission of the recommended do not entail punishment. Instead, their omission and commission, respectively, entail a reward, assumed to await the individual in the hereafter. Similarly, the category of the neutral prescribes neither permission nor prohibition,

[16] On *zinā*, see chapter 10, section 2 (i), below.

leaving these up to the preferences of the individual. The neutral, it must be stressed, is a strictly legal category rather than an area in which the Sharīʿa failed, or did not care, to regulate human acts. Put differently, categorizing an act as neutral is both a deliberate choice and a conscious commitment not to assign particular values to particular acts.

Neither Muslim jurists nor Muslim intellectuals at large have – until the twentieth century – made any distinction between the legal and moral components of Islamic law. The punitive character of the obligatory and forbidden and the absence of this characteristic from the other three categories failed to engender a distinction between the moral and strictly legal, a phenomenon that should prompt us to wonder why Muslim jurists failed (if indeed they did) to realize the typological significance of this fact. To answer this question we must first understand that, by its very nature, Islam – both as a worldview and as an intellectual system – made no real distinction between the legal and the moral on the grounds that morality and ethics were never perceived as anything less than integral to the law.[17] (Indeed, what begs explanation is the modern separation between the two, a divide that can hardly be described as normative or natural in the long stretch of human history.)[18] The categories of the recommended and the disapproved do entail punitive consequences, but they are not earthly consequences. That they are distinctly theological and eschatological does not *relegate* them to a category below, and thus outside, the law. In fact, in the Muslim system of thought, the force of heavenly retribution is far graver than any earthly punishment, since the latter involves lighter physical suffering and certainly is of shorter duration. Hell, or any department thereof, is by dramatic contrast the eternal abode of those who violate the law, particularly the more serious of its injunctions. Historically, the genuine belief in this eschatological reality – inculcated in the individual by a complex and lengthy process of acculturation and socialization – explains the seemingly incredible, yet authentic, reports of people voluntarily approaching the Muslim court to confess to committing (among other offenses) *zinā*, a crime that entails the death penalty if the adulterer is married.[19] This penalty, however harsh and violent, was deemed lighter than eternal consignment to Hell. The impending reality of hellish punishment was thus as grave as, and in fact graver than, any that a judge or a state could mete out.

[17] Hallaq, "Fashioning the Moral Subject."

[18] See, e.g., Max Weber on the evolution of "rational" rules in the West, as discussed by Lassman, "Rule of Man," 83–98.

[19] El-Nahal, *Judicial Administration*, 28. The morality of admission before the *qāḍī* was enshrined in a Prophetic report, known as *ḥadīth* Māʿiz. See this and similar *ḥadīth*s in Ibn Abī Shayba, *Muṣannaf*, V, 540–41.

This essentially psychological phenomenon also explains the force of the oath as a substantive procedural element. If the plaintiff cannot produce convincing evidence, the defendant must swear by oath that the plaintiff's claim is unfounded, an oath that releases him from liability. Refusal to take such an oath in effect constitutes admission of guilt, resulting in a decision in favor of the plaintiff, notwithstanding his shaky evidence. For such a system to work – as it without doubt did for centuries – moral considerations must be assumed to play an indubitable role in the formation of human behavior. Accordingly, Muslim jurists had no good reason to exclude the categories of the recommended and disapproved from the realm of legality, or to assign them to an exclusive realm of morality. The distinction, therefore, is patently Occidental, emanating from both the death in western and central Europe of transcendentalism and the (resultant) separation between law and religion, or, more specifically, between the nation-state's law (of "Caesar") and the church law (of "God"). It is incorrect, therefore, to impose this distinction between the legal and the moral on Islamic law, for it is liable to give birth, as it did, to unwarranted assumptions, thus distorting several features of this law and its history.

Meshing the moral with the legal, these norms were subject to a great deal of articulation and discussion. The impact of epistemological distinctions is felt here as elsewhere. The Ḥanafite school, for instance, distinguished two categories of the obligatory, the *wājib* and the *farḍ*. The former, based on probable evidence, is itself inevitably probable, whereas the latter is certain, since it is based on clear and authentic textual indications, which is to say that it is grounded in a language that not only admits of a single interpretation but also is transmitted by means so reliable that no doubt can be cast on its provenance.

The obligatory also raised questions about the precise time of performance. The issue at stake was whether such an act must be performed instantaneously or whether a delay within a predetermined stretch of time might be tolerated. If I command my butler to iron my shirt "today," is he under the obligation to perform the task instantaneously or can he perform it later today? Some jurists argued that, rationally, the butler would fulfill his obligation if he were to iron the shirt anytime during the day. But as we have just seen, rationality by itself is insufficient in legal argument. The answer to this question was instead made to rest on a juristic consensus with regard to the penance due upon the violation of certain rules, which penance required the freeing of a slave, feeding sixty of the poor, or feeding one of the poor for sixty days. Although performing penance is obligatory, the violator is entirely free to choose one or another of these forms of expiation. So the obligatory category does, after all, involve a choice as to the time the act should be performed, as long as it is performed within the limits of the prescribed period.

We have alluded to the recommended category as one that entails reward for performance, but which upon omission requires no punishment. As the purpose here is to encourage piety, omission does not constitute violation of the law, since obedience to the lawgiver is in any case rendered. Similarly, obedience is also attained in the category of the permissible, or the so-called indifferent, whose commission or omission is equally legitimate. That neither reward nor punishment is prescribed should not be taken to mean that the law has failed to take a position on this category of acts, as some "rationalist" theologians have thought. Indeed, as we have already noted, it is a standing legal principle that the law deliberately offers the Muslim individual a free choice between the two.

Finally, legal theory also laid down another taxonomy related not to the acts themselves, but to the status of their performance. For example, an obligatory act, having been predetermined as such, must be performed; but its performance is one thing while having been performed correctly is another. Thus an act can also be valid or invalid, such as a contract or a transaction of sale. When a contract is valid, it is binding and productive of full legal effects; when invalid, it ceases to be so binding. But being invalid does not mean that it is null and void, which is to say that it has no legal effect whatsoever. In respect to an invalid marriage contract, for instance, the law still recognizes the children of the union as legitimate, having, *inter alia*, rights of inheritance.

4. Legal language

But how does the jurist arrive at a legal norm or a ruling regarding a specific act? In other words, what are the materials and interpretive tools at his disposal that permit him to derive one rule or opinion but not another? To answer these questions, we begin with a brief account of legal language and the hermeneutical principles that govern its use.[20]

In attempting to find a solution to a hitherto unresolved legal problem (or to evaluate a preexisting legal opinion in a fresh effort of *ijtihād*), the jurist begins with texts that constitute his frame of reference, texts that he intuitively deems relevant to the case befalling him. His analysis of these texts comprises, first, the identification of the precise passage(s) applicable to the case at hand and, second, the determination of the semantic

[20] For concise statements of the theory on linguistic interpretation (*kalām*, *alfāẓ*), see Shīrāzī, *Luma'*, 6–35; Ḥillī, *Ma'ārij al-Uṣūl*, 51–121.

force and implication of this textual material as it bears on that case. This latter activity constitutes part of *qiyās*, which we shall take up later. The former, however, involves a linguistic interpretation in preparation for *qiyās*, with a view to determining whether words within the relevant text are univocal, ambiguous, general, particular or metaphorical. In other words, before any inference is made, the text must be interpreted and understood to be substantively relevant and fit as the basis of legal reasoning.

The theory of legal language conceives of words as either clear or ambiguous. Ambiguous words that can in no way be clarified remain non-functional and hence unproductive of legal norms. On the other hand, equivocal language that can be disambiguated (i.e., rendered clear), as well as intrinsically clear language, are fit for the task of legal construction. Yet, despite its problematic nature, language often does contain univocal, clear expressions that engender certitude in the mind. For instance, when we hear the word "four" we understand, without a shade of doubt, that it is not five, three or seven. To comprehend the meaning of "four," we need not resort to any principles of interpretation, nor to other explicative language. The language is self-evident and thus belongs to the category of necessary knowledge (discussed in section 2, above). The clarity and certitude that it generates renders it the most evincive, a textual category labeled as *naṣṣ*.

But most expressions are not so clear, even when they appear to be so. One such linguistic type is the metaphorical. It is the general assumption of jurists that words are originally coined for a real meaning, e.g., "lion" signifies a member of the species of big cats. A word is used in a metaphorical sense when applied by extension to something that is not the original referent; thus, the expression "lion" may be applied in the Arabic language to a man who is courageous. Legal examples of this use of language include words such as "today" or "tomorrow," which may be used metaphorically when promising to perform a duty at a certain time. In their real usage, the expressions "today" or "tomorrow" can include late night hours, but they normally mean – in business transactions, for instance – daytime hours. The challenge for the jurist here is to determine whether a particular word in legal language is being used metaphorically or in its real sense.[21]

Of prime importance to such a determination are the contextual indications (*qarāʾin*; sing. *qarīna*)[22] associated with the use of the real or metaphorical term. To say in Arabic that "I met a lion on my flight from

[21] Shāshī, *Uṣūl*, 42–50. [22] On *qarāʾin*, see Hallaq, "Notes on the Term *Qarīna*."

Paris to Montreal" is to provide sufficient contextual indications as to make it clear that on my flight I made the acquaintance of a human being whom I thought to be courageous. Similarly, when I refer to a tall man as a "palm tree," I am merely substituting this flora for his name or for his person as a referent. In complex cases, however, it takes more than common sense to determine whether a usage is real or metaphorical. Such terms can be tested by the method of coextensiveness, namely, whether the real usage would apply to all trees of the family *Palmea*, but would not so apply to all tall things in the world. The exception, in this case tall men, is metaphorical. Furthermore, the word would have to satisfy all ordinary uses. Thus, if we proceed to refer to the arms of the tall man as branches (ordinary for a tree but not for a human being), we would be deemed to have gone too far, and this excess is evidence of the metaphorical use of "palm tree."

Metaphorical or otherwise, words may also be either clear or ambiguous. When ambiguous, they can brook different interpretations, due to the fact that the referent of such words includes several attributes or different genera. One such ambiguity is found in homonymous nouns, which refer to more than one object, such as the word "spring," which may refer to the season of the year, an artesian well or a coil of wire. Yet, a word may not be a homonym and still retain ambiguity. For example, Quran 17:33 reads: "And he who is killed wrongfully, we have given power to his heir." The term "power" here is markedly ambiguous, since it may include: (1) the power to pardon; (2) the right to retaliate; or (3) the right to levy monetary compensation. If the ambiguity can be resolved by seeking the help of another text, then the ambiguity is disentangled in favor of one meaning or another. If not, the rule would by necessity encompass all possible meanings, as is in fact the case with Quran 17:33. Here, in the absence of further clarification, the heirs in the event of homicide are given the full range of the term "power," granting them the free option of choosing which of the three "rights" they should exercise.

General terms are also problematic in the sense that they can refer to two or more individuals, as in the case of plural nouns and general statements that include more than one genus. When confronted with such language, the jurist is faced with the task of particularization, namely, determining which genus or genera is meant by the general statement. A classic example of particularization occurs in Quran 5:3, where it is stated: "Forbidden unto you [for food] is carrion." This was particularized by a Prophetic *ḥadīth* allowing the consumption of dead fish. That the Quran can be particularized by a *ḥadīth*, as this example illustrates, is obvious; so can a *ḥadīth* be particularized by the Quran, epistemologically a more secure source of law.

Particularization may be effected through a condition that is attached to, or brought to bear upon, a general and thus ambiguous statement. In 3:97, the Quran states: "And pilgrimage to the House is a duty unto God for mankind, for him who can find a way." This language makes it clear that the obligation to go on pilgrimage is waived for those who lack the means to perform it. Particularization may also be effected through qualifying general statements. This is known as the qualification of unrestricted language. For instance, if a man solemnly promises not to resume marital relations with his wife (a declaration known as *ẓihār*), but later reneges on his promise, the prescribed Quranic penalty or atonement (58:3) is "freeing a slave." But the Quran (4:92) also stipulates "freeing a believing slave" as a punishment for unintentional homicide. The latter verse, possessing specific language, was taken to restrict and further define the meaning of "slave" in Quran 58:3. This restriction in meaning represents a human transference, namely, an inference that the jurists recognized to be their best guess at God's intention, but far from the necessary *linguistic* dictates of the revealed texts.

As a system of obligations, law depends heavily on prescriptive textual expressions of the type "Do" or "Do not do," known, respectively, as imperative and prohibitive commands.[23] Such expressions were not devoid of interpretive problems, and much ink was spilled in constructing a theory of this category. The very definition of the imperative mood was itself open to wide disagreement. Some theoreticians saw it as language demanding of a person that he/she perform a certain act. Others insisted that the element of the superiority of the requester over the person ordered must be present for the form to qualify as an imperative. Against the objection that one can command one's equal, they argued that such a command, though it may take the imperative form, is merely a metaphoric usage and should not be treated as a command in a real sense.

Essential to accurately construing the imperative is the determination of the legal effects of language. When someone commands another, telling him "Do this," should this command be regarded as falling only within the legal value of the obligatory norm, or could it also be within that of the recommended and/or the indifferent? The position of the majority of legal theorists seems to have been that imperatives, as a rule, are assumed to engender obligation, unless shown otherwise by circumstantial or contextual evidence (*qarīna*). In 2:43, the Quran says: "Hold the prayer," using language that was construed as eminently obligatory. But when the same source, on the matter of freeing slaves, states: "Write them

23 For the imperative, see Ghazālī, *Mustaṣfā*, I, 411–35; Shīrāzī, *Sharḥ al-Luma'*, I, 199–219. See also Wakin, "Interpretation of the Divine Command," 33–52.

[a contract of manumission] if you detect in them any good," the language was taken to be a recommendation.[24] Furthermore, the seemingly imperative form pertaining to the permissibility of hunting outside the sacred territory of the Kaʿba (Q. 5:2) was understood and adjudged to be an indifferent act.

To make sense of these varied interpretations of what appears an integral linguistic form, some jurists argued that the imperative is a homonym, equally signifying obligation, recommendation and indifference. Others begged to differ, espousing the view that the imperative form always engenders obligation, and when it does not there must be contextual evidence, thereby making its construal as recommendation or indifference possible, even necessary. Otherwise, standing on its own, an imperative form must, perforce, impart obligation.

These varied, but mutually exclusive, exegetical positions do not seem to have offered a satisfactory and consistent solution to the problem, for none, on its own, could account for the range of uses that the imperative form generated. Ghazālī seems to have been one of the first to advance a comprehensive theory that, I think, successfully resolved the issue. He pointed out that the significations of linguistic forms, including the imperative, must be understood in light of what has been established by convention, which is known by means of widespread usage (*tawātur*)[25] of the language. Through this pervasive usage, which cannot be falsified, we know from past authorities what the convention is with regard to the meaning of a word, or we know that the Lawgiver has accepted and confirmed the meaning as determined by that convention. Such reported usage also informs us of the existence of any consensus in the community on how these words are to be understood or, in the absence of a consensus, of how they were understood by authorities whose erudition, rectitude and integrity would have prevented them from remaining silent when an error in language was committed. It was through one or more of these channels that words – as a linguistic convention – acquired their meaning.[26]

Like their imperative counterparts, prohibitive forms are seen as commands issued from a superior to an inferior. Whereas the imperative requires the commission of an act, the prohibitive calls for omission. But unlike the imperatives, which do not require immediate performance, prohibitions require immediate and constant omission of the act, for

[24] Although the historical evidence suggests that in practice ex-slaves often carried with them a document of manumission, notarized and witnessed by the court. See Peirce, *Morality Tales*, 283.

[25] For a definition, see further below.

[26] See Weiss, "Language and Tradition," 92 ff.

failure to refrain immediately from performance itself constitutes an act of performance, and this in turn necessarily entails an infraction.[27]

Some theorists viewed prohibitives as encompassing commands not to do either of two types of acts: sensory and legal. An example of the former is, "Do not drink wine," and of the latter, "Do not sell one gold coin for two gold coins" (since this would involve prohibited usury, *ribā*). The sensory acts are prohibited because they are inherently evil, whereas the legal acts are prohibited for a reason external to themselves. Drinking wine or fornication are inherently evil acts, but selling gold is not, since it is prohibited only when it is transacted in a particular fashion resulting in unlawful consequences.[28]

Is the opposite of a prohibited act obligatory? The jurists argued that if the prohibited act has no more than one opposite, then it would be an obligation to perform that opposite act. If the prohibited act has more than one opposite, then the performance of any one of these opposites would in effect constitute an omission of the prohibited act, rendering performance obligatory. Arguably, being involved in the laudable acts of prayer, fasting, working, etc., is oppositional to the prohibited act of adultery.

This opposition raised a central debate in legal theory as to the difference between meaning and implication. The meaning inheres in the very language of the texts. By the imperative "sit down," we normally understand a command that someone take a seat. Implication, on the other hand, is understood not directly from the semantic force of language but rather from what can be inferred from it. In addition to the *meaning* that requires one to be seated when told "sit down," there is also the *implication*: "do not stand up." This debate was relevant to the imperative and prohibitive forms, but no less so to two forms of reasoning subsumed under the category of *qiyās*. We shall, therefore, take up this debate again when dealing with *qiyās*.

5. Transmission and abrogation of texts

The jurist's interpretation of legal language would be meaningless without the knowledge that this language has been transmitted with a certain degree of credibility. A text that has been passed down via a dubious or defective chain of transmitters, or transmitters who are known to be untrustworthy, was held to lack any legal effect even though its language might be clear and unequivocal. Thus all texts must pass the test of both linguistic analysis and transmission before they are employed as the raw material of legal reasoning.

[27] Rāzī, *Maḥṣūl*, I, 338. [28] Hallaq, *History*, 57–58.

The general principle with regard to the duality of interpretation/transmission is that probable conclusions of legal reasoning are the result of lack of certainty in either the denotation of a term or the transmission of the text encompassing that term. A particular language sample may thus be univocal (*naṣṣ*) in meaning, but reported through a chain of transmission that is merely probable, rendering its overall legal effects likewise only probable. Univocal language can also be transmitted by weak or even highly dubious transmitters, thus making it useless in legal construction. On the other hand, certainty can be gained in transmission but lost through a lack of linguistic clarity. For example, a text transmitted by a multiplicity of channels will, despite this epistemic advantage, generate no more than probability if its language is not univocal.

In its entirety, the Quran is regarded as certain in terms of transmission, since the entire community of Muslims was involved in its transmission from one generation to the next. The foundational argument here stems from the theory of consensus, namely, that it is inconceivable for the entire Muslim community to conspire in either forging or distorting it. Thus, for a text to be deemed credible beyond a shadow of doubt (i.e., to have certainty), it must meet this requirement of multiple transmission, or recurrence, known as *tawātur*. For certainty to obtain through multiple transmission, three conditions must be met: first, the text must be conveyed from one generation to the next through channels of transmission sufficiently numerous as to preclude any possibility of error or collaboration on a forgery; second, the first class of transmitters must have had sensory perception of what the Prophet said, did, or did not do; and third, the first two conditions must be met at each stage of transmission beginning with the first class and ending with the last narrator of the text.[29]

Multiple, recurrent transmission brings about necessary knowledge, which we have defined as immediate, uninferred knowledge that is imposed on the mind and that needs no reasoning or reflection. Upon hearing the recurrent report, the mind has no choice but to admit the contents of the report *a priori*, as true and genuine. But this report is lodged in the mind spontaneously. Hearing the report for the first time will no doubt engender probability, but hearing it countless times, from different sources, will ultimately lead to a point where one accepts the contents as authentic. The hearer does not know how and when he reaches such knowledge. Those who have never visited Mecca, for instance, know with certainty of its existence, and this is effected by the endless "reporting" of those who have seen it while on pilgrimage. But no

[29] Ibn Barhān, *Wuṣūl*, II, 141–50; Shīrāzī, *Sharḥ al-Luma'*, I, 572 ff.; Hallaq, "Inductive Corroboration," 9–19; Weiss, "Knowledge of the Past," 81–105.

one can identify the exact report by which he or she reached this certainty about Mecca, or at what point knowledge ascended from the realm of probability to that of certainty. The theoreticians argued that this intellectual transition from probability to certainty is as difficult to pin down as determining the exact moment that night ends and the light of day begins. And this point of transition may change from one person to another, rendering the *tawātur* a largely subjective category. It is only when necessary knowledge obtains that the number of channels of transmission heard can be determined, not the other way around.[30]

Any text transmitted through channels fewer than *tawātur* is termed *āḥād* (literally: solitary), although the actual number of channels can be two, three or even more. The majority of theoreticians saw this category as leading to probability, although a minority distinguished circumstances under which some solitary reports may lead to certainty of the acquired type.[31]

With the possible exception of a few reports, the *ḥadīth* is generally considered solitary, and, unlike the Quranic text, it does not possess the advantage of *tawātur*.[32] As we saw in chapter 1, there were far more fabricated, and thus weak, *ḥadīth*s than there were sound ones. But even these latter did not always engender certainty, since most were of the solitary kind and therefore yielded only probable knowledge. If all this points to anything about Islamic law, it is its insistence that, as a practical field, *fiqh* law (mostly a *ḥadīth* derivative) does not have to enjoy certainty. The latter is a category necessary only when the issue is either the epistemic status of the four sources *qua* sources or a higher order of belief, such as God himself.

Yet, to be fit for practical application, a probable report must have transmitters who, from beginning to end, are known for their reliable and trustworthy character, and each must have met the next link in person, so as to make it credible that transmission did occur. Throughout the third/ninth century, and probably the fourth/tenth, the jurists held that interrupted *ḥadīth*s are nonetheless sound, "interrupted" meaning that one or more transmitters in the chain are unknown. But this was predicated on the assumption that the transmitter with whom the report resumes after the interruption had the reputation of transmitting only those *ḥadīth*s that are sound. This assumption rests on another, namely, that such a person would not have transmitted the *ḥadīth* had he known it to be inauthentic or fabricated. The later jurists, however, seem to have rejected such *ḥadīth*s, classifying them as unsound or defective.

[30] Ghazālī, *Mankhūl*, 245 ff.; Shīrāzī, *Sharḥ al-Luma'*, II, 578.
[31] Hallaq, *History*, 62–63. [32] See Hallaq, "Authenticity," 75–90.

It is thus clear that the trustworthiness of individual transmitters played an important role in the authentication of *ḥadīth*s. The attribute that was most valued, and in fact deemed indispensable and determinative, was that of being just (*ʿadl*), namely, being morally and religiously righteous. A just character also implied the attribute of being truthful (*ṣādiq*) which made one incapable of lying. This requirement was intended to preclude either outright tampering with the wording of the transmitted text, or interpolating it with fabricated material. It also implied that the transmitter could not have lied regarding his sources by fabricating a chain of transmitters or claiming that he had heard the *ḥadīth* from an authority when in fact he had not. He had also to be fully cognizant of the material he related, so as to transmit it with precision. Finally, he must not have been involved in dubious or "sectarian" religious movements, for if this were the case, he would have been liable to produce heretical material for the sake of the movement to which he belonged. This last requirement clearly suggests that the transmitter must be seen to be loyal to Sunnism, to the exclusion of any other community.[33]

Transmitters were also judged by their ability to transmit *ḥadīth*s verbatim, for thematic transmission ran the risk of changing the wording, and thus the original intent, of a particular *ḥadīth*. Furthermore, it was deemed preferable that the *ḥadīth* be transmitted in full, although transmitting one part not thematically connected with the rest was acceptable.

By the early fifth/eleventh century, Sunnite legal theory came to acknowledge a category of *ḥadīth* representing a cross between the solitary and recurrent types. The recurrent report is one that has the same wording, irrespective of how widespread its transmission may be. It is a text transmitted verbatim throughout all the channels in a recurrent fashion. But the jurists discovered that some *ḥadīth*s do not have the same wording, although they all reflect the same meaning or theme (*maʿnā*). Taken altogether, they are so frequently transmitted that they are in effect tantamount to *mutawātir*. Because they are recurrent in their meaning, yet lack identical language, they became known as *tawātur maʿnawī*. The most renowned examples in point are a dozen or so *ḥadīth*s to the effect that the community of Muslims will never agree on an error, providing in the process the authority for consensus (*ijmāʿ*).[34]

After having been transmitted in a solitary fashion, some *ḥadīth*s gained recurrence three or four generations after the Prophet. Known as widespread (*mashhūr*), these reports were deemed to occupy an epistemic

[33] On the Twelver-Shīʿite view, see section 9, below.

[34] On establishing consensus as a source of Sharīʿa, see Hallaq, "On the Authoritativeness of Sunni Consensus."

grade combining certain and acquired knowledge, which is to say that this knowledge is neither immediate nor necessary. The knowledge engendered by such reports is certain because of the multiplicity of reporting during the later centuries of Islam, but it is not of the necessary type because some reflection and analysis were needed to verify their authenticity at the early stages of their transmission.

In attempting to arrive at a solution to a particular case, the jurist may encounter more than one *ḥadīth* relevant to that case. The problem that arises is when these *ḥadīth*s are contradictory or inconsistent with one another. If he cannot reconcile them, the jurist must seek to make one *ḥadīth* preponderant over another by establishing that the former possesses attributes superior to, or lacking in, the latter. The criteria of preponderance depend on the mode of transmission as well as on the subject-matter of the *ḥadīth* in question. For example, a *ḥadīth* transmitted by mature persons known for their prodigious ability to retain information is superior to another transmitted by young narrators who may not be particularly known for their memory or precision in reporting. Similarly, a *ḥadīth* whose first transmitter was close to the Prophet and knew him intimately is regarded as superior to another whose first transmitter was not on close terms with the Prophet. The subject-matter also determines the comparative strength or weakness of a *ḥadīth*. For instance, a *ḥadīth* that finds thematic corroboration in the Quran would be deemed preponderant over another that finds no such support. But when preponderance proves to be impossible, the jurist resorts to the procedure of abrogation, whereby one of the *ḥadīth*s is made to repeal, and thus cancel out the effects of, another.

But what if the jurist encounters Quranic verses that bear upon the case he is considering but nonetheless appear to him to be inconsistent or contradictory? Here, abrogation (*naskh*) was unanimously held as one of the authoritative methods of dealing with contradictory texts. Just as Islam as a whole came to abrogate earlier religions without denying their legitimacy, abrogation among and between revealed Islamic texts was also admitted and in fact practiced, without this entailing the diminution of the status of the repealed texts as divine scripture. This method was specifically approved in Quran 2:106: "Such of Our Revelation as We abrogate or cause to be forgotten, We bring [in place of it] one better or the like thereof." Yet, the theory of *naskh* does not imply that the texts themselves are actually abrogated – only the legal rulings embedded in these texts. For to admit that God revealed contradictory and even conflicting statements would mean that one of the statements is false and that God, therefore, revealed an untruth.

The fundamental principle of abrogation is that one text repeals another contradictory text that was revealed prior to it in time. But abrogation may result from a clearer consideration, especially when the text itself is made to supersede another. An example in point is the Prophet's statement: "I had permitted for you the use of the carrion leather, but upon receipt of this writing [epistle], you are not to utilize it in any manner." Yet another consideration is the consensus of the community as represented by its scholars. If one ruling is adopted in preference to another, then the latter is deemed abrogated, since the community cannot agree on an error. However, in the post-formative period, a number of jurists tended to object to this principle, arguing that a consensus that lacks textual support does not possess the power to abrogate. Consensus, they asserted, must rest on revealed texts, and if these texts contain no evidence of abrogation, then consensus cannot decide the matter. Consensus, in other words, cannot go beyond the evidence of the texts, for it is only the texts that determine whether or not one ruling can abrogate another. If a ruling subject to consensus happens to abrogate another conflicting ruling, then the assumption is that the abrogation must be due to evidence existing in the texts, not to consensus.

The epistemological strength of texts also plays a central role in abrogation. A text deemed presumptive or probable cannot repeal another having the quality of certitude. On the other hand, texts that are considered of equal epistemological value may abrogate one another. This principle derives from Quran 2:106, which speaks of abrogating verses and replacing them by similar or "better" ones. Hence, Quranic verses, like recurrent *ḥadīth*s, can repeal each other. The same is true of solitary *ḥadīth*s. Furthermore, by the same principle, the Quran and recurrent *ḥadīth*s may abrogate solitary *ḥadīth*s, but not vice versa.

That the Quran can abrogate *hadīth*s is evident, considering its distinguished religious and epistemological stature. And it is perfectly understandable, on the basis of the epistemological principles just outlined, why solitary *ḥadīth*s cannot abrogate Quranic verses (although a minority of jurists permitted this type of abrogation). However, the question that remained controversial was whether or not recurrent *ḥadīth*s can abrogate Quranic verses. Those who denied this power to the *ḥadīth* argued their case on the basis of Quran 2:106, in effect claiming that no *ḥadīth* can ever acquire a status equal to the Quran. Their opponents, on the other hand, couched their arguments in epistemological terms, maintaining that both recurrent *ḥadīth*s and Quranic materials enjoy the status of *mutawātir*, and since this rank yields certainty, they are both equal in status and thus can repeal one another. (It must be said, however, that in practice there are a few cases where both solitary and recurrent *ḥadīth*s have abrogated Quranic verses.)[35]

[35] For a detailed discussion of recurrent and solitary traditions, see Weiss, "Knowledge of the Past," 81–105; Hallaq, "Inductive Corroboration," 3–31.

6. Consensus

The third source of law, consensus (*ijmāʿ*), guaranteed not only the infallibility of those *fiqh* rulings (opinions) subject to juristic agreement but also the entire structure of law. It is by virtue of consensus guaranteeing the entire structure of law that Sunnism defines itself versus the "Muslim Other." The community to which Sunnism by definition belongs is that of *al-sunna wal-jamāʿa*, i.e., those upholding: (1) the Sunna of the Prophet as a wholly authoritative source (without making the sanctioning authority of the Imam necessary [in reference to Twelver-Shīʿism]);[36] and (2) the institution of consensus, which makes them: (a) a unitary group that shares a well-defined set of principles; and (b) willing subjects to a political and, generally, religious practice or a set of practices defined and determined by these principles. It is noteworthy that these macro-functions of consensus were simply assumed, and never subjected to the analytical categories of the jurist-theoreticians.

What was thoroughly expounded was consensus as a micro-instrument, defined as the agreement of the community as represented by its *mujtahid*s living in a particular age or generation, an agreement that bestows on those rulings or opinions subject to it a conclusive, certain knowledge. But this nearly universal understanding of consensus was not to be reached until the end of the fourth/tenth century, if not later.

We saw earlier that by the end of the second/eighth century practice-based *sunna* was intertwined with the local consensus of scholars.[37] This consensus, in turn, was frequently based on the idea that unanimous legal practice issued, and continued with regularity, from the conduct and ways of the Companions. The traces of this sort of consensus may be found in the legal theory of the early fourth/tenth century, which represents a middle point between the un-theorized second/eighth-century practice and the fully mature and developed theory of the post-formative period. The later theory granted the instrument of consensus the authority of certitude, no matter how or by whom consensus is reached.

Later Mālikite legal theory continued to integrate the history of the school in Medina as a part of its theoretical rationalization. This theory insisted that the consensus of the scholars of Medina, the hometown of Mālik, constituted a binding authority, an insistence that gave rise to a discussion of whether or not any region in the world of Islam could independently, and validly, form a consensus. Against the Mālikites, theorists of other schools argued that the Quran and, particularly, the Sunna attest to the infallibility of the entire community, and that there is

[36] See section 9, below. [37] See chapter 1, section 4, above.

nothing in these texts to suggest that any segment of the community can alone be infallible. Furthermore, they maintained that the recognition of the consensus of a particular geographical area would lead to a paradox, since the opinion of a *mujtahid* who partook, say, in a Medinese consensus would be authoritative in Medina but not so once he left the city. The Mālikite claims, these jurists argued, gave rise to another objectionable conclusion, namely, that a particular geographical locale possesses an inherent capacity to bestow validity and authority upon the products of *ijtihād*, the cornerstone of consensus. This claim not only makes no sense rationally, but also cannot be justified by the revealed texts: either consensus is that of the entire community (as represented by all its *mujtahid*s who live in a particular generation), or it is not a consensus at all.[38]

The universal validity of consensus must thus be justified, not by reason or geographic privilege, but by nothing short of revelation. Consensus, like *qiyās*, is a source of law, but it is a derivative source nonetheless. The Quran and the Sunna were revealed, but not so consensus, whose justification must rest with the available indicants (*dalīl*s) in the two material sources.

The argument that an entire community cannot agree on an error could not be supported on purely rational grounds because, it was noted, both the Christian and the Jewish communities did, after all, agree on many falsehoods. The proof for the authority of consensus had therefore to be sought from either the Quran or the Sunna. But early attempts by theoreticians to articulate a Quranic basis for consensus failed, since the Quran (even its verse 4:115)[39] did not offer evidence bearing directly on authoritativeness. No less disappointing were the recurrent Prophetic reports which contained virtually nothing to this effect. All that was available were solitary reports speaking of the impossibility of the community on the whole ever agreeing on an error. "My community shall never agree on a falsehood" and "He who departs from the community ever so slightly would be considered to have abandoned Islam" are fairly representative of the themes conveyed by these solitary reports. While a dozen or more of these reports are relevant to the issue of authoritativeness, they give rise to an epistemological problem. Solitary reports are probable and thus cannot prove anything with certainty. Consensus is one of the four sources of the law, and must as such be shown to have its basis in nothing short of certain evidence.

[38] On this theoretical discussion, see Hallaq, *History*, 80.

[39] "And he who opposes the Messenger after the guidance has been manifested unto him, and follows other than the believers' way, We ... expose him unto Hell, a hapless journey's end."

To solve this quandary, the jurists turned to the reports that are thematically recurrent (*tawātur maʿnawī*). Although solitary, these reports not only are numerous but, despite the variation in their wording, possess in common a single theme, namely, that through divine grace the community as a whole is safeguarded against error. The large number of transmissions, coupled with their leitmotif, transforms these reports into the *maʿnawī* concurrent type, thus yielding certain knowledge of an infallible nature.

Conclusively established as a source of law, consensus ratifies as epistemically certain any particular rule that may have been based on probable textual evidence. The reasoning advanced in justification of this doctrine is that if consensus on probable evidence is attained, the evidence cannot be subject to error as the community cannot err in the first place. Thus, consensus may be reached on the basis of the inferential methods subsumed under *qiyās*, all of which are deemed probabilistic: it is consensus that renders their conclusions certain. The proponents of this doctrine, the majority, held the view that if consensus is reached on what appears to be probable evidence, then the fact that consensus was possible makes it necessary to believe that this evidence was certain after all.

Whatever the nature of textual evidence, there remained the question of how consensus is determined to have occurred. Much theoretical discussion was devoted to this issue, but in practice knowledge of the existence of consensus on a particular case was determined by looking to the past and by observing that the *mujtahid*s were unanimous with regard to its solution. And such cases were relatively few.[40]

7. Legal reasoning

Before embarking on inferential reasoning, the jurist must establish the meaning and relevance of the text employed, and ascertain its validity insofar as it was not abrogated. Knowledge of cases subject to consensus was required in order to ensure that his reasoning did not lead him to results different from, or contrary to, the established agreement in his school or among the larger community of jurists. The importance of this requirement stems from the fact that consensus bestows certainty upon the cases subject to it, raising them to the level of the unequivocal texts in

[40] Ibn Ḥazm (d. 456/1063) collected the legal rules subject to consensus in a small tome, *Marātib al-Ijmāʿ*. However, Ibn Taymiyya (d. 728/1327) accused Ibn Ḥazm of an overly expansive definition of consensus. In *Naqd Marātib al-Ijmāʿ* he resummarized legal rules that he deemed to be subject to no juristic disagreement whatsoever. In a modern edition, the *Naqd* consists of fewer than two dozen pages.

the Quran and the recurrent *ḥadīth*; thus, reopening such settled cases to new solutions would amount to questioning certainty, including conclusive texts in the Quran and recurrent *ḥadīth*. Yet, as I have already noted, the cases determined to be subject to the certainty of consensus remained numerically insignificant as compared to those subject to *khilāf*, or juristic disagreement.[41] The point remains, however, that inferential reasoning is legitimate only in two instances, namely, when the case in question had not been subject to consensus (having remained within the genre of *khilāf*) or when it was entirely new.

The theorists recognized various types of legal reasoning, some subsumed under the general term *qiyās*, and others dealt with under such headings as *istiṣlāḥ*, *istiḥsān* and *istidlāl*. We begin with *qiyās*, considered the fourth source of law after consensus.

Qiyās. The characterization of this category as a "source of law" need not imply that it is a material source on the *substance* of which a jurist can draw. Instead, it is a source only insofar as it provides a set of methods *through* which the jurist arrives at legal norms. The most common and prominent of these methods is analogy. As the archetype of all legal argument, *qiyās* was seen to consist of four elements, namely: (1) the new case that requires a legal solution; (2) the original case that may be found either stated in the revealed texts or sanctioned by consensus; (3) the *ratio legis*, or the attribute common to both the new and the original cases; and (4) the legal norm that is found in the original case and that, due to the similarity between the two cases, must be transposed to the new case. The archetypal example of legal analogy is the case of wine. If the jurist is faced with a case involving date-wine, requiring him to decide its status, he looks at the revealed texts only to find that grape-wine was explicitly prohibited by the Quran. The common denominator, the *ratio legis*, is the attribute of intoxication, in this case found in both drinks. The jurist concludes that, like grape-wine, date-wine is prohibited due to its inebriating quality.

Of the four components of *qiyās*, the *ratio legis* (*ʿilla*) occasioned both controversy and extensive analysis, since the claim for similarity between two things is the cornerstone and determinant of inference. Much discussion, therefore, was devoted to the determination of the *ratio*, for although it may be found to be explicitly stated in the texts, more often it is intimated or alluded to. Frequently, the need arose to infer it from the texts. For instance, when the Prophet was questioned about the legality of bartering ripe dates for unripe ones, he queried: "Do unripe dates lose

[41] See previous note.

weight upon drying up?" When he was answered in the affirmative, he reportedly remarked that such barter is unlawful. The *ratio* in this *ḥadīth* was deemed explicit since prohibition was readily understood to be predicated upon the dried dates losing weight; hence, a transaction involving unequal amounts or weights of the same object would constitute usury, clearly prohibited in Islamic law. On the other hand, the *ratio* may be merely intimated. In one *ḥadīth*, the Prophet said: "He who cultivates a barren land acquires ownership of it." Similarly, in 5:6, the Quran declares: "If you rise up for prayer, then you must wash." In these examples, the *ratio* is suggested in the semantic structure of this language, reducible to the conditional sentence "If... then..." The consequent phrase "then..." indicates that the *ratio* behind washing is prayer, just as the ownership of barren land is confirmed by cultivating it. It is important to realize here that prayer requires washing, not that washing is consistently occasioned by prayer alone. For one can wash oneself without performing prayer, but not the other way round. The same is true of land ownership. A person can possess a barren land without cultivating it, but the cultivation of, and subsequent entitlement to it, is the point.

*Ratio*s may be applicable to a class of cases or to an individual case subsumed under a genus. In homicide, for example, capital punishment is meted out when the elements of both intentionality and religious equality (i.e., where the murderer and victim, for instance, are both Muslim or both Christian) are present. But it must not be assumed that capital punishment is applicable only where homicide is involved. For example, apostasy and *zinā* committed by a married person also elicit this penalty.

The *ratio* may also consist of more than one attribute, all of which must be considered as "causing" a normative rule to arise from them. For instance, the *ratio* of the theft penalty encompasses five attributes: (1) the taking away of something by stealth; (2) the stolen object must be of a minimum value (normally set at 10 *dirham*s or their equivalent); (3) the object must in no way be the property of the thief; (4) it must be taken out of custody (*ḥirz*); and (5) the thief must have full legal capacity.[42] All of these attributes must obtain for an act to qualify as theft (*sariqa*) punishable by cutting off the hand. Each attribute is necessary; no single one by itself suffices to produce the *ratio legis*.

In this case, the rationale behind the rule is comprehensible: stealing a particular object under certain conditions qualifies as *sariqa*; and as a punishment and deterrent, the penalty of cutting off the hand is prescribed. Likewise, the intoxicating attribute of wine renders it prohibited

[42] For a detailed account of theft (*sariqa*), see chapter 10, section 2 (iv), below.

because intoxication incapacitates the mind and hinders, among other things, the performance of religious duties. In this example, we comprehend the reason for the prohibition. Some properties, however, do not disclose the reason. We do not know, for instance, why edibility should be the *ratio legis* for the prohibition of usury; all we know is that no object possessing the property of edibility can be the subject of a transaction involving usury.

The attributes comprising the *ratio*, once identified, must be confirmed as the entirety of the attributes that give rise to the rule in the original case. But again, there is a distinction between an explicitly stipulated *ratio* and one that is inferred. An example of the former may be found in the *ḥadīth* related to the barter of unripe dates cited above. In this *ḥadīth*, the language of causation is deemed clear: prohibition is instituted due to the fact that unripe dates lose weight upon further maturity, a fact that precludes their usurious barter for ripe dates.[43]

The *ratio* may be causally connected with its rule in a less explicit manner, however. From Q. 17:23, "Say not 'Fie' to them [parents] neither chide them, but speak to them graciously," the jurists understood that uttering "Fie" before one's parents is prohibited due to the lack of respect the expression entails. If the utterance of "Fie" is prohibited, then striking one's parents is *a fortiori* prohibited. The prohibition on striking is indirectly engendered by the prohibition to utter "Fie," and is not explicitly stated in the texts. At times, the sequence of events may also help unravel the *ratio*, for the sequence is interpreted causally. The Prophet, for instance, tersely commanded a man to free a slave upon hearing that the man had sexual intercourse with his wife during the fasting hours of Ramadan. Although the connection between the infraction and the command was not made clear by the Prophet, the sequence of events nonetheless renders them causally so connected. The Prophet would not have behaved in this manner without the occurrence of a particular event that precipitated his particular command.

The *ratio legis* may also be known by consensus. For example, it is the universal agreement of the jurists that the father enjoys a free hand in managing and controlling the property of his minor children. Here, minority is the *ratio* for this unrestricted form of conduct, and property the new case. Thus, the *ratio* may be transposed to yet another new case, such as the unrestricted physical control of a father over his children.

A significant method for discovering and evaluating the *ratio* is that of suitability (*munāsaba*). The Quran prohibits the consumption of wine

[43] Baṣrī, *Muʿtamad*, II, 775–77; Juwaynī, *Burhān*, II, 774 ff.; Shīrāzī, *Sharḥ al-Lumaʿ*, II, 844–45.

because it possesses the attribute of inebriation, leading the intoxicated person to neglect his religious duties. The theorists argued that even if the Quran did not allude to the reason for the prohibition, we would still come to the understanding that the prohibition was pronounced due to inebriation's harmful consequences. This is reasoning on the basis of suitability, since we, independently of revelation and through our rational faculty, are able to recognize the harmful effects of intoxication and thus the rationale behind certain sorts of prohibition.

In light of our discussion in section 2, above, there are limits to rationality within and without the method of suitability. Since the law cannot always be analyzed and comprehended in (exclusively) rational ways, reason and its products are not always in agreement with the legal premises and their conclusions. Suitability, therefore, may at times be relevant (*mulā'im*) to the law, and irrelevant (*gharīb*) at others. No *ratio* may be deemed suitable without being relevant; and any irrelevant *ratio* becomes, *ipso facto*, unsuitable, which precludes it from any further juristic consideration. In the case of divorced women who are of the age of majority, male guardianship is waived by virtue of the life experience that such divorcees have gained. Thus, such divorcees may remarry without the need for a guardian's approval. Logically, this reasoning would apply to divorcees who are minor, but rationally this is inappropriate since it runs counter to the aims of the law in protecting the welfare and interests of minors.

Suitability's goal is to offer "relevant" ways of rational reasoning that serve the public interest (*maṣlaḥa*) as defined through the fundamental principles of the law. In other words, interpreting law in the light of suitability is accomplished independently of the revealed texts, since the *ratio* is not, in the first place, textual.[44] Rather, it is rational and seeks to conform to the spirit of the law, which is known to prohibit what is harmful and promote what is good for this life and for the hereafter. The systematic exclusion of harm and inclusion of benefit are the aims (*maqṣūd*) of the law, and it is to these goals that the rational argument of suitability must conform. Protection of life, religion, private property, mind and offspring are the most salient of these goals. These are known as the indispensable necessities (*ḍarūriyyāt*), for without them no society or legal system can meaningfully exist. Then there are other supportive goals that fall under the heading of needs (*ḥājiyyāt*). While these are not regarded as indispensable necessities, they are *needed* for maintaining an orderly society and for laying the grounds to achieve the successful implementation of the

[44] For a detailed account of *maṣlaḥa*, see Kamali, *Principles*, 338–56.

ḍarūriyyāt. An example of the *ḥājiyyāt* is the necessity to appoint a guardian for the purpose of giving a female of a minor age in marriage. Here, neither life nor offspring is threatened, but only the protection of the interests of minors, a protection that is *needed* for ensuring the orderly and just functioning of society.

The third and final category in the "aims of the law" is that termed "improvements" (*taḥsīniyyāt*), which includes legal elements related to issues not directly connected with the *necessary* and *needed* aims. Barring slaves from giving testimony in a court of law does not directly serve the *ḍarūriyyāt* and *ḥājiyyāt*, but does serve the general aims of the law in that it purports to maintain the high standards of social status on which testimony rests. The menial social status of slaves was understood to impede their independent testimony. Thus, while suitability is a rational method, it must conform to the spirit of the law, a spirit that dictates to what extent and under what circumstances suitability is to be accepted or not. This spirit distinguishes between relevant and irrelevant suitability, for what is irrelevant is compatible not only with this spirit, but ultimately with the letter of the law.

Once the *ratio* in analogical *qiyās* is identified and confirmed to be the *relevant* and *complete* common factor between the original case and the new one, very little else is involved in the transference of the legal norm from the former to the latter case. Analogy, however, is not the only method of inference subsumed under *qiyās*. Another important argument is that of the *a fortiori* type. From Quran 5:3, "Forbidden unto you are carrion, blood, flesh of the pig," the jurists took the last four words to include all types of pork, including that of wild boars, although the original reference was to domestic pigs. Technically, the *a fortiori* consists of two types, the *a minore ad maius* and the *a maiore ad minus*, thought to be the most compelling forms of *qiyās*. An example of the former type may be found in the language of Quran 99:7–8: "Whoso has done an atom's weight of good shall see it, and whoso has done an atom's weight of evil shall see it." From this verse, it was understood that the reward for doing more than an atom's weight of good and the punishment for doing more than an atom's weight of evil are greater than that promised for simply an atom's weight. An example of the latter type, the *a maiore ad minus*, can be seen in judgments based on the Quranic permission to kill non-Muslims who engage in war against Muslims. From this permission, it was understood that acts short of killing, such as confiscation of the belligerent unbeliever's property, are also lawful.

A number of jurists argued that the *a fortiori* is not an inferential argument in the first place, for a proposition such as "the flesh of wild boars is forbidden" needs no inference since the very language of the Quran engenders necessary knowledge of its own meaning and requires no processes of inference whatsoever. The distinction, therefore, was one between inferential and linguistic means of acquiring knowledge. In contradistinction to a higher linguistic category containing statements that are expressly revealed in order to specify the rule of a particular case, this category of *a fortiori* propositions is intended to legislate in matters that have not been explicitly specified but which are clearly understood from the language of these propositions. Points of law in this category are *denoted* in the texts but not specifically stated. Yet, the denotation is so strong that the *ratio* embedded in the language is grasped by the mind, if not imposed on it, without any inference. However, while accepting the strong denotational-linguistic force of the *a fortiori*, the majority of theorists insisted on subsuming it under the general category of *qiyās*.

A third type of argument is the *reductio ad absurdum*, a line of reasoning in which the converse of a given rule is applied to another case on the grounds that the *ratio legis* of the two cases are contradictory. The cornerstone of this argument is the determination of a rule by demonstrating the falsehood or invalidity of its converse. In other words, if a rule standing in diametrical opposition to another is proven invalid or unwarranted, then the latter emerges as the only sound or valid rule. Of the same type is the argument that proceeds from the assumption that the non-existence of a *ratio* leads to the absence of the rule that must otherwise arise from that *ratio*. For example, in the case of an unlawfully appropriated animal, the wrongdoer (*ghāṣib*) – according to the Ḥanafites – is not liable for damages with regard to the offspring of the animal since the offspring, unlike its mother, was not usurped.[45]

The foregoing account has presented *qiyās* from the perspective of logical structure, only one, though significant, way of analyzing this category. The importance of this sort of analysis lies in the fact that ever since modern scholarship began to turn its attention to *qiyās*, it has systematically managed to reduce it to its analogical form, thereby neglecting its other components. The tenacity of this misconception is evidenced in its undiminishing force despite the glaring fact that corrections of this misconception were made in the 1980s.[46]

Be that as it may, and in addition to an analysis of its logical structure, *qiyās* may also be typified according to the type of *ratio legis* involved and the latter's epistemic strength. From this perspective, *qiyās* is classified into two major types of inference, the causative and the indicative. In the causative type, the *ratio* and the rationale behind it are readily identifiable,

45 See chapter 9, section 3, below.
46 Hallaq, "Non-Analogical Arguments in Sunni Juridical *Qiyās*."

but in the indicative type, the rationale is merely inferred or not known at all. Wine is declared prohibited because of its intoxicating quality, and the rationale behind the prohibition is that intoxication leads to repugnant behavior, including carelessness and neglect in performing religious duties. Here the rationale is known. In indicative inferences, however, the rationale is known merely by conjecture, such as by positing that the *ratio* behind the prohibition of usury is edibility (according to the Shāfiʿites) or measurability by weight (according to the Ḥanafites). But no revealed text clearly states that one or the other (or both) constitutes the rationale behind the prohibition. Nonetheless, the difference between the two types of *qiyās* is often one of form, not substance. God could have said "Pray, because the sun has set," or He could have said "When the sun sets, pray." The former injunction gives rise to a causative inference, whereas the latter merely allows for an indicative one. The relationship between prayer and sunset is not, at any rate, causal but rather a matter of concomitance.

Istiḥsān. In chapter 1, we saw that second/eighth-century Iraqian reasoning was not always directly based on the revealed texts, a fact that prompted Shāfiʿī to launch a scathing criticism of what he labeled "human legislation." A substantial part of this reasoning – which originally fell under the rubric of *raʾy* – became known as *istiḥsān*. With the traditionalization of the Ḥanafite school, a process whose beginnings seem to have been associated with the contributions of Muḥammad b. Shujāʿ al-Thaljī, Ḥanafite theorists after the third/ninth century endeavored to dissociate themselves from any reputation connecting them with *raʾy*, now synonymous with arbitrary reasoning. Following the normative practice that had evolved as the unchallenged paradigm of juridical reasoning, they insisted that no argument of *istiḥsān* can rest on any grounds other than the texts of revelation. In fact, they never acknowledged that discretionary reasoning had ever existed in their jurisprudence. The resulting technical modifications that were introduced into *istiḥsān*, however, rendered it acceptable to other schools, notably, the so-called conservative Ḥanbalites.

In legal theory, *istiḥsān* was little more than another form of *qiyās*, one that was deemed to be – in some cases – "preferred" to the standard form. Simply stated, *istiḥsān* is reasoning that presumably departs from a revealed text but leads to a conclusion that differs from one reached by means of *qiyās*. If a person, for example, forgets what he is doing and eats while he is supposed to be fasting during the month of Ramadan, *qiyās* dictates that his fasting becomes void, since food has entered his body, whether intentionally or not. But *qiyās* in this case was abandoned in favor of a Prophetic *ḥadīth* which pronounced the fasting valid if the act of eating was the result of a mistake. The *qiyās* reasoning here is one that typically falls within a large area of the law where no exceptions are allowed. If the fasting during Ramadan is broken on any given day, then *qiyās* requires compensation. Yet, despite the fact that *istiḥsān* is based on a text, the very choice of this text represents the juristic intention to create an exception to the law. If a mistake does not invalidate fasting, then no atonement or compensation is required.

Some, but by no means all, *istiḥsān* exceptions were justified by sacred texts. Many were in fact based either on consensus or on the principle of necessity, the latter of which earned it Shāfiʿī's wrath. For instance, to be valid, any contract involving the exchange of commodities requires immediate payment. But some contracts of hire do not fulfill this condition, a fact that would render them void if *qiyās* were to be invoked. The common practice of people over the ages has been to admit these contractual forms in their daily lives, and this is viewed as tantamount to consensus. As an instrument that engenders certainty, consensus becomes tantamount to the revealed texts themselves, thereby bestowing on the reasoning involved here the same force that the Quran or the *ḥadīth* would bestow.

Likewise, necessity often requires the abandonment of conclusions reached by *qiyās* in favor of those generated by *istiḥsān*. Washing with ritually impure water would, by *qiyās*, invalidate prayer, but not so in *istiḥsān*. Here, *qiyās* would lead to hardship in view of the fact that fresh, clean water is not always easy to procure. The acceptance of necessity as a principle that legitimizes departure from strict reasoning is seen as deriving from, and sanctioned by, both the Quran and the Sunna, since necessity, when not acknowledged, can cause nothing but hardship. Thus, *istiḥsān* in the context of necessity is viewed as legitimized by the revealed texts, reflecting the reasoned distinction of textual evidence.[47]

This distinction is ultimately one between two *ratio*s, one establishing a commonality between the original case and the new one, and the other – while taking note of the rule generated by the first *ratio* – forming an exception to this rule based upon a more suitable and relevant text. This suitability leads to what has been termed "a preferred *qiyās*,"[48] a category to be distinguished from *qiyās* proper. An example in point is the analogy between predatory birds and predatory animals. The human consumption of the former's flesh is deemed prohibited because the latter are stipulated by the revealed texts to be ritually impure, and therefore prohibited. The *ratio* here is the impurity of the flesh of both kinds of animals. Consequently, food left by predatory birds is also considered impure,

[47] Makdisi, "Legal Logic," 85. [48] Sarakhsī, *Uṣūl*, II, 204.

rendering its consumption prohibited, just as is the case with carcasses left by predatory animals. By *istiḥsān*, however, food left by predatory birds is permissible for humans. For when predatory animals eat, they secrete saliva that comes in touch with their food, making it impure for humans. Birds, on the other hand, do not transmit saliva when they feed, since their beaks, made as they are of bone, remain dry while picking on food. Here, we know that bones are ritually pure from revealed texts which permit the use of the bones taken from dead animals. But all this textual support and legal reasoning should not hide the essential fact that the real need to create an exception to food touched by predatory birds boils down to the principle of necessity. If all food that such birds touch becomes legally inedible, then society is bound to face severe hardship, and this is contrary to the fundamental spirit and wishes of the law.[49]

Maṣlaḥa. Like the Iraqian Ḥanafites of the second/eighth century, the Medinese, including their chief jurist Mālik b. Anas, resorted to reasoning that did not appear to be directly based on the revealed texts. This procedure became known as *istiṣlāḥ/maṣlaḥa*, loosely translated as "public interest." Later Mālikite theory nonetheless denied that their Medinese predecessors had ever reasoned without textual support. They argued that to proceed thus on the grounds of public interest must, at the end of the day, boil down either to a universal principle of the law or to a specific, revealed text.

We have already taken note of the important role that public interest plays in determining the *ratio*'s suitability (*munāsaba*) in *qiyās*. It is because of this relationship between the *ratio* and suitability that *maṣlaḥa* is deemed an extension of *qiyās*. As such, most theorists do not devote to it an independent section or chapter but treat it under the category of suitability. This fact attests to the heavy emphasis *qiyās* places upon the non-literal extrapolation of rules, a phenomenon insufficiently appreciated by students of legal theory.

Thus, on the basis of a comprehensive study of *fiqh*, the jurists came to realize that there are five universal principles that underlie the Sharīʿa, namely, protection of life, mind, religion, private property and offspring. The reasoning was that the law has come down explicitly to protect and promote these five areas of human life, and that nothing in this law can conceivably run counter to these principles or to any of their implications, however remotely. If the feature of public interest in a case can be shown to be indubitably connected with the five universals, then reasoning must proceed in accordance with *istiṣlāḥ*. The condition of

[49] For an expanded discussion of the *ratio legis* in *istiḥsān*, see Hallaq, *History*, 110–11.

universality is also intended to ensure that the interests of the Muslim community at large are served.[50]

8. *Mujtahid*s, *muqallid*s and *fatwā*s

Central to the entire edifice of the Sharīʿa is the idea that the human intellectual faculty mediates between God's will and human reality. This faculty, termed *ijtihād*, is preeminently individualistic and juristic. Upon the occurrence of an unprecedented case, it is called upon to provide a solution, represented in the form of an opinion. *Ijtihād*, one of the most salient elements and defining features of Islamic law, is just that, an opinion. It does not claim monopoly on jural truth, nor does it instigate any powers of enforcement. It is precisely here where the "law" of the Sharīʿa, the *ijtihād*ic opinion, differs fundamentally from the law of the modern state. Islamic law, from at least this perspective, is not law, in the modern sense, at all.[51]

Now, the jurist in possession of this faculty is the *mujtahid*, he who exerts to the utmost his intellectual faculties with a view to arriving at a solution that was, in all probability, intended by God for that particular case. But what are the conditions that a jurist must fulfill in order to qualify as *mujtahid*? Put differently, what legal qualifications are required to allow a jurist to perform *ijtihād*? It must first be stated that, although theory formalized both the question and the answer to the issue of qualifications, there was no formal procedure by which jurists were tested for meeting these requirements. Exercising *ijtihād* remained a matter of juristic practice, regulated by the prevailing local or regional norms of that practice. Put differently, a jurist claiming the competence to practice *ijtihād* is one who has been latently sanctioned as such by the scholarly community.

With this caveat in mind, the first condition expected to be met is that a jurist should have expert knowledge of the 500 or so Quranic verses that touch on legal subject-matter. Second, he should know all legal *ḥadīth*s and must acquire proficiency in *ḥadīth* criticism, so as to be able to sort out credible and sound *ḥadīth*s from those that are not. But he may also rely on those canonical works that have already recorded the *ḥadīth*s that are considered sound. Third, he must be knowledgeable in the Arabic

50 Ghazālī, *Mustaṣfā*, I, 284–315.

51 While it is true that many modern legal systems (including that of the US) rely on private legal opinion – making this latter an integral part of judicial practice – modern legal doctrine does not derive from such a body of opinion. In the Sharīʿa, opinion/*ijtihād* is the exclusive foundation of legal doctrine.

language so that he can understand the complexities involved, for example, in metaphorical usages, in general and particular language, and in equivocal and univocal speech. Fourth, he must possess a thorough knowledge of the theory of abrogation and of those verses that have been abrogated by others. Fifth, he must be deeply trained in the art of legal reasoning, in how *qiyās* is conducted and in the principles of causation (i.e., establishing the *ratio legis* and using it in inferences). Sixth, he must know all cases that have been sanctioned by consensus, as he is not permitted to reopen any of these cases and subject them to fresh legal reasoning. However, he is not required to know all rulings of *fiqh*, although this is recommended – especially those cases subject to disagreement. Nor is he required to be of just character, even though the absence of the quality of rectitude does have an effect on the authoritativeness of his opinions, for judges and laymen are perfectly entitled to ignore them.

Once a jurist rises to the rank of a *mujtahid*, he can no longer follow the *ijtihād* of others and must exercise his own reasoning and judgment. This requirement stems from the assumption that all *mujtahid*s in principle are correct in their legal reasoning, and that his opinion is as valid as that of any other. Yet another rule that follows from the principle of equality of *ijtihād* is that a *mujtahid* must never follow the opinion of another less learned than he is.

Anyone who is not a *mujtahid* is, by definition, a *muqallid*, someone who practices *taqlīd*. A *muqallid* is a jurist who follows the *mujtahid* and who cannot perform *ijtihād* by himself. In the terminology of legal theory, *muqallid*s are also laymen and laywomen. It is their inability to reason independently on the basis of the revealed texts that consigns them to the same camp as jurist-*muqallid*s. The layman's access to the law can be had only through referring to the opinion of the *mujtahid*; this opinion is transmitted to them by the jurist-*muqallid* and they have no choice but to follow it.

The theorists agree that laypersons must follow a *mujtahid* as their sole reference. The layperson is charged with the responsibility of enquiring about the credentials and reputation of the jurists he or she consults. The enquiry, usually conducted by "asking around," amounts to soliciting the testimony of witnesses, as happens, for instance, in the case of establishing the rectitude of court witnesses.

In theoretical juristic discourse, the *mujtahid* is generally equated with the *muftī*, or jurisconsult, who issues expert legal opinions (*fatwās*). Whatever scholarly credentials the *mujtahid* must possess, the *muftī* must possess too, but with a single difference: the *muftī* must be pious and of just character and must take religion and law seriously. A person who meets all these requirements falls under the obligation to issue a legal opinion to anyone who solicits it from him. As a master of legal science, he is even under the obligation to teach law to anyone interested, this being considered as meritorious as the issuing of *fatwā*s.

It is a remarkable feature of legal theory that its discourse typifies nearly all legal categories, creating thereby distinct and neatly ordered classifications of such categories. Thus, interpretive legal activity or creative legal reasoning is seen to belong exclusively to the *mujtahid*, but by no means to the *muqallid*; nor, consequently, can a *mujtahid* be a *muqallid* or vice versa, even when the *muqallid* is a jurist – i.e., not a layman – on his own. In the mundane realities of law, however, such neat classifications did not prevail, as the functions of theory and applied jurisprudence understandably stood apart. To conduct its mission effectively, legal theory had to categorize and typify. The category of the *mujtahid* could not be confused with that of the *muqallid*. As types, these two had to stand each on its own. In reality, however, serious difficulties would have arisen if legal culture and juristic activity were to be divided into such black-and-white categories. The *mujtahid*, in the typology of legal practice, thus can be a *muqallid*, and vice versa.

To explicate the spectrum of interpretive legal practice, the jurists elaborated a juristic taxonomy whereby the entire community of legists was divided into types according to levels of hermeneutical engagement. Thus, in the majority of these taxonomies, the master-jurists ranked first, followed as a second by major jurists who adhered to the masters' methodologies by virtue of the major jurists' *independent* conviction of the masters' methodological superiority. These two classes would have been one, identical category had the master-jurists, the founders of the schools, not preceded them in chronological terms. The other categories, variously defined as being anywhere from three to five in number, classified jurists according to varying capabilities of *ijtihād*, ranging from those who could reason by *ijtihād* on the basis of the legal methodologies of the master-jurists to those who could only apply the doctrines of the *mujtahid*s in their respective schools.

The analytical value of these taxonomies is exceptional and wide-ranging,[52] but for our purposes here we can read them only as serving to illustrate the range of activities of a single jurist. The more accomplished the jurist, the greater the number of activities in which he might be involved. Needless to say, jurists operated within a system of authority, which means that *taqlīd* constituted the great majority of cases with which they had to deal. But jurists of a high caliber did deal with less common

[52] See Hallaq, *Authority*, 1–23.

and "hard" cases which required competence of a more specialized and sophisticated type. Such jurists functioned at several levels, but to the exclusion of the first two types – i.e., the founding masters and their "independent" followers – which became, historically, unique phenomena. The *taqlīd* of later jurists was of the best type, so to speak, for it involved the reproduction of the masters' opinion through careful reasoning and interpretation that at times were qualitatively superior to those the masters produced. This *taqlīd*, therefore, is an intellectually independent affirmation of authority and in no way involves "blind" adherence to the legal doctrines of the masters. It is preeminently of the methodological type, having nothing to do with the acceptance of *fiqh* conclusions at face value. Yet, the great majority of cases handled on a daily basis by the judges and jurisconsults involved simpler forms of *taqlīd*, such as the application of legal doctrine – generally much in the same way that a Western judge applies the law in his or her court.[53] Thus, all these forms of *taqlīd* maintained a positive image since they amounted to an assertion about affiliation and loyalty to the school. For no school, in the first place, could have come into existence and survived without this doctrinal loyalty. This loyalty, popularly summed up in Western legal systems by the expression "law is conservative," is nothing if not the lynchpin of all legal systems in complex societies.

9. Twelver-Shīʿite legal theory

As Sunnite legal theory found its complete, but by no means final, expression during the second half of the fourth/tenth century, it would be unreasonable to expect that Twelver-Shīʿite legal theory could have developed into a complete, structured form before then. In fact, an extensive, elaborate and highly abstract formulation of Twelver *uṣūl al-fiqh* was not to appear until much later, but by the middle of the fifth/eleventh century a few works had already advanced a basic but complete exposition of its subject-matter. The persecution of the Shīʿites at the hands of the Sunnite ruling elites meant that law in Shīʿism was long an incomplete project, not least because of the absence of crucial institutional structures and the general lack of public financial and other forms of support for the jural class and its intellectuals. This deprivation continued to hold until the Būyids came to rule over Iran and Iraq around the middle of the fourth/tenth century, a dynasty that sponsored Twelver-Shīʿism as its official creed (though the legal administration of the population in both

[53] Subject, that is, to our discussion in chapter 4 (below), namely, to the unique ways the *qāḍī* dealt with the social, moral and other facets of local Muslim societies.

regions continued to be largely, if not entirely, Sunnite). Būyid sponsorship may in part explain the flourishing of a Twelver juristic and intellectual class, but together with the Ismāʿīlī Fāṭimids in North Africa and Egypt, it certainly gave Shīʿism in general a tremendous boost.

The early Shīʿite works display an ever-present consciousness of Sunnite legal theory as a theoretical, methodological and hermeneutical force to be reckoned with, but more so to be distanced and set apart from what was being constructed by these authors as a separate hermeneutical and discursive identity. On the first page of his somewhat pioneering work, Shaykh al-Ṭā'ifa al-Ṭūsī (d. 460/1067) nicely illustrates the conscious attempt not only to set the Twelver-Shīʿite legal methodology apart, but also to begin a counter-discourse of considerable intellectual weight. "I am writing this book," he states,

> in accordance with the requirements of our ways of thinking (*madhāhib*) and the dictates of our precepts (*uṣūl*). For, those writing on this subject would each follow the dictates of his own *madhhab*'s precepts. None of our associates (*aṣḥāb*) has written on this matter except our Shaykh Abū ʿAbd Allāh in his short work on *uṣūl al-fiqh*, a terse work containing irregularities that need to be corrected and (weak) expositions that need improvement. Our Great Master, al-Murtaḍā ... did not author anything on this subject that one can cite or use as a backing [to one's arguments and exposition].[54]

Twelver-Shīʿite legal theory, as well as its applied law, came to differ from its Sunnite counterpart on a number of essential points and, obviously, on countless details. Even those differences that appear, according to many modern scholars, to be minor, are not really minor when their ramifications and consequences are fully considered. On some determinative issues, the differences are considerable, and so are their effects. Shīʿite jurisprudence rests on several major premises (very much as in a syllogism), three of which are of immediate concern to us here. The first relates to the divine appointment of the Imamate, which begins with the foundational assumption that there exists a qualitative dissimilitude between human and divine qualities. Man's intelligence is ultimately defective: God's is perfect. He is all-knowing; we are not. We do not know what He has in mind, and therefore possess incomplete knowledge of His Law. All this of course presumes that obligations (*taklīf*) of worship and obedience imposed on humans create another obligation on the part of God Himself, that is, to make these very obligations known to the human mind, for otherwise there would be no *taklīf*. As a means of communicating His signs (*āyāt*) that embody His Will and Law, God

[54] Ṭūsī, *ʿUddat al-Uṣūl*, 2. See also Abisaab, "Ulama of the Jabal ʿAmil," 115.

chose a number of persons who possessed superior qualities and made them Prophets and Imams. The Imam is neither a second-class Prophet nor a deputy, as the early Sunnite caliphs were conceived by the Sunnites. He is a substitute for the Prophet, taking on the tasks and functions of the Prophet in his absence (*qā'im maqām*).[55]

The second premise takes the Imam to be a sinless, infallible and perfect being. By virtue of having been chosen as an Imam, he combines qualities that are superior (*al-afḍal*) to any other human living in his age. If it were not for the convention of religious texts, the Imam would be no less a prophet than the Prophet Muhammad himself. The distinguished al-Shaykh al-Mufīd observed that "it is divine law that forbade our Imams being given the name of prophecy, not reason."[56] The Twelver-Shīʿite Imams are thus not subordinate to the Prophet Muhammad but rather his peers. Nay, whereas he is deemed to be a fallible human, they are deemed immune from error. On the other hand, the Prophet was an instrument of revelation, whereas none of the Imams was chosen for this task. But since their knowledge is infallible, their ability to convey the divine Law to their followers has the status of certitude. (This divine empowerment of the Imams must be kept in mind when we turn, in a later chapter, to the jural-political developments in modern Iran, for the Imamic ennoblement appears to run counter to the claim that the jurist-master, the Marjaʿ al-Taqlīd, can replace and fully represent the Imam in the latter's absence. In fact, the Imams did not delegate their powers to anyone, and were reported to have condemned as fraudulent any political governance in their name.)[57]

The third premise was constituted by historical events. Around 260/874, the twelfth Imam disappeared, and since then he has been presumed to be in hiding (*ghayba*) as a result of the persecution he suffered. Yet, while hiding, he continues to bear the knowledge of law in its best, infallible and most perfect form. In many ways, he in effect takes on a divine status, since – according to a number of Twelver-Shīʿite jurists – there can be no access to God's mind without resort to the Imam. Indeed, it seems that with the exception of some jurists of the Uṣūlist school, the Imam represents for Twelver-Shīʿism the locus of the law, if not its probative source. At the end of time, the Imam will reappear, implementing his just law with full force, but until then, several functions that the Imams had fulfilled must somehow be dispensed. As we just noted, the delegation of political rule was, until the twentieth century, out of the

[55] Eliash, "Ithnā ʿAsharī-Shīʿī Juristic Theory," 22–23. [56] Cited in *ibid.*, 24.
[57] See Halm, *Shiʿa Islam*, 88, and Eliash's arguments in this regard, "Ithnā ʿAsharī-Shīʿī Juristic Theory," 24.

question, but other local communal functions were, by virtue of necessity and with the passage of time, taken on by the chief jurists, the *faqīh*s. As in Sunnism, the running of the community's affairs required knowledge of the law, knowledge whose sources were the Quran and the narrative of the Prophet, his Sunna. But the Imam counts just as much, so his Sunna must be included. The Shīʿites have always held that the hegemonic power of the Sunnites since the earliest phases of Islamic history has created a system of knowledge that amounts to no more than a colossal lie, one that is primarily political, but also theological, legal and otherwise. Accordingly, no Sunnite *ḥadīth* is to be trusted. The only trustworthy *ḥadīth* is that narrated by the Imams and their Companions, which *ḥadīth* came to be recorded in the Four Books (*al-Kutub al-Arbaʿa*), very much emulating the Six Books of *ḥadīth* compiled earlier in Sunnite Islam. These four are: Kulaynī's (d. 328/939) voluminous *Kāfī*, said to contain the majority, if not all, of the Imams' *ḥadīth*; Ibn Bābawayh al-Qummī's (d. 381/991), *Man lā Yaḥḍuruhu al-Faqīh*; and al-Shaykh al-Ṭūsī (d. 460/1067, later known as Shaykh al-Ṭāʾifa), who supplied two of the four works, *al-Istibṣār* and *Tahdhīb al-Aḥkām*.[58]

During the third/ninth century, vehement controversies erupted in Sunnite circles over the role of human reason in determining the intellectual and practical affairs of society. As a general rule, the more reason was validly ascribed to human agency, the more humans were bestowed with the authority to determine their own affairs and, correlatively, the lesser authority the divine will had over the conduct of such affairs. The solution to this intense intellectual debate came after a century, in the form of a synthesis, dividing in more or less equal portions the competence between reason and revelation. *Qiyās* was to constitute a counter-balance to the weight of revelation, and consensus itself was the very manifestation of this rational–textual balance.

A similar dispute that acquired no less a sectarian dimension within Twelver-Shīʿism was that which erupted between the so-called Akhbārists and Uṣūlists. Intellectual ingredients in the claims of the two camps may be found in works written as early as the fifth/eleventh century, and so the origins of the formation of the camps has been a point of disagreement among Shīʿites themselves as well as among modern Western scholars.[59] But it seems plausible to assert that while the seeds – and thus potential differences between jurists – were planted from the very early centuries, the culmination and final articulation of two clearly opposing positions

[58] For these four works, see Bibliography, below.

[59] Gleave, *Akhbārī Shīʿī Uṣūl al-Fiqh*, 26; Modarressi, "Rationalism and Traditionalism," 154 f.

came to the fore only by the end of the tenth/sixteenth century. The confrontation is said to have begun when Muḥammad Amīn al-Astarābādī (d. 1036/1626) wrote in criticism of *ijtihād* and the use of *ʿaql* (reason) as a basis of juristic authority.[60]

On the whole, the Uṣūlist camp had the upper hand, and won majority support among the Persian- and Arab-speaking jurists, the latter mostly coming from what have today become southern Lebanon, Iraq and Bahrain. For most of the time, the Akhbārist stronghold was outside of Iran,[61] and this was no coincidence. In the early tenth/sixteenth century, the rulers of the recently ascendant Ṣafavids sought to legitimize their rule in Iran by carving for themselves a dynastic governance (and an anti-Ottoman identity) based on Twelver-Shīʿism, thus replacing the largely Ḥanafite traditions that had prevailed in those regions for centuries. To accomplish this, they, like all pre-modern dynasties, needed the collaboration of the ulama, the *mulla*s who represented the populace. The scarce presence of Shīʿite scholars in Iran compelled them to import some of the most distinguished theologian-jurists from the Arab-speaking areas just mentioned.[62] Al-Karakī, among others, was a major contributor to this process of legitimation, having argued that a secular leader, a *sulṭān*, may represent the Imam in carrying on the latter's tasks in the temporal world. Without, as a first step, arrogating to human reason the ability to partake in the determination of the law, a human agency representing – and represented by – the Imam would not have been possible. The theoretical, intellectual and thus religious-cultural foundations having been laid down, the Ṣafavids not only claimed to speak on behalf of the Imam, but in fact declared themselves his lineal representatives by virtue of being, so they claimed, descendants from the ʿAlid family.

To map out the chief elements of this Akhbārist–Uṣūlist dispute, I shall in part draw on a list that Samāhijī (d. 1135/1723) compiled in his *Munyat al-Mumārisīn* (without necessarily following his arrangement).[63] Samāhijī significantly lists *ijtihād* as the first point of disagreement, and as an indication of the centrality of this axial differential, he gives the name *Mujtahid*s (Ar. pl.: *Mujtahidūn*) to the Uṣūlist camp, which latter designation he does not use. For the Uṣūlists/Mujtahids, *ijtihād* during the

[60] See his *Fawāʾid*, 90 ff.; Gleave, *Inevitable Doubt*, 6 f. For a different viewpoint, see Newman, "Nature of the Akhbārī/Uṣūlī Dispute," pt 2, 250–61.
[61] Modarressi, "Rationalism and Traditionalism," 156–57.
[62] On this "conversion," see Abisaab, *Converting Persia*.
[63] The relevant Arabic text was edited and translated into English by Newman in "Nature of the Akhbārī/Uṣūlī Dispute," pt 1, 24–38. Henceforth, all references to Samāhijī are based on the Newman Arabic edition.

absence of the Imam[64] is regarded as an indispensable jurisprudential method, whereas the Akhbārists reject it altogether on the grounds that it leads, as everyone admits, to no more than probable knowledge.[65] Banning *ijtihād* also meant a rejection of the (Uṣūlist and Sunnite) belief that in the Hereafter a *mujtahid* will be rewarded twice if he is correct in his *ijtihād* and once if he errs (because he expended his utmost effort, the very meaning of the term *ijtihād*). The Akhbārists believe that he sins in either case, merely by exercising *ijtihād*. If he does not base himself on an Imam's *ḥadīth* (this being precisely what *ijtihād* is), and if he happens to be right, then he must be punished because he has, in effect, feigned the truth; and if he has erred, he should also be punished for "lying in the name of God."[66] The Akhbārists regard the *akhbār* (Prophetic Sunna as transmitted through the infallible Imamic narrative) as the exclusive source of knowledge, since, by the very nature of this narrative, it yields certainty.

The Uṣūlists'/Mujtahids' position can by no means be regarded as having been newly introduced to Shīʿite thought, since the influential al-ʿAllāma al-Ḥillī (d. 726/1325) had already adopted a theory of *ijtihād* resembling its Sunnite counterpart and holding much of *fiqh* rulings to be probable, certainty being assigned only to the sources of the law.[67] Juristic disagreement (*ikhtilāf*) is thus admitted by the Uṣūlists/Mujtahids, much as it is recognized by the Sunnite jurists themselves. But the Akhbārists reject juristic *ikhtilāf*, the truth for them being only that which is embedded in the infallible reports of the Imams.[68] The admission by the Uṣūlists/Mujtahids of *ijtihād* does not, however, automatically mean that *qiyās* is also incorporated as part of the package. In fact, it was, after discussion in almost every Twelver *uṣūl* work, largely rejected, although in hermeneutical practice it was inescapable and was subsumed under a different guise.[69] This adamant avoidance of the very word *qiyās* was perhaps due to the Imams' condemnation of it, a tradition that has its Sunnite equivalent in Ibn Idrīs al-Shāfiʿī's scathing attack on *istiḥsān*, a method the later Shāfiʿites came to use in substance, but whose Ḥanafite terminological designation they avoided at any cost.[70]

Second, the Uṣūlists/Mujtahids adopt four sources of the law: the Quran, the Sunna of the Prophet as culled by the Imams, the consensus

[64] Which is his sixth point in Samāhijī, 26. [65] Calder, "Doubt and Prerogative," 59.
[66] The issue of rewards represents point 18 in Samāhijī, 29–30.
[67] Halm, *Shiʿa Islam*, 100–02; Gleave, *Inevitable Doubt*, 4–5.
[68] This being point 23 in Samāhijī, 31.
[69] See further below, and Modarressi, "Rationalism and Traditionalism," 148.
[70] Ṭūsī, *ʿUddat al-Uṣūl*, II, 82–89 where he nonetheless discussed *qiyās* and its substance, and 89 ff. where he declares it objectionable. See also Gleave, *Inevitable Doubt*, 103; Calder, "Doubt and Prerogative," 59–60.

of the jurists, and the rational indicant (*dalīl al-ʿaql*). Most of the Akhbārists accept only the first two, and some reject even the Quran.[71] But what do the two camps mean by these source-designations? The Uṣūlists/Mujtahids, assigning to human reason a significant role, hold that the Quranic meanings are intelligible to the jurist who has mastered the art of interpretation and whose hermeneutical tools permit sound analysis. The Akhbārists, on the other hand, are suspicious of human reason, and thus invoke higher forms of interpretive competence than those possessed by even the most skilled jurists. For them only the interpretation and explicatory commentary of the Imam can unravel the meanings of the Quran, and this commentary is abundantly found in the Imam's narrative, the *akhbār* collected in the Four Books. This is why a group of jurists among the Akhbārists subordinate the Quran to the Sunna, deeming the Sunna the only source of the law.

Twelver-Shīʿite jurists generally disagreed on consensus and on the extent of its validity, some holding it to yield certitude, others deeming it to be merely probable.[72]

It is admitted by the Uṣūlists/Mujtahids as a valid source of law as long as it includes the opinion of the Imam, for it is this inclusion that guarantees its certitude, not the collective weight of the jurists. "Our rational and revealed indicants," al-Shahīd al-Thānī (d. 966/1558) declares,

> demonstrate that at no time will legal obligation (*taklīf*) be devoid of an Imam who will preserve the Sharʿ and whose opinion must be the frame of reference. Should the [Twelver-Shīʿite] Community reach a consensus on any opinion, the Imam's opinion would inevitably be included in it, because he is its Lord and as such he is infallible. Only then will that consensus constitute an authoritative opinion (*ḥujja*). In our doctrine, the authoritativeness of consensus rests in its ability to uncover that authoritative opinion, the opinion of the Infallible. It is precisely to this notion that al-Muḥaqqiq [al-Ḥillī] referred ... saying that "consensus is the revealer of the opinion of the Imam (*kāshif ʿan qawl al-Imām*), not that it is an authority in and of itself."[73]

Bihbahānī, however, adduces another argument, akin to that which the early Mālikites advance in justification of Medinese consensus.[74] The early community of the Imam's Companions knew the ways of the Infallible One and lived by his guidance, and these ways have been transmitted from one generation to the next with certainty. Thus any opinion that is subject to the consensus of the jurists must be grounded in this

71 Astarābādī, *Fawāʾid*, 14–18.
72 Al-Shahīd al-Thānī, *Maʿālim*, 199. See also generally Cole, *Sacred Space*, 66 f.
73 Al-Shahīd al-Thānī, *Maʿālim*, 199–200; Ṭūsī, *ʿUddat al-Uṣūl*, II, 75–76.
74 On Medinan consensus, see section 6, above. See also Hallaq, *Origins*, 110–12.

knowledge of Companions' practice, knowledge that is in turn free of any doubt or probability.[75]

An obvious Muʿtazilite influence, the fourth source of law, *dalīl al-ʿaql*, appeals to human reason to adjudicate good from bad, and harm from benefit. Acknowledging *ʿaql* as inherently sound and in consonance with Divine Reason, the Twelver-Shīʿites adopt the maxim – also well known in Sunnite theology – to the effect that there is nothing in sound rational valuation that can run against authentic revelation, this having been expressed in the maxim "*kullu mā ḥakama bihi al-ʿaql ḥakama bihi al-Sharʿ*" (and in Sunnism as "*ʿadam taʿāruḍ al-ʿaql wal-naql*").[76] Reason thus has the ability to operate on the basis of rational principles through which the revealed indicants and legal norms can be deduced. Muʿtazilite or not, *dalīl al-ʿaql* never led, until the dawn of modernity, to any legal formulation that failed to be grounded in the deontology of revelation.[77]

The most basic of rational principles are the Law of Excluded Middle and the Law of Non-Contradiction, but, more specifically, Twelver-Shīʿite jurisprudence recognizes three rational principles that have a direct bearing on matters legal, namely, (a) the Assumption of an Original State (*al-Barāʾa al-Aṣliyya*), (b) the Assumption of Unaffected Continuity (*Istiṣḥāb al-Ḥāl*), and (c) what we might call rational linguistics.

The Assumption of an Original State requires that if an act was decided neither by reason nor by revelation to belong to any of the legal norms, then it must be the case that it is licit, because if it were reprehensible or injurious, it would have been prohibited or curtailed by one means or another. In other words, the *modus operandi* of divine law, like processes of reasoning themselves, is subject to a meta-reason that explains and rationalizes not only divine jural wisdom but also the rational order itself.

The second principle operates under a similar assumption: once an act is given a legal value (norm), then we continue to uphold this norm as long as we do not observe any change in the relevant circumstances that had given rise to the rationale of the value.[78] For example, having failed to find water, a person may perform ablution with sand. Suppose that in the middle of his prayer the believer happens to discover that water is or has become available, then, by virtue of the Assumption of Unaffected Continuity, the person must continue to pray because it has been *a priori*

[75] Gleave, *Inevitable Doubt*, 79–80.

[76] Modarressi, "Rationalism and Traditionalism," 142; and see, among others, Ibn Taymiyya's work *Darʾ Taʿāruḍ al-ʿAql wal-Naql*.

[77] For an interesting discussion of this theme, see Dahlén, *Islamic Law, Epistemology and Modernity*, 82 ff.

[78] For a detailed juristic analysis of *istiṣḥāb*, see Ayatullah Khomeini (Khumayni), *Istiṣḥāb*, but for an introductory account, see pp. 1–16.

admitted – also as a juristic precept – that ablution with sand fulfills the prerequisite of a sound prayer performance.[79]

Finally, the third principle holds that through rational means one understands language and its signification without inference, i.e., without *qiyās*. In the Quranic verse we encountered earlier (17:23), we know rationally and *a priori* that hitting parents has been subsumed in the language of the verse although it is not clearly stated therein. Whereas many Sunnite jurists have espoused the same position, many others have claimed this sort of understanding to be inferential, involving perforce a transition (*taʿdiya*) from one premise to another. It was precisely to this transition – which entailed the identification and "bringing out" of an unstipulated, inferential *ʿilla* – that the Twelver-Shīʿites objected. And because this mode of causation was identified as *qiyās*, it was rejected as a "source." Otherwise, the Twelver-Shīʿites would find *qiyās* based on *al-ʿilla al-manṣūṣa* (textually stipulated) to be admissible since the third rational principle involves *a priori* (and thus apodictic) proof, but not an inferential one.[80] (It must also be noted that both the first and the second of these Assumptions were entirely admitted by Sunnite jurisprudence.)

The third point of disagreement – and as intimated under the first point – is that the Uṣūlists/Mujtahids accept probability (*ẓann*) in *fiqh* rulings, whereas the Akhbārists insist on certainty (*ʿilm*, *qaṭʿ*) since their texts, having come down from the infallible Imam, are consequently infallible.

Fourth, the Uṣūlists/Mujtahids adopt a fourfold typology of *ḥadīth*, also likely to have found its origins in the writings of al-ʿAllāma al-Ḥillī and his mentor Ibn Ṭāwūs (d. 664/1266):[81] (1) a sound report (*ṣaḥīḥ*) which has an unbroken chain of transmission going back to the Prophet or an Imam; (2) an acceptable report (*ḥasan*) that goes back to the same authorities but that does not have a sound chain of transmission (*isnād*); (3) an enhanced report (*muwaththaq*), transmitted through a complete chain in which one or more of the narrators is not a Twelver-Shīʿite but nonetheless regarded as a reliable transmitter; and (4) a defective (*ḍaʿīf*) and thus unusable report. The differences on this point, Samāhijī notes, are largely nominal since the Akhbārists do admit the validity of the second and third types if they deem them as sound basis for practice (*in jāza al-ʿamal bi-hi*).

[79] Al-Shahīd al-Thānī, *Maʿālim*, 262–63; Ṭūsī, *ʿUddat al-Uṣūl*, 124 ff. See also Gleave, *Inevitable Doubt*, 87–88.

[80] Al-Shahīd al-Thānī, *Maʿālim*, 261–62; Hallaq, "Non-Analogical Arguments in Sunni Juridical *Qiyās*," 289 ff., 300 ff.

[81] Gleave, *Inevitable Doubt*, 39; Samāhijī, 25.

Fifth, and as a result of their attitude toward the role of human reason, the Akhbārists adopt the position that the community in its entirety must practice *taqlīd* of the Infallible Imam and that in this context the need for a *mujtahid* cannot arise. The Uṣūlists/Mujtahids, much like their Sunnite counterparts in this respect, divide the community into *mujtahid*s and laypersons, the latter falling entirely under the category of *muqallid*s.

Sixth, the Uṣūlists/Mujtahids permit only the *mujtahid* to be in charge of the affairs of *iftā'*, judgeship, and market-inspection (*al-umūr al-ḥisbiyya*). The Akhbārists, abjuring the *mujtahid*, expectedly assign these tasks to the *rāwī*, expert in the *akhbār* narrated from the 'Alid line and in the methods of their transmission. For these *akhbār* contain and stipulate, according to Akhbārist theory, all necessary rulings and legal norms (with their infallible safeguards), this by implication rendering speculative *ijtihād*, *ipso facto*, profoundly superfluous. Related to this is another difference, namely, that the Akhbārists permit the layperson (*'āmmī*) to act on the basis of *ḥadīth*, if that layperson deems it to be a sound *ḥadīth*, transmitted with assurance on the authority of the Imam. The Uṣūlists/Mujtahids, on the other hand, do not arrogate such a privilege to the layperson, deeming *taqlīd* of a *mujtahid* an absolute requirement.[82]

Seventh, unlike the Uṣūlists/Mujtahids, who recognize both absolute and partial *mujtahid*s (*muṭlaq* and *mutajazzi'*), the Akhbārists deny that an absolute *mujtahid* can or does exist. The only type of *ijtihād* possible is a partial one, and the partial *mujtahid* is one who is adept in some of the *fiqh* rulings (*aḥkām*) through textual transmission, not legal reasoning. The point is that no one, except the Imam himself, knows all the derivations of the law, this including some of the eponyms of Sunnism. Mālik b. Anas, Samāhijī argues, often refrained from issuing *fatwā*s as he was hesitant to indulge in speculation.

Stemming from the foregoing juristic disagreement is yet another difference, namely, that the Uṣūlists/Mujtahids are not reluctant to infer rulings even when the Imam was silent on the issue in question, whereas the Akhbārists take the position that, in the event of such silence, abstention from formulating a ruling is necessary.[83]

Eighth, the Uṣūlists/Mujtahids espouse the view that for a jurist to attain the rank of *muftī* and *ḥadīth* specialist he must master six sciences: (1) scholastic theology (*kalām*) and the science treating the foundations of religion (*uṣūl al-dīn*);[84] (2) grammar; (3) syntax; (4) literature; (5) logic;

[82] This sixth point combines points 8 and 12 in Samāhijī's account, 26, 28.
[83] This seventh point combines points 9 and 17 in Samāhijī, 26, 29.
[84] Newman mistranslated "*al-kalām wal-uṣūl*" as "theology, legal methodology" (p. 42) since Samāhijī counts the sciences as six and lists *uṣūl* at the end, specifically qualifying

and (6) legal theory (which includes the four sources of the law, the Quran, the Sunna, consensus and the rational indicant). Some Uṣūlists/Mujtahids are reported to require mastery of as many as fifteen sciences (which Samāhijī does not enumerate). In sharp contrast, the Akhbārists modestly require mastery of no more than Arabic literature, syntax and grammar, and some of them even limit the requirement to the first of this triad.[85]

Ninth, the Uṣūlists/Mujtahids resort to rational and speculative reasoning to determine which *ḥadīth* is preponderant over another, whereas the Akhbārists conduct the operation of preponderance through textual evidence, playing texts against each other; the Uṣūlists/Mujtahids resort to equivocal *ḥadīth*s whereas the Akhbārists restrict themselves only to *ḥadīth*s of the unequivocal type (*ṣarīḥ*) and Quranic verses of the unambiguous (*muḥkam*) category. The Uṣūlists/Mujtahids resort to weak *ḥadīth*, if any revealed texts are used at all, as a basis for the legal norms of recommended (*mustaḥabb*) and reprehensible (*makrūh*), whereas the Akhbārists employ the same textual standard for all five norms. Moreover, Uṣūlists/Mujtahids accept as the basis of their legal reasoning ambiguous Quranic subject-matter, even when this subject-matter is not supported or sanctioned by *ḥadīth*, their reasoning being that certainty of the Quran's transmission constitutes at least one safeguard against uncertainty and doubt. By contrast, the *ḥadīth* lacks such an assurance since its transmission is uncertain, and its meaning, on the whole, is by no means univocal. The Akhbārists, on the other hand, admit Quranic subject-matter only insofar as it is sanctioned by the Imams' exegesis, explanations and commentary, for the Quran cannot be subject to the whims of exegetes and interpreters who are not truly assured of infallible knowledge.[86]

Tenth, the Uṣūlists/Mujtahids view as valid the adoption of the Sunnite juristic principles by which legal indicants are inferred (*qawāʿid addilat al-fiqh*), whereas the Akhbārists, having rejected *ijtihād* altogether, disallow the use of any such principles, even more so if they happened to be of Sunnite pedigree.

Last, but not least, although the Uṣūlists/Mujtahids acknowledge the *mujtahid* to be fallible (but not so the Imam), they regard as obligatory the

them as "the four sources" and calling them by name. Thus, the first reference to "*uṣūl*" must be to some other *uṣūl*, namely, the "non-speculative," non-scholastic theology of the sort advocated by the Ḥanbalites. See Ibn Qudāma on the distinction between *kalām* and *uṣūl al-dīn*, as two distinct theological discourses; *Taḥrīm al-Naẓar*, xiv–xviii; Arabic text, 7 ff.; trans. 5 ff.

[85] This point brings together points 10 and 28 in Samāhijī's list, 27, 33.

[86] This tenth point combines points 11, 13, 14 and 16 in Samāhijī's account. For the five norms, see section 3, above.

layperson's obedience to both, and to the same extent. The jurist not only must be the highest legal authority in the manner of a *muftī* or a *qāḍī*, but must lead Friday prayer (whose attendance by the layperson is mandatory) and is entitled to levy the alms-tax. And as if to affirm the total loyalty of laypersons and indeed the masses to the Mujtahid-*faqīh*s, the Uṣūlists insisted that these Mujtahid-*faqīh*s must execute the *ḥudūd* ("penal law"), conventionally the function of the political sovereign.[87] As we have already seen, the Akhbārists by contrast accept allegiance only to the Imam,[88] and refuse to extend that authority to the jurist. The latter's competence is not questioned on the grounds of functioning in the capacity of a legist, be it a judge, *muftī*, professor or author-jurist, but rather in the very principle of delegation; or, as the Akhbārists saw it, appropriation of what can belong to no one but the Imam.[89] (This Uṣūlist position, it must be noted, constituted the means by which the doctrine of *wilāyat al-faqīh*, and thus Khomeini's form of governance, were to emerge after the 1979 Revolution.)

By the end of the eighteenth century, and at the hands of Muḥammad Bāqir al-Bihbihānī (d. 1205/1791), the Akhbārist school lost all ground and was ousted from the scene entirely, leaving the Uṣūlists to reign supreme in law and jurisprudence. Two centuries later, they would command the spheres of politics and governance as well.[90]

[87] Calder, "Legitimacy and Accommodation," 96. [88] Samāhijī's thirtieth point, 34.
[89] Litvak, *Shi'i Scholars*, 14; Gleave, *Inevitable Doubt*, 7.
[90] On this development, see chapter 16, section 4 (D), below.

3 Legal education and the politics of law

1. Introduction

It is impossible to speak of legal education over the course of Islamic history without having to deal with issues of politics and political legitimacy; hence the conjunction of both realms within the confines of this chapter. Yet, during the first two or three centuries, education was largely and deliberately disconnected from politics, being limited to private scholarship which the rulers sought to influence without much success. The story of this chapter is that of the transformation of legal scholarship from a highly independent enterprise to a markedly subordinate system that came to serve the ruler and his administration. However, a significant aspect of this story must not escape emphasis, namely, that despite this eventual subordination the content of the law and its application remained uncompromised by any political accommodation. In fact, it was the ruler who – from the beginning of Islam until the middle of the nineteenth century – consistently had to bow to the jural wishes of the Sharīʿa and its representatives in governing the populace. As a moral force, and without the coercive tools of a state, the law stood supreme for over a millennium.

In mapping out the history of legal education in Islam, one must begin with the study circle (*ḥalaqa*; variant: *ḥalqa*), the essential unit of legal scholarship until the early nineteenth century. But the *ḥalaqa*, as an eminently educational institution, did not remain intact for long. Sometime during the late fourth/tenth century, the *madrasa* came into being, exhibiting a strong tendency to superimpose itself over the *ḥalaqa*, and in the long run changing some of its features. The *ḥalaqa* differed from the *madrasa* in one crucial respect: it was largely a free scholarly gathering of a professor and his students, for the most part without political interference and unfettered by financial considerations beyond the small fees that the students might have paid their teacher or the occasional and *ad hoc* gifts these teachers received from members of the political elite. The *madrasa*, on the other hand, was as much, if not more, a financial and a political phenomenon as it was an educational one, and it subjected legal education to increasingly systematic control by rulers. It was established as a charitable trust through the law of *waqf*, whereby a mosque would be dedicated to the teaching of law and the professor and students were provided with, among other things, stipends, food, a library and dormitories. While ordinary men and women founded many such *madrasa*s, these remained limited educational projects usually having no effect or influence beyond the local neighborhood. What gave rise to the complex relationship between law and politics was the important fact that those who founded the largest, most affluent and most prestigious *madrasa*s were the rulers and their immediate entourage (viziers, commanders, mothers, wives, brothers and daughters).[1] Legal education and the *ḥalaqa* could not, in other words, escape the beleaguering effects of political control. An account of the development of pre-modern Muslim education is therefore important not only for its own sake, but also, as we shall later see, for explaining the foundational and dramatic changes that befell Islamic law during the modern period.

To weave the historical outline of legal education, a number of threads must be brought together. First, in line with the developments described in chapter 1, we must trace the dynamics of the early relationship between the legal scholars and the caliphate, for in these dynamics lie the seeds of the political elite's interest in the jurists, judges and their law; second, a brief account of legal education within the *ḥalaqa* is in order, for it was this forum of legal scholarship that remained, until the nineteenth century, the most enduring mechanism of transmitting knowledge in Islam; third, we describe the rise of the *madrasa* and its patronage, a line of enquiry that can hardly be separated from the law of *waqf*, which was in turn vital to the *madrasa*'s very establishment; and finally, we return to the dialectical relationship that obtained in the middle and pre-modern ages between the legal profession and the ruling elite.

2. Law and politics during the formative period: an equilibrium

During most of the first century of Islam, the main representatives of the law were the proto-*qāḍī*s who, to all intents and purposes, were not only government employees and administrators of sorts but also laymen who – despite their experience in adjudication and knowledge of customary law – had no formal legal training of the sort that came to prevail later. As we saw in chapter 1, their appointments as *qāḍī*s were most often conjoined with other functions, including posts as provincial secretaries

[1] For a useful account on royal endowments in Morocco, see Shatzmiller, *Berbers*, 87–113.

and story-tellers. In these capacities, they functioned as the provincial governor's assistants, if not – on rare occasions – as governors-cum-*qāḍīs*. In the near absence of a class of private, legal specialists at this time, these proto-*qāḍīs* constituted the bulk of what may roughly be termed a legal profession, and as such they were an integral part of the ruling class. During this phase, therefore, no noticeable distinction can be made between government and law, since both functions resided in the same hands.

Despite the formal inseparability of the proto-*qāḍī*'s office from that of government administration, the government in this early period rarely, if ever, interfered in determining what law was applied. The caliphate was by no means a distinct or a comprehensive source of law. No edicts regulating law are known to have come down from caliphs; there were no constitutions, and certainly no legal codes of any kind. Even when no class of legal specialists had yet appeared, neither the caliphs nor their viziers or provincial governors made any effort to control or appropriate the province of the law, which was largely customary. The legal role of the caliph was one of *occasional* legislative intervention, coming into play when called for or when special needs arose. But this intervention must be understood to have been harmonious with those laws and rules propounded by the proto-*qāḍīs*, for the caliphs drew on the same sources. The caliphal legislative function was thus minimal, falling well short of their role as *sunna*ic-exemplars. In this latter role, some – but by no means all – caliphs were seen by the proto- and later *qāḍīs* as providing a good example to follow, but this was not because of royal edicts or intrusive policy. The occasional invocation, or even application, of a caliph's *sunna* was an entirely private act, the free choice of a *qāḍī* or a scholar. On the other hand, caliphal orders enjoining a judge to issue a particular ruling were a rare occurrence and ephemeral to boot. Such orders did not represent "secular" or "royal" law as opposed to religious law, but rather a different interpretation of the same sources of authority. In such cases, caliphs were themselves pronouncing on law as jurist-*qāḍīs* or acting on the advice of legal specialist or *qāḍīs* sitting in assembly with them. Thus, the proto-*qāḍī* was principally a government administrator who acted largely according to his normative understanding of how disputes should be resolved – guided, as he was, by the force of social custom, Quranic values and the established ways of the forebears (*sunan māḍiya*).

The early caliphs, on the other hand, saw themselves as equally subject to the force of these *sunan* and the then dominant religious values. True, they were God's and the Messenger's deputies on earth, but they were distinguished from other world leaders by the fact that they acted within the consensual framework of a distinct and largely binding social and legal (though not always political) fabric. Like their predecessors – the Arab tribal leaders and even Muhammad himself – they viewed themselves as part not only of their communities but also, and primarily, of the social and political customs that had come down to them across the generations and from which they were unable to dissociate themselves, even if they wanted to. The proto-*qāḍī*s' relative judicial independence was therefore due to the fact that social, customary and evolving religious values governed all, but were no more known to, or incumbent upon, the caliph than his judges. If the judges queried the caliphs with regard to difficult cases, it was also true that the caliphs queried the judges. That knowledge of the law – or legal authority – was a two-way street in the early period is abundantly clear; the caliph of Islam was far from an exclusive source of law, and not even a distinct one. Rather, his legal role was minimal and partial, mostly enmeshed – and selectively at that – in the body of exemplary precedent that Muslims came to call *sunan* (but not Sunna, later to become the preserve of the Prophet alone).

The emergence, after the 80s/700s, of a class of private legal specialists, signaled a new phase in Islamic history, one characterized by the spreading in Muslim societies of a new religious impulse accompanied by an ascetic piety that became the hallmark of the learned religious elite in general and of the jurists (*fuqahā'*) and later mystics in particular.[2] The importance of this piety in Muslim culture cannot be over-emphasized, either at this early time or in the centuries that followed. If anything, its increasing force was to contribute significantly to later developments. Yet, even in this early period, ascetic piety took many forms, from dietary abstinence to abhorrence of indulgent lifestyles (with which the middle and later Umayyad caliphs were, with some exceptions, partly associated). Above all, this piety called for justice and equality before God – the very emblem of Islam itself.

By the end of the first century and the beginning of the second, it had become clear that a wedge existed between the ruling elite and the emerging religio-legal class. This wedge was to make itself evident with two concurrent developments, the first of which was the spread of a new religious ethic among the ranks of the legal specialists, who increasingly insisted upon ideal human conduct driven by piety. In fact, it is nearly impossible to distinguish this ethic from the social category of legal scholars, since the scholars' constitution was, as we have said, entirely defined by this ethic of piety, mild asceticism and knowledge of the law and religion. The second wedge was the increasing power and

[2] On this important theme, see Hurvitz, "Biographies and Mild Asceticism."

institutionalization of the ruling elite, who began to depart from the egalitarian forms of tribal leadership known to the early caliphs and according to which they had conducted themselves. Whereas the Caliph ʿUmar I, for instance, led a life that many Arabs of his social class enjoyed, and mixed with his fellow believers as one of them, the Umayyad caliphs lived in palaces, wielded coercive powers, and gradually but increasingly distanced themselves from the people they ruled. This gap was further increased by the growth in the size of Muslim populations. Thus, while earlier, smaller communities were easily accessed by the ruler, the later communities were large enough to prevent him from forging personal alliances and ties at a local level.

The religious impulse, permeated with ethical and idealistic values and inspired and enriched by the proliferation of the religious narratives of the story-tellers and traditionists, began to equate government and political power with vice and as infested with corruption as the religious impulse of the pious was virtuous. This attitude originated sometime around the end of the first century (c. 700–715 AD), and was reflected in the multitude of accounts and biographical details speaking of appointments to the office of judgeship. As of this time, and continuing for nearly a millennium thereafter, the theme of judicial appointment as an adversity, even a calamity, for those so designated became a topos and a recurring detail of biographical narrative. Jurists are reported to have wept – sometimes together with family members – upon hearing the news of their appointment; others went into hiding, or preferred to be whipped or tortured rather than accept office.[3]

Suspicion of political power and of those associated with it was so pervasive that the traditionists – and probably the story-tellers amongst them – managed to find a number of Prophetic traditions that condemned judges and rulers alike, placing both ranks in diametrical moral and eschatological opposition to the learned, pious jurists. On the Day of Judgment, one tradition pronounces typically, the judges will be lumped together with the sultans in Hellfire, while the pious jurists will join the prophets in Paradise.[4] Yet, this profound suspicion of association with the political did not mean that the legists predominantly refused judgeships, nor even that they did not desire them. In fact, by and large, they accepted appointment and many junior legists must even have viewed it as a high point in their careers. At the same time, the ruling elite could not dispense

[3] Dhahabī, *Siyar*, IV, 534; Wakīʿ, *Akhbār*, I, 26; III, 25, 37, 130, 143, 146, 147, 153, 177, 184, and *passim*; Ibn Saʿd, *Ṭabaqāt*, VII, 183; Ibn Khallikān, *Wafayāt*, II, 18; III, 201, 202; Zaman, *Religion*, 78 ff.

[4] Al-Shaykh al-Niẓām, *al-Fatāwā al-Hindiyya*, III, 310; Ibn Khallikān, *Wafayāt*, II, 18. On actual refusals to serve in the judiciary, see Kozlowski, "Imperial Authority," 356 and sources cited therein.

with the jurists, for it had become clear that legal authority, inasmuch as it was epistemically grounded, was largely divorced from political authority. Religion and, by definition, legal knowledge had now become the exclusive domain of the jurist, the private scholar. It is precisely because of this essentially epistemic quality that the ruling elite needed the legists to fulfill the Empire's legal needs, despite its profound apprehension that the legists' loyalties were not to the government but to their law and its requirements, which frequently conflicted with the views of the ruling class. But the fact remained that each side needed the other, and thus both learned to cooperate – and cooperate they did.

Many legists were paid handsome salaries when appointed to a judgeship, but they also often received generous grants as private scholars. Throughout the second/eighth century, the remuneration for judicial appointments was steadily on the increase, reaching by the end of the period levels of income that made judgeships in large cities highly coveted.[5] The *qāḍīs*, however, were not alone in benefiting from government subsidies. The leading private scholars were no less dependent on the government's financial favors,[6] and this, as we shall see, was for a good reason.

The rulers, on the other hand, were in dire need of legitimization, which they found in the circles of the legal profession. The latter served as an effective tool for reaching the masses from whose ranks they had emerged and whom they represented. As we will see in more detail later in the chapter, it was one of the salient features of the pre-modern Islamic body-politic (as well as of those in Europe and the Far East) that it lacked control over the infrastructures of the civil populations it ruled. Jurists and judges emerged as the civic leaders who, though themselves a product of the masses, found themselves, by the nature of their profession, involved in the day-to-day running of civic affairs. We have seen that the *qāḍīs* were not only justices of the court, but the guardians and protectors of the disadvantaged, the supervisors of charitable trusts, the tax collectors, the foremen of public works, and the informal mediators in social and family quarrels.[7] They resolved disputes, both in the court and outside it, and established themselves as the intercessors between the populace and the rulers. Even outside of the courtroom, jurists and judges felt responsibility toward the common man, and on their own frequently initiated action without any formal petition being made.[8] As a product of their own social environment, the legists' fate and worldview were inextricably intertwined with the morality and interests of their societies.

[5] Wakīʿ, *Akhbār*, III, 233, 235, 242; Kindī, *Akhbār*, 421, 435.
[6] Ibn Khallikān, *Wafayāt*, III, 315. [7] See also chapter 4, sections 2 and 3.
[8] *Ibid.*, III, 203–04; Kindī, *Akhbār*, 440.

Hence the religious scholars in general and the legists in particular were often called upon to express the will and aspirations of those belonging to the non-elite classes. They not only interceded on their behalf at the higher reaches of power, but also represented for the masses the ideal of piety, rectitude and fine education. Their very profession as Guardians of Religion, experts in religious law and exemplars of the virtuous Muslim lifestyle made them not only the most genuine representatives of the masses but also the true "heirs of the Prophet," as one Prophetic *ḥadīth* came to attest.[9] They were the locus of legitimacy and of religious and moral authority. A pious and erudite man could attract adulation by virtue of his piety and erudition, whereas a caliph could do so only by the threat of coercion. Thoroughly familiar with the ways of earlier caliphs, like Abū Bakr, ʿUmar I and ʿUmar II, the later Umayyad and early ʿAbbāsid caliphs realized that brute power could not yield legitimacy, which they were striving to attain. Legitimacy lay in the preserve of religion, erudition, ascetic piety, moral rectitude, and, in short, in the *persons* of those men who had profound knowledge of, and fashioned their lives after, the example of the Prophet and the exemplary forefathers. Thus, the caliphs *ab initio* understood that, inasmuch as the pious scholars needed their financial resources, they in turn needed the scholars' cooperation, for the latter were the ruler's only source of political legitimacy.

Increasing Islamicization among the masses, and the legitimacy with which the legal scholars were invested, left the caliphs no option but to endorse a religious law whose authority depended on the human ability to exercise hermeneutic. Those who had mastered this science were the jurists, and it was they and their epistemological and juridical domains that set restrictions on the absolute powers of the rulers, be they caliphs or provincial governors. When the Persian secretary Ibn al-Muqaffaʿ (d. c. 139/756) suggested to the ʿAbbāsid caliph that he, the caliph, should be the supreme legal authority, promulgating laws that would bind the courts, his suggestion was met with complete disregard.[10] For while his proposal insinuated that legal authority could have been appropriated by the caliph – in keeping with the ancient Persian ways of governance – the fact that nothing whatsoever came of it is a strong indication that the jurists' control over the law was, as before, inviolable. The legal specialists and the popular religious movement that had emerged by the 130s/750s were too well entrenched for any political power to expunge or even

9 Ibn ʿAbd al-Barr, *Jāmiʿ*, I, 34.

10 A fine analysis of this proposal may be found in Zaman, *Religion*, 82–85. See also Goitein, "Turning Point," 120–35.

replace them. Indeed, it was precisely this movement and its representatives that drove the wedge between religious authority and political power.

Later epistles and treatises written in the way of advice to the caliphs confirm the ascendancy of religious law as represented by the jurists and their social and hermeneutical authority. No longer could anyone propose a caliphal appropriation of legal power. In the letter of ʿAnbarī (d. 168/785) to the Caliph al-Mahdī and in Abū Yūsuf's (182/798) treatise to Hārūn al-Rashīd, the subservience of the caliph to the religious law and to the Sunna is a foregone conclusion.[11] The caliph and the entire political hierarchy that he commanded were subject to the law of God, like anyone else. No exceptions could be made. The *raison d'être* of the caliph himself, and the caliphate with him, was to enforce the religious law, not to make it.

Yet, ʿAnbarī and Abū Yūsuf did not conceive of themselves or of their profession as adversaries of the caliphs. Their writings clearly exhibit the cooperation that the jurists were willing to extend to the rulers; both authors were financially dependent on the caliphs, although both also hailed from a background entirely defined by religious law and religious morality. This cooperation, coupled with the realization that rulers too, not so long ago, were counted among the ranks of jurists, justified ʿAnbarī and Abū Yūsuf in their decision to treat the caliphs as peers of legists and judges. Their writings call on the caliphs to act as guides to their judges when faced with difficult cases, a measure not only of the role that the legal scholars wanted to assign to caliphs as religious leaders but also of the caliphs' need to portray themselves as legitimate rulers standing guard over the supreme law of God. It is clear then that in the legal sphere the caliph did not act with, or think himself to embody, an authority superior to that of the jurists, be they judges appointed by him or private legal scholars. If the caliph occasionally involved himself in resolving legal problems, he did so on a par with the legists, and not as one superior to them in their roles as judges and jurists. His engagement was an integral part of, and no more than a supplement to, the legists' professional and hermeneutical activities. The result was not a struggle over religious authority, where the caliphs competed with the legal scholars, for the caliphs did not challenge the legal scholars in their own domain of competence. Rather, caliphal engagement in the law represented an effort to gain political legitimacy through a demonstration of juristic competence that the jurists and the early caliphs (who were set up as a model to be emulated) possessed.

As caliphs increasingly grew detached from what had become a specialized field of legal knowledge, they were expected to surround themselves

[11] Zaman, *Religion*, 85–100.

with competent jurists who would assist them in addressing difficult legal matters. This, being conducive to their legitimacy, they duly observed in practice. So whereas the earliest caliphs could acquire legitimacy by virtue of their own knowledge of the law, it later became necessary to supplement the caliphal office with jurists who routinely sat in royal courts (*jalasa fī ṣuḥbati al-ʿulamāʾ*) and who, in effect, constituted the legitimacy that the caliphs (and later all sultans and emirs) desperately needed. In these royal–juristic assemblies, not only were matters of religion, law and literature discussed, but so were scholarly disputations (*munāẓara*) held between master-jurists.[12] Almost every caliph of the second, third and fourth centuries was known to have befriended the *fuqahāʾ*, and later emirs and sultans did much the same.[13]

The privileges and favors the jurists acquired not only brought them easy access to the royal court and to the circles of the political elite,[14] but also rendered them highly influential in government policy as it affected legal matters, and perhaps in other matters of state. Beginning in the middle of the second/eighth century, almost all major judicial appointments were made on the recommendation of the Chief Justice at the royal court or the assembly of jurists gathered by the caliph, or both. And when the provincial governor wished to find a qualified judge, he too sought the advice of jurists.[15] Some jurists, throughout Islamic history, were immeasurably influential in legal as well as political matters.[16]

Caliphal patronage of the jurists and of their assemblies at the royal court was one source of garnering legitimacy. Another was caliphal participation in the pilgrimage to Mecca, which almost invariably involved the company of distinguished legal scholars. And when a leading jurist died, the funeral prayer was performed by the caliph himself (just as it was normally the distinguished jurists who performed this prayer when a caliph died). Moreover, the caliphs continued to display an interest in religious learning in an attempt to maintain the image of erudition for which some early caliphs were known. Thus, they dabbled in legal matters and studied and memorized *ḥadīth* that were usually effective as tools of legitimization when cited in courtly audiences.[17]

[12] Later to become a specialized field on its own, generating much writing and theory. See generally Hallaq, "Tenth–Eleventh Century Treatise," and Miller's dissertation, "Islamic Disputation Theory."

[13] Wakīʿ, *Akhbār*, III, 158, 174, 247, 265, and *passim*; Ibn Khallikān, *Wafayāt*, II, 321, 322; III, 204, 206, 247, 258, 389; Kindī, *Akhbār*, 388.

[14] In addition to the sources cited in the preceding note, see Baghdādī, *Tārīkh*, IX, 66.

[15] Kindī, *Akhbār*, 393.

[16] An example of this is the career of Yaḥyā b. Aktham b. Ṣayfī (d. 242/856). See Ibn Khallikān, *Wafayāt*, III, 277 ff.

[17] Baghdādī, *Tārīkh*, IX, 33, 35–6; Zaman, *Religion*, 120–27.

All this, however, cannot mask the fact that there always remained points of friction between political power, secular power and religious law. The relationship between the two was constantly negotiated, and it was never devoid of sporadic challenges mounted by the ruling elite against, not the law, but its application by its representatives.[18] Such challenges seem to have occurred mostly at the provincial and periphery courts, but the caliphs themselves also appear, on rare occasions, to have interfered in the judiciary and the judicial process.[19] Yet, if these anecdotes illustrate caliphal abuses of the law, they are still exceptions to an overwhelming pattern, displayed in the sources, of caliphal reluctance to overstep their limits in judicial intervention. Thus, when the Caliph Abū Jaʿfar al-Manṣūr (r. 136–58/754–75) wrote to his Baṣran judge, Sawwār, with regard to a case, the latter treated the caliph's request (the details of which we do not know) as legally unwarranted and thus dismissed it. Offended by this verdict, Manṣūr resorted to threats, but never acted upon them, for an advisor or a confidant of his is reported to have told him: "O Commander of the Faithful, Sawwār's justice is, after all, an extension of yours."[20] The moral imperative, as we shall see later, was integral to the ethic of caliphal governance, for supreme power morally required unbounded forbearance.

That the caliphal office was thought to uphold the highest standards of justice according to the holy law was undeniable, and the caliphs themselves felt such responsibility, generally conducting themselves in accordance with these expectations.[21] Inasmuch as the law in and of itself possessed authority, the caliph and his office were seen not only as another locus of the holy law, but also as its guarantor and enforcer. As a rule, the caliphs and their provincial representatives upheld court decisions and normally did not intervene in the judicial process. They generally complied with the law, if for no other reason than in order to maintain their political legitimacy, represented in their subservience to the commands of the religious law. In other words, their compliance stemmed from their acceptance of religious law as the supreme regulatory force in society, coupled with the conviction that they were in no way rivals of the religious legal profession. Instances of judges deciding in favor of persons who litigated against caliphs and governors are well attested in the literature, with the caliphs and governors accepting and submitting to such verdicts in the vast majority of cases.[22] The literary accounts suggest that even the

[18] For instances of this challenge, see Kindī, *Akhbār*, 328, 356, 367; Wakīʿ, *Akhbār*, III, 232.
[19] Kindī, *Akhbār*, 410–11; Wakīʿ, *Akhbār*, III, 271–72.
[20] Wakīʿ, *Akhbār*, II, 60. [21] *Ibid.*, II, 59.
[22] See, e.g., Ibn Khallikān, *Wafayāt*, III, 392; Ibn ʿAbd Rabbih, *al-ʿIqd al-Farīd*, I, 38–48; ʿAsqalānī, *Rafʿ al-Iṣr*, 508.

highest political and military offices in the land found it necessary to resort to the law and to submit to its (sometimes lengthy) procedures, even when they easily could have accomplished their ends through sheer coercion.

From the early Umayyads until the later Ottomans, Islamic political culture displayed a particular, if not unique, pattern of governance. As a rule, monarchs and their lieutenants acted with remarkable fairness and justice when arbitrating disputes and conflicts to which they were not parties. Their occasional infringements were usually associated with, and limited to, cases in which their own interests were involved. Although this in no way means that encroachment occurred whenever such interests were present, it does suggest that whenever rulers staked their interest in the judicial process, they had to weigh their overall gains and losses. To have accomplished their ends through coercion would have meant that their legitimacy had failed the test. On the other hand, total compliance with the law at times meant that their quest for material gain or will to power would be frustrated. It was this equation that they attempted to work out and balance carefully, at times succeeding but at others not. The post-formative centuries of Islamic history suggest that rulers generally preferred to maintain an equation in favor of compliance with the religious law, since compliance was the means by which the ruling elite could garner the sympathies, or at least tacit approval, of the populace.

Yet, compliance with the law was a relatively passive act, insufficient on its own to promote and augment the much coveted goal of political legitimacy. As it happened, the sphere of legal education proved to be fertile ground, allowing the ruling dynasties not only to garner legitimacy but also to implement, during the nineteenth century, fundamental and everlasting changes in the legal system. It is to legal education then that we now turn.

3. From *ḥalaqa* to *madrasa*

The informal financial patronage offered to the legists during the early period was in due course to be systematized and institutionalized. It so happened that the law college (*madrasa*) became the chief means by which the legists were coopted by the ruling elites. The fairly sudden appearance of the *madrasa* on the scene and its rapid diffusion make it impossible to imagine the legal and educational history of Islam without the presence of this institution. Similarly, it is impossible to make sense of the demise of Islamic law during the modern period without taking into account this educational institution. Yet, as a legal and educational institution, the *madrasa* continued to operate in ways thoroughly rooted in the pedagogical tradition that had existed prior to its appearance. This tradition was represented in the *ḥalaqa*, at once a pedagogical, legal and sociological phenomenon. The *ḥalaqa* was in effect the engine that ran legal education; indeed, the *madrasa* would not have been viable had it not been for the existence of the *ḥalaqa*.

The *ḥalaqa*'s origins must have been tribal, functioning as the normative form of assembly for members of the clan or tribe. As such, it may have been brought by the Peninsular Arabs to the garrison towns of Iraq, Syria and Egypt, where the assemblies moved from the chief's tent to the central mosque. Just as tribal affairs had been the subjects of discussion in these *ḥalaqa* assemblies, in the garrison towns it was now the affairs of the religious communities that became the focus of discussions and debates. The first discussions about law that were ever to arise in Islam occurred precisely within these *ḥalaqa*s. Those individuals who distinguished themselves as knowledgeable about law attracted audiences who listened to them discoursing on matters related to *sunan*, *sīra* and various types of stories (*qiṣaṣ*) displaying proper exemplary conduct (again: *sunna*) as their main theme. It was from these *circles* (literally: *ḥalaqa*) that the legal specialists of the end of the first century emerged (see chapter 1); and it was these circles that continued to serve as the chief fora of Islamic pedagogy. Beginning as early as the second/eighth century, the circle began to spread to Iran and Transoxiana in the east, and North Africa and Andalusia in the west. Later, it was to spread into all regions and towns that adopted Islam, from Mogadishu to Aceh.

A remarkable setting, the *ḥalaqa* began as a slightly open circle.[23] At the deep end of its circumference and facing the opening that formed its entrance sat (*jalasa*) the tribal chief and, later, the legal specialist or the law professor. The point of entry was at times left vacant, so as to allow people to join. Generally, the farther the students sat from the professor, the less advanced they were deemed to be. Beginners sat in the rear rows, when the circle was formed of more than one row. A student who showed rapid progress would be moved to a position closer to the professor. It was at times the case that delinquent students would be moved (or themselves take the initiative of moving) to the back.[24]

Just like its tribal predecessor, the pedagogical *ḥalaqa* manifested a certain hierarchy, where the professor would be flanked by his senior students who themselves would soon become teachers or legal specialists of some sort. At times, they were accomplished scholars in other fields, attending the *ḥalaqa* in order to gain mastery in law. These advanced students also functioned as teaching assistants (*muʿīd*s; lit. repetitors). In

[23] Pedersen, *Arabic Book*, 26. [24] Ephrat, *Learned Society*, 77.

short, the early *ḥalaqa* reflected a graded hierarchy that, at its highest point, began with the professor and moved away from him, on both sides of the circle, to the less advanced students. The most remarkable feature of this circular hierarchy was the perfect continuity between the teacher and students. There was, in other words, no pedagogical rupture between teacher and student, but rather a graded, transitive continuity. The teacher was the epistemological pinnacle, the advanced students his subordinates, and the less advanced students, the subordinates of the latter. In due course, we will see how later – albeit minor – changes in the physical constitution of the *ḥalaqa* reflected fundamental changes in both legal education and, indeed, the legal profession as a whole.

Until about the eighth/fourteenth century, the *ḥalaqa* exhibited an intimate relationship between professor and students, especially advanced ones. The professor was not merely a teacher of a technical science, as modern university professors are. He was an educator, a companion, a supporter and a moral mentor. Instilling a deep sense of morality based on the concept of *ʿadāla* (rectitude) was as much part of the curriculum as any substantive subject (if there was ever a curriculum in our sense of the word). As we shall see in the next chapter, the application of law presupposed a system of social morality, a system upon which the efficacy of law depended and from which it could not be separated. The professor, among others, cultivated in the student the elements of this moral system. Professor–student relationship was often akin to that of father and son, and many students not only resided in, and dined at, the homes of their professors but married their daughters too. And it was precisely this institution of marriage that fostered close ties between the ulama in one city or region and between and among them in distant locales. A remarkable case in point are those networks that developed through the *pesantren* over the expanses of Sumatra, Java and Madura, and between these and the (geographically distant) scholarly communities of the Hejaz.[25]

The intimate relationship between professor and student was exemplified in the concept of *ṣuḥba* (companionship),[26] a central pedagogical and social institution in Islam. Generally cultivated over many years, *ṣuḥba* signified a close personal and intellectual companionship between student and teacher, or between any two or more scholars. To obtain, there had to be *mulāzama*, a long-term association involving study and "sitting together." Modeled after the *ṣuḥba* between the Prophet and the many individuals who befriended and supported him (collectively known as the *Ṣaḥāba*; the Companions), the later *ṣuḥba* meant a life-long intellectual

[25] See, for example, van Bruinessen, "Tarekat and Tarekat Teachers," 91–118.
[26] Chamberlain, *Knowledge and Social Practice*, 120–22.

friendship that crossed over rank. *Ṣuḥba* could exist between a professor and a student, but it could also be established between two scholars of equal rank who could learn from each other in terms of their respective fields of specialization.[27] Thus, a professor leading a *ḥalaqa* of *ḥadīth* or Quranic exegesis might well be a student in a *ḥalaqa* of law, and vice versa.

The *ḥalaqa*, as with all aspects of Islamic education, was a highly informal entity. There was no administrative process of admission beyond the need to obtain the professor's oral permission to join. Nor was there any restriction on the size of the *ḥalaqa*, or on who could join. There is no evidence of any kind in our sources to show that social or economic background or ethnic origin played a role in admission to *ḥalaqa*s. Indeed, the *ḥalaqa* was an open forum, even for transient students as well as passers-by. Most legal *ḥalaqa*s were small, not exceeding twenty or thirty students, but those led by distinguished jurists and professors were said to have been exceptionally well attended, at times attracting three or four hundred students.[28] *Ḥalaqa*s of *ḥadīth* generally attracted much larger audiences, but this subject was not considered a "graduate" or advanced discipline, as law was.

Nor was there any unity in the "curricular" structure between one *ḥalaqa* and the next. Each professor was free to teach the treatises of his choice, a freedom later mildly restricted by the appearance of authorized texts that the four schools produced over time. Although any type of treatise – of any length – could be taught, abridgments (*mukhtaṣar*s) were generally preferred after the fifth/eleventh century when they became abundant. Some of these abridgments were specifically produced by professors for teaching purposes, their intent being to sum up *fiqh* doctrine by invoking legal principles and alluding to "cases" that supported these principles. The professor explained the terse statements of the *mukhtaṣar* by appealing to the large compendia and *fatwā* collections on which these abridgements were based. The students had to memorize the *mukhtaṣar*, not for its own sake but as an outline of the law embedded in the comprehensive and extensive works. The professor's function in the *ḥalaqa* was to make the abridgment intelligible and comprehensible. Repetition and further explanation of the day's lesson were performed by the *muʿīd* after the professor had left the *ḥalaqa*. The *muʿīd* also listened to the students recite what they had learned, his task being to ensure that the lesson was understood before the next *ḥalaqa* was held.

The teaching was manifestly oral. The student did not read the work for himself in silence but listened to the professor, who would recite the work

[27] See, generally, Berkey, *Transmission of Knowledge*, 34–37; Jacques, *Authority, Conflict and Transmission*, 120–39.

[28] See, e.g., Ibn Khallikān, *Wafayāt*, II, 81.

for all to hear. This reading was accompanied by commentary, the true contribution of the teacher. Learning was also conducted on the initiative of the student: he read the work out loud before the professor, who queried him on difficult points. The two processes of instruction were at times combined. A professor might teach his students a text he had authored himself, and the students would write down the lectures, thereby producing a copy of the book. Reading the copied text back to the professor constituted a process of certification that ensured that the work conformed in every detail to the demands of the professor. While this process constituted an integral part of the activity of publishing (namely, making copies of an author's work accessible to the public), it was often an important ingredient in advanced legal education. The last stage of this education was the writing of the *taʿlīqa*, a dissertation or "commentary" that showed the mastery of the student in a specialized field of law. One of the most monumental *taʿlīqa*s was Abū Ḥāmid al-Ghazālī's *Mankhūl*, an *uṣūl al-fiqh* treatise that he wrote under the distinguished jurist and theologian Imām al-Ḥaramayn al-Juwaynī.

The course of study in the *ḥalaqa* culminated in the *ijāza*, a license amounting to a diploma. Literally meaning "permission," the *ijāza* represented the teacher's certification that a student had mastered and, therefore, could transmit a particular text. Thus, legal education was largely about reading, writing and transmission of texts through memorization, though transmission had at its core the fundamental task of maintaining the legal authority of the school (*madhhab*). Such a license might attest to the ability of the student merely to transmit the book, or it might also confirm his competence to teach it to students. Advanced students who had accumulated several *ijāza*s, especially in the books of the *madhhab*, were awarded *ijāza*s to teach (*tadrīs*), to issue *fatwā*s or to engage in scholarly disputation (*munāẓara*), three of the most advanced *ijāza*s that could be obtained.

Yet, the *ḥalaqa* was also a place where *fatwā*s were issued and where legal disputation between scholars was conducted. Oftentimes, a professor held a *ḥalaqa* for teaching, to be followed by another *ḥalaqa* for issuing *fatwā*s or for "sitting" as a judge to adjudicate disputes. Thus, a jurist's *ḥalaqa* reflected his juridical competences, for when he engaged in all these roles he would be said to wear many hats, so to speak. Accomplished jurists could attain the highest ranks in their profession by combining four roles: namely, those of teaching, issuing *fatwā*s, writing legal works (*taṣnīf*), and sitting as judges.[29] Students in a teaching *ḥalaqa* might go on to join the next *ḥalaqa* of their professor over which he would preside as

[29] A detailed treatment of these roles may be found in Hallaq, *Authority*, 167–74.

judge. At times they sat in the audience as observers, but at others they might act as scribes or as witnesses (*shuhūd*) attesting to the court procedure. These same students might still be present at the next *ḥalaqa*, held for issuing *fatwā*s, and their participation was one way in which they would gain, from their professor-cum-*muftī*, experience in the art of *iftā*ʾ. It is thanks to these students that we have numerous useful *fatwā* collections of distinguished jurists, for it was they who recorded and "published" such collections on behalf of their masters.[30] Thus, the informality of the *ḥalaqa* also permitted the integration of apprenticeship in a variety of legal subfields, for apprenticeship was the standard method of acquiring skills in any craft or profession.

The *ḥalaqa* was therefore the established forum of legal education in Islam and its locus was usually the mosque or grand mosque, although homes less frequently hosted such an activity. Every grand mosque hosted numerous *ḥalaqa*s, some dedicated to the study and disputation of law, and others to grammar, *adab* literature, Quranic exegesis, *ḥadīth*, logic, medicine, mathematics, astronomy and other subjects. Fusṭāṭ's Mosque of ʿAmr, for instance, hosted forty *ḥalaqa*s in around 700/1300.[31] A professor might teach one, two or more subjects, usually in different *ḥalaqa*s. Some professors were known to hold *ḥalaqa*s in more than one mosque, but whatever specific subject they taught was restricted to a single *ḥalaqa* session. Thus, it was in the very nature of the *ḥalaqa* to offer instruction in a specialized field of knowledge, or to involve a specific activity, such as issuing *fatwā*s or disputing legal doctrine.[32]

For centuries, therefore, the *ḥalaqa* – as a set of pedagogical, social and moral relationships between professor and students – defined Muslim education. It was and remained until the nineteenth century the only Islamic form of imparting and receiving knowledge, despite the introduction of the *madrasa*. The latter, it must be emphasized, did not constitute a new form of education but rather bestowed on the *ḥalaqa* an external legal framework that allowed pedagogical activity to be conducted under the auspices of endowments. The *madrasa*, in other words, affected neither the curriculum of the *ḥalaqa* nor its modalities in transmitting knowledge. It was the professor, not the *madrasa*, who decided the curriculum, and it was he who continued to have an exclusive monopoly over the granting of *ijāza*s. The pre-modern *madrasa*s, as "institutions" that possessed no juristic personality, bestowed not a single *ijāza*.

The embryonic stages of the *madrasa* appear to have developed toward the end of the second/eighth century, when provisions and salaries began

30 Hallaq, "From *Fatwā*s to *Furū*ʿ," 43.
31 Berkey, *Transmission of Knowledge*, 86; Makdisi, *Rise*, 20.
32 Makdisi, *Rise*, 12–16.

to be made in favor of the staff of certain mosques, including the professors who taught law there. Once professors began to receive salaries, it meant that students were exempted from whatever "tuition" they used to pay. Soon thereafter, some mosques were enlarged to include dormitories for transient students and even for the professors themselves. Eventually, the salaries, tuition, shelter and food were paid by endowments (*waqf*). The *madrasa*, the last stage of this development, came to meet all the other needs of professors and students, and this included an endowed, fully furnished building for the meeting of *ḥalaqa*s, sleeping quarters for staff and students, food, a library, paper, ink and much else.[33]

The early stages of this development appear to have occurred in Khurāsān where, in addition to endowing mosques, private homes hosting legal *ḥalaqa*s were converted into hostels for transient scholars and students.[34] From Khurāsān, the idea of such endowments spread throughout the eastern domains of Islam during the Sāmānid period (ending in 395/1005), southward during the rule of the Ghaznawids, and then westward during the dominion of the Saljūqs. The founding in Baghdad of eleven imposing *madrasa*s during the second half of the fifth/eleventh century by the Saljūq vizier Niẓām al-Mulk (455–85/1063–92) was in fact the most significant event that brought the *madrasa* onto the center stage of Islamic history.

By the end of the sixth/twelfth century, Baghdad could claim more than thirty *madrasa*s on its eastern side alone, and at least a few more on the western side.[35] Egypt's first *madrasa* may have been established in Fusṭāṭ as early as 491/1097, but Saladin (r. 564–89/1169–93) appears to have been the first to found *madrasa*s on a scale similar to that of Baghdad's Niẓāmiyyas. By the time the Mamlūks came to power in the middle of the seventh/thirteenth century, Cairo had thirty-two *madrasa*s, and Alexandria could claim several more.[36] According to one count, Cairo would increase its *madrasa*s to seventy-three by the early ninth/fifteenth century.[37] At the end of the eighth/fourteenth century, there were thirteen *madrasa* endowments in Ottoman Edirne and twenty-five in Bursa. By the end of the tenth/sixteenth century, Edirne had increased its share of *madrasa*s to thirty-one and Bursa to thirty-six, while Istanbul claimed 142. By 1869, the active *madrasa*s of Istanbul had reached, by the lowest estimate, 166, with no less than 5,370 students.[38] Altogether, the

[33] *Ibid.*, 31, 32. [34] Lapidus, *History*, 165. [35] Ephrat, *Learned Society*, 30.
[36] Berkey, *Transmission of Knowledge*, 8–9. [37] *Ibid.*, 45.
[38] According to Zilfi, *Politics of Piety*, Istanbul had 120–200 *madrasa*s in the eleventh/seventeenth century, a number that was to increase dramatically over the next century. By Zilfi's estimates, nineteenth-century Istanbul would have claimed somewhere around 300 *madrasa*s.

*madrasa*s of the Ottoman Balkans numbered in the hundreds, and by the twelfth/eighteenth century, the city of Bukhāra could boast over 110 *madrasa*s[39] while Ṣafavid Iṣfahān reportedly had forty-eight.[40] In short, by the middle of the eighth/fourteenth century, the *madrasa* had reached all corners of the Muslim world, from Kilwa in Somaliland to Transoxianian Bukhāra and Malacca in the Malaysian Peninsula. Three centuries later, the *madrasa*s numbered in the thousands.

The significance of this astounding proliferation of *madrasa*s will be addressed later. But in order to appreciate fully the meaning and ramifications of this increase, especially in light of modern reforms, it would be better to dwell further on the nature and constitution of the *madrasa*. Pedagogically, the most fundamental ingredient of the *madrasa* was its *ḥalaqa*, that feature which had preceded the *madrasa* and coexisted with(in) it throughout the entire history of Islamic education. Physically, the *madrasa* was constituted of a building that at times was the mosque itself, but at others was a special structure built as an annex to a mosque. The *khān*, in effect an inn, was also built in the vicinity of the mosque, separate from the *madrasa*, but at times it constituted a part of the annex that was the *madrasa*. Yet, the *ḥalaqa* and the buildings, and even the wealth that was needed to sustain them, were not enough in themselves for "raising up" a *madrasa*. This was because fundamental to the entire enterprise was the law and practice of *waqf*, a defining aspect of the cultural and material civilization of Islam.

The law of *waqf*, therefore, represented the glue that could bind the human, physical and monetary elements together. Essentially, *waqf* was a thoroughly religious and pious concept, and as a material institution it was meant to be a charitable act of the first order. One gave up one's property "for the sake of God," a philanthropic act which meant offering aid and support to the needy. The promotion of education, especially of religious legal education, represented the best form of promoting religion itself. A considerable proportion of charitable trusts were thus directed at *madrasa*s, although *waqf* provided significant contributions toward building mosques, Ṣūfī *khānqāh*s, hospitals, public fountains, soup kitchens, travelers' lodges, and a variety of public works, notably bridges. A substantial part of the budget intended for such philanthropic enterprises was dedicated to the maintenance, daily operational costs and renovation of *waqf* properties. A typical *waqf* consisted of a mosque and rental property (e.g., shops), the rent from which supported the operation and maintenance of the mosque.

[39] Lapidus, *History*, 428. [40] Chardin, *Voyages*, 82; Cole, *Sacred Space*, 59.

Once the founder (*wāqif*) alienated his or her property as a *waqf*, the act was legally deemed irrevocable, entailing as it did the complete transfer of the right to ownership from the hands of the *wāqif* to those of God. The purpose, after all, was to do good "for the sake of God." Once alienated, the property could not be bought, sold, inherited, gifted, mortgaged or transferred in any other manner. The only exception was when the property ceased to serve its intended purposes. Only then was it permissible to sell it in order to purchase another, usually equivalent, property (*istibdāl*) that would serve the same purpose.[41] The property was usually immovable, but some movables, such as books, were at times the object of *waqf*s. In fact, as a rule, libraries constituted an essential part of endowed *madrasa*s. Immovability was more a matter of practice than a point of law, and the fact that practice was at times confused with law says much about the Muslim preference for immovable property. Legally, the property must not be perishable in the sense that it should be "something whose benefit is long lasting,"[42] a category under which were subsumed such items as agricultural tools and cooking wares.

The law granted the *waqf* founder extensive freedoms in setting up the trust, the assumption being that one has virtually unlimited rights over one's own property. Since the assumed purpose of endowments is charity and piety, the founder, as long as he or she intended to perform a philanthropic act, had unrestricted rights in specifying the conditions by which the *waqf* should operate. He appointed trustees (*mutawallī*s) to manage the property, designated beneficiaries, and determined the *ratio* of benefit for each beneficiary. He could appoint himself or a member of his family as the trustee of the *waqf* and could stipulate that he and/or one or more of his descendants could alter, in the face of changing circumstances, the terms of the *waqf* deed (*waqfiyya*). However, once the deed was certified and witnessed (usually before a judge), the founder could no longer effect any substantive changes to its stipulations. If, for instance, he failed to include in the original deed a provision to the effect that he, or a descendent, had the future right to alter the terms of the endowment, then he and the *waqf* itself were, once and for all, bound by the stipulated terms. However, this finality could not stand in the way of the continuing operation and welfare of the endowment. Thus, if the founder did not set up a proper administration for the *waqf*, such as by failing to designate a trustee or to have a salary paid to a trustee, then the *waqf* deed remained valid but a judge had the power to intervene to designate a trustee as well as an appropriate remuneration. In theory and in practice, the judge had

[41] Hanna, "Administration of Courts," 52. [42] Nawawī, *Rawḍa*, IV, 380.

the ultimate power to supervise and oversee the *waqf*'s administration, intervening whenever a situation not covered by the deed arose or whenever he felt his intervention was necessary or called for.[43]

A doctrine central to our concerns here is the unfettered right of the founder to reserve the power to appoint himself – and/or a descendant upon his own death – as a trustee of the *waqf*.[44] The centrality of this doctrine becomes even more apparent when conjoined with the precept that the trustee himself or herself had near unlimited powers in the administration of the endowment. He or she could not be dismissed (even by the founder himself, when the latter was not the trustee) unless the founder had stipulated in the deed his right or competence to change trustees. In due course, we will observe the effect of these powers in the cooptation of the legal profession by the ruling elites, who founded through *waqf* the most influential *madrasa*s.

A trustee still could not be dismissed without cause, even if the founder reserved for himself or herself the right to dismiss the *waqf*'s officers. In theory and in practice, the most common valid grounds for dismissal was embezzlement, which usually involved deriving profit from the *waqf* beyond the amount of salary allotted by the deed.[45] The administrative backbone of the endowment, the trustee (indispensable to any *waqf*) was required to be of just character and impeccable rectitude (*ʿadl*). This was the single most important legal requirement. If for any reason this quality was lost or diminished to any degree, the trustee might be dismissed or placed in a co-trusteeship with another person of just character.[46] In all cases, the judge had the competence to audit the financial and administrative functioning of the *waqf* at any time.

The trustee had the right of *taṣarruf*, namely, of administering the *waqf* in a manner by which he might fulfill his or her designated duties, responsibilities and powers. He could appoint assistants or deputies (usually known as *nāẓir*s or *mushrif*s) to help him in the dispensation of these responsibilities, the most important of which were: maintenance of the *waqf* properties; appointing and dismissing staff whose duties included cleaning and repairing; leasing property and collecting rent for the sake of the beneficiaries and for payment of salaries; farming land and selling its

43 Makdisi, *Rise*, 36.
44 The Mālikite school was, among the four schools, singular in disallowing a founder to designate himself a trustee. George Makdisi, *Rise*, 37–38, argued that this prohibition led to the decline of the school in Baghdad and discouraged members of the school from creating *madrasa* endowments in North Africa, where the school gained dominance.
45 Although trustees were also fired on grounds of mismanagement of, or neglecting to maintain, *waqf* properties. See El-Nahal, *Judicial Administration*, 55.
46 Makdisi, *Rise*, 44–45, 54.

produce to generate supporting income; and resolving disputes and representing the endowment's interests in any litigation. In mosque endowments, the function of trustee was frequently conjoined with that of the imam, and in that capacity the trustee was charged with the added duty of leading the public prayer.

In view of the eminently charitable purpose of endowments, the most important responsibility of the trustee was to ensure the procurement of income so that it could be allocated to the beneficiaries in accord with the terms of the deed. These terms could specify that the allocation be paid in the form of either a wage, a gift or alms, each having a different legal effect. If an employee paid upfront with a lump sum did not complete the term of his appointment, he would not have to refund the prorated difference of the remaining portion of the term if his income was deemed a gift or alms. However, he would have to make a refund if the income was considered a salary.[47]

The charitable nature of the *waqf* dictated that the rich could not benefit from charitable endowments, and this was the understanding of the majority of jurists. A minority of later Shāfiʿites, however, came to approve of establishing endowments for the benefit of the well-to-do,[48] a modification of doctrine that appears to have reflected the practice on the ground.

Drawing near to God (*qurba*) was certainly the prime motive of many – if not most – *waqf* founders.[49] The average pious Muslim founded mainly the smaller, local and less significant endowments. On the other hand, it was almost a universal pattern that the founders of those major endowments that supported, among other things, *madrasa*s and Ṣūfī *zāwiya*s, were the rich and powerful, in particular the ruling elite and their retinue. Their endowments dwarfed not only all other endowments, but even the large buildings in Muslim cities. An example in point is the *madrasa* of the Mamlūk Sultan Ḥasan, built in Cairo at the end of the eighth/fourteenth century. Of colossal dimensions, it featured a spacious inner courtyard, flanked by four large halls that hosted the *ḥalaqa*s of four professors, each representing one of the *madhhab*s. Multistoried edifices lying between these halls supported other *madrasa*s, each *madrasa* offering its students separate accommodation and a mosque. The endowment's student population exceeded 500, all but about 100 of whom studied law. Those who did not specialize in law studied, among other things,

[47] *Ibid.*, 58. [48] Nawawī, *Rawḍa*, IV, 385.
[49] On *qurba* and philanthropy in the context of fashioning the moral subject, see Hallaq, "Fashioning the Moral Subject."

Quranic exegesis, *ḥadīth*, language, logic, mathematics and medicine. Several imams led prayers in the various mosques of the college, and over a hundred Quran readers maintained an uninterrupted recitation of the Quran. All building and personnel expenses were paid by endowed revenues, as were the costs of construction itself. Typically, all major *madrasa*s included such facilities, not to mention other features such as primary schools and a tomb chamber for the founder and his family.[50]

4. The *madrasa* and political cooptation of the legal profession

Clearly, it was the powerful ruling elite that established the most imposing and prestigious endowments, be these *madrasa*s or otherwise. It is also true that the colleges endowed by this elite were far fewer in number than the countless smaller endowments made by Muslim (and non-Muslim) merchants and less affluent persons.[51] Nevertheless, these towering and awe-inspiring royal buildings outlived the more modest *waqf*s and, more importantly, projected the ruler's munificence and political power. This projection is a nearly universal characteristic of rulers, and as such it must have been partly on the mind of the sultans, emirs and their political dependents when they embarked on establishing these endowments. ("Nearly universal" because, under the Tīmūrids of India, grants of titles and stipends were preferred over institutional *waqf*s.)[52] Yet, this consideration was not the prime motive behind their seemingly auspicious acts. Uppermost in their minds was their crucial (even desperate) need to find a group or an entity that could represent their rule to the masses and represent the masses before their rule. If the latter part of the equation was important, it was so because it served the imperatives of the former, which at the end of the day amounted to little more than an anxious search for legitimacy.

The question that inevitably arises here is: Why this search? The answer lies partly in the universal nature of pre-modern government, and partly in the specific circumstances of the Muslim context – in contradistinction, for instance, to those of China and Europe. (I have advisedly avoided the use of the term "state" to designate pre-modern government or rule, for it

50 Berkey, *Transmission of Knowledge*, 47, 67–69. See also Leiser, "Notes on the Madrasa," 22.
51 Çizakça, *History*, 15.
52 Kozlowski, "Imperial Authority," 355–63. The chief reason for this divergence in practice appears to have been the absence of major "urban" centers such as the cities of the Ṣafavids and the Ottomans, on the one hand, and the resultant diffusion of religious classes and of Ṣūfī orders throughout small, outlying villages, on the other (*ibid.*, 361–62).

is evident that the state is a modern phenomenon, exclusively the product of Europe until the end of the nineteenth century.)[53]

It was a near-universal characteristic of pre-modern governments that they exercised their power through small ruling elites, with a limited sphere of direct influence. They could not penetrate the societies they ruled, nor could they regulate the internal affairs of their subject populations. Their rule was generally concerned with their monopoly over military and political power, and their legislative interference did not go beyond the need to establish order in the form of quelling political competition and suppressing disruptive criminal behavior. These areas, together with launching wars and levying taxes, constituted the chief activities of rulers and governments. In establishing their control (which was nearly always personal, as compared to the impersonal and corporate nature of the modern state), a ruler was faced with a pernicious dilemma: if he wished to extend his dominion beyond his immediate realm, he had no choice but to increase his army and the numbers of his commanding officers; and once these officers took up their governorships, they almost invariably became independent or semi-autonomous, depriving the ruler of provincial revenues. On the other hand, if he wished to reduce the numbers of his officials, he would risk decentralization due to shortage of soldiers and staff, and this too exposed him to weakness or diminution in revenues.[54]

More importantly, rulers failed to penetrate the societies they governed because they lacked the mechanisms necessary to administer the smallest units of which these societies were made. This is another way of saying that the pre-modern state lacked the bureaucratic organization that provided the tools for establishing particular relations of power, relations that are the cornerstone of all modern political regimes (what Foucault aptly characterized as biopolitics).[55] Once firmly rooted in a society, impersonal bureaucracy tends to replace personal rule. Unlike bureaucratic rule, therefore, pre-modern forms of governance depended upon personal loyalty rather than obedience to abstract, impersonal regulations.[56]

The absence of intrusive bureaucracies from such pre-modern forms of governance meant that the ruler was navigating at the surface of the societies he ruled. Even if he had a staff that could be hierarchically deployed to reach the lowest social strata, loyalty to him progressively

[53] On the development of the state, see van Creveld, *Rise and Decline*; Corrigan and Sayer, *Great Arch*. For a critique of the discourse on the role of the colonial state in shaping, or failing to shape, the modern state, see Chatterjee, *Nation and its Fragments*, 14–34. See also chapter 13, below.

[54] Crone, *Pre-Industrial Societies*, 42–44, 56.

[55] Foucault, *Ethics, Subjectivity and Truth*, 72–79.

[56] Lassman, "Rule of Man," 94.

dissipated as it traveled away from the center. In other words, in the absence of the modern rule of bureaucracy (with all its attendant props, including nationalism and surveillance), the farther the pre-modern official found himself from the center of power, the less loyalty he had to the ruler, and, in turn, the more loyalty he had to the social group from which he hailed. Thus, the ruler could neither penetrate nor control or integrate these societies. He merely sat atop a pyramid of what one historian has aptly termed "self-help" groups[57] consisting of linguistic and religious communities, guilds, clans, village assemblies, city councils, and literate elites whose internal ties of loyalty were unsurpassable, and whose daily lives were barely touched by whatever administrative machinery the ruler could muster.

In the specifically Islamic context, there were at least three features in the exercise of political power that further intensified the gap between the ruling elite and the populace. First, the rulers and dynasties of the Islamic world, at least from Transoxiana and India to Egypt (but to a certain extent also in South-East Asia), were not native to the territories they ruled. In general, they and their armies neither shared the cultures of the populations they governed nor spoke their languages. Arguably, this alone was a formidable obstacle. Second, until the Mamlūks, Islamic dynasties did not last long enough to establish genuine roots among the subject populations, in terms either of creating a "rule of bureaucracy" (as had been achieved in Europe)[58] or of building institutionalized mechanisms that tied them in a particular relationship of power to these populations. Due to the fluid nature of political loyalty, no policy that may have aimed at creating such mechanisms could have outlasted a ruler's death, for loyalty was to the person, not to a policy enshrined in "corporate" governance.[59] Third, and despite the ancient secretarial traditions of the Near East, Muslim rulers could never command powerful and intrusive bureaucracies such as those developed in Europe or Sung China.[60] With the partial exception of the Ottomans (a semi-European empire), the Muslim ruling elites saw no need to develop the surveillance–bureaucratic mechanisms which Europe later excelled at producing.

Thus, the warlords who ruled Muslim lands after the third/ninth century could not administer their domains directly, having constantly to appeal to the legal profession who served as representatives of the

[57] Crone, *Pre-Industrial Societies*, 45, 56.
[58] See, e.g., Corrigan and Sayer, *Great Arch*, 15 ff.
[59] The corporation being one of the most fundamental components of the modern state. See the illuminating introductory discussion in van Creveld, *Rise and Decline*, 1.
[60] Chamberlain, *Knowledge and Social Practice*, 17.

"self-help" groups referred to above. This appeal, as we saw in section 1, was also characteristic of the ʿAbbāsid caliphate, although the latter differed from the warlords in one important respect: hailing from the Prophet's tribe, the ʿAbbāsid dynasty possessed the politico-religious authority to speak and act in the name of Islam, whereas the later foreign rulers did not. The authority of the ʿAbbāsids did of course require the complementary attribute of legitimacy, which was obtained through subordinating their rule to the Sharīʿa, and this they achieved successfully.[61] The warlords, on the other hand, were mostly foreigners and, as if this were not enough to alienate them from the populace, they were in want of authority as well as legitimacy. Accordingly, they stood in dire need of local, indigenous support. It was the legal profession that provided this support, but not readily and not without much reluctance, for a substantial investment had first to be made on the part of these rulers in order to successfully coopt this profession.

An even stronger reason for their greater authority was that the ʿAbbāsids did not need to insert themselves in the midst of the cultural, social and educational practices of the relatively small communities they ruled, since they possessed – by virtue of their ethnic association with these communities – the tools of cultural communication to cultivate political legitimacy. The succeeding effective rulers, however, did not. The gulf that the Shīʿite Būyids and Fāṭimids created between themselves and the Sunnite masses did not permit any considerable penetration into the existing social institutions. They could not have, in the first place, sponsored the Sunnite religious elites and legal scholars to any significant extent, for this would have amounted to sapping their own strength. The result was that these elites were pushed down into society and were thus largely disconnected from the ruling circles.[62]

The first major dynastic warlords to sweep through Iran and the Middle East were the Saljūqs, committed Sunnites who defeated the Būyids, but otherwise lacked both religious authority and political legitimacy. Toward solving this problem, the Saljūqs set in motion a pattern of governance that was to be emulated and reinforced until the nineteenth century. Their first experiment was in the province of Khurāsān, where – after a failed policy initiated by their grand vizier ʿAmīd al-Mulk al-Kundurī –[63] they turned to a policy that we may term horizontal sponsorship. Kundurī's policy of vertical sponsorship had been to adopt the cause of one party

[61] An interesting commentary on this success may be found in Mottahedeh, *Loyalty*, 180.
[62] *Ibid.*, 184.
[63] On al-Kundurī's sponsorship of the Ḥanafites and persecution of the Ashʿarite-Shāfiʿites, see Ibn Khallikān, *Wafayāt*, III, 71–73; Makdisi, "Ashʿarī and the Ashʿarites," 47.

against another, in his case the Ḥanafites against the Ashʿarite-Shāfiʿites, thereby destroying the political power of the latter in the city of Nīshapūr. His policies led to enough civil unrest as to cause the Saljūqs great concern. His successor, Niẓām al-Mulk, reversed this policy and worked to sponsor the various groups evenly. It was from this point onwards that the *madrasa* system began to flourish on a massive scale, since the founding of educational institutions gave the dynasty the long-desired venue to promote itself as a legitimate government among the populace; and it was the influential legal profession that staffed the *madrasa*s which afforded the tool for achieving this end.

Deriving their moral authority and social standing from the religious law, the legists were the only civilian elite that could represent the foreign ruler and the indigenous subjects to each other. Yet, there was more to this elite than its professional association with the religious law, however important this association was. In the fifth/eleventh century, the social backgrounds of the legists were still quite varied, representing all segments of society. They hailed as much from the lowest strata of tradesmen and farmers as from affluent merchant families and politically influential secretarial classes.[64] Their socio-economic connections – deeply embedded in their own societies but also in relative proximity to the ruling classes – thus allowed them to fulfill a variety of functions in mediating the relationship between the government and the subject population.

Drawing on these connections, Niẓām al-Mulk embarked on constructing and endowing a series of *madrasa*s, first in the province of Khurāsān, then moving westward to Baghdad, where, as we have mentioned, eleven major institutions were established. These *madrasa*s were effectively used to recruit the loyalties of the major jurists in Nishāpūr, Baghdad and elsewhere. Probably the first to exploit so skillfully the minutiae of the law of *waqf* for political gains, Niẓām al-Mulk personally took charge of appointing, with handsome pay, well-known jurists and law professors. He retained exclusive powers over appointment and dismissal, for this guaranteed his leverage to bestow *personal* favors and thus acquire the loyalty of the legal profession. As political loyalty was not institutional, Niẓām al-Mulk's personal involvement was indispensable. With the partial exception of the later Ottomans, this personal involvement was invariably the rule. It was the sultan, emir, vizier or (often) influential female member of the ruling elite who founded *madrasa*s, named them after themselves, and took a personal interest in how they were run and who taught in them. It was in this way that the foreign rulers and military

[64] Cohen, "Economic Background"; Ephrat, *Learned Societies*, 126. Ephrat estimates that almost half of Baghdad's scholars she surveyed came from a merchant background (96).

commanders, who characterized the political scene in the Muslim world for centuries, could insert themselves into social networks, thereby fitting their political strategies into the populations they ruled.

The appearance of richly endowed *madrasa*s in the middle of the fifth/eleventh century proved to be a crucial factor in the economic and professional make-up of the legal elite. By the time that century drew to a close, a substantial segment of this elite was in the pay of government. In Baghdad, nearly a third of the Ḥanafites and Shāfiʿites – the two most sizable schools in the city – were either professors or judges, financially dependent on the Saljūq government.[65] The official judicial class had been associated with the political, and was, as we have seen, morally and ethically distinct from the private class of jurists, law professors and *muftī*s. With the incorporation of the professors into the *madrasa* system, the political domain encroached further into the terrain of the law, subordinating a considerable segment – even the elite – of the professorial profession and contributing to the increasing diminution of the "moral community" of the legists. Some of the best professors were now in the company of the judges. This was why many jurists refused to accept teaching posts, just as many others had refused judgeships. The money that paid the judges' salaries came from the same coffer as that which built the towering *madrasa*s and which hired the most accomplished professor-jurists. But the coffer was generally regarded as suspect, having been filled through dubious means. No wonder then that, like the honorable jurists who refused judgeships, professors who did likewise were lauded and praised.

Yet, the legal elite ultimately succumbed to moral compromise, and increasingly so. By the seventeenth century, most legists were in the employ of the government,[66] and the professors and author-jurists who held out had to function within a diminishing "moral community" created by the financial and material dependence of their less independent peers on the ruling powers. The judges – or many of them – were promised eternal damnation because they were unlucky enough to have transgressed in a period when the Prophetic traditions were still fluid enough to make them fit any occasion. The *madrasa* professors, on the other hand, escaped universal condemnation only because nearly the entire profession – itself the source of the discourse on heaven and hell – became engaged in government service; at any rate, their moral compromise came late enough to escape the wrath of Prophetic traditions or other paradigmatic discourse.

The governmental *madrasa* thus attracted the community of legal scholars, for it afforded them a wide spectrum of career options, often

[65] Ephrat, *Learned Societies*, 138. [66] Zilfi, *Politics of Piety*, 28.

with handsome pay. The Saljūq experiment in fact met with phenomenal success, and was emulated throughout the Muslim world. Within less than a century after its appearance in Baghdad, the *madrasa* was introduced into Syria, where it was efficiently used by Nūr al-Dīn Zanghī (549/1154–570/1174) to accommodate his rule in Damascus.[67] From that point on, *madrasas* rapidly multiplied and increasingly dominated the legal culture in that city. Like Baghdad a century or two before, Damascene *madrasas* attracted accomplished jurists and law professors from all corners of the Muslim world, scholars who contributed to the internationalization of scholarship in the city and outside it. The Ayyūbids continued the *madrasa* expansion into Egypt, suppressing the Fāṭimids and rejuvenating the much-needed Sunnite scholarship through the founding of law colleges. The Mamlūks carried on by building on the efforts of their predecessors, creating some of the largest *madrasas* and entrenching their control of the population deeper and with more lasting effect than any dynasty had done hitherto.

From Khurāsān, the *madrasa* traveled to India, and quickly became a means of recruiting the Sharīʿa specialists in government service. Under the Delhi Sultanate (603/1206–933/1526), the legists were no less beholden to the government than their western counterparts in Baghdad, Damascus and Cairo. Under the Mughal Sultan Akbar (964/1556–1014/1605), as under his contemporaries – the Ottomans, the Ṣafavids, the Shaybānid Khānate, and the Mangits – the legal profession's cooptation was near complete. (As far as I know, the only exception to this generalization was the Mataram Kingdom of East Central Java, where the jurists and religious scholars remained independent of the ruling dynasty, and operated at the level of local village communities.)

On the whole, however, an equilibrium did exist between the men of the sword and those of the law: the ruling elite received the cooperation of the scholars and their promotion of its legitimacy, while the scholars received a salary, protection, and the full right to apply the law as they saw fit. The office of the judge was, and continued to be, the prototype of what was becoming an increasingly complex and interdependent relationship: the government appointed, dismissed and paid the judge, but the judge applied the *fiqh* as the Sharīʿa and its author-jurists and *muftīs* required. If there was one constant in this relationship between rulers and legists, it was that the *fiqh* and its application to the population were not compromised.

[67] For an excellent study analyzing this city under the Ayyūbids and Mamlūks, see Chamberlain, *Knowledge and Social Practice*, 69–90 and *passim*.

5. The *madrasa* and centralization policies

The *madrasas*, we have said, created for the legists abundant career opportunities. Enterprising students from modest economic and social backgrounds found in the endowed and subsidized colleges auspicious opportunities to pursue their education that in turn opened the door to professional and social mobility.[68] The advanced student soon became a *muʿīd* to his professor, then perhaps moved on to work as a court scribe or a court witness. These steps could be immediately followed by an appointment to a judgeship that could in turn culminate in a chief magistracy if the candidate had sufficiently extensive credentials and, at times, connections. Yet, such a career path did not necessarily preclude the student's concomitant engagement in the more complex and sophisticated fields of legal scholarship that would lead him, usually somewhat later in life, to the two highest ranks in the profession: namely, those of *muftī* and author-jurist. While both areas of expertise were the most prestigious in the legal profession, they did not guarantee economic or material privileges. By the fifth/eleventh century, only the *qāḍī* and his court subordinates – the scribe and witness – had routinized incomes. Studying and teaching in the *madrasa* was to become part of this routinization.

Yet, the *madrasa* had no monopoly over legal education, and many legists who served as judges did not acquire their education in a *madrasa*. Furthermore, a tiny minority of *madrasa* graduates ended in government service,[69] mainly as administrative secretaries or viziers, which leads us to the conclusion that the *madrasa* was neither intended nor perceived as a tool for training government administrators and bureaucrats, but rather instituted in order to generate and augment political legitimacy.[70] The *madrasa*'s function of training bureaucrats was only to be introduced in later centuries, as we will see in due course.

The *madrasa*'s proliferation after the fifth/eleventh century created another venue of income. Now, not only could students benefit from free and subsidized education, but so could jurists gain paid employment as professors. The more *madrasas* that were founded, the more teaching jobs became available and, in turn, the larger the number of legists who benefited from them. The growth in these numbers also meant a dramatic increase in the competition between and among the legists. The competition intensified particularly where the major *madrasas* (founded by sultans

[68] Leiser, "Notes on the Madrasa," 22–23. [69] Ephrat, *Learned Society*, 117–18.

[70] Cf. Tibawi, "Origin," who argues that one of Niẓām al-Mulk's reasons for founding *madrasas* was to cultivate a class of administrators and bureaucrats. Richard Bulliet rightly observes that this consideration was not likely to have been on Niẓām al-Mulk's mind. See his "Shaikh al-Islam," 65.

and grand viziers) were involved, as professorial salaries offered there were usually higher than anywhere else.

The accrual of income from judgeships and professorships – not to mention scribal and witnessing functions – allowed a class of legists to make service in the law a full-time, life-long career. By the middle of the fifth/eleventh century, many legists came from the merchant class, while a majority appears to have issued from various other backgrounds, most of which were economically modest. Many of them had only a part-time engagement in law, its study and practice, for, in order to earn a living, they still had to combine their legal careers with other crafts or skills, such as book copiers, tanners, market inspectors and, increasingly, administrators of sorts. This state of affairs persisted for some time. But once a legist could secure all his income from a judgeship or a *madrasa*-professorship, he would attempt to do what everyone else had done, be he professor, carpenter, janitor or jeweler, namely, pass on the profession to his male children. In this context, it is noteworthy that professions were as much a hereditary affair as wealth.

Thus, by the middle of the sixth/twelfth century, retaining certain teaching positions within the family began to emerge as a rudimentary pattern, as had already happened somewhat earlier with judgeships. Whereas the pursuit of knowledge in the earliest centuries was, generally speaking, done for its own sake, or, more accurately, for the sake of epistemic and social prestige (and no doubt propelled by a sense of religiosity), it had now come to pass that knowledge was being acquired for the sake of a competitive edge, which in part led back to the acquisition of social prestige. This is to say that the increasing professionalization of the legal profession rendered it – in unprecedented fashion – a venue for garnering political, economic and social capital. Furthermore, once knowledge itself became (as a source of income) commodified, its standards were manipulated as the need arose. And the more posts became available, the more commodified the entire profession appeared to be. In every corner of the Islamic world, the rise and spread of the *madrasa* was causally accompanied by this process of "familial professionalization."

Between the seventh/thirteenth and eleventh/seventeenth centuries, this process of professionalization grew steadily, but the legist families could not achieve a complete monopoly over the social background of the legal profession. Conversely, while these families were able to increase their numbers in the legal profession,[71] merchant and other families continued to have access to it, albeit gradually less so. A complete

[71] Mandaville, "Muslim Judiciary," 20.

monopoly by the legist families over the profession had to await the early twelfth/eighteenth century, when in the Ottoman Empire not a single legist from a merchant background occupied high office.[72] By all indications, this development in the legal profession during the later phases of the Ṣafavid and Mughal empires appears to have generally followed the same pattern, although detailed study of such phenomena has yet to be undertaken.

The legists' family-centered monopoly over the legal profession, and especially over prominent governmental posts, was the result of a deliberate and systematic centralization policy that the Ottomans had begun to pursue as early as the sixteenth century. Whereas Niẓām al-Mulk founded two or three dozen *madrasa*s throughout the Saljūq Empire, the Ottomans built a *madrasa* in every city and town they conquered, and the larger the population conquered, the bigger the *madrasa*. But the largest and most prestigious colleges were reserved for Istanbul, where a succession of sultans – as well as other influential men and women – poured much of their wealth into these colossal foundations. More important is the crucial fact that whereas provincial and smaller *madrasa*s within and without Istanbul continued to train students and produce legists and scholars of all sorts, the men of law who ran the Empire were consistently graduates of the Istanbul sultanic *madrasa*s. In other words, entry into government service was predicated upon completing the required course of study in these imperial *madrasa*s, which were increasingly staffed by the children of the legist families. Smaller, non-imperial and provincial *madrasa*s continued to train students, but their graduates never came to be part of the professional hierarchy that regulated society and, in certain respects, government.

Control over the *madrasa* was integral to a centralizing scheme by which the legists were streamlined into an official hierarchy. This Ottoman policy probably began during the latter half of the ninth/fifteenth century, but can only be documented from the middle of the next century onwards. Under Mehmet II, eight *madrasa*s were established as part of this sultan's grand mosque, and their graduates were guaranteed the highest positions in the Empire. Later, under Bayezid II (886–918/1481–1512) and Suleyman I (927–74/1520–66), new *madrasa* systems were established, superseding in prestige all *madrasa*s built by previous sultans. Later still, Selim II and Murat III, among other sultans, endowed colleges that were

[72] Zilfi, *Politics of Piety*, 45, 55. This development began earlier, during the last few decades of the Mamlūks. See Mandaville, "Muslim Judiciary," 20, who rightly observes that there is "some justification that a local judicial aristocracy existed at this period in Damascus." There is little doubt that during the same time Cairo would have developed the same pattern.

to challenge the preeminence of previous imperial *madrasa*s. Nonetheless, these *madrasa*s remained altogether superior to other colleges founded by viziers and members of the dynasty in the capital city. And even within their ranks, the sultanic *madrasa*s were generally differentiated by their age, the newer ones partaking more than the others in reproducing the official legal hierarchy.

The hierarchy within the government-controlled *madrasa*s was organized according to income from the functions the graduates would fulfill. Thus, one *madrasa* would produce functionaries for positions carrying salaries of 300 *qurūsh*, while another, more prestigious *madrasa* would train judges or professors for positions paying 500 *qurūsh*. It was usually from within the latter's graduates that the highest legal posts in the Empire were filled.

From the tenth/sixteenth century onwards, and with the increase in the number of *madrasa*s and students, the course of study was expanded to five years, whereas earlier it had consisted of an average of four years.[73] Generally, students attended classes several hours a day, five days a week, Thursdays and Fridays being holidays. Each government-controlled *madrasa* specialized in a different level of education, the highest level being that which concentrated on various areas of law, especially *fiqh* and *uṣūl al-fiqh*. At the lower levels were taught, among other things, Arabic grammar, syntax, geometry and astronomy. Intermediate levels specialized in *adab*-literature, rhetoric, logic and other "rational" sciences. Students now sat in an open semi-circle facing the professor, a change reflecting the professionalization of legal education and the development of a formal hierarchy within the legal profession. Now, the professor was more distant from his students, who were generally more uniform in terms of their educational level. The notion of *ṣuḥba*, which involved the presence – within close physical proximity to the professor – of advanced students and scholars in the *ḥalaqa*, is hardly present, thereby exacerbating the epistemic disconnection between professor and student.

Be that as it may, upon graduating from such a *madrasa*, the student would become a *mulāzim*, i.e., a candidate for office. As in the old *ḥalaqa* system, the career of the *mulāzim* depended first on the certification of the professor, since the *madrasa* itself, even under the later Ottomans, never acted as an entity possessing a juristic personality, and thus could not grant degrees. With an *ijāza*, the *mulāzim* would then become dependant on an office-holder, who might be his own professor or some other functionary. How these *mulāzama* ties were forged is thus not altogether clear,

[73] Makdisi, *Rise*, 96.

but it seems that family connections played a part. At any rate, this association with an office-holder rendered the *mulāzim* eligible for appointment, *inter alia*, in the government judicial bureaucracy. In the middle of the tenth/sixteenth century, an official register began to be kept for recording the names of *mulāzims* in the order of their entrance into this category. The office-holders had the right to designate a *mulāzim* once every seven years, and the eligible *mulāzim* would wait his turn until a post became available.[74] The more prestigious the *madrasa* from which a candidate graduated, the more highly ranked the post assigned would be. Thus, beginning toward the end of the ninth/fifteenth century, and for the first time in Islamic history, the *madrasa*, not the professor, would determine the rank of the student and his professional capabilities.

The absorption of legal education into the political and bureaucratic structure of government was nowhere more manifest than in the legal hierarchy that the Ottomans constructed as part of their general policy of governance. One of the curiosities about this hierarchy is that, beginning with the end of the ninth/fifteenth century, the Shaykh al-Islām – whose epistemic and legal capacity was strictly defined within the institution of *iftā'* – became the supreme religious figure in the Empire, who alone was responsible for appointing and dismissing provincial judges, and for a long time possessed the *de facto* power to depose sultans.[75] Until the eleventh/seventeenth century, he enjoyed life appointment, and could not be dismissed even by the sultan himself. He at times adjudicated disputes upon appeal from litigants before provincial Sharī'a courts, but more often ordered judges to conform to the religious law, which he usually stated for them.

The functions of the Ottoman Shaykh al-Islām were not entirely consistent with the earlier judicial history of Islam, where the chief justice, a *qāḍī* himself, was the official who would appoint and dismiss provincial *qāḍī*s and who would hear judicial appeals. Nor were they consistent with the earliest phases of Ottoman legal history itself, as the two highest judicial positions in the Empire were the two Qāḍī 'Askars who controlled, respectively, the European and Asian jurisdictions of the Empire. The explanation for this departure from past experience appears to have been closely connected with an evolving policy that had vague beginnings during the Saljūq period of Transoxiana and that eventually culminated with the Ottomans – a policy formed specifically to increase the ruling elite's control over legal education. From the initial stages of the Saljūq state of Rūm (r. 470–707/1077–1307), the forerunner of the Ottoman

[74] Repp, *Mufti of Istanbul*, 51–55. [75] Gerber, *State, Society*, 80.

Empire, a Shaykh al-Islām was appointed as head of the scholarly group involved in legal education in each city. Professors and colleges fell under his supervision.[76] He was a *muftī*, but he had neither monopoly nor preeminence in this field, for his real powers lay in his office as supervisor of the colleges and their professors. While he would be the only Shaykh al-Islām in the city, he might be only one among several *muftī*s and legal scholars. Thus, in their bid to make of Istanbul a centralizing and centralized capital, the Ottomans did with the Shaykh al-Islām what they had done with regard to creating a monopoly of sultanic *madrasa*s: they made the Shaykh al-Islām of Istanbul the supreme head directly responsible for the provinces. This step in the policy of centralization was not only as decisive as that which led to the creation of sultanic *madrasa*s, but also in fact an integral part of the overall policy to appropriate into the political realm the legal profession, utilizing it in the administration of the Empire. And that is precisely what the Ottomans managed to accomplish. Yet, in doing so, they also resolved once and for all the problem of legitimacy. In the nineteenth century, as we will see, the Ottomans were to multiply their gains, since the absorption of the legal profession into the government hierarchy allowed them to decapitate it, and decapitate it they did.[77]

[76] Bulliet, "Shaikh al-Islam," 55, 61.

[77] See chapter 15, sections 1–2, below.

4 Law and society

1. Introduction

That the Muslim world, from Egypt to western Iran, was predominantly and for centuries ruled by foreign dynasties is a fact that bore directly on the complex relationship between the rulers and the legists,[1] on the one hand, and on the ways in which jurists' law was interpreted and applied in the social context, on the other. An important, if not crucial, feature resulting from the political, military, cultural and linguistic disjunctions between ruler and ruled was the preservation and, indeed, enhancement of ancient forms of social and economic autonomy and local self-rule. This disjunction only bolstered the dominant characteristic of pre-modern forms of rule, namely, the considerable degree of separation between the populace and the ruling regime. The latter quite simply lacked the necessary surveillance mechanisms that would permit direct control of the social groupings by which society organized itself. Whereas the great majority of disputes in industrial societies are resolved by state courts of law or arbitration regulated by state law, typically pre-industrial societies, and certainly those of Islam, were only marginally subject to government intervention. To put it slightly differently, in pre-modern Islamic societies, disputes were resolved with a minimum of legislative guidance, the determining factors having been informal mediation/arbitration[2] and, equally, informal law courts. Furthermore, it appears to be a consistent pattern that wherever mediation and law are involved in conflict resolution, morality and social ethics are intertwined, as they certainly were in the case of Islam in the pre-industrial era. By contrast, where they

[1] Important aspects of which have been discussed in chapter 3, above.

[2] Whereas in modern law there is a clear difference between mediation and arbitration, in pre-modern tribal law and custom the boundaries of the two at times overlapped, giving the mediator a certain authority to arbitrate (necessarily and teleologically integral to the process of mediation) and, more importantly, to bestow on the arbitrator mediative powers. The practice still survives in many tribal and rural areas in the Middle East; e.g., in the context of *ṣulḥa*s among Arabs of Upper Galilee and the West Bank.

are absent, as they are in the legal culture of Western and, increasingly, non-Western modern nation-states, morality and social ethics are strangers. Morality, especially its religious variety, thus provided a more effective and pervasive mechanism of self-rule and did not require the marked presence of coercive and disciplinarian state agencies, the emblem of the modern body politic.

2. Mediation and arbitration

In speaking of "legal system," as several legal anthropologists have asserted,[3] it would be neither sufficient nor even correct to dwell on the law court as the exclusive vehicle of conflict resolution. In any system, what goes on both outside the court and prior to bringing litigation before it are stages of conflict resolution that are just as significant to the operation of the legal system as any court process. This is particularly true in closely knit social structures, such as traditional Islamic societies, where groups tended to manage conflicts before they were brought before a wider public forum, mainly the law court. It was within these groups, from Malaya to Morocco,[4] that the initial operation of the legal system began, and it was through the continued involvement of such groups that the Muslim court was able to accomplish its task of conflict resolution. For, as we shall see, it was inconceivable for the Muslim court in particular to process claims regarding disputes without due consideration of the moral sensibilities and communal complexities of the social site from within which a dispute had arisen.

Disputes occurring prior to and outside the court's involvement thus centered in the various micro-communities which made up Muslim societies. The extended family (the typical, though not exclusive, family unit known until the nineteenth century),[5] the clan and the tribe constituted the core and kernel of social existence, even when they happened to be intersected by other social orderings. Small villages predominantly consisted of these units, but in towns and cities other units of social coherence shared the demographic landscape. The neighborhood (*ḥāra*), a perduring unit of social organization, constituted a sort of corporate group that was at times based on kinship, but at others on religious or other unifying

[3] See, e.g., Gulliver, "Dispute Settlement without Courts," 24 ff., and references cited therein; also, generally, the various discussions in Gulliver, *Cross-Examinations*.

[4] For the Mediterranean region, see the multiple sources below. For the less-studied Malay world, see the important works of Sadka, *Protected Malay States*, 264, and Peletz, *Islamic Modern*, 49–50.

[5] Marcus, *Middle East*, 197, partly disputes the universal prevalence of the extended family in late twelfth/eighteenth-century Aleppo.

ties. The neighborhoods of the Christians, Jews and immigrant communities (Armenians, Maghrebites, Franks),[6] as well as the guilds (*ṭawā'if*; sing.: *ṭā'ifa*) of the tanners, soap-makers, porters, physicians, copper merchants and the like were fixed presences in Muslim cities.[7] Each neighborhood consisted of dozens, even hundreds, of families and houses,[8] with shops, public facilities, a house of worship, a school, a public bath, a public fountain, and several small streets or alleys connected to a main road. The neighborhood was usually contained within walls, with guarded gates at the points leading to the main roads of the city. That interaction between the various neighborhoods was extensive goes without saying,[9] but this in no way obscures the glaring fact of each neighborhood's separate and independent religious, filial or professional identity. Yet, it was the extended family that constituted the unshakable foundation of social existence and, as such, its members always stood in a relationship of solidarity with each other. The family not only constituted an economic unit of production, but provided lifetime security for its members. The family, in other words, defined much of human relationships.[10] And this was as true of Malayan societies as it was of Mediterranean Islam. The family and the immediate community made an investment not only in the well-being of their individual members but also in ensuring their jural compliance; for "it was commonly accepted that they could suffer when a member of the group offended ... In the words of a Malay text, 'Parents and children, brothers and sisters, share the same family fortune and the family repute. If one suffers, all suffer.'"[11]

[6] All of which occupied quarters in Cairo. The Palestinian city Nazareth provides another example. Traditionally, and largely still today, it consisted of quarters belonging to the Greek Orthodox, the Roman Catholics (Latin quarter) and the Copts, while the rest was occupied by Muslims (known as al-Ḥāra al-Sharqiyya).

[7] Marcus, *Middle East*, 158–59, observes that some professions had several guilds, such as the porters, dyers and silk spinners who were organized around their locations in Aleppo or, in the case of the tanners, around the colors they produced. The same was true of Cairene merchants who formed a guild for each market in which a group of them operated. Hanna, *Making Big Money*, 19–20. For some details on the construction guild, see Hanna, *Construction Work*, 7–10. For a useful overview of modern scholarship on guilds, see Ghazaleh, "Guilds," 60–74.

[8] Raymond, "Role of the Communities," 39; El-Nahal, *Judicial Administration*, 52.

[9] In sixteenth- and seventeenth-century Cairo, for example, interaction between and among professional and religious neighborhoods was extensive. It was not uncommon for a member of a confessional group to bail out a person from another neighborhood or another religious denomination, or for a Muslim to testify in favor of a Christian against another Muslim. In business, the interaction was most extensive. Muslims and non-Muslims, carpenters and builders, went into partnership with each other and, as empowered legal agents, represented each other. See Nahal, *Judicial Administration*, 56.

[10] Ortaylı, *Studies*, 125–26.

[11] Peletz, *Islamic Modern*, 30, citing Barbara Andaya, "States, Laws, and Gender Regimes in Early Modern Southeast Asia" (unpublished paper).

Even before the appearance of corporate professional guilds under the Ottomans of the ninth/fifteenth and tenth/sixteenth centuries[12] (guilds which further enhanced the inner groups' dynamics of mediation and conflict resolution), the extended family, the clan, religious communities, neighborhoods and the various loosely organized professions all provided extensive social networks for informal conflict resolution.[13] Many private disputes, such as spousal discord and disagreements over joint family property, were often mediated by the head of the household or an authoritative figure in the clan or neighborhood. Village imams, as well as the elders of nomadic, semi-nomadic and settled tribes, commonly appear in court records as having intervened as arbitrators in disputes prior to the arrival of the case before the judge. As much under the Ottomans as under the Malayan Laws of 1667 (Dato Sri Paduka Tuan), village elders were to report to authorities any and all crimes that might disrupt public order or the life of the community.[14] But these elders also played a crucial role in mediation and conflict resolution. Indeed, many court cases in which the claimants' evidence was inconclusive were resolved (often at the recommendation of the judge)[15] by such mediators during the process of litigation, and before the judge passed sentence. At times, the "peacemakers" would be relatives of the claimant and/or defendant or simply residents of the same neighborhood. At others, these peacemakers were officials of the court, specifically appointed to carry out this particular task.[16] Cases were often dismissed by the judge when mediators from within or without the court were successful in settling the dispute.[17]

The legal maxim "amicable settlement is the best verdict" (*al-ṣulḥ sayyid al-aḥkām*)[18] represents a long-standing tradition in Islam and Islamic law, reflecting the deep-rooted perception, both legal and social,

[12] Baer, "Guilds," esp. at 16–17, 27. However, Baer's account of the appearance of guilds around the tenth/sixteenth century must be questioned, for his argument almost exclusively rests on an alleged absence of pre-sixteenth-century evidence explicitly referring to guilds. The persistent reference in guilds' discourse to the "ancient laws" that regulated their professional life is sufficient to problematize Baer's supposed absence of pre-sixteenth-century evidence. See Gerber, *State, Society*, 114–16; Kuran, "Islamic Influences," 44. See also the references to ʿAbbasid guilds in Omar, "Guilds,"198–217, and to their presence around the sixth/twelfth-century in South-East Asia: Federspiel, *Sultans*, 19–20.

[13] Akarlı, "Law in the Marketplace," 249 ff.; Hanna, "Administration of Courts," 54; Raymond, "Role of the Communities," 39–40; Starr, "Pre-Law Stage," 120; Marcus, *Middle East*, 109.

[14] Peletz, *Islamic Modern*, 30. [15] Marcus, *Middle East*, 111.

[16] On this "institution" in Muslim Spain, see Fierro, "Ill-Treated Women," 331 ff.

[17] Peirce, *Morality Tales*, 123, 185–86; Hanna, "Administration of Courts," 54; El-Nahal, *Judicial Administraion*, 19–20, 30; Gerber, *State, Society*, 51; Marcus, *Middle East*, 111.

[18] In the Ottoman tradition, the prevailing maxim appears to have been "*al-ṣulḥ khayr*" (amicable settlement is a good work). See Peirce, *Morality Tales*, 186.

not only that arbitration and mediation are integral to the legal system and the legal process but that they even stand paramount over court litigation, which was usually seen as the last resort.[19] There are a number of reasons why mediation constituted a preferred mode of conflict resolution. First, and historically speaking, extended households (large families, clans or tribes), with ramified authority structures, were the most typical feature of early societies, be they Arab, Berber, Persian or central Asian. Hailing from what anthropologists term "simple societies," these households provided the internal dynamics and processes to resolve disputes within them in a context where the ruling power and its proxies were either weak or non-existent. Thus, clan-centered and localized conflict resolution of the informal type historically preceded any extra-filial, formal and exogenous modes of adjudication. Second, and until the dawn of modernity, Islamic rulers not only depended on this tradition of micro-self-regulation, but indeed encouraged it, for it facilitated efficient and low-cost governance that simultaneously ensured public order. Third, in a society that viewed as sacrosanct all family relations and affairs, disputes involving intimate and private matters were kept away from the public eye and scrutiny. For every case that went to court – and these were countless – many more were informally resolved at the local level, with the intervention of the elders, the imam, the household matriarch, or others of equal prestige and authority. Fourth, and in some cases this was a decisive factor, informal mediation was indispensable for avoiding the escalation of conflict. In communities that heavily depended on group solidarity and in which the individual was defined by his or her affiliation to larger group-units, private disputes had great potential of becoming "expandable into political disputes between competing groups."[20] If the sanctity of family was paramount, it was so also because it constituted an integral part of a larger consideration, namely, the maintenance of social harmony. Attending to and eliminating dispute at the most local level preempted the escalation of disputes that might have disrupted such harmony.

Some anthropologists have rightly argued that the fundamental distinction between arbitration (-cum-mediation) and adjudication is the distinct absence from the former of authoritative decision-making. For such arbitrators are usually third parties who, because they are not burdened with a decision-making competence, are invariably inclined toward flexibility by virtue of the fact that each party is dependent on the other for obtaining a positive outcome (negotiation here being a central feature).[21] Arbitration thus becomes a viable option if the interests of the two parties

[19] Also see the closing lines of n. 23, below.
[20] Starr, "Pre-Law Stage," 130. [21] Gulliver, "Process," 33, 42.

are partially overlapping, and not totally incompatible. A typical case in point is homicide. In modern state criminal systems, no negotiation or mediation of the penalty is possible (once a plea bargain is entered), for one penalty or another must be meted out, and exclusively at the hands of the state to boot. By contrast, in a tribal (and in this case Islamic) system, where blood-money is often substitutable for retaliation, arbitration is rendered feasible by virtue of the possibility of settlement for monetary payment, a possibility enhanced by the mutual desire to avoid both further costly feuding and non-compensable loss. Furthermore, and quite significant in this context, pardon granted by the next of kin is at times a distinct possibility, especially if the victim was clearly the one who spurred the trouble causing his own death.[22] Thus, another significant feature of mediation/arbitration is the win-some-lose-some mode of conflict resolution, which avoids all-or-nothing solutions at any cost. When the latter mode asserted itself as the only option, arbitration would be *a priori* precluded, and adjudication would remain as the only resort.

3. The *qāḍī* and his court

Yet, evidence from the world of Islamic legal practice does not support the anthropological observation that, at the level of adjudication, the main, if not only, option available was that of "all-or-nothing." Nor does it entirely support the rigid distinction between the roles of judges and arbitrators insofar as judges, because they possess the power of decision-making, are inclined to the all-or-nothing mode. It is true that, in some cases, the Muslim judge was faced with black-and-white juristic options, and it was precisely in such instances that mediation had no role in the first place. Nevertheless, in many, if not the great majority of cases, the *qāḍī* or his representatives would be acting in an adjudicatory-cum-mediatory role. At least in one important respect, the successful result of his mediation was often regarded at the social level as a judgment.[23] Moreover, the *qāḍī* oftentimes played the exclusive role of mediator in cases that were not of a

[22] Without self-defense (as we understand, say, in American law) being involved. It must also be stressed that such options provided for in the Sharīʿa law of homicide have their genealogical origins in a logic of arbitration. Further on this, see chapter 10, section 3, below.

[23] This aspect still survives even in modern Sharīʿa courts. Drawing on his study of a Jordanian court, Richard Antoun observes that the judge's role as an agent of reconciliation is institutionalized in the ideology of the court and its procedure. Judges "use their personal authority to reconcile the parties … The aim is to give reconciliation, whether through the litigant's own efforts or the efforts of intermediaries, the force of judgment. The importance of compromise in the judicial process can be more readily assessed by the degree to which compromise is institutionalized than by the percentage of court

strictly legal nature. Not only did he arbitrate disputes, and reconcile between husbands and wives,[24] but he listened, for example, to the problems between brothers who might need no more than an outsider's opinion.[25]

More important, however, was the social context in which the *qāḍī* and his court were positioned. As Gluckman and Rosen have observed – in two different cultural sites – judges invariably sought to unravel the wider relational context of the litigating parties, often attempting to resolve conflicts in full view of the set of present and future social relationships of disputants.[26] Like arbitrators, but unlike modern judges,[27] the *qāḍī* tried, wherever possible, to prevent the collapse of relationships so as to maintain a social reality in which the litigating parties could continue to live together amicably.[28] Such a *judicial* act required the *qāḍī* to be familiar with, and willing to investigate, the history of interaction between the disputants. No facts could be determined by the court without reference to what I here call social biography, which comprises data relative to the litigant as a socially constituted entity. Nor did the *qāḍī*'s adjudication allow for a narrow application of legal doctrine, certainly not without allowing the full range of social biography to enter into the thinking and discourse of the court. Rosen's apt description of modern-day Morocco is expressive of a systemic feature in Islamic court justice:

> The predominant goal of the [Islamic] law is not simply to resolve differences but to put people back into a position where they can, with the least adverse implications for the social order, continue to negotiate their own arrangements with one another ... even though the specific content of a court's knowledge about particular individuals may be both limited and stereotypical, the terms by which the courts proceed, the concepts they employ, the styles of speech by which testimony is shaped, and the forms of remedy they apply are broadly similar to those that people use in their everyday lives and possess little of the strange formality or professionalized distortions found in some other systems of law.[29]

compromise decisions. Frequently ... the aim of the litigants is not to receive a judgment from the court but rather to effect a compromise back in the village guest house, simply using the Islamic court as one more recourse toward that end. Thus litigation itself does not contradict the goal of compromise." Antoun, "Islamic Court," 463; see also Mir-Hosseini, *Marriage*, 61.

24 A long-standing Quranic injunction (4:128).

25 Hanna, "Administration of Courts," 54; Peirce, *Morality Tales*, 186, 387. Court records from the Ottoman period are replete with references to cases that were terminated prior to rendering a court decision because the mediators (*muṣliḥūn*) had intervened and reconciled differences. El-Nahal, *Judicial Administration*, 19–20; Gerber, *State, Society*, 51. This "non-legal" involvement continues to flourish in today's Middle East societies, as several Sharīʿa judges tell me. See also Antoun, "Islamic Court."

26 For Max Gluckman, see Gulliver, "Process," 46; Rosen, *Anthropology*, 16–19.

27 Gulliver, "Process," 42.

28 Haviland, *Cultural Anthropology*, 331.

29 Rosen, "Justice," 39–40. Cf. Davies, "Local Participation," 48–61, esp. at 55–61.

That the Muslim court is, *inter alia*, both a specific and a specialized social unit that has been carved out of society at large is accurately captured in the centuries-old and highly recurrent prescription that a *qāḍī*, to qualify for service, must be intimately familiar with the cultural context of his jurisdiction and the range of social customs and habits prevailing therein.[30]

The Muslim adjudicatory process, therefore, was never remote from the social world of the disputants. Like the arbitrative process, the Muslim court was embedded in a social fabric that demanded a moral logic of social equity rather than a logic of winner-takes-all resolutions. Restoring parties to the social roles they enjoyed before appearing in court required social and moral compromise, where each party was allowed to claim at least a partial gain. Total loss was avoided wherever possible, and was usually only countenanced when a litigant had caused an irremediable or serious breach of social harmony and/or the moral code. Nearly all else was subject to what one perceptive commentator labeled as "separate justices," whereby judges cared less for the application of a logically consistent legal doctrine or principle than for the creation of a compromise that left the disputants able to resume their previous relationships in the community and/or their lives as these had been led before the dispute began.[31] But even when this was not possible, and even when the victim recovered all damages, the wrongdoer was also usually allowed a partial recovery of his moral personhood, for by the informal nature of the Muslim court, the parties and their relatives, neighbors and friends were allowed to air their views in full and without constraint, defending the honor and reputation of one litigant or the other. Such a collective and public expression permitted even the loser to retain some moral dignity, for this defense explained and *justified* the compelling circumstances under which wrongdoing had taken place. This amounted to a moral exoneration that could, in the community's imagination, border on the legal. For although the jural punishment here may have been inevitable, the circumstantial compulsion under which the wrongdoing occurred left the loser and, particularly, his relations (who were both the moral extension and moral predicate of the culprit and who would have to leave the court to resume their communal lives) able to retain sufficient dignity to allow them to function in the normative and morally structured social world. The moral foundations of such a reinstatement constituted the means by which the court – with its socially oriented structure – fulfilled one of its chief tasks, namely, the preservation of social order and harmony.

[30] Ibn al-Humām, *Sharḥ*, VII, 259–60; Māwardī, *Ḥāwī*, XVI, 26.
[31] Peirce, *Morality Tales*, 387. See also Petry, "Conjugal Rights," 227–38.

The task of preserving social order presupposed a court that was deliberately and subtly attuned, by the nature of its own social make-up, to the entire system of social and economic cleavages. But predicating the maintenance of the social order on the universal and "ecological" balance of a moral system posed for the court a challenge, for while cleavages, and thus "class" and other prerogatives, existed and constantly asserted themselves, morality was the lot and intrinsic right of everyone, the poor, the rich, women, men, religious minorities and even slaves. Social equity, the unquestionable mission of the court, was thus defined in moral terms, and it demanded that the morality of the weak and underprivileged be accorded no less attention than that attributed to the rich and mighty. As the former undoubtedly saw themselves (and were seen) as equal members of the moral community, the court had to afford them the same kind of treatment it did the latter, if not even more attentively. It was particularly the court's open and informal forum that permitted the individual and defenders from within his or her micro-community to argue their cases and special circumstances from a moral perspective. But it was also the commitment to universal principles of law and justice that created a legal culture wherein everyone expected that injustices against the weak would be redressed and the wrongdoing of the powerful curbed. This was an expectation based on a centuries-long proven practice where peasants almost always won cases against their oppressive overlords, and where Jews and Christians often prevailed in court not only over Muslim business partners and neighbors but also against no less powerful figures than the provincial governor himself.[32]

The Muslim court thus afforded a sort of public arena for anyone who chose to utilize that space for his or her defense. The highly formalized processes of the modern court and its structure of legal representation (costly and tending to suppress the individual voices of the litigants, let alone their sense of morality) were unknown to Islam. So were lawyers and the excessive costs of litigation that prevent the weak and the poor from pressing their rights. The Muslim court succeeded precisely where the modern court fails, namely, in being a sanctified refuge within whose domain the weak and the poor could win against the mighty and the affluent. A case in point was women. Considerable recent research has shown that this group received not only fair treatment in the Muslim court but also even greater protection than other groups,[33] a tradition that

[32] Marcus, *Middle East*, 112; Gerber, *State, Society*, 56–57. On the use by Jews and Christians of the Muslim court, see al-Qattan, "*Dhimmīs* in the Muslim Court," 429–37.

[33] Jennings, "Women," 61–62, 98, 112; Peirce, *Morality Tales*, 7; Zarinebaf-Shahr, "Women," 84.

survives in some Muslim societies even today.[34] Taking advantage of largely unrestricted access to the court in litigating pecuniary and other transactions, women asserted themselves in the legal arena in large numbers and, once there, they argued as vehemently and "volubly" as men, if not more so.[35] Protected by a moral sense of honor and sanctity, they asserted their rights and privileges within the court as well as outside it. That they were empowered by virtue of the sanctity of their honor was a crucial fact that allowed them to assert their rights against men and against each other. And when legal doctrine proved restrictive toward them – as it at times did – they developed strategies in response.[36] The female moral code and sanctity, as well as the strategies that were developed in response to the vagaries of legal doctrine, were all understood and accommodated in the law court.[37] For the latter, emerging from within a centuries-long tradition of moral and socio-legal praxis, understood that no social order and its prerequisite of moral "ecology" could be maintained without an equitable justice.

That the court was embedded in both society and social morality is attested to by the nature of the court's social constitution on the one hand, and by the legal-mindedness of the very society the court was designed to serve on the other. The *qāḍī* himself was typically a creature of the very culture in which he adjudicated disputes – a practice that pervaded almost the entire Muslim world. A partial exception to this rule occurred under the Ottomans, who shuffled *qāḍī*s on average every two years or so,[38] and often sent them from one province to serve in another. Nevertheless, generally speaking, they did not themselves adjudicate disputes in their jurisdictions, leaving this task mostly to their local and native deputies. Embedded in the moral fabric of social relations, the *qāḍī* could have no better interest than to preserve these relations. He operated within established modes of mediation and arbitration, modes that preceded and defined his professional involvement. If mediation and arbitration sought to achieve social equity and to preserve the individual's sense of morality, the *qāḍī* had to absorb these imperatives into his court and accommodate them within a normative legal framework. Every case was considered on its own terms, and defined by its own social context. Litigants were treated not as cogs in the legal process, but as integral parts of larger social units, structures and relations that informed and were informed by each litigant. The *qāḍī*'s accommodation of litigants-as-part-of-a-larger-social-relationship

[34] Hirsch, "Kadhi's Courts," 218; Mitchell, "Family Law," 201–02.
[35] Peirce, *Morality Tales*, 176; Marcus, *Middle East*, 106.
[36] See in more detail section 5, below. [37] Jennings, "Women," 61–62.
[38] For a one-year duration, see Rafeq, "Application of Islamic Law," 411.

was neither the purely customary mode of negotiation (prevailing in the pre-trial stage) nor the black-and-white, all-or-nothing approach (mostly prevailing in systems where the judge is socially remote from the disputants).[39] Rather, the *qāḍī* mediated a dialectic between, on the one hand, the social and moral imperatives – of which he was an integral part – and, on the other, the demands of legal doctrine which in turn recognized the supremacy of the unwritten codes of morality and morally grounded social relations. And it was this dialectic that culminated in one of the most striking features of Muslim judiciary throughout North Africa and the eastern Mediterranean (at least under the Ottomans), namely, an impressive consistency in judicial decisions.[40]

That the law took social and moral imperatives for granted should not obscure the fact (which has nonetheless largely escaped modern scholarship) that while this law does formally declare itself to be divine and thus, by implication, above the seemingly petty concerns of human affairs, it in no way disregards its worldly function. From this perspective, then, jurists' law operated in a dual capacity: first, it provided an intellectual superstructure that positioned the law within the larger tradition that conceptually defined Islam, thereby constituting a theoretical (and profoundly psychological) link between metaphysics and theology on the one hand, and the social and physical world on the other; and second, it maintained the discrete goal of infusing a given social and moral order with legal norms – an infusion whose method of realization was not imposition but rather mediation. At this level, jurists' law guided and promoted, but did not superimpose itself upon, social morality. Because the *qāḍī* was an immediate product of his own social and moral universe, he was constituted – by the very nature of his function – as the interpretive agency through which *fiqh* law was mediated and made to serve the imperatives of social order and harmony. Procedurally too, the work of the court appealed to social constructions of probity and moral rectitude that immediately derived from the local site of social practice. Thus, the shared communal values of honor, integrity, shame and religio-social virtue entered the arena of the court as part of a dialectic with the assumptions of *fiqh* law.

[39] Gulliver, "Process," 42: In modern judicial systems, "all or nothing is a characteristic feature of the ordinary judicial method. *An action is proven and sustained or not proven and dismissed* ... [The] verdict of the court has an either/or character; the decision is based upon a single, definite conception of what has actually taken place and upon a *single* interpretation of legal norms" (emphasis mine).

[40] This is clearly attested in the various Ottoman court records from Egypt, Syria and Anatolia, some of which are published and studied. See, e.g., Cohen *World Within*, and the third volume of *Wathā'iq al-Maḥākim al-Shar'iyya al-Miṣriyya*. See also Marcus, *Middle East*, 111; Hallaq, "*Qāḍī*'s *Dīwān*."

Yet the *qāḍī* was not the only socially linked official in the court. All other functionaries, most notably the witnesses and the court examiners, shared the same social and moral landscape. Much of the work of the court related to the investigation not only of events but also, and perhaps more importantly, to that of the integrity and rectitude of the persons involved in litigation or in these events. Just as the *qāḍī*'s primary concern in recruiting witnesses for the court was their moral integrity (*ʿadāla*), it was the concern of these witnesses to assess the moral worth of people involved in litigation, primarily witnesses appearing on behalf of the litigants. The function of witnesses would have been rendered impossible without local knowledge of existing customs, moral values and social ties. Impossible not only because their knowledge of others would be inadequate and insufficient but, more importantly, the credibility of the testimony itself – the bedrock of adjudication – would cease to be both testable and demonstrable. For rectitude and trustworthiness – themselves the foundations of testimony – constituted a personal moral investment in social ties. To lie meant in effect to sever these ties and, in turn, to lose social prestige, honor and all that was productive of life's networks of social obligations.

As we have already noted, each case was inscribed into the minutes of the court, and attested at the end of the entry by witnesses whose number ranged from two to several. Some were officials of the court, and some relatives of the litigants, whereas others were no more than bystanders who happened to be present on account of another matter.[41] Although witnesses, retained and paid by the court, hailed usually from the higher social classes – some of them being prominent jurists and provincial magnates – other witnesses who accompanied the litigants obviously represented the entire spectrum of social classes in the wider population, particularly the lower strata. As an aggregate act, their attestation at the end of each record summing up the case amounted not only to a communal approval of, and a check on, court proceedings in each and every case dispensed by the court,[42] but also to a depository of communal memory that guaranteed present and future public access to the history of the case. In many ways, therefore, these witnesses functioned as community inspectors of the court's business, ensuring the moral integrity of its procedures, just as their counterparts, the court's legal experts (*ahl al-ʿilm*), ensured the soundness of the application of law.[43]

[41] Peirce, *Morality Tales*, 97; Marcus, *Middle East*, 112. [42] Marcus, *Middle East*, 112.

[43] Ḥaṭṭāb, *Mawāhib*, VI, 117; Māwardī, *Ḥāwī*, XVI, 47–50; Nawawī, *Rawḍa*, VIII, 125–26; al-Ḥusām al-Shahīd, *Sharḥ*, 59; Serrano, "Twelve Court Cases," 477–78. This practice continued in many parts of the Muslim world until the present, even in countries that underwent significant modernization. For the case of Jordan, for instance, see Antoun, "Fundamentalism," 373.

Like judges and witnesses, the scribe (*kātib*) of the court was invariably a member of the local community and himself a jurist of some sort. His ties to the community enhanced the already strong connections between the court and the surrounding population, and provided a stabilizing constant that offset the effects of the Ottoman policy of shuffling judges. The scribe, by virtue of his role, was indeed instrumental in preserving the relationships of social and epistemic continuity between court and society (and it was oftentimes the case that senior scribes were appointed as deputy-*qāḍī*s). Under Ottoman rule, and probably before, this usually happened when the Istanbul-appointed *qāḍī* would delegate his function to a local deputy, or when there was a gap between the departure/death of a judge and the arrival of a newly appointed one. The ability of Istanbul-appointed judges to administer justice on the local level, and to maintain (and exploit) continuity, depended largely on their access to the scribe's knowledge of local ties and customs. As one scholar aptly noted: "[J]udges and scribes seem to have developed an interdependency that sustained their cooperation, particularly since lower-ranking judges often also shared a similar social background with the scribes."[44]

Furthermore, the consumers of law and of the court's services were themselves the loci of the moral universe. That those who initiated litigation at the court were the social underdogs is now beyond debate. They were women versus men, non-Muslims versus Muslims, and commoners versus the economic and political elite. That they won the great majority of cases and that they found in the court a defender of their rights is likewise clear from the evidence.[45] They appeared before the *qāḍī* without ceremony and presented their cases without needing professional mediation. They spoke informally, unhampered by anything resembling the discipline of the modern court. They employed the discursive and rhetorical techniques that, according to individual capacity, each could muster. That they could do so was testimony to a remarkable feature of Muslim justice, namely, that no gulf existed between the court as a legal institution and the consumers of the law, however economically impoverished or educationally disadvantaged the latter might have been. Yet, it was not entirely the virtue of the court and *qāḍī* alone that made this gap non-existent, for some credit must equally be given to these very consumers. Unlike modern society, which has become estranged from the legal profession in multiple ways, traditional Muslim society was as much engaged in the *sharʿī* system of legal values as the court was embedded in the moral universe of society. It is a salient feature of that society that it

[44] Agmon, "Social Biography," 106. [45] Gerber, *State, Society*, 56–57, 139.

lived legal ethics and legal morality, for these constituted the religious foundations and codes of social praxis. To say that law in pre-modern Muslim societies was a living and lived tradition is merely to state the obvious.[46]

The culture of the law court was, by itself, neither authoritative nor influential enough to spread legal norms throughout the social order and ranks. Instead, the agencies that enabled this spread lay outside of the court. First, as we saw in chapter 3, legal education was informal and accessible to all interested individuals. The *ḥalaqa*, where legal education took place, required no formal application or any institutional approval for admission. This permitted the curious and the interested to "sit in," thereby contributing to the spread of legal knowledge, to one degree or another, among non-professionals. The neighborhood imams who spoke of religious matters and who delivered the Friday sermons were agencies of popularizing law, and the many students aspiring to a legal career played a similar role. Similarly, the notary (*shurūṭī*), a private scholar who drafted legal documents for a fee, also provided advice and expertise, often without remuneration.[47] But it was the *muftī* who perhaps more than anyone else contributed to the spread of legal knowledge among the masses. From minor experts to major legal scholars, *muftī*s were routinely accessible to the masses, free of charge or nearly so.[48]

The social underdogs thus knew their rights before approaching the court, a fact that in part explains why they won the great majority of cases when they happened to be plaintiffs.[49] Their counsels were neither lawyers who spoke a different, incomprehensible language, nor higher-class professionals who exacted exorbitant fees that often made litigation and recovery of rights as expensive as the litigated object. Instead, their

[46] It is in this context that a major revision of Schachtian doctrine can be made. Schacht and his followers accept the historicity of a "living tradition" during the second/eighth century, a tradition that allegedly lost momentum and disappeared with the disjunction that occurred between law, on the one hand, and society and politics, on the other. That law continued to be a living and lived tradition, and that society was the carrier of this tradition, are propositions that were dismissed out of hand by Schacht and his ilk. It is now beyond question that the living and lived tradition continued to flourish, with ever increasing force, centuries after the formative period of Islam had ended. For Schacht, see *Origins*, 58 ff.

[47] Hallaq, "Model *Shurūṭ* Works," 109–34.

[48] Serrano, "Twelve Court Cases," 478. This "free legal advice" was noted even by early colonialist officers in India, whose commentary on Islamic justice was otherwise negative. See Strawson, "Islamic Law and English Texts," 34. It is to be noted, however, that the introduction of *muftī*s to certain areas of Malaya (e.g., Naning and Rembau) was a relatively late one, ironically coming upon the heels of British colonization. See Peletz, *Islamic Modern*, 30–31.

[49] Marcus, *Middle East*, 111–13.

counsel on the technical and more difficult points of law were the largely free-of-charge *muftīs* whose opinion the court took very seriously, as we shall see shortly.

But the spread of the legal ethic and legal knowledge in the social order was also the function of a cumulative tradition, transmitted from one generation to the next, and enhanced at every turn by the vibrant participation of the aspiring law students, the greater and lesser *muftīs*, the imams, and the occasional advice that the judge and other learned persons gave while visiting acquaintances, walking in the street or shopping in the market. Thus when the common folk appeared before the court, they spoke a "legal" language as perfectly comprehensible to the judge as the judge's vernacular "moral" language was comprehensible to them.[50] Legal norms and social morality, if they could be at all separated, were symbiotic beings, one feeding on and, at the same time, sustaining the other. As much a social as a legal institution, the Muslim court was eminently the product of the very community which it served and in the bosom of which it functioned.

Trials were typically opened by a *muddaʿī*, a plaintiff or claimant, who was more frequently an illiterate peasant or a small shop owner than a merchant or a government official. To be substantiated, the claim (*daʿwā*) required evidence in support of any allegations made.[51] Thus, the burden of proof lay with the plaintiff. But if the plaintiff failed to provide evidence against the defendant, then the latter would be required to take an oath to the effect that he or she was innocent of the charges. Although the judge could request such an oath from the plaintiff as well, it seems that in most cases it was the plaintiff who determined whether or not such an oath was to be taken by the defendant.[52] In such an instance, the case would be concluded, and a decision rendered, upon either acceptance or refusal to take the oath. If taking the oath was accepted, the case would be decided in favor of the defendant; if refused, the case would be resolved in favor of the plaintiff.[53]

The requirement of an oath from the defendant was not merely a legal formality, but rather a religious act that carried with it a major transcendental liability. In a religiously charged society, taking an oath of innocence (e.g.,

[50] See, e.g., Ṭaḥāwī's comments on the accessibility of legal documents (*shurūṭ*) to the average person, in Wakin, *Function*, 10–29.

[51] See chapter 12, below.

[52] In her study of a year's worth of litigation in Aintab, Peirce (*Morality Tales*, 186, 427, n. 34) found that there were thirty cases involving oaths, twenty-five of which were required by the plaintiff against the defendant, and five requested by the defendant against the plaintiff. For an example of the latter, see *Wathāʾiq al-Maḥākim al-Sharʿiyya al-Miṣriyya*, I, 16–17 (1). See also chapter 12, below.

[53] See chapter 12, section 3, below; El-Nahal, *Judicial Administration*, 28; Peirce, *Morality Tales*, 102–03.

against a charge of stealing an object) amounted to a decision on the part of the guilty to opt for the more considerable, indeed everlasting, punishment: the scorching fire of Hell.[54] This threat, far more effective and pervasive than the worldly coercion of the modern state, sustained the *qāḍī*'s or plaintiff's position in assigning or requesting the oath. When demanded of a litigant, the oath reflected the likelihood that he knew more about the case at hand,[55] and was not demanded simply because he happened *formally* to fall into the category of "defendant." Some micro-historians have noted the rarity of decisory oaths in legal proceedings, but observed the corresponding high frequency of confession, production of alibi, or pleas for extenuating circumstances.[56] It is perhaps fairly safe to conclude from this evidence that an oath did not constitute a convenient way to escape liability and that it was, as a rule, accepted as a genuine attestation of innocence.

The claim and subsequent defense were typically made in the vernacular, and recorded in the court register, at times also in the vernacular, but often in a modified form usually determined by the scribe and perhaps reflecting his level of education.[57] Some cases required the assistance of the court experts who, as we have noted, might be sent by the judge to investigate the

[54] It is profoundly important here to note that coercive divine power was not a category detached from other divine attributes. In the conception of the believer, God is omnipotent and omniscient, the One who endures through eternity, who does not sleep, who knows the most minute particulars of worldly occurrences, who keeps accounts, and yet is all-merciful, compassionate, loving and forgiving. He is everything in their contradictions. If one seeks nearness to Him, one seeks those attributes desired, avoiding those that are not. It is not merely a fear of punishment that compels the believer to do the right thing, but the desire for, and allure of, His love, compassion, generosity and eternal comfort. He is not a unidimensional entity of terror and fear, the Inquisitor, the Inspector of Bad Deeds, awaiting the slightest fault or misdemeanor to jump at the opportunity to punish. He is, before anything else, the Compassionate and the Merciful ("*al-Raḥmān al-Raḥīm*"), the two names by which He is famously and universally known, two attributes that announce Him in all human speech and mundane action. Divine punishment may, by analogy, be easily elided into the coercion of the modern state. But Allah cannot be subjected to this analogy. For the deserving, His punishment is indeed horrendous and eternally painful, to an extent and quality that cannot even be imagined by the human mind. To the petty, and not so petty, wrongdoers, He is forgiving and merciful. Repentance pays. Not only some, nay many, bad deeds can be forgiven, but good deeds also are rewarded. The reward is thus exponential. Doing good and performing good deeds increases one's credit, meticulously noted in one's transcendental ledger. And everyone has a ledger. By contrast (and excepting selective, if not relatively rare, honors such as those bestowed on scientific, literary and military achievers), no such credit is awarded the state's citizen, not even an acknowledgment, however much good one may do. Thus, to do good is by definition to be "near God" (*qurba*) in this life and in the hereafter, to be loved and in receipt of His grace and bounty. "There is no god but God" ultimately epitomizes, but does not mask, the totality of these relationships with the Creator, in their threat and promise. For more on the role of religious morality in the functioning of the law, see Hallaq, "Fashioning the Moral Subject."

[55] Rosen, "Justice," 39. [56] Peirce, *Morality Tales*, 103.

[57] On the scribe, see chapter 1, section 6, above; Hallaq, "*Qāḍī*'s *Dīwān*," 422–23.

matter. These were usually professionals or guild chiefs who determined, for instance, if a person's window violated his neighbor's right to privacy, or if a man found dead in a public street had been murdered or not. Just as the chief builder and chief surgeon would, respectively, be involved in these two cases, so too would many other professionals be called upon to testify about aspects of the life of the community in which they lived and which they expertly understood. Upon completing their enquiry, the experts reported to the judge, who made the final decision. The claim, the defense, the expert's findings and the judge's decision would all be succinctly recorded by the court, attested to by two or more witnesses, and copies of this record were often issued to the litigating parties.[58]

The court was by no means restricted to operating as a site of conflict resolution, and quite frequently performed the all-important function of confirming rights and ownership through the registration and issuance of documents. Transfers of real and movable property, loans, manumissions, bonds of surety, acknowledgments and business partnerships were all recorded at court and copies of the registry issued to the concerned parties.[59] Marriages, divorces, estates of deceased persons, divisions of inheritance, religious conversions, and many other transactions and events were also often recorded at court. Likewise, a verbal or physical assault would at times end up in the court record, without this event resulting in any claim, suit or damages prescribed by the judge. The wronged would merely demand that the assault be noted and recognized by the court, and an attested copy of the entry be given to him for possible use in the future. Also, as it was common for slaves to flee their masters' households, no legally manumitted slave wished to be caught without being in possession of either the "book" of manumission or a confirmation/certificate received from the court in attestation of his freedom.[60] All in all, it is certain that the role of the court as a judicial registry was as important as, if not more important than, that of conflict manager. One survey of mid-eighteenth-century court business in Aleppo reveals that no more than 14 percent of all cases were lawsuits, whereas the rest mostly involved notarial attestation.[61] The practice of courts in other locales and regions could not have strayed much from this ratio, much less reversed it.

[58] Hanna, "Administration of Courts," 53; Hallaq, "*Qāḍī*'s *Dīwān*," 420.
[59] Lutfi, "Study of Six Fourteenth Century Iqrārs"; *Wathāʾiq al-Maḥākim al-Sharʿiyya al-Miṣriyya*, I, 35 (23), 44–46 (4–5), 65 (19), and *passim*.
[60] Peirce, *Morality Tales*, 194, 283; *Wathāʾiq al-Maḥākim al-Sharʿiyya al-Miṣriyya*, I, 34–35 (22–23).
[61] Marcus, *Middle East*, 107. Of those not involving litigation, almost half of the court entries were related to registration of houses or of other real property sold, while nearly one quarter dealt with divorces, child support, estates, debts and acknowledgments.

Nonetheless, it is clear that not all transactions or events were recorded at the court, for it appears that the need for the court's attestation possessed one common feature, namely, the perceived possibility that a claim or an event might arise again in the future. A recorded verbal offense established "a case history" which might be crucial for the wronged party to prove his or her claim if the aggression were to escalate in the future. A recorded divorce guaranteed for the wife future benefits in the way of alimony, delayed dower, or entitlement to her portion of any property she might have gained before or during the marriage. Similarly, recording the terms and shares of inheritance with regard to common property would guarantee the rights of a brother or a sister who could not prove a permanent physical presence on that property. For it was a common occurrence that a sibling would argue before the court that he or she enjoyed full ownership of a property by virtue of exclusive residence in said property over a long duration. The frequency of recordings at the court confirms the remarkable fact that Muslims of every walk of life understood not only their rights but also the far-reaching ramifications of the transactions and events in which they engaged in their daily existence.[62]

4. The jurisconsult (*muftī*) and the author-jurist (*muṣannif*): society and legal change

We have already intimated that, pedagogically and juridically, the *muftī* was instrumental in propounding legal norms and legal knowledge at grassroots level. An integral part of his activity related to mediation, in a manner similar, but not identical, to those mediators who were involved in the pre-trial stages of conflict resolution. Unlike the latter, whose role as negotiator depended upon a win-some-lose-some mode of resolution, the *muftī* stated what the law was in a particular factual situation. As he constituted an accessible center of legal and moral authority, his opinion,

[62] Nelly Hanna, who studied the courts of Ottoman Cairo, observes that "the procedures of the courts of Cairo were simple and easy to understand; almost unimaginable today, they generally handed down decisions or notarized documents the very day the case or the document was brought before them. Even the local doctrines of the four schools of law seem to have been understood by the people. What we regard today as a very formidable and specialized area of knowledge – the various distinctions between the Hanafi, Shafiʿi, Maliki, and Hanbali schools of law, in matters, for instance, of personal status or transactions – seems to have been common knowledge at that time. It was not unusual for one person to buy a house one day according to Hanbali law and get married next day according to Maliki or Shafiʿi law. By assessing the specific differences between the schools of law ... people deliberately chose the school that best defended their interests in any particular case or transaction." Hanna, "Administration of Courts," 53.

though non-binding, settled many disputes "on the spot."[63] For as we shall see, the *fatwā* represented an authoritative statement of law, a statement that the courts routinely upheld and applied. A disputant who failed to receive a *fatwā* in his favor was not likely to proceed to court, and would instead abandon his claim altogether or opt for informal mediation.

The informal accessibility of the *muftī* to the masses represented only one side of his involvement in conflict resolution. The other side was the formal role he played in the courts of law. From its early stages, the Islamic legal tradition has insisted on the presence of *muftī*s, at times described as "the people of knowledge" (*ahl al-ʿilm*), in the courts of law,[64] both as advisors for the *qāḍī* on difficult points of law and as overseers-cum-witnesses of court proceedings. In the Mālikite courts of Muslim Spain the presence of these experts (known as *mushāwirūn*) was a requirement.[65] Somewhat like the Ottoman Shaykh al-Islām, but politically less powerful, they often issued *fatwā*s bearing on the policies and conduct of the sovereign, who appointed them to various jurisdictions after consultation with judges.[66] In the eastern lands of Islam, not all courts had a "sitting" *muftī*, a fact bearing more on form than on content.[67] Massive evidence suggests that the physical absence of *muftī*s from the courts in no way changed the dependence of the latter upon the former, for difficult cases were routinely referred to *muftī*s, local or distant.[68] The bulk of *fatwā* literature at our disposal attests to the now well-established fact that *fatwā*s were requested by judges from *muftī*s who, at times, lived hundreds of miles away.[69] The great majority of *fatwā*s thus originated in the

[63] A telling example of the *fatwā*'s legal power is the case of a Damascene individual who, sometime toward the end of the ninth/fifteenth century, appealed a Sharīʿa court's decision by traveling to Cairo in order to obtain a *fatwā* that showed the decision to be erroneous. On the basis of this *fatwā*, the Mamlūk Sultan, presumably presiding over a *maẓālim* court in his Dār al-ʿAdl (see chapter 5, section 2, below), issued a decree (*marsūm*) that dismissed the decision of the Damascus court. See Mandaville, "Muslim Judiciary," 71. On appeal and the state of scholarship on it, see the useful article of Gradeva, "On Judicial Hierarchy."

[64] Māwardī, *Ḥāwī*, XVI, 47–52; Qalqashandī, *Ṣubḥ*, X, 267, 284, 288.

[65] Masud, *Islamic Legal Interpretation*, 10–11.

[66] *Ibid.*, 11. [67] Mandaville, "Muslim Judiciary," 11.

[68] Ibn ʿĀbidīn, *ʿUqūd*, I, 3; Ibn ʿĀbidīn, *Ḥāshiya*, V, 359, 360, 365, 370; Ibn Abī al-Damm, *Adab*, 71, 75–76; Ibn al-Munāṣif, *Tanbīh*, 67, 68; Heyd, "Ottoman Fetva," 51–52; Jennings, "Kadi, Court," 134; *al-Fatāwā al-Hindiyya*, III, 312, 313. In his study of Bursa's court, Gerber, *State, Society*, 81–82, observes that the party armed with a *fatwā* always won the case. For Ḥafṣid North Africa, see Powers, "Legal Consultation," 93, 94, 96. Powers notes that, generally, the more serious the dispute, the greater the number of *muftī*s consulted. For the Mamlūks, see Mandaville, "Muslim Judiciary," 11.

[69] The *fatwā* collections of Ibn Rushd (*Fatāwā*) and Wansharīsī (*Miʿyār*) are two cases, among many, in point. The latter consists of a multitude of *fatwā*s belonging to numerous major and less renowned *muftī*s.

actualities of social and economic practices, even when they were not solicited by the court.[70]

The court's juristic dependence on the *muftī* and his authoritative opinions belies, in one important sense, the dictum that the *fatwā* is a non-binding opinion. While it is true that the *fatwā* is formally non-binding, because of the obvious reason that it does not qualify as a *qāḍī*'s decision (*ḥukm*), it was nonetheless commonly accepted as the basis of court rulings, and rarely, if ever, ignored. When on occasion a *fatwā* was disregarded, it was usually because another *fatwā* constituted a more convincing and authoritative opinion, which meant that the latter received the doctrinal support of the school's prominent authorities. In other words, and to put it conversely, it was rare for a judge to dismiss a *fatwā* in favor of his own opinion, unless he happened to be of a juristic caliber higher than that enjoyed by the *muftī* from whom the *fatwā* was solicited.

That the *fatwā*, reflecting the authoritative doctrine of the school, normatively constituted the basis of the *qāḍī*'s ruling also explains why court decisions were not deemed authoritative or binding precedent, as is the case in common law legal systems. This phenomenon also explains why the Muslim court decisions were neither kept nor published in the manner practiced by common law courts. In other words, law was to be found not in precedent, or in a doctrine of *Stare Decisis*,[71] but rather in the juristic corpus of the school, a corpus elaborated by the author-jurist (*muṣannif*) and extracted for difficult and complex cases by the *muftī*. The law of those (standard) cases that did not call for the specialized expertise of the *muftī* was found by the *qāḍī* himself, either in the works of the author-jurist or in the *fatwā* compilations – or in both.[72]

Thus, emanating from the world of legal practice, the *fatwā*s rather than court decisions were collected and published, particularly those among them that contained new law or represented new legal elaborations on

70 For a detailed discussion of this issue, see Hallaq, *Authority*, 174–80.

71 Essentially defined as a "[p]olicy of courts to stand by precedent and not to disturb settled point." It is a "[d]octrine that, when court has once laid down a principle of law as applicable to a certain state of facts, it will adhere to that principle, and apply it to all future cases, where facts are substantially the same." *Black's Law Dictionary*, 1261; Hardisty, "Reflections on Stare Decisis," 41 ff., 64–69. Further on *Stare Decisis* in British India, see chapter 14, section 1, below.

72 Particularly after the sixth/twelfth century, there appeared a genre of short manuals intended for the use of judges, normally consisting of one or two volumes. Marghīnānī's *Hidāya* and Ḥalabī's *Multaqā* are two cases in point. But the *qāḍī*s, especially those trained in advanced jurisprudence, did refer to expanded works, known as the "School's Compendia" (*kutub al-madhhab*); e.g., Nawawī's *Rawḍat al-Ṭālibīn* or his *al-Majmūʿ*. Yet, it was by no means uncommon for the *qāḍī* to use the *fatwā-fiqh* collections, such as *al-Fatāwā al-Hindiyya* by al-Shaykh al-Niẓām *et al.*, and Ḥaṭṭāb's *Mawāhib*.

older problems that continued to be of recurrent relevance.[73] The collected *fatwās* usually underwent a significant editorial process in which legally irrelevant facts and personal details (e.g., proper names, names of places, dates, etc.) were omitted.[74] Moreover, they were abridged with a view to abstracting their contents into strictly legal formulas, usually of the hypothetical type: "If X does Y under a set of conditions, then L (legal norm) follows." Whether abstracted, edited or not, these *fatwā* collections became part and parcel of the authoritative legal literature. In Ḥanafite law, for example, they formed the third tier of authoritative legal doctrine, reflecting the contributions made by jurists who flourished after the first masters of the school, Abū Ḥanīfa, Abū Yūsuf, Shaybānī and al-Ḥasan b. Ziyād, who contributed the first and second tiers.[75] In sheer size and in the daily reality of legal practice, however, the third tier was the most dominant, as it reflected the multiple accretions and successive modifications to the "basic legal corpus" of the first masters. In the Mālikite school, no formal hierarchy of substantive law was articulated, but the absorption of *fatwās* into the works of author-jurists was as prominent and systematic as that exhibited in the Ḥanafite school.[76]

This integration of *fatwās* into the equation provided the world of the Sharīʿa with a fully developed and comprehensive account of the law, with all of its juristic disagreements (*ikhtilāf*), dialectical subject-matter and authoritative opinion. The author-jurist's activity extended from writing the short but specialized *risāla* to compiling longer works, be it the *mabsūṭ* (lit. extended) or the *sharḥ* (commentary). It was mainly these two types of discourse that afforded the author-jurist the framework (and full opportunity) to articulate a modified body of law, one that reflected both the evolving social conditions and the state of the art in the law as a technical discipline. The overriding concern of the author-jurists was the incorporation of points of law or "cases"[77] that were deemed relevant and necessary to the age in which they were writing. This is evidenced not only in their compilation practices, but also in their untiring insistence on the

[73] For a list of important *fatwā* collections, see Hallaq "From *Fatwās* to *Furūʿ*," 31 ff.

[74] For a detailed account of this editorial process, see Hallaq, *Authority*, 183–88.

[75] Samarqandī, *Fatāwā*, 1; Ibn ʿĀbidīn, *Ḥāshiya*, I, 69.

[76] Cases in point are Ḥaṭṭāb, *Mawāhib*; and Khurashī, *Ḥāshiya*.

[77] Not to be confused with cases in the common law legal system. A typical mode of exposition is the following: "When X bequeaths something to Z, a particular individual, the ownership of the article bequeathed is suspended, meaning that if Z accepts it after X's death, even if after some time has passed, then Z has owned it from the moment X died; but if Z declines to accept it, then X's heirs own it. If Z accepts it, but then refuses it before having taken possession of it, this cancels his ownership of it, though if he refuses after having taken possession of it, it does not cancel his ownership." Ibn Naqīb, *ʿUmda*, 465.

necessity of including in their works "much needed cases"[78] deemed to be relevant to contemporary exigencies and those cases of "widespread occurrence" (*mā taʿummu bi-hi al-balwā*), whereas cases that had become irrelevant to the community and its needs were excluded.[79] Many, if not the majority, of the cases included were acknowledged as belonging to the "later jurisprudents" who elaborated them in response to the emerging new problems in the community.[80] Reflecting the "changing conditions of people and of the age" (*li-ikhtilāf al-ʿaṣr wa-taghayyur aḥwāl al-nās*), the author-jurists opted for later opinions that were at variance from the doctrines of the early masters.[81] It is also instructive that the *fatwā*s that formed the substance of later doctrine were those that answered contemporary needs and had at once gained currency in practice.[82] On the other hand, those opinions that ceased to be of use in litigation were excluded as weak or even irregular.[83]

Despite these exclusions, the author-jurist's subject-matter was multi-layered, comprising the fundamental and foundational principles of the law – principles overlaid by the technical contributions of successive generations of jurists, ranging from the founders' disciples down to his own immediate predecessors. His main source for elaborating the basic law and foundational principles was the *fatwā* literature, which intimately reflected legal practice within the courts and outside them, as well as the general practical concerns of the community. Each generation of these longer works maintained the general principles of substantive and procedural law while simultaneously incorporating all current and relevant subject-matter, whether found in older or newer works.

These longer works, or abridged versions thereof, constituted the jurisprudential basis of legal practice and adjudication, which itself gave rise to these works and furthered their continuous development. Thus the movement was at once circular and dialectical, one that may aptly be described as a "dialectical wheel": society's legal disputes ended up before the courts of law; judges encountered hard cases which they took to the *muftī* for an expert opinion (though the *muftī* was queried by laypersons too); the *muftī* provided solutions to these hard cases, thereby preparing them for

78 Qāḍīkhān, *Fatāwā*, I, 2; ʿAlamī, *Nawāzil*, I, 18.

79 See, for example, Ramlī, *Fatāwā*, I, 3; Khushanī, *Uṣūl*, 44.

80 Zaylaʿī, *Tabyīn*, I, 2; Kurdarī, *Fatāwā*, IV, 2; Mūṣilī, *Ikhtiyār*, I, 6; Nawawī, *Majmūʿ*, I, 6; Bāʿalawī, *Bughya*, 8–9; Qāḍīkhān, *Fatāwā*, I, 2–3; Ramlī, *Fatāwā*, I, 3; ʿAlamī, *Nawāzil*, I, 18; Ramlī, *Nihāya*, I, 9–10, 45; Ḥaṭṭāb, *Mawāhib*, I, 31; Baghdādī, *Majmaʿ*, 2. See also the detailed discussion in Hallaq, *Authority*, 188–89.

81 Ibn ʿĀbidīn, *Ḥāshiya*, I, 69; Qāḍīkhān, *Fatāwā*, I, 2–3; Ramlī, *Fatāwā*, I, 3.

82 Khushanī, *Uṣūl*, 44; Ramlī, *Fatāwā*, 3; Ḥaṭṭāb, *Mawāhib*, I, 33.

83 Khushanī, *Uṣūl*, 44; Hallaq, *Authority*, 190.

integration into the law works of his school; students usually copied, collected, edited, abridged and finally published such *fatwās*; the author-jurist, the author of the school's authoritative *fiqh* work, incorporated most of these *fatwās* into his compendium; this he did while: (1) strictly maintaining the body of principles governing his school's legal corpus; (2) weeding out opinions that had fallen out of circulation; and, conversely, (3) retaining opinions that had newly arisen or those that continued to be relevant to legal practice. The product of this juristic activity was the *fiqh* work that continued to gauge and be gauged by legal practice. In sum, while legal practice was guided by *fiqh* discourse, the latter was shaped and modified by the former. Dialectically, one issued from, yet also fed, the other.

By the time that it came to be applied in the court, legal doctrine would have already undergone a long and complex process. The *qāḍī*'s doctrinal reference might have been the long compendium, the so-called *mabsūṭ*, but it might just as well have been the abridgment (*mukhtaṣar*) he had studied in the college of law (*madrasa*), where he acquired knowledge of it by memorizing and understanding the legal text. The *mukhtaṣar* is by necessity adroitly exiguous, dense and often exhibiting an elliptic economy of words. Often impenetrable, it elicits the commentary of the law professor, without whose expert intervention the text would remain inaccessible to the student. Something of a medium-size or a thin volume, the *mukhtaṣar* represents a condensation of the *corpus juris* as expounded in the *shurūḥ* or *mabsūṭāt* – multi-volume works of exquisite but enormous detail.[84] Defying the human capacity to retain information by rote, the *shurūḥ* and *mabsūṭāt* were abridged in a manner that allowed the student to recall mentally – through citing from the *mukhtaṣar* a clause or a sentence – a principle plus a host of cases and examples illustrating the law applicable to a particular case.

The student's memorization of the abridgment was integral to the process of commentary received from the professor in the study circle (*ḥalaqa*). The oral commentary in the *ḥalaqa* reflected the contents of the long commentaries and the abridgments, but did not necessarily duplicate them. Examples of a casuistic nature were constantly introduced to illustrate substantive legal principles, but the source of these examples might have been either a long text or the professor's own legal practice.[85] For it

[84] See, for example, al-Bāqir al-Majlisī's *Biḥār al-Anwār*, a work consisting of 111 volumes.

[85] A highly misunderstood phenomenon is the so-called casuistic method employed in Islamic law. That it is a "method" and that it is characterized as "casuistic" are due to the taxonomy of modern Western scholars. What the latter find striking (and often objectionable) is the oftentimes hypothetical nature of the cases adduced in legal works, a nature that comports with the received but utterly unfounded notion that Islamic law

was quite common, if not the norm, that a professor of law was also a *muftī* or a judge, and when he engaged in the role of teacher he would bring his *iftā᾽-qaḍā᾽* experience to the *ḥalaqa* where it would be brought to bear upon his students' course of study.[86]

Beginning in the early fourth/tenth century, every school adopted a *mukhtaṣar*, not only as a standard pedagogical text, but also as an authoritative summary of its substantive law.[87] The utility of these *mukhtaṣars* could at times last up to two centuries before needing to be replaced by another abridgment, but such a substitution never meant that the older *mukhtaṣars* became obsolete. In fact, the process of replacement itself was gradual, slow and, strictly speaking, never complete, for while new *mukhtaṣars* did become standard and "canonical," the old ones, as a rule, never totally faded away.

This continuing relevance of the *mukhtaṣar* was typical of all other legal genres, beginning with those basic works written down on the authority of the founding masters during the second/eighth century and ending with the magisterial compendia of the last great jurists of the thirteenth/nineteenth century. It was the remarkable structural continuity of Islamic legal culture that made this tradition possible. Yet, and equally remarkable, it was a salient feature of this culture that legal works – the basis of legal practice in the law courts, in *iftā᾽* and in document drafting (*shurūṭ*)[88] – were constantly updated, rewritten and modified in a number of ways. No work was identical to another, and significant differences could indeed be observed between and among successive works of the same genre and in the same school. For the past century, and until quite recently, Western scholarship viewed this cumulative textual activity as a hair-splitting exercise, where the piling of commentary upon commentary yielded nothing

"has lost touch with reality," be it social, political or otherwise. The hypothetical cases of substantive law thus become the proof of this disconnection, if not dislocation. (In his "Defining Casuistry in Islamic Law," Walter Young provides an in-depth critique of modern writings on the subject, and calls for the dismissal of this essentially European concept as a useful category for *fiqh* analysis). From a strictly juridical perspective, however, this "method" is both legally efficient and intellectually cautious. Its purpose is: (1) to lay down legal principles and precepts, usually through the presentation of several illustrative cases; and (2) to do so without engaging in the authoritative practice of *laying down* deductive definitions that are by nature fixed and that might cause these principles and precepts to become rigid. Accordingly, when "real" cases did not meet the needs of illustration, hypothetical cases were created. The overall effect finally turns out to be both structural and heuristic flexibility rather than the assumed impracticality of the Sharī῾a. Cf. Johansen, "Casuistry," 135–56.

[86] Further on this, see chapter 3, section 3, above. [87] Fadel, "Social Logic."

[88] On the *shurūṭ* as reflecting practice and as a part of the "dialectical wheel," see Hallaq, "Model *Shurūṭ* Works," 115–34.

of substance worth studying.[89] More recent scholars came to appreciate the output of Muslim legal scholarship and indeed took delight in studying its rich and varied scholarly texture; yet their verdict remained that the juristic tradition, with all its massive corpus of texts, commentaries and super-commentaries, represented no more than "intellectual play," having little, if anything, to do with society and its problems.[90] This brand of scholarship is associated with the academic but predominantly political doctrine espousing the Sharīʿa's stagnation – a doctrine that justifies and rationalizes the latter's eradication as part of the colonizing and modernizing project (the subject of Part III).[91] In fact, there has thus far been no research that shows such stagnation ever existed. The latest scholarship has demonstrated exactly the opposite, namely, that Islamic legal discourse constituted the vehicle through which legal change – as a response to changing social reality – was modulated.[92]

It must be stressed that legal change during the pre-modern period was characterized by two qualities, the first of which was its imperceptible nature. No sudden mutability was required, no ruptures, violent or otherwise, but rather a piecemeal modification of particular aspects of the law, and only when general and wide-ranging circumstances (*mā taʿummu bi-hi al-balwā*) demanded such modifications. The change, therefore, was always eminently organic, naturally arising, as it were, from the adaptive experiences of the past and, most importantly, from within the legal sub-culture of a particular region. (After the third/ninth century, some of the main regions that developed legal sub-cultures were Transoxiana, Iran, Iraq, Greater Syria, Egypt, western North Africa, and Andalusia. By that time, the Hejaz and the Yemen had become legally marginal.) The second quality lay in the fact that a modern notion of change (which tends to signify qualitative leaps and at times violent physical and epistemic ruptures from the past) was clearly absent from the conceptual world and discourse of the jurists. The famous dictum that "the *fatwā* changes with the changing of times and places" certainly did not indicate the presence in traditional Islamic law of this modern notion of change but instead stated a working principle of accommodation and malleability. Change, however it was understood, was both evolutionary and organic.

[89] See, e.g., Coulson, *History*, 84.
[90] See, e.g., Calder, "Law." See also n. 85, above.
[91] Hallaq, "Quest for Origins."
[92] Udovitch, *Partnership*, 5 ff.; Hallaq, *Authority*, 121–235; Hallaq, "Model *Shurūṭ* Works," 109 ff.; Johansen, *Islamic Law*; Johansen, "Legal Literature," 29–47; Powers, *Law, Society*; Mundy, "Ownership or Office."

5. Women, society and legal practice

It is not mere chance that the body of modern legal and quasi-legal scholarship on Ottoman women has recently come to surpass in quantity the total sum of twentieth-century scholarship on either the formation of Islamic law throughout the first four centuries of Islam or the subsequent middle period, lasting half a millennium, leading up to the Ottoman ascendancy. In fact, it is quite likely that it has surpassed or will soon outstrip the total sum of scholarship on the two periods combined. And it is not fortuitous that the upsurge of scholarship on Muslim women occurred only in the 1990s, slightly after the proliferation in the West (Australia included) of writings on feminist jurisprudence. Even less fortuitous is the substantive connection between these two bodies of scholarship and their criteria of analysis. Most striking is the unrelenting similitude not only in the categories of analysis but in the fairly inflexible application of these categories to the subject of Muslim women during the pre-modern past. The aporia generated as a reaction to Western feminist discourse has been largely confined to the Indian and African post-colonial feminist critique, Islam having largely remained on the margins of both the latter critique and the attendant theoretic consequences.[93]

Historians have paid attention to the gendered fabric of the Muslim social order, of family, marriage and divorce, but this very attention has been driven – on nearly all methodological and interpretive levels – by modernly defined frames of analysis where, for instance, power at large (itself a foundational, pre-determinative and prejudicial principle of analysis) is delimited by, and inferred from, material, economic and political structures. These are the very notions and structures upon which capitalist and power-defined modernity rests, but these also become the enshrined parameters and substrates of historical analysis. While it is undeniable that such approaches to the history of the Other are highly productive, they cannot suffice in gauging either the spectrum or the magnitude of privilege, prestige, status, rank or epistemic authority. For moral, religious, epistemic and other types of socially based powers operated with equal efficacy but have received, in current scholarship, next to marginal attention.[94] If the underlying common concern of this Islamicist scholarship is to measure the extent of female legal power in the gendered world of Islam, it has greatly neglected the moral, the religious and to some extent the socio-structural foundations of power, aspects that the

[93] For some powerful voices in the post-colonial feminist critique, see Mohanty, *Third World*; Donaldson and Kwok, *Postcolonialism*; Narayan, "Project"; Chatterjee, "Colonialism."

[94] A partial exception in the category of moral analysis is Peirce, *Morality Tales*.

modern analysis of power has, perforce, left largely underdeveloped. Yet, this is in no way to argue that women's acquisition of moral and other forms of power liberated them any more from the clutches of a patriarchal system whose legal doctrine discriminated against them in more than one way. But what it does argue is that, within the context of this subordination and because of it, women's strategies of resistance extended to spheres beyond the tangible discrimination against them as – for example – witnesses, or as heirs to the estates of their parents.

In the absence of scholarly attention to women's moral, religious and epistemic capital, one is ill equipped to provide a general portrait of such areas where women made an investment on terms that were normative to their *own* societies. Gaining and maintaining power did not stem only or directly from economic or material status, nor even from formal rights in the law, for these latter constituted only a part of the process by which rights, on the ground, were defined and finally determined. Earlier stages in the process that influenced the qualitative accumulation or depletion of rights were mutative and inflectional, determined by a variety of factors that spanned social/familial status, moral standing in the community, rank, economic power, class and much else. But this is not to say that these are discrete categories that can stand independently; in a society where status (social or legal) intersects, in a unique way, with a number of material and non-material considerations, these categories will have to remain for the historian as artificial and arbitrary as any historical exercise of periodization. In other words, they are invented categories designed to assist us in the control of our subject but are not located in a precisely delimited object in the real world of the past.

With this realization, women can be said to have gained or lost power – if that is what we have to assess – while standing at the nexus of a variety of intersecting factors, and as they succeeded or failed to employ strategies in the overall context of this nexus. Put differently, women's power was, by the nature of the closely knit social fabric, derivative.[95] Derivative, however, not in the sense that it tended to be different from the supposedly non-derivative power of men (which in fact was also derivative, albeit in different ways) but rather in the sense that such power mostly depended on interrelated and complex webs of personal contacts and social–familial relations. These relations were in turn collectively permeated by values and systems of morality that at once empowered and constrained social individuals, be they men or women. (Again, this is not to suggest that, in a clearly patriarchal system, women and men were constrained to an equal degree.)

[95] The underlying premise here is that power is always derivative, as it cannot wholly stem from a single, discrete source.

In illustration of non-materialist and non-economic augmentation of power, take, for instance, women of no economic means who dedicated their lives as *shaykhāt* of Ṣūfī female *khānqāh*s, where worship, *dhikr*, and leading a pious and charity-dedicated way of life could bestow on them enough socio-religious prestige as to make them exemplary and influential leaders in their communities. And as we saw, communities were the site in which the court and the functioning of the law were embedded. The court, to put it differently, represented that domain in which the community functioned in legal ways. Thus with attaining social prestige or with making similar moral "contributions" to the social order, there might be combined an *effort* (the much commended *jihād*) to increase one's net worth in religious morality, by, for instance, performing pilgrimage. While the power that accrues from such "contributions" to the moral-religious order is utterly non-materialistic and may continue to be so, it may nonetheless intersect with, or even generate, financial means or benefits that can augment the actor's power. Yet, even when no materialist power accrues, social power or other non-economic forms of power may still obtain and similarly enhance the position of a woman in the very absence of economic power. For instance, in some parts of the Muslim world, forgoing shares of inheritance is seen as strengthening the position of women, in that such a material concession guaranteed her family's support by providing security against the breakup of a marriage or the death of a husband.[96] Similarly, non-economic power may be derived from what we may call the epistemic field, where women of learned families acquire social – and at times eventually financial – power by virtue of their own erudition as well as the erudition of their fathers, brothers or mothers. The relative disconnection of learning from upper-class wealth was true for most of the Islamic centuries, and could be said to have changed only in the Anatolian and Balkan regions of the Ottoman Empire after the sixteenth century, when the learned class there – and more specifically in Istanbul – was finally incorporated into the imperial administration.[97]

Thus women-scholars who taught *ḥadīth*, educated children and engaged in literary circles within their "invisible" spheres[98] neither drew nor aimed at acquiring financial benefits or economic power; nevertheless, their social prestige, enhanced by the scholarly reputation of their families, augmented their investment in the larger religious-moral order. Yet, although this investment immediately translated into social (i.e., non-economic) forms of power, it often intersected with financial and

[96] Moors, "Gender Relations," 69–84; Moors, "Debating," 159.
[97] See chapter 3, section 5, above, and Zilfi, *Politics of Piety*, 45, 55 and *passim*.
[98] For examples, see Rapoport, *Marriage*, 10–11.

other material terrains that benefited women. The prospect of marriage to a well-to-do husband, with the attendant promise of a large dower, a generous trousseau, and a lucrative style of marital life is only one case in point. The largely independent status of women in the marital households, coupled with such financial and non-economic privileges – including the initial prestige emanating from erudition, learning and religiosity – would amount at the end of the day to a significant sum of power.

I noted earlier that this so-called social power could often translate into legal power. Our sources, which largely consist of court records, tell us little[99] about the social background of the women involved in court proceedings, how they were viewed by the individual members of their social group, how they were perceived and positioned in the larger group making up their immediate community, and, more importantly, how influential women who capitalized on the largely non-economic social power could reap, in the province of the law, the benefits of their socio-moral and religious investments. But it is clear that personal rectitude played a decisive role in legal proceedings, a fact that translated into decisions and injunctions in favor of women who themselves were of such a character or supported by female witnesses seen to have an equally charged moral character. If judicial evidence is the thread by which justice hangs, then rectitude and moral character are the filaments from which the thread is made. And rectitude and morality were no less the province of women than they were of men.

Moral and economic wealth, coupled with a foundational and thoroughgoing legal conviction that women possess full legal personality, largely explains the by-now not-so-striking phenomenon that women enjoyed as much access to the Muslim courts as did their male counterparts.[100] Like men, they approached the courts not only with prior knowledge of their rights, but with the apparent conviction that the courts were fair, sympathetic and operating with the distinct inclination to enforce their rights.[101] They often represented themselves in person,[102] but when

99 Other documentary evidence, such as the petitions of the Imperial Council for Complaints (*şikāyet defterleri*), has no noticeable advantage over the court records in revealing social, economic or legal data.

100 Zarinebaf-Shahr, "Women," 86–95; Jennings, *Studies*, 115–99; Gerber, "Social and Economic Position," 231–44; Marcus, "Men, Women," 137–63; Seng, "Invisible Women," 241–68.

101 For the spread of legal knowledge in society at large, see chapter 5, above, as well as the cases studied by Peirce, *Morality Tales*, 372–73; Seng, "Gates of Justice," 203; Petry, "Class Solidarity," 133–35. For a comparative perspective, see Davies, "Local Participation," 61.

102 On the basis of her work on Istanbul's court records, Zilfi ("We Don't Get Along," 278, 281) states that a minority of women sent a deputy to represent them in court.

not – and this being typical in the case of women (and many men) of the higher classes, including non-Muslim women[103] – they normally had a male relative, a servant or their business manager represent them. By all indications, when they approached the court in person, they did so on the same terms as did men, and asserted themselves freely, firmly and emphatically.[104] The courts allowed for a wide margin of understanding when women were assertively forthright, giving them ample space to defend their reputation, honor, status and material interests. They approached the court as both plaintiffs and defendants, suing men but also other women. Muslim women sued Christian and Jewish men and women, and these latter sued them in turn (though litigation between religious denominations appears to have been substantially less frequent than within each respective denomination). Manumitted female slaves took their former masters to court[105] as often as they sued others for defaulting on a debt owed to them, or for a breach of pecuniary or other contracts. Women sued for civil damages, for dissolution of their marriages, for alimony, for child custody plus expenses, for remedies against defamation, and brought to trial other women on charges of insolvency and physical assault. But women were also sued by men on charges of physical abuse.[106]

Of course, women were used and abused far more frequently than men, though not all of them waited to fall victim to such circumstances. A recent study of court records from sixteenth-century Cairo has shown that both Ḥanafite and Mālikite judges adjudicated cases in which the marriage contracts routinely included contractual terms otherwise thought to be permissible only in the Ḥanbalite school.[107] In their marriage and remarriage contracts (which accounted for 47 out of a total of 361 cases), women inserted conditions to varying effects, including a woman's right to dissolve the marriage contract if her husband took another wife (34/41%);[108] if he were to force her to move to a residence not of her choice (26/24%); if he were to take a concubine (14/24%); were he to default on spousal or child support (11/18%); or if he were to beat her (6/29%). (Needless to say, such protections had been common practice centuries before the Ottomans, a proposition that undermines the widespread claim among legal historians of the modern period to the

[103] Seng ("Invisible Women," 249) is right in remarking that agents were used by men too, Muslim or otherwise.

[104] Jennings, "Women," 53–114; Gerber, "Social and Economic Position," 231–44; Seng, "Standing," 189–203; Göçek and Baer, "Social Boundaries," 60.

[105] Seng, "Standing," 196, 203; Christelow, *Muslim Law Courts*, 91.

[106] Seng, "Invisible Women," 247; Seng, "Standing," 199.

[107] Zantout, "*Khulʿ*," 38–45.

[108] The second percentage is that of remarriage contracts.

effect that in 1917 and thereafter the nation-states resorted to such contractual stipulations to effect an improvement in women's status.)[109] Any breach of these terms on the part of the husband permitted the wife to enter, by force of the marriage contract, into a divorce settlement of *khulʿ* whereby she would free herself in return for payment deemed symbolic when compared to the dower owed to her.[110]

It is certainly true that Islamic law, reflecting the social make-up of the great majority of Islamic communities, promoted gendered social and legal structures. Equally true, as some historians have observed, is the fact that "the court language privileged the social status of men and Muslims over women and non-Muslims."[111] But nothing in this language or in the court itself could diminish the rights of women or even discourage them from approaching the court, much less take away from them the full rights of property ownership, of juridico-moral rectitude or of suing whomever they pleased. This was equally true of non-Muslim women, who, in the language of the court, were doubly unprivileged by the facts of being women and non-Muslims. Yet, their rights, as well as their actual legal and social powers, were no more disadvantaged than their Muslim counterparts – as we shall see in some detail in due course.

It is also true that in legal doctrine a woman's testimony, in most areas of the law, carried half the weight of that of a man.[112] However, we have few data on the actual effects that such juristic discrimination had on the actual lives and experiences of women. How, in other words, did this evidentiary rule affect their marital, familial and property rights – among others – and, equally important, how were these effects perceived and interpreted by Muslim women themselves? Judging by the available evidence, the overall and relative effect of such discriminatory evidentiary rules certainly compares not unfavorably to the experience of their contemporary European counterparts.

Evidence of the innocuousness involved in women's diminished evidentiary value is the glaring fact that women appeared in court as plaintiffs or defendants in every sphere of legal activity, ranging from criminality to civil litigation. Although the majority of cases bringing them to the court (admittedly not the only province of law) were economic in nature,[113] they were active on several other fronts. It may even be said that courts

109 See chapter 16, section 3, below. 110 Zantout, "*Khulʿ*," 49–52.
111 Göçek and Baer, "Social Boundaries," 63.
112 For a useful commentary on the issue, see Fadel, "Two Women, One Man."
113 For example, Zarinebaf-Shahr, "Women," 261, estimates that close to 89 percent of women's petitions to the Imperial Council of Complaints related to economic issues. Although this figure seems high, it gives a rough indication of the economic role women played in society as well as in the life of the law.

often preferred women as guardians of minors, asking (and paying) them to manage the orphans' financial affairs and the wealth they inherited.[114] They were no less hesitant to sue on behalf of these minors than they were with regard to their own farms, agricultural tools, weaving equipment, livestock and slaves.

Much litigation about property related to lapsed *ṭalāq* payments and inheritance settlements,[115] although the distribution (*taqsīm*) of estates was usually taken up by the courts as a routine procedure, not by virtue of litigation. In either case, the common presence of women in court, mostly as plaintiffs, attested to the relatively advantageous positions in which they stood. *Ṭalāq*, as the jurists understood very well,[116] and as legal practice testifies,[117] was a very costly financial enterprise for the husband, let alone that in many cases it was effectively ruinous (a fact which may explain the rarity of polygamy).[118] Upon *ṭalāq*, the ex-wife was entitled to maintenance for at least three months (*ʿidda*), delayed dower, children's maintenance, any debts the husband incurred to her during the marriage (a relatively frequent occurrence),[119] and, if the children were young, a fee for nursing. And if the husband had not been consistent in paying for marital obligations (also a relatively frequent occurrence), he would owe the total sum due upon the initiation of his *ṭalāq*. In this context, it must be clear that when women entered marriage, they frequently did so with a fair amount of capital, which explains why they were a source of lending for many husbands and why so many of them engaged in the business of money-lending in the first place.[120] In addition to the immediate dower and the financial and material guarantees for her livelihood, the wife secured a postponed payment, but one that she could retrieve at any time she wished (unless otherwise stipulated in the contract). But more financially significant was the trousseau that she received from her parents, customarily consisting of her share of her natal family's inheritance paid in the form of furniture, clothing, jewelry and at times cash.[121]

114 Zarinebaf-Shahr, "Women," 260; Meriwether, "Rights of Children," 219–35.

115 Seng, "Standing," 202.

116 See chapter 8, section 2, below.

117 Zilfi, "We Don't Get Along," 269–71; Rapoport, *Marriage*, 70.

118 See Zilfi, "We Don't Get Along," 269, and the many sources cited in n. 15 therein. Nor does *ṭalāq* appear as common (269). In the 1880s, for example, the rate of polygamy in Istanbul marriages was 2.52 percent. See Yilmaz, "Secular Law," 124. Also Gerber, "Social and Economic Position," 232; Jennings, *Christians and Muslims*, 29, 36, 385 ("Polygamy was almost unknown"); Tucker, "Marriage and Family," 165–79.

119 The practice of husbands borrowing from their wives was frequent, as was that of women engaging in the business of money-lending at interest. See Rapoport, *Marriage*, 24.

120 See Marcus, "Men, Women," 145, for Aleppine women who were money-lenders and whose customers often included their own husbands. See also Jennings, "Women," 97–101.

121 On the size of many a trousseau, see Rapoport, *Marriage*, 12–22; e.g., a sultan's manumitted slave-girl commanded a trousseau worth 100,000 gold *dīnars*.

Many women, before or during marriage, were endowed with a *waqf* portion, giving them further income. Whatever the form of the trousseau and the total wealth they could accumulate, women were entirely aware of their exclusive right to this wealth, and understood well that they were under no obligation to spend any portion of it on others or even on themselves. They apparently spent their own money on themselves only if they chose to do so, since such expenses as pertained to sustenance, shelter and clothing (in the expansive meaning of these terms if the husband was prosperous) were entirely his responsibility, not hers. In other words, unlike that of husbands, the property of wives was not subject to the chipping effect of expenditure, but could instead be saved, invested and augmented.

Considering the unassailability over the centuries of these rights – which on balance availed women of property accumulation – it is not surprising that, in the historical record, *ṭalāq* appears to be less common than *khulʿ*, the contractual dissolution of marriage.[122] The relative frequency of the latter in Istanbul, Anatolia, Syria, Muslim Cyprus, Egypt and Palestine has been duly noted by historians.[123] It is a phenomenon that explains – in this context – three significant features of Muslim dissolution of marriage. First, while *ṭalāq* was the unilateral prerogative of the husband, there was also a "price" that he paid for this prerogative. In other words, *ṭalāq* may appear in the manuals of *fiqh* to be an unrestrained prerogative (though a careful examination of these manuals falsifies such a perception), although in reality it was constrained (for the average husband) by hefty financial deterrents, coupled with legal and moral deterrents installed by jurisprudential doctrine to boot. Second, *ṭalāq* in effect also amounted to a unidirectional transfer of property from the husband to the wife, beyond and above all that he was – for the duration of the marriage – obliged to provide his wife by default. In fact, an important effect of this transfer was the fact that many repudiated women purchased the husband's share in the matrimonial house, funneling the *ṭalāq* payment due to them toward such a purchase.[124] Third, *khulʿ*, within the economic equation of Muslim marriages, was in a sense less of a depletion of the woman's property as a concession on the part of the woman to due privileges. The case of Ayşe who petitioned the court to dissolve her marriage by *khulʿ* – which

[122] See chapter 8, section 2, above.

[123] Rapoport, *Marriage*, 4; Peirce, "She Is Trouble," 281–82; Marcus, *Middle East*, 205–06; Jennings, "Women," 82–87; Jennings, "Divorce," 157; Ivanova, "Divorce," 121; Tucker, "Revisiting Reform," 11–12; Zilfi, "We Don't Get Along," 272, and sources cited in n. 22 in this article.

[124] Marcus, "Men, Women," 155.

amounted to her delayed dower plus her waiting period allowance –[125] was a typical one. So typical was it that the juristic manuals reflected this practice as a normative doctrine.[126] The point, however, remains that it was the very financial promise made by the groom (i.e., delayed dower) and the financial guarantees he had to make for the three months of the *ʿidda* that were used as the bargaining chip for *khulʿ*.[127]

Khulʿ provides an auspicious context to assess domestic violence against women, an area of marital discord on which we have virtually no data. In chapter 8, we will discuss the irregular marital behavior termed *nushūz*, a behavior that, under certain circumstances, gives rise to a right whereby the husband is permitted to "beat his wife lightly."[128] "Light beating," however, may not be light at all in the context of a violent and highly abusive husband who, adding insult to injury, might refuse to grant his wife the right to *khulʿ*. Having fairly easy access to the courts, however, abused women had the option of addressing themselves to the *qāḍī*, who would assign officials of the court to investigate the abuse. If abuse was proven, the court had the power to dissolve the marriage, as it often did. The law also allowed the woman the right to self-defense, including, under certain circumstances, the killing of her abusive husband.[129]

This formal legal perspective on such situations may be coupled with another social perspective that acted independently or conjointly. Obviously, the ties of the wife/woman to her original family were not, upon marriage, severed, and her parents, brothers and even sisters (especially the unmarried ones) continued to watch closely as the marriage of their daughter/sister unfolded. It was, after all, the parents of the wife who had usually arranged the marriage, and to some variable extent were responsible not only for it, but for the well-being of their daughter. This sense of involved responsibility intersected with two other elements, one having to do with their status in the surrounding community and their sense of dignity and honor, the other with teleological considerations: the former would be seriously jeopardized should their daughter suffer abuse (assuming it was publicly known, which was a very likely possibility in such intimate, closely knit communities), and the latter would promote

[125] Zilfi, "We Don't Get Along," 276, 284. Zilfi does not argue that eighteenth-century marital dissolution necessarily resulted in reducing the economic status of women which is "axiomatic in the contemporary world." But, she says, *khulʿ* divorcees "could not have been better off economically immediately upon divorce" (284). While this may be true, the two cases in support of her argument are uncharacteristically speculative and severely lacking in detail to constitute evidence.

[126] ʿAynī, *Bināya*, V, 511; Ḥiṣnī, *Kifāya*, II, 79; Ibn Muftāḥ, *Sharḥ*, V, 394–99. See also chapter 8, section 3, below.

[127] A similar point is made by Zilfi, "We Don't Get Along," 295.

[128] Miṣrī, ʿ*Umda*, 541–42; Ḥiṣnī, *Kifāya*, II, 77–79.

[129] Tucker, *House*, 65–66.

their constructive involvement so as to avoid having to "take back" their daughter when the marriage collapsed – with all the economic consequences this "taking back" might entail. This tripartite, but multi-layered, interest in the success of a daughter's marriage explains the close scrutiny many families exercised (and still do) to prevent abuse by the husband of their daughter (including such Levantine measures as the brothers of the wife beating the abusive husband).[130] Unlike the situation of many women who, in the nuclear family of today, must fend for themselves,[131] the average woman in earlier Islamic societies continued to have the psychological and social – and when necessary economic – backing of her original family. This obviously did not prevent abuse in all cases, but it contributed significantly to its reduction. However, when all attempts had failed, the wife's original family, often with the collaboration of the husband's own family, would exercise the necessary pressures to bring the marriage to an end, before the *qāḍī* or not.

I earlier noted that the majority of our evidence about women relates to economic and property rights, although I also emphasized that non-material experiences and socio-moral contexts of Muslim women could be as useful in determining their status and "power." But if economics is a significant measure, and it is, then Muslim women's involvement in the law of property was considerable. Constituting up to 40 percent of the real estate dealers in some cities, they approached the court to register their sales and purchases, recording in this way the fact that, in Aleppo, they were involved in as much as 67 percent (and in Kayseri, 40 percent) of transactions related to house transfers.[132] As court litigation and registries show, women owned both residential and commercial properties, mainly rent-earning shops. They oftentimes owned their own houses, and frequently jointly purchased houses with their husbands, during, but also before, the marriage.[133] And when they were repudiated by their husbands, they often bought the latter's share in the matrimonial house with the very money their husbands owed them as a result of *ṭalāq*.

130 A practice that survives even today in many Palestinian villages. On the other hand, the urban tradition of "brotherly protection" seems to have ceased after the 1980s.

131 Duly noted here are the somewhat exaggerated claims, recently emerging in scholarship, that the nuclear family was more widespread than "had previously been thought." Exactly what is meant by what "had previously been thought" has never been defined. See, for instance, Zilfi, "We Don't Get Along," 289.

132 Marcus, "Men, Women," 144, who further observes (146) that "[w]omen need to be reckoned as a major actor in the urban real estate market." For a more general account of the economic role of women in earlier Middle Eastern history, see Goitein, *Mediterranean Society*, III, 312–59.

133 Marcus, "Men, Women," 154.

Women were also participants in one of the most powerful economies in Muslim lands, namely, the real property dedicated as *waqf*, which, by the dawn of colonialism, constituted 40–60 percent of all real property. Except for the largest endowments, usually established by sultans, kings, viziers and emirs, many of the founders of medium-size and smaller *waqf*s were women. They often founded and managed endowments alone, and to a lesser extent they were co-founders, with males and other females.[134] A relatively impressive number of *waqf*s were established by manumitted female slaves associated with the political and military elites, and these too established *waqf*s independently as well as with their (former) masters[135] (a fact that attests to the financial, and even political, power of female slaves). *Waqf*s of modest range appear to have been established by men and women in equal numbers.[136] Women's participation in the important *waqf* economy began early on,[137] and steadily increased throughout the centuries. By the eighteenth century, women constituted 40–50 percent of *waqf* founders in Aleppo,[138] and, according to one estimate, about 25 percent of those of Cairo in the same period.[139] Another estimate for this century shows proportionately more women establishing endowments than men.[140] In some cities, a significant number, and at times more than half, of endowments established by women were public, dedicated to religious and educational purposes or to caring for and feeding the poor.[141] And like men, at least in Aleppo, about 60 percent of women creating endowments purchased their properties for this purpose.[142]

It is only reasonable to assume that more women benefited from *waqf* endowments as beneficiaries than there were women who founded such endowments. Quantitative evidence of the proportions of men and women who were *waqf* beneficiaries has still to be tabulated, but the general evidence thus far points to well-nigh equal numbers. The theory that the juridical instrument of *waqf* was used to deprive females of their entitlements to inheritance no longer stands, for it appears, to the contrary, that the *waqf* was more often used as a means to avoid the laws of inheritance to accomplish the opposite effect:[143] not only to allocate

[134] Deguilhem, "Consciousness of Self," 102–15. [135] Fay, "Women and Waqf," 35.
[136] Meriwether, "Women and Waqf Revisited," 135.
[137] See, for instance, Seng, "Invisible Women," 245–46.
[138] Meriwether, "Women and Waqf Revisited," 132. Cf. Marcus, "Men, Women," 147.
[139] Fay, "Women and Waqf," 34. [140] Crecelius, "Incidence of Waqf," 176–89.
[141] See, for instance, the numbers for Aleppo in Meriwether, "Women and Waqf Revisited," 133–34. For obvious reasons, however, more men than women founded endowments in the capital city of the Ottomans.
[142] *Ibid.*, 134.
[143] Depriving females of Quranic inheritance was deemed, in the social discourse of morality, a reprehensible act that diminished the prestige of families who did or entertained doing so.

bigger shares for female heirs than what they would have inherited by Quranic rules, but also to create a sort of matrilineal system of property devolution.[144] Equally important, however, was the crucial factor of avoiding the partition of family property, frequently an economically harmful act which was curbed by having recourse to the *waqf* instrument. It should therefore not be surprising to find many *waqf* deeds that allocate to the beneficiaries the same proportional entitlement to the estate as the Quranic shares.[145]

One historian has found that in eighteenth- and nineteenth-century Aleppo women were disadvantaged as inheritors in less than 1 percent of the 468 *waqf* deeds she examined.[146] Women generally designated more females than males as beneficiaries, while some 85 percent of men designated their wives and/or daughters, a situation that obtained in sixteenth-century Istanbul as well. The same pattern occurs with regard to rights of residency in the family dwelling of the founder. The great majority of deeds – in Aleppo, Istanbul and elsewhere – did not discriminate against females, nor did they limit their rights in any way. But when they did, the restriction did not preclude the right to live in the house until marriage, or to return to it when they became orphaned or divorced. Nor did preclusion apply to female descendants, a fact that "left the door open for married women and their spouses and their offspring to claim their rights to live in the house."[147]

Women were also deemed to be as qualified as men in their capacity as managers of endowments, an influential administrative and financial position.[148] Although there were more men than women performing this function, a large number of women appear as administrators of *waqf*s established by their fathers, mothers, grandparents and distant relatives. In the eyes of the court too, women manifestly had precedence over younger males as administrators.[149] And like men, women reserved for themselves the right to be the first administrators of their own endowments. They also reserved and used the right to sue against infringements of *waqf* rights, on behalf of themselves as well as others.[150]

In sum, Muslim women were full participants in the life of the law. As Y. Seng puts it with regard to Ottoman women, they

[144] Tucker, *Women in Nineteenth-Century Egypt*, 95–96.
[145] Meriwether, "Women and Waqf Revisited," 138; Rapoport, *Marriage*, 27.
[146] Meriwether, "Women and Waqf Revisited," 138.
[147] *Ibid.*, 138–39. [148] Also see Zarinebaf-Shahr, "Women," 260.
[149] Meriwether, "Women and Waqf Revisited," 140–50.
[150] Tucker, *Women in Nineteenth Century Egypt*, 95–96.

used their right of access to the courts to promote their interests, in which a manumitted slave could restrict the claim of her past master to her estate, where a farm woman could challenge the claim of a creditor upon the expensive livestock she had purchased, where a widow could assert her priority right to buy her husband's share in real property, and where a woman traveling alone from one village to another could charge a police officer with obstructing her path.[151]

But if the law depended, in its proper functioning, on the moral community, then women – just as much as men – were the full bearers of the very morality that the law and the court demanded. And as moral denizens, or denizens who aspired to the power that was generated by moral character, they engaged in the law, losing and winning on the way. But when they lost or won, it was *not necessarily because they were women*, but rather because they were full legal persons responsible – morally and otherwise – for their actions. They understood their rights, and they approached the courts with the full knowledge that they would receive fair treatment. When the law was, by our modern standards, unfair to them (whether they perceived it as such or not), they developed strategies to counteract its effects, and in doing so drew on the moral and social resources available to them. They no doubt lived in a patriarchy, but the inner dynamics of this patriarchy afforded them plenty of agency that allowed them a great deal of latitude. That "Islamic modernity" has proven to be oppressive of women, as we shall see in chapter 16, cannot take away from the fact that for a millennium before the dawn of modernity they compared favorably with their counterparts in many parts of the globe, particularly in Europe.

[151] Seng, "Standing," 202. The historical scholarship on "women in Islam" may be usefully complemented by recent anthropological work on contemporary Muslim women. See Abu-Lughod, *Veiled Sentiments*; Abu-Lughod, "Romance of Resistance," 41–55; Wikan, *Behind the Veil*; Mahmood, *Politics of Piety*.

5 The Circle of Justice and later dynasties

1. The political background of justice

After the decline of the caliphate of Baghdad, the Muslim world witnessed the rise of kingship in the shape of foreign dynasties hailing from the steppes of Central Asia. After the military power of the Būyids, Qarakhānids, Saljūqs, Ayyūbids and Mamlūks was spent, the two dynasties that ruled the majority of Muslim lands during the eighteenth and nineteenth centuries were the Ottomans (1389–1922) and the Qājārs (1779–1924). The latter were preceded by the Ṣafavids (1501–1732), who converted Iran to Twelver-Shīʿism from what was mostly Sunnite Ḥanafism.[1] The Qājār rule was politically and militarily weak, and its system of organization decentralized and bureaucratically thin.[2] The Ottomans, on the other hand, were preceded by the Mamlūks, who in turn might never have come into existence, much less sustain themselves as a ruling dynasty, without the military manpower supplied by the Mongols or by the peoples the latter had conquered, most notably the Kipchaks. An important element of this manpower was the Mamlūk purchase from merchants of kidnapped or enslaved boys – a system that was adopted and developed by the Ottomans. It is thus remarkable that – unlike the European populations that were engaged by their nobility in a constant state of warfare[3] – the local populations of the Middle East rarely faced military conscription. More remarkable, and causally connected with the administration of justice, was the resultant fact that an enormous cultural, linguistic and ethnic wedge separated the ruling dynasties from the populations they ruled.

The longest-ruling dynasty in Islam, the Ottomans governed vast territories from the Hejaz to eastern Europe. By 1517, the three holiest cities of Islam – Mecca, Medina and Jerusalem – had fallen under their rule, while

[1] On this process of conversion, see Abisaab, *Converting Persia*.
[2] For more on the Qājār regime in a legal context, see chapter 15, below.
[3] Parker, *Military Revolution*, 1–2.

at the same time the ʿAbbasid caliphate had been moved to Istanbul to lend the regime a semblance of legitimacy. Yet, in a strictly Sharīʿa-minded sense, Ottoman rule had already begun with Bayezid I (r. 791–804/1389–1401) who, far more than any of his predecessors, sponsored the religious elite, both Ṣūfīs and legists. But his patronage differed somewhat from that of Niẓām al-Mulk and the dozens of Muslim rulers that had come and gone in the interval. For Bayezid invited the legists to assist him and, in effect, to enter into an active ruling partnership with him. As it happened, his venture became an entrenched paradigm of governance for the two centuries after his death, and continued to have a marked, though less significant, influence on the style of Ottoman rule until the end of the Empire.

Engaging the legists in the administration of justice within the body politic was a model of governance that answered the political exigencies that arose after the decline of the ʿAbbasid caliphate. In the Muslim worldview, kingship represented a morally repugnant form of political governance that Islam had originally come to replace. The Arabic language reserves the terms *malik* and *mulk* to designate, respectively, "king" and "kingship," with the distinct meanings of "possessor" and "possession." To be a king is to possess that over which one rules. Yet, the foundational Quranic language and the Sharīʿa assign categorical possession exclusively to God who is recognized as, and given the name, Owner of the Universe in both of its spheres, the here and the hereafter.[4] Any human claim to earthly possession must thus be either metaphorical or a plain usurpation of the divine Kingdom or a portion thereof.[5] For a man to rule without incriminating himself in the irredeemable sin of usurpation, he must act as the guardian and administrator of the Law, just as the caliphs had done earlier. They claimed to possess nothing of God's world, and stood as administrators of, and thus beneath, His Law.

This perception of divine sovereignty lay at the foundations of the relationship between the ruling dynasties and the civilian populations they had come to rule.[6] As we saw in chapter 4, gaining and holding on to legitimacy was the prime challenge that every ruler and dynasty had to face. The imperative of upholding justice as embodied in the Sharīʿa thus had to be reconciled with the demands and expediency of political rule,

[4] On this conception in the context of the theory of property, see chapter 9, section 1, below. See also Quran 24:42; 57:2; 59:23.

[5] See chapter 9, section 1, below; Mottahedeh, *Loyalty*, 185.

[6] In fact, this conception of governance continues to lie at the ideological foundations of the modern Islamist movements, as advocated, among others, by the influential Muslim Brother Sayyid Quṭb and the Pakistani ideologue Mawdūdī. Qutb, *Milestones*, 87–116; Adams, "Mawdudi and the Islamic State," 111 ff.

for it was widely recognized that the latter's failure would be assured without the backing of the former. Yet, it was equally and fully recognized that, without the sovereign's juridico-political administration (*siyāsa sharʿiyya*), the Sharīʿa would also become a hollow system. The Sharīʿa thus defined the substance and form of legal norms, while the sovereign ensured their enforcement. Hence the formula – adopted by both the Sunnites and the Shīʿites – that the *qāḍī*s were appointed and dismissed by the ruler, and their independent judgments enforced by him, but without any interference on his part in the substantive law that was applied.[7]

From the perspective of the rulers, the desideratum of governance was the maintenance of their own sovereignty and its tool, legitimacy. The religious law, long established and impossible to alter, constituted not only an efficient tool of governance but an effective means through which sovereignty and legitimacy were achieved. It would be a mistake, therefore, to assume that Muslim rulers merely tolerated the Sharīʿa and its servants, for the latter, in the absence of a state machinery of bureaucracy and surveillance,[8] were indispensable to any form of political rule.

From the perspective of rulers, therefore, the theory of the Circle of Justice has come to reflect accurately the *modus operandi*, if not *modus vivendi*, of political rule in Islam, perhaps more so than it did pre-Islamic forms of rule (whence the Circle is said to originate). The Circle begins with the idea that no political sovereignty can be attained without the military; yet no military can be sustained without financial resources. These resources furthermore can be raised only through levying taxes, which presupposes continuous economic productivity on the part of the subjects; but to maintain a level of prosperity that can sustain taxable income, justice needs to be ensured, and this in part means controlling the excesses of provincial officials whose vision of justice may be overshadowed by personal power and rapacity. Thus, to be attained, justice requires public order, the all-important social harmony, and control of abusive and greedy government servants. To achieve all this, the Sharīʿa, clearly the axis of governance, points the way. But the Sharīʿa cannot be implemented without political sovereignty, and this cannot be attained without the military. Here, the Circle is joined.[9]

From the perspective of the legists, on the other hand, this version of the Circle conceptually begins at the wrong point, since the emphasis is placed on the justice of the ruler and his authoritative and military standing, rather than on the Law. The legists would stress instead the

7 Hallaq, *Origins*, 79–85; Floor, "Change and Development," 114.
8 Here defined in a modern sense. 9 İnalcık, "Suleiman the Lawgiver," 107–08.

attainment of justice through implementation of the Sharīʿa, which in turn requires public order and social harmony. Here, the sovereign's function is to ensure stability and prevent internal fractiousness at any cost, and to this end he raises legally prescribed taxes to support his regime and implements *siyāsa sharʿiyya*. Political authority thus becomes at once subservient to, and necessary for, the legal order. As we saw in chapter 4, and as the present chapter further attempts to show, the reality on the ground was a synthesis between the two readings of the Circle, although during the later periods, especially during the Mamlūk and Ottoman regimes, the balance of influence stood in favor of the sovereign's mode of realizing the Circle. The ultimate question that confronts us is, hence, the scope of *siyāsa sharʿiyya* and its diachronic mutations.

2. Self-rule, government and the *sharīʿa*

In theory, and largely in practice, *siyāsa sharʿiyya* represented the discretionary legal powers of the ruler to enforce the *qāḍī*'s judgments and to supplement the religious law with administrative regulations that mostly pertained to the regime's machinery of governance, including powers to limit jurisdiction to certain areas of the law or to particular types of cases,[10] as well as to curb and discipline abuses by government officials. (This latter function came to be identified in both Sunnism and Shīʿism with the courts of grievances, discussed earlier.)[11] The dilemma that every regime faced was its inability, due to distance from the center, to control the excessive violence of provincial governors and their men, violence mostly wrought for the sake of extorting taxes. In addition, *siyāsa sharʿiyya* regulations normally included matters related to tax collection, public order, land use, and at times criminal law and some aspects of public morality that could affect social harmony. The qualification "*sharʿiyya*" in this compound expression is intended to convey the notion that exercise of the powers of *siyāsa* was not only permitted, but in fact insisted upon by *sharʿī* juristic theory and judicial practice. Such powers were not only consistent with the dictates of religious law, but could in no way constitute an infringement thereof if properly exercised.[12]

Under the Mamlūks, for example, the *ḥājib* or viceroy tried emirs and soldiers, government clerks and tax-farmers at times independently, at

[10] See, e.g., the late eighteenth-century Ottoman–Syrian practice of allocating lawsuits involving more than a certain amount to the Main Court, where the Ḥanafite Chief Qāḍī presided. Knost, "*Waqf* in Court," 429. See also Serrano, "Twelve Court Cases," 476–77, and Ibn ʿĀbidīn, *Ḥāshiya*, V, 419.

[11] In chapter 1, section 5, above.

[12] Māwardī, *Aḥkām*, 3.

others in consultation with the sultan. But, apart from relatively very few – if not isolated – exceptions,[13] the jurisdiction of the viceroy did not extend to the civilian population, which was governed entirely by the Sharīʿa and the *qāḍī*. Even when a clerk or a tax-farmer would escape the viceroy's *maẓālim* justice and seek refuge in a Sharīʿa court, it was usually left to the *qāḍi* to adjudicate the matter. On occasion, these Mamlūks would place themselves for prolonged periods of time in the custody of *qāḍī*s in an attempt to escape the surely less merciful punishment of the *ḥājib*.[14]

In the judicial hierarchy of the Mamlūks – as was the case with the Ghaznawids and the Qājārs of Iran – the highest court was that of the *maẓālim*, held in the so-called *Dār al-ʿAdl* (something of a pre-modern *palais de justice*). The site of this court was the palace or residence of the sultan in the capital, Cairo, or of his viceroy, the provincial governor who, as the sultan's representative, enjoyed all the *siyāsa sharʿiyya* prerogatives of the latter. Always present in the hearings at *Dār al-ʿAdl* were the chief-justices of the capital or the province, serving as representatives of the four legal schools. Present also was a distinguished *muftī* (or *muftī*s) whose erudition and legal knowledge earned him (or them) what might be termed epistemic charisma. The role that these jurists played is not entirely clear, but it could not have been merely formal. Anyone, including private individuals, brought cases before this body, often against high and low officials of the regime, and infrequently against the decisions of Sharīʿa courts. Although criminal cases were traditionally within the purview of Sharīʿa courts, they seem to have been tried more often at the *Dār al-ʿAdl* than by these courts.[15] Furthermore, the *muḥtasib* was not the function of the *qāḍī* but rather a position occupied by Mamlūk officials.[16] Yet, the default tribunal of justice was the Sharīʿa court which tried the great majority of cases, and almost all those of the civilian population. As we shall see in some detail, a similar situation obtained under the Ottomans, although this dynasty allocated even a greater role than did the Mamlūks to the Sharīʿa and its courts.

In Ṣafavid and Qājār Iran, we find a comparable state of affairs. The judicial system was divided into Sharīʿa and *ʿurf* courts, the former being the standard courts of general jurisdiction, and the latter discharging the functions of the *maẓālim* tribunals of the ruler. And since the ruler's concern was to institute a sort of public order that permitted the efficient

13 As we shall see in due course in this chapter.

14 Ayalon, "Great Yāsa," IVa, 105, 115; IVd, 108. It is perhaps instructive that, in today's Saudi Arabia, an appeal to the Sharīʿa court on matters falling within religious law is not normally subject to change of venue, that is, to the Board of Grievances, still known as *dīwān al-maẓālim*.

15 Mandaville, "Muslim Judiciary," 67, 69–71.

16 *Ibid.*, 3, 67, 85.

raising of taxes, the *ʿurf* courts attended to abuses by government officials as well as to capital crimes, theft, highway robbery, and any violation that disrupted social or public harmony. The Sharīʿa courts dealt with almost everything else. The appointment of the *qāḍī*s was the function of the Shaykh al-Islām, who was a salaried government official appointed as head of the judiciary in every city, not only in the capital. At the provincial level, the *ʿurf* tribunals were administered by the governor or his officials, but the capital's tribunal (*dīvān-e shāh*) was normally presided over by the Shah himself. As in the Ottoman case, the *dīvān-e shāh* heard any and all appeals from the lower Sharīʿa and *ʿurf* courts, and its decisions were final (without this being a consciously formulated doctrine).[17] But unlike the Ottomans – who were ardent centralizers and who developed and then absorbed into their government administration a legal aristocracy – the Ṣafavids and Qājārs continued to operate on the earlier model of maintaining a degree of separation between the military/political sovereign and the Sharīʿa establishment. Nor did they subsume their Empire's administration under a unified legal system, as the Ottomans did in placing even the smallest administrative unit under the *qāḍī*'s care. Nevertheless, Persia's Ṣafavid, Zand and Qājār rulers unfailingly continued to uphold their duties as prescribed to them by *siyāsa sharʿiyya*.[18]

So did the Mughals of India between 1556 and 1757, when the British appropriated for themselves the administration of justice. As elsewhere, the legists under the Mughals operated in part privately – in their college-mosques and all dealings associated with their functions therein – but they also worked in the service of the ruler. Adopting the judicial systems laid down by the Delhi sultanate, the administration of the judiciary was assigned to a *qāḍī* (known as the *Ṣadr*), not a chief *muftī*. The provincial *Ṣadr* appointed and supervised local *qāḍī*s, *muḥtasib*s and *waqf* administrators. Some *muftī*s were also appointed in an official capacity by the *Ṣadr*, and these functioned as legal advisors for both the government and their judge-colleagues. The *Ṣadr* determined judicial salaries and had the power – unknown in the western domains of Islamdom – to allocate lands as fiscal remuneration for judicial service.[19]

Be that as it may, the ruler's legitimate intervention, seemingly unimpeded, was nonetheless complicated by several factors that intruded upon both universes of law and polity. In other words, the lines of authority were never separate from each other, and, if anything, they intersected,

[17] See Floor, "Change and Development," 113–15, for a good, albeit somewhat stereotypical, survey.
[18] Generally on the Ṣafavids, see Halm, *Shiʿa Islam*, 106–12.
[19] Siddiqi, "Muhtasib," 113–19; Singha, *Despotism*, 9–10.

overlapped and enmeshed with each other. To begin with, neither the Sharīʿa nor *siyāsa sharʿiyya* penetrated deeply enough within the social fabric as to regulate, to any exclusive degree, all aspects of social life. This is not to deny, however, that the Sharīʿa was far more successful than the sovereign in asserting its legal norms within that fabric, for after all it did constitute itself as the hegemonic moral and legal discourse in the lives of Muslims everywhere. But while the social system of values was heavily permeated by Sharīʿa-mindedness[20] (which was never the case with any political discourse), custom and customary law were considerably and conjointly responsible for the operation of the social order and for providing conflict-resolution mechanisms within it. Having evolved over the millennia, and adapting to every political, dynastic and legal turn, these customs absorbed, and indeed influenced, the Sharīʿa in multiple and particular ways, depending on the specific local context. Custom and customary law thus stood in a dialectical relationship with religious law, but never lost their independence from this law or, especially, from political intervention – until, that is, modernity and the dawn of the nation-state changed the scene in structural ways during the nineteenth century and thereafter.

In the context of mediation – discussed in the preceding chapter – we noted the importance of self-ruling groups in effecting conflict resolution.[21] Their ability to negotiate and effect mediation was an integral part of the system of self-governance that they developed over time, a system that was embedded in both custom and morality. Furthermore, in the village, often far more remote from direct political control than the city, the dominant group was the extended family, clan or tribe. In the city, on the other hand, the communal groups were mainly the professional guilds and neighborhoods, which enjoyed a large measure of self-rule, even with regard to security and public order.[22] Once constituted as a clan, quarter or guild,[23] these units came to serve crucial administrative functions, most notably as instruments for governing the local populations.

20 Discussed in the preceding chapter, section 2.

21 For a micro-illustration of this, see Akarlı, "Law in the Marketplace," 245–70.

22 See Marcus, *Middle East*, 108–09; al-Qattan, "*Dhimmīs* in the Muslim Court: Legal Autonomy," 429 ff.

23 Gaining the status of a neighborhood or a guild was a desideratum, since such a status bestowed a corporate position of autonomy on the group. Raymond, "Role of the Communities," 37–38, reports that when the Syrian Melkites arrived in Cairo around 1138/1725, they strove to organize and to settle as a cohesive group in a single geographical location in an effort to gain recognition as a community and thereby enjoy an autonomous status. A similar effort was made a few decades later by the Palestinian community arriving in the same city.

Clearly, the use of guilds in a distinctly administrative capacity was an Ottoman innovation, just as the *qāḍī* and *qaḍā'* became, with the Ottomans, nearly as much a central apparatus of administration as they were a central judicial institution.[24] The residential neighborhoods and guilds were headed by a *shaykh* (at times himself a patriarch or chief rabbi) who represented the community and its concerns to the ruling classes as well as to the *qāḍī*. Such leaders not only were in regular contact with the authorities, but many of them regularly attended the assembly (*dīwān*) of the provincial governor, together with *qāḍī*s and *muftī*s.[25] At times, representation of a single neighborhood was the responsibility of a group of *shaykh*s, although it was often the case that all but one in the group acted in the supporting role of deputy-*shaykh*s or community elders.[26] We are not clear as to how the *shaykh*s attained this position of representation, but it seems highly likely that their social prestige, personal qualities and seniority in years played crucial roles in the emergence of a consensus among the neighborhood's elders and notables. In the case of guild *shaykh*s, whose appointment lasted from several months to a couple of years,[27] good professional standing and proficient knowledge of the craft or trade were no doubt essential.[28] The process, in other words, was not elective, but one that involved informal negotiations and a slowly emerging consensus. Yet, guilds did at times encounter difficulties in choosing their *shaykh*s, in which case – under the Ottomans at least – the court interfered with a view to settling disagreement and assisting in the selection of a head.[29]

Over time, and long before the Ottomans, the professional guilds had developed their own, independent rules of conduct, and neither the government nor the *qāḍī* dictated or interfered in these rules.[30] They set

[24] The rise, under the Ottomans, of the guild as an administrative entity perhaps explains why its mention in the sources becomes more frequent and detailed. Baer's argument that the guild is a seventeenth-century phenomenon largely rests on an *e silentio* argument. See chapter 4, n. 12, above, for sources pointing to much earlier origins. The appearance of multiple references to the guild in early seventeenth-century sources may well be explained by the rise of guilds as administrative tools, a function that must have brought them for the first time into a direct relationship with the organs of government.

[25] Marcus, *Middle East*, 82–83. [26] El-Nahal, *Judicial Administration*, 56.

[27] Akiba, "From Kadı to Naib," 45; Marcus, *Middle East*, 175.

[28] However, according to N. Hanna, in the construction guild, the *shaykh* was not always an expert builder but acted in the capacity of an administrator. If this was the case, then we see here the beginning of a tendency to create of the guild *shaykh* an office that was partially governmental. In other words, the *shaykh* would not only be the guild's chosen representative to the government, but also the regime's official who is the administrator of the guild's operation. See Hanna, *Construction Work*, 8.

[29] Raymond, "Role of the Communities," 34.

[30] Gerber, *State, Society*, 114, 116. Cf. Marcus, *Middle East*, 104–05.

for themselves production standards and prices, and regulated dealings among their members and between these and outside individuals, be they members of other guilds, the *qāḍī* or government officials. They at times imposed fines and penalties upon their own members who violated these rules, especially those engaging in fraudulent practices with regard to quality of products, weights and measures.[31] Of course, violations by and against guild members were oftentimes taken to court by the *muḥtasib*, the market inspector, and less frequently by the guild *shaykh* himself.[32] This tendency appears to have increased under the Ottomans, who exercised, more than any preceding dynasty, a higher level of surveillance over their populations. But even when infractions were brought to the *qāḍī*, the court's "expert witness" – the one who evaluated the factual basis of alleged infractions – was none other than the guild *shaykh* himself. While the *qāḍī*'s and *muḥtasib*'s interventions represented the watchful eyes of the regime, the standard of judgment regarding violations was set by the guild itself. For the problems that arose in such contexts were not just legal in nature; indeed, in the first instance, they were moral. As a corporate entity the guild was as much responsible to the public as it was accountable before the religious law or "secular" government. A baker's fraudulent reduction in the weight of the bread he produced was primarily a shameful act to be morally censured by the community, even when the *qāḍī* might do no more than rebuke the baker for his misdeed.[33] Guild infractions thus constituted not only legal but moral violations against the very community in which the guild as a collectivity, and guild members as individuals, lived and participated as social and moral beings. The fact that even in court the guild was allowed to evaluate its own actions and infractions underscores the considerable communal trust in the higher principles of morality that effected self-regulation, self-rule and what we euphemistically call conscientiousness.

The utility of the guild and neighborhood for the government lay in the economy of rule, for the government had to deal mainly with the *shaykh* as representative of an autonomous unit that was hierarchically structured. In consultation with the senior members of the guild (who themselves represented apprentices and other junior members),[34] the *shaykh* fixed prices, licensed new members in the profession, acted as an expert witness

[31] Gerber, *State, Society*, 116–17; Peirce, *Morality Tales*, 189; Hanna, *Construction Work*, 10.

[32] See, in some detail, Baer, "Administrative, Economic and Social Functions," esp. at 36–44.

[33] Peirce, *Morality Tales*, 189–90.

[34] On the hierarchy of professional guilds, see El-Nahal, *Judicial Administration*, 58. Guilds normally consisted, from bottom to top, of apprentices, journeymen, masters, deputy-*shaykh*s and *shaykh*s. At times, two guilds specializing in similar businesses – e.g., punch-makers and sweet-makers – had one *shaykh*.

in court litigation involving his own guild, and was consulted by the *muḥtasib* on numerous professional matters. Most importantly, the *shaykh*s of guilds and neighborhoods performed three functions, all of which were indispensable to any ruler: they maintained a register bearing the names and personal details of guild members or of residents in the neighborhood, organized the collection of taxes on the basis of this register, and maintained, with the help of the police or janissaries, public order in their own guilds or neighborhoods.[35] That this was the most economic and efficient form of rule for the time is beyond question.

It was particularly with the coming of the Ottomans that the guilds and neighborhoods became more closely tied to the law court, the smallest unit of administration in the Empire. Although the *shaykh* continued to be elected by the members of the guild or the residents of the neighborhood, he was henceforth to be confirmed by the court, confirmation consisting in the *qāḍī*'s recognition of the new *shaykh* and the registering of the new appointment in the court record.[36] The court also confirmed and registered the prices charged by the guild, usually after the *muḥtasib* and the *shaykh* agreed on them. Upon violation of these prices, or upon commission of fraudulent acts involving weights and measures, the *muḥtasib* brought the accused to court for trial.

The same procedure was followed in determining the taxes owed by the guilds and neighborhoods to the government. Both the tax-collector (*multazim*) and the *shaykh* would agree on a yearly lump-sum, to be approved and recorded by the court. When the tax-collector levied more taxes than the agreed-upon sum, the *shaykh* (accompanied at times by senior members of the guild or neighborhood) would normally bring a suit against him before the *qāḍī*.[37] But when it was the neighborhood or guild that defaulted on payment, the tax-collector would appear before the court as plaintiff. In such cases, it often came to pass that the *qāḍī* would arrange a schedule of payments that the neighborhood or guild was obliged to meet.[38]

In the preceding chapter we had occasion to note that many, if not most, disputes and instances of social discord were resolved at the local level through mediation. The senior members of the family were the natural negotiators and arbiters, but in expanded disputes, the *shaykh* and the

[35] Raymond, "Role of the Communities," 35; Gerber, *State, Society*, 113–26.
[36] El-Nahal, *Judicial Administration*, 58–60; Gerber, *State, Society*, 119–20; Marcus, *Middle East*, 173.
[37] Marcus, *Middle East*, 176.
[38] El-Nahal, *Judicial Administration*, 61–62, 67; Raymond, "Role of the Communities," 39; Gerber, *State, Society*, 124. For examples of cases in which tax-collectors transgressed the rights of peasants, see Peirce, *Morality Tales*, 328–29.

senior-ranking members of the guild or the neighborhood played such roles. The latter were also representatives of the collective public interest of their constituency. In the rare case of a homicide occurring in their neighborhoods, they, as representatives, were liable for the *qasāma*, the blood-money owed the family of the victim if the murderer could not be found.[39] The amount of the *qasāma* would then be levied from the households of the neighborhood. But the *shaykh*s also acted as the representatives of the corporate interests of their neighborhoods when they could not resolve a problem arising in their midst. They often appeared in court as plaintiffs against certain members of their own community, members deemed to be of an undesirable nature and with whom negotiation was not an option. Habitual liars, incorrigible gossipers, criminals, belligerent individuals, prostitutes, liquor consumers, noisy and loud residents who disturbed the peace, and residents who permitted dubious mixing of men and women and who habitually partied or engaged in unseemly behavior were often taken to court.[40] If the charges were proved, the court usually ordered these to move out of the neighborhood, a course of action that seems to have been usual in such instances.[41] Banishment for a period of one year was typical.

Problems between guilds or between neighborhoods were also brought to court for resolution. On behalf of his neighborhood's interests, the *shaykh* would demand protection, among other things, against misconduct, negligence or transgression. For example, he might petition the judge to block a road permitting access to one neighborhood from another, on the grounds that the residents of the latter offended the mores of the former. He might also seek the closure of windows in an adjacent neighborhood that invaded the privacy of residents in his own quarter. But it was also often the case that the *shaykh* would appear in court seeking redress against the mismanagement of a bath-house keeper or requesting permission to repair a run-down mosque or a collapsing wall that threatened the safety of his quarter's inhabitants.[42]

The point is that the communities – be they constituted as neighborhoods, guilds or villages – found representation in the circles of government, cultivating with their *shaykh*s an extensive working relationship that yielded a successful form of administration (a system that, incidentally, was

[39] See chapter 10, section 3, below.

[40] Peirce, *Morality Tales*, 90; Raymond, "Role of the Communities," 40; El-Nahal, *Judicial Administration*, 21, 55; Gerber, *State, Society*, 39. For a different view of prostitution under the Mamlūks, see Muṣaylihī, "al-Bighā' fī Miṣr."

[41] At times, however, the charges could not be proved, and the case would be dismissed. El-Nahal, *Judicial Administration*, 27.

[42] Raymond, "Role of the Communities," 40–41.

to collapse in the early nineteenth century). Between these two parties there always stood the *qāḍī*, without whom the entire equilibrium of cooperation would have fallen apart. In this context, A. Raymond's description of Ottoman Cairo can be taken, *mutatis mutandis*, as representative:

> The existence of communities ... allowed management of the city at widely varied levels: security, moral control, administration, micro-urbanism. The insertion of these communities in the city geography ensured their efficiency and complementarity. They enabled the Ottoman rulers – at little cost and without resorting to a specific administration – to govern the population of the city whose basic needs, in terms of security and public services, were thus assured ... Far from being isolated individuals, left to face oppressive and arbitrary rule, the inhabitants of Cairo were involved in a system of networks covering all the facts of their professional, religious and private lives ... [T]he collective administration of the city was efficiently carried out without any visible administrative apparatus. One hundred *shaykhs* of quarters and communities, and two hundred and fifty *shaykhs* of guilds, were involved in the process. They collectively fulfilled the objective of running a system which combined election and cooperation, and which ensured the submission and cooperation of the subjects under the ever-vigilant eye of the authorities in general and the qadi in particular.[43]

3. The limits of executive authority

Although this picture is entirely true of the Ottoman experience, it is also largely applicable to other dynasties and regions, the exceptions being either minor or short-lived. The Ottomans' perfection of this system was largely due to one of their reforms, namely, the abolishment of the *maẓālim* court, the extra-judicial tribunal of grievances. Instead of placing a political/military body in a position to judge the misconduct of government officials, the Ottomans located this function firmly within the jurisdiction of the Sharīʿa judge. The *qāḍī* became the only government official empowered to hear cases and to adjudicate them, and, more importantly, to decide on the legality of conduct of the highest provincial officials, including the governor. It is the *qāḍī* who supervises the transfer of the governor's office: he is the one who calls on the outgoing governor to surrender his documents, weapons, gunpowder, and everything else related to his office; he is the one who confirms the new governor and his subordinates, such as guards, tax-farmers, canal janitors, etc.[44] In fact, in order to ensure the compliance of the governor, the lines of communication between Istanbul and provincial *qāḍī*s were kept open, unconstrained by any intermediary official. Obviously, curbing the abusive powers of the provincial governors depended, at the end of the day, on

[43] *Ibid.*, 41. [44] El-Nahal, *Judicial Administration*, 65–66.

Istanbul's military might, as evidenced by its failure to control provincial separatism in the late twelfth /eighteenth century.[45]

On the other hand, Mughal and Mamlūk rule represented a spectrum of judicial experience that ranged, respectively, from the different to the oppositional when contrasted with Ottoman practice. While the Mughals shared with the Ottomans the ethic of sultanic protection of the weak against *ẓulm* – a term that bore, among other connotations, the meaning of tyranny – they assigned all criminal jurisdiction in the countryside to the *faujdār* who controlled public order and the excesses of the powerful *zamindārs*. In urban centers, the *qāḍī* assumed extensive judicial responsibility, although he did bear a share of administrative responsibility. But it was not uncommon that the regional governor, the *nāẓim*, took over the *qāḍī*'s jurisdiction, for he frequently decided which cases should be transferred to the *qāḍī* and which he would adjudicate himself or hand over to some other official.[46] The point is that under the Mughals the *qāḍī* remained subordinate to the high executive officials, although "what the Nazim ... decides should be done in accord with the judges."[47]

Under Mamlūk rule, especially in Syria, the *maẓālim* courts (presided over by *ḥājib*s, not legally trained judges) were raised to the top of the judicial hierarchy, a remarkable practice but not uncommon.[48] But then they went even further. With the growth in power of some *ḥājib*s, the Mamlūks expanded the function of the *maẓālim* tribunals. Sometime during the reign of the Sultan al-Malik al-Kāmil b. Qalāwūn (r. 678–89/ 1280–90), certain emirs began the unprecedented practice of acting as judges over the civilian population, thus clearly encroaching upon Sharīʿa's domain. Even the occasional practice of Mamlūk officials petitioning the *qāḍī* was barred, and for the first time such petitioners were dragged out of Sharīʿa courts, beaten and made to pay heavy fines.[49] And while interference in the jurisdiction of Sharīʿa courts must have been halted soon afterwards, the operation of the *maẓālim* tribunals continued well into the late sixteenth century before the Ottomans replaced them by strictly Sharīʿa institutions. Pronouncement on the conduct of executive officials was henceforth the province of the *qāḍī*, not of other executive officials.

It was first the *qāḍī* and, indirectly, the *muḥtasib* who overtook the *maẓālim* functions. But before we proceed, a few remarks about the *muḥtasib* may be

[45] Marcus, *Middle East*, 73–74, 113.
[46] Siddiqi, "Institution," 240–59; Singha, *Despotism*, 4–7.
[47] Cited from Akbar's *Firmān* of Justice (1672), in Singha, *Despotism*, 14–15.
[48] Peirce, *Morality Tales*, 347, citing the work of Mandaville on Damascus.
[49] Ayalon, "Great Yāsa," IVd, 108.

in order. Deriving from the moral notion of "commanding good and forbidding wrong" (expressed in the term *ḥisba*, hence *iḥtisāb* and *muḥtasib*), the function is probably pre-Islamic, having acquired distinctly religious connotations by the second/eighth century. According to Māwardī's *al-Aḥkām al-Sulṭāniyya* – not entirely a theoretical work – the *muḥtasib* shared with the *qāḍī* the function of hearing disputes in three specific domains, to which he was strictly limited: (1) foul play with respect to weights and measures; (2) fraud in the sale and pricing of merchandise; and (3) refusal to pay back debts when the debtor was solvent. He could not hear any other types of case, even though they might be closely connected with commercial transactions and sales, such as pecuniary contracts. Nor could he take on cases that required for their solution hearing evidence and testimony, even within the tripartite jurisdiction assigned to him. This last delimitation clearly defines further the scope of the *muḥtasib*'s function, namely, disciplining transgressors who were caught red-handed, in cases where outright commercial fraud and obvious market malpractices were involved. In addition to these, he was charged with urging neighborhood residents to attend Friday prayers, and generally to conform to good conduct. But he had the competence neither to pass a judicial decision (*ḥukm*), nor to imprison any person on the charge of non-payment of a debt. And herein lies another difference between the *qāḍī*'s and the *muḥtasib*'s duties: the *qāḍī* was passive in that he presided in his *majlis*, awaiting litigants to appear before him, whereas the *muḥtasib*'s function was proactive, in that he could suddenly appear on site, reining in malpractice while it was being committed. Yet, insofar as executive competence was concerned, the *muḥtasib* ranked lower than the *qāḍī*, just as the *qāḍī* ranked lower than the judge presiding over *maẓālim* tribunals.[50] This ranking, it must be clear, was a matter of normative practice, sanctioned by no formal hierarchy.

The *muḥtasib* may also have brought government officials to court on charges of corruption or abuses of the powers delegated to them by the sultan, but it was the *qāḍī* who passed the verdict on such infractions. In certain regions, and it seems only under the Ottomans, the *qāḍī* himself acted in the capacity of a *muḥtasib*.[51] El-Nahal reports that in seventeenth-century Cairo, the *qāḍī* himself toured the market, performing the tasks of the *muḥtasib*.[52] Charging the *qāḍī* with these tasks may have

[50] Māwardī, *Aḥkām*, 208–09.

[51] Mandaville, "Muslim Judiciary," 85, reports that under the Mamlūks, the *qāḍī*s never functioned as *muḥtasib*s. Yet, in twelfth/eighteenth-century Aleppo the *muḥtasib*'s function seems to have become defunct altogether. See Marcus, *Middle East*, 173.

[52] El-Nahal, *Judicial Administration*, 26. Cf. Gerber, *State, Society*, 69.

been due to the temporary lack of an official qualified to serve in that capacity, or because in some areas the *muḥtasib* was charged with collecting taxes, a function that may have been seen as an extension of his capacity as inspector of guilds and markets, both of which were sources of tax income.

That the *qāḍī* occasionally took over the *muḥtasib*'s inspectorial functions in the area of tax-collecting underscores a fundamental policy of the Ottomans, namely, that in fulfillment of the philosophy embedded in the Circle of Justice, the power of government officials was to be curbed and checked at every point. Until the very end of the eighteenth century, the system worked, and worked well, because a number of factors combined to produce these curbing effects. First, the civilian population was subject to the law of the Sharīʿa, an unwavering standard of justice. The people thus enjoyed immunity from the sovereign's crude power whether with regard to life or property. The government's servants, by contrast, were subject to a less merciful code which may aptly be called sultanic. We have here a unique feature of justice in the lands of Islam, for while no man or woman, Muslim, Christian or Jew in the civilian population could be punished without a Sharīʿa court trial – largely independent of the sovereign's will – the sultanic code was absolute with regard to the sovereign himself and his men.[53]

The sovereign himself was expected to observe not only his own code but, more importantly, the law of the Sharīʿa. Forbearance, mercy and near infinite forgiveness were expected, standards of governance that, when violated, could result in his dismissal or even assassination, a frequent event in later Ottoman times. For political power to acquire any legitimacy, it had to meet these standards, and conduct itself in a morally and legally responsible way. Even highly unsympathetic European observers of the Islamic legal system felt compelled to acknowledge this feature. Describing the late Mughals of India, the eighteenth-century English scholar Alexander Dow observed that the Sharīʿa "circumscribed the will of the Prince" and "the House of Timur always observed [the law]; and the practice of ages had rendered some ancient usages and edicts so sacred in the eyes of the people, that no prudent monarch would choose to violate either by a wanton act of power."[54]

Siyāsa, therefore, was in no way the unfettered power of political governance but in a fundamental way the exercise of wisdom, forbearance and prudence by a prince in ruling his subjects. In the case of the civilian

[53] İnalcık, "Suleiman the Lawgiver," 111, writes that this form of dual justice "was the essence of what we call the Middle Eastern state." See also Mardin, "Just and the Unjust," 116.
[54] Cited in Strawson, "Islamic Law and English Texts," 35.

population, these qualities manifested themselves in the recognition of the *qāḍī* as the final judge and as representative of the religious law, for in each and every case referred by the sultan to the *qāḍī*, it came with the unwavering sultanic command of applying the Sharīʿa law and the *qānūn*.[55] While the imperial servants, on the other hand, also frequently benefited from the sultanic virtue of forgiveness – especially upon first or less grave infractions – they were ultimately subject to the sultanic code that was absolute, swift and harsh. The right of summary judgment was reserved for the sultan against his own men and, by extension, their official representatives, all of whom owed complete allegiance to him.[56] For, after all, these men, who were brought up from childhood as the servants of the state, literally belonged to the *salṭana* ("sultanship"). They themselves, and all the wealth that they would accumulate in their lives, were the property of the salṭana; and this property was to revert to whence it came at the discretion of the sultan.

Having reigned over centuries, from Iran to the Maghreb, this system of governance also explains the largely misunderstood phenomenon of *muṣādara*, namely, the confiscation of the property of statesmen upon their death or dismissal from office, a phenomenon that reached its apex under the Mamlūks but seems to have decreased under the Ottomans. While it was rare for a sultan to confiscate the property of a civilian, even that of a rich merchant,[57] it was the norm for these statesmen to lose all their wealth when their office was terminated (hence the practice of alienating major properties as *waqf* before, and in anticipation of, an almost inevitable act of confiscation). What had been given through the good offices of the *salṭana* was retrieved by the same offices, and this included property and life as well. Thus, under the Ottomans as well as under earlier dynasties, rule and governance entailed a unique logic whereby the civilian population and ordinary folk enjoyed the rights of due process and full range of Sharīʿa law and procedure, whereas those who ruled over them did not, being subject to another law altogether.[58]

Government employees, including *qāḍīs*, thus represented the sultan who, as the overlord, was responsible for any commission of injustice by his servants. With the virtual abolition of the *maẓālim*, the Ottomans augmented the powers of the *qāḍī*, making him the judge of these servants' conduct and affirming the supremacy of the Sharīʿa's jurisdiction. But the

[55] Jennings, "Limitations," 164, 166, 167. [56] *Ibid.*, 164.
[57] Even under the Mamlūks, who were notorious *muṣādara* practitioners, seizing private property was rare. See Mandaville, "Muslim Judiciary," 77. For the Ottomans, see Mardin, "Just and the Unjust," 116.
[58] Peirce, *Morality Tales*, 315, speaks of this phenomenon as a "paradox."

function itself continued at the same time to operate through means that were now more direct than before. Misconduct of government servants and of *qāḍī*s could be referred directly to the sultan or the Porte's Office of Complaints. What is remarkable about this conception and practice of governance is that, far from depending on an ethic of desirable and fair conduct of institutions (or constitutions), it was grounded in a different ethic seen as indispensable for political legitimacy and for the well-being of "state" and society. In other words, it was a culture. For the sultan himself and his Imperial Council and Office of Complaints were all as accessible to the peasant as to the urban elite. It was thus by design that a line of communication was always left open between the tax-paying subjects and the imperial order.[59] The symbiotic existence of government and society fulfilled the requirements of a Sharīʿa-based political community, without which the aims of the Circle of Justice could not be accomplished.

Second, the imperial officials working on the ground were themselves members of the very communities to whom they were appointed as the ruler's representatives, or as the representatives of his regional representative, the governor. The local officials were the only administrative staff who knew their environment, since the highly frequent reshuffling of provincial governors – which, in the first place, was intended precisely as insurance against establishing local connections and a power-base – rendered them incapable of intimately understanding, and therefore dealing with, the local population. This is also why the governor's assembly (*dīwān*), which met regularly to discuss local problems, included the *qāḍī*s, the tax-collectors, the notables, the leading *muftī*s, the neighborhood and guild *shaykh*s, and a host of other figures from the populace.[60] These local officials were therefore subject to intersecting interests whereby the loyalties they may have otherwise shown to the sultan and empire would be mitigated and counterbalanced by the local stakes they had in maintaining their own social, economic and moral networks.[61] Indeed, the local *qāḍī*s, *shaykh*s, *muftī*s and even tax-farmers sat in the assembly as defenders of their communities' interests, which latter had justified their appointment to that assembly in the first place.

[59] Zarinebaf-Shahr, "Women," 85. [60] Marcus, *Middle East*, 82.

[61] Peirce, *Morality Tales*, 330. Marcus, *Middle East*, 79, 82, observes that these local officials were essential for the central government's rule over the provinces. "Unlike the transient Ottoman officials, the local leaders had roots and followings in the city, and were familiar with the inner workings of the community. Their local networks of control gave them the means to assist the government or to undermine it ... While they participated in the Ottoman system of rule as loyal auxiliaries accountable to higher authority, the local leaders were not submissive creatures given to total control from above" (*ibid.*, 84).

Third, and hardly dissociated from the two foregoing considerations, the loyalty of government servants to the sovereign was itself enshrined in the imperatives of the Circle of Justice. Yet, in order to realize these imperatives, *siyāsa* required that a supplement be made to the Sharīʿa in what was known as the *qānūn*. The latter often merely asserted the provisions of religious law in an effort not only to place emphasis on such provisions but also to depict the sultanic will as Sharīʿa-minded. In these instances, the bid for legitimacy is unmistakable. But the *qānūn* did add to the religious law, especially in areas having to do with public order, the bedrock of any successful regime. Public order was enforced by extra-*sharʿī* legislation pertaining to highway robbery, theft, bodily injury, homicide, adultery and fornication (and accusation thereof), usury, taxation, land tenure, and categorically all "disturbers of the peace."[62] With a view toward a strict enforcement of these extra-*sharʿī* laws, the *qānūn* permitted torture (mainly to extract confession from thieves) and the execution of highway robbers by the Sultan's executive authority. Legalized usury, extra-judicial taxes and torture were perhaps the most objectionable pieces of legislation in the view of the jurists. The latter, along with several Şeyhülislams (Ar. Shaykh al-Islāms), often militated against the *qānūn*, and particularly, it seems, against these three provisions.[63] The jurist's objections notwithstanding, the *qānūn* – in its thin but diverse substance – was mostly seen, and accepted, as an integral part of the legal culture, and as an extra-judicial element that was required – after all – by the *siyāsa sharʿiyya* itself.[64]

The Sharīʿa and the *qānūn* had far more in common than they differed upon. True, substantive *qānūn* transgressions upon the Sharīʿa did occur,[65] but the *qāḍī*s and *muftī*s ignored them whenever they could.[66] More remarkable, however, were the similarities between the two. As Peirce has perceptively noted, both the *qānūn* and Ḥanafite law recognized, each in its own sphere but also mutually, a cumulative tradition: the later school texts (and in particular those of the Ḥanafite school, adopted as the official *madhhab* of the Ottomans) never abrogated the earlier ones, and the founding fathers' doctrines continued to be enmeshed in the much later *fatwā* literature and author-jurist compilations.[67] The *qānūn* too was a cumulative discourse, each sultan propounding his own decrees while largely maintaining the sultanic laws of his predecessors. To be

[62] Gerber, *State, Society*, 62–63. For a similar situation in Java, see Ball, *Indonesian Legal History*, 37–39.
[63] Heyd, *Studies*, 152–57, 192–93; Gerber, *State, Society*, 63.
[64] Gerber, *State, Society*, 64–65, 77. [65] Heyd, *Studies*, 180–83.
[66] Gerber, *State, Society*, 64–65; Heyd, *Studies*, 191–92. [67] Hallaq, *Authority*, 57–120.

sustainable, it was in the nature of these cumulative legal traditions to integrate into their structure the viability and necessity of juridical difference. The concept of individual *ijtihād* in the legal schools constituted an analogue to the individual sultanic will that produced different *qānūn*s at different times and places. The internal differences exhibited by the two traditions were clearly intended to accommodate the local and regional differences throughout the Empire. Just as the Sharīʿa insisted on local custom as a guiding principle of the *fiqh*'s application, the *qānūn*, in its various compilations, catered to the needs of particular towns, districts and provinces. *Qānūnnāme*s were issued at each of these levels, as well as at the universal level of the Empire. And like the Sharīʿa law, the *qānūn* developed structural mechanisms to accommodate change and to respond to diachronic and synchronic geographical variations. Finally, and no less importantly, both systems viewed their own laws as a "statement of the limits of the tolerable rather than a set of inflexible rules to be imposed regardless of circumstances."[68]

What is striking about the *qānūn*, and consistent with the Ottoman policy of allowing the widest scope for Sharīʿa justice, is the fact that the *qāḍī* stood as the exclusive agent of the *qānūn*'s enforcement. On the ground, he was the ultimate administrator and final interpreter of the *qānūn*, which was unwavering in reiterating the decree that no punishment could be meted out without a trial by a *qāḍī*; and indeed, evidence from court records overwhelmingly shows that the decision to punish was exclusively the *qāḍī*'s, and that the meting out of penalties was normally the province of executive authority. The *qānūn*'s decree, frequently restated in the *qānūnnāme*s of several succeeding sultans, in effect constituted a direct prohibition against conduct by government servants that might lead to injustice being inflicted upon the civilian population.[69] The *qānūn* of Suleyman the Lawgiver,[70] for example, states that the "executive officials shall not imprison nor injure any person without the cognizance

[68] Peirce, *Morality Tales*, 122.

[69] Heyd, *Studies*, 177: To achieve the aim of preventing oppression of executive authority, the *qānūnnāme*s "had to be brought to the knowledge of the people, so that every citizen would be aware of his rights or, more correctly, of the limits to the rights of the authorities. For this reason the cadis or governors to whom they were sent were often explicitly ordered to have them read out to the public. For 120 *akçe* people could, in the sixteenth and seventeenth centuries, obtain a copy of a *qānūnāme* from the Central Government, and any citizen could, for a smaller fee, ask the local law-court for a certified copy of a *ʿadāletnāme* [a sultanic rescript of justice], so that he might present it wherever necessary to prove his rights." In the *ʿadāletnāme*, a new sultan confirmed his "wish to see justice done to all his subjects, particularly the poor and the helpless, and strictly forbidding all sorts of oppression by government officials" (*Ibid.*, 150, n. 4). Also see İnalcık, "Suleiman the Lawgiver," 105.

[70] İnalcık, "Suleiman the Lawgiver," 111–26.

of the [Sharīʿa] judge. And they shall collect a fine according to [the nature of] a person's offense and they shall take no more [than is due]. If they do, the judge shall rule on the amount of the excess and restore it [to the victim]."[71] The *qānūn* therefore upheld the Sharīʿa by enhancing and supplementing its position and provisions, while the Sharīʿa, on the other hand, required the intervention of sultanic justice. This complementary duality was endlessly expressed in various decrees and letters in the judicial discourse of the Ottoman authorities, be they Sultans, Şeyhülislams, viziers or *qāḍī*s: justice had always to be carried out "according to the Sharʿ and *qānūn*."[72]

4. Judicial administration under the Ottomans

The Ottoman regime saw itself as the legatee of Islamic Turco-Persianate political culture on the one hand, and, more pronouncedly, of the Arabicate legal tradition on the other.[73] It is also less acknowledged, but nonetheless significant, that a considerable portion of the manpower recruited to operate the Royal Palace originally hailed from south-east Europe, particularly the Balkans. The first two elements directly, and the third obliquely, combined to produce an Empire and a legal system that shared much in common with their predecessors, but also differed from them in some important, if not fundamental, respects.

The differences were mostly the result of conscious and highly deliberate efforts to implement changes, although some of these differences may have been the by-products of other forces. A central change that was characteristically effected by the Ottomans, but not by other dynasties of the Sunnite world, was that they adopted the Ḥanafite school as the official law of the Empire. The other schools never vanished of course, and retained followers – albeit decreasingly – in the population as well as in the judiciary. The farther a province lay from Istanbul, and the less strategic it was, the less influenced it was by this policy. But provinces and regions adjacent to the capital were affected significantly. Every major city or provincial capital in the Empire was headed by a Ḥanafite *qāḍī al-quḍāt*, a chief justice, who appointed deputies in several quarters of the city as well as throughout the province (appointment of such deputy-judges by the chief *qāḍī* of the city or region was a common practice).[74] Some of

[71] Peirce, *Morality Tales*, 119, 327.
[72] Jennings, "Limitations," 166, 168; Peirce, *Morality Tales*, 119.
[73] İnalcık, "Suleiman the Lawgiver," 107–08; Kozlowski, "Imperial Authority," 356–57. On the incorporation of Mamlūk and Dhul-Qādir criminal and other codes in Ottoman *qānūnnāme*s, see Heyd, *Studies*, 38–53.
[74] For the North African Mālikites, see, e.g., Ḥaṭṭāb, *Mawāhib*, VI, 107.

these deputy-judges were non-Ḥanafites who held court in neighborhoods and large villages whose inhabitants were either Shāfiʿite, Ḥanbalite or Mālikite. But the official system and government apparatus were Ḥanafite to the core, and any advancement in a government legal career (under the Ottomans the most prestigious and powerful of all legal arenas) presupposed Ḥanafite legal education as well as membership in the Ḥanafite school. If the chief *qāḍīs* appointed from Istanbul were all Ḥanafites, it was because the legists who ran the judiciary were products of the exclusively Ḥanafite royal *madrasas* of Istanbul. And in order to rise to the highest levels of judicial and government careers, they had to stay Ḥanafite through and through. The effects of this policy were clear: the legal profession, law students and legists of non-Ḥanafite persuasion were encouraged to, and indeed did, migrate to the Ḥanafite school in search of career opportunities. For instance, in Greater Syria, the majority of the population in general and the population of the legists in particular were Shāfiʿites at the time of the Ottoman conquest in 922–23/1516–17,[75] whereas by the end of the nineteenth century only a tiny minority of Shāfiʿites remained in that region, the rest having become Ḥanafites.

Such effects constituted the culmination of a deliberate effort to create uniformity in the subject populations, and to streamline the administration of justice throughout the Empire if possible, but certainly throughout each of its main provinces.[76] The age of uniformity had begun, in the Ottoman Empire no less than in Europe.[77] Uniformity, in other words, entailed low costs of governing, management and control, for, after all, economic efficiency of domination was a desideratum of any form of rule.

An indirect effect of adopting the Ḥanafite *madhhab* as the official school of the Empire was the considerable marginalization of legists

[75] Mandaville, "Muslim Judiciary," 7–8, 67–68, 68a (no pagination), 85, speaks of the predominance of Shāfiʿite judges and deputy-judges in the Mamlūk judiciary of Syria and Egypt. The Shāfiʿites also obtained a monopoly over the *imāma* of the Umayyad Mosque of Damascus, a politically sensitive public office. Furthermore, when "posts were filled by members of the judiciary, it was done by members of the leading families usually belonging to the Shāfiʿī school." Yet, the Mamlūks never made of Shāfiʿism what the Ottomans made of Ḥanafism. Each city had chief justices belonging to the four schools, and no Shāfiʿite hierarchy was developed in legal education and judicial administration, all of which are characteristic Ottoman developments.

[76] Peirce, *Morality Tales*, 287.

[77] Although achieving a higher form of uniformity in Europe required higher levels of coercion and violence, which the Ottomans tried to avoid. But it must be stressed that the forms and level of uniformity that the Ottomans attempted to achieve, and largely did achieve in the fifteenth and sixteenth centuries (and Europe between the early seventeenth and nineteenth centuries), were undoubtedly unprecedented in Afro-Eurasia. Arguably, during much of the sixteenth and seventeenth centuries, the Ottoman Empire and Europe mirrored each other in terms of administration and bureaucracy (which in Europe continued to develop exponentially as the foundations and defining features of modernity).

from the Arabic-speaking provinces, for they had little, if any, role to play in the administrative bureaucracy centered in Istanbul.[78] The same appears to have been true of the Balkans. Not only were the high-ranking administrators in the capital all "Turks" (*Rūm*), raised by the Istanbul elites and educated in the royal *madrasa*s of the same city,[79] but so was virtually every chief *qāḍī* appointed to run the judicial affairs of the Arab provinces, including Syria and Egypt. Syrian and Egyptian *muftī*s and *qāḍī*s received their education locally, particularly in Egypt. These *muftī*s, while enjoying local prestige by virtue of their erudition and religious–social standing, remained outside the pale of officialdom just as the locally trained *qāḍī*s could aspire to no higher position than that of deputy-*qāḍī* under the "Turkish" chief justice.

Placing the administration of the Empire's affairs in the hands of "Turks" was not a nationalist act, however. Of distinctly European origin, nationalism was not on the minds of Ottomans before the second half of the nineteenth century, and even then just dimly so. Rather, the Turkification of Ottoman administration aimed at creating a unified and centralized bureaucracy that could efficiently manage a diverse Empire with multiple ethnicities, religious denominations, languages, cultures and an endless variety of sub-cultures. The model of a "Turkish," Istanbul-educated chief justice dispatched to run a province's judiciary with the indispensable assistance of local and locally trained *qāḍī*s was one that found a telling parallel in the multi-layered *qānūnnāme*s that the Ottomans excelled in promulgating. The "universal" *qānūn*s aimed to create an overarching unity within the Empire as a whole, while those *qānūn*s issued for cities or even specific courts (usually termed *resim*s or *firmān*s) were intended to impose law and order while according great sensitivity to the cultural uniqueness of the recipients. The provincial *qānūn*s represented a middle stage between the two, striving to balance both the local context of the city and that of the Empire as a whole. Just as the universal *qānūn*s operated in conjunction with the Istanbul-based legal education (both emitting centralized values of "Turkish" administration), the regional–local *qānūn*s and the indigenous deputy-*qāḍī*s represented Istanbul's awareness of, and attention to, regional differences and local variety. It was these macrocosmic and microcosmic pulls, a seeming paradox, that created a dialectic of justice which made Ottoman rule unique when compared not only to its Islamic predecessors, but also to its contemporary neighbors to the east (including the Far East) and the west.

[78] Gerber, *State, Society*, 86. [79] Zilfi, *Politics of Piety*, 61.

Centralized bureaucracy, judicial administration and legal education in the capital were momentous developments that served the Ottomans well during the first three centuries of their rule and they had considerable effects on the course of events leading to the Empire's encounter with the modern West. We shall deal with the impact of these effects in Part III, but here we need only stress the newness and tenacity of Ottoman centralization at all levels of judicial administration.

First, the fixing of a geographical locale for administration was more characteristic of the Ottomans than of any of their Muslim predecessors or counterparts. Most, if not all, dynasties changed the location of their capitals every so often. But once Istanbul was taken from the Byzantine emperor in 857/1453, it became the Ottomans' capital until the termination of their caliphate in 1342/1924. This same pattern may be observed in the case of law courts. The Ottomans were the first in Islamic history to commit the court to a particular residence, a courthouse so to speak. *Qāḍī*s could no longer hold their *majlis* in the yards of mosques, in *madrasa*s or in their residences.[80] Existing "public" buildings were modified for this purpose, and the number of courts was increased significantly when compared to the pre-Ottoman period.[81] Whereas it was typical for Mamlūk and pre-Mamlūk cities to have in or around the commercial city-center a total of four courts, each representing one of the four schools,[82] the Ottomans had several around the city, usually in large neighborhoods. The Ottomans were also the first, it seems, to bestow on the *qāḍī*'s *dīwān*, the court's register, a public status. No longer could the *qāḍī*s keep these registers in their private custody, a fact which explains why so many *dīwān*s have managed to survive from the Ottoman era but precious few from earlier periods.[83]

Fixing the physical site of the court was an administrative act of the first order. The court had become at one and the same time the smallest unit and the core of the Empire's administration. For it was the court that became the destination of sultanic *qānūn*s and *firmān*s, and it was from the court that these decrees were promulgated in the name of the sovereign.[84] The court was also the locus of fiscal administration, where taxes paid and

[80] As was the practice under the late Mamlūks and since the first/seventh century. For court location under the Mamlūks, see Mandaville, "Muslim Judiciary," 71–72.

[81] Hanna, "Administration of Courts," 50, reports that tenth/sixteenth-century Cairo had fifteen courthouses throughout the city, allocating on average one courthouse for every 20,000 inhabitants; Hanna, *Making Big Money*, xxi.

[82] Mandaville, "Muslim Judiciary," 72. Deputy-*qāḍī*s did at times hold their court in their neighborhoods, especially in their own houses, but this was not an institutionalized practice, as these deputy-judges could change the location of their *majlis* at will.

[83] Hallaq, "*Qāḍī*'s *Dīwān*," 434–36.

[84] Heyd, *Studies*, 151–52.

taxes due were recorded and monitored. And in order to commit the provincial court system to a regularized contact with the capital – a centralizing act – the provincial chief justice not only was an Istanbul man and a "Turk," but was also rotated every one to three years to work in various cities, including the capital.[85] This policy ensured that the top provincial judge was nearly always from Istanbul or, at the very least, thoroughly inculcated in its political and legal culture, and thus loyal to the dynasty that ruled from it. This structured practice was unprecedented, having been made possible by another unprecedented process, namely, coopting the legal training of the Empire's judicial servants from the private sphere of the jurists and concentrating it in a permanent, affluent, powerful and ever-growing capital.[86]

Furthermore, the court became, probably for the first time, financially independent and a source of income for the imperial treasury. Whereas pre-Ottoman *qāḍīs* received salaries from the government, as well as public stipends which they disbursed to the officials that staffed the courts, the Ottoman judges depended on fees that were paid directly by court users, including, probably, litigants.[87] Most probably for the first time in Islamic history, *qāḍīs* were forbidden from hearing cases that did not involve formal petitioning of the court, the purpose being that fees had first to be paid and a formal record of the case maintained. Also for the first time, at least in Egypt, and almost certainly in most other provinces, all marriages were to be recorded in court, and a fee was to be levied.[88] At work here was a double-pronged policy of introducing writing as a means of control, and of regularly replenishing the central treasury.

In newly conquered Egypt and Crete, among other places, fees began to be levied on those marriage contracts that were attested and registered at court. Gradually, and within a few years of Egypt's occupation, fees came to apply to many more transactions, such as certification of divorces, manumission, business partnerships, transferring testimony, and so on.

[85] Rotating chief justices was to some extent a Mamlūk practice, although it was neither regular nor limited to a fixed period. See Mandaville, "Muslim Judiciary," 21–22, 62. It seems that, with the passage of time, the average length of judicial appointment under the Ottomans became shorter, reaching one year by the end of the twelfth/eighteenth century. See Marcus, *Middle East*, 79.

[86] See chapter 3, above.

[87] Whereas Peirce, *Morality Tales*, 285, does not think that in Aintab of the 950s/1540s legal fees were charged for routine use of the court, Hanna ("Administration of Courts," 47) argues otherwise with regard to Cairo of the tenth/sixteenth and eleventh/seventeenth centuries. See also Marcus, *Middle East*, 106, who reports that in twelfth/eighteenth-century Aleppo, the court claimed 10 percent of all sums contested in legal suits. These exorbitant fees, which were seen as such by the city's population of that time of crises, are not documented in earlier centuries.

[88] Hanna, "Administration of Courts," 46–47, 50; Heyd, *Studies*, 153.

By various imperial decrees, the scribes of the Empire's courts, who themselves wrote these attestations, were to charge graded fees depending on the document drafted. The fees paid to the court were distributed – according to ratios specified in the *qānūn*s – among the *qāḍī*, the scribe, the court treasurer and other officials of the court. A portion was allocated to the chief justice of the province, and another was sent to the imperial treasury.[89] Thus, the Ottoman systematic and systemic policy to centralize was at once combined with the policy of optimizing revenues for the capital. Expanding the authority, prestige and scope of the law courts was an essential step toward streamlining not only revenues but also, and no less importantly, the administrative mechanisms without which, after all, revenues could never have been generated either systematically or regularly.

It is difficult to assess what the imposition of court fees meant for the average individual. For the poor these fees must have meant less accessibility to the law courts and perhaps prevented them from obtaining necessary legal documents, although we have no direct evidence of this other than the occasional and short-lived critique initially voiced by some observers upon the introduction of these fees.[90] Yet, the fees could not have been exorbitant due to the undeniable fact that the number of courts as well as the volume of business they handled were dramatically increased under the Ottomans, which attests, if anything, to the success of the Ottoman policy of making the law court the vehicle of government control and taxation, and the hub of social and economic conflict-resolution. But if the courts were the government's choice and medium of control, the government itself was bound by the court's rules which were paradigmatically Sharīʿa-based. The highest manifestation of this rule of law was that, when the government aimed to take action against individuals, confiscate property or assert for itself any right, it addressed itself to the court and sought the *qāḍī*'s permission to do so.[91] And the law of the court was, with minor *qānūn* supplements, that of the Sharīʿa. It was the Sharīʿa, and nothing but the Sharīʿa, that constituted the overarching and permanent law of the Empire and the highest authority by which to rule.[92]

89 Hanna, "Administration of Courts," 46–47.
90 *Ibid.*, 47, 55: "The fact that fees were paid for the services the court offered meant that the lower strata of the population were probably either excluded from or at least not encouraged to use the services as readily as others."
91 Gerber, *State, Society*, 139. 92 See the apt description in Marcus, *Middle East*, 102–03.

Part II

The law: an outline

6 The legal pillars of religion

1. Introduction

Islam, according to one important Prophetic tradition, "was built upon five [foundations]: [a] the double-testimony that there is no god but God and that Muhammad is the Messenger of God (*shahādatayn*); [b] performance of the prayer (*ṣalāt*); [c] payment of alms-tax (*zakāt*); [d] performance of pilgrimage (*ḥajj*); and [e] fasting (*ṣawm*) during the month of Ramadan."[1] Apart from the first, a foundational theological pronouncement of faith accompanied by neither substantive nor procedural rules, the rest occupy a prominent place in the legal literature, having for the entire history of Islam been regarded as the bedrock of religion and religious practice, melding the theological with the legal. It is not without good reason that they, together with purification (*ṭahāra*) – a preface to prayer – have come to constitute the opening chapters of legal works, occupying as much as one-quarter to one-third of the entire body of these works (see Appendix A).

These performative works are constructionist, in that they are constituted and created by the believers as devotional acts for the purpose of fulfilling a covenant with God. In this sense they stand apart from the rest of the law, where acts relate to worldly objects and persons, to Muslims and non-Muslims, where the intention and *raison d'être* is to acquire or sell property, marry, divorce, free slaves, sue for damages, etc. Their priority in the overall corpus of the law is reflected in their universal placement at the beginning of legal treatises, a long-standing tradition of arranging legal subject-matter that no jurist has ever violated. But the placement was not merely an emblem of symbolic importance and priority; rather, it had a function which made this ritualistic grouping a logical and functional antecedent. The function was subliminal as well as psychological, laying as it did the foundations for achieving willing obedience to the law that was

[1] Ṣanʿānī, *Muṣannaf*, III, 42; Māwardī, *Ḥāwī*, IV, 4; [Miṣrī, *Reliance*, 278, 659]. See also various Shīʿite versions of this *ḥadīth*, in ʿĀmilī, *Wasāʾil*, I, 25–27.

to follow, that is, the law regulating human affairs. Prayer, with its ever-changing bodily positions, signals submission to a higher power, and its recitals, invocations and incantations, expresses the need for that power's contentment and pleasure with the deeds and comportment of the believer. By the same token, fasting compels identification with the suffering of others, generating compassion for, and humility before, other human beings. It represents an acknowledgment of gratitude to God for the bounties He bestowed and continues to bestow on humankind, enabling people to enjoy earthly and material pleasures. So too does almsgiving engender empathy toward the needy and the poor, reminding the believers of the nominal ownership that whatever earthly wealth they possess, its real Owner can claim it back at His own discretion. This cumulative enhancement of the recognition of God's generosity is crowned by the demanding act of pilgrimage, which exhibits the believer's humility before God and His creation.

Modern scholarship, in the West as well as in the Muslim East, has drawn a line of separation between the legal pillars of religion and the rest of *fiqh*, regarding the former as "merely" ritualistic, pertaining to the "private sphere" of religious belief, and the latter as constituting the law "proper." As we saw in chapter 4, the Sharīʿa cannot be understood, nor could it have operated in any social context, without its moral bearings. And Islamic morality, legal, social or otherwise, traces its sources in large measure to the performative force of the five pillars. The morality that activated willing submission to the authority of the law was constituted and constructed by these performative acts.[2] That they were given prime weight and precedence is testimony not only to their ritualistic religious significance, but also, if not primarily, to their grounding moral force. To oust these pillars from the *fiqh* is to disengage the moral foundations of the law, to render it devoid of the most compelling impulse for jural observance.

At the foundation of all *fiqh* norms lies the general concept of *taklīf*,[3] a charge of duty, responsibility and right that constitutes the lot of all humans. Every human being is assumed to be a *mukallaf*, that is, subject to *taklīf*, unless there is a lawful impediment that gives rise to an exemption. But in order to account for the differences in the human state – for instance, between an embryo and a mature adult, or between the healthy and the infirm, the sane and the insane – the *fiqh* elaborated general concepts that typify these states in a system of categories. The locus and substrate of *taklīf* is *ahliyya*, the general capacity to oblige and be obligated

[2] Further on this theme, see Hallaq, "Fashioning the Moral Subject."
[3] [Miṣrī, *Reliance*, 40–46.]

by other humans (e.g., in contractual transactions) as well as before God (e.g., in ritual performances). This general capacity is known as *ahliyyat al-wujūb*, the quality that enables humans to be subject to the entire range of rights and duties, privileges and obligations.[4] General capacity, assumed to emanate from the *dhimma* of persons (that is, persons who are charged with a duty of care, fiduciary trust, observance, liability, etc.), is however subject to "natural" impediments. The embryo (*janīn*), being a soul (*nafs*), is potentially a subject of general capacity, but the lack of complete formation and of physical independence as a person disqualifies it from the full status of *ahliyyat al-wujūb*. This explains why an embryo is not subject to obligations, but is capable of inheriting. *Ahliyyat al-adā'*, on the other hand, is a full legal capacity that entitles an individual to the entire range of rights, and permits engagement in obligations and their execution.[5] This "performative" capacity presupposes mental and physical maturity, the two essential prerequisites that, when jointly present, define the notion of majority (*bulūgh*). Although physical maturity is a substrate of its mental counterpart, it is taken as the measure of mental development that shows the person to be responsible for her acts, capable of constructive act-performances in her own interest and in the interest of her family, group, community, etc. This ability, *rushd*, is a desideratum, a state of being that is distinguished from prior stages of development that require guardians to act on behalf of their charges, those who lack *rushd*. The absence of *rushd* may thus be the function of minor age, or it may also connote insanity, foolhardiness and stupidity (*sufh*). The absence of *rushd* is furthermore subsumed under discernment (*tamyīz*), i.e., the ability to comprehend legal obligations but without the attainment of a full performative capacity. Thus, *tamyīz* is said to begin at the age of seven, at which time one attains a level of obligation that is absent in earlier years of life. For example, a child can be disciplined by members of his family at the age of ten if he refuses to pray.[6]

2. Purification and prayer (*ṭahāra*, *ṣalāt*)

Purification, wrote one jurist, is the "key to prayer," prayer being "the most certain of Islam's pillars after the *shahādatayn*."[7] Although it is not itself one of the pillars (*arkān*) of religion, purification as a juristic subject occupies a relatively prominent position, amply attested by the fact that its treatment in legal works occupies space roughly equal to that of each of the

[4] [*Ibid.*, 43–44.] [5] [*Ibid.*, 44–46.] [6] [*Ibid.*, 109.]

[7] Buhūtī, *Rawḍ*, 15. [For *ṭahāra*, see Miṣrī, *Reliance*, 49–100; Ibn Rushd, *Distinguished Jurist's Primer*, I, 1–95; Marghīnānī, *Hidāya*, I, 5–77.]

four "pillars,"[8] namely, prayer, alms-tax, fasting and pilgrimage (see Appendix A). A prerequisite for the performance of prayer and a condition for its validity, purification's juristic prescriptions rest on the core Quranic verse 5:6: "O you who believe: when you rise up for prayer, wash your faces, your hands up to the elbows, and lightly rub your heads and wash your feet up to the ankles. And if you are unclean, purify yourselves."[9] Juristic works differ greatly in their detailed prescriptions as to how and what to wash. It is generally agreed, however, that washing the face must cover (vertically) the skin beginning from the hair-line of the forehead down to the chin and the curve of the lower jaw, and (horizontally) the frontal surface between and including the earlobes. No more than a quarter of the beard need be washed, if it is long. However, short or long, the beard where it meets the chin must certainly be cleansed. Elbows and ankles, most jurists insist, must be included.[10] "Washing" in the Quranic verse is construed as letting water flow over a surface; it does not involve "scrubbing," or "rubbing." It merely requires water to be in touch (*iṣāba*) with the surface.[11]

Purification is not limited to the believer's body, but rather extends to his clothing, the place in which he intends to pray, and the very body of water used for washing, including the vessels (*āniya*) that carry it. Bodily excretions, including fluids secreted with or without sexual arousal, as well as pus and vomit, are agents of impurity, and thus must be washed away. So are blood and wine, unless the latter has fermented into vinegar. The hides of unlawfully slaughtered animals, and of dead animals that have not been slaughtered, including that of the dog, are impure, unless they have been tanned[12] (though tanning, considered a purifying agent because it removes from the hide traces of blood, fat and hair, is ineffective in eliminating the inherent and irremovable ritual impurities of pig hide). Vessels made of tanned leather as well as all metal containers are deemed pure, unless they are made of, or plated with, gold or silver.[13] The use of these is prohibited, for men and women, be it for purposes of prayer or otherwise.

Impurities are of two types, one caused by bodily secretions (*ḥadath*), and the other by external factors, generally termed *najas*.[14] The *ḥadath* is

8 For example, in Maqdisī's *ʿUdda*, the chapter of purification occupies about 40 (21%) out of the 190 pages devoted to the "pillars," whereas in Ḥalabī's *Multaqā*, the proportion is 43 (19%) out of 225 pages.

9 For an extensive analysis of this verse and of purification more generally, see Katz, *Body of Text*, esp. 59–99.

10 Ḥalabī, *Multaqā*, I, 11–12.

11 *Al-Fatāwā al-Hindiyya*, I, 3.

12 Māwardī, *Ḥāwī*, I, 57.

13 Shaʿrānī, *Mīzān*, I, 134; Buhūtī, *Sharḥ*, I, 25; [Miṣrī, *Reliance*, 56].

14 [Miṣrī, *Reliance*, 70 ff., 95 ff.; Marghīnānī, *Hidāya*, I, 14–19, 69–75; Ibn Rushd, *Distinguished Jurist's Primer*, I, 32–40, 79–88.]

in turn divided into major (*akbar*) and minor (*aṣghar*) impurities, the former including those caused by spermatic excretion, sexual penetration, sexual fluid from the woman, post-natal bleeding and menstruation. Minor impurities, on the other hand, include urine, feces, gas, spermatic excretion without sexual arousal, and vaginal excretion. Both *ḥadath* and *najas* can be purified, unless they are part of a substance that is inherently incapable of purification, e.g., urine and pig.

Water is the sole agent of purification.[15] In its naturally clean state, it is the supreme agent, for it is both pure in itself and capable of purifying (*ṭahūr*) when applied to other objects. A second-class agent is the *ṭāhir* water, considered thus because while it is pure in itself it cannot purify other objects (according to the Mālikites, Shāfiʿites and Ḥanbalites).[16] The *ṭāhir* category also includes *ṭahūr* water that has already been used for purification, as well as water that has changed in color or odor due to its commingling with pure substances, such as rose water. The Ḥanafites are alone in regarding *ṭāhir* water as capable of purifying other objects. The third major agent is polluted water, deemed ritually impure. The Ḥanafites classified water in terms of its movement, flowing water being superior, *ṭahūr* and incapable of being polluted in strong currents. On the other hand, water from a slow current – where a straw thrown into it does not move – is not *ṭāhir*.[17] Generally, there is a relationship between impurity and the volume of water involved, as anything less than two *qulla*s (a total of 216 litres) is made ritually impure by filth having fallen into it. Large bodies of water, including running water, are not affected. This explains why one of the methods of purifying water is to augment it with larger amounts of purifying (*ṭahūr*) water.

The foremost condition for the validity of ablution – as in all forms of worship – is intention (*niyya*), according to the majority of jurists.[18] The worshiper must have the intention to purify herself when embarking upon washing the face, the first step in the performance. *Niyya* occurs in the heart (*qalb*), and need not be accompanied by verbal pronouncements, although some jurists require verbal confirmation. It is an internal state, giving acts of worship their identity and separating them from other identical acts that do not belong to the category of worship, e.g., washing the face or handing over money. The latter might be either an act of paying *zakāt* (requiring *niyya*) or simply paying for a purchased object, just as the former might be either an act of *ṭahāra* or just a mundane act of refreshing

15 [Miṣrī, *Reliance*, 52 ff.; Marghīnānī, *Hidāya*, I, 25–42, 69–75; Ibn Rushd, *Distinguished Jurist's Primer*, I, 20–31.]

16 Shaʿrānī, *Mīzān*, I, 128–29. 17 Qāḍīkhān, *Fatāwā*, I, 4.

18 Māwardī, *Ḥāwī*, I, 87–92; [Miṣrī, *Reliance*, 60; Ibn Rushd, *Distinguished Jurist's Primer*, I, 3–4].

oneself. *Niyya* constitutes an awareness of, and confidence in, the individual act as fulfilling a particular purpose that is categorized as an act of worship. Acts that cannot be mistaken for any other actions do not require *niyya*.[19]

A constitutive element of prayer, and without which prayer can never be valid, *niyya* is required to affirm one's consciousness of the obligatory nature of prayer and to make clear which of the five daily prayers one means to perform.[20] Another constitutive element is the Opening Invocation (*takbīrat al-iḥrām*), consisting of the declaration "God is Great," which is intended to remind the performer of the gravity of this act of worship, of the exalted and magnificent status of the One to whom one is praying.[21] It is recommended that one pronounce the Opening Supplication (*du'ā' al-istiftāḥ*), which announces one's monotheistic faith and loyalty to the One and only God.[22] This pronouncement may be followed by another, seeking refuge in God against Satan (*ta'awwudh*).[23] At this point, and upon every act of bowing down, the *Fātiḥa*, the opening chapter of the Quran, is recited in full, and concluded with the *ta'mīn*, the solemn ratification "Amen." Upon the first and/or second act of bowing down, it is recommended for the believer to recite a Quranic chapter, however short it may be. Bowing down (*rak'a*), in its minimal form, requires as much bending as one needs to place one's palms on one's knees, this being followed by a pause, then praise to the Lord (*tasbīḥ*). When standing up, the body's posture must be perfectly straight, so that this position is not confused with bowing. Prostration (*sujūd*), on the other hand, requires the exposed part of the forehead to touch the ground, pausing in this position for at least a moment. To validly qualify as a prostration, the head must be lower than one's lower back. Any physical impediment preventing full prostration, e.g., pregnancy or a back injury, waives the requirement inasmuch as one is unable to perform it. "Stacking up pillows so that one can place his forehead on them is not necessary. One bows to the extent that one can."[24] At the end of the prayer, one must sit back to perform the Testimony of Faith (*tashahhud*), with one's posterior on the ground and the left leg crossed over beneath and beyond the right leg.

Intended to establish a certain connection and closeness (*qurba*) between the worshiper and her God, prayer, as I have already intimated, is the most important of all religious acts after the *shahādatayn*. Anyone

[19] Powers, *Intent*, 32–33, 49–50; Hallaq, "Fashioning the Moral Subject."
[20] [Miṣrī, *Reliance*, 127 ff.; Marghīnānī, *Hidāya*, I, 104–05; Ibn Rushd, *Distinguished Jurist's Primer*, I, 132.]
[21] [Miṣrī, *Reliance*, 129 f.; Ibn Rushd, *Distinguished Jurist's Primer*, I, 133–35; Marghīnānī, *Hidāya*, I, 109–11.]
[22] [Miṣrī, *Reliance*, 130 ff.] [23] [*Ibid.*, 132.] [24] [*Ibid.*, 138]; Ḥiṣnī, *Kifāya*, I, 109–10.

who deliberately desists from praying stands accused of renouncing his religion. Anyone who is lazy enough to neglect the performance of this duty must be disciplined, with repeated failures on this account amounting to an act of heresy.[25] Prayer is so fundamental that it has the distinction of being the only ritual performance that can claim to be the constant companion of the believer. Requiring a minimum of five performative acts a day for the entire duration of adult life, prayer exceeds any of the other four obligations: the *shahādatayn*, pilgrimage (required once in a lifetime), fasting (once a year in Ramadan plus some optional periods) and alms-tax (once a year). Each and every sane Muslim adult must begin this regimen of prayer, for all practical and educational purposes, starting from ten years of age – even though adulthood technically begins at puberty.[26]

3. Alms-tax (*zakāt*)

Among all the "branches" of the law, *zakāt*[27] is unique in that it has a dualistic character: on the one hand, it is an integral part of religious ritual and one of the five "pillars" of religion; on the other hand, it functions as a substantive legal sphere, constituting itself as a "tax law." Literally meaning growth, *zakāt* bears the extended connotation of paying out of the growth on one's property with a view to purifying that property. In one sense, *zakāt* is the financial/material parallel of ritual *ṭahāra*: just as washing removes ritual filth, *zakāt* removes the moral burden that accompanies the garnering of wealth.[28] In other words, to be wealthy is potentially a moral liability that requires dispensation, and the means of such dispensation is the sharing of that wealth with those who are in need. The sharing of excess in wealth with the Quranically specified beneficiaries (the poor, the needy and the wayfarers) not only is seen as such a means of purification, but reflects, among other things, the belief that all things ultimately belong to God and that Muslims are the trustees of earthly wealth, accountable for the ways in which they dispose of it. Hoarding wealth is a cause for divine condemnation as well as punishment in the Hereafter.[29]

Zakāt is due on property that is (a) fully owned, precluding freely grazing, wild animals as well as property that is not in the possession (*yad*) of the owner (e.g., an unlawfully appropriated herd, *maghṣūb*).[30]

25 [Miṣrī, *Reliance*, 109; Ibn Rushd, *Distinguished Jurist's Primer*, I, 98–99.]
26 On the same point in fasting, see section 4, below.
27 [Miṣrī, *Reliance*, 244–76; Marghīnānī, *Hidāya*, I, 245–302; Ibn Rushd, *Distinguished Jurist's Primer*, I, 283–329.]
28 [Miṣrī, *Reliance*, 246.] 29 Q. 3:180.
30 On unlawful appropriation in the context of *zakāt*, see Mawāq, *Tāj*, II, 296–97; Ḥaṭṭāb, *Mawāhib*, II, 296.

Derivative from this requirement is the capability of making payment at the time payment is due, since property can perish between the end of the "fiscal" year and the time payment is required (capability, *imkān*, being a legal condition applicable to all the "pillars"). It is also due on property that is (b) capable of growth, such as cattle, agricultural lands and commercial goods. Goods for personal consumption, e.g., animals intended for food, personal clothing and furniture, are exempt. On the other hand, precious metals, such as gold and silver, are taxable since they are commonly used in profit-based enterprises; (c) in excess of subsistence (e.g., food, shelter, household furniture, etc.); or (d) productive for a minimum of one full lunar year, with the exception of agricultural crops and minerals extracted from underground (in which case, *zakāt* is due upon "harvesting" since this in itself constitutes "growth"). Finally, it is due on property that is (e) free of impediments, such as a debt.

Given these conditions, the payment of *zakāt* is obligatory upon every Muslim, male and female, including – according to Mālikites, Shāfiʿites, Ḥanbalites and Twelver-Shīʿites – minor and insane individuals.[31] To be valid, it must be accompanied by *niyya*.[32] Generally, it is levied at the rate of 2.5 percent on the growth of one's wealth, above and beyond the amounts needed for subsistence; however, this rate could reach 10 percent on some agricultural produce according to some jurists. A *niṣāb* is an amount of property below which no *zakāt* can be levied, and it varies according to the genus of property. A property that is between two *niṣāb*s, namely, one that has not reached the next *niṣāb*, is exempt from levy on the differential. For example, the *niṣāb* of camels is five, so a person who owns nine camels would be paying *zakāt* on only the first five. The *niṣāb* of cattle is thirty; of goats forty; of gold twenty *mithqāl*s;[33] of silver a hundred *dirhams*; of crops five *awsāq*;[34] of profit on trade a hundred *dirhams*. The Shāfiʿites and Ḥanbalites require that the *niṣāb* be maintained throughout the year, without interruption. Should a cattle owner have, say, thirty head, one of which dies during the eleventh month of the taxation year, even if only a few hours later a calf is born, she would owe no *zakāt* on her herd for that year. She would owe *zakāt* on this *niṣāb* a year after the birth of that calf, provided there is no diminution in the number for any duration.

The Ḥanafites, Shāfiʿites and Ḥanbalites require the payment of *zakāt* on grazing animals (*sāʾima*) but not on those that subsist on fodder

[31] Saḥnūn, *Mudawwana*, I, 308; Mawāq, *Tāj*, II, 292; Nawawī, *Rawḍa*, II, 3; Ḥalabī, *Multaqā*, I, 169. Ṭūsī, *Khilāf*, I, 316, requires *zakāt* on minors' productive property. [Miṣrī, *Reliance*, 246–47.]

[32] Ṭūsī, *Khilāf*, I, 321; [Miṣrī, *Reliance*, 266].

[33] A *mithqāl* is 4.68 grams. [34] A *wasq* is about 16 kilograms.

(*maʿlūfa*). To be regarded as *maʿlūfa*, the animals must live on fodder for at least six months of each year. The cost of maintaining such animals considerably diminishes the rate of "growth" on them, making the collection of *zakāt* unwarranted. Yet, the Mālikites make no such distinction, and require *zakāt* on all livestock, whether subsisting on fodder or on pasturage. They also differ from the rest of the schools in imposing *zakāt* on labor animals (e.g., those used for plowing and milling).[35]

The rate of *zakāt* paid on camels is as follows: up to twenty-four camels, one goat or sheep for every five camels. In this case, there are four *niṣāb*s as a person who owns twenty-four camels pays on only twenty of them, since the fifth *niṣāb* is not complete; between twenty-five and thirty-five camels, one female camel in its second year (*bint makhāḍ*); between thirty-six and forty-five, one female camel in its third year (*bint labūn*); between forty-six and sixty, one female camel in its fourth year (*ḥiqqa*); between sixty-one and seventy-five, one female camel in its fifth year (*jadhaʿa*); between seventy-six and ninety, two *bint labūn*s; between ninety-one and 120, two *ḥiqqa*s; and exceeding 120, one *bint labūn* for every forty, or one *ḥiqqa* for every fifty.[36]

In all *zakāt* on livestock, the levied animals must be of "average" quality and size, and should not be the best of the herd. The *zakāt* levy on gold and silver is generally 2.5 percent, and so is the production of all types of mines.[37] The rate on agricultural produce[38] is 10 percent if the crops are irrigated by natural resources, but 5 percent if they are irrigated artificially, whether the water is purchased or ported in by paid labor. In *muḍāraba* partnerships,[39] the sleeping partner pays *zakāt* on the principal, but jurists disagree as to who must pay on the profits. The Shāfiʿites assign responsibility entirely to the sleeping partner, whereas the Ḥanafites require the worker to pay for his own share of the gains. In commonly owned and commingled property (*māl mushtarak*), the majority of jurists hold that *zakāt* is due not on the *niṣāb* of the total property owned, but rather on each partner's share.[40] The Shāfiʿites, however, take the position that the *niṣāb* must be based on the total aggregate of property.[41]

35 Mawāq, *Tāj*, II, 256; [Miṣrī, *Reliance*, 250–51].

36 Saḥnūn, *Mudawwana*, I, 252–53; Maqdisī, *ʿUdda*, 122–23; Ḥalabī, *Multaqā*, I, 173; Ṭūsī, *Khilāf*, I, 300–01.

37 Maqdisī, *ʿUdda*, 132; Ḥalabī, *Multaqā*, I, 183–85; [Miṣrī, *Reliance*, 257].

38 The jurists generally agree that dates, grapes, wheat and barley are subject to *zakāt*, but they disagree about most other crops. Cf. Ḥiṣnī, *Kifāya*, I, 176 ff.; Ḥillī, *Sharāʾiʿ*, I, 111 f.; [Miṣrī, *Reliance*, 254 ff.; Marghīnānī, *Hidāya*, I, 283 f.; Ibn Rushd, *Distinguished Jurist's Primer*, I, 291, 294].

39 On the law of *muḍāraba*, see chapter 7, section 4, below.

40 Ṭūsī, *Khilāf*, I, 314.

41 Nawawī, *Rawḍa*, II, 27 ff.; [Miṣrī, *Reliance*, 254].

Finally, another alms-tax, levied on persons and not on property, is the *zakāt al-fiṭr*, due upon breaking the Ramadan fast, and intended to provide food for all the poor to celebrate the occasion. It is obligatory on every financially capable[42] free Muslim, adult or minor, male or female; but this tax does not have the same status as a "pillar," namely, those who abjure it are not deemed to be apostates.[43] Having in part the status of *ṣadaqa*,[44] this *zakāt* may be delayed or advanced by a day or two, according to most jurists. Due to the nature of its purpose and function, the levy is usually in foodstuffs.

4. Fasting (*ṣawm*)

Although fasting[45] is usually associated with the month of Ramadan, it plays other roles in religious acts, most notably as penance or expiation. In Ramadan, fasting – which consists of abstinence from food, drink and sex – is obligatory, by universal agreement. During certain other times of the year, it is recommended and performed on a voluntary basis (*taṭawwuʿ*). The voluntary fast must not be undertaken on Saturdays or Sundays (or any other non-believers' holidays, Naurūz included), but is most recommended on the Day of ʿArāʾ,[46] the Day of ʿArafa,[47] Mondays and Thursdays of every week, any three days of every month (minding the reservations about Saturdays and Sundays), six days in Shawwāl, or the entirety of Shaʿbān, Muḥarram and/or Rajab.[48]

Underlying fasting there lie various rationales, all of which aim to train the self to acquire and augment compassion, self-control, self-discipline and gratitude toward the Creator. Experiencing hunger and thirst through fasting restrains the soul and trains the body to control physical and

[42] I.e., he who has, on the eve of the Day of Breaking the Fast (*ʿĪd al-Fiṭr*), any food that is in excess of what he and his family can consume. Nawawī, *Rawḍa*, II, 203; Maqdisī, *ʿUdda*, 135; [Miṣrī, *Reliance*, 261 ff.; Marghīnānī, *Hidāya*, I, 297–302; Ibn Rushd, *Distinguished Jurist's Primer*, I, 324–29].

[43] Nawawī, *Rawḍa*, II, 3, 152 f.

[44] Although the term *ṣadaqa* is often used to indicate *zakāt* proper, technically it is different in that it is supererogatory, is entirely voluntary, and may be used for a wide variety of purposes. While *zakāt* must be collected and managed through a public office, *ṣadaqa* is more of an individual, private, and possibly discreet, philanthropic act. [Miṣrī, *Reliance*, 275 f.]

[45] [Miṣrī, *Reliance*, 277–96; Marghīnānī, *Hidāya*, I, 303–46; Ibn Rushd, *Distinguished Jurist's Primer*, I, 330–65.]

[46] Falling on the 10th of Muḥarram, and celebrated in honor of Moses and his victory over the Pharaoh. Further on this, see Goitein, *Studies*, 95 f.

[47] Falling on the 9th of Dhū al-Ḥijja, the Day of ʿArafa is designated as a special time to seek forgiveness.

[48] [Miṣrī, *Reliance*, 291–93; Marghīnānī, *Hidāya*, I, 338–40; Ibn Rushd, *Distinguished Jurist's Primer*, I, 361–65.]

mental desires. It teaches compassion for the poor in whose life hunger is a common experience. No less important, however, is that experiencing thirst and hunger functions as a strong reminder of God's blessings, of the bountiful existence He created for us. It is an instrument to thank the Giver (*Mun'im*).

Those exempted from the duty to fast include the sick, pregnant women, nursing women, the elderly, travelers on long-distance and arduous trips, and persons whose health may be threatened if subjected to fasting. All others must fast during Ramadan. To be valid, abstinence must aggregately and concurrently include food, drink and sex, and must begin at dawn and end at sunset. The subject must be a Muslim individual of major age, without the impediments of insanity or uncleanliness, either of which can invalidate fasting. Majority, for purposes of fasting, begins at around ten years of age, the early start in this case being viewed as necessary to inculcate the practice in children who will have to fulfill this demanding obligation in the most complete fashion when they reach puberty. Menstruation and post-natal bleeding, among other impurities, invalidate the fast.[49] So does the absence of prior intent (*niyya*) to fast, which constitutes an important requirement for validity. During Ramadan – or any voluntary period of fasting – the intention regarding the next day must be declared each preceding day between *ifṭār* (breaking the fast) and the light of dawn (when fasting resumes). Intent must be present until the end of the fasting day. Failure to maintain intent, even for the shortest period, is cause for the fast's invalidity.[50]

Interruption in intent, the occurrence of menstruation, having sex, ejaculation, masturbation, sexual touching by hand, thigh, etc., all invalidate the Ramadan fast. So does female sexual activity if vaginal excretions (*inzāl*) are involved. Smelling of tobacco smoke does not invalidate fasting, unless it is a "heavy smelling" which allows the entry of smoke into the throat. The Shāfi'ites regard medication that has been inserted in the ear to be an invalidating factor, but the Mālikites require, for invalidity, the medicine to reach the throat. Any rectal suppositories that are not dry also invalidate the fast. Should fasting be unintentionally interrupted by invalidating acts (including mistakes or forgetfulness), the believer must make up (*qaḍā'*) for those days in their entirety, even though the invalidity may have occurred shortly before breaking the fast. Intentional acts of eating, drinking and having sex clearly invalidate the fast and incur penance (*kaffāra*) in addition to *qaḍā'*. *Kaffāra* requires the freeing of a Muslim slave in good bodily health, failing which, fasting for two consecutive

[49] Ḥalabī, *Multaqā*, I, 196; Nawawī, *Rawḍa*, II, 230–31; [Miṣrī, *Reliance*, 288].
[50] Nawawī, *Rawḍa*, I, 214–15; [Miṣrī, *Reliance*, 282–83; Marghīnānī, *Hidāya*, I, 305–09].

months, failing which, feeding sixty of the poor. Women who engage in sexual acts during fasting must make up the fasting, but are absolved of the duty to do penance.[51]

The consensus on the obligation to fast throughout Ramadan is based on Quranic verses 2:183 and 185 as well as on Prophetic *ḥadīth*. Ramadan begins when the crescent moon is sighted, and if the crescent is not sighted (i.e., due to cloud cover), it is deemed to begin thirty days from the start of Shaʿbān, the preceding calendar month. If a person sights the crescent moon, then he is under obligation to begin the fast; otherwise, the testimony of two persons who attest to seeing it suffices to initiate that obligation.[52]

5. Pilgrimage (*ḥajj*)

A "pillar" of religion,[53] pilgrimage (as well as *ʿumra*, in the opinion of some jurists)[54] is obligatory at least once in a lifetime, that is, if the believer is able (*istiṭāʿa*) to perform it.[55] Except for the Twelver-Shīʿite school, all jurists regarded belief in Islam as a condition for pilgrimage.[56] In addition, the believer must be sane, of major age, and free. *Istiṭāʿa* consists of the following elements: (a) the ability to provide sustenance for oneself as well as for the dependent family members whom the pilgrim leaves behind; (b) the means to afford travel costs, food, lodging, etc.; (c) being healthy enough to travel and endure the hardships involved in the journey; and (d) the concomitant feasibility of *a*, *b* and *c* during the season of pilgrimage.[57] Some jurists added the condition of travel safety and security on pilgrimage routes.[58] Women are subject to the additional conditions of: (i) having to be accompanied by a family member; and (ii) not being subject to the *ʿidda* (for either *ṭalāq* or her husband's death).[59] The legal duration of pilgrimage extends over the months of Shawwāl and Dhū al-Qaʿda, and the first ten days of Dhū al-Ḥijja.[60] The inclusion in this duration of the

[51] [Miṣrī, *Reliance*, 286.] [52] Nawawī, *Rawḍa*, II, 207–08; Ḥillī, *Sharāʾiʿ*, I, 154.

[53] As always, the implication being that he who abjures it is declared an apostate. Further on this matter, see Buhūtī, *Kashshāf*, II, 456–57.

[54] The so-called "minor pilgrimage" which, unlike *ḥajj*, can be performed any time of the year. Shāfiʿī and Ibn Ḥanbal considered it obligatory, while Abū Ḥanīfa and Mālik deemed it to be recommended. Shaʿrānī, *Mīzān*, II, 38. [For pilgrimage in general, see Miṣrī, *Reliance*, 297–370; Marghīnānī, *Hidāya*, I, 347–471; Ibn Rushd, *Distinguished Jurist's Primer*, I, 374–453.]

[55] For an encyclopedic exposition of *istiṭāʿa*, see Māwardī, *Ḥāwī*, IV, 7–15.

[56] Ṭūsī, *Khilāf*, I, 411; [cf. Miṣrī, *Reliance*, 301.]

[57] Ḥalabī, *Multaqā*, I, 208–09; [Miṣrī, *Reliance*, 301–05; Marghīnānī, *Hidāya*, I, 349–52; Ibn Rushd, *Distinguished Jurist's Primer*, I, 374–78].

[58] Nawawī, *Rawḍa*, II, 282–84.

[59] Marghīnānī, *Hidāya*, I, 135; [Marghīnānī, *Hidāya*, I, 352 f.]. [60] [Miṣrī, *Reliance*, 310.]

Day of Immolation (Yawm al-Naḥr, being the 10th of Dhū al-Ḥijja) is subject to juristic disagreement.[61] Also subject to disagreement is whether the obligation to perform pilgrimage/*ʿumra* becomes effective immediately (*ʿalā al-fawr*) after one has fulfilled all conditions of *istiṭāʿa* or whether it can be delayed (*ʿalā al-tarākhī*) to a subsequent year. It appears that the majority of the jurists were in favor of immediacy, but Shāfiʿī and a number of others allowed for delay.[62]

The first of the four essential components (*arkān*) of pilgrimage is that of entering a state of ritual consecration (*iḥrām*). This state begins with the *niyya*[63] to perform pilgrimage in a specific form, namely, to perform *ḥajj* alone, *ʿumra* alone, or both together.[64] A ritual bath (*ghusl*) is then taken, also accompanied by the *niyya* that the act is performed specifically for the purpose of entering *iḥrām*. Shaving pubic hair, plucking the underarms, clipping the mustache and trimming nails are then in order.[65] Clothes that have any sewing on them are exchanged for a white garment, and footwear for sandals that must not cover the toes or the heel. The body should be perfumed, for both men and women, and for women it is recommended that they dye their hands with henna. Finally, a prayer consisting of two *rakʿa*s is performed, the first requiring the reading of Q. 109, and the second Q. 112. Once all this is done, and the believer begins journeying toward Mecca, he or she is said to have entered the state of *iḥrām*.[66] During the entirety of the *iḥrām* period, it is forbidden to wear sewn garments, to remove hair or clip nails, to engage in sexual activity, or to hunt.[67]

The second component involves being present at Mount ʿArafa on the 9th of Dhū al-Ḥijja. *Ghusl* is performed, followed by chanting, prayer, even weeping, while standing in full humility.[68] At sunset, the pilgrim proceeds to Muzdalifa, again chanting and praying.[69] The third component is the circumambulation (*ṭawāf*) of the Kaʿba, to take place on the next day, the 10th of Dhū al-Ḥijja, while the fourth and final one is a

61 Marghīnānī, *Hidāya*, I, 159.
62 Buhūtī, *Kashshāf*, II, 469; Nawawī, *Rawḍa*, II, 307; Ṭūsī, *Khilāf*, I, 417; [Miṣrī, *Reliance*, 304].
63 Counted by some jurists as a fifth component. See Ḥiṣnī, *Kifāya*, I, 219–20.
64 For the relevance of *niyya* in asserting the performance of certain acts, see section 2, above, and Hallaq, "Fashioning the Moral Subject."
65 Ḥalabī, *Multaqā*, I, 212–13; [Miṣrī, *Reliance*, 311–12].
66 [Miṣrī, *Reliance*, 312–13; Marghīnānī, *Hidāya*, I, 357–59; Ibn Rushd, *Distinguished Jurist's Primer*, I, 397–400.]
67 [Miṣrī, *Reliance*, 314–22; Marghīnānī, *Hidāya*, I, 360–61; Ibn Rushd, *Distinguished Jurist's Primer*, I, 384–90.]
68 Nawawī, *Rawḍa*, I, 375–76.
69 Ḥalabī, *Multaqā*, I, 216; [Miṣrī, *Reliance*, 337; Marghīnānī, *Hidāya*, I, 374–78; Ibn Rushd, *Distinguished Jurist's Primer*, I, 412–14].

rapid walk (*sa'y*) between Ṣafā (one of the gates to Masjid al-Ḥarām) and Marwa (a hill), departing from Marwa and making the trip seven times.[70] The Ḥanafites consider only the second and third components to be essential.

Those who cannot perform pilgrimage for lack of *istiṭā'a* may send a proxy. Conversely stated, *istiṭā'a* renders pilgrimage by proxy null and void. The grounds must be a permanent infirmity, caused, for instance, by old age or chronic disease. The proxy, to qualify as such, must have already performed pilgrimage on his/her own behalf.[71]

The law of pilgrimage, like the law pertaining to all the other "pillars," is complex and detailed. Yet, the rationale behind this juristic complexity, behind the discursive and actual practices, is comprehensible to laymen and jurists alike: through the performance of *ḥajj*, a relationship of submission is reenacted, submission to and presence before the greater power of God. These acts are enhanced by the shedding of earthly luxuries, by wearing the most basic of clothing and footwear, by abandoning all worldly concerns, and by focusing the heart (*qalb*), the mind and the soul on the graceful, generous, merciful, compassionate and creative God. It is the last performative "pillar" that crowns the acts of worship and seals them into a cogent and complete body of works ensuring the final act of submitting to the will and power of the Lawgiver. In their aggregate force, these performative acts provide the modalities through which the moral foundation and moral dimension of the law are constituted and constructed.[72]

[70] Nawawī, *Rawḍa*, 369–72.

[71] Māwardī, *Ḥāwī*, IV, 9, 16–23; Maqdisī, *'Udda*, 161; [Miṣrī, *Reliance*, 304–05; Marghīnānī, *Hidāya*, I, 457–62; Ibn Rushd, *Distinguished Jurist's Primer*, I, 375–477].

[72] For a detailed discussion of the role of rituals as props of substantive law, see Hallaq, "Fashioning the Moral Subject."

7 Contracts and other obligations

1. Contractual principles in general

i. Constitutive features

In *fiqh*, contracts do not stand as a separate category, in the manner, say, American or French law articulates them in textbooks and treatises. Rather, Islamic conceptions of contract are implicit in juristic discussions pertaining to pecuniary and commercial transactions, among others.[1] They are constituted by three essential elements (*arkān;* sing. *rukn*), namely: (a) the parties; (b) the form (*ṣīgha*) of offer and acceptance; and (c) the object, or subject-matter.[2] The Ḥanafites held form to be the only essential element, as the acts of offer and acceptance presuppose the presence of both the parties and the subject-matter.[3]

(a) *The contracting parties*: A person qualified to enter into a contract on behalf of oneself or another must be of major age (*bāligh*) and have attained *rushd*, namely, the capacity to behave in a responsible and constructive manner (*muṣliḥan*), and without this capacity being subject to interdiction (*ḥajr*).[4] Minors and the insane cannot enter into a contract without a guardian acting in their interest, except for discerning minors (*mumayyiz*) who can, *inter alia*, receive gifts and be the beneficiaries of a *waqf*.[5]

(b) *Offer and acceptance* (ījāb *and* qabūl): The majority of jurists associate offer with the owner (*mālik*) of the object, and acceptance with the party to whom ownership or possession of that object (or usufruct) is transferred. The Ḥanafites placed greater importance on the order of

1 See Appendix A, below.

2 [Miṣrī, *Reliance*, 377; Ibn Rushd, *Distinguished Jurist's Primer*, II, 204–07.]

3 Ibn ʿĀbidīn, *Ḥāshiya*, IV, 504; Ḥalabī, *Multaqā*, II, 6.

4 Ramlī, *Nihāya*, III, 373. *Ḥajr* is defined as a legal restriction imposed on the pecuniary acts of persons who are insane, minor, foolhardy (*safīh*), insolvent (*muflis*) or enslaved, among a few others.

5 [For contracting parties, see Miṣrī, *Reliance*, 379–80; Ibn Rushd, *Distinguished Jurist's Primer*, II, 206 f.]

occurrence, declaring the first proposition seeking to contract to be the offer, and the second in chronological order to be the acceptance.[6]

Key to any contract is the presence of *riḍā*,[7] i.e., wholehearted consent without any trace of coercion whatsoever.[8] The expression and manifestation of *riḍā* can take many forms, ranging from spoken or written language to deeds and actions. For instance, a contract will be concluded should A say to B "I give you this object for such-and-such amount," and should B accept. The term "give" in the offer is to be interpreted according to the intent behind the transaction, which is the sale of the object as evidenced by the pecuniary consideration specified. Thus, generally speaking, *fiqh* admits of a wide variety of expressions and ways in which a contract can be concluded, the sole exception being the marriage contract, where explicit language – such as "*zawwaja*" and "*nakaḥa*," both bearing the unequivocal meaning "to marry" – is required.

In most contracts, considerations of intent are paramount, determining as they do the meaning and contents of the words used.[9] Conversely, the power of words to determine intention is limited (see the example in the preceding paragraph), although some jurists favor adopting the apparent meaning of words when contractual language exhibits clarity. A telling illustration of intent in Ḥanafite jurisprudence is the so-called *bayʿ al-wafāʾ*.[10] Technically, such sales are binding, but intention bestows on the contract a function that differs from that of a regular sale. Intended as security (*rahn*) against debtors, the *bayʿ al-wafāʾ* is treated as temporary, for it is dissolved upon repayment of the debt. For the Ḥanafites, however, the supremacy of intent is not universal; hence a gift will not be valid should it be stated in the form of a sale contract that fails to specify the consideration. Nor is a loan valid if drawn up in the contractual language of hire-and-lease (*ijāra*) while omitting mention of the fee/rent.[11]

The Mālikites assign intentionality a wider scope than do the Ḥanafites. A contract is thus deemed binding even if it involves only a silent interaction

[6] Ibn al-Humām, *Sharḥ*, VI, 248–49; [Miṣrī, *Reliance*, 377–79; Ibn Rushd, *Distinguished Jurist's Primer*, II, 204 ff.].

[7] *Riḍā* is prescribed in Quran 4:29: "O you who believe, do not devour each other's property in vain, except it be a trade by mutual consent" (*riḍā*).

[8] The central notion of *riḍā* permeates all Sunnite juristic discussions but the Zaydite Shawkānī seems to dwell on it throughout his work more than any other. See his *al-Sayl al-Jarrār*, II, 575 ff., 586 ff., 641 f., 744 ff., and *passim*. By contrast, see Nawawī, *Rawḍa*, III, 5; Māwardī, *Ḥāwī*, V, 13.

[9] Bāz, *Sharḥ*, I, 19 (3); Powers, *Intent*, 97–121.

[10] Baghdādī, *Majmaʿ*, 242–43; Bāz, *Sharḥ*, I, 19 (3), 67 (118).

[11] Marghīnānī, *Hidāya*, III, 221.

or a silent pursuit of contractual activity (*muʿāṭāt*),[12] such as when a person, without any verbal pronouncement, pays a shopkeeper the price of an item and the latter accepts the sum. While the Shāfiʿites generally adopt toward intentionality a position located somewhere between the quasi-formalist Ḥanafites and the Mālikites, the Ḥanbalites seem to go beyond the latter in according paramount importance to intention and meaning versus form and language. For language is the conduit of meaning, not the other way around, and meaning is paramount in contracts. But language is imperfect, and its use even more so, making the determination of intention the primary goal of interpreting contracts. Should, therefore, a contract whose language represents a meaning not intended by the parties be deemed altogether invalid, or should its language be taken as allusive (*kināya*), intending to accomplish other lawful ends? The answer, even in the Ḥanbalite view, must rest on a balance between the language, on the one hand, and meaning and intention, on the other. Some Ḥanbalite jurists held a loan contract, even when accompanied by specification of consideration, to be an altogether invalid transaction, since loans do not involve the transfer of ownership. Other Ḥanbalites held it to be a valid contract of loan of non-fungibles, and the pecuniary consideration a security.[13]

Although explicit language no doubt reduces the ambiguity of contractual intent, it does not guarantee intent's clarity. In some contracts, however, explicit language is essential, in that its absence will invalidate the contract altogether, such as in marriage contracts. In attempting to pin down a general rule as to where allusive language would – or would not – be contractually valid, the later Shāfiʿites held the view that unilateral actions and actions whose validation does not require witnesses – such as manumission and rent, respectively – are contractually binding if they combine allusive language with a proper intention. The determination of intention rests on circumstantial evidence (*qarāʾin al-aḥwāl*),[14] without which, in turn, no intention can be established. On the other hand, actions that entail witnesses, such as marriage, require only explicit language, since witnesses, *qua* witnesses, cannot decipher intention. The Ḥanbalites, on the other hand, allow for allusive language in a limited sphere, mainly in manumission and *ṭalāq*.[15]

Written contracts and contracts concluded through the medium of writing[16] are, again with the exception of marriage, also valid, by virtue

[12] Ibn al-Ḥājib, *Jāmiʿ*, 337; Buhūtī, *Sharḥ*, II, 141; Zarqā, *Madkhal*, I, 411, 418–19; Ṣanʿānī, *Tāj*, III, 72; Shawkānī, *al-Sayl al-Jarrār*, II, 670.
[13] See section 10, below. [14] Hallaq, "Notes on the Term *Qarīna*."
[15] Ibn Rajab, *Qawāʿid*, 51 (39). For a useful analysis of intent, see Powers, *Intent*.
[16] That is, contracts that were negotiated and agreed through written instruments between and among parties geographically distant from each other – this being one of the reasons for committing contracts to paper.

of Quran 2:282: "O you who believe, when you contract a debt for a fixed term, record it in writing." Whether stipulated in writing or not, the present tense of the verb in contracts of sale is generally deemed allusive, requiring a confirmatory oath on behalf of the party using that form. Whereas the past tense in the Arabic language indicates complete action and thus the certainty of intention to enter the contract, the present tense denotes incomplete action that could extend into the future. The uncertainty inherent in the future, be it immediate or distant, calls for further clarification, requiring the affirmation that an actual sale is indeed intended, not, for instance, a promise of sale.[17]

Now, since intention is the chief desideratum of a contract,[18] it may be conveyable through signs (*ishārāt*), including those of the mute. Contracts entered into by these persons, including those made in writing, are all valid and binding.[19] The Mālikites accept as valid any contract concluded through signs even when the parties are neither dumb nor mute.[20] In the same vein, silent interaction (*muʿāṭāt*) expressing consent and intention constitutes – except in marriage – an instrument through which offer and acceptance may be made in contracts involving consideration.[21]

A further requirement for valid contracts is the correspondence of offer and acceptance. For instance, an offer relating to a particular commodity must not, for the contract to be valid, be accepted either partially (in price, volume, weight or number) or by substitution of a different commodity.[22] Moreover, in the majority of contracts, offer and acceptance must be made in the same session (*majlis*), the reasoning being that acceptance in the same session guarantees that no change will occur in the offer.[23] Yet, the offer in and of itself is not binding, and therefore can be withdrawn, as long as the withdrawal occurs before acceptance is made. An acceptance made after withdrawal of the offer is not contractually productive. However, the Mālikite Ibn Rushd (the Grandfather) rejected the majority position, and took the view that once an offer is made, it cannot be withdrawn: only non-acceptance of the other party can render the offer non-productive.[24]

17 Marghīnānī, *Hidāya*, III, 21; Qārī, *Majalla*, 118, art. 224; on promises, see Hassan, "Promissory Theory," 45–72.
18 Further on intent (*niyya*), see chapter 6, section 2, above.
19 Ibn Qudāma, *Mughnī*, IV, 9; Qārī, *Majalla*, 49 (70); Ramlī, *Nihāya*, III, 373.
20 Ḥaṭṭāb, *Mawāhib*, IV, 228.
21 Buhūtī, *Sharḥ*, II, 141. For a useful discussion of *muʿāṭāt*, see Zarqā, *Madkhal*, I, 411, 414–16.
22 Qārī, *Majalla*, 119, art. 227.
23 Ibn ʿĀbidīn, *Ḥāshiya*, IV, 526; [Ibn Rushd, *Distinguished Jurist's Primer*, II, 204 ff.]. Some jurists went as far as to hold the view that if the session in which the offer is made was interrupted by discourse not directly related to the contract, or by periods of long silences, the agreement would be nullified. See, e.g., Ramlī, *Nihāya*, III, 369–70; [Miṣrī, *Reliance*, 380].
24 Ḥaṭṭāb, *Mawāhib*, IV, 241.

The requirement of the "unity" of the contractual session does not mean that contracts may not be concluded by parties who cannot physically meet. Since writing, as we saw, is an instrument through which offer, acceptance, consent and intention can be expressed, acceptance of a written offer is deemed to be as binding as an oral one made in the "same session." The written offer is thus considered to be a true representation of the will and intention of its author, as if she had appeared in person. Still, the acceptance must be made within the same session, namely, after the written offer is made known in the session at which the other party is present. Complete absence of hesitation, of reluctance or of disapproval is essential for the acceptance to be deemed valid and binding. Obvious exceptions to the "unity of session" are, *inter alia*, contracts of bequest (where acceptance is made after the testator's death), and designation of trustees and guardians for the management of financial affairs and care of children after a parent's death.

(c) *The locus of the contract*: It is largely because of the existence of a variety of contractual objectives and aims that several types of contract have come to be recognized. These range from objects to be sold and bought, to those gifted, pawned, loaned, hired or rented. As we shall see, in contracts of sale, not only must the object be in existence (with the single exception of the *salam* contract)[25] but its characteristics must also be known with a great deal of specificity.[26] The requirement of existence must likewise be potentially present in contracts involving the lease and hire of usufruct. The condition of potentiality in rentable and hirable objects cannot be avoided, since land, for instance, cannot yield a usufruct until its actual rent causes its cultivable potential to be realized. Moreover, whatever the object or the usufruct contracted for, it must be lawful in nature. For example, contracting the sale of ritually impure substances, such as wine, pork, insects, etc., is forbidden.[27]

Some jurists distinguished between contracts of exchange (*ʿuqūd muʿāwaḍa*) and donative contracts (*ʿuqūd tabarruʿāt*), deeming the latter valid even though the object contracted for has not yet come into existence. The Mālikites, for instance, consider valid a gift by A to B of A's share in C's inheritance, when the value of the inheritance is not known and when C has not yet died.[28] As a rule, however, the object must be known to the contracting parties to be in existence and must lend itself to

[25] See below, section 3.
[26] Māwardī, *Ḥāwī*, V, 14 ff.; Buhūtī, *Sharḥ*, II, 141–53, especially at 146; [Miṣrī, *Reliance*, 383; Ibn Rushd, *Distinguished Jurist's Primer*, II, 187–88].
[27] Ramlī, *Nihāya*, III, 380–84. [28] Ḥaṭṭāb, *Mawāhib*, VI, 51.

a fairly exact description.[29] Lack of knowledge (*jahāla*) in these regards can lead to *gharar*, namely, uncertainty that is liable to engender dispute. Minor uncertainty (*gharar yasīr*), regarded as inevitable, is not sufficient to invalidate contracts. But not so a major uncertainty (*gharar fāḥish*), such as selling pearls that are still in the sea.

Yet, *gharar* is to be distinguished from *jahāla*, lack of knowledge as to the subject-matter of the contract. *Gharar* involves ontological possibilities, such as the very existence or inexistence of the thing contracted. Buying a certain number of adult mackerel tuna still in the sea is a prime example. *Jahāla*, on the other hand, presumes existence but involves lack of reasonable knowledge of the thing's characteristics. An example in point would be the purchase of a stone after having seen it, but without knowledge as to whether it is glass or diamond, or of the flawless or included diamond types.[30] Buying an unspecified pearl in the sea combines both *jahāla* and *gharar*, since not just the quality but the very existence of the pearl cannot be ascertained. Thus, while *jahāla* and *gharar* overlap in part (since some *jahāla* is *gharar* and some *gharar* is *jahāla*), they are distinct in other respects (e.g., the tuna example). Now, although the notion of *gharar* dominates in all contractual types, its presence is deemed permissible in certain contracts which society finds indispensable, e.g., *salam* and *istiṣnāʿ* contracts, whereby an immediate payment is made for the future delivery of a product, such as a yacht to be built in accordance with certain specifications. The specifications must include details as to the time of delivery, the exact characteristics, measures and weight of the product, and descriptions sufficiently detailed to preclude misunderstanding and future dispute.[31] However, the benchmark of *gharar* and *jahāla* is the fundamental principle that when their presence has the potential to produce discord and dispute (*mufḍī ilā al-nizāʿ*), the contract is deemed invalid.[32]

Finally, the object of the contract must be capable of immediate delivery, namely, it must be, at the time of concluding the contract, in the possession of the owner and free of all encumbrances. For example, a misappropriated house[33] or a stray animal cannot be rented or sold, respectively.[34] As seen

29 Ramlī, *Nihāya*, III, 392. 30 See n. 32, below.

31 Ḥalabī, *Multaqā*, II, 45–49; Bāz, *Sharḥ*, I, 219–21 (art. 388–91); Buhūtī, *Kashshāf*, III, 325–48.

32 However, Nawawī holds the view that *jahāla*, at least in the case of buying glass that was thought by the buyer to be diamond, does not invalidate the contract, because the buyer did not exercise due diligence in having the stone inspected by experts before purchase. *Rawḍa*, III, 132; [for an account of sales proscribed due to *gharar*, see Ibn Rushd, *Distinguished Jurist's Primer*, II, 179–87].

33 On unlawful appropriation (*ghaṣb*), see chapter 9, section 3, below.

34 Buhūtī, *Sharḥ*, II, 145–46; Mawāq, *Tāj*, IV, 269; Ramlī, *Nihāya*, III, 386–87; [Miṣrī, *Reliance*, 382–83].

earlier, the Mālikites allow for exceptions in donative contracts, permitting, for instance, gifts of runaway slaves or stray cattle.[35]

ii. *A typology of contracts*

The legal effects of a contract depend on whether it is binding (*lāzim*) or non-binding (*jāʾiz*).[36] In the former, a party possesses no right to annul the contract without the permission of the other party or parties (thus, a mutual agreement to rescind the contract is known as *iqāla*).[37] Neither the death of the parties nor their insanity (after concluding the contract) constitutes cause for annulment. Contracts of sale, *salam*, rent and hire, and agricultural leases belong to this type. Partnership (*sharika*), agency (*wakāla*), loan (*qarḍ*) and deposit (*wadīʿa*) are, on the other hand, *jāʾiz* contracts that may be annulled unilaterally. Some contracts, such as those involving liability (*ḍamān*), guaranty and suretyship (*kafāla*) are deemed binding on one party but non-binding on the other. For instance, partnership is a *jāʾiz* contract for all partners, but if misconduct incurs damages, then the liable party enters into a *lāzim* relationship with the other(s), in that she is obliged to compensate her partners for the resulting loss.[38]

Contracts are also classed as pecuniary (*mālī*) and non-pecuniary (*ghayr mālī*), the *mālī* including, among many others, gifts, sleeping partnerships (*muḍāraba*) and all types of sale, while the *ghayr mālī* contracts are represented by agency and suretyship. Some contracts, such as marriage, are considered to be quasi-pecuniary, as they involve a consideration from one contracting party. Lease/hire (*ijāra*), on the other hand, is among those contracts involving usufruct, acknowledged as having a pecuniary value in all schools except that of the Ḥanafites.[39]

As we saw earlier, contracts may be of the exchange or donative type, the gift (*hiba*) being a prime example of the latter. This distinction becomes relevant insofar as *gharar* is concerned. Since contracts of exchange give rise to mutual rights and obligations, and are intended to secure fair trading as well as fair conduct, the principle of *gharar* applies in its entirety, whereas in donative contracts, a lesser degree of certainty is allowed with regard to the specific characteristics, value, weights and measures of the object or service contracted.

Contracts may be valid (*ṣaḥīḥ*; lit. "sound") or invalid (*ghayr ṣaḥīḥ*). Unlike the latter, the former type satisfies the legal requirements of offer and acceptance, the capacity and competence of the contracting parties

[35] Ḥaṭṭāb, *Mawāhib*, VI, 51; *al-Mawsūʿa al-Fiqhiyya*, XXX, 227.
[36] Nawawī, *Rawḍa*, III, 100. [37] Marghīnānī, *Hidāya*, III, 54–55.
[38] Qārī, *Majalla*, 87 (60), 549–50 (1829–30). [39] See chapter 9, section 2, below.

(majority, sanity, etc.), the existence and availability of the contract's subject-matter, etc. Invalid contracts, on the other hand, involve a deficiency in one or more of its *arkān*, such as when a party is proven insane (before concluding the contract) or when the object is deemed unlawful, e.g., wine or carcasses. A valid contract is deemed effective (*nāfidh*) when its execution does not depend on the consent of another who has *wilāya* insofar as the object of the contract is concerned. A servant may contract on behalf of his master (*ʿaqd al-fuḍūlī*), but, for the contract to be effective, his consent must be seconded by that of the master; otherwise the contract is said to be *mawqūf* (lit., "suspended").[40] Without *wilāya*, therefore, a contract remains ineffective, which is to say that effective contracts do not hinge on the approval of anyone other than the parties directly concluding them.

iii. Conditions, effects and termination

Contractual terms (*shurūṭ*) introduced with the view of restricting or defining rights, or predicating the contract's effects upon a future event or a third party's consent, may be valid or invalid.[41] Stipulations in a contract of sale with regard to payment are valid, for instance, but an invalid condition would be one that runs counter to the contract's objectives, or one that involves uncertainty (*gharar*) or usury (*ribā*). Conditions of these types invalidate the contract itself; e.g., the sale of a pearl in its sealed shell violates the contractual rule that the precise characteristics of the object transacted must be known. Other conditions that fall in between the valid contractual terms and *gharar–ribā* stipulations can be deemed invalid without necessarily invalidating the contract. For instance, should it be stipulated that part of the profits of a partner be gifted to a third party, the condition pertaining to the gifting will alone be annulled, leaving the contract to stand. The Twelver-Shīʿites, among all schools, adopt the most lenient position with regard to inserting contractual conditions, allowing any condition that is not explicitly prohibited by the Quran and/or the Sunna.[42]

Be that as it may, every sound contract must have an effect (*athar*), the very *raison d'être* of contracting. In sales and gifts, for instance, the *athar* is the transfer of property, whether or not a consideration is required. The same applies to contracts of rent and loans, which may not always involve a consideration, but have an *athar* in the transfer of usufruct. Several other

[40] Ḥalabī, *Multaqā*, II, 44; Marghīnānī, *Hidāya*, III, 68–70.
[41] Buhūtī, *Sharḥ*, II, 160–66; [Miṣrī, *Reliance*, 388–89].
[42] Ṭūsī, *Khilāf*, I, 511, 516–17; [cf. Ibn Rushd, *Distinguished Jurist's Primer*, II, 192–98].

types of contract do not yield the *athar* of transfer: in marriage, the *athar* is mutual enjoyment, whereas in *kafāla*, the *athar* consists in acquiring an additional liability for the debt.

Finally, contracts of the *lāzim* type cannot be terminated unless both parties agree or unless certain conditions obtain, such as the perishment of the object rented or loaned. The Ḥanafites admit the termination of *ijāra* contracts upon the death of either party.[43] *Lāzim* contracts can also be annulled during the option period (*khiyār*), as we shall see in the case of sales. In *jā'iz* contracts, termination may be effected by one party (without permission of the other) or by both. The mutual annulment of *lāzim* contracts is termed *iqāla*, whereas the annulment of *jā'iz* contracts is known as *faskh*. Unilateral annulment is permitted with the proviso that no harm, due to *faskh*, shall come to the other party or parties; otherwise, *faskh* gives rise to damages.

2. Sales (*buyū'*)

Together with marriage contracts, commutative contracts[44] are regarded as the "pillars" on which the social order rests.[45] The contractual principles discussed in the previous section constitute the general bases of commutative contracts (*buyū'*), where consideration is tendered by one party in return for an equivalent delivered by the other party. The form must also be made whole and complete before the two parties leave the "contractual session" (*majlis al-bay'*) and before the object of sale is altered in such a way that the terms of the buyer no longer apply to it (e.g., grape juice turning into vinegar). The language of offer and acceptance may employ any tense of any verb that has the sense of buying, although the past tense is preferable since in the Arabic language this tense implies more certainty than do others, including the imperative form (sell me such-and-such), but entirely excluding the interrogative. Notwithstanding these general guidelines, most expressions are deemed valid as long as they express *riḍā*.[46]

For any commutative contract to be valid, a number of conditions must come into being. The Ḥanafites distinguish between conditions relative to the validity of the contract (*shurūṭ al-ṣiḥḥa*) and conditions that must

[43] Ḥalabī, *Multaqā*, II, 168.
[44] [On *buyū'*, see Miṣrī, *Reliance*, 371–459; Ibn Rushd, *Distinguished Jurist's Primer*, II, 153–231.]
[45] See Ḥaṭṭāb, *Mawāhib*, IV, 221, who also reports on the authority of other jurists that "sales" constitute a "quarter of all religious works." On the general importance of sales, see also Buhūtī, *Kashshāf*, III, 167; Māwardī, *Ḥāwī*, V, 11–12.
[46] Marghīnānī, *Hidāya*, III, 21. For a useful analysis of *riḍā*, see Zarqā, *Madkhal*, I, 438–39, 449 ff.

obtain for the contract to come into being *qua* contract (*shurūṭ al-inʿiqād*). *Shurūṭ al-inʿiqād*, being the most fundamental, are prerequisites for *shurūṭ al-ṣiḥḥa*, since that which is not integral to the very essence of a contract cannot be admitted as integral to a given contract's validity. *Shurūṭ al-inʿiqād* are all related to the object which must: (a) be in existence; (b) have a monetary value (*māl*) capable of lawful use; (c) be owned by the party selling it; and (d) be capable of delivery.[47] By contrast, the condition that the object must be known to the two parties is one of validity, for if this condition were not met during the contractual session, the contract would be defective (or voidable; *fāsid*) but not null and void (*bāṭil*). Knowledge of the object encompasses genus, species, type, quantity and other specifications that distinguish it from others similar, but not identical, to it. Fixtures and attachments are normally included in the object automatically, unless customary usage excludes such fixtures. The sale of *uṣūl*,[48] such as land, trees and cattle, includes attachments customarily deemed an integral part of the *uṣūl*, but does not include the fetuses in pregnant animals, the fruits on trees or valuable natural resources underground, e.g., petroleum and precious stones.[49]

The price or consideration may be anything that legally qualifies as an object of sale, for that which can be sold can be a price. A price is distinguished from the sold object as follows: money is always a price. Likewise, fungibles are always regarded as a price when exchanged for non-fungibles. If both are fungibles, then the price is that which is named in the contract in conjunction with the preposition "bi," as in the common formula "I sell you a hundred pounds of rice for (*bi*) two hundred pounds of wheat." Here, the wheat is the price. If, on the other hand, both are non-fungibles, they are deemed interchangeably a price and an object, one being the price of the other.

Commutative contracts, among others, may include conditions stipulated by either or both parties, which conditions are termed *khiyārāt irādiyya* (lit., voluntary options). *Khiyār al-sharṭ* and *khiyār al-taʿyīn*, discussed below, are two major forms of this category. The majority of options to rescind or ratify, however, arise out of the operation of the law, which is to say that they need not be specified in a contract in order for certain rights and obligations to arise subsequent to contractual dealings. *Khiyār al-ʿayb* and *khiyār al-ruʾya* are of this type, although the Mālikites

47 For a detailed treatment of these conditions, see Buhūtī, *Kashshāf*, III, 169–99.

48 In this context, *uṣūl* are cultivable agricultural entities that are inherently productive, such as trees bearing fruit and cattle that yield milk, meat and offspring.

49 Marghīnānī, *Hidāya*, III, 25; Ibn al-Humām, *Sharḥ*, VI, 282.

deem *khiyār al-ru'ya* to be a voluntary option that, to have an effect, must be stipulated in the contract. Some of these options are as follows.[50]

Khiyār al-'ayb: The seller must inform the buyer of any defects known to him in the object of sale; otherwise, he will be deemed to have committed *ithm* (a moral wrong punishable in the hereafter). Within one or two days of discovering the defect,[51] the buyer has the option of rescinding the contract provided that: (a) the buyer was not aware of the defect at the time he bought the object; (b) the seller did not incorporate in the contract any provisions exempting him from possible or actual defects; and (c) the defect must be deemed "efficient" (*mu'aththir* or *mu'tabar*; that is, of a nature that affects the value of the object contracted). This defect is judged to be so by customary usage. Two further conditions must apply: (i) the value of the object must be deemed to have decreased upon the discovery of the defect; and (ii) the buyer must be incapable of mending the defect with reasonable effort. This option also applies to lease and hire (*ijāra*) as well as to the consideration women pay in *khul'* contracts.[52]

Khiyār al-ru'ya: The right to rescind a contract upon the inspection of the object bought was acknowledged, provided that the buyer did not see the object during or before the contractual "session." Shāfi'ī deemed this option invalid, as it involves *gharar* due to the fact that the object bought is unknown (*majhūl*; or subject to *jahāla*). Upholding the validity of this option, the Ḥanafites reasoned that an inspection within the period of option removes the element of *jahāla*, thereby preempting the causes of dispute after the contractual period of option comes to an end.[53]

Khiyār kashf al-ḥāl: Resembling the previous option, this *khiyār* arises when a difference exists between the units of measure and weight customarily used by the two parties. Should the buyer, upon inspection, discover that the 200 *raṭl*s he bought are in fact 180 of the standard *raṭl* measure known in his town, he has the right to rescind.[54]

Khiyār al-sharṭ (var. *al-khiyār al-sharṭī* and *khiyār al-tarawwī*): A contractually stipulated right to rescind within no longer than three days.[55]

50 For a detailed discussion of a large variety of *khiyārāt*, see *al-Mawsū'a al-Fiqhiyya*, XX, 41–184; [Miṣrī, *Reliance*, 380–81; Ibn Rushd, *Distinguished Jurist's Primer*, II, 250–55].

51 Some jurists hold the period of this *khiyār* to be no longer than one day, preferring immediate notification. Others admit as long as two days, provided that the notification is accompanied by an oath. Ḥiṣnī, *Kifāya*, I, 252–53.

52 Māwardī, *Ḥāwī*, V, 22–23; Marghīnānī, *Hidāya*, III, 35–36; Buhūtī, *Kashshāf*, III, 245–47.

53 Marghīnānī, *Hidāya*, III, 32–33; Ṭūsī, *Khilāf*, I, 505–06; Wichard, *Zwischen Markt und Moschee*, 153 ff. On an actual court case involving this type of *khiyār*, see Messick, "Commercial Litigation."

54 Ibn Ḥajar al-Haytamī, *Fatāwā*, II, 157.

55 Marghīnānī, *Hidāya*, III, 27.

Khiyār al-taʿyīn: A stipulated option to choose an object, within a certain period of time, from amongst a number of objects in the same class; e.g., purchase of any three bulls from the herd.[56]

Khiyār al-majlis or *khiyār al-mutabāyiʿayn*: Held to be valid by a few jurists, this option spans the period between the pronouncement of the acceptance and the termination of the contractual "session" when the seller and buyer part company.[57]

Khiyār al-ghabn: This option arises when unjustified enrichment occurs without the knowledge of the buyer. *Ghabn* (or *ghubn*) must be of the *fāḥish* type, namely, a major, not a minor, unjustified enrichment, defined by the Ḥanbalites and Mālikites as profiteering, i.e., profiting to the extent of one third or more of the value of the object transacted. The determination of such enrichment is normally the task of expert witnesses whose standards of judgment are the customary local practices. Should *ghabn* be determined to have occurred, the buyer has the option of rescinding the contract and of retrieving the price upon return of the object. But she cannot claim damages amounting to the difference between the actual value of the object and the price paid.[58] (Very similar to this option is *khiyār al-tadlīs*, the option arising from fraud or fraudulent misrepresentation, whereby the object of sale is subjected to an intentional act of temporary improvement or embellishment with the aim of securing a higher price from the buyer.)[59]

3. Sales of *salam* and *istijrār*

Explicitly sanctioned by the Quran and the Sunna,[60] *salam* is a particular contract of sale whereby a price is paid at the contractual session for delivery of a lawful object at a future date.[61] To qualify as a *salam* transaction, a contract must meet the following conditions: (a) the object of the contract must not be in existence at the time of the contract;[62] (b) the object of the contract must lend itself to a reasonably exact description that is deemed capable of precluding dispute, e.g., a garment or a carpet woven in a well-known village or town can be specified by make and size, but not so a fetus in a mare; (c) the contract must also describe in detail the characteristics of the object in question, including type, size, color, weight, shape, etc.; (d) the time of delivery must be stipulated; (e) the

[56] *Ibid.*, III, 24.
[57] Māwardī, *Ḥāwī*, V, 22–23; Ibn Qudāma, *Mughnī*, III, 482; Ṭūsī, *Khilāf*, I, 506–07.
[58] Buhūtī, *Kashshāf*, III, 240–42. [59] *Ibid.*, III, 242–44. [60] Māwardī, *Ḥāwī*, V, 388 ff.
[61] [Miṣrī, *Reliance*, 400–02; Ibn Rushd, *Distinguished Jurist's Primer*, II, 240–49.]
[62] Shīrāzī, *Muhadhdhab*, III, 162; Ṭūsī, *Khilāf*, I, 591.

price must be delivered immediately, i.e., at the contractual session; and (f) the object must be commonly found (*ʿāmm al-wujūd*) at the agreed time of delivery; e.g., buying a ton of a particular fruit to be delivered at a time it is known to be in season.[63]

Another type of contract that may involve *salam* and *muʿāṭāt*[64] is the so-called *bayʿ al-istijrār*, a continuous series of transactions involving the purchase of objects, including perishables, with a payment made at a future date. Since the payment is made at a time when the object is no longer in existence, and since the price was not known at the time the object exchanged hands, the Ḥanafites deemed this contract contrary to *qiyās*, but they declared it to be a valid transaction according to *istiḥsān*. Acknowledging the role of prevalent customary practices, where such a transaction was made routinely in daily household purchases, they argued that this transaction does not involve a contract of sale but represents a reimbursement for damages (*ḍamān al-mutlafāt*) made with the permission (*idhn*) of the object's owner. However, when purchases are made with initial agreement on the price to be paid at a later time, it is considered a valid sale of *muʿāṭāt*. Also valid is the form of *istijrār* whereby a price is paid in advance for a series of purchases to be made in the future.[65]

4. Partnerships (*sharikāt*)

The term *sharika* applies to two distinct types of partnerships, known as *sharikat milk* (joint ownership) and *sharikat ʿaqd* (contractual partnership).[66] The former, frequently involving indivisible property, is defined by what it is not: it is not formed through the parties' meeting of the minds (*irādatayn*) and it lacks the element of offer and acceptance, and so it is not contractual. An example of this *sharika* is two sisters inheriting a house left to them by their father. Moreover, it differs from the *sharikat ʿaqd* in a central way: it lacks the element of the fiduciary duty that partners owe each other, including the constitutive element of agency which is assumed to exist in all contractual partnerships (hence the designation *sharikat ʿaqd*). Thus, a partner in *sharikat milk* has no right of disposal whatsoever without the explicit permission of the other partner.[67]

In contrast, contractual partnership is formed through offer and acceptance, although, being *jāʾiz*, it can be dissolved at will by any of the

[63] Ibn al-Ḥājib, *Jāmiʿ*, 370–73; Shīrāzī, *Muhadhdhab*, III, 164–65; Buhūtī, *Kashshāf*, III, 325–48; Ḥalabī, *Multaqā*, II, 45–49; Bāz, *Sharḥ*, I, 215–19 (art. 380–87); Ṭūsī, *Khilāf*, I, 591–92.
[64] See section 1, i, above. [65] *Al-Mawsūʿa al-Fiqhiyya*, IX, 43–47.
[66] [Miṣrī, *Reliance*, 417–19; Ibn Rushd, *Distinguished Jurist's Primer*, II, 301–06].
[67] Qārī, *Majalla*, 539–43 (art. 1788–1809); Nawawī, *Rawḍa*, III, 507.

partners.[68] Since the Ḥanafites define it as a contract formed in respect of both the capital and the profit, they exclude from it the so-called sleeping partnership (*muḍāraba*), since the latter is formed in respect of the profit alone, not the capital.[69]

An important taxonomy of partnerships is that which distinguishes between *sharikat mufāwaḍa* and *sharikat ʿinān*. In the former, the entire partnership, including both capital and labor, is entirely equal between the two or more partners, whereas in the latter it is not. Should a change, therefore, occur in the partners' proportions in *sharikat mufāwaḍa*, the partnership would automatically be transformed into *sharikat ʿinān*. The Mālikites, Shāfiʿites and Ḥanbalites deemed contractual partnerships to embody a relationship of agency (*wakāla*), whereby each partner owes a fiduciary duty of trust toward the other partner(s). On the other hand, the Ḥanafites were alone in holding the principle that the *mufāwaḍa* partnership in addition incorporates suretyship (*kafāla*) by operation of the law, whereas *kafāla* is not so incorporated in *ʿinān* partnerships unless it be contractually stipulated by the partners themselves.[70] This explains why the Ḥanafite contract of *mufāwaḍa* permits unrestricted freedom for the partners to act on behalf of each other, whereas the remaining three Sunnite schools not only limit this freedom to what is deemed customary business practice within each trade, but also require the permission (*idhn*) of the partners in dealings that lie outside such normative practices.[71] Yet, all jurists agree that, because fiduciary duty (*amāna*) is integral to any contractual partnership, partners do not bear liability for each other's property except when they commit negligence (*taqṣīr*) or cause damage through a fault of their own (*taʿaddī*). Furthermore, the presumption of fiduciary duty does not require of partners more than an oath (*yamīn*) with regard to the declaration of profits they made and the losses they incurred in conducting the business of the partnership.[72]

The Ḥanafites hold the contract of *mufāwaḍa* to be null and void should it stipulate labor to be the exclusive lot of one partner, while the Mālikites insist that labor be divided equally. Furthermore, because the profit is unknown, it must, in all contractual partnerships, be stipulated as a percentage or proportion – e.g., a half, a quarter, etc. – and not as an absolute number. Any lack of clarity as to the division of profits, after all the objective

[68] A few jurists, like Abū Ḥanīfa, state that, for the unilateral dissolution of partnership to take effect, the other partner must be informed. Furthermore, in order for the dissolution of the contract to be effective (*nāfidh*), the capital must be capable of liquidation (i.e., if it is tied up in an obligation whose cancellation may cause damage or harm, the dissolution will not be effective).

[69] Ḥalabī, *Multaqā*, II, 135 ff. [70] Bāz, *Sharḥ*, II, 712 (art. 1334–35).

[71] See, e.g., Buhūtī, *Sharḥ*, II, 321–23. [72] *Ibid.*, II, 337.

of partnership, will invalidate the contract. The Ḥanafites insist on equal shares of profit in *mufāwaḍa*, as well as complete equality of the partners in the capital invested, in legal competence, and in duties of agency and suretyship toward each other. On the other hand, the other three Sunnite schools do not hold this equality to be necessary, while the Twlever-Shīʿites reject the *mufāwaḍa* contract altogether.[73]

Another taxonomy divides partnerships according to the nature of capital invested. A "financial partnership" (*sharikat amwāl*) requires each partner to bring in a given portion of capital, it being immaterial whether they work the capital jointly or separately. On the other hand, when partners own no capital but offer their labor as joint venture, they are said to be engaged in *sharikat aʿmāl* (labor partnership), also known as *sharikat abdān* (lit., bodily partnership),[74] *sharikat ṣanāʾiʿ* (partnership of craftsmanship) or *sharikat taqabbul* (partnership of procuring contracts). On the other hand, *sharikat wujūh*[75] is a partnership that involves purchase of property with delayed payment, a debt that is paid upon procurement of profit. Because of the absence of any capital which constitutes the locus (*maḥall*) of the contract, the Shāfiʿites do not recognize the second and third forms, whereas the Mālikites reject only the third.[76]

To be valid, *sharikat amwāl* must be formed – in the majority's opinion – with existing, free capital (*ʿayn*), i.e., capital that must consist of *naqd*, such as gold and silver, and not with a debt (*dayn*). The majority of the Ḥanbalites and some Shāfiʿites require this *naqd* to be in the form of minted coins, but the Mālikites accept these metals in any form. Goods (*ʿurūḍ*), in contrast to *nuqūd* (sing. *naqd*), have no fixed value and therefore were not admitted as valid forms of partnership capital by the majority of later jurists, the Shāfiʿites being a noteworthy exception.[77] The Shāfiʿites and Twelver-Shīʿites also require commingling of the partners' shares of capital, the reasoning being that if the capital of one of the partners happened to perish, the loss might be invalidly deemed to fall upon him alone.[78] This is also why they deem invalid any partnership in which the capital invested by one partner is different from that invested by the others, e.g., gold versus silver coins.[79]

The Ḥanafites require *sharikat aʿmāl* to involve the labor of all partners, since they construe this type of partnership as similar to contracts for hired labor (*ijāra*), summing up the matter in the maxim: "What is deemed

[73] Ṭūsī, *Khilāf*, I, 644; [Miṣrī, *Reliance*, 418–19].
[74] Entirely rejected by the Twelver-Shīʿites. See Ṭūsī, *Khilāf*, I, 644–45.
[75] Bāz, *Sharḥ*, II, 709–11 (art. 1329–32). The Twelver-Shīʿites reject this form of partnership. See Ṭūsī, *Khilāf*, I, 644–45.
[76] Nawawī, *Rawḍa*, III, 511–12; Ibn al-Ḥājib, *Jāmiʿ*, 395; [Miṣrī, *Reliance*, 418].
[77] Nawawī, *Rawḍa*, III, 510. [78] Ṭūsī, *Khilāf*, I, 643. [79] Nawawī, *Rawḍa*, III, 509.

invalid in *ijāra* cannot be the locus of *sharikat a'māl.*" The Ḥanbalites and Mālikites accept as valid a contract whereby a partner invests his labor while the other supplies tools and equipment, the latter deemed a valid substitute for labor and thus deserving of a share in the profits. But the Ḥanafites and Twelver-Shī'ites regard this form of partnership as invalid, awarding all profits to the laborer, who would simply be obligated to pay the other partner the customary value of rent for his tools.[80]

In *sharikat wujūh*, the Ḥanafites stipulate that the profit is divided between and among the partners in proportion to each of their shares, and thus of their liability (*ḍamān*) in incurring the debt. If the contract includes a provision specifying the distribution of profits in a proportion that is at variance with their actual shares of the debt, the provision would be null and void. The Ḥanbalites, on the other hand, accept such a provision, since a debt liability of one partner that is smaller than his proportionate share of profits may represent compensation for additional labor he might have invested in the business.[81]

The last, but by no means least, type of partnership is *muḍāraba*, defined as a contract whose aim is to make profit through the association of capital from one party (*rabb al-māl*; sleeping partner) and labor from another (*'āmil*; "worker" or agent).[82] The Ḥanafites do not deem it a complete society because it violates the principles of *qiyās*: the agent is hired for an undetermined fee that, furthermore, did not exist at the time of the contract. Instead, the juristic basis of this partnership lies in *istiḥsān*, in turn grounded in the Quran (73:20), the *ḥadīth* and the continuing practice of the community at large.[83]

The *muḍāraba* contract may or may not specify in detail the type of investment the agent must undertake, the specific location, the duration, or the third parties with whom business is permitted. As in other partnerships, agency (*wakāla*) is assumed to exist between the sleeping partner and the agent, a relationship whose lynchpin is trust. Thus, unless otherwise stipulated in the contract, the agent is assumed to be free to travel with the capital – the implication being that trust is of the essence, since it is not an easy matter to find and arrest a person who has fled with capital. The capital must be: (a) *naqd*, silver and/or gold; (b) known in quantity, for otherwise the profit cannot be determined, rendering the contract *ab initio* void; and (c) free and not subject to a debt.

[80] Ḥillī, *Sharā'i'*, II, 387.
[81] Buhūtī, *Kashshāf*, III, 559–60; Bāz, *Sharḥ*, II, 742 (art. 1400–02).
[82] "Agent," here, is to be distinguished from *wakīl*, discussed in section 8, below.
[83] Qāḍīzādeh, *Natā'ij*, VIII, 446–48.

The agent cannot borrow an amount larger than the capital, and any excess in borrowing would constitute a debt against the agent alone. Since a fiduciary duty (*amāna*) is assumed to exist between the two partners, the agent is liable for the loss of the capital only if he is deemed negligent or if he commits a wrongful act (*taʿaddī*). The agent is also liable for any use of the capital that goes beyond the contractual provisions and customary norms, since this act, in the language of jurists, would amount to *ghaṣb*, whose defining feature is the taking of property from its lawful owner without her permission. The centrality of permission – here and elsewhere – is so pronounced that if the agent buys, with the capital or a portion thereof, an object without the contractual or implied permission of the sleeping partner, and should he make a profit as a result of trading with that object, the profit belongs entirely to the sleeping partner, again analogous to growth on unlawfully appropriated property while in the hands of the *ghāṣib*. Should he, on the other hand, suffer a loss, he alone would be liable.[84]

As in *sharikat ʿinān*, the profit in *muḍāraba* must be clearly stipulated in the contract and, furthermore, according to percentage/ratio. In the absence of such clarity and in the case of a dispute, the assumption is that profit will be divided into equal shares. Any provision to the effect that the entire profit belongs to one partner renders the entire contract invalid according to the Shāfiʿite school, whereas the Ḥanafites regard the contract as one of loan (*qarḍ*), and the Mālikites as a donative (*tabarruʿ*) instrument.

The Ḥanbalites allow the sleeping partner to contribute work as well, since they acknowledge labor – and tools – as valid forms of investment. Most other jurists, however, regard this provision as a cause of defect in the contract, the reasoning being that a *muḍāraba* contract rests on a fiduciary duty and this, as in deposit (*wadīʿa*), cannot come into being until the capital is delivered to the agent; thus, if the so-called sleeping partner engages, like the agent, in the business of the partnership, then he cannot be said to have "delivered" (or parted company with) the capital, thereby barring the essential elements of the contract from being realized.

Finally, the agent is entitled to his stipulated share of the profit as well as to out-of-pocket expenses (food, shelter, travel costs, etc., but not medical expenses) spent while conducting the business of the partnership. If he himself pays for these expenses, the amount becomes a debt against the profit, or the capital if profit is not achieved. Any dispute as to the proper amount of these expenses is adjudicated by expert witnesses who assess

84 Qārī, *Majalla*, 556; see also chapter 9, section 3, below.

the amount owed on the grounds of customary practices. The net profit, in the majority opinion, is divided between the two partners after liquidating the assets and freeing the capital from partnership obligation (*tanḍīḍ*).[85]

5. Hire and lease (*ijāra*)

A contract of exchange (*muʿāwaḍa*),[86] *ijāra* combines both the rent of objects and the hire of human labor and animals.[87] Terminologically, the western Mālikites often distinguish between these two categories, applying the terms *ijāra* to the hiring of human labor and *kirāʾ* to the rent of objects as well as to the hire of animals.[88] This contract, of the binding (*lāzim*) type,[89] may be concluded through language that directly or indirectly connotes the meaning of rent and hire, including language of "loan" or "gift," as long as such expressions are accompanied by stipulations to the effect that a usufruct is exchanged for consideration. It may also be concluded through *muʿāṭāt*, although the Shāfiʿites before Nawawī (d. 676/1277) are said to have rejected this form of offer and acceptance.[90] In all major respects, this contract conforms to the general prerequisites outlined above (section 1). However, it differs from the contract of sale in that it does not, according to some jurists, go into effect if a cancellation option (*khiyār al-sharṭ*) is stipulated, but it can do so in the case of *khiyār al-ʿayb*.

The locus of *ijāra* is rent or hire of a usufruct for consideration, with the proviso that the substance (*ʿayn*) hired or rented must be of value (*mutaqawwim*), lawful for use, capable of delivery and incapable of perishing or diminishing. Thus, contracts of *ijāra* involving dogs, runaway animals and unlawfully appropriated objects (*maghṣūbāt*) are invalid. The usufruct must not involve *gharar*, and must thus be known and definable for the contracting parties in such a way as to reasonably preclude dispute.

By the agreement of all schools, the services rendered in *ijāra* are largely defined by customary usage, which constitutes the benchmark of the parties' expectations. In the rent of objects, specification of duration (*mudda*) is deemed conducive to clarity and avoidance of *gharar*. But as duration in

85 Qārī, *Majalla*, 538, 558–59.
86 Shāfiʿī considered *ijāra* a type of sale. Māwardī, *Ḥāwī*, V, 14.
87 [Miṣrī, *Reliance*, 439–45; Ibn Rushd, *Distinguished Jurist's Primer*, II, 264–81.]
88 Ḥaṭṭāb, *Mawāhib*, V, 389. The Egyptian Mālikite jurist Ibn al-Ḥājib (*Jāmiʿ*, 434–41) seems less consistent in applying different terms to the two types. The Ḥanbalites use *ijāra* and *kirāʾ* interchangeably. See Ibn Qudāma, *Mughnī*, VI, 4; Qārī, *Majalla*, 205.
89 Māwardī, *Ḥāwī*, VII, 393; *al-Fatāwā al-Hindiyya*, IV, 412; Ṭūsī, *Khilāf*, I, 710.
90 Qārī, *Majalla*, 207; Zarqā, *Madkhal*, I, 411, 418–19; *al-Mawsūʿa al-Fiqhiyya*, I, 255 ff.; Ṣanʿānī, *Tāj*, III, 72.

some *ijāra* contracts cannot be *ab initio* fixed, a specification of performance must be substituted. A contract for hiring a horse for the stipulated purpose of transporting Zayd from location A to location B can be constrained not by predetermination of a duration, but rather by the accomplishment of the task, namely, the arrival of Zayd in location B. The Ḥanbalite Ibn Qudāma held the view that *ijāra* must involve the options of duration and/or performance of a specific task. If the locus of usufruct is labor, then the contract can be based on either option; however, if labor is not present, as in the rent of real estate, then only the fixing of time-limit is allowed.[91]

The hired person (*ajīr*) may be common (*mushtarak*) or exclusive (*khāṣṣ*), the former being one who works for two or more hirers, whereas the latter works for a single employer. In the case of the former, who may perform a variety of services within his or her own profession, a precise prescription of the work in *ijāra* is a requirement of a valid contract. In the case of the latter, specification of duration is deemed sufficient. But the specification of both work and duration is controversial among jurists, for the opponents of this specification argue that the imposition of a time-limit on the completion of a task may result in undue hardship. Furthermore, they argue, a contradiction will ensue from this combination, for the specification of duration makes the hired person an exclusive employee, whereas the specification of completion makes him a common one.[92]

The general principle governing compensation is that whatever lawfully constitutes a price or a consideration in a contract of sale can constitute a fee in rent and hire. The stipulation of fee must be made clear and in advance, and can, according to many jurists, be in cash as well as in a usufruct of the same genus, such as when two persons rent each other's residences, or when a laborer or artisan is paid a percentage of his production. The absence or excessive lack of clarity in the specification of a fee in advance may render the contract null and void, as the contract would be deemed to involve *gharar*. The Ḥanafites distinguish between invalid (*bāṭil*) and voidable (*fāsid*) contracts, the former being defective due to the absence of a specification of performance or fee. In the event that a fee is not stipulated, the contract will remain binding and effective but the fee will be determined after the completion of the work by an expert on the basis of the going customary rate.

Since enjoyment of usufruct is the locus of *ijāra* contracts, the fee becomes due upon the owner's surrender of the *ijāra* object to the lessee,

[91] Ibn Qudāma, *Mughnī*, VI, 8–9.

[92] Buhūtī, *Sharḥ*, II, 365. The two types of *ajīr* differ in significant ways in one other area, namely, their liability (*ḍamān*) for damages they caused their employers; [Ibn Rushd, *Distinguished Jurist's Primer*, II, 278].

and, according to some jurists, suspended when such enjoyment ceases to exist due to a defect in the substance, e.g., unlawful appropriation of the rented property. In such a case, the tenant has the right to wait for recovery or, according to many jurists, to cancel the contract. The unlawful appropriator (*ghāṣib*) would then be liable for the rent value of the period in which the tenant was unable to exercise her right of enjoyment. Thus, if misappropriation neither affects nor interrupts enjoyment, then rent continues to be due to the landlord notwithstanding.

The *ijāra* contract is terminated upon the exhaustion of the time-limit or of the work, or the perishing of the object hired or rented (e.g., death of the animal or destruction of the house). Being a *lāzim* contract, it may be brought to an end by the agreement of the parties to the contract – an act known as *iqāla*. According to the Ḥanafites and Twelver-Shīʿites, the contract is terminated upon the death of one of the parties,[93] but all schools agree that termination comes into effect should the contracted usufruct or object perish or become impossible to use.[94]

6. Guaranty, suretyship (*kafāla*)

Defined as the joining of the guarantor's liability (*dhimma*) to that of the principal (*aṣīl*), *kafāla* may be contractual or donative, the latter involving unilateral commitment. In law books, it appears under *kafāla* and/or *ḍamān*, although the Mālikites also recognize it as *zaʿāma* and, more frequently, *ḥamāla*.[95] The majority of jurists deem *kafāla/ḍamān* to be a unilateral obligation, requiring only an offer since no transactional reciprocity is entailed. A minority, including some Ḥanafites and Shāfiʿites, hold it to be a contract since the principal enjoys the right of demanding the guarantor to fulfill the terms of her guaranty. Therefore, in the conception of the majority, *kafāla/ḍamān* is, strictly speaking, guaranty, whereas the minority view it as suretyship.[96] Some jurists limit the scope of *kafāla* to guaranty of another person's appearance before the court (failing which the guarantor may be imprisoned),[97] and use the term "*ḍamān*" for pecuniary suretyship/guaranty.[98] Unlike *ḥawāla*, which

93 Some Twelver-Shīʿites deem the contract terminated with the death of the tenant/hirer. Ṭūsī, *Khilāf*, I, 711.
94 *Ibid.*
95 Ḥaṭṭāb, *Mawāhib*, V, 96; Mawāq, *Tāj*, V, 96; [Miṣrī, *Reliance*, 414–16; Ibn Rushd, *Distinguished Jurist's Primer*, II, 355–59].
96 Nawawī, *Rawḍa*, VI, 433–34; Qārī, *Majalla*, 355 (art. 1068). See also Schacht, *Introduction*, 158, who lumps both under the term suretyship. Cf. *Black's Law Dictionary*, 634.
97 Marghīnānī, *Hidāya*, III, 87.
98 Qārī, *Majalla*, 368 (art. 1130), and sources cited therein.

requires the transfer of liability from one person to another, *kafāla/ḍamān* places liability with two or more persons at once (i.e., the principal, the guarantor and possibly the guarantor's guarantor), making them jointly responsible for the payment of a debt or for the presence of a third party before the law. Moreover, while *ḥawāla* acquits the "principal" of any liability, the same cannot be said of *kafāla/ḍamān*.

In addition to assuming responsibility for another's debt, *kafāla/ḍamān* is operative, *inter alia*, in financial compensation for bodily harm, payment of *mahr*, wifely support, and "merchants' guaranty" (*ḍamān al-sūq*; a variety of debt suretyship whereby merchants are guaranteed – usually by each other – for their purchases on credit). However, guaranty was universally deemed unacceptable in matters involving capital and physical punishment (e.g., lashing or cutting off the hand).[99]

Liability for the *kafāla* of personhood is extinguished upon the death of the guaranteed (*makfūl*), but not so liability for pecuniary *kafāla/ḍamān* since property rights cannot be extinguished.[100] The rights arising from guaranty are inherited, so that the death of the guarantor does not acquit her heirs from claims made by the principal or by his own heirs. In other words, the heirs – and, theoretically, their heirs how-low-so-ever – possess inalienable rights against the guarantor's estate.[101]

Anyone who is not a minor, a madman, a *safīh*[102] or a slave can lawfully stand as a guarantor. Even a person interdicted (*maḥjūr*) for insolvency (*iflās*) may undertake liability in *kafāla/ḍamān*, but he cannot be deemed to fall under obligation until he is released from interdiction. A *ḍamān* made during mortal illness is invalid if the amount involved is larger than one-third of the person's total estate. So is the *ḍamān* of married women according to the Mālikite school, which is singular in limiting her capacity to stand as a guarantor (*ḥamīl*) to an amount greater than one third of her wealth without the permission of her husband.[103]

The capital offered in *kafāla/ḍamān* may be in any form that is permitted in a pledge (*rahn*), including a loan given out to a third party by the guarantor, a rent of property, or an advance payment made in a sale of *salam*. The effect of the *ḍamān* may be immediate, or it may be delayed to a future time, even, say, to a year or more subsequent to the date on which

99 *Ibid.*; Marghīnānī, *Hidāya*, III, 89.
100 Therefore, in principle, there is no "statute of limitations" in the Sharīʿa. The Ottoman–Ḥanafite juristic discourse, which stipulates such time limitations on land claims and related issues, belongs to the *qānūn* and otherwise stands contrary to the spirit and general principles of the Sharīʿa. For the Ḥanafite justification of time limitations, see Ibn ʿĀbidīn, *Ḥāshiya*, V, 419–22.
101 Marghīnānī, *Hidāya*, III, 88–89.
102 On the *safīh* (n. *sufh*), see previous chapter, section 1.
103 Mawāq, *Tāj*, V, 97.

the debt becomes due. Generally speaking, vagueness as to the duration or amount of the guaranty does not invalidate the overall guaranty as long as it is deemed of a minor nature, representing *gharar yasīr*, not *gharar fāḥish*. The Mālikites accepted a higher level of uncertainty in both duration and the sum guaranteed. If, without any further specification, A says to B: "if C does not pay to you what he owes you, I shall do so," then A's guaranty is both valid and binding.[104] The Twelver-Shī'ites and some Shāfi'ites rejected this position on the grounds of *jahāla*.[105]

Finally, the acquittal (*ibrā'*) of the principal effectively absolves all guarantors, both primary and secondary (since the principal's guarantor may be guaranteed by another); but acquittal of the secondary guarantor no more absolves the primary guarantor than the acquittal of the latter absolves the principal. In *ḍamān/kafāla*, then, acquittal is effective only insofar as the person acquitted and his functional derivatives are concerned, not vice versa.[106] However, the principal's claim against his guarantors is not governed by this principle, as he has the right to seek payment from any of the guarantors, primary and/or secondary.[107]

7. Transfer (*ḥawāla*)

Ḥawāla is a contract whereby liability for a debt (*dayn*)[108] is transferred from the debtor (*muḥīl*; literally, he from whom the liability is removed) to a third party (known as *muḥāl 'alayh*, since he is said to have accepted the liability to pay the debt).[109] The creditor, or owner of the right to the debt, is the *muḥāl lahu*, and the debt itself is *muḥāl bihi*. For example, if A owes a debt to B, and C owes a debt to A, then A can assign C's debt to B, thereby freeing himself of that liability.[110] According to the Ḥanafites, the parties to the contract are the *muḥāl 'alayh* and the *muḥāl lahu*,[111] and need not involve the consent of the *muḥīl* since he can in no way be harmed but stands to gain as a beneficiary of the contractual effects.[112] The Mālikites, on the other hand, do not regard the consent of the *muḥāl 'alayh* as necessary.[113] Other jurists, as well as the Twelver-Shī'ites, deem the consent of the *muḥīl* to be a condition for the contract's validity.[114] Once such a

[104] Ḥaṭṭāb, *Mawāhib*, V, 101. [105] Ṭūsī, *Khilāf*, I, 640–41.
[106] Qārī, *Majalla*, 370 (art. 1145). [107] Māwardī, *Ḥāwī*, VI, 436.
[108] Included in the concept of *dayn* is the right or obligation to return of an object, such as those arising from options of sale (*khiyārāt*). Ibn al-Ḥājib, *Jāmi'*, 390. On these *khiyārāt*, see section 2, above.
[109] Ṭūsī, *Khilāf*, I, 634; Ibn al-Ḥājib, *Jāmi'*, 390; [Miṣrī, *Reliance*, 412–13; Ibn Rushd, *Distinguished Jurist's Primer*, II, 360–62].
[110] Jazīrī, *Fiqh*, III, 169. [111] Sha'rānī, *Mīzān*, II, 105; Ḥalabī, *Multaqā*, II, 66.
[112] Ṭūsī, *Khilāf*, I, 634; Bāz, *Sharḥ*, I, 373 (art. 681). [113] Ibn al-Ḥājib, *Jāmi'*, 390.
[114] Nawawī, *Rawḍa*, III, 462; Ṭūsī, *Khilāf*, 634; Jazīrī, *Fiqh*, III, 172–76.

contract is concluded, and provided that it is not predicated on another contract that may be proven invalid, the *muḥīl* would be free of any and all liability.[115] For example, if merchant A contracts with merchant B to buy certain goods and A arranges for a *ḥawāla* by which the amount he owes to B is assumed by C, and at a later date it transpires that the sale contract is null and void, then the *ḥawāla* contract is rendered void as well. However, if the contract presumed by the *ḥawāla* is not void but rather was cancelled by one or both parties (*faskh* or *iqāla*, respectively), then the *ḥawāla* remains binding. For instance, if A rents an apartment from B, and A transfers his liability of paying rent to C, then the obligation of C continues to hold even if A and B cancel their contract. Any claims C may have with regard to, say, over-payment to B, he will have to take up against A.[116]

Unlike the other schools, the Ḥanafites do not require for the validity of the *ḥawāla* that the *muḥāl ʿalayhi* (C in the examples above) be considered indebted to the *muḥīl* (A). Therefore, acceptance by C of the obligation to pay on behalf of A does not create a presumption of debt.[117] The *muḥāl bihi*, the amount transferred, must in all cases be well defined and known in order for the contract to be deemed valid.[118]

The *ḥawāla*'s effect is the acquittal of the *muḥīl* (A) and his guarantor, if any. Therefore, once the contract is concluded, the *muḥāl ʿalayh* (C) must not pay the *muḥāl bihi* to the *muḥīl*, for if he does he will stand liable to the *muḥāl lahu* (B) to the extent of the amount concerned. Nor will the *muḥāl ʿalayh*'s duty to pay be extinguished should he die, for the duty remains outstanding against his estate and heirs. The acquittal of the *muḥīl* also means – except for the Ḥanafites – that the *muḥāl lahu* will cease to have any claim against the *muḥīl* regarding the debt (*muḥāl bihi*). [119]

8. Agency, procuration (*wakāla*)

Agency may either arise by implication, such as in the context of partnerships, or be created by an independent contract, the contract type being the concern of this section.[120] It represents a *jāʾiz* contract[121] between a principal (*muwakkil*) and an agent (*wakīl*; less frequently *muwakkal*) whereby the former endows the latter with a capacity to act on his behalf – during the principal's lifetime – in undertaking lawful and reasonably defined acts.

[115] Bāz, *Sharḥ*, I, 371 (art. 673), 373 (art. 681). See also Ḥaṭṭāb, *Mawāhib*, V, 90; Mawāq, *Tāj*, V, 90.
[116] Bāz, *Sharḥ*, I, 379–80 (art. 693). [117] *Ibid.*, I, 375 (art. 686).
[118] *Ibid.*; Qārī, *Majalla*, 377 (art. 1167). [119] Jazīrī, *Fiqh*, III, 176–77.
[120] [Miṣrī, *Reliance*, 419–23; Ibn Rushd, *Distinguished Jurist's Primer*, II, 363–67.]
[121] Shaʿrānī, *Mīzān*, II, 111.

Should the agency continue after the principal's death, it would cease to be *wakāla* and be automatically converted into a *waṣiyya* (bequest).[122]

The principal must be legally competent to dispense with his own property and affairs, which is to say that he cannot be a minor, a slave or permanently insane. According to some Ḥanafites, intermittent insanity (*junūn mutaqaṭṭiʿ*) does not constitute a disqualification, for during periods of sanity (*ṣaḥw*) – when such periods can be clearly identified – he can function as an agent; and if he is qualified to do so, then he can validly act as a principal.[123] The agent, on the other hand, though he cannot be a slave, can be either an adult or a minor, but, if a minor, he must have demonstrated maturity of behavior (*rushd*).[124] The agent's knowledge of his designation as an agent is a condition of validity, since the lack of such knowledge would invalidate all his actions on behalf of the principal. Furthermore, whether he is working for a fee or not – both being valid options[125] – the agent has a fiduciary duty (*amāna*) toward the principal, and thus can be held liable for damages caused by his negligence (*taqṣīr*) or transgression (*ʿudwān* or *taʿaddī*).

The subject-matter of agency (*muwakkal fīhi*), be it a right (*ḥaqq*) or an object (*ʿayn*), must be fully owned by the principal at the time the agency contract is concluded. For instance, since agents can be appointed for the purpose of divorcing the principal's wife, an agent's mandate to do so in the case of a woman whom the principal has not yet married is invalid. The subject-matter must also be specified and cannot be an unknown, leading to excessive *gharar*. Appointing an agent to purchase an object without sufficient description constitutes excessive uncertainty (*gharar fāḥish*) that will invalidate the agency, as contrasted with appointing him to buy a house of a medium size in a particular neighborhood – a valid assignment. Nor can the subject-matter be in an area of the law where deputizing is inconceivable, such as ritual law (except pilgrimage, alms-taxes, etc.)[126] – *liʿān*,[127] *qasāma*[128] and testimony (*shahāda*). Except for the Ḥanafites, all Sunnite schools seem to agree that an agency may involve procurement of common, freely available property, such as water from un-owned land and wood in the forest. But it is transactional contracts that are the real

[122] Ḥaṭṭāb, *Mawāhib*, V, 181; Jazīrī, *Fiqh*, III, 135–36; Qārī, *Majalla*, 387 (art. 1207).

[123] Jazīrī, *Fiqh*, III, 138. Cf. Ibn ʿĀbidīn, *Ḥāshiya*, V, 511, who excludes the insane categorically. See also Nawawī, *Rawḍa*, III, 530.

[124] Marghīnānī, *Hidāya*, III, 137. Further on *rushd*, see previous chapter, section 1.

[125] Although the default opinion appears to have been in favor of paying a fee, like *ijāra*. Ibn al-Ḥājib, *Jāmiʿ*, 399.

[126] See chapter 6, sections 3 and 5, above.

[127] On *liʿān*, see chapter 10, section 2, ii, below.

[128] On *qasāma*, see chapter 10, section 3, below.

substance of agency, including, but not limited to, sales, rent-and-hire, marriage, divorce, gift, deposit, pledge and court-room "litigation" (*khuṣūmāt*). The Mālikite school, however, requires special specific agency for the divorce of the principal's wife, marrying off his daughter or selling his domicile. In other words, universal agency would not be deemed valid if it were to cover these three domains merely by implication.[129]

Being fully accountable to the principal, the agent would be deemed a *fuḍūlī*[130] should he operate without the principal's approval. The sole exception is when the agent's operation is deemed to be consistent with customary practices, where it is presumed that the agent has the implicit approval of the principal.[131] If the agent buys an object while being aware of a defect in that object, he, as we already saw, forfeits his right to *khiyār al-ʿayb* and thus cannot return it to the seller. In this case, and unless the agent has the explicit approval of the principal, the principal may hold the agent liable for damages. If the agent sells an object for a price lower than that specified by the principal, the agent will also stand liable; but if he sells it for profit, then that profit is the principal's.[132]

Two of the most common areas in which agency was actually put to use were in the business of trading and representation in courts of law. For this representation to encompass receiving funds (including debts owed) and monetary damages awarded by the court, a special agency – specifying these tasks – must be issued, and only a single agent can be appointed at a time.[133] In contrast, an agent whose appointment specifies the receiving of such funds is presumed to have the power to represent the principal at court, even in disputed matters of sale as well as in other pecuniary transactions. But representation at court does not extend to disputes unrelated to that for which the agent had originally received the power of agency.[134]

Being a *jāʾiz* contract, *wakāla* may be cancelled by either party or through mutual agreement.[135] However, the agent does not possess the

129 Mawāq, *Tāj*, V, 191; Jazīrī, *Fiqh*, III, 146.
130 I.e., acting without authority. See further at the end of section 1, ii, above.
131 Qārī, *Majalla*, 398 (art. 1253).
132 Ḥalabī, *Multaqā*, II, 100–06; Qārī, *Majalla*, 395 (art. 1233–34); Jazīrī, *Fiqh*, 150.
133 Mawāq, *Tāj*, V, 182. 134 Ṭūsī, *Khilāf*, I, 651; Ḥaṭṭāb, *Mawāhib*, V, 183.
135 Maqdisī, *ʿUdda*, 249. Termination of the agency by the principal may confirm the appointment of the agent if the agency is *wakāla dawriyya* (literally: circular agency). This *wakāla* is usually formulated by the following language: "I empower you as my agent to carry out such-and-such business, and in every instance I discharge you, I in effect reappoint you as such an agent." The termination of this type of agency must be formulated in the following terms, known as *ʿazl dawrī*: "I (the principal) discharge you, and in every instance in which I appoint you, I discharge you." See Qārī, *Majalla*, 382, 390 (arts. 1189, 1219).

power to discharge himself (*ʿazl*) should his assignment regarding a particular transaction be incomplete, and should his resignation as an agent cause harm to the principal. Some jurists, including Shāfiʿites and Twelver-Shīʿites, opine that discharging the agent without his knowledge will render null and void all transactions he undertakes on behalf of the principal subsequent to dismissal.[136] The death or insanity of either party is likewise a cause for termination, as is the placement of interdiction (*ḥajr*) against either one of them. Termination is also automatic upon the destruction of the subject-matter. The death of the principal is cause for termination as of the time of death, even though the agent may not be aware of this fact.[137] The implication of this precept is that the agent's action after the principal's death would become contestable, thus giving rise to claims for damages against him by the principal's heirs.

9. Deposit (*wadīʿa*)

Resting on a relationship of fiduciary duty, deposit is a type of agency that is confined to the elements of property and safe-keeping.[138] Except in Ḥanafite doctrine,[139] the law of agency is thus seen to constitute the juridical basis of deposit, this being defined as a procuration contract for the safe keeping of an object (*tawkīl ʿalā ḥifẓ māl*).[140] As a *jāʾiz* contract, *wadīʿa* involves the depositor (*mūdiʿ*), the depositary (*wadīʿ*) and the object deposited (*ʿayn*).[141] As in all pecuniary contracts, the language of offer and acceptance may be explicit or allusive (*kināya*), or it may be a verbal offer from one side and silence accompanied by action from the other. If one asks a neighbor to keep one's automobile in her driveway for a week and hands her the keys, her acceptance of the latter constitutes a contract of deposit.

Both depositary and deposit must be known in that the depositary cannot be an indistinguishable group of individuals, but rather a certain individual or individuals; the deposit must be quantifiable with precision, for the lack of knowledge about either of these two elements may constitute *gharar*, which can in turn void the contract.

Being a fiduciary relationship, deposit does not give rise to damages if the deposit perishes or diminishes in value while in the custody of the

136 Ṭūsī, *Khilāf*, I, 649. 137 Maqdisī, *ʿUdda*, 249–50.
138 Nawawī, *Rawḍa*, V, 285–86; [Miṣrī, *Reliance*, 424–27; Ibn Rushd, *Distinguished Jurist's Primer*, II, 375–78].
139 Who deem that it rests solely on fiduciary duty (*amāna*). Marghīnānī, *Hidāya*, III, 215; Qāḍīzādeh, *Natāʾij*, VIII, 485.
140 Mawāq, *Tāj*, V, 250; Ibn al-Ḥājib, *Jāmiʿ*, 404; Buhūtī, *Kashshāf*, IV, 165; Jazīrī, *Fiqh*, III, 198–99.
141 Nawawī, *Rawḍa*, V, 286, 289; Buhūtī, *Kashshāf*, IV, 165.

depositary, unless it be due to his negligence or transgression.[142] The depositary's oath (*yamīn*) suffices to vindicate him. Any provision in the contract that assigns damage liability to the depositary when he is neither negligent nor transgressive is deemed an invalid condition (*sharṭ bāṭil*). The depositary's use of the deposit, including traveling with it, without the permission of the depositor, gives rise to damages. So does commingling the deposit with a species different in quality, such as mixing corn with barley.[143] Furthermore, the depositary's surrendering the deposit to a third party is cause for liability, unless such surrender becomes necessary in order to safeguard the deposit, e.g., when an object is moved to the depositary's neighbor's residence due to the outbreak of fire in her own house. Moreover, failing to provide proper housing for the object may also be cause for damage claims, at least for the Ḥanbalites; e.g., the failure of the depositary to lock up a gold ring, leaving it for instance on a book shelf.[144]

The expenses incurred to maintain the object while in custody are the depositor's burden, including storage fees and servicing. Even if the contract does not stipulate such expenses, they are nonetheless due to the depositary by operation of the law, and calculated by customary usage. Non-payment of these expenses, such as in the case of the depositor's long absence, is cause for the depositary to go to the court and seek a loan against the depositary's assets, a procedure identical to the failure to pay wifely support (*nafaqa*). But if the deposited object is divisible, the depositary may petition the court to sell a part of the object in order to maintain the rest.

As in all fiduciary-based contracts, attestation (*wathīqa*) constitutes evidence of agreement. If the depositary denies (*jaḥada*) having received a deposit, he is not liable without evidence. Should he admit to having acted as a depositary and yet claim to have returned the object, he would be liable for damages unless he can provide proof of return. Should he admit having returned the deposit after having denied being a depositary, then he would be deemed liable for damages despite any evidence he may adduce.[145]

The termination of the contract by the depositor becomes effective only upon informing the depositary. Death or insanity is automatic cause for terminating the contract. In the event the depositary dies, his heirs are obliged to return the deposit immediately, and will be held liable for any

142 Nawawī, *Rawḍa*, V, 289–99, for causes of negligence and transgression.
143 Ḥalabī, *Multaqā*, II, 144; Qāḍīzādeh, *Natā'ij*, VIII, 488–89; Qārī, *Majalla*, 426 (art. 1368).
144 Buhūtī, *Kashshāf*, IV, 167.
145 *Ibid.*, IV, 176–78; Marghīnānī, *Hidāya*, III, 219; Jazīrī, *Fiqh*, III, 208.

delay. The same obligation falls upon the depositary if he unilaterally terminates the contract. Unlike other contracts, transgression (*taʿaddī*, e.g., using the deposit without permission of the owner) constitutes an automatic cause for termination, requiring the immediate return of the deposit (plus damages, if any).[146]

10. Loans (*ʿāriya, qarḍ*)

A free loan of non-fungible things, *ʿāriya* (pl. *ʿarāyā*) is a revocable (*jāʾiz*), non-contractual obligation amounting to a gift of usufruct.[147] On the scale of the five legal norms, it is deemed a recommended act that, according to some jurists, becomes obligatory when the borrower (*mustaʿīr*) stands in dire need of the loan. The lender (*muʿīr*) must own the right to use, but need not be the owner of, the object.[148] The Ḥanafites and Mālikites charge the borrower with a fiduciary duty, thus exempting him from damage liability when destruction or diminution in the value of the borrowed object is not caused by his negligence or transgression. The Shāfiʿites and Ḥanbalites, on the other hand, hold the borrower liable in all events, charging him with a fiduciary duty only in the case of borrowing *waqf* books.[149] Revocation may be effected by both borrower and lender, but the lender must, under penalty of damages, forgo his right to restoration of the object if interrupting its use by the borrower results in harm. Yet, when revocation by the lender does not result in the immediate return of the object, the borrower is liable for compensation equal to the value of proper rent. A deposit (*wadīʿa*), for the use of which the depositary received permission from the depositor, is deemed a loan.

The *ʿāriya* may be unlimited in both scope and duration (*iʿāra muṭlaqa*), and restricted by either or both. One can lend a piece of land to someone for a year in order to cultivate wheat, or to someone to do whatever she wishes, or to cultivate wheat indefinitely (namely, until revocation by the lender) or to use it for whatever (lawful) purpose a person may wish for as long as he/she likes. The borrower can lend the object to a third party, provided that the use of the object by the third party is identical to his (e.g., cultivating wheat on the borrowed land).[150] Should the use be different, permission of the original lender must be obtained on penalty

[146] Qārī, *Majalla*, 417 (arts. 1328, 1330); Nawawī, *Rawḍa*, V, 297–98.
[147] Ibn Qudāma, *Kāfī*, II, 272; [Miṣrī, *Reliance*, 427–29; Ibn Rushd, *Distinguished Jurist's Primer*, II, 379–82].
[148] Nawawī, *Rawḍa*, IV, 71.
[149] *Ibid.*, IV, 76–77; Marghīnānī, *Hidāya*, III, 220–21; Jazīrī, *Fiqh*, III, 229; Ibn Qudāma, *Kāfī*, II, 272–73.
[150] Marghīnānī, *Hidāya*, III, 221.

of damages. In all cases, the costs of returning the object to the lender must be borne by the borrower alone.[151]

Another kind of loan is the *qarḍ*, which differs from the *ʿāriya* in that in this latter the object itself must be returned, whereas in *qarḍ* there must be a consideration (*ʿiwaḍ*), as with sales.[152] It also differs from *ʿāriya* in being a contract, but whereas the Shāfiʿites considered it of the *jāʾiz* type, the Ḥanbalites deemed it *jāʾiz* on the part of the borrower (*mustaqriḍ*) and *lāzim* on the part of the lender (*muqriḍ*). Because of its (mostly) *jāʾiz* character, no option (*khiyār*)[153] can be exercised. It is of the essence that: (a) the value of the *qarḍ* be known with precision; and (b) the contract not be predicated upon garnering an added benefit – this amounting to *ribā*. Yet, since *qarḍ* represents a commended pious activity involving charitable works, the borrower may voluntarily elect to return the borrowed value plus an additional sum.[154]

11. Pledge, security (*rahn*)

Involving offer and acceptance, *rahn* is defined as a contractual withholding (*ḥabs*) of property until an obligation, such as a debt, has been satisfied.[155] All schools seem to agree that the debtor's pledge of property as security becomes binding once the pledgor/debtor (*rāhin*) receives the loan for which he has pledged from the creditor/pledgee (*murtahin*). The pledged property may remain in the possession (*bi-yad*) of the pledgor/debtor or may alternatively be deposited in escrow with a third party who must be trustworthy (*ʿadl*). Unless the third party transgresses or acts with negligence, liability for damage to the pledged property is the creditor/pledgee's alone. Should the creditor/pledgee maintain custody of the pledged property, he is entrusted with a fiduciary duty (*amāna*) and the debt to him would thus be considered satisfied should that property perish due to negligence on his part.[156] The debtor/pledgor must likewise take due care to maintain the pledged property should it remain in his possession. Each party is liable to the other for any surplus remaining in their possession if the debt and the pledge are not of equal value. Such eventualities make it a condition for contractual validity that the debt and the pledged property be known and quantifiable. Except in Ḥanafite doctrine,

151 *Ibid.*, III, 220–23; Nawawī, *Rawḍa*, IV, 70–91.

152 [Miṣrī, *Reliance*, 402–03.] 153 On options, see section 2, above.

154 Shīrāzī, *Muhadhdhab*, III, 183–87; Maqdisī, *ʿUdda*, 235–36; Qārī, *Majalla*, 269–71 (arts. 729, 742).

155 Ṭūsī, *Khilāf*, I, 602; [Miṣrī, *Reliance*, 404–06; Ibn Rushd, *Distinguished Jurist's Primer*, II, 325–33].

156 Ḥillī, *Sharāʾiʿ*, II, 347.

the growth and fruits of the pledged property belong to the debtor/pledgor, unless the creditor/pledgee contractually stipulates otherwise. However, the Ḥanafites hold the position that the debtor/pledgor must secure the permission (*idhn*) of the creditor/pledgee in order to benefit from such by-products, even though this benefit may in no way diminish the value of the pledged property.[157]

Payment of the debt terminates the pledge contract, whereas invalidation of the debt contract automatically renders the pledge invalid. Failure to pay the debt places the debtor/pledgor under obligation to sell the pledged property. Failure to sell is cause for action, which requires the *qāḍī* to order the sale and satisfaction of debt.[158]

Slaves are subject to being pledged, but sale of a slave woman resulting from the need to satisfy the master's debt must include her children if she has any. (The Mālikites, Shāfiʿites and Ḥanbalites prohibit family separation, and the Ḥanbalites in particular add the prohibition of separating minors from their families.) Any sale that separates mother and children is deemed by the greatest majority of jurists to be null and void.[159]

12. Gift (*hiba*)

This is a contract lacking any stipulation of consideration, but continuing to qualify as a contract of sale if price is specified.[160] It is concluded through offer and acceptance, as well as through *muʿāṭāt*.[161] The jurists disagree as to whether it is *lāzim* or *jāʾiz*: those who hold it to be of the latter type deem withdrawal by the donor (*wāhib*) to be reprehensible (*makrūh*). The gift must be: (a) the property of the donor; (b) in existence; and (c) capable of delivery. Some jurists require the gift to be known and well defined, but others, especially the Ḥanbalites, allow the gift of an unknown, vaguely defined object because the contract is donative. Any contractual stipulation that purports to restrict the freedom of the recipient in dispensing of the gift (e.g., that he cannot sell it or donate to someone else) is null and void. The Shāfiʿites deem the gift to be binding upon the conclusion of the contract, but for the Mālikites the binding effect ensues from delivery (*qabḍ*).[162]

Even those jurists who hold gifts to be permanent and irrevocable accept two sub-types that are temporary. The first is the *ʿumrī* (life) gift

[157] Ḥalabī, *Multaqā*, II, 271.
[158] *Ibid.*, II, 270–76; Qārī, *Majalla*, 325–33; Jazīrī, *Fiqh*, 272–85.
[159] Ḥalabī, *Multaqā*, II, 273. Cf. Nawawī, *Rawḍa*, III, 285.
[160] Ṭūsī, *Khilāf*, II, 13; Ḥaṭṭāb, *Mawāhib*, VI, 49; [Miṣrī, *Reliance*, 457–58; Ibn Rushd, *Distinguished Jurist's Primer*, II, 397–404].
[161] Mawāq, *Tāj*, VI, 53; Qārī, *Majalla*, 303 (art. 870).
[162] Mawāq, *Tāj*, VI, 56–57.

that reverts to heirs of the donor upon his death. The second is the *raqbī* gift which reverts to the donor upon the recipient's death if he dies before him. Both are valid forms for gifting real property, although the *ʿumrī* allows for animals as well.[163]

13. Acknowledgment, confession (*iqrār*)

Non-contractual yet *lāzim*, acknowledgment can create an abstract obligation but usually functions as an affirmation of an actual right owed to another.[164] To be valid, acknowledgment must (a) be made by a person of full legal capacity; (b) represent consent (*riḍā*) that is devoid of any compulsion; (c) involve a thing in existence as well as in the possession – and at the disposal – of the owner; and (d) not be predicated upon a future condition, e.g., if Y happens, a party will owe X amount. The acknowledgment will not be deemed void should it fail to specify accurately the object or thing acknowledged; rather, the maker of the acknowledgment will be asked to explicate her intention precisely. Acknowledgment is irrevocable in matters of property, lineage and crime, with the obvious exception of those *ḥudūd* offenses that are overturned by the slightest of doubts (*shubuhāt*).[165] Acknowledgment, however, cannot establish the culpability of second parties in criminal matters; so a man's admission that he committed *zinā* with a particular woman results in the punishment of the man alone.[166]

14. Amicable settlement (*ṣulḥ*)

Intended to resolve a dispute, *ṣulḥ* is a contractual obligation that differs from arbitration (*taḥkīm*) in that the latter results in a decision by an arbiter, not in a contract, and does not necessarily require one or both parties to concede certain of their rights, an element essential in *ṣulḥ*. The Mālikites are singular in permitting parties to agree to enter into amicable settlement before any dispute arises, this being conceived as a preventive measure.[167] The majority of jurists do not regard *ṣulḥ* as a distinct type of contract, with its own principles and rules, but rather define it by the

[163] For such rules on gifts, see Marghīnānī, *Hidāya*, III, 224 ff.; Ḥalabī, *Multaqā*, II, 152, 167 f.; Buhūtī, *Sharḥ*, II, 522–23; Qārī, *Majalla*, 302 ff.; Ḥaṭṭāb, *Mawāhib*, VI, 50 ff.; Mawāq, *Tāj*, VI, 51 ff.; Jazīrī, *Fiqh*, III, 230 ff.

[164] Such as: "I owe you such-and-such" or "I borrowed (or took) from you such-and-such." Ibn al-Ḥājib, *Jāmiʿ*, 400–01.

[165] On this obligation, see Ṭūsī, *Khilāf*, I, 656 ff., Qāḍīzādeh, *Natāʾij*, VIII, 318–20; Ḥalabī, *Multaqā*, II, 120–24; Nawawī, *Rawḍa*, IV, 3 ff.; Qārī, *Majalla*, 512–18.

[166] Nawawī, *Rawḍa*, IV, 6–7.

[167] Ḥaṭṭāb, *Mawāhib*, V, 79; Mawāq, *Tāj*, V, 81; Ibn al-Ḥājib, *Jāmiʿ*, 388–89; [Ibn Rushd, *Distinguished Jurist's Primer*, II, 353–54].

nature of the dispute that it intends to settle. Thus, if *ṣulḥ* comes in the wake of a dispute over a sale, then it would be constituted according to the sale contract, in which case the rights of option (*khiyār*), prohibition against usurious interest and *gharar*, etc., must be observed. If, on the other hand, the *ṣulḥ* over a sale involves benefit from a usufruct, then the contract is one of *ijāra*.

The *ṣulḥ* contract amounts to *ibrā*ʾ (acquittance), to *isqāṭ* (relinquishment), or both. For instance, a *ṣulḥ* contract that reduces the size of a debt owed by one-third combines both concessions, since the creditor absolves the debtor of the obligation to pay one-third of the amount and, simultaneously, relinquishes his right to that third. Although the thrust of this contract is pecuniary transactions, it is applicable to areas of the law related to easements, liens, family law, slaves and bodily harm. There is obviously no amicable settlement in *ḥudūd* crimes.[168]

[168] Shīrāzī, *Muhadhdhab*, III, 287–90; Ḥalabī, *Multaqā*, II, 127–34.

8 Family law and succession

1. Marriage

A sanctified social and legal institution, marriage (*nikāḥ*) was seen in Islam as the cornerstone of social order and communal harmony, for as an institution it simultaneously regulated sexual, moral and familial relationships.[1] In quasi-legal literature, its goals were said to have been preservation of pedigree and sexual fulfillment for both men and women. Since the only conceivable way of bringing children into this world and of raising them properly was through marriage, and since sexuality was equally inconceivable outside a lawful framework (which included lawful concubinage), the marriage institution thus became key to maintaining social harmony, the cornerstone of the entire Islamic order.[2] Yet, in strictly legal terms, marriage as *nikāḥ* was a contract with a narrow scope, one that did not pretend to regulate the entirety of relationships that normally existed within marital life. Reduced to its essential contractual components – which make up the entirety of juristic formal discourse – the *nikāḥ* contract excluded what we might call the elements of companionate marriage (as widely defined),[3] and limited itself to regulating, in strictly contractual ways, only those aspects of the matrimonial institution that pertained to the lease of services.

Together with habitual infractions of the law and illicit violence, sexuality outside marriage (*zinā*) is regarded as the primary cause of social discord, to be avoided at virtually any cost.[4] Fornication and adultery, both subsumed under *zinā*, thus do not merely constitute the diametrical moral and logical opposites of marriage, but stand *vis-à-vis* this institution

[1] [On *nikāḥ*, see Miṣrī, *Reliance*, 508–53; Ibn Rushd, *Distinguished Jurist's Primer*, I, 473–546.]
[2] See the commentary of Māwardī, *Ḥāwī*, IX, 3–7.
[3] For such discourse as may bear on non-contractual relationships of marriage, see Nasā'ī, *'Ishrat al-Nisā'*, 86–92, 300–02, and *passim*.
[4] This being reflected in the severity of punishment as compared to the punishment of other infractions also belonging to the same *ḥudūd* class. See Ibn Mufliḥ, *Furū'*, VI, 56; Jawzī, *Aḥkām*, 77–82 and chapter 10, section 2, below.

as mutually exclusive.[5] Nor is this exclusivity limited to the logical and the moral, for the law consciously sets out to combat *zinā* through marriage. This explains, for instance, the juristic stance which upholds marriage to be wholly obligatory in the case of individuals whose sexual desires are uncontrollable or nearly so.[6] In such cases, failure to marry entails a sort of sin (*ithm*), to be punished in the Hereafter. However, for those with average sex drive, marriage is deemed recommended, and indeed for those incapable of marriage – due to an infirmity or to marked disinclination toward it – it is deemed outright reprehensible. This relativist stance, characteristically and interchangeably comprising the moral and the legal, reflects a great deal of sensitivity toward differences among social persons, differences that need to be individually dealt with through commensurate legal mechanisms. But whatever type of control is called for, it is intended to serve a single, ultimate imperative: social harmony.

In an effort to bolster this harmony, marriage becomes regulated and delimited by a network of rules, at the forefront of which stands the concept of a permanent contract.[7] Grounding marriage in contract guarantees the permanency of rights and obligations, a substantive permanency that conduces to the stability of the social order. And like this substantive permanency, contractual permanency serves to fortify this stability. For, among other things, anything short of a permanent contract will *perforce* entail a temporary arrangement that might, in turn, constitute *zinā*.[8] Falling into this category is the Twelver-Shīʿite *mutʿa* marriage which is characterized by its fixed duration expressed in terms of (for instance) months, seasons or the duration of a sojourn. Several early legists admitted it, but Sunnite Islam soon came to reject it altogether during and after the first/seventh century.[9]

Marriage, then, rests on an indefinite contract that may be written or oral, but in all cases must involve at least two contracting parties, two witnesses, and a guardian.[10] The foundational elements (*arkān*) necessary

[5] Jawzī, *Aḥkām*, 89.

[6] See Kāsānī, *Badāʾiʿ*, III, 311–17, for a detailed discussion of various juristic positions on the obligatory or recommended character of marriage. See also Ibn Qudāma, *Mughnī*, VII, 334–37.

[7] Kāsānī, *Badāʾiʿ*, III, 465, 479. Avoiding temporary contractual arrangement at any cost led some jurists, mainly the Ḥanbalites, to outlaw any marriage contract in which the husband has harbored the intention of terminating his marriage prior to entering it. The Shāfiʿites considered it repugnant.

[8] However, a valid marriage contract in which a duration is stipulated continues to hold; only the stipulation is nullified. See Saḥnūn, *Mudawwana*, II, 130.

[9] Ṭūsī, *Khilāf*, II, 179–80. On the practice of *mutʿa* marriage in modern Iran, see Haeri, *Law of Desire*.

[10] Ibn Qudāma, *Mughnī*, VII, 337.

to effect a valid marriage must involve a language (*ṣīgha*) of offer by one party and acceptance by the other.[11] The guardian represents the woman in concluding the contract, and the witnesses attest to it as a legal fact, but their function is also to advertise that fact in society so as to preclude any suspicion of *zinā*.[12] The witnesses thus fulfill the requirement of social sanction, since it is this sanction that marks the difference between secretive, illicit acts and lawful behavior.

The language of offer and acceptance generated detailed juristic discussions, as divergent customary practices posed for judges and legists alike questions that intersected the languages of the social and the legal. In other words, their mission consisted of the effort of sorting out the language that, in its widest definition, could be accepted as formulas befitting contractual agreements. The Ḥanafites permitted the widest linguistic latitude, accepting such metaphorical terms as "gifting" (*hiba*), selling and "surrendering ownership" (*tamlīk*). The Shāfiʿites, Ḥanbalites and Twelver-Shīʿites adopted a more literal and formal approach, rejecting such terms and confining the language of offer and acceptance to the terms *nikāḥ*, *tazwīj*[13] and their derivatives.[14] Their rejection was based on the argument that the marriage contract does not involve gifting, nor does it amount to a sale or surrendering of ownership (viz., of the woman), but rather it is an act whereby two persons are brought, fitted or paired together (*talfīq*; *ḍamm*) due to the suitability (*mulāʾama*) of one to the other.[15] This "fitting or pairing together," they argued, is wholly inconsistent with gifting and "taking ownership," since the "owner" (with a distinct reference to slavery) can never stand with that which is "owned" in such a relationship of pairing.

Although it was normative that the offer be made by the man, some jurists permitted the woman's guardian to do so. The Ḥanafites deemed the offer to be the first statement pronounced, even though it might also take on the form of acceptance.[16] Whatever the terms accepted by each school, they all had to entail clear offer and acceptance of entering into a marriage contract. Certain linguistic formulas – such as the past tense of the Arabic verb – were preferred, because this tense indicated finality and thus less ambiguity in conveying readiness for commitment. But clarity of

[11] See previous chapter, section 1; [and Miṣrī, *Reliance*, 517–23; Ibn Rushd, *Distinguished Jurist's Primer*, II, 3–58; Marghīnānī, *Hidāya*, I, 475–78].

[12] Ibn al-Humām, *Sharḥ*, III, 199; Ibn Qudāma, *Mughnī*, VII, 434–35; Ibn Abī Shayba, *Muṣannaf*, III, 484.

[13] *Tazwīj*, having the connotation of "pairing off," technically means "marrying."

[14] Shams al-Dīn Ibn Qudāma, *Sharḥ*, VII, 370–71; Ṭūsī, *Khilāf*, II, 157.

[15] Ibn al-Humām, *Sharḥ*, III, 193; Māwardī, *Ḥāwī*, IX, 152; Ḥiṣnī, *Kifāya*, II, 36.

[16] See previous chapter, section 1, i, b. Cf. Shams al-Dīn Ibn Qudāma, *Sharḥ*, VII, 375–76.

intent was the desideratum, whatever its means of expression. Even silence, in the case of acceptance, was deemed sufficient if in a context in which refusal would have evoked a clear reaction.[17]

Either of the two contracting parties could be represented by a person acting on his/her behalf as a legally empowered agent (*wakīl*). But this was to be distinguished from the guardian (*walī*) who, in the doctrine of most jurists, was a constituent element of the contract and who was normally, but not always, the father of the woman. The agent *qua* agent was not a guardian. The Ḥanafites were alone in permitting a free woman, who is *compos mentis* and who has reached the age of majority, to conclude her own marriage contract without a guardian.[18] The Twelver-Shīʿites largely shared the Ḥanafite doctrine, but some of their jurists added the condition that the woman, in order to enjoy this right, could not be a virgin (i.e., she must previously have been married).[19] In the case of minors or mentally infirm individuals, a guardian acting on their behalf was mandatory. On this all schools agreed, but the Mālikites, Shāfiʿites and Ḥanbalites required a guardian to represent every woman, even those who were free, *compos mentis* and of legal age.[20]

The Ḥanbalites, moreover, bestow on the father-guardian extensive rights, thereby allocating significant weight to the collective family interests he represents.[21] In their doctrine, he is permitted to act unilaterally, without the approval of the charge (except in the case of a previously married woman [*thayyib*] whose explicit approval is required according to all jurists of all schools).[22] Yet, when the guardian exercises such a right over a virgin ward who has come of age, he – especially the father[23] – is limited by a number of conditions that must be fulfilled for his guardianship to survive the quashing of the court. First, there cannot be any apparent discord between the woman and her guardian, for the presence of such a discord is sufficient grounds to annul his competence to marry her off without her permission. Second, the guardian must ensure that the prospective husband be compatible (*kafʾ*; *kafuʾ*) in every relevant way,

17 Ibn Qudāma, *Mughnī*, VII, 386–87.
18 Marghīnānī, *Hidāya*, I, 196; Ḥalabī, *Multaqā*, I, 243; [Marghīnānī, *Hidāya*, I, 491].
19 Ṭūsī, *Khilāf*, II, 140. 20 Maqdisī, *ʿUdda*, 354–60; Nawawī, *Rawḍa*, V, 397.
21 Ibn al-Laḥḥām, *Qawāʿid*, 24; Ibn Qudāma, *Mughnī*, VII, 346.
22 Ibn Qudāma, *Mughnī*, VII, 386; Shams al-Dīn Ibn Qudāma, *Sharḥ*, VII, 389. Strictly speaking, *thayyib* is a woman who has lost her virginity, the assumption being that normally this happens by virtue of her having been married. However, all other means leading to loss of virginity, including rape and *zinā*, are also causes that engender this status. A woman who is not a *thayyib* is *bikr*.
23 In the absence of a father, the paternal grandfather, then the paternal uncle, then the paternal uncle's son, etc. The hierarchy follows that employed in the rules of inheritance (*mīrāth*). In the absence of all these relations, the *qāḍī* must undertake this role.

compatibility being defined in terms of socio-economic status and personal suitability, i.e., his personality and attitudes should in no way cause her any harm, and, *inter alia*, he should be "neither old nor blind."[24] (The Twelver-Shīʿites limit compatibility to the husband's competence to support his wife [*nafaqa*] and his sharing with her the same religious creed. Accordingly, they permit the marriage of a slave to a free woman.)[25] Finally, the guardian must secure for his charge not only an amount of dower befitting her status but also a prospective husband having the means to pay any delayed dower.[26]

In sum, a guardian was regarded by the majority of jurists as a necessary component of the marriage contract. Except for the Ḥanbalites,[27] all schools insisted on the need for the guardian to secure the approval of the bride, thus creating what they termed *wilāyat mushāraka*, namely, a "guardian-partnership," whereby the woman and her guardian function as partners in deciding on the marriage.[28] The guardian thus had to heed even the most subtle signs of disapproval exhibited by the woman, for there was not supposed to be any form of coercion[29] – itself grounds for seeking annulment of marriage at court. In social reality, however, while this partnership was constituted by the father/guardian and the woman/daughter/charge, they were simply the formal legal actors through whom various family members channeled their opinions and feelings about the proposed marriage, including the mother, brothers and sisters, uncles and aunts, cousins and friends. Typically, the guardian/father represented the interests of the family as a social collectivity, whose priorities were dictated by an acute sense of social status and honor. The woman/charge, on the other hand, represented her own interest, which at the same time coincided with the interest of the group in her own well-being. Thus, the conflation and reconciliation of the interests of the two groups, represented formally by two individuals, were designed to secure the collective well-being of the family at large, including its daughters.

[24] On the concept of *kafāʾa*, see Ziadeh, "Equality," 503–17; Bravmann, *Spiritual Background*, 301–10; [Miṣrī, *Reliance*, 523–24; Marghīnānī, *Hidāya*, I, 500–04; Ibn Rushd, *Distinguished Jurist's Primer*, II, 17 ff.].

[25] Ṭūsī, *Khilāf*, II, 149–50.

[26] Saḥnūn, *Mudawwana*, II, 105–07, 113–15; Ḥalabī, *Multaqā*, I, 246. Cf. Nawawī, *Rawḍa*, V, 426.

[27] Ibn Qudāma, *Mughnī*, VII, 353. But Shams al-Dīn Ibn Qudāma, *Sharḥ*, VII, 378–79, speaks of division in the ranks of the school over this matter.

[28] Or "*wilāyat sharika*," contrary to *wilāyat istibdād* where the permission of the ward is not taken. Kāsānī, *Badāʾiʿ*, III, 358–59; Ṭūsī, *Khilāf*, II, 140. [On guardians in general, see Miṣrī, *Reliance*, 518–23; Marghīnānī, *Hidāya*, I, 491–500; Ibn Rushd, *Distinguished Jurist's Primer*, II, 8–19.]

[29] Marghīnānī, *Hidāya*, I, 197; Kāsānī, *Badāʾiʿ*, III, 360–65; [Marghīnānī, *Hidāya*, I, 492].

Marriage was not an individualistic venture but a family matter. Even the Ḥanafites deemed guardianship socially – though not legally – a necessary symbolic gesture since the presence of a guardian was a matter of prevailing custom and a norm that pervaded the very fabric of society. The distinguished Ḥanafite jurist Marghīnānī explained that this norm arose out of the social need to avert a situation in which women embarking on such a venture without male-relative representation might be seen as insolent and impudent (*waqāḥa*).[30] The Shāfiʿites and Mālikites in particular held that a male guardian was indispensable for the validity of the marriage *qua* contract.[31] Some reasoned that all contractual transactions, including marriage, fall within the domain of public affairs, a male province where women are not fit to engage. But the argument does not hold water by the very standards set by both juristic theory and socio-juridical practice, for women did enjoy rights equal to those of men when it came to engaging in trade, partnership, and investing in real property, as well as nearly every sort of commercial activity involving the private and public spheres. What is more, these were rights that women exercised fully.[32] Thus, we would do well to think of mandated marriage guardianship in terms of ensuring conformity to a sexual and social morality that set the priorities governing both social status and the well-being of the community.

We have already noted the moral significance of attesting to the marriage. Two male witnesses or one male and two female witnesses constituted the minimum requirement for the validity of the contract, but ultimately fulfilled the purpose of advertising the marriage as well. This explains the Mālikite preference for the marriage contract being concluded in the mosque, since such a locale represented a public arena where most communal activities took place.[33] This may also explain why Mālik, the Twelver-Shīʿites and a number of other scholars did not consider the witnesses integral to the validity of the contract if knowledge of the marriage were truly made public.[34] The witnesses were thus deemed representatives of the community at large, representatives who attested to the fact that the marriage had come into existence and that no *zinā* was involved. The witnesses were generally required to be free persons, *compos mentis*, and of majority age. Slaves and non-Muslims could not attest to Muslim marriages,

[30] Marghīnānī, *Hidāya*, I, 196. See also Ibn al-Humām, *Sharḥ*, III, 257; [Marghīnānī, *Hidāya*, I, 491].

[31] Māwardī, *Ḥāwī*, IX, 148. [32] See chapter 4, section 5, above.

[33] Ḥaṭṭāb, *Mawāhib*, III, 408; Ibn al-Humām, *Sharḥ*, III, 199. Mālik does not consider the witnesses integral to the validity of the contract if knowledge of the marriage was made public. See also Kāsānī, *Badāʾiʿ*, III, 390–93; [Miṣrī, *Reliance*, 518; Marghīnānī, *Hidāya*, I, 476 f.; Ibn Rushd, *Distinguished Jurist's Primer*, II, 19 f.].

[34] Kāsānī, *Badāʾiʿ*, III, 390–93; Ṭūsī, *Khilāf*, II, 145.

although Abū Ḥanīfa and Abū Yūsuf did accept non-Muslims (those who had attained majority and who were free and *compos mentis*) as witnesses to marriages between a Muslim man and a non-Muslim woman.[35] Nor did the Ḥanafites require the witnesses to be upright (*ʿadl*), contrary to the Mālikites, Shāfiʿites and Ḥanbalites.[36]

A prominent feature of marriage was the dower (*mahr*), paid by the husband to the wife, which was normally divided into two parts, immediate and delayed, but could also be paid in yearly installments.[37] Immediate dower, paid upon conclusion of the contract, remained the wife's property throughout the marriage, and she was not obliged to spend it on anything or anyone other than herself, not even her children (who were, in full measure, the responsibility of the father). The delayed dower was normally stipulated as protection, becoming due to the wife from the husband if he repudiated her through *ṭalāq* or if either of them died. If repudiation took place before the marriage was consummated, then she would be entitled to half of the dower. Except for the Ḥanafites, all schools permitted payment of dower in the form of usufruct, such as rent on a particular real property or (the value of) agricultural produce.[38]

The dower may not be stipulated in the marriage contract, "nor is it the point of marriage,"[39] but both theory and practice required that it be paid. The Ḥanafites were alone in regarding the contract invalid when no dower was stipulated,[40] but the other schools – while admitting the validity and effectiveness of dowerless contracts – demanded that it be paid whether or not it was stipulated. When not stipulated, it became due to the wife in an amount appropriate to her status (*mahr al-mithl*; defined by the court in terms of her personal and physical attributes, her character, and her familial, social and material status before marriage).[41] If a smaller dower – i.e., less than that to which her overall status entitled her – was stipulated, the stipulation might be invalidated and an appropriate dower imposed.[42]

As is well known, Islamic law permits a free man to marry up to four wives, and a male slave up to two wives (except for the Mālikites who allowed him four).[43] However, with the notable exception of Dāwūd

35 Ibn al-Humām, *Sharḥ*, III, 203. 36 *Ibid.*, III, 201; Ḥaṭṭāb, *Mawāhib*, III, 408.

37 See, e.g., *Wathāʾiq al-Maḥākim al-Sharʿiyya al-Miṣriyya*, I, 203, 224, 225.

38 ʿAynī, *Bināya*, V, 137; Ḥiṣnī, *Kifāya*, II, 64. For historical practice, see Rapoport, *Marriage*, 15.

39 ʿAynī, *Bināya*, V, 131; Kāsānī, *Badāʾiʿ*, III, 484; Ḥaṭṭāb, *Mawāhib*, III, 421.

40 See Kāsānī, *Badāʾiʿ*, III, 480–81; but also see Sarakhsī, *Mabsūṭ*, V, 62–63.

41 Saḥnūn, *Mudawwana*, II, 147; Ibn al-Ḥājib, *Jāmiʿ*, 280; Ḥiṣnī, *Kifāya*, II, 60–64.

42 ʿAynī, *Bināya*, V, 137; [Miṣrī, *Reliance*, 533–36; Marghīnānī, *Hidāya*, I, 507–28; Ibn Rushd, *Distinguished Jurist's Primer*, II, 20–36].

43 Saḥnūn, *Mudawwana*, II, 132–33; Māwardī, *Ḥāwī*, IX, 193; Ibn Qudāma, *Mughnī*, VII, 436–37.

b. Khalaf al-Ẓāhirī (whose school died out), the jurists agreed that monogamy was preferable.[44]

Marriage to one's female ascendants and descendants, one's sister's and brother's ascendants and descendants, one's paternal and maternal aunts, and the ascendants' aunts was forbidden. If a man engaged in polygamy, he had to abide by a further list of prohibited relations, who included the following: any of his wives' mothers, sisters, aunts, grandmothers, grandmothers' daughters how low so ever, and daughters of her sons how low so ever.[45] (The Twelver-Shīʿites, however, permitted marriage to the wives' paternal and maternal aunts.)[46] Furthermore, a marriage was not permitted between a man and a woman who "suckled from the same breast," and this impediment extended to relatives too. It was thus forbidden to marry the sister of one's foster-mother.[47] All schools deemed marriage to be valid between a Muslim man and a woman of the People of the Book, except some Twelver-Shīʿite jurists who forbade such a marriage categorically.[48]

Integral to the marriage contract is a set of operative conditions, whether specified in the contract itself or not. Taken for granted are terms requiring cohabitation, sexual intercourse, and the wife's rights to financial and material support. Other conditions that may validly be stipulated in the contract are, for instance, an increase in dower or support over and above the amount proper to the wife and her status; or, the wife may stipulate that there will be no change of matrimonial residence or that she will not be forced to relocate to another city or town.[49]

Stipulating an invalid condition in the marriage contract does not, in Ḥanafite doctrine, nullify the contract; only the condition itself would be regarded as void. The Mālikites void such contracts before consummation of the marriage, but not subsequently, whereas the Shāfiʿites and Ḥanbalites void only conditions deemed harmful to marriage, such as the stipulation that no dower shall be paid; that sexual intercourse between husband and wife be limited to, say, once a year; or that they will not inherit from each other.[50]

Mutual sexual enjoyment is mandatory in that both spouses must make themselves available for the sexual pleasure of the other;[51] the husband,

[44] Ṭūsī, *Khilāf*, II, 326; [Miṣrī, *Reliance*, 530; Marghīnānī, *Hidāya*, I, 485–86; Ibn Rushd, *Distinguished Jurist's Primer*, II, 47].
[45] Marghīnānī, *Hidāya*, I, 191–92; [Marghīnānī, *Hidāya*, I, 480–81].
[46] Ṭūsī, *Khilāf*, II, 160. [47] *Ibid.*, II, 163.
[48] *Ibid.*, II, 166; [Miṣrī, *Reliance*, 527–30; Marghīnānī, *Hidāya*, I, 478–89; Ibn Rushd, *Distinguished Jurist's Primer*, II, 37–58].
[49] Ibn Qudāma, *Mughnī*, VII, 448. [50] *Ibid.*, VII, 450–52.
[51] Kāsānī, *Badāʾiʿ*, III, 614–15. On the Mālikite judicial definition of harm resulting from sexual deprivation, see Powers, "Four Cases," 398 f.

however, has more extensive rights in this respect than his wife, who has the right to have sex with him at least once every four months.[52] Mutual also is the right of one to inherit from the other insofar as their shares are determined by the pool of living eligible heirs.[53] But the wife, like her husband, maintains an independent financial status throughout the marriage. Any inheritance or gift she may receive before or during the marriage remains hers exclusively, and so does her dower and all property that accrues to her.[54] Marriage does not create community property. For her obligations within the matrimonial home, she receives maintenance (including food, shelter, clothing, and sometimes cash) which must be equal to that to which she had been accustomed, or of a standard at least befitting a woman of her status, before marriage. As in the case of dower, she is under no obligation to spend any of this support or any portion of her own property on others, including her own children whose needs are, in their entirety, looked after by the father. If the husband does not fulfill his obligations toward his wife or children (due, *inter alia*, to negligence, insolvency or abandonment), the wife can sue for child and/or spousal maintenance.[55] Ordinarily, the husband's assets, if there are any, are sold by the *qāḍī* in order to pay the costs of such maintenance, and in the absence of assets the *qāḍī* will direct the wife to borrow against her husband's credit.[56] This protection afforded to Muslim women perhaps explains, in part, why independent property ownership was historically so widespread and extensive among them. They invested in real estate, went into business ventures with relatives and non-relatives, and often sued (on these and other matters), and won suits against, husbands, brothers and others.[57]

Wives who have insolvent husbands from whom financial support is impossible to obtain can petition the court for an irrevocable dissolution

[52] This being reasoned on the grounds that *ilā'* (see below) requires, insofar as the woman's rights are concerned, the resumption of sexual intercourse after a minimum period of four months. See Najdī, *Ḥāshiya*, VI, 437. Cf. Ṭūsī, *Khilāf*, II, 185, to the effect that an impotent husband has one year to resume sexual relations, failing which the wife can petition for dissolution of the marriage. [Also cf. Miṣrī, *Reliance*, 525 f.]

[53] See section 6, below. [54] See further on this chapter 4, section 5, above.

[55] [Miṣrī, *Reliance*, 542–47; Ibn Rushd, *Distinguished Jurist's Primer*, II, 63–65.]

[56] For exceptions in the Mālikite doctrine, see Saḥnūn, *Mudawwana*, II, 181–82.

[57] Summing up important scholarship on this matter, A. Moors writes that women's "involvement in property deals was considerable. In Aleppo, for instance, women constituted one-third of the dealers in commercial real estate, and one-third of these women were buyers; also, more than one-third of the founders of religious endowments were women. Within the family, the majority of women were buyers, whereas most men were sellers, resulting in family shares in houses moving from men to women. More generally, the fact that women were involved in from 40 percent (in Kayseri) to 63 percent (in Aleppo) of all property sales points to their widespread access to property." Moors, "Debating," 146–47.

of the marriage, a judicial order known as *tafrīq* (lit. to separate the spouses from each other). Likewise, this order may be obtained if her husband has not availed himself once every four months of her bed. Sexual grounds for *tafrīq* are also constituted by the husband's absence for more than six months, unless he produces evidence (*bayyina*) to show that his return within the period in question was impossible.[58]

2. *Ṭalāq*

Divorce in modern Western law finds no exact parallel in *fiqh*. The latter produced a variety of forms of marital dissolution that are qualitatively distinct from each other. Furthermore, these forms acquired a juristically discursive ordering that was not necessarily matched by practices on the ground. We have as yet no empirical means to measure which form of dissolution was more widespread, when and where (not to mention why). The term "divorce" has thus far been used to characterize *ṭalāq*, a form of dissolution entirely emanating from the will and action of the husband. Thus, assigning the term "divorce" to mean *ṭalāq* unduly predetermines a paradigmatic meaning of what divorce represents in Islam. Yet, there is nothing compelling in this assignment, not even the fact that *ṭalāq* is at times discussed by jurists in the opening sections of chapters on matrimonial dissolution (although several influential works begin by discussing other forms).[59] Furthermore, the unilateral nature of *ṭalāq* has never been a feature in modern Western laws of divorce, rendering the term "divorce" highly equivocal and useless for our purposes here.

In a patriarchal society where men, not women, initiate marriage, the husband's rights in dissolution (*ṭalāq*) generally receive, as earlier noted, first attention. *Ṭalāq*, in other words, is one form of repudiation – among others – that is the husband's exclusive right. The husband, and only the husband (or his proxy), can effect it, provided he is *compos mentis*, chooses to do so freely, and has attained the age of majority. In other words, repudiation by minors, and by individuals under coercion or undue duress,[60] is not deemed valid or effective. Nor is repudiation by the insane and anyone whose mental faculty has been temporarily impaired by a

[58] Exceptions permitting a period of absence longer than six months are military service and pilgrimage. Najdī, *Ḥāshiya*, VI, 437–38.

[59] See Appendix A, as well as Shīrāzī, *Muhadhdhab*, IV, 253, 277; Buhūtī, *Kashshāf*, 229, 249; Najdī, *Ḥāshiya*,, VI, 459, 482; Ḥaṭṭāb, *Mawāhib*, IV, 18; [for *ṭalāq* in general, see Marghīnānī, *Hidāya*, I, 557–614; Miṣrī, *Reliance*, 554–77; Ibn Rushd, *Distinguished Jurist's Primer*, II, 71–120].

[60] Mild coercion that does not justify bowing to pressure is deemed insufficient to invalidate an act of repudiation. See Shīrāzī, *Muhadhdhab*, IV, 278.

narcotic or medicinal substance. The Shāfiʿites and some Ḥanafites also subsume intoxicants under the causes of "temporary insanity," but the Ḥanbalites and Mālikites – apparently motivated by a more stern attitude against the consumption of inebriants – deem effective any *ṭalāq* pronounced under the influence of alcohol.[61] Extreme anger that causes drastic behavioral changes in one's character is also seen as rendering *ṭalāq* ineffective. Ineffective too is deemed the utterance of repudiation by mistake, although the Ḥanafites uphold the contrary. Their position hinges on the argument that there is no objective means of determining mistake; hence, they hold the view that exonerating someone who claims to have made a mistake but who in fact had repudiated his wife with full intent – yet then wished to retract – would likely open the door for abuses.[62]

The terms used to effect *ṭalāq* may at times be unequivocal and clear (e.g., when employing the verbal form of *Ṭ.L.Q.*) but at others ambiguous (e.g., when using one colloquial formula or another indicating such meanings as "go!" or "I want you to go," etc.). Unambiguous language (*ṣarīḥ*) is sufficient to effect *ṭalāq* repudiation without the need for showing intention, as linguistic clarity *ipso facto* both comprises and reveals intention.[63] Ambiguous language (*kināʾī*), on the other hand, is deemed to have no legal effect without also showing intention, as equivocal language may bear meanings having nothing to do with repudiation. A *kināʾī* term may nevertheless become conventionally used in a region or locale exclusively to designate *ṭalāq*, in which case it will be treated as *ṣarīḥ*.[64]

A man may repudiate his wife in either of two ways: one through a succession of three utterances of *ṭalāq*, each made during a phase of purity from menstruation; the other through making three such utterances at once. The former type is known as revocable *ṭalāq* (or minor separation; *al-baynūna al-ṣughrā*), since the first and second pronunciations may be withdrawn, in which case marriage resumes without the need for any legal action. Irrevocable, three-in-one *ṭalāq* (leading to *al-baynūna al-kubrā* or major separation), however, terminates the contract once and for all. Once marriage is terminated, resumption of the marital relationship by the same couple requires the woman first to remarry another man, which marriage must be consummated and then dissolved. In other words, no man can remarry his wife after repudiating her unless another

[61] Ibn ʿĀbidīn, *Ḥāshiya*, III, 240–41; Shīrāzī, *Muhadhdhab*, IV, 277–78.
[62] Ibn ʿĀbidīn, *Ḥāshiya*, III, 241–42. Cf. Ibn Qudāma, *Mughnī*, VIII, 254–62.
[63] Ḥalabī, *Multaqā*, I, 263. On intention, see chapter 6, section 2, above.
[64] Māwardī, *Ḥāwī*, X, 150–51; [Miṣrī, *Reliance*, 559–60; Marghīnānī, *Hidāya*, I, 569–85; Ibn Rushd, *Distinguished Jurist's Primer*, II, 88–97].

consummated marriage, to another man, has first been undertaken. In a society where sexual honor is paramount, such an intervening marriage constitutes a powerful deterrent to men who might rush into repudiating marriages they otherwise want to keep. The message the jurists wished to urge upon men was that they should not resort to *ṭalāq* unless there is a compelling cause, and even when such a cause appears to exist, they should proceed with caution. This is why the so-called triple-*ṭalāq* is deemed *bidʿa ṭalāq*, a reprehensible form, whereas the revocable *ṭalāq* is viewed with relative favor as it only allows the man to effect final *ṭalāq* after having contemplated it for three months. Furthermore, the moral–legal restrictions on the husband's *ṭalāq* are expressed through assigning the legal value of "unlawful" or "reprehensible" to repudiations not motivated by a compelling cause such as the impossibility of cohabitation due to protracted and irreconcilable conflict.

These legal and moral limitations placed on *ṭalāq* are largely equivalent to the formal laws that modern Muslim states are currently imposing on men with a view to confining their freedom to dissolve marriages. For while women in Islamic law are invariably required to produce arguments as to why they wish to be released from their marriages, men are not so queried as to their motives. The pre-modern jurists reasoned that obliging men to produce, presumably in a court of law, reasons for repudiating their wives might expose family secrets and affairs to public scrutiny that would ultimately hurt the reputation of the wife far more than that of the husband.[65] This consideration, they argued, is to be coupled with the inextricable difficulties involved in determining the real causes of dispute in marriage. But more important was the consideration that husbands were generally seen as having no interest in repudiating their wives without a good cause because they were the ones that stood to lose most from marital dissolution through *ṭalāq*: They had to bear the burden of paying the delayed dower, the alimony (*mutʿa*),[66] and costs of child custody. These costs appear to have constituted a sufficient deterrent that gave rise to the operative assumption that when husbands repudiate their wives, they have good reasons for doing so.[67]

A husband can repudiate his wife by proxy,[68] a right that he can delegate to the wife herself, enabling her to dissolve her marriage on his behalf.

65 The woman's right to divorce her husband in a court of law (usually through *khulʿ*) was seen as less damaging to the reputation of the husband since bringing the faults of men to the public sphere was not as sensitive as bringing to light the faults of women. For *khulʿ*, see next section.

66 For various juristic views on *mutʿa*, see Sarakhsī, *Mabsūṭ*, VI, 61–70; [Miṣrī, *Reliance*, 536; Ibn Rushd, *Distinguished Jurist's Primer*, II, 117–18].

67 Further on this, see chapter 4, section 5, above.

68 On assigning agents, see chapter 7, section 8, above.

This delegation of powers may be terminable (*ṭalāq tawkīl*) or irrevocable (*ṭalāq al-tafwīḍ*). The former is accomplished by means of agency (*wakāla*), which permits the husband to terminate the powers of the agent before acting on his behalf in ending the marriage.[69] In *tafwīḍ*, however, the powers bestowed on the agent cannot be withdrawn, and are terminated by operation of the law only after repudiation has been effected by the agent. The chief difference between the two forms is the addition of such conditionals as "if you wish" to the language of *tafwīḍ*, conditionals that still assign repudiation powers without depriving the husband of the same powers.[70] The instrument of *tafwīḍ* was useful, among other things, for wives who secured it as a valid condition in their marriage contract. *Tafwīḍ*, therefore, was an equalizer, giving men and women the same rights to *ṭalāq*.

Every *ṭalāq* within a consummated marriage entails an obligation on the wife's part to observe the so-called "waiting period" (*ʿidda*), the length of which is three menstrual periods. Other circumstances likewise require the wife to observe *ʿidda*, including *liʿān*,[71] judicial and contractual dissolution,[72] or the death of the husband. In the case of the husband's death, the waiting period becomes mandatory even if the marriage was not consummated. The *ʿidda* of a pregnant woman extends until delivery, while the *ʿidda* of a woman whose husband has died must be observed for four months and ten days after his death. Slave women need observe only half of this period.[73]

3. *Khulʿ*

Another form of marital dissolution, apparently more widespread than *ṭalāq*,[74] is *khulʿ*.[75] "If a woman dislikes her husband due to his ugly appearance or as a result of discord between the two, and she fears failure to fulfill her [marital] duties toward him, she may rid herself of him for consideration. But even though she may not dislike anything [about him], and they amicably agree to separate [through *khulʿ*] without a reason, it is

69 Marghīnānī, *Hidāya*, I, 243; [Marghīnānī, *Hidāya*, I, 601].
70 Ibn Qudāma, *Mughnī*, VIII, 287–88; [Miṣrī, *Reliance*, 557; Marghīnānī, *Hidāya*, I, 593–605].
71 See chapter 10, section 2, ii, below.
72 The first arising from the *qāḍī*'s pronouncement, the second by virtue of *khulʿ*. See the section on *khulʿ*, below.
73 Ḥalabī, *Multaqā*, I, 290–92; [on *ʿidda*s, see Miṣrī, *Reliance*, 566–71; Ibn Rushd, *Distinguished Jurist's Primer*, II, 106–17].
74 See Tucker, "Revisiting Reform," 11. Rapoport, *Marriage*, 4; Marcus, *Middle East*, 205–06; Jennings, "Women," 82–87; Ivanova, "Divorce"; Zilfi, "We Don't Get Along," 272, and sources cited in n. 22.
75 [Miṣrī, *Reliance*, 562–63; Ibn Rushd, *Distinguished Jurist's Primer*, II, 79–84.]

also permissible."[76] Yet, despite this legal permissibility, the jurists are unanimous in their view that it is morally reprehensible to dissolve a marriage for no compelling reason.[77] Thus *khulʿ* is classified by many jurists into three types: permissible (arising out of discord), reprehensible (without a compelling cause) and forbidden. The forbidden type is one that arose out of a situation where a husband deliberately oppressed his wife with a view to accomplishing dissolution of the marriage through *khulʿ* and still be compensated for it.[78] If such an ambition is proven in a court of law, the dissolution would still took effect, but the husband's compensation would be forfeit.[79]

Khulʿ is an offer made to the husband by the wife in respect of marital dissolution, and accompanied by some material consideration. If the husband accepts the offer, he will then repudiate his wife once, considered to be an irrevocable utterance (*bāʾin*). The finality of the single utterance stems from the fact that payment renders the repudiation contractual,[80] thus making the acceptance of the offer binding upon conclusion of the session – which is not the case in unilateral, non-contractual *ṭalāq*. The unilateral nature of *ṭalāq* also leads to another difference in the opinion of many jurists, namely, that *khulʿ* constitutes *faskh* (dissolution), not *ṭalāq*. The *ṭalāq* is said to annul the *effects* (*āthār*) of the marriage contract, whereas *khulʿ* annuls the contract itself.[81] This explains why remarriage between the repudiated spouses is possible in *khulʿ* without the requirement of an intermediary consummated marriage to another man, whereas remarriage following *ṭalāq* does require it.[82] An intermediate marriage is intended to deter whimsical and capricious husbands from repudiating their wives unilaterally, whereas this need does not apply in mutually consensual *khulʿ*.

The juristic presumption is that while *ṭalāq* is usually precipitated by the wife's irregular behavior (*nushūz*), *khulʿ* is caused by that of the husband, in which case, at least according to the Ḥanafites, it is reprehensible for him to receive any consideration.[83] The majority of jurists seem to relate *nushūz* to sexual inaccessibility of the wife, although the husband can be subject to the charge of *nushūz* as well.[84] A wife's "leaving the matrimonial residence without his permission" constitutes *nushūz*; however, its juristic

[76] Shīrāzī, *Muhadhdhab*, IV, 253–54. Similarly, see the Ḥanafite ʿAynī, *Bināya*, V, 506; Jawzī, *Aḥkām*, 92.
[77] Ibn Muftāḥ, *Sharḥ*, V, 383. [78] Buhūtī, *Kashshāf*, V, 230–31.
[79] Marghīnānī, *Hidāya*, II, 14. [80] Najdī, *Ḥāshiya*, VI, 465.
[81] Ibn Rajab, *Qawāʿid*, 118. [82] Sarakhsī, *Mabsūṭ*, VI, 171–72; [Miṣrī, *Reliance*, 563].
[83] Marghīnānī, *Hidāya*, II, 14.
[84] "*Nushūz* of the husband" (acknowledged in the Quran 4:128) figures prominently in juristic discussions, albeit less so than that associated with the wife. See, e.g., Azharī, *Ẓāhir*, 343.

rationale is not the desire to keep women in seclusion but rather to make them sexually available to their husbands. A necessity requiring women to leave home does not, for instance, constitute "leaving without permission," including such occasions as meeting daily needs (shopping for food, etc.), attending to their own business interests,[85] consulting a jurisconsult, bringing suit in a court of law, etc.[86] Refusal to perform domestic chores, such as preparing food, cooking, baking, cleaning, washing, etc., does not constitute *nushūz* "because these are not part of her contractual duties, for all she is obligated to fulfill is (the husband's right to) sexual enjoyment."[87]

The husband's inability to fulfill his marital duties also constitutes *nushūz*, in which case the great majority of jurists and schools require the husband to grant his wife *khulʿ* without remuneration. It is reasoned that the failure to deny the husband this remuneration would result in a double injury to the wife.[88] *A fortiori*, the husband would be deprived of any remuneration if he is proved, in any manner, to have coerced (*yukrih*; n. *ikrāh*) his wife into seeking *khulʿ*, including intentional withholding of payments of marital alimony (*nafaqa*).[89] The jurists disagree, however, with regard to a case in which the husband forces his adulterous wife to request *khulʿ*. Some espouse the view that he is entitled to financial consideration by virtue of the fact that she was at fault, while others deem it to be an unlawful coercion nonetheless.[90] Be that as it may, the great majority of jurists hold the view that the amount involved in *khulʿ*, even when the wife is at fault, should not exceed the amount of her dower.[91]

As a contract, *khulʿ* is constituted by five elements. The first is a husband or his agent, while the second is a wife who is in possession of, and able to pay, consideration, and who is competent to transact. For example, a husband who repudiates his minor wife in response to her request for *khulʿ* (with the provision that the consideration be equal to her dowry) will have effected the dissolution of the marriage without him being entitled to any consideration. Her status as a minor renders her incapable of lawfully possessing and, therefore, alienating property. The

[85] On women leaving their homes to conduct business during the Mamlūk period, see Rapoport, *Marriage*, 35.

[86] On the latter point in particular, see Peirce, *Morality Tales*, 153.

[87] Shīrāzī, *Muhadhdhab*, IV, 236. [88] ʿAynī, *Bināya*, V, 510–11.

[89] Buhūtī, *Kashshāf*, V, 230. [90] Shīrāzī, *Muhadhdhab*, IV, 254.

[91] ʿAynī, *Bināya*, V, 511. The general agreement on this principle probably stems from the reliance on a well-nigh paradigmatic *ḥadīth* in which the Prophet permitted a woman to leave her husband as long as she returned to him the garden/land he gave her as dowry. See Ḥiṣnī, *Kifāya*, II, 79. See also Ibn Muftāḥ, *Sharḥ*, V, 394–99.

third element is an intact marriage where no repudiation or separation of any form has yet been effected. Fourth is consideration (*ʿiwaḍ*) equal to the amount of dower, for "what is acceptable as dower is acceptable as consideration in *khulʿ*."[92] The consideration may consist of: (a) actual property or cash; (b) a debt owed by the husband to the wife (apparently a common situation in many Muslim marriages);[93] (c) a usufruct, including her work/service in suckling their children for a specified duration; (d) a non-existent object, such as "pearls in the sea" or "unripe fruits on a tree." In this regard, the jurists, except the Shāfiʿites, reasoned that, if stipulating hypothetical conditions is permissible in *ṭalāq* (i.e., that it will take effect if X or Y events take place), then it is likewise permissible in *khulʿ*. The Shāfiʿites, however, were logically consistent in their rejection of this last form of consideration, since it entails excessive *gharar*, an uncertainty that invalidates any contract. Finally, there is the fifth element, i.e., the contractual language which consists of offer and acceptance, and which may involve, as in *ṭalāq*, the use of clear (*ṣarīḥ*) or ambiguous (*kināʾī*) terms.[94]

4. *Īlāʾ* and *ẓihār*

A Muslim husband who is *compos mentis* and sexually capable can take an oath (*ḥilf*, *qasam*), if his wife is not nursing their child, to the effect that he will abstain from having sexual intercourse with her for at least four months.[95] The language of the oath must be unequivocal (*ṣarīḥ*) and stated with a clear sense of purpose; otherwise, if it is ambiguous or allusive (*kināʾī*) it must be accompanied by intent (*niyya*). The minimum duration for slaves is two months. Should the period of *īlāʾ* lapse without resumption of sexual intercourse, the oath will have the force of a final *ṭalāq*. Should, on the other hand, the husband resume intercourse with his wife prior to the lapse of the "statutory" period, he will be obliged to perform penance (*kaffāra*). The latter penalty is imposed on the grounds that the husband has caused his wife undue hardship by depriving her of sexual enjoyment without having intended or succeeded in effecting the dissolution of the marriage.[96]

Associated with *īlāʾ* is the oath of *ẓihār*, which a husband may pronounce in any manner to the effect that his wife is as sexually forbidden to him as any intimate part of his mother's body, e.g., abdomen, thighs or

92 Ḥiṣnī, *Kifāya*, II, 80. 93 Rapoport, *Marriage*, 25, 55.
94 Buhūtī, *Kashshāf*, V, 229–32, 235–38.
95 Shāshī, *Ḥilya*, VII, 135; Najdī, *Ḥāshiya*, VI, 621–22; Ibn al-Ḥājib, *Jāmiʿ*, 306–07; [on *īlāʾ*, see Miṣrī, *Reliance*, 565–66; Ibn Rushd, *Distinguished Jurist's Primer*, II, 121–26].
96 Buhūtī, *Kashshāf*, V, 379–80; Marghīnānī, *Hidāya*, II, 13–14.

lower back (*ẓahr*; hence *ẓihār*).[97] The oath does not itself lead to dissolution of the marriage, but is deemed reprehensible, involving – if *ṭalāq* is not effected[98] – both the commission of a sin (to be punished in the Hereafter) and doing penance before he can resume sexual relations with his wife. Penance may take one of three alternative forms: (1) freeing a slave, and if this is not within his means, then (2) fasting for two consecutive months, or, barring this (e.g., for medical reasons), then (3) feeding sixty of the poor for one day each.[99]

5. Child custody and family maintenance

Mothers have an unqualified right to custody (*ḥaḍāna*) over their minor children.[100] Failing the availability of the mother, custody rights pass in the following order of priority to: the mother's mother, the father's mother, the father's full sister, his half-sister on the mother's side, the maternal aunts, etc. The mother's marriage to an *ajnabī*[101] is sufficient cause for her to lose the right to custody, although this right is restored upon dissolution of the marriage. Jurists differ as to the age at which the mother's custody over boys must terminate, seven or nine years being generally the Ḥanafite position. At these ages, it is reasoned, children become self-sufficient in terms of personal care, for they are assumed to be able to eat on their own and wash by themselves. The Mālikites, however, extend the mother's custody until majority for boys and marriage for girls. The Ḥanbalites limit it to the first seven years for both sons and daughters.

Even while having custody, the father is not permitted to take his minor children to live in another town or locale, for this is seen as encroaching on the rights of the mother. Only when the boys reach the "age of sufficiency," and girls the age of puberty, can he do so. Nor can the mother take the children away to live in another locale, unless it is to her home town (*waṭan*), i.e., where she lived before marriage. Upon the dissolution of a marriage with her children's father, she is under no compulsion to stay where her married home was. However, her freedom to return to her home town and family is entirely proscribed if that home town is part of *dār al-ḥarb*.[102]

97 Ibn al-Ḥājib, *Jāmiʿ*, 308–10; [Ibn Rushd, *Distinguished Jurist's Primer*, II, 127–39].
98 Shāshī, *Ḥilya*, VII, 172; but also see Sarakhsī, *Mabsūṭ*, VI, 223–24.
99 Ḥiṣnī, *Kifāya*, II, 115; Marghīnānī, *Hidāya*, II, 17–19; Ibn Qudāma, *Mughnī*, VIII, 574–77.
100 [Miṣrī, *Reliance*, 550–53; Ibn Rushd, *Distinguished Jurist's Primer*, II, 66–67.]
101 In this context, an *ajnabī* is a man who is not a relative. In the context of contractual obligations, the *ajnabī* is a third party.
102 Mūṣilī, *Ikhtiyār*, IV, 14–16. On *dār al-ḥarb*, see chapter 11, below.

Once the husband consummates the marriage, he owes his wife a duty of support (*nafaqa*).[103] The socio-economic status of the woman before marriage is decisive in determining the level of *nafaqa* a husband must provide his wife, in terms ranging from the quality of food to that of clothing and housing. If she had a servant/slave before marriage, he must provide one at his own expense, as well as lodging that – in all cases – affords privacy and is separate from his extended family. Some jurists did not regard as relevant her status and material comfort before marriage, and imposed on the husband the duty to provide his wife with a servant if he is of a middle income, and two if he is more prosperous. Only if he is poor is he absolved of this responsibility. Technically, according to many jurists, the wife is entitled to own the substance (*'ayn*) of her food but not the usufruct (*manfa'a*) of clothing and shelter. But in all cases, the husband owes this support upon consummation of the marriage.[104] If food is not supplied on a daily basis, he is to pay this expense to her once a month. Support for her clothing (including soaps and beauty accessories)[105] is to be paid once every six months. In addition, he is responsible for providing support to her servants, for both food and clothing.

The wife is obliged neither to cook for the family nor to clean the home, but she may choose to do so at her will and pleasure. If she chooses not to do so, he must provide her, at his expense, with someone to cook and clean. However, he is not obliged to cover medical expenses. Failure to provide wifely support is grounds for the wife to petition the *qāḍī* for an injunction to borrow against the husband's estate. According to some jurists, should she fail to turn to the court at the time he defaults, she cannot claim any arrears.[106] These rules are, in their entirety, applicable equally to Muslim and non-Muslim women, whether free or not.[107]

During their waiting period, women whose marriage was terminated are also entitled to maintenance, unless they were at fault in the dissolution of marriage (e.g., for reasons of infidelity or apostasy). Fathers are also responsible to provide maintenance to their young children, including the payment for a wet nurse whose task it is to suckle the infant at its mother's domicile. A mother, therefore, is not obligated to nurse her child unless a wet nurse cannot be found, or if the infant is refusing to suckle from all but her. The Mālikites, however, oblige the mother to nurse if she

[103] Ḥiṣnī, *Kifāya*, II, 65; Ibn al-Humām, *Sharḥ*, IV, 385. Cf. Ṭūsī, *Khilāf*, II, 339–40 (nos. 56–57); [Miṣrī, *Reliance*, 542–50; Ibn Rushd, *Distinguished Jurist's Primer*, II, 63–66].
[104] Ṭūsī, *Khilāf*, II, 327–28.
[105] For a list of these items, see Nawawī, *Rawḍa*, VI, 459–60.
[106] See, however, *ibid.*, VI, 488.
[107] Ṭūsī, *Khilāf*, II, 326, 329; Mūṣilī, *Ikhtiyār*, IV, 3–8; Nawawī, *Rawḍa*, VI, 449 ff., 486.

comes from a lower social class,[108] the assumption apparently being that she is used to hard work.

The jurists discuss at length other types of support, the most important of which is what might be called family support, owed by certain family members toward others. Parents and grandparents have priority to receive attention immediately after wife and children. If in need, parents are owed support by their adult children, male and female. Stepmothers are to be maintained by their husband's son, and the maintenance of the son's wife, if in need, is the responsibility of her husband's father.[109] Other family members, whether agnates or cognates, are entitled to support from their relatives if in need or if afflicted by a physical or mental infirmity that prevents them from earning a living. The general rule for support in this category is that those relatives who stand to inherit from the person in need must offer support in proportion to the share of each in his or her estate.[110] Although the size of these shares cannot be exactly determined until death, the idea is that those who stand to inherit the most should bear the greater burden of support.

Finally, masters are under a legal obligation to provide *nafaqa* to their slaves. Should a master decline to provide maintenance, his or her slaves are legally permitted to seek work and gain income sufficient to support themselves. This allowance is significant, as it frees the slaves from providing services (*manfaʿa*) to the master or mistress during the time of independent employment. If they should fail to find such employment, then the master or mistress is compelled to sell them to one who can afford their maintenance.[111] The master of a married female slave cannot have sexual access to her, but continues to benefit from her services (*manfaʿa*; usufruct). The majority of jurists held the master or mistress responsible for the slave's support during the time of service, whereas the slave's husband would be responsible for the time she spends with him (assumed to be the nighttime hours). Mālik opined that the husband is liable for payment of the entire amount of support.[112]

6. Estates, bequests and succession

Upon death, the estate (*tarika*) of the deceased is subject to three types of deduction before being distributed to the heirs: (a) funeral expenses; (b) any and all outstanding debts; and (c) the value of any bequest the

[108] Ṭūsī, *Khilāf*, II, 335. [109] *Ibid.*, II, 330–33.
[110] Mūṣilī, *Ikhtiyār*, IV, 9–11; Ṭūsī, *Khilāf*, II, 333–34. [111] Mūṣilī, *Ikhtiyār*, IV, 13.
[112] Māwardī, *Ḥāwī*, XI, 525–32; Ibn al-Humām, *Sharḥ*, IV, 426–28; Buhūtī, *Kashshāf*, V, 504–09.

propositus may have made. The Ḥanbalites and some Ḥanafites require that preparations for burial (*takfīn, tajhīz*) be made and paid for first, followed by payment of debts, the latter taking precedence over dispensation of the bequest. The other schools' and the authoritative Ḥanafite doctrine is that payment of debts stands first on the ladder of priorities.[113] For obvious reasons, debts incurred before the death-illness (*dayn al-ṣiḥḥa*) must be paid before debts incurred during that illness (known as *dayn al-maraḍ*). Furthermore, included in the category of debt are all financial liabilities arising from homicide, whether the blood-money (*diya*) is due to intentional or unintentional murder. Should the estate be insufficient to pay all debts, then its value is prorated according to the size of each creditor's share,[114] and the costs of burial (according to the Shāfiʿites, Mālikites and most Ḥanafites) must fall upon those who are legally charged with providing maintenance (*nafaqa*) to the propositus (a duty in turn determined by their fractional shares in what they would have inherited from the latter's estate). As a general rule, and as we saw above, those who stand to inherit from a person are obligated to provide maintenance in old age or in case of physical or mental incapacity.

Once debts have been satisfied and burial expenses covered, the bequest must be discharged. To respect God's will in the proportional sharing-out of the inheritance, and to prevent unwarranted augmentation of wealth, the Sunnite jurists held the position that "no bequest can be made to an heir," a golden rule represented in the legal maxim and *ḥadīth* "*lā waṣiyyata li-wārith*."[115] By contrast, the Twelver-Shīʿites allowed such bequests.[116]

The legator must be *compos mentis*, of major age and free, and can be a Muslim or non-Muslim. According to the Shāfiʿites and Twelver-Shīʿites, a slave cannot leave bequests because he or she is the property of his/her master; thus, any act of bequeathing on the slave's part amounts to alienating the property of the master, and by extension, the slave's very self – a legal impossibility. Nor can the legator bequeath anything to his own slave, since the slave is part of the estate itself. A bequest can, however, be made in favor of another's slave, but in this case the actual legatee is the master, not the slave.[117]

[113] Mūṣilī, *Ikhtiyār*, V, 85; [for a general treatment of inheritance, see Miṣrī, *Reliance*, 460–505; Ibn Rushd, *Distinguished Jurist's Primer*, II, 411–42].
[114] Pearl and Menski, *Muslim Family Law*, 440. See further on prorated shares in Maqdisī, *ʿUdda*, 295.
[115] Mūṣilī, *Ikhtiyār*, V, 63; Ṣanʿānī, *Muṣannaf*, VIII, 371–72.
[116] Ṭūsī, *Khilāf*, II, 89. For other doctrines, see Nawawī, *Rawḍa*, V, 103.
[117] Ṭūsī, *Khilāf*, II, 100.

The jurists were divided over whether a legatee convicted of homicide or of the murder of the legator can legally inherit. As we shall see, such convictions would bar all rights to inherit through Quranic succession (*mīrāth*), but the Shāfiʿites, Mālikites and Twelver-Shīʿites held the opinion that such a killer can be a beneficiary of a legacy.[118] The Shāfiʿites held that a Muslim can lawfully bequeath to non-Muslims, be they protected *dhimmī*s or *ḥarbī*s of the "Abode of War."[119] Against the Ḥanafites who opposed this position, the Shāfiʿites reasoned that such a legacy should not be treated differently from gifting (*hiba*) to the *ḥarbī*s and marrying *ḥarbī* women, both of which are licit acts.[120]

A bequest can also be made in favor of maintaining objects and public works, such as hospitals, mosques, colleges or bridges.[121] The usufruct of property, as distinct from the property itself, may also be bequeathed, including the services of slaves. According to the Shāfiʿites and Ḥanbalites, alimony or maintenance (*nafaqa*) for the slave must be provided by the legatee, but other jurists held the owner to be responsible. The sale of the slave does not affect the right of the legatee to the enjoyment of the usufruct.[122]

Finally, and as a rule, the bequeathed wealth should not exceed one-third of the estate after payment of debts and covering burial expenses. If one's Quranic sharers are poor, the bequest should be less than one-third, the full one-third being morally desirable when they are prosperous. Should the legator bequeath more than one-third, it is up to the heirs to approve; if not, the bequest will be reduced to one-third.[123] Should there not be any heirs, most jurists argued that the bequeathed amount should be reduced to one-third, and the remainder escheats to the Public Treasury (*bayt al-māl*). Abū Ḥanīfa objected, however, permitting the entire estate to be bequeathed in the absence of heirs, and excluding any special privileges for the Public Treasury.

After dispensing with the legatee's entitlement, the heirs (*wurathāʾ*), if any, plus their shares, must be determined. Heirs acquire their status by virtue of blood relationship to the propositus, as well as through marriage and patronage (*walāʾ*). We already noted that committing homicide (be it intentional, quasi-intentional or accidental)[124] bars one from inheriting as an heir, but not as a legatee. Some jurists opined that only killing the propositus acts as a bar. So does difference in religion (*ikhtilāf al-dīn*) and

[118] *Ibid.*, II, 98; Māwardī, *Ḥāwī*, VIII, 191.
[119] Nawawī, *Rawḍa*, V, 102; Ṭūsī, *Khilāf*, II, 98.
[120] Māwardī, *Ḥāwī*, VIII, 193. [121] Nawawī, *Rawḍa*, V, 102.
[122] *Ibid.*, V, 112 ff., 173–74; Mūṣilī, *Ikhtiyār*, V, 70. [123] Ṭūsī, *Khilāf*, II, 93.
[124] On these types of homicide, see chapter 10, section 3, below.

being a slave (*riqq*), on both of which there is juristic agreement. Some jurists also added apostasy. The exclusion of slaves is justified by the fact that whatever they inherit would be the property of their master, who is the propositus himself. That Muslims and non-Muslims can have no mutual rights of inheritance is a position justified by Prophetic *ḥadīth* which are in turn grounded in the reasoning that such rights would permit the transfer of property, and therefore strength, to non-Muslim communities. That bequests can be made in favor of non-Muslims is justified according to some jurists by the legal fact that a bequest is a contract, whereas inheritance is not.[125] For the same reason, apostates cannot inherit from Muslims, but according to Ḥanafite jurists their Muslim heirs can inherit from them. The Mālikites, Shāfiʿites and Ḥanbalites objected and held the opinion that all the apostate's estate must be dispatched to the Public Treasury, as if it were war-time booty.

The Quran apportions estates according to mathematical shares in terms of half, quarter, eighth, two-thirds, one-third and one-sixth. Those who inherit one-half of the estate of the deceased are his/her daughter if she is an only child; the husband if there are neither children nor a son's children; and the full sister if the propositus has no children. Those who inherit one-quarter are the husband if he has children or a son's children, and the wife if the deceased husband has no children or a son's children. Those who receive one-eighth are the wife (and should there be more than one, the one-eighth is divided equally), if the propositus has children or son's children. Those who receive two-thirds are daughters if they are more than two in number. The mother of the propositus receives one-third if the propositus has no children, but one-sixth if there are children. The mother's half-brothers and half-sisters, if respectively two or more in number, receive in toto one-third, divisible equally amongst them irrespective of gender. But if the mother has only one half-brother or half-sister, then he or she inherits one-sixth. The same share belongs to the father of the propositus if there are children or a son's children, as well as to the son's daughter or daughters (divisible equally between or amongst them). Each of these Quranic heirs is positioned in relation to the other relatives surviving the propositus, be they of the same group or agnatic. In all possible configurations, the father, for instance, inherits in one or more of three ways, and so does the mother. Sisters, however, may inherit in one of seven ways, while half-brothers and half-sisters from the mother's side inherit in one of three ways.[126]

[125] Ḥillī, *Sharāʾiʿ*, II, 481; [Miṣrī, *Reliance*, 462].

[126] For juristic accounts of succession rules, see Mūṣilī, *Ikhtiyār*, V, 86–110; Ḥiṣnī, *Kifāya*, II, 17–31; Buhūtī, *Rawḍ*, II, 384–94. For a lucid modern account of the rules of inheritance, see Pearl and Menski, *Muslim Family Law*, 439–87.

The following is a list of heirs, the first seven categories of whom are male, the rest female: (1) husband; (2) son or son's son how low so ever; (3) father or father's father how high so ever; (4) full brother or half-brother; (5) son of full brother or son of half-brother from the same father; (6) father's full brother or father's half-brother from the same father; (7) son of the deceased's father's full brother or father's half-brother from the same father; (8) daughter; (9) son's daughter, son's son's daughter how low so ever; (10) mother; (11) grandmother and great-grandmother how high so ever; (12) full sister or half-sister; and (13) wife. This list includes those who are entitled to a Quranic share (known as *aṣḥāb al-farāʾiḍ*), as well as the agnates (*ʿaṣaba*), those males that are related to the propositus without a female link, with precedence going to the immediate agnates, namely: (a) the male descendants how low so ever; (b) male ascendants how high so ever; (c) brothers and sons of brothers; (d) paternal uncles; and (e) the *mawlā*s (clients through patronage). The Mālikites and Shāfiʿites included in this list of agnates the Public Treasury. Unless the Quranic sharers have exhausted the entire estate, the agnates inherit along with them, taking the residue. These two groups take precedence over any other, excluding cognates (*dhawū al-arḥām*), *mawlā*s, acknowledged relationships (through *iqrār*)[127] and the Public Treasury, in the case of jurists who do not deem this as belonging to the agnatic group. But the agnatic group is not strictly agnatic, as females do enter into its orbit. The jurists recognize not only the *ʿaṣaba* as defined above (known as *ʿaṣaba bil-nafs*, i.e., *ʿaṣaba* in and by itself), but also an *ʿaṣaba bil-ghayr*, namely, an agnatic extension. Female heirs, such as the daughter of the son, acquire the status of *ʿaṣaba bil-ghayr* through their brothers who are immune heirs. Also recognized is the *ʿaṣaba maʿa al-ghayr*, namely, females who become *ʿaṣaba* by standing in conjunction with another female, such as the full or half-sister(s) on the father's side.[128]

Yet, the two primary groups of Quranic and agnatic heirs are not mutually exclusive, as certain male members qualify as both Quranic sharers and agnates. For example, the father of the propositus, depending on who the other heirs are, may inherit a fixed share or an agnatic portion or both. But neither he nor any other beneficiary can exclude male descendants or ascendants, who are always protected. The only exception is the son of a predeceased son, who will not inherit the share that his dead

[127] I.e., acknowledgment by the propositus that a certain person is related to him through blood, paternity claims included. On *iqrār*, see previous chapter, section 13. On paternity and "marriage bed" in both *fiqh* and the modern nation-state, see chapter 16, section 3, below.

[128] Nawawī, *Rawḍa*, V, 10–11; Mūṣilī, *Ikhtiyār*, V, 92–94; Ibn Qudāma, *Kāfī*, II, 386.

father would have inherited since Sunnite law does not acknowledge the right of representation.

Quranic heirs may exclude either agnatic or cognatic heirs or both (*ḥajb ḥirmān*), or they can reduce their shares (*ḥajb nuqṣān*).[129] Yet, some of the Quranic sharers themselves may be subject to partial or total exclusion, partial meaning a reduction in their shares due to the presence of a certain configuration of living relatives. Those who are always immune from any exclusion are the parents, the surviving spouse, and sons and daughters. Those who are subject to a partial exclusion are the spouses, the mother, the son's daughter and the maternal aunt. But some of those who are subject to total exclusion may, by virtue of being so excluded, cause other heirs to suffer reduction in their shares. For example, if the propositus leaves behind a father, a mother and brothers, the presence of the brothers in the configuration causes a reduction in the share of the mother to the value of one-sixth. The point of reduction is of course to make the total sum of fractions come to one. It happens that certain configurations create a situation in which the Quranic rules may produce an aggregate of shares that is larger than one, in which case the mathematical arrangement is maintained but each share is reduced proportionately (through the so-called *ʿawl*), so one-sixth might become one-seventh or two-fifteenths. Conversely, in other configurations, especially when no distant agnates remain alive at the death of the propositus, the Quranic sharers do not exhaust the entire estate, in which case the residue is divided among the heirs proportionate to their shares. This method, known as *radd* (lit. return),[130] was not acknowledged by the Mālikites, who held the residue to be the share of the Public Treasury.

Finally, it must be said that the complexity of the Sharīʿa system of inheritance may be explained by the fact that the new religion of Islam came, through the Quranic revelation, to affirm a number of positions that constituted what it is to be a Muslim and what it is that distinguishes this religion from others. One of these distinguishing reforms was a concerted attempt to reduce the power of tribalism and to chip away at its structures. Tribal conceptions stood in diametrical opposition to the Islamic notions of community (*umma*), whereas the family, in its extended form, did not. Reportedly, in pre-Islamic Arabia only male agnates inherited, but Islam incorporated into the religious community the women of the nuclear family, privileging them over agnates outside of the nuclear framework. The Quranic legislation of share-based inheritance must thus be seen as the sphere in which the Quran modified the tribal system of agnatic

[129] Nawawī, *Rawḍa*, V, 26–29; Ibn Māza, *Muḥīṭ*, XXIII, 306.
[130] Nawawī, *Rawḍa*, V, 45 ff.; Ibn Māza, *Muḥīṭ*, XXIII, 318 ff.

succession, relegating it to a virtual secondary status, but certainly not disposing of it altogether since some agnates themselves stood within the family bounds that Islam wished not only to maintain but to promote.

In light of particular political circumstances having to do with claims to the caliphate, the Twelver-Shīʿite interpretation of the Quran and the law entirely excluded from succession the category of agnates. Except for the son, all other agnates within the Sunnite group of Quranic heirs inherit less according to Twelver-Shīʿite law. The heirs stand in three different classes, each of which entirely excludes lower classes. Parents and lineal descendants constitute the first class, whereas grandparents, brothers, sisters and their descendants make up the second. The third class is made up of paternal and maternal uncles and aunts as well as those of parents and their issue.[131] The nearer to the deceased in the first two classes exclude the less near within each of these classes, and the nearest members within both of these classes inherit together, irrespective of their relative degree of proximity to the propositus. The Twelver-Shīʿite arrangement into classes, coupled with the rule of exclusion, leads to results that drastically differ from those at which Sunnite law arrives. For example, under the latter, the estate of a deceased person survived by a daughter, a mother and a brother will be divided as follows: one-half for the daughter, one-sixth for the mother, and one-third for the brother (as an agnate). Under Twelver-Shīʿite law, by contrast, the daughter and the mother, being heirs in the first class, exclude the brother altogether, as he belongs to the second class. Through *radd*, the brother's share is proportionately divided between daughter and mother. Furthermore, and significant to legal changes in the twentieth century,[132] in Sunnite law the estate of a propositus who is survived by a full brother and a daughter's son (but not the daughter herself), will be entirely inherited by the brother. But not so in Twelver-Shīʿite law, where the daughter's son will be the one to inherit the entire estate.[133] Finally, as we recall, while the Shīʿite jurists, like their Sunnite counterparts, limit bequests to one-third of the estate, they depart from Sunnite law in giving the testator complete freedom to allocate it to an heir.[134]

131 Ḥillī, *Sharāʾiʿ*, IV, 261 ff. 132 See chapter 16, sections 3–4, below.

133 Ṭūsī, *Khilāf*, II, 33–36, 42–55. For these and other examples, see Ḥillī, *Sharāʾiʿ*, IV, 271–85. For Shīʿite *ḥadīth* related to this ruling, see Ṭūsī, *Istibṣār*, III, 166–68. See also Pearl and Menski, *Muslim Family Law*, 470–72. See also Khan, *Islamic Law of Inheritance*, 100–26.

134 For a reevaluation of the legal history of Quranic succession, see Kimber, "Qurʾanic Law"; Powers, *Studies*.

9 Property and ownership

1. Introduction

The Islamic juristic categories of ownership and property are grounded in the theological conception that God is the sole and ultimate Owner (*Mālik*) of the universe. *Mālik*, a name and an attribute of God, is the active participle denoting "one who owns," while *milk*, the verbal noun, represents a state in which ownership obtains. God is thus the true Owner of everything,[1] including human beings and all they possess. Strictly speaking, therefore, human beings own nothing. And so it is only by divine generosity that it becomes possible for human beings to claim, and only in a metaphorical (*majāzī*), not a real (*ḥaqīqī*),[2] sense, rights of ownership over parts of the world.[3] This generosity manifested itself as an act of delegation and subsidiary empowerment. Quran 57:7 states: "Believe in Allah and His Messenger, and spend (*anfiqū*) of that with regard to which he made you [his] deputies" (*mustakhlafīna fīhi*). Human ownership, put in legal terms, is empowerment by agency (*wakāla*), and it is constrained by the terms of good conduct expected of humans in dispensing of God's wealth.[4] Good conduct in dispensation is linguistically funneled through the imperative form "spend" which, throughout centuries of legal discourse, consistently refers to spending in the way of care and charity, including on one's family, relatives, and the poor, all of which translate into a duty to care for one's community.[5] While "spending" was generally left, by virtue of this agency, to the individual's

[1] Ibn Manẓūr, *Lisān*, X, 492.

[2] For the distinction between real and metaphorical uses of language, see chapter 2, section 4, above.

[3] Ghazālī, *Mukhtaṣar*, 109.

[4] This conception stands in stark contrast to the modern notion of the "conquest of nature," a notion that defines not only modernity's exploitation of the natural environment but the very intractable problems that have arisen as a result of this intrusive exploitation. In this context, see also Wichard, *Zwischen Markt und Moschee*, 91–93.

[5] Ṭabarī, *Tafsīr*, XI, 671–72; Ibn Kathīr, *Tafsīr*, IV, 476–77.

discretion and sense of good conduct,[6] those parts of spending which pertained to family and the poor were retained as the "Rights of God." Thus, agency is not absolute but rather limited by a direct covenant whose terms require that part of God's wealth remains with Him so that He can ensure that the prosperous give to those who are not. This theological–social conception of property and wealth is both Quranic and paradigmatic, constituting an essential part of Muslim belief.

The concepts of ownership and property (*māl*) are complementary in that together they provide the entire gamut of parameters for the relationship between things, on the one hand, and those who are competent to possess rights over them, on the other. Thus, ownership is the lawfully unencumbered right of exclusive enjoyment of the substance of the thing and/or its usufruct, be this in the way of benefiting from its produce, services or rent. It is a "legal relationship between a person and a thing that permits him, to the exclusion of others, to dispense with it [within the boundaries of the law]".[7] Conversely, property is that substance which is lawfully made, together with its usufruct, the object of ownership rights.

2. Concepts and categories

A theory of property represents the sum total of typological oppositions that arise from various rights attached to property in diverse transactional contexts. The Ḥanafites classified property into two types, one possessing value (*mutaqawwim*), the other not (*ghayr mutaqawwim*).[8] The *mutaqawwim* is deemed subject to the full range of lawful transactions, including sale, rent, pledge and gift. Valueless property, on the other hand, is barred from such transactions as it is deemed unlawful. Prime examples of this type of property are wine and pork, considered lawful for the *dhimmī*s but not for Muslims. The functional relevance of this distinction pertains, *inter alia*, to the law of damages, since the act of destroying wine or pigs owned by a Muslim does not give rise to any compensatory rights, irrespective of the religious identity of the transgressor. However, such a transgression would warrant full compensation when the pig or wine is owned by Christians, since property here is deemed *mutaqawwim*.[9] The Mālikites do not recognize this Ḥanafite typology, but uphold the compensatory rights of *dhimmī*s on the grounds that these denominations themselves regard pigs and wine as property, strictly speaking. For the

[6] Such discourse on the ethics of spending constituted a preoccupation of manuals on ethical conduct. See, e.g., Ḥasanī, *Tahdhīb al-Akhlāq*, 68 ff., 101 f.
[7] Aḥmadnagarī, *Jāmiʿ al-ʿUlūm*, III, 322. [8] Bāz, *Sharḥ*, I, 70.
[9] Baghdādī, *Majmaʿ*, 130–31; Ṭūsī, *Khilāf*, I, 679.

Shāfiʿites and Ḥanbalites, however, the relevant consideration is not the value attached to property by the law of a particular denomination, but rather the very lawfulness of its use in the Sharīʿa. Accordingly, wine and pork, whose consumption is illicit in Islam, are considered to be of no value, a doctrine that bars payment of any compensation when pigs or wine, owned by *dhimmīs*, are destroyed or damaged.[10]

The same Ḥanafite typological distinction applies to animals in the wild, such as free birds and fish in the sea.[11] In their natural habitat, these animals are deemed to have no monetary value until they are captured. Again, this distinction finds its origins and relevance in the law of damages, for the destruction of fish in the sea does not give rise to any claims for compensation since ownership does not exist. Furthermore, the Ḥanafites do not recognize value as residing in every form of property of the *mutaqawwim* type, such as a single or a few grains of wheat or a miniscule slice of bread. Thus, technically, while sampling a small quantity of foodstuff in a grocery store might constitute theft under one or another legal system, in Ḥanafite doctrine it does not.

Unlike the other three Sunnite schools,[12] the Ḥanafites also hold that usufruct is not a *mutaqawwim* property since it is not a thing, but a contingent (*ʿaraḍ*).[13] In other words, a property may or may not yield a usufruct, such as a horse which might not be put to any use. Only when the usufruct becomes the object of an actual pecuniary transaction, such as rent, does its potential come to be realized, thereby acquiring the status of property.[14]

Property is also classified into fungible (*mithlī*) and non-fungible (*qīmī*).[15] Fungibles are defined as property the kind of which is "commonly available in the market, without there being an appreciable difference [between and among its individual members]." Such property may be of the type that can be measured by volume (e.g., barley and wheat), by weight (e.g., silver, iron and gold), by surface (e.g., silk and wool garments), or by number (e.g., money and eggs). Non-fungibles are properties the likes of which are not to be commonly found available in the market, and even if they are to be found, the members of each species would be so different from each other so as to affect their individual value appreciably. Examples of these are houses and pieces of jewelry, each of which is considered unique, thus requiring individual valuation. Also belonging to this category are fungibles that have become rare or gone out of common circulation, such as antiques.[16] This typology is highly relevant for at least two important spheres in

[10] Ibn al-Laḥḥām, *Qawāʿid*, 54; Buhūtī, *Rawḍ*, II, 341; Ṭūsī, *Khilāf*, I, 679.
[11] Bāz, *Sharḥ*, I, 70, 101; Shaʿrānī, *Mīzān*, II, 84. [12] E.g., Buhūtī, *Sharḥ*, II, 140.
[13] Aḥmadnagharī, *Jāmiʿ al-ʿUlūm*, III, 188; Bāz, *Sharḥ*, I, 69–70.
[14] Kāsānī, *Badāʾiʿ*, III, 494; Qārī, *Majalla*, 112.
[15] Bāz, *Sharḥ*, I, 71–72. [16] *Ibid.*, I, 620.

the law: (1) determining the forms of compensation when claims of damages arise; and (2) determining whether or not usurious interest was levied in transactions involving them.

Property is likewise divisible into productive (*nāmī*) and non-productive (*qunya*) types. Inherent in the former is the capability to grow, either physically (as in raising cattle), by procreation (as in breeding) or by means of investment (as in commercial dealings and rent). An example of non-productive property is an ordinary utensil used for household purposes; it can be neither rented nor traded for purposes of commercial gain. Again, the chief purpose of this distinction is to determine the value of compensation in damage claims, for, as we shall see, productive property that was misappropriated must be restituted (either in kind or in cash) along with the growth that the appropriator enjoyed while it was in his possession.

Misappropriation and loss also give rise to the distinction between property that is deemed likely to be regained (*māl marjuww*) and property of which there is no hope of return (*māl ḍimār*). Property whose owner fails to produce evidence both of his entitlement and of its misappropriation is not likely to be won back. Similarly, a runaway slave or a purse that fell from a sailing ship is considered *māl ḍimār*.

In addition to the distinction between freehold and encumbered property (e.g., pledged property with regard to which the owner's rights of enjoyment are restricted), a major distinction is one between movable (*manqūl*) and immovable property (*ʿaqār*). All commodities measurable by weight, volume and number are of the movable type; so are cattle and currency. Buildings and land constitute the main objects of the immovable type, in turn divisible into covered structures (*musaqqaf*; e.g., houses, shops, public baths) and that which is measurable (*mudharraʿ*, *madhrūʿ*; e.g., vineyards, pastures, cultivable fields).[17]

The foregoing typologies define property *qua* property. Ownership, on the other hand, defines the legal relationships between persons and property insofar as rights are concerned. For this reason, the notion of ownership rights is best expounded through typification. Accordingly, ownership may be complete (*tāmm*) or incomplete (*nāqiṣ*, *ḍaʿīf*), complete meaning rights over both the substance and usufruct of the property, and incomplete consisting of rights over either of the two, but not both at once. The jurists moreover assert that when the term "ownership" (*milk*) is used without qualification, the default referent is complete ownership, which must include the rights to usufruct. But usufruct may be owned

[17] *Ibid.*, I, 71–72, 105–07.

indefinitely, to the exclusion of the substance, as happens in the case of *waqf*, where enjoyment never entails ownership of the trust's substance.

Ownership rights to usufruct are in turn divided into (a) rights of enjoyment (*milk intifāʿ*) that – by operation of the law – bar the owner from leasing or selling these rights, and (b) rights that can be shared with others (*milk manfaʿa*). An example of *milk intifāʿ* would be the right to enjoy the benefits accruing from residing in a law college or *khānqāh*, where such a right cannot be transferred in any fashion for any type of remuneration.[18] The distinction has come to be expressed by the maxim: "He who owns *manfaʿa* owns the right to rent out and to loan" (*Man malaka al-manfaʿa fa-lahu al-ijāra wal-iʿāra*).

On another level, the difference between complete and incomplete ownership lies in the fact that the former gives the owner the right to dispose of his property in any lawful manner, including renting it or alienating it, whether in the form of gift or sale. This is why incomplete ownership is not a *real* one, since the owner is limited, within his rights to usufruct, either to enjoyment only (in the case of *milk intifāʿ*) or to rent or loan (in the case of *milk manfaʿa*). Furthermore, complete ownership is distinguished by indefiniteness, in that this type of ownership must not, by definition, be contingent upon any limitation of time. Incomplete ownership, on the other hand, is restricted by duration, place, or aspects of usufruct. For instance, a person (having ownership rights to usufruct) may rent a horse for a year to transport logs from a particular village to another.

The manner by which property accrues to persons lies behind another classification of ownership rights, divided into so-called voluntary (*milk ikhtiyārī*) or involuntary acquisition (*milk qahrī*). The voluntary type accrues by initiative; for example, by purchase, by raising certain animals and hunting others, or by cultivating dead land. The other is involuntary in the sense that the property devolves upon a prospective owner by virtue of the act of another; e.g., by receiving shares in inheritance or benefits from a *waqf* endowment.

Ownership is further constrained by three considerations, namely, mode of acquisition, use and transfer. For it to be lawful, ownership must accrue through legal means which preclude, among other things, unlawful appropriation (*ghaṣb*),[19] theft (*sariqa*)[20] or usurious interest (*ribā*).[21] The use of property within the confines of lawful ownership is moreover predicated upon sound use, where moderation in "spending" (*infāq*) is required. In certain instances, lawful ownership combines with

[18] *Ibid.*, I, 318–19. [19] See next section. [20] See chapter 10, section 2, iv, below.
[21] Shaʿrānī, *Mīzān*, II, 88–89; [Miṣrī, *Reliance*, 384–87].

sound use so as to produce a derivative constraint. For example, while the acquisition and ownership of silk may be lawful, men are not permitted to wear it.[22] Similarly, productive property accruing by lawful means must not lie idle, for the law morally demands that it be worked, traded, manufactured or cultivated. Working to increase wealth is therefore deemed a duty incumbent upon every individual Muslim capable of fulfilling it (*farḍ kifāya*).[23] Finally, as in the manner of acquisition, transfer must not involve fraud, unjustifiable enrichment (*ghabn*), or absence of mutual satisfaction (*riḍā*).[24]

Although private ownership and private property are sacrosanct, the interests of the community as a public collectivity are deemed superior. Accordingly, the ruler can expropriate individual property – at a fair market price – for the purpose of constructing public facilities, such as expanding streets or enlarging college-mosques. The ruler can also force an individual to sell his property at a fair market price if there is a dire public need for it. A classic example of this is the ruler's intervention to prevent *iḥtikār*, a sort of monopoly whereby a product on the market is hoarded for the purpose of increasing its price at a later date when supply diminishes and demand rises. Private property can also be sold by the judge in order to satisfy unpaid debts, or outstanding wifely or child support in the case of husbands or fathers who abandoned their family but left assets behind, or for payment of damages, whether arising from criminal offenses (e.g., blood-money) or pecuniary transactions (*ḍamān*).[25] So too can jointly owned property be sold by the judge upon petition by one of the partners, on the grounds that the petitioner would incur a loss if he were to sell only his share in the joint property. The governing principle here is that private property is sacrosanct as long as it does not prejudice the rights of others.

3. Unlawful appropriation (*ghaṣb*)

Property and ownership are distinguished from possession (*yad*), for a person can lawfully or unlawfully possess the property of others, such as in

[22] Ibn al-Laḥḥām, *Qawāʿid*, 52.

[23] In the same vein, work (with or without property, capital or assets being involved) is deemed *farḍ kifāya* proportionate with the needs of the individual. An adult male is thus expected to work hard enough to support his wife, children and poor parents. But it is preferable that such earnings be in excess of what is needed to support immediate family and distant relatives, for that excess ought to be spent on the poor at large. This form of piety is deemed superior to that which manifests itself in the form of performing prayers and other rituals in excess of the number required by law. See Ibn Mufliḥ, *Ādāb*, III, 423–42, 452–59.

[24] For *riḍā*, see chapter 7, section 1, i, above.

[25] Buhūtī, *Sharḥ*, II, 141.

a relationship of fiduciary duty (*yad amāna*) or one of unlawful appropriation (*yad ghāṣiba, yad bāṭila, yad ʿudwān*), respectively. Fiduciary relationships (*amāna*) constitute the backdrop to the laws of custody, agency, pledge and much else that is discussed in other chapters in this Part. A discussion of unlawful appropriation, however, belongs here, as it directly pertains to the "civil" sphere of misappropriation, and is distinct and separate from theft and related felonious offenses against property.

Unlawful taking of property[26] violates one of the five universals upon which the Sharīʿa is deemed to rest, namely, right to life, religion, mind, procreation and property. The Quran warns against taking the property of others unlawfully (2:188), and the Prophet is reputed to have said, among other things in this regard: "He who unlawfully takes a foot of land will be punished in the Hereafter with seven pieces of land collapsing upon him."[27]

The elements constituting unlawful taking vary from one school to another. Many Ḥanafite jurists tend to restrict the scope of misappropriation by a number of requirements: for them, to qualify as such, misappropriation must entail dispossession, namely, the "removal of the owner's hand"[28] from his property openly (*jahran*) and by way of transgression (*ʿudwānan*). In other words, public seizure must obtain, while the requirement of openness is intended to differentiate between criminal theft and non-criminal ("civil") misappropriation. None of the other schools, however, seems to have required the element of openness, and they confined their definition to the unlawful taking of property, which ultimately rests on lack of the owner's permission (*idhn*).[29] Furthermore, none of the other schools, nor even Shaybānī or Zufar (two of Abū Ḥanīfa's most prominent disciples), required the "removal of the owner's hand," which means that, according to the rest of the Ḥanafites, the property itself not only must transfer hands in terms of possession but must also be capable of being transferred physically. This is why Abū Ḥanīfa and Abū Yūsuf, whose joint opinion was adopted as the authoritative doctrine in the Ḥanafite school, did not deem immovable property to be capable of *ghaṣb*.[30] The other schools, including the Twelver-Shīʿites, defined "unlawful taking" (*istīlāʾ*) to mean depriving the owner of his property without this necessarily involving the removal or transfer of the property itself.[31] Thus, *ghaṣb* occurs when, for instance, a residence is taken

[26] [On *ghaṣb* in general, see Miṣrī, *Reliance*, 429–32; Ibn Rushd, *Distinguished Jurist's Primer*, II, 383–93.]
[27] Cited in Buhūtī, *Sharḥ*, II, 400. [28] Ibn Māza, *Muḥīṭ*, VIII, 200.
[29] *Ibid.*; Ibn al-Ḥājib, *Jāmiʿ*, 409 ff.
[30] Ibn Māza, *Muḥīṭ*, VIII, 200; Ṭūsī, *Khilāf*, I, 675. [31] Nawawī, *Rawḍa*, IV, 98–99.

unlawfully and when the taker places his possessions and furniture in it, an act that constitutes *istīlā'*.[32]

Except for the Ḥanbalites, all schools allow the judge the discretion to inflict a term of imprisonment and a measure of beating in cases of intentional and pernicious *ghaṣb* (deemed similar to theft according to the Shāfiʿites, Ḥanafites and Twelver-Shīʿites).[33] None, however, sets pecuniary punitive damages.[34] Since *ghaṣb* can occur without intent to take property unlawfully, most jurists did not deem intention to be a definitional part of what constitutes *ghaṣb*.[35] Unintentional misappropriation – as when a partner (*sharīk*) unknowingly uses and disposes of the other partner's property, thinking it to be his own – does not create *ithm*, a sort of moral sin, punishable, if committed, in the Hereafter. Representing this lenient view, the Ḥanafites and Ḥanbalites – as well as jurists of other schools – left the determination of *ithm* and its potentially malevolent effects to God and the Hereafter.[36] What mattered was restoring rights, not punishment of an act where *niyya*, being a hidden matter (*fil-bāṭin*), cannot be determined.

It was universally agreed that property must be returned to the same place from which it was taken, since the market value was deemed to be affected by location.[37] Any and all costs involved in restoring the property are entirely the responsibility of the *ghāṣib*, for, so goes the reasoning, if he is under the obligation to restore the property, then he is under obligation to incur all expenses entailed by restoration.[38] In the event the misappropriated object perishes or is lost (or escapes, as in the case of a runaway slave), then, if the property is fungible, a like object – equivalent in shape, color, size, value, etc. – must be offered instead, and if it is non-fungible, then its fair market price.

The misappropriated property must furthermore be returned in the same condition it was taken.[39] The *ghāṣib* is liable for any changes that he made to the property in a manner that affects its value. The owner is entitled to have the *ghāṣib* destroy, at his own expense, any structure he built on the misappropriated property, or uproot any trees or plants that have grown there. But the jurists differ as to the manner of compensation

[32] Ḥillī, *Sharā'iʿ*, IV, 204; Ṭūsī, *Khilāf*, I, 675. [33] Ṭūsī, *Khilāf*, I, 675.
[34] With the possible exception of Ibn Taymiyya. See his *Mukhtaṣar*, 341.
[35] However, see the Zaydite Shawkānī, *al-Sayl al-Jarrār*, III, 83.
[36] Ibn Māza, *Muḥīṭ*, VIII, 200.
[37] Nawawī, *Rawḍa*, IV, 111; Ibn Māza, *Muḥīṭ*, VIII, 205; Shaʿrānī, *Mīzān*, II, 120.
[38] And if the owner happens to incur any expense in the process of restoring the misappropriated object, then the *ghāṣib* is held responsible for such costs. See Nawawī, *Rawḍa*, IV, 111; Yanagihashi, *History*, 98 ff.
[39] Ḥillī, *Sharā'iʿ*, IV, 207.

when the misappropriated object is subjected to conditions that bar a straightforward recovery. The case of a misappropriated wooden beam used in the construction of a house poses the question of feasibility of recovery in that the destruction of the house might cause more damage or harm than had been caused by the misappropriation of the beam. In this case, some Ḥanafites opine that, upon embedding the beam in the structure, the beam ceases to be the property of the owner, and the *ghāṣib* becomes liable for its value. Other jurists, including some Ḥanafites, argue that if the misappropriated property is of a higher value than the object in which it has been embedded, then the object may be destroyed with a view to returning the property intact to its legitimate owner.[40] Still other jurists hold the view that, regardless of the relative value of the two properties being wedded, the owner loses the right to the misappropriated object itself and becomes instead entitled to its value.[41]

The Twelver-Shīʿites, however, do not oblige the owner to accept the equivalent value of the misappropriated property, but instead demand that the *ghāṣib* extract it from the structure within which it is embedded, whatever the loss to his property may be.[42] The Mālikites bestow on the owner this entire range of options, but with limitations: he may have the trees planted or structures built on the misappropriated property uprooted or destroyed by the *ghāṣib*; or he may keep them, but must compensate the *ghāṣib* for the value of improvements the latter made to the property.[43]

When land is unlawfully taken and the structure built on it by the *ghāṣib* has a higher value than the land itself, then the *ghāṣib* has the right to become owner of the land but must compensate the victim for its fair market value. The Shāfiʿites and Ḥanbalites, on the other hand, would compel the *ghāṣib* to destroy, at his own expense, all accretions to the property. He must compensate the owner for any damage caused to the land by such destruction, and must also return the land in the same condition as had obtained at the time of misappropriation. He is further liable for the highest possible estimate of its usufruct, whether actually realized or not.[44] The Ḥanafites, on the other hand, do not award damages for usufruct on the grounds that usufruct, regarded as non-*mutaqawwim* property, is incapable of *ghaṣb* in the first place.[45] Thus, should someone unlawfully take another's land or house, and should he plant seeds in the land or rent the house, the *ghāṣib* is entitled to the crop or rent, not the owner. Only if the property diminishes in value due to his

[40] Ibn Māza, *Muḥīṭ*, VIII, 211. [41] For still more opinions, see Nawawī, *Rawḍa*, IV, 142.
[42] Ḥillī, *Sharāʾiʿ*, IV, 207–08. [43] Ibn al-Ḥājib, *Jāmiʿ*, 412–13.
[44] Nawawī, *Rawḍa*, IV, 103. [45] Kāsānī, *Badāʾiʿ*, III, 494.

ventures will he be liable to compensate the owner for the amount of his loss. All other schools, including the Twelver-Shīʿites, award damages for the full value of misappropriated usufruct.[46]

Changes to the nature of the misappropriated object raises another set of rules. In the case of change by force of nature, such as grapes turning into raisins, the owner has the right either to recover the object itself in its changed state or receive its value. But if the change was effected through the *ghāṣib*'s work on the misappropriated object (e.g., dyeing a dress or mixing unlawfully taken barley with his own), the owner, in Ḥanafite jurisprudence, is given an option: he can receive damages equaling the value of the object before it was transformed, or take the transformed object and compensate the usurper the difference of any increased value. However, the Shāfiʿites, Ḥanbalites and Twelver-Shīʿites disagree with this Ḥanafite position, holding the view that if the *ghāṣib* invested only labor and workmanship in the transformation of the object, then the *ghāṣib* is entitled to no compensation whatsoever, and all increases in the value of the misappropriated object must revert to the owner. They ground this doctrine in the Prophetic report: "The sweat of the transgressor shall not be rewarded."[47] If, however, the *ghāṣib* also invested in material improvements to the misappropriated object, then both receive shares proportionate to the value of their property.[48]

The Shāfiʿites, the Ḥanbalites and the Ḥanafite Shaybānī hold that the *ghāṣib* is liable for the value of growth accruing to the property while in his custody, whether this growth is an integral part of the property (*muttaṣil*; e.g., a calf becoming a cow) or separate from it (*munfaṣil*; e.g., growing crops or breeding cattle).[49] Unless destroyed by *force majeure*, the *ghāṣib* is liable for restoring them or their value, irrespective of whether or not he was responsible for their destruction. (In case of destruction by a third party, the *ghāṣib* is liable to the owner, while the third party becomes liable to the *ghāṣib* to the extent of the value of damages he caused.) This opinion is rejected by Abū Ḥanīfa and Abū Yūsuf, who award damages only when the *ghāṣib* transgresses against the property, in which case the damages do not arise on account of *ghaṣb* but only from aggression (*taʿaddī*) and negligence (*taqṣīr*). Their reasoning rests on the premise that the growth occurred while the property was in the custody of the *ghāṣib*, which is to say that the owner of the misappropriated property cannot be the owner of a *post factum* growth. In other words, "removal of the owner's hand," a constitutive element of the Ḥanafite definition, cannot be said to have taken place insofar as growth is concerned.

[46] Ṭūsī, *Khilāf*, I, 674; Ḥillī, *Sharāʾiʿ*, IV, 214. [47] Buhūtī, *Kashshāf*, IV, 80–81.
[48] Buhūtī, *Rawḍ*, II, 344–45. [49] Qārī, *Majalla*, 434; Ṭūsī, *Khilāf*, I, 681–83.

The Shāfiʿites, Ḥanbalites and Twelver-Shīʿites also award the victim of *ghaṣb* the usufruct or its value. The rent of a misappropriated object during the period of unlawful taking must be paid to the owner irrespective of whether or not the *ghāṣib* derived these profits himself. In other words, unlike the Ḥanafites and Mālikites, the Shāfiʿites and Ḥanbalites (and at least some Twelver-Shīʿite jurists) fully allow for the recovery of lost profits on rentable and hirable things[50] *plus* the misappropriated substance itself.[51] The Mālikites, however, make the *ghāṣib* liable only for profits actually made, not for missed opportunity.

Based on Abū Ḥanīfa's opinion, authoritative Ḥanafite doctrine deems the rights to compensation for misappropriated fungibles to arise as of the date of litigation, namely, when a suit is brought before the *qāḍī*. The majority of the jurists, including other major Ḥanafites, hold liability to arise as of the day misappropriation took place, whether the object misappropriated was fungible or not. In Mālikite doctrine, the value of the property is determined on the day of misappropriation, and is not subject to varying valuation according to price fluctuation. The Shāfiʿites and Ḥanbalites, on the other hand, measure the value of the property from the day of misappropriation but consider, for purposes of determining the amount of damages, its maximum value.[52] They are quite distinct in their unqualified stance against *ghaṣb*, insisting that the owner is entitled to this maximum, plus any damages for defects caused during the period of misappropriation, plus all rent and growth actually incurred or lost.

4. Pre-emption (*shufʿa*)

In jointly owned property, each party enjoys a prior option to purchase the share(s) of his co-owner(s).[53] Only upon refusal to exercise this right can a third party (*ajnabī*) purchase the property. The Ḥanafites appear to be alone in extending the same right to neighbors as well.[54] A majority of jurists allow only immovable property and fixtures (e.g., trees, though not their fruits)[55] to be subject to *shufʿa*, but a few admit movables, such as ships, tools and animals.[56] Some Mālikites permit exercising the right of *shufʿa* in ownership of usufruct (*manfaʿa*), such as in the case of renting

[50] As defined by custom, dwellings being a universally rentable property, while certain agricultural tools may be deemed so in some regions but not in others. On these customary variations, see Hallaq, "Prelude to Ottoman Reform," 51–53.
[51] Nawawī, *Rawḍa*, IV, 103; Ḥillī, *Sharāʾiʿ*, IV, 214. [52] Nawawī, *Rawḍa*, IV, 110–11.
[53] This basic doctrine is said to be subject to consensus. See Shaʿrānī, *Mīzān*, II, 124; [Miṣrī, *Reliance*, 432–34; Ibn Rushd, *Distinguished Jurist's Primer*, II, 307–16].
[54] Nawawī, *Rawḍa*, IV, 159–60; Ḥillī, *Sharāʾiʿ*, III, 223.
[55] Cf. Ibn al-Ḥājib, *Jāmiʿ*, 416. [56] Ḥillī, *Sharāʾiʿ*, III, 221.

agricultural land.[57] Right of *shufʿa* ceases if the purchaser is unable to provide full and immediate payment (*ʿala al-fawr*).[58]

5. Slavery (*riqq*)

Captivity was the single means by which slavery could come into existence, provided that the captive was not Muslim at the time of capture.[59] Once falling into this status, slaves could be sold, leased out for services or freed. They were treated as property and as persons, depending on the situation.[60] For example, they could be pledged and sold, but like free men and women they were under the obligation to fulfill some religious duties. Within the field of ritual laws, they were not obliged to perform pilgrimage yet they had to fast during Ramadan, the reason being that fasting does not affect the rights of their masters over them, but pilgrimage does, in that the slave's traveling to Mecca, and consequent absence, were liable to deprive his/her master of the services (usufruct) the slave owed him by duty.

Slaves could own property but ultimately it belonged, as they themselves did, to their masters or mistresses. From this arose the exemption from paying alms-tax (*zakāt*), which some jurists made to be the master's obligation. Although contracts of sale that attach a condition limiting the future use or ownership of the buyer were deemed null and void (since such limitations contravened full rights of ownership, the purpose of the contract in the first place), it was permissible, in the case of selling slaves, to insert the condition that they be freed by the buyer upon or after purchase.Together with feeding the poor, freeing slaves was the chief means of penance (*kaffāra*).[61]

[57] Ibn al-Ḥājib, *Jāmiʿ*, 416; Ibn ʿAbd al-Rafīʿ, *Muʿīn*, II, 573–74.

[58] Ḥiṣnī, *Kifāya*, I, 298–99; Ḥillī, *Sharāʾiʿ*, III, 223.

[59] *Fiqh*'s juristic presumption is that people are born free and that their status as slaves is a contingent (*ʿāriḍ*). A foundling (*laqīṭ*) whose parentage is unknown, or cannot be proven to originate in slavery, is deemed free. See Ibn al-Ḥājib, *Jāmiʿ*, 460. Similarly, if a slave who has attained the age of majority claims he is a free person, the onus of proof (*bayyina*) is upon him who claims otherwise, and any evidence to the effect that the slave had, in the past, served him as a slave, is irrelevant. Ownership must be established, since the presumption is that people are free unless proven otherwise. Ibn Mufliḥ, *Furūʿ*, IV, 579–80; Subkī, *Fatāwā*, I, 381; II, 504.

[60] While obedience to the master or mistress is of the essence, the latter cannot force their slaves to commit illegal acts, such as drinking alcohol, theft, or any other behavior damaging or harmful to others. Nor can they force them to adopt Islam if they are non-Muslims, or, if they are Muslims, forbid them from performing religious works to which they are entitled, such as prayer and fasting. Furthermore, a slave owner is prohibited from forcing his or her adult male slave to marry a woman, free or not, without the slave's consent. [On slavery in general, see Miṣrī, *Reliance*, 458–59; Ibn Rushd, *Distinguished Jurist's Primer*, II, 443–77.]

[61] See chapter 6, section 4, above.

10 Offenses

1. Introduction

It is for good reason that this chapter is not entitled "criminal law" or "penal law." The concepts of criminality and, in particular, penal justice are at the forefront of what Foucault characterized as a carceral system symptomatic of an epistemic transformation that overtook Europe between the seventeenth and nineteenth centuries, but which later became standard in the great majority of non-European legal and political systems. To term that Sharīʿa branch which deals with offenses against life, body, morality, public conduct and property "criminal" or "penal" is to be conceptually imprecise, since far from all of its infractions can be subsumed under modern notions of criminality. Even more importantly, the modern conceptualization of crime and penal law was not shared, in any marked way, by the Muslim jurists of the pre-modern era, for their notions served epistemic imperatives that fundamentally differed from those enshrined in and by the modern state and its systems. While the state's conceptions of criminality and penal codification were integral to its formation as a political-legal culture, the Sharīʿa obviously was not a state and never partook in the construction of such an entity.[1] To speak of criminality and penal law in the Islamic context is not just to inject into the pre-modern Sharīʿa notions that belonged to it only in part, but also to attribute to it notions that were conceived differently in terms of both function and structure.

Penal law in the world of modernity exercises both systemic and systematic violence[2] – the exclusive right of the state – with a view to instilling the subservience that is variably called good citizenry, a sense of service to the fatherland (or motherland) and material productivity, all of which serve the nation as a tool of the commanding state. The ultimate goal is therefore to

[1] Further on this, see the Introduction to Part III, below.
[2] Including the threat of violence which is an integral part of the definition of violence. See Aijmer and Abbink, *Meanings of Violence*, xi and *passim*.

produce as much docility as can be achieved; hence, the need for the development of the various tools that Foucault might well have called carceral epistemology (an epistemology that transcended the penal system and in fact permeated the fabric of the modern social order).[3] Systemic surveillance by the modern state, as well as its exclusive right to exercise violence, served as compensation for the collapse of social and religious morality in the new European order of state, polity and society. Where once God – or the church – commanded loyalty and willing obedience, it is now the state and the ideological nation, nationhood and nationalism that demand such devotion.[4] The world of the Sharīʿa, by contrast, lived under the full shadow of an omniscient God who – by one of the most cardinal tenets of Islam – knew each and every particular of human conduct and misdemeanor.[5] The sanctioning and controlling power of a social morality, backed by a mighty divine omnipresence, required less coercion and less penalization than what the modern secular state can today command or muster. God, it would seem, proved to be a more successful commander and ruler than the state, which found it necessary to develop – in order to compensate – a highly coercive and punitive system in order to ensure obedience. Still, obedience to the state is seldom willing or deeply psychological and spiritual, all of which qualities largely defined and shaped the relations between the Islamic social order and the Sharīʿa. It is this difference in the quality of obedience that engenders structural, functional and epistemological distinctions between the Islamic conception of offenses (and its conceptual and linguistic world), on the one hand, and its modern and Western counterparts, on the other.

The reason this is so is that Muslim jurists did not conceive of offenses as ultimately falling into a single unifying category, as happens in modern legal cultures where they are placed under the general designation "criminal law" or "penal law." In as much as there was not, strictly speaking, a family law (as opposed to a law of marriage, a law of *ṭalāq*, a law of *khulʿ*, a law of custody, a law of spousal support, a law of inheritance), there was no single umbrella category equal in scope and taxonomical grouping to the modern notion of criminal or penal law. Instead, the *fiqh* works recognized separate categories, each horizontally equated with the others. If there was a standard, it was the underlying and fundamental concept of compensation for life, limb and property.

[3] Foucault, *Power: Essential Works*, 326–48; 382–93; and on the carceral system in particular, Foucault, *Discipline and Punish*, 283–308, and *passim*.

[4] See chapters 13 and 16, below.

[5] On this doctrine and on the significant philosophical debate it generated in Islam, see Marmura, "Some Aspects," 299–312; Leaman, *Introduction*, 108–20; Hallaq, "Fashioning the Moral Subject."

Although this concept of compensation emerged out of the old Semitic and ancient Near Eastern tradition of "an eye for an eye and a tooth for a tooth," it was largely (though not totally) transformed under the Sharīʿa and its judicial practice into a system of monetary awards for the victim or his/her family to be paid by the culprit or his/her family, this amounting in effect to a form of remuneration in place of revenge. Thus, whereas in most modern legal systems homicide and bodily harm are primarily criminal offenses punished by the state as a matter of correction and retribution, in the Islamic system they were to be remedied largely – though not exclusively – through material compensation for the victim and his or her kin group. Even when the so-called retaliation was resorted to, it was not exclusively an act of revenge but represented rather the considered and measured equalization (supervised, in all cases, by the *qāḍī*) of loss of either limb or life. This law, no doubt of tribal origin, was intended to reduce the power of the transgressing tribe by the same amount and extent suffered by the transgressed tribe, for the balance of power and strength, essential for survival, had to be maintained. It might be even tempting to describe this regime as conducing to an ecological balance. Whether it was retaliation or compensation, the effect was not primarily to punish, but rather to restore loss, which in itself contributed to recreating such a balance. This in part explains the Sharīʿa's heavy reliance, incomparable to any modern penal system, on financial compensation in offenses against life (*diya*) and limb (*arsh*). It also explains why this branch of the law, like most other branches, remained in the Sharīʿa largely within the realm of private wrongs, where the ruler merely implemented punishments but himself seldom prosecuted the criminals as a part of his independent jural duty. He had, of course, the exclusive right to prosecute such criminals when they offended against him and his prerogatives, a phenomenon that enhanced further the private nature of wrongs.

As we saw earlier, offenses recognized by the Sharīʿa ranged from the moral to the pecuniary and homicidal. Some of these happened to be regulated by the Quran and the Sunna, as they appear to have acquired special importance in the life of the early Muslim community. Thus, those offenses which were regulated – to one extent or another – by the founding texts came to be known as *ḥudūd* (sing. *ḥadd*), literally, the limits prescribed by God, and technically, offenses whose punishments are fixed and are God's right. *Zinā*, wrongful accusation of *zinā* (*qadhf*), drinking alcohol (*shurb al-khamr*), theft (*sariqa*) and highway robbery (*qaṭʿ al-ṭarīq*) were accepted by all jurists as *ḥudūd* offenses.[6] The Shāfiʿites also

[6] Including the Twelver-Shīʿites. See Ḥillī, *Sharāʾiʿ*, IV, 394.

acknowledged *qiṣāṣ* as a *ḥadd*, which they saw as encompassing both homicide (*qatl*) and bodily harm (*jināyāt*).[7] The Mālikites, on the other hand, rejected the qualification of *qiṣāṣ* as a *ḥadd*, but instead included in this category insurrection (*baghy*) and apostasy (*ridda*). In addition to the offenses thus far enumerated, discretionary punishment (*ta'zīr*) was an independent category reserved for offenders who neither were guilty of homicide or bodily harm, nor had transgressed against the *ḥudūd*. Thus, if we were to exclude *qiṣāṣ* and *jināyāt* from *ḥudūd*, which is the majority position, we would be left with only three categories of offenses: (a) *ḥudūd*; (b) homicide and bodily injury; and (c) discretionary punishment.[8]

2. *Ḥudūd*

The severe sanctions applied to *ḥudūd* offenses were intended to deter (*zajr*) and were thus infrequently implemented in practice. This is exceedingly clear from the strict evidential procedures required to prove them. Yet, the harsh penalties inflicted on *ḥudūd* transgressors represented only one element of their value as deterrence, the other being their enshrinement in a moral code that bestowed on them a prohibitory force far more powerful and effective than their judicial enforceability in the here and now. Their commission, when not punished in this world, landed the offender in eternal Hellfire, an eschatological notion that tended to engender moral compliance on a deep psychological level.

The extreme economy with which the *ḥudūd* were invoked was motivated by the maxim, generated from a Prophetic *ḥadīth*, that they had to be "averted at the existence of the slightest doubt."[9] In fact, standard legal rules, otherwise invoked in all other branches of *fiqh*, were applied differently where the *ḥudūd* were concerned. For instance, in any other area of the law, confession (*iqrār*) was irrevocable, but not so in the *ḥudūd* (except in *qadhf*) where a *ḥadd* proven by confession was cancelled upon the withdrawal of that confession. In the same vein, the testimony of a secondary witness (*shahāda 'alā al-shahāda*),[10] otherwise admissible in law in general, was inadmissible in *ḥudūd*, as was any written communication between judges (*kitāb al-qāḍī ilā al-qāḍī*).[11] As we shall see in due course, while each *ḥadd* was bounded by relevant evidentiary rules, these rules were highly constricting, exclusionary and demanding. It would not be an

[7] Nawawī, *Rawḍa*, VII, 4.
[8] For a useful study of the application of these laws in Muslim Spain, see Serrano, "Twelve Court Cases."
[9] Māwardī, *Ḥāwī*, XIII, 210, 241.
[10] On this form of testimony, see chapter 12, section 2, below.
[11] On this important instrument, see Hallaq, "*Qāḍī*s Communicating."

exaggeration to state that cases of *zinā* and theft, the only offenses that required, respectively, capital punishment or mutilation – aside from highway robbery – were, short of confession, nearly impossible to establish.

*i. Fornication/adultery (*zinā*)*

Zinā is defined as sexual intercourse that (a) involves actual penetration, (b) by persons of full legal competence, (c) outside of a man's right to such intercourse, and (d) without there being any doubt whatsoever (*shubha*) with regard to these rights, even when defined broadly.[12] Having sex during the *ʿidda* is a case in point, since marriage during that period is not dissolved beyond any point of return. The waiving of the *ḥadd* punishment, moreover, does not extinguish the husband's financial liability to the wife in the amount of a fair dower (*mahr al-mithl*). A *shubha* exists even if a man merely claims, without any proof, that he had married the woman with whom he was accused to have committed *zinā* (provided, of course, that the woman is single). Likewise, if a person claims, under oath, that because of darkness he thought the woman with whom he is charged with committing *zinā* was his wife, he is vindicated.[13]

Generally, married individuals who are convicted of *zinā* are punishable by stoning and their marriages are annulled (according to some jurists). The penalty for unmarried adulterers is a hundred lashes[14] (plus banishment for one year, according to some jurists).[15] The distinction is in fact between *muḥṣan* and non-*muḥṣan*, *muḥṣan* being a free person, *compos mentis*, who has attained majority and who has consummated his marriage to a *muḥṣan* spouse (this existing in a state known as *iḥṣān*). Thus, slaves, minors and the insane are not subject to the *ḥadd*.[16] The Ḥanafites and Mālikites include in the definition of *muḥṣan* the element of membership

[12] Nawawī, *Rawḍa*, VII, 305–07; Mawāq, *Tāj*, VI, 290–91; Ḥillī, *Sharāʾiʿ*, IV, 394; [Miṣrī, *Reliance*, 610–11; Ibn Rushd, *Distinguished Jurist's Primer*, II, 521–30].

[13] Mūṣilī, *Ikhtiyār*, IV, 89–90; Māwardī, *Ḥāwī*, XIII, 217–20.

[14] Lashing by the whip must be applied in moderate force where the armpit of the person administering the whipping must not come in public view. The lashes should not be inflicted on the same location, but should be distributed so as to lessen the harm to the skin. Sensitive areas, such as chest, groin, neck, head, etc., must be avoided. The culprit must not be tied and must not be stretched on a board. Women are allowed to be whipped while seated and fully clothed. Some jurists required men to be divested of the clothing on their upper body, while others required only thick clothing to be taken off. Mūṣilī, *Ikhtiyār*, IV, 85–86; Māwardī, *Ḥāwī*, XIII, 203–04. The Ḥanbalites held the position that the lashing must be graded according to the offense, *zinā* requiring the most severe form, followed by *qadhf* (see below) and drinking alcohol, this last commanding the mildest form. See Ibn Mufliḥ, *Furūʿ*, VI, 56.

[15] See the Shāfiʿite jurist Ḥiṣnī, *Kifāya*, 178.

[16] Ḥillī, *Sharāʾiʿ*, IV, 396.

in the Islamic faith, which means that no person belonging to other confessions is subject to this penalty.[17] The Twelver-Shīʿite doctrine condemns to death anyone who commits incest or rape, whether or not they are *muḥṣan*, free, "old or young."[18] The same applies to a *dhimmī* who commits *zinā* with a Muslim woman.[19]

A charge of *zinā* must be proven by four trustworthy (*ʿadl*) male witnesses who must all appear in the same court session to testify, in extreme detail and in unambiguous (*ṣarīḥ*) language, that they saw the couple engage in sexual activity and that the man penetrated the woman to the extent that "his penis has entirely disappeared from sight."[20] The Twelver-Shīʿites admit the testimony of three men and two women or two men and four women.[21] The Ḥanafites, Mālikites, Ḥanbalites and Twelver-Shīʿites require all witnesses to appear in court simultaneously, failing which requirement, their testimony will be rejected and all of them will be charged with *qadhf*, or wrongful accusation of *zinā*. Upon cross-examination by the *qāḍī*, any discrepancy in their testimonies (with regard, *inter alia*, to the place in which the act occurred and the manner of their being "with each other") will vindicate the accused and, furthermore, expose the witnesses themselves to the charge of *qadhf*, an offense punishable by eighty lashes.

False testimony that leads to conviction and the death penalty will entail the right to damages against the witness. The Ḥanafites allow for blood-money[22] payment, while the Shāfiʿites would condemn the false witness to death.[23] Should the witness or witnesses prove to be untrustworthy, the financial damages (*diya*) will be the responsibility of the Public Treasury, although the Shāfiʿites and Ḥanbalites require the *qāḍī*, in addition, to pay for bodily injury in the case of non-*muḥṣan* victims. The Ḥanafites and Ḥanbalites require the witnesses to begin the punishment of stoning, if they can be present, and refusal by any of the witnesses to engage in the punishment is sufficient cause for dismissal and release of the accused, although none of the witnesses will be charged with *qadhf*. The Ḥanbalites find it preferable (*mustaḥabb*) that the witnesses begin meting out the punishment,[24] whereas the Twelver-Shīʿites do not require the witnesses to be present.[25]

Confession of *zinā*, however, is a more realistic and apparently a more common method of proof. To be admissible, it should be made four times

[17] Mūṣilī, *Ikhtiyār*, IV, 88. [18] Ḥillī, *Sharāʾiʿ*, IV, 399. [19] *Ibid.*
[20] *Ibid.*, IV, 394: *wa-yataḥaqqaq dhālika bi-ghaybūbat al-ḥashafa.* [21] *Ibid.*, IV, 397.
[22] [Miṣrī, *Reliance*, 588–93; Ibn Rushd, *Distinguished Jurist's Primer*, II, 495–505.]
[23] Māwardī, *Ḥāwī*, XIII, 236–37. [24] Ibn Mufliḥ, *Furūʿ*, VI, 59.
[25] Ḥillī, *Sharāʾiʿ*, IV, 402.

by a person who is of age, *compos mentis* and free (i.e., not a slave); and he or she must do so without compulsion (i.e., by choice, *ikhtiyār*).[26] However, if a confessor identifies an alleged partner in *zinā*, and if the latter denies the act (under oath), the confessor will be punished for both fornication and *qadhf*, according to the majority opinion.[27] Obviously, in the case of confessed *zinā*, denial is sufficient vindication because otherwise four male witnesses are required to prove that the act indeed occurred.

The requirement of four witnesses also obtains if a man kills his wife's lover after having found him with her in bed. Unless the husband procures three male witnesses (according to the Mālikites) or unless the murdered man admits to *zinā* before his death, the husband will be charged with murder and punished accordingly. The other schools, deeming the husband an involved party and thus prone to suspect testimony (*muttaham*), require four independent witnesses to prove that the man committed adultery with the murderer's wife. Only then will the husband's punishment for homicide be dismissed.

The Ḥanbalites and Mālikites regard childbirth out of wedlock as proof of *zinā*. However, should the woman claim that the pregnancy was the result of rape, she must produce evidence to this effect. The admissible evidence, however, can be of the circumstantial type (*qarīna*) and does not require the procurement of any witnesses to the act itself.[28] For instance, she can produce two witnesses to attest to the fact that they heard her, at one point in time, screaming. She can also claim, without witnesses, that she was impregnated during her sleep or that the pregnancy was induced due to heavy fondling, without this involving penetration. The Ḥanafites and Shāfiʿites deem sufficient a claim by a pregnant unmarried woman that she was raped. Pregnancy out of wedlock is not proof of adultery if four witnesses do not testify against her and if she does not confess.[29] In any case, the rapist, should he be identified and arrested, must face the *ḥadd* punishment, and must furthermore be responsible for the child and pay to the woman financial compensation equal to her dowry.[30] It is noteworthy and instructive that juristic discussions of rape do not usually appear under the chapter of *zinā* but instead under that of *ikrāh* (compulsion).[31]

[26] Māwardī, *Ḥāwī*, XIII, 206–07; Ḥillī, *Sharāʾiʿ*, IV, 396.
[27] Qāḍīkhān, *Fatāwā*, III, 470. [28] Ḥaṭṭāb, *Mawāhib*, VI, 294; Ḥillī, *Sharāʾiʿ*, IV, 395.
[29] Māwardī, *Ḥāwī*, XIII, 227.
[30] Mawāq, *Tāj*, VI, 294; Peters, *Crime*, 15; Jazīrī, *Fiqh*, V, 80–81.
[31] E.g., Ḥalabī, *Multaqā*, II, 181.

Homosexual *zinā* is treated like its heterosexual counterpart by all schools except the Ḥanafites, who deem it a *taʿzīr* offense, thus requiring only two witnesses and involving a discretionary punishment short of death. But they impose the death penalty in the case of repeat offenders.[32] The Twelver-Shīʿites require four male witnesses, and, like other non-Ḥanafites, prescribe the death penalty, irrespective of *iḥṣān*.[33]

*ii. Slanderous accusation (*qadhf*)*

False accusation of *zinā*,[34] even against deceased individuals, gives rise to the application of the *ḥadd* penalty, with or without the victim's willingness or ability to prosecute. This, in other words, is the only strictly *ḥadd* offense that need not await prosecution by the victim but can be tried and punished on the instigation of the general public or authorities. *Qadhf* is also constituted by any statement of offense or a curse, such as "You, son of an unchaste woman."[35] The penalty is eighty lashes, unless the accused produces four male witnesses proving his claim to be true. The only exception to this law is *liʿān*, whereby the husband affirms under oath that his wife committed adultery and/or that her child is not his. Upon the wife's denial under oath, the marriage is dissolved but the accusing husband is not subjected to the charge of *qadhf*.[36] No one other than the husband can accuse the wife of *zinā* with impunity. The husband is not under obligation to produce any witnesses because he, as well as his children and extended family, are presumed to be severely harmed by the accusation itself. The shame to which he and his relatives are exposed amounts to proof provided by disinterested testimony. In other words, if his accusation is malicious, he would be hurting himself and his own family first.

iii. Drinking alcohol

With the exception of a minority of jurists, *shurb al-khamr* is deemed a *ḥadd* offense and punished as such.[37] Evidence of drinking includes intoxication, but the act of drinking must be voluntary. As an offense, it

32 Qāḍīkhān, *Fatāwā*, III, 469; Zarkashī, *Sharḥ*, VI, 284. 33 Ḥillī, *Sharāʾiʿ*, IV, 404.

34 This includes any and all verbal insults to the effect that a person is illegitimate. On the law of *qadhf*, see Māwardī, *Ḥāwī*, XIII, 253–65; Mūṣilī, *Ikhtiyār*, IV, 93–96; Mawāq, *Tāj*, VI, 298 ff.; [Miṣrī, *Reliance*, 611–13; Ibn Rushd, *Distinguished Jurist's Primer*, II, 531–34].

35 Ḥillī, *Sharāʾiʿ*, IV, 408–09.

36 Unlike in the case of rape, the child implicated in *liʿān* dissolution belongs to, and inherits from, the mother. As in *ṭalāq*, the mother continues to be entitled to her *mahr*.

37 [Miṣrī, *Reliance*, 617–18; Ibn Rushd, *Distinguished Jurist's Primer*, II, 534–36.]

is regulated by the Sunna, not the Quran.[38] It is also deemed less grave than *zinā* and *qadhf*[39] since it represents aggression primarily against oneself and not others. The Shāfiʿites impose as penalty forty lashes, but the other three Sunnite schools apply eighty.[40] As almost everywhere else in the law of offenses, slaves receive half of this penalty. Likewise, the Shāfiʿites do not require the punishment to be applied using an actual whip, accepting instead such other devices as slippers, palm-tree leaves or bare hands (perhaps suggesting the slapping of the culprit's shoulders or back).[41]

iv. *Theft (*sariqa*)*

The *ḥadd* punishment of amputation is applied in cases of *sariqa*, a type of theft that must meet a particular set of conditions. If only some of these conditions are met, the offense is not regarded as *sariqa* and is therefore punished by a mitigated penalty within the spectrum of *taʿzīr*, not *ḥadd*. The distinction comes across clearly in the jurists' technical language: a person convicted of *ḥadd* is described as having been *ḥudda* (present tense: *yuḥaddu*), whereas a person convicted of *taʿzīr* is said to have been *ʿuzzira* (present tense: *yuʿazzaru*). Strictly speaking, a person convicted of *taʿzīr* is not a thief of the *sariqa* type, i.e., not a *sāriq*.[42]

Sariqa is thus technically defined as the taking of the property of another by stealth (*khufya*; antonyms, *mujāhara*, *ʿalāniya*), where the property must be of licit character (e.g., not pork or wine), imperishable, and in excess of a minimum value (*niṣāb*). It must also have originally been lodged in a *ḥirz*, a place of custody, such as a safe, a cupboard, a house or a shop. A person who robs a house whose door was left unlocked is not regarded as having breached a *ḥirz*, and cannot therefore be charged with *sariqa*. The charge is also dropped if the act was not done by stealth. (This explains why *nahb*, according to most schools, stands as a different category of theft, since it is open and public, and accordingly does not call for the *ḥadd* penalty.) However, like so much else in the Sharīʿa, the final definition of *ḥirz* rests with customary, local practices (*ʿurf*). A barn, for instance, is deemed a *ḥirz* for cattle, but not for jewelry or silverware; the beast is a *ḥirz* for that which it transports; and the human body is a *ḥirz* for the clothing on it and all that is stored in the pockets.

[38] ʿAsqalānī, *Bulūgh*, 279–81. But see an interpretation of the Quran's condemnation of it (at verse 5:91) in Māwardī, *Ḥāwī*, XIII, 391.
[39] Ibn al-Mundhir, *Iqnāʿ*, 285.
[40] Māwardī, *Ḥāwī*, XIII, 412; Ibn al-Mundhir, *Iqnāʿ*, 285. [41] Māwardī, *Ḥāwī*, XIII, 415.
[42] Cf., e.g., Ḥillī, *Sharāʾiʿ*, IV, 394; [Miṣrī, *Reliance*, 613–15; Ibn Rushd, *Distinguished Jurist's Primer*, II, 536–46].

Further qualifiers of *sariqa* relate to the thief, who must be of major age, *compos mentis* and accepting of the rule of Islam, which is another way of excluding minors, the insane, and *ḥarbīs*, i.e., those who are not Muslims and who have no permanently protected status under the rule of Islam (unlike, e.g., *dhimmīs* or *musta'mins*).[43] The accused cannot be convicted of *sariqa* should there be any shade of doubt (*shubha*) that he or she has a right of ownership in the property, however insignificant, which precludes persons from being convicted of *sariqa* after stealing from their parents. The jurists also agree that the *ḥadd* penalty is inapplicable to the poor who steal food, nor is it implemented in the case of "foreigners" (*a'ājim*), meaning here those who are unfamiliar with the teachings of Islam and thus unaware of this *ḥadd* law.[44]

It bears repeating that a conviction for theft that falls short of the conditions of *sariqa* is still punishable by *ta'zīr*. Thus, if the theft involved property in excess of the stipulated minimum (*niṣāb*), but the thief stole the property in stages, each of which involved values lesser than the *niṣāb*, then the *ḥadd* penalty does not apply. The same principle is applicable to theft carried out by a group of thieves. If the value stolen, when divided by their number, does not amount to the *niṣāb*, they will be exonerated from *ḥadd* but will be punished by *ta'zīr*.[45] The Mālikites also upheld this position if the theft could have been carried out by an individual acting alone. They dissented from the other schools, however, in cases where it would have been impossible to implement the theft without the cooperation of a group. In this case, all the thieves would be punished by *ḥadd*. Similarly, a *ḥadd* will not apply to thieves if one of them entered, say, a house, and handed over the stolen property to his collaborators outside the house, because the person inside did not commit *sariqa*, while the one(s) outside did not steal from a *ḥirz*. Again, the Mālikites make crucial distinctions here. If the thieves outside extend their hands into the interior of the house to receive the stolen property, they become subject to *ḥadd*, but if the insider hands over the property by holding it outside the walls (through windows, doors, etc.), then he is the one who should be so punished.[46]

The penalty for *sariqa* on first conviction is severing the right hand at the wrist, applicable equally to free men, women, slaves, Muslims and *dhimmīs*. Repeat convictions are punished by severing the left leg for the second conviction, the left hand for the third, and the right leg for the fourth.[47]

43 Shīrāzī, *Muhadhdhab*, V, 418–20. On *musta'mins*, see chapter 11, section 2, below.
44 Jazīrī, *Fiqh*, V, 149. 45 Ḥillī, *Sharā'i'*, IV, 421.
46 Ḥaṭṭāb, *Mawāhib*, VI, 309; Jazīrī, *Fiqh*, V, 159–61.
47 Mawāq, *Tāj*, VI, 306; Mūṣilī, *Ikhtiyār*, V, 109–10.

Procedurally, two witnesses are required to prove *sariqa*. False testimony entails payment of pecuniary damages on the part of the witness. But should this testimony be intentionally mendacious and malicious, the witness's hand must be severed.[48]

v. Highway robbery

Known as *qaṭʿ al-ṭarīq* or *ḥirāba*, this type of theft is armed and "open" (*jahr*), namely, it does not involve stealth. Subject to it in terms of legal competence are Muslims and *dhimmī*s, but not *ḥarbī*s or *mustaʾmin*s, since they are presumed to abide neither juridically nor willingly by the Sharīʿa. As in all *ḥudūd*, only sane persons of major age can be convicted. This type of robbery is punished by severing the right hand and left leg, but if it is accompanied by murder the robbers are killed by sword and crucified. If murder is involved without the taking of any property, the punishment is death. If the amount stolen falls short of *niṣāb* and neither murder committed nor bodily harm inflicted, the convicted are sentenced to banishment.[49]

*vi. Rebellion (*baghī*) and apostasy (*ridda*)*

Only the Mālikites categorize these two infractions as *ḥudūd*, but the rules governing them are similar in all schools. *Bughāt* are not just any rebels, but ones who have articulated a particular creed that is rationally comprehensible (*taʾwīl ṣāʾigh*). The distinct implication of this requirement is that the imam must deal with the *bughāt* as rivals to his authority, and not as common criminals or highway robbers.[50]

The imam must, however, enquire as to the causes of the rebels' discontent, and must attempt to remove any and all injustice from which they suffer. This is grounded in the Quranic injunction: "And if two parties of believers fall to fighting, then make peace between them. And if one party of them did wrong to the other, fight ye that which did wrong till it return unto the ordinance of Allah; then, if it returns, make peace between them justly, and act equitably" (Q. 49:9).[51] But should the rebels think their demands to be lawful when in fact they are not (something that was often determined by the elite jurists surrounding the imam),[52] the imam must

48 Further on evidence, see chapter 12, section 2, below.
49 Maqdisī, *ʿUdda*, 554–56; Mūṣilī, *Ikhtiyār*, IV, 114–16; [Miṣrī, *Reliance*, 616; Ibn Rushd, *Distinguished Jurist's Primer*, II, 547–51].
50 [Miṣrī, *Reliance*, 593–94.]
51 Māwardī, *Ḥāwī*, XIII, 99, 102–03; Najdī, *Ḥāshiya*, VII, 392–93.
52 On the rule of law within the context of the Circle of Justice, see chapter 5, above.

attempt to dissuade them by inviting them to the "right path" which is argued for and demonstrated through rational evidence and textual proof. Should they persist, and should they fail to repent,[53] he must then fight and kill them, but he must in no way harm either their family members or the rebels' own private property, which should devolve upon their lawful heirs in accordance with the laws of inheritance. Those who hold a dissenting doctrine/"ideology" (*khawārij*) but are peaceful in their conduct must be left alone and must be treated like the rest of the community.[54]

In a culture whose lynchpin is religion, religious principles and religious morality, apostasy is in some way equivalent to high treason in the modern nation-state. Accordingly, a Muslim of a major age and *compos mentis* cannot abandon Islam with impunity, and is charged with heresy if he does. To be deemed an apostate, one has to have acted willingly (*mukhtār*), and no element of coercion could be present.[55] From this it follows that a *dhimmī* or a *musta'min* coerced into converting to Islam, and who subsequently renounces the new religion that was imposed on him, is not deemed an apostate. The element of intent is also regarded as a requirement in the Ḥanafite school as well as in the opinion of some Shāfi'ite jurists, rendering, for instance, a drunkard's renunciation of Islam ineffective.[56]

Acts constituting apostasy include: (a) denying the truth of the Quran; (b) accusing the Prophet of mendacity; (c) cursing God, the Prophet Muhammad or any messenger whose prophethood is undoubted (e.g., Abraham, Jesus Christ and Moses); (d) abandoning prayer (*salāt*) on principle or denying the validity of a legal matter subject to consensus (e.g., the prohibitions on fornication and drinking wine); and (e) worshiping idols.

Some jurists allow three days after apostasy is proven for the apostate to repent,[57] this latter consisting simply of uttering the two *shahāda*s.[58] Failing such repentance, according to some jurists, the apostate is killed and his property confiscated by the Treasury. Other jurists, who seem to be a minority, hold that the property devolves upon the apostate's legal heirs. Apostasy is also cause for dissolution of the apostate's marriage.[59]

[53] Repentance is admitted in the law of highway robbery and in apostasy, but in none of the other *ḥudūd*.
[54] Najdī, *Ḥāshiya*, VII, 397. For a detailed study of the laws of rebellion, see Abou El Fadl, *Rebellion and Violence in Islamic Law*.
[55] Ḥillī, *Sharā'i'*, IV, 395; [Miṣrī, *Reliance*, 595–98; Ibn Rushd, *Distinguished Jurist's Primer*, II, 552].
[56] Ibn 'Ābidīn, *Ḥāshiya*, IV, 224. [57] Sha'rānī, *Mīzān*, II, 212.
[58] Namely, that there is no god but God and that Muhammad is the messenger of God. Mūṣilī, *Ikhtiyār*, IV, 146.
[59] *Ibid.*, IV, 147–48.

The Ḥanafites and Twelver-Shīʿites exempt women from capital punishment and substitute for it a term of imprisonment for life.[60]

3. Homicide and bodily harm (*qiṣāṣ*)

Homicide is a private wrong, prosecuted only upon the demand of the victim's next of kin. Minors and the insane are exempt from punishment, but their next of kin become liable for financial damages.[61] There are at least five types of homicide, all graded on a scale of intentionality. The degree of intentionality involved is measured by external criteria, as the jurists deemed knowledge of inner motives (*mā fil-bāṭin*) to be well-nigh impossible. Gauging intent was therefore predicated upon the type of implement used in murder, although the Mālikites seem to have given some weight to the psychological state of the killer during the time leading up to the act of murder (e.g., anger, rage, malicious intent, etc.).[62]

Liability for punishment or damages is inextinguishable, giving the kin of the victim an eternal right to inflict appropriate retaliation or collect damages. The first type, intentional homicide (*qatl ʿamd*), involves, by definition, not only the intent to kill but also the use of a lethal implement or an instrument that is customarily used to kill. Furthermore, an integral element of intentionality is the uncoerced will of the murderer, for anyone who kills under duress is not deemed to fall into this category and therefore would not be liable for the death penalty.

The second type, quasi-intentional killing (*shibh ʿamd*), is where the element of intention to exercise violence is present but the instrument used is neither regarded as lethal nor customarily construed as a murder weapon (e.g., a small stick). The Shāfiʿites and Ḥanbalites hold the position that if someone repeatedly struck another with a stick, then the killer would be deemed to have committed his act with full intent, as opposed to causing death by striking once or twice. Likewise, a quasi-intentional killing is said to occur when someone pushes another into a body of water infested with sharks or alligators, provided that the killer did not know of the presence of these predators, and even though he may have done so playfully. Compensation in this form of murder consists of extensive blood-money[63] (or pardon by the victim's family), but capital

[60] *Ibid.*, IV, 149; Ḥillī, *Sharāʾiʿ*, IV, 426; Māwardī, *Ḥāwī*, XIII, 155; Shaʿrānī, *Mīzān*, II, 212.

[61] Ḥiṣnī, *Kifāya*, 159–60; Ḥillī, *Sharāʾiʿ*, IV, 456–57; [Miṣrī, *Reliance*, 585–88; Ibn Rushd, *Distinguished Jurist's Primer*, II, 479–521].

[62] [Miṣrī, *Reliance*, 583–88; Ibn Rushd, *Distinguished Jurist's Primer*, II, 480–82.]

[63] Known as *diya mughallaẓa*, amounting to a hundred camels delivered over a three-year period. In customary usage, blood-money may consist of pecuniary payments of various amounts, usually determined through a process of mediation (*ṣulḥ*). See next note.

punishment is waived. A lesser amount of damages[64] arises in the third type, known as *qatl khaṭa*ʾ, i.e., accidental homicide, such as in shooting someone while hunting for game. The fourth type, requiring the same amount of (mitigated) damages, is homicide that is "treated as a *qatl khaṭa*ʾ" (*majrā al-khaṭa*ʾ), such as when someone rolls over another in sleep and kills him. Fifth, and finally, is indirect killing (*qatl bi-sabab*), best exemplified by someone digging a well (say, in search of water) into which another accidentally falls and dies. This last type, though requiring a lesser amount of blood-money, is deemed qualitatively different from all the preceding types, as evidenced in the legal stipulation that, except in indirect killing, the murderers in all the former types are barred from inheriting from their victims.[65]

When the murderer is unknown, homicide falls under the rubric of *qasāma*. This procedure is followed when a person is found dead outside his neighborhood, village or tribal territory. His next of kin can sue the inhabitants of the locale in which the body was found for *diya*, on the grounds of *lawth*, namely, an evidentiary "indicant" (*amāra*) to the effect that animosity between these inhabitants and the victim's clan or tribe constitutes motive. It is an "indicant" but not a "proof" because it has the weight of only a single witness, not the necessary two witnesses.[66] If *lawth* is established, then the defendant, the collectivity, must pay the *diya* after having sworn fifty oaths to the effect that they have not murdered the man and do not know who has done so. Should there not be a sufficient number of persons, then they must repeat the oaths until fifty have been sworn. If *lawth* is not established, a defendant may swear an oath and will not owe a *diya*. In this case, the *diya* becomes the responsibility of the Public Treasury.[67]

Liability for the death penalty is not universal, however. The Ḥanafites are alone in accepting the equality of Muslims and non-Muslims and free persons and slaves. Accordingly, a Muslim person is subject to retaliation if he kills a non-Muslim, and a free Muslim is likewise punished if he kills a slave. There is a consensus, however, to the effect that liability for homicide is gender-free within the Muslim community. Accordingly, a free male Muslim may be punished by death for intentionally killing a free Muslim woman, and vice versa.

[64] *Diya mukhaffafa*, amounting to a thousand (or about four kilograms of) gold *dīnār*s or a hundred camels of a lower quality than that required in the extensive *diya*. For a detailed account of *diyāt*, see Mūṣilī, *Ikhtiyār*, V, 35–45; Qāḍīzādeh, *Natāʾij*, X, 270–78.

[65] Māwardī, *Ḥāwī*, XIII, 70–71; Ḥalabī, *Multaqā*, II, 282–85.

[66] On testimony and witnesses, see chapter 12, section 2, below. See also Ḥillī, *Sharāʾiʿ*, IV, 464.

[67] Buhūtī, *Rawḍ*, 546; Ḥiṣnī, *Kifāya*, 175; Ḥillī, *Sharāʾiʿ*, IV, 464; [Ibn Rushd, *Distinguished Jurist's Primer*, II, 515–21].

The principle of *qiṣāṣ* also applies to bodily harm, where the offender may be subjected to the same injury he inflicted on the victim. The principle of an eye for an eye holds in its full meaning, which is to say that the principle insists on a good eye for a good eye, but not on a good eye for a bad eye or vice versa. Yet, just like homicide, pardon or, especially, financial compensation (*arsh*) stands as a distinct possibility. The measure of *arsh* is the full *diya*, the blood-money that is paid in homicide.[68]

Bodily harm is seen to fall into three categories: wounds (*jurūḥ*), severance of members (*ibānat ṭaraf*) or functional incapacitation of bodily organs (*izālat manfa'a*).[69] Depending on their depth and location in the body, wounds are awarded different damages. Head wounds and deep wounds are compensated by one-third of the *diya*, while moderate wounds to the body, or lighter wounds, are compensated by three-twentieths and one-twentieth, respectively. The general rule in the loss of bodily members is that, where there is only one, payment of a full *diya* is required, but where they come in pairs, only half is paid for each. Loss of the nose, tongue or sex organ, for instance, entails payment of the full blood-price, but an eye, a hand or a (woman's) nipple is worth half as much. A finger or a toe is worth one-tenth, and of a tooth, one-twentieth.[70] Incapacitating the mind requires the full *diya* and cannot be punished by retaliation. Sensory members that come in pairs require half a *diya* if incapacitated, e.g., seeing and hearing. Lesser injuries causing dysfunction incur a graded pecuniary compensation.[71]

4. Discretionary punishment (*ta'zīr*)

Any offense not classified under *ḥadd* or *qiṣāṣ* punishments is deemed to fall within the category of *ta'zīr*. Theft involving amounts below the *niṣāb* or without breaching a *ḥirz*, or false accusation of unchastity other than fornication, are all offenses punishable by *ta'zīr*. Although the range of discretionary punishment is wide and more varied than those stipulated in *ḥudūd* and *qiṣāṣ*, it cannot exceed or even match the *ḥudūd* in severity.[72] Death or bodily injury resulting from a *ta'zīr* punishment will give the kin of the victim the right to demand pecuniary damages from the sovereign (since it is one of his officials who is normally charged with implementing this punishment).[73]

[68] Mūṣilī, *Ikhtiyār*, V, 35; Zarkashī, *Sharḥ*, VI, 153. [69] Nawawī, *Rawḍa*, VII, 125.
[70] *Ibid.* [71] *Ibid.*, VII, 125–64; Zarkashī, *Sharḥ*, VI, 153–89.
[72] Thus, lashes range from a minimum of three to a maximum of thirty-nine. Mūṣilī, *Ikhtiyār*, IV, 92.
[73] Shīrāzī, *Muhadhdhab*, V, 462–64; [Miṣrī, *Reliance*, 619].

In practice, *ta'zīr* appears to have been the most common of all punishments, though often entirely lacking in obvious physical violence. Since personal honor was a precious commodity, with higher stakes at the upper levels of the social order, besmirching this honor was – and remains so in many parts of the Muslim world today – an effective method of inflicting punishment.[74] Social and moral standing within the community would be a central consideration in punishing the offender. It is reported, for instance, that the Mughal emperor Akbar once instructively commented: "Punishment of everyone should be befitting his status ... a severe glance at a man of lofty nature is equivalent to killing him, while a kick is of no avail to a man of low nature."[75] In the Malay Peninsula, even in the twentieth century, the *ta'zīr* punishment – even for certain serious crimes – was often non-physical, frequently consisting of shaming and humiliation in public. For example, a man seducing another's wife would be forced to bow before the husband in the presence of a large gathering.[76] This was normatively regarded as sufficient punishment.

[74] Singha, *Despotism*, 11–12. [75] *Ibid.*, 11.

[76] Sometime in the 1880s, Sir Hugh Clifford observed that the punishment of public humiliation consisted in placing the criminal on a beast, smeared with soot and turmeric. This punishment, he remarked, "was far more dreaded by Malay thieves than fine or mutilation, and I can well believe that this was the case, for a fear of open shame and a fierce self-respect are two of the strongest feelings in the breast of the average Malay in his natural condition." In the Malay world, this punishment was deemed so severe that it seems to have been resorted to even as a substitute to the penalty for theft. Peletz, *Islamic Modern*, 37, 42, 43.

11 *Jihād*

1. Introduction

In the entire repertoire of legal concepts, there is today no more ambiguous and multi-layered term than *jihād*. The concept is charged with religious, legal, cultural and political connotations, and has proven to be even more controversial than such concepts and practices as polygamy. Its potential and outward militancy invariably provokes hostile reactions from Western observers, even when they are in full cognizance of the fact that *jihād* is a theory that belongs to the past. The fear of Islam and of its alleged aggressiveness – in itself a constitutive ingredient of Western culture since at least the European Middle Ages – has led even the more prominent scholars to view the theory as if it were an applied reality and – as if this were not problematic enough – to attach to the theory the most negative interpretations. What is even more problematic is a third complicating factor, i.e., the projection of an overcharged negative interpretation of the remote past upon a contemporary reality that bears no resemblance whatsoever to that former era. It appears that paradigmatic Western scholarship – not to mention mass media – has allowed itself to succumb to all three problematics. In this chapter, I will briefly discuss the classical theory of *jihād*, how it was reinterpreted in light of European colonialism, and – by way of conclusion – its significance today.

2. The classical theory

As in all manners of conduct, the theory of *jihād* was expounded (at times under the title *siyar*)[1] in legal works, either within the parameters of a chapter in a comprehensive law book or in treatises wholly dedicated to the subject. Such independent treatises were also allotted to other

[1] Deriving from the root *s-y-r*, which carries the notion "to walk," the term *siyar* connotes the act of marching with the assumption that the march embodies a military expedition directed toward the enemy. In non-legal works, the term commonly used was *al-maghāzī*, indicating the act of raiding. [Miṣrī, *Reliance*, 599–605; Ibn Rushd, *Distinguished Jurist's Primer*, I, 454–87.]

subjects, such as charitable trusts (*waqf*), taxation (*kharāj*), damages (*ḍamānāt*) and the rules regulating judgeship and *muftī*ship (*adab al-qaḍā'*, *adab al-muftī wal-mustaftī*). It is, however, remarkable that whereas the number of independent treatises on *jihād* declined after the third/ninth century, those specializing in the other individual topics significantly increased, most notably in the *waqf* and *adab al-qāḍī* genres.

In legal works, *jihād* and *siyar* always referred to military campaigns by the Abode of Islam against the Abode of War, this latter defined as territory inhabited and ruled by non-Muslims, be they Christians, Jews, Zoroastrians or pagans of all sorts. One influential technical dictionary defined *jihād* as "a call to the right religion and fighting to implement it when the unbelievers refuse to accept it or refuse a protected status" (under Muslims).[2] Remarkably, the juristic works did not define the term at the outset of chapters dealing with the subject, the practice having been to begin with the statement that *jihād*, by universal agreement,[3] was a duty of the *kifāya* type, namely, that if a number of persons happened to perform the obligation it would cease to be incumbent upon the others. This stood in stark contrast to a duty of the *ʿayn* type, which represented an obligation on each and every Muslim, irrespective of whether or not others are or were able to perform it.[4]

However, under certain circumstances, the obligation did become binding upon each and every Muslim who happens to find himself in such circumstances. First, if a battle broke out, those who were already present on the field were all obliged to remain therein and fight. The assumption here was that the battle would not be initiated by the Muslim side since there can have been no intent on the Muslim side to have begun the fight in the first place. Second, the inhabitants of any town or locale had, to a man, to fight an army that invades their territory. Third, all those whom the imam called upon to participate in the *jihād* had to comply. These three exceptions, it must be said, were not intended to circumvent the general principle of *kifāya* obligation, but rather to carve out particular situations in which *jihād* cannot be successful without the participation of all *jihād*ists.[5] Generally, offensive *jihād* was deemed *farḍ kifāya*, whereas defensive *jihād*, especially in a state of weakness, was unanimously regarded as *farḍ ʿayn*. *Jihād* by proxy was permitted only by the Twelver-Shīʿites who permitted individuals to hire others to conduct *jihād* on their behalf for a fee (*ujra*).[6]

[2] Aḥmadnagarī, *Jāmiʿ al-ʿUlūm*, I, 424. [3] Ṭūsī, *Khilāf*, II, 500.
[4] Ḥalabī, *Multaqā*, I, 354; [Miṣrī, *Reliance*, 599–600].
[5] Ibn Qudāma, *Mughnī*, X, 364–66; Ramlī, *Nihāya*, VIII, 42. [6] Ṭūsī, *Khilāf*, II, 500.

To qualify as a *jihādist*, one had to be a Muslim male, an adult, free, and of sound body and mind. These conditions were intended to exclude non-Muslims, women, minors, slaves, handicapped persons and the insane. The handicapped were defined as those who were seriously ill or blind, and all those who suffered from any physical ailment or weakness that rendered them unable to fulfill military obligations.[7] In addition to these personal specifications, circumstantial conditions could bar a person from qualifying: in the event that the *jihād* was a *farḍ kifāya*, the permission of parents of young volunteers constituted a requirement for qualification, as did the permission of a lender (*mudayyin*), unless a guarantor had been secured.[8] Finally, provisions and support had to be afforded to the *jihādist* and to his family for the entire duration of the war. These provisions had to include weapons and other necessities that the *jihādist* needed during the campaign and on the battlefield.[9]

Yet, the conditions that a *jihādist* had to meet are neither fixed nor universal. The public interest of Islam and Muslims, and various contingencies, may have required enlisting the aid of non-Muslims in *jihād* wars. In such cases, the majority of jurists allowed unbelievers to join the *jihādist* army, even if these unbelievers happen to be of the same "ideological" persuasion as those against whom the Muslims intended to wage war. A minority of jurists reject the possibility of enlisting unbelievers, while another minority espouse this possibility while insisting that the recruited fighters differed from the enemy in religious belief.[10] These unbeliever-*jihādists* could be persons of protected status (*dhimmī*s), or persons from a land with whom Muslims had struck a peace treaty, or even *ḥarbī*s, namely, persons from the Abode of War.[11]

Thus while the universal distinction is between the Abode of Islam and the Abode of War, there conceptually stands in between them an intermediate territory with which the Abode of Islam may live in peace. Again, as in recruiting non-Muslim soldiers, the public interest (*maṣlaḥa*) of the Abode of Islam may justify striking peace treaties with unbelievers for as long as it is deemed appropriate by the imam. However, the majority of jurists restrict the duration of peace treaties to ten years, finding their

[7] Nawawī, *Rawḍa*, VII, 411–12; [Miṣrī, *Reliance*, 601–02; Ibn Rushd, *Distinguished Jurist's Primer*, I, 455].

[8] That is to say that if a debtor has failed to satisfy the debt before leaving on *jihād*, he must obtain permission (*idhn*) from the lender to do so, or he must secure a guarantor. Sha'rānī, *Mīzān*, II, 241; Nawawī, *Rawḍa*, VII, 413; [Ibn Rushd, *Distinguished Jurist's Primer*, I, 455].

[9] Ibn Qudāma, *Mughnī*, X, 366, 382, 384; Ramlī, *Nihāya*, VIII, 55; *al-Mawsū'a al-Fiqhiyya*, XVI, 137–39, on the authority of Saḥnūn, Nawawī, Ibn 'Ābidīn, Ibn Qudāma, Buhūtī and Dasūqī.

[10] Nawawī, *Rawḍa*, VII, 441; Ibn al-Ḥājib, *Jāmi'*, 244.

[11] Ramlī, *Nihāya*, VIII, 59–60; [Miṣrī, *Reliance*, 602].

precedent for this in the diplomatic practices of the Prophet.[12] On the other hand, if the public interest of the Abode of Islam permits, *jihād* expeditions should be launched at least once a year, unless any of a number of conditions obtain. *Jihād* may thus be suspended, with or without a peace treaty, if, for instance: (1) Muslims are too weak to fight, either because of depleted manpower or insufficient weapons and equipment; (2) Muslims deem it necessary to wait for the arrival of support or munitions from external sources; (3) the way to the battlefield is inhospitable, replete with obstacles or lacking in supplies; or (4) there is reason to believe that the Abode of War has shown positive signs that it might convert to Islam.[13]

In all juristic discussions, it is assumed that *jihād* is organized and conducted by the imam, who is also regarded as the chief military commander (*amīr*, emir).[14] The imam, or his deputy, has the exclusive powers to call for *jihād*, to prepare and equip the army, give orders, decide how the attack is to be carried out and how the booty is to be distributed, and whether or not a peace treaty should be struck and under what terms. He is also charged with the specific duty of ensuring that the weak-hearted and those who promote the spirit of defeatism are identified and ousted from the *jihād*ist army. Raids conducted without the permission of the imam or his deputy are seen as legally reprehensible, though not outright forbidden.[15] *Jihād* is therefore conceived as taking place under the leadership of the imam, even though he may be deemed unjust or lacking in ethical or moral conduct.[16] In Twelver and Zaydite Shīʿism, it is the imam – a member of the ʿAlid family – who has the sole prerogative to order *jihād*.[17] Accordingly, in theory, no *jihād* of the expansionist type has technically been possible since the Occultation of the last Imam in 260/873, but of course the events of history were not as neat as this theory prescribes.

If the goal of *jihād* is to subdue the Abode of War to the dominion of the Abode of Islam, this dominion was neither categorical nor indiscriminate. The Christians, Jews and Magians were to be fought with the view of either converting them to Islam or subjecting them to Islamic rule while allowing them to maintain their religious beliefs. If the latter, then they were under the obligation to pay the poll-tax (*jizya*). However, pagans enjoyed no such options, having been obliged to convert to Islam or fight to the death. In other words, they were allowed neither to pay the poll-tax

[12] Ibn Qudāma, *Sharḥ*, X, 368. [13] *Ibid*., X, 367. [14] Nawawī, *Rawḍa*, VII, 440.
[15] Ḥaṭṭāb, *Mawāhib*, III, 348–49; Ramlī, *Nihāya*, VIII, 57.
[16] Ibn Qudāma, *Sharḥ*, X, 371. Aḥmad Ibn Ḥanbal disapproved of this, however. Yet, he did not regard it as prohibited.
[17] Ibn Muftāḥ, *Sharḥ al-Azhār*, X, 432.

nor to convert to another monotheistic religion.[18] (Historical reality, however, differed greatly from this theory, as evidenced in the willing acceptance of Hindus, Jains, Buddhists and other non-monotheists in the Indian Sub-Continent – not to mention centuries-old cooperation between them and Muslims).

From a religious perspective, the more challenging the *jihād*, the more commendable it was considered. Just as, historically, fighting naval wars was held in the highest esteem (since "riding the Sea" was universally considered to be fraught with mortal danger),[19] fighting the People of the Book commanded the highest respect and reward.[20] But an interpretive caution is called for here. The added respect and reward was not due to any particular animosity toward Christians and Jews, for they, after all, are singled out as having special rights of protection under Muslim rule. Rather, the underlying assumption is that, because the People of the Book are presumed to fight with conviction (due to their firm religious commitment to another form of monotheism – with which the Muslims obviously identified), *jihād* against them is markedly more difficult, just like the dangers encountered at sea are significantly more serious than in land warfare.

Muslim jurists expended a great deal of energy expounding in detail the conditions under which *jihād* wars can be initiated, conducted and brought to conclusion. According to all legal schools, no *jihād* war can be launched without prior notice, which usually involves calling the enemy to accept Islam or suffer the consequences of refusal. According to the Mālikites, the call is to be repeated thrice, over three days, and upon consistent refusal the attack may begin on the fourth day.[21] According to the Ḥanbalites, such a warning is required only in the case of those who are not familiar with Islam, such as peoples whose territories lie at a distance from the Abode of Islam.[22] In all cases, however, as long as the battle has not begun, the enemy continues to have the opportunity to save life and property even after refusal of the threefold warning.[23]

Once fighting ensues, all males who are capable of fighting are legitimate targets, although the jurists do not state the matter in these terms. The great majority of jurists espouse the opinion that it is strictly forbidden to kill anyone who cannot fight, or is not trained in the use of weapons, such as women, children, farmers, the handicapped, the elderly, the chronically ill,

[18] Ibn Qudāma, *Mughnī*, X, 387; Ṭūsī, *Khilāf*, II, 509. [19] Ibn Qudāma, *Mughnī*, X, 369.

[20] *Ibid.*, X, 370, reports that the Prophet informed one Umm Khallād that her son was killed in *jihād* and that he would have two rewards, instead of the usual one. When the Prophet was queried as to the reason, he said: "Because he was killed by the People of the Book."

[21] Ḥalabī, *Multaqā*, I, 355–56; *al-Mawsū'a al-Fiqhiyya*, XVI, 144; [Ibn Rushd, *Distinguished Jurist's Primer*, I, 461–62].

[22] Ibn Qudāma, *Mughnī*, X, 385–86. [23] Ibn Qudāma, *Kāfī*, IV, 164–65.

hermaphrodites, monks and all "church folk" of the monastic kind.[24] Nor is it permissible to kill the enemy's envoy (*rasūl*).[25] The only exclusion from amongst these exceptions is women who directly engage in the war effort, such as by preparing weapons or transporting munitions and food to the enemy fighters on the battlefield.[26] Some Twlever-Shīʿite jurists permit the killing of hermits and monks, because of their active engagement in propounding the enemy's heretical religion.[27]

Ambushing enemy troops, cutting off their water supplies, destroying their forts and catapulting fireballs on their ranks are deemed legitimate practices, though perfidy, treachery, torture and mutilation are forbidden.[28] So are burning crops and bee hives, uprooting trees and plants, and the killing of animals that the enemy does not utilize for fighting purposes, although eating the products of the enemy's fauna and the fruits of flora is permissible when Muslim supplies fall short of need.[29] The Twelver-Shīʿites go so far as to forbid the destruction of enemy horses and cattle seized by Muslims even when the enemy army is about to retrieve them from Muslim hands.[30] In this context, the jurists' main concern is the minimizing of harm to human life and property, two principles of the Sharīʿa that along with three others (preservation of religion, offspring and mind) constitute the universals upon which law is founded.[31] The underlying principle governing the Muslim conduct of warfare is that no loss of life or damage to property is permitted to take place behind enemy lines unless it is essential, and directly related, to defeating the enemy's army. Needless devastation also resembles the highly condemned practice of "spreading harm and evil on earth" (*al-fasād fil-arḍ*), punishable by death. Thus, if the enemy is subdued or if the Muslims have good reason to believe that victory is within reach, major assaults, bellicosity, and particularly the use of fire, are impermissible. On this all jurists are in agreement.[32] These principles of avoiding harm to life and property also explain why all activities that might cause such harm must immediately cease upon the enemy's surrender.[33] From this it also follows that, even

[24] Ḥalabī, *Multaqā*, I, 358; Shams al-Dīn Ibn Qudāma, *Sharḥ*, X, 389–90, 392, 400; *al-Mawsūʿa al-Fiqhiyya*, XVI, 148; [Miṣrī, *Reliance*, 603–04; Ibn Rushd, *Distinguished Jurist's Primer*, I, 456–61]. The reason why hermaphrodites are included in this group is that their sex cannot be determined, and thus they may be subsumable under the category of women.

[25] Nawawī, *Rawḍa*, VII, 445. [26] Shams al-Dīn Ibn Qudāma, *Sharḥ*, X, 402.

[27] Ṭūsī, *Khilāf*, II, 501. [28] Ḥalabī, *Multaqā*, I, 358.

[29] Ibn Qudāma, *Sharḥ*, X, 390–95; *al-Mawsūʿa al-Fiqhiyya*, XVI, 156, on the authority of Ibn ʿĀbidīn, Ibn Qudāma, Buhūtī and others.

[30] Ṭūsī, *Khilāf*, II, 500. [31] Hallaq, *History*, 167 ff.

[32] Ibn Qudāma, *Sharḥ*, X, 396; *al-Mawsūʿa al-Fiqhiyya*, XVI, 152.

[33] Ibn Qudāma, *Sharḥ*, X, 396; Ibn Qudāma, *Kāfī*, IV, 164–65.

during war-time, attacks on enemy civilian targets (with the intention of weakening the enemy or otherwise) are forbidden.

The principle of avoiding harm is reconciled with the demands of reality through the deployment of the concomitant principle of "opting for the lesser of two evils."[34] As it was the practice in pre-modern warfare to use an enemy population or prisoners as a human shield in battles, Muslim jurists were faced with the legal problems to which such a situation gave rise. A minority of jurists categorically rejected the killing of Muslim individuals who were used by the enemy as a frontal shield, but the majority permitted such an act when necessary. The reasoning of the majority in justification of Muslim troops killing their own "brothers in religion" is diverse, but it comes down to the argument that if the Muslim army does not fight – in an attempt to save the lives of those forming the human shield – then *jihād* will cease, the enemy will win, and many more Muslims will be killed and subjugated.[35] (To sacrifice the lives of a minority to save those of a majority happens to be the most cited example in illustration of the principle of "opting for the lesser of two evils.") Yet, if this were to occur, many jurists argued, blood-money should be paid and penance performed.[36] Abū Ḥanīfa dissented, waiving any liability toward the victims forming the human shield.[37]

What of prisoners? The elderly, the handicapped, the chronically ill and monks are not to be taken as prisoners. Women and children may be taken into captivity, but the jurists are in universal agreement that no harm should befall them at the hands of Muslims. Furthermore, it is not permitted to torture or mutilate adult male prisoners,[38] nor is it permitted to kill them without first presenting them before the imam, who has the power to do one of four things. In the case of prisoners who are willing to accept a protected status under Muslim rule, the imam has the power to order them killed, enslaved, exchanged for Muslim prisoners in enemy hands (or for ransom) or simply freed. In the case of those who refuse a protected status, the option of slavery is excluded, as their coexistence with Muslims under the rule of Islam becomes impossible.[39] If a prisoner converts to Islam before the imam exercises his options, the prisoner can no longer be killed, exchanged or freed. Slavery remains the sole option, though he can always purchase his own freedom.[40] Slavery is also the fate

[34] Bāz, *Sharḥ*, I, 29–30.
[35] Nawawī, *Rawḍa*, VII, 447; Ibn Qudāma, *Sharḥ*, X, 402–03.
[36] On blood-money, see chapter 10, section 3, above. On penance, see chapter 6, section 4, above.
[37] Ibn Qudāma, *Sharḥ*, X, 403. [38] *Al-Mawsūʿa al-Fiqhiyya*, XVI, 151.
[39] Shams al-Dīn Ibn Qudāma, *Sharḥ*, X, 403–05, 409; Ramlī, *Nihāya*, VIII, 65.
[40] Shaʿrānī, *Mīzān*, II, 287 ff.

of women who happen to fall into captivity, whether they convert or not, but like their male counterparts who are willing to convert, they can purchase their freedom through a manumission contract. For the pagan prisoner to convert, the pronouncement of the *shahāda* ("There is no god but God") is sufficient, but for the People of the Book, they must utter the second *shahāda* ("And Muhammad is the Messenger of God").[41]

The marriage contract of two captives continues to be valid and binding, but that of a woman who is taken prisoner without her husband becomes null and void. As a slave, she becomes sexually lawful to her Muslim master.[42] Parents are not to be separated from their children when sold as slaves, nor a person from his or her grandchildren, since they possess, in effect, the same status as parents.[43]

By the same token, Muslim prisoners are likewise subject to the law of Islam. A Muslim prisoner who was granted freedom on the condition that he should continue to live amongst the unbelievers must honor the enemy's terms, and must not try to escape. Nor is he permitted to betray the unbelievers or be treasonous in any manner.[44] Should the enemy release him without specifying any conditions for his freedom, he may escape and even kill while attempting to do so. The underlying reasoning here is that neither a contract nor a relationship of trust (*yu'amminūhu*) is said to have been created between him and the enemy.[45] If a male prisoner is released by the enemy on the condition that he should return to them with a payment of ransom, he is under obligation to fulfill his end of the agreement. If he agrees that he will return if he fails to raise the amount of ransom, he is indeed obliged to do so according to some jurists. Other jurists, however, did not deem this commitment to be binding on him. On the other hand, all jurists agree that a woman is under no obligation to return to the enemy, whether or not she made promises to that effect or any other.[46] If, on pain of death, a Muslim prisoner is coerced to convert to the enemy's religion, he must do so to escape death, but must do so outwardly, not "in his heart." Outward conformity is also permitted if the Muslim prisoner is requested to prostrate before the enemy's king or leader (prostration in Islam being an act to be performed only before God).[47]

In general, booty is distributed in five parts: one-fifth belongs to the imam, one-fifth to foot soldiers, and three-fifths to horsemen. Among the

[41] Qāḍīkhān, *Fatāwā*, III, 569; [Miṣrī, *Reliance*, 604].
[42] Ramlī, *Nihāya*, VIII, 67; Ibn Qudāma, *Sharḥ*, X, 412.
[43] Ṭūsī, *Khilāf*, II, 506–07; Shams al-Dīn Ibn Qudāma, *Sharḥ*, X, 415–17; Nawawī, *Rawḍa*, VII, 455. See also chapter 9, section 5, above.
[44] Ibn Qudāma, *Kāfī*, IV, 209. [45] *Ibid.* [46] *Ibid.* [47] Qāḍīkhān, *Fatāwā*, III, 571.

latter, the share of the horse itself (or, for that matter, mule or camel) is said to be two-fifths. According to many jurists, the imam's share is spent on one or all of three groups, namely, orphans, the poor and wayfarers. Other jurists permit the imam to dispose of his fifth, especially if it consists of land, on other communal philanthropies, such as establishing public charitable trusts (*waqf*).[48]

The People of the Book who fall into a protected (*dhimmī*) status after a *jihād* war must pay the poll-tax, the so-called *jizya*. This tax is incumbent upon all adult males, but women, children, freedmen, slaves, the insane, the chronically ill and the poor are exempted. Payable at the end of each year, the tax is exacted as a lump sum according to three levels of prosperity: rich, modest and middle. The poor, as we have seen, are exempted. The proportion comes to 48 *dirhams* for the rich, 24 for those of middle income, and 12 for those of modest means (or four, two and one *dīnār*, respectively). If a *dhimmī* converted to Islam at any time during the year, even during the final week, he would owe no poll-taxes whatsoever for that year.[49]

When a *jihād* war is over or no longer possible, a peace treaty (*hudna*) may be struck with the enemy.[50] Most jurists allowed ten years as a limit for such a treaty, but others opined that if the public interest of Muslims is served by further extension, then the ten-year specification ceases to hold. At all events, Muslims, once signatories to a treaty, must honor it however long its duration may be. The death of the contracting imam does not absolve his successors from the treaty's terms, by which they are fully bound. Under *hudna*, Muslims who damage the unbelievers' property are liable to pay full damages, and vice versa. If unbelievers violate the terms of a treaty by launching a war against the Muslims, then the peace treaty is automatically rendered null and void.[51]

Individuals from the Abode of War may visit, trade or stay in the Abode of Islam under *amān*, a contract of safe-conduct whereby these "guests," in their persons and property, are fully protected. Unlike their counterparts who live under a protected status and for which they must pay the poll-tax, the receivers of *amān* (known as *musta'mans*) are under no obligation to pay taxes. Some jurists, especially the Shāfiʿites, limited the

48 Ibn Qudāma, *Kāfī*, IV, 179–80, 199; Qāḍīkhān, *Fatāwā*, III, 567; [Miṣrī, *Reliance*, 606; Ibn Rushd, *Distinguished Jurist's Primer*, I, 466–83]. For an outline of the law of *waqf*, see chapter 3, section 3, above.

49 Ramlī, *Nihāya*, VIII, 81; Ḥiṣnī, *Kifāya*, II, 217; Ibn al-Mundhir, *Iqnāʿ*, 385; Ibn Qudāma, *Kāfī*, IV, 217; [Miṣrī, *Reliance*, 607–09; Ibn Rushd, *Distinguished Jurist's Primer*, I, 483–87].

50 [Miṣrī, *Reliance*, 604–05; Ibn Rushd, *Distinguished Jurist's Primer*, I, 463–64.] For a brief history of capitulatory rights given, under terms of *hudna*, by Muslim rulers to European rulers and merchants, see Leibesny, "Development of Western Judicial Privileges," 312–27. See also van den Boogert, *Capitulations and the Ottoman Legal System*.

51 Ibn Qudāma, *Kāfī*, IV, 210–13.

period of *amān* to four months, whereas many Ḥanbalite jurists allowed up to one lunar year (eleven or twelve days shorter than a Gregorian year). Others argued for an indefinite *amān*. What is striking, from the viewpoint of the practices of the modern state, is the fact that any private Muslim individual, whether man, woman or slave, has the juridical competence to grant an *amān* to as many as ten unbelievers who are otherwise denizens of the Abode of War.[52] The imam, of course, also has the same competence, but he is permitted to grant an *amān* to any number, including entire populations. Furthermore, he and his military commanders alone are judicially empowered to grant an *amān* to prisoners.[53]

The *amān* contract may be concluded in writing, by oral agreement, or by any other means, including what may be termed course of conduct. Thus, the customary practice of merchants entering the Abode of Islam for the purpose of trading is by itself sufficient to constitute evidence of approval of their stay, it being as if the merchants have obtained an explicit *amān* from the Muslim population. In effect, in this particular context, an implied contract may be said to exist. Similarly, and under the same principle, foreign envoys and emissaries are automatically protected by *amān*.[54] In stark contrast to modern international and nation-state law, the considerable tolerance in the law of non-Muslim denizens in Muslim lands is quite remarkable.

Now, in light of the remarkably high level of sensitivity in Western culture toward *jihād*, it is important to understand a number of characteristics with regard to the theory as found in juristic treatises and as outlined in the foregoing pages. First, this theory is narrowly driven by a single concern, namely, the conversion of unbelievers to the Islamic faith. It is a religious duty to be performed only when possible, for, as we have said earlier, if public interest contradicts *jihād*, it need not be performed. By all indications, material gain *in this theory* is a minor consideration, if at all.[55]

Second, the theory is partial in that it deals only with conflict between Muslim and non-Muslim sovereignties. Nowhere in the entirety of juristic discourse do the legists deal with wars and conflict between and among Muslim principalities themselves, a feature of considerable importance given the fact that, historically, wars between these principalities were as frequent, if not more so, as wars between Muslims and non-Muslims.[56]

52 Ramlī, *Nihāya*, VIII, 76; Qāḍīkhān, *Fatāwā*, III, 564; Ibn Qudāma, *Kāfī*, IV, 205.
53 Ibn Qudāma, *Kāfi*, IV, 205.
54 Ramlī, *Nihāya*, VIII, 76; Ibn Qudāma, *Kāfi*, IV, 207.
55 See the informative discussion in *al-Mawsūʿa al-Fiqhiyya*, XVI, 140–42. This is not to say, however, that in historical reality material gain was less than a considerable motive.
56 In what ways these intra-Muslim wars were juristically justified, especially after the third/ninth century, is a question that forms a significant topic for research.

Third, the theory is partial in yet another way, in that it regulates the conduct of the Muslim side alone, however thoroughly, but has nothing to say about how the enemy should conduct itself. International law is (in theory) universally and mutually applicable, but Islamic law is not, having been uninterested in proffering a parallel system. Thus, it is this feature of the Islamic juristic theory that makes it difficult for one to speak of the *jihād–amān* discourse as international law.

Fourth, and inextricably related to the preceding characteristic, the theory entirely overlooks the possibility of Muslim defeat, and more importantly, the possibility of Muslim sovereignty being reduced or subjugated. Throughout every discussion of each and every law book, the assumption is one of always winning: first comes the qualifications of the *jihād*ist, then his conduct on the battlefield, how the enemy prisoners should be treated, spoils divided, and conquered populations ruled. There is very little comment about Muslim prisoners in enemy hands, and virtually no provision made for the enemy's victory and rule over Muslim populations.

Fifth, the theory of *jihād* is just that – theory. As in all branches of substantive law, such as pecuniary transactions, adultery and criminal law, it is one thing to speak of legal doctrine but quite another to speak of how this law interacts with the mundane context. A consideration of particular importance here is the proximity of *jihād*'s normative law to the interests of the rulers. As we have frequently argued throughout this book, the larger the investment of the ruling elite in a particular sphere of law, the more likely that the application of this sphere will be tinged with non-Sharīʿa, government-dictated, elements.

Sixth, and finally, the theory directly arose from specific historical experiences originating mainly in the first Muslim century, but was considerably enhanced by successive historical events stretching down to the Siege of Vienna in 1095/1683. For most of the period between the appearance of the Arabian Prophet and that siege, Islam was mostly triumphant, and its ruling dynasties often rose to become world imperial powers. Conversely, Muslims had little reason to change or significantly modify this theory, until, that is, they encountered modern Europe.

3. Reinterpretation and political uses

The aforementioned fourth characteristic of *jihād* theory, at first sight obscure, nonetheless proved in at least one way a source of interpretive flexibility for Muslim thinkers who faced the unprecedented phenomenon of massive European colonialism. For the first time in their long history, Muslims encountered this reality in India, where entire Muslim populations fell first under Dutch, and later under prolonged British occupation. The reality of colonialism on the one hand subverted the theory of *jihād*, and, on the other, provoked unprecedented reactions on the part of many Muslims, those whom we will call here the Islamists.[57] The subversion was conducted by the so-called modernists, who thought that adopting Western modern ideas and institutions was wholly in the interest of Muslims. And the facts of recent history and the present were on their side: *jihād*, like slavery and much else in Islamic legal doctrine, has come to represent no more than an obsolete idea, lacking judicial and jurisprudential relevance in the practices of the modern Muslim world. The relevance, instead, has become political, and in this case entirely severed from both the legal systems of Muslim states and the principles of international law. In other words, at the hands of modernity and its political, military and other processes, *jihād* has metamorphosed into an ideological and political discourse, as opposed to legal or jurisprudential.[58] Some Islamists, within a staggeringly diverse camp, rebounded with a generally extreme political interpretation of the theory and applied it, as recent history has shown, with commensurately extreme violence. It would seem that the modernist camp tamed the classical theory beyond recognition, while the Islamist side radically altered both its form and content.[59] In either case, therefore, *jihād* as Muslims conceived it in theory and practice for over a millennium no longer exists.

The ideological positions of both the modernists and the Islamists retained the same textual inventory on which the classical theory rested, but the differences between them lay in their respective interpretive approaches to this inventory. Muslim tradition is clear about the core Prophetic events that formed the interpretive basis of the theory, events that are structured in a patently chronological fashion. Mirroring the Prophetic experience, the Quran during the early Meccan period promoted a defensive stance that in turn reflected the still precarious position of the Prophet *vis-à-vis* the hegemonic aristocracy of the Quraysh. During this period, the Quran seldom calls upon Muslims to fight the unbelievers, a fact that was retrospectively interpreted by the classical jurists as warranted in light of the need to "warn" and "preach" the new message.[60] But the Prophet's entry into Medina and his victory over the Meccans in 8/629–30 transformed the otherwise passive stance into a more aggressive

[57] For an attempted definition of this group, see chapter 16, section 4 (A), below.

[58] On *jihād* in current international politics, see Kelsay, *Arguing the Just War*, especially chapters 4–6.

[59] As exemplified in ʿAbd al-Salām Faraj's *al-Farīḍa al-Ghāʾiba*. See Sagiv, *Fundamentalism*, 52–58.

[60] Ramlī, *Nihāya*, VIII, 41.

one. Illustrative of the new approach is Q. 2:190, revealed in Medina, which states: "Fight in the way of God against those who fight against you, but do not begin the hostilities. God does not love the aggressors." While in the next verse the Quran commands Muslims to fight the unbelievers "wherever you find them," a subsequent verse states: "But if they desist, then God is indeed forgiving" (2:192). Q. 9:5 goes further: "When the sacred months have passed, slay the unbelievers wherever you find them, and take them captive, and besiege them, and set for them an ambush everywhere. But if they repent and establish worship and pay the alms-tax, then leave their way free. God is forgiving, merciful." Sometime in the year 8/629–30, the Prophet removed the restriction on fighting during the sacred months, and the Quran seems to have reflected this in Sūra 9:29, which commands Muslims to fight the unbelievers "until they pay the *jizya* readily, being brought so low." The culmination of this process appears in 9:36, a verse that has become known as the Verse of the Sword.[61] The second part of it reads: "And wage war on all the idolaters as they wage war on all of you, and know that God is with those who keep their duty."[62]

This wide spectrum of Quranic discourse on *jihād* permitted the Muslim Indian thinker Sir Sayyid Aḥmad Khān (1817–98) to introduce a new theory whose basis was a new interpretation of the Quran. Drawing on those verses that speak of the need for *jihād* when Muslims are attacked, he argued that the true purpose of *jihād* is the defense of the faith, not the conversion of the enemy. A *jihād* must be conducted against those who obstruct the faith and its performance, particularly when the pillars of Islam – i.e., profession of faith, prayer, alms-tax, fasting and pilgrimage – are threatened. He asserted that the Muslims of India were not obliged by their religion to fight the British, as there was no evidence that the British had attempted as much as to undermine these pillars. By arguing thus, Khān excluded various grounds that might otherwise justify *jihād*. Not the least of such excluded grounds was conquest of the Abode of Islam by the unbelievers. And by insisting on such a restrictive interpretation, he, unwittingly or not, introduced a sharp division between the religious and the political. *Jihād* was thus made a predicate of the religious, having nothing to do with the political.[63]

Expunging from *jihād* all political and even military considerations became the emblem of the modernist project, characterized by an intensely apologetic tone. Aḥmad Khān may have been one of the first, if not the first, to offer a new interpretation, but he was followed, at least in

[61] *Ibid.*, VIII, 42. [62] On this transition in attitude, see Firestone, *Jihād*, 50–65.
[63] Peters, *Islam*, 125, 160–61.

tenor, by the majority of the modernist thinkers, some of whom can hardly be identified as Sharīʿa legal experts. In all cases, however, the modernists adopted the stance that the Quranic verses on *jihād* do not bear upon all circumstances and all times. The verses that call for unconditional fighting are episodic, arising as they did from the hostile and militant environment surrounding the Prophet and his nascent community. The true message of the Quran, the modernists insist, is to be located in the spirit of earlier verses, such as 2:190 (quoted above). Muslims are to fight only those who provoke hostility or who threaten the religious foundations of Islam. The Egyptian scholar Muḥammad Rashīd Riḍā (d. 1935) could proffer little more than did his Indian counterpart, Aḥmad Khān. But unlike Khān, who reduced the grounds on which *jihād* might be launched to the essentials of the faith, Riḍā was unable to resolve the issue of how Muslims should react in the face of proactive aggression as exemplified by British colonialism in Egypt and elsewhere.

Perhaps the most salient feature of the modernists' discourse on, and reinterpretation of, *jihād* is its reengineering from an active quest to convert the unbelievers into a passive mechanism that may be adopted as self-defense in the face of aggression against Islam and Muslims. One of the most vocal proponents of such a position is the Egyptian scholar Maḥmūd Shaltūt (d. 1963), whose exegetical sojourn through the Quranic text led him to the conclusion that Islam does not aim at converting unbelievers by force but only through peaceful debate and inner conviction. An inductive survey of history, he argued, also confirms this to be true. The aggressive language of Q. 2:190–94 (cited above) is particular to a specific situation in which the nascent Muslim community was reacting in self-defense against persecution. Thus, he concluded, "there is not a single verse in the Quran which could support the opinion that the aim of fighting in Islam is conversion."[64] The significance of this conclusion is clear: if *jihād*'s goal is not conversion, then it ceases to be offensive and is thereby altered into a defensive method.

One of the most articulate modernists to proffer a new interpretation of *jihād* has been Muḥammad Saʿīd ʿAshmāwī, a lawyer, professor of law and Chief Justice of the Criminal Court of Egypt. His discourse on *jihād* is part of a larger theory that attempts to provide a new method for interpreting Islamic law in a modern context.[65] An essential element of his theory is the crucial distinction between religion as a pure idea and religious thought, including law, as an elaboration of that idea. Religion is supra-human, immutable and objective. Religious thought is merely human, and thus

[64] Shaltūt, "Koran and Fighting," 79. [65] See chapter 17, section 7, below.

changeable according to place, time and circumstance. This idea – which ʿAshmāwī takes up at length – is intended to absolve today's Muslims from any commitment to a tradition that was by definition constructed and elaborated by their predecessors. Religion is eternal and belongs to God, but what each generation or age constructs for itself is binding on that time and place, not on their fellow believers down through the centuries. To be perfect for each age, the Sharīʿa must be brought to bear upon the social and human exigencies which are in a state of continuous flux.[66] It is within this context that ʿAshmāwī addresses the problem of *jihād*.

ʿAshmāwī's treatment starts from the foundational premise that neither the Quran nor the Sunna prescribed any form of Islamic governance, since religion was sent to people as a human, not a political, entity. If government can never be Islamic, then *jihād* (traditionally conceived as part of religion) cannot be construed as a means to protect this government. And if *jihād* in the Quran was not decreed to promote the political interests of the Abode of Islam, then the *raison d'être* for the *jihād* prescription must be sought in the very circumstances and realities with which revelation stood in a dialectical relationship. Like Shaltūt, ʿAshmāwī sees Q. 2:190–93 as a reaction to persecution and aggression, justifying in turn the fight in self-defense. He asserts that nowhere does the Quran enjoin Muslims to launch *jihād* against those who believe in other scriptures, unless these first attack the Muslims. Nor does the Quran command Muslims to war against others in order to convert them, for if God's plan were to do so, he would have created all mankind as Muslims in the first place. The Quran itself, after all, averred that "Had God willed He would have made you one community" (5:48). Thus, the classical Muslim jurists had erred in their interpretation of Q. 9:29, 9:123 and similar verses, for one cannot conclude from these verses that the People of the Book must be fought until they convert. If anything, the Sharīʿa urges peace, as attested in a number of verses, including 8:61: "If they incline to peace, you should incline to it as well." *Jihād*, ʿAshmāwī concludes, was intended as no more than self-defense.[67]

Whereas the modernists view *jihād* as defensive, and as such compatible with modern notions of warfare and the nation-state system generally, some Islamists insist, going beyond the classical juristic theory, that the purpose of *jihād* is the propagation of Islam and the conversion of non-Muslims to Islam. Their programs go further in articulating the rationale that justifies this type of *jihād*, proceeding with elaborate criticism of

[66] ʿAshmāwī, *Uṣūl*, 52–85. For a more detailed discussion of ʿAshmāwī's reformist method in law, see Hallaq, *History*, 231–41.

[67] ʿAshmāwī, *Uṣūl*, 89–98.

Western cultures and institutions. The classical jurists were in no way concerned with the nature of the unbelievers' ways of life or the governments under which they lived. They viewed it as a religious duty that should be performed whenever possible. Nowhere do they even allude to *jihād* as a struggle that should be waged to change oppressive rule or tyrannical regimes against which Islam, as a way of life, affords a remedy. But this is a dominating theme of some Islamist programs. For instance, Abū al-Aʿlā Mawdūdī (d. 1979), a Pakistani intellectual, argued in precisely these terms. His concept of *jihād* is part and parcel of an ideology that constructs the world in terms of equality and fairness, of human happiness and contentment. Islam, for him, offers a practical program that leads to human happiness and is wholly about and for people, not about governments, nation-states or their selfish interests. If Islam, through *jihād*, aims to dominate the world, it is not because it covets material resources and wealth, or in order to appropriate these from other groups or nations in the interest of a particular elite. Islam's claim to global governance, Mawdūdī implies, shares none of the attributes of Western colonialism which plundered the natural and material resources of the majority of non-European lands. Rather, Islam "wants and requires the earth in order that the human race altogether can enjoy the concept and practical program of human happiness."[68] And in order to achieve this goal, an all-embracing revolution and a far-reaching struggle are needed. For Mawdūdī, then, these are precisely the elements that constitute *jihād*, a revolutionary struggle against both oppression and inequality.[69]

It should not come as a surprise that the ideology of the anti-Marxist Mawdūdī echoes more the basic platforms of nationalist and Marxist liberationist movements than anything the classical jurists espoused, nor should it be surprising that he calls his proposed revolution *jihād*. In their quest for political activism, the majority of the Islamists have effectively resorted to *jihād* as a discursive strategy. A leading Egyptian Islamist, Sayyid Quṭb, capitulated – knowingly or not – to the Weberian notion of "the rule of man over man,"[70] arguing that such a Western method of governance leads to the subjugation of one man or class to another. This sort of regime enslaves people and obscures their vision as to justice and equality. Islam, on the other hand, frees man from such shackles and oppression to acknowledge only the supremacy of one God. *Jihād* is to be launched with a view to liberating humankind from these tyrannies, but it

[68] Cited from a translation by Peters, *Islam*, 130. [69] *Ibid.*

[70] Lassman, "Rule of Man." Further on Quṭb's ideas in this regard, see Euben, *Enemy in the Mirror*, 56–62, especially at 61.

is not to be deployed toward converting people by force. It merely "sets the individual free to choose the creed according to his free will, after having liberated him from the political pressures."[71] But it is clear that Quṭb's assumption is that this liberated individual will ultimately opt for Islam.

By the 1970s, social and intellectual protests in the Islamic and Arab countries were beginning to take a new direction. Although the West continued to be regarded as the main culprit, the ruling elites and dictators of the Muslim world were identified as incorrigible agents of Western imperialism, especially of the United States. The struggle, then, was no longer to be carried out solely in the international arena, but had to begin at home. The national regimes now became the first targets and the means to resisting and combating Western encroachments. The way to liberating Jerusalem was through liberating Cairo and Amman (originally a Marxist Palestinian slogan, notably espoused by none other than the Christian leaders George Ḥabash and Nāyif Ḥawātmeh). Many Arab, Iranian and South-East Asian Marxists have called for revolutionary struggle, and some still do. But an increasing number of individuals and organizations have opted for an Islamic frame of reference, and have called upon the Muslim masses to take up *jihād* against the political regimes of their respective countries.[72] Marxian discourse of revolution was transformed into Islamic vocabulary, but the political content is much the same. Two out of many groups adopting such discourse are the Organization of Islamic Liberation and the Association for Muslims (better known by the title *Jamāʿat al-Takfīr wal-Hijra*), both established around the mid-1970s by a scientist and an agricultural engineer, respectively.[73] To what extent these two figures were knowledgeable, if they were at all, in any aspect of the Islamic sciences is a question that remains open.

Any sensitive and intelligent analysis of these movements and ideologies makes it abundantly clear that the uses of the concept of *jihād* in the twentieth and twenty-first centuries are not only widely varied, but also qualitatively different from the consistent pre-modern juristic doctrine. To reduce these differences between the modern and pre-modern concepts of *jihād* to mere differences of style and language, as some scholars have argued, is not only to miss the point but also to conflate the social, economic, political and legal realities of the second/eighth century with those of our own time, thereby producing a "historical Islam" that is

[71] Cited from a translation by Peters, *Islam*, 131.

[72] See, for example, Faraj, *al-Jihād: al-Farīḍa al-Ghāʾiba*. See also Bassiouni, "Evolving Approaches," 136–46.

[73] Sagiv, *Fundamentalism*, 52–58.

reducible to one abstracted essence. It is remarkable that Christian Arab leaders have invoked the vocabulary of *jihād* in their support of Arab national movements, just as ʿAbd al-Ḥalīm Maḥmūd, none other than the Rector of Al-Azhar himself, insisted that *jihād* is a *national* duty no less incumbent upon Christian Arabs than on their Muslim counterparts.[74]

[74] Peters, *Islam*, 158.

12 Courts of justice, suits and evidence

Almost every work of *fiqh* contained three chapters or "books" that, from a modern perspective, may be characterized as belonging to the law of procedure.[1] The first of these chapters usually dealt with the *qāḍī* and his *adab*,[2] namely, the conditions and terms of his appointment, conduct and work while in tenure.[3] The prescriptions extend from personal characteristics and state of mind to the procedure he must follow in his court, all of which, as always, are subject to the multiplicity of legal opinion (*khilāf*; *ikhtilāf*). The second traditionally deals with the obligations and rights of plaintiffs and defendants, and how a suit (*daʿwā*) must open, proceed and end. The third chapter addresses evidence, especially oral testimony (*shahādāt*), but it also deals with written instruments, oaths, confessions and related matters.

1. Lawsuits

Although the greater bulk of the matters handled by the Muslim court did not involve litigation,[4] an important function of the court was obviously the resolving of disputes.[5] The *qāḍī* was under the legal and moral obligation to hear and adjudge all disputes (except for those which involved conflict of interest), and was forbidden to turn away claimants or disputants, even if they appeared before him outside his schedule.[6] "Razing

[1] See Appendix A, Books 51–53, below.

[2] These chapters also commanded a special treatment in independent works commonly titled *adab al-qāḍī* or *adab al-qaḍāʾ*. For a list of such works, see Hallaq, "*Qāḍī*'s *Dīwān*," 418–19, nn. 15–20.

[3] The majority of jurists, including the Twelver-Shīʿites, espoused the view that only a man can be a *qāḍī*. Abū Ḥanīfa held the opinion that women can serve in this capacity in all areas of the law where their testimony is deemed valid, namely, in all areas except *ḥudūd* offenses and *qiṣāṣ* (see chapter 10, above). The eponym of the defunct Jarīrite school, Ibn Jarīr al-Ṭabarī (d. 310/923), reasoned that because women can exercise *ijtihād* like men, they can serve as judges in the entire gamut of the law. Ṭūsī, *Khilāf*, II, 590.

[4] See chapter 4, sections 2–3, above. [5] See also chapter 1, section 5, above.

[6] It was normative that *qāḍī*s designated at least one or two days a week to hear disputes. Only during times of prayer or eating could the *qāḍī* turn away claimants, and even then only temporarily. See Nawawī, *Rawḍa*, VIII, 139–40; Māwardī, *Ḥāwī*, XVI, 273.

injustice" was the *qāḍī*'s unqualified duty, to be fulfilled effectively and without undue delay.[7] Protracted adjudication and postponements in the judicial process were thus abhorred, and deemed to aggravate injustice.[8]

Much of the discourse in this literature was dedicated to the ethics of litigants' treatment by the *qāḍī*. Equity was of the essence, beginning with the litigants' physical approach to the *majlis al-ḥukm* (the court as it sits in session).[9] Queues were to be maintained, and when claimants and disputants would arrive at the court simultaneously, or when the queue was lost, lots were to be drawn. The *qāḍī* was commanded to maintain respectful treatment of the litigants, to greet them, to invite them to sit in his *majlis*, to be serious yet polite, economic in speech and firm yet gentle, giving them his undivided attention.[10] Most jurists, especially of the later centuries, strongly advised against a judge relying, in formulating his decision, on prior knowledge of the litigants.[11] Those who permitted such reliance did so with caution, precluding any and all cases within the sphere of *ḥudūd*.[12] Gifts and bribes were forbidden, but if the *qāḍī* did not receive income from the public treasury[13] he could charge the litigants (as well as all other users of the court) an appropriate fee.[14] He was not to adjudge cases in which a relative or a friend of his was involved,[15] and, to ensure his integrity, he had to have a group of legal scholars attend his court sessions.[16] He could, upon request, review his predecessor's decisions, just as his successor could review his.[17] Once out of office, he could be called upon by his successor to account for any misconduct during his tenure, and had to face justice like any other defendant.[18]

7 *Al-Fatāwā al-Hindiyya*, III, 306.

8 Ḥiṣnī, *Kifāya*, II, 256; Ramlī, *Nihāya*, VIII, 224; [Miṣrī, *Reliance*, 624–30; Ibn Rushd, *Distinguished Jurist's Primer*, II, 553 f.].

9 It was only under the Ottomans, and after the sixteenth century, that the court in towns and cities was to be held in a building specifically designated for that purpose. Hallaq, "*Qāḍī*'s *Dīwān*," 435–36; [Miṣrī, *Reliance*, 630–32; Ibn Rushd, *Distinguished Jurist's Primer*, II, 568–72].

10 Nawawī, *Rawḍa*, VIII, 147; Māwardī, *Ḥāwī*, XVI, 273; Ibn Mufliḥ, *Furū'*, VI, 442.

11 Ibn 'Ābidīn, *Ḥāshiya*, V, 423; Māwardī, *Ḥāwī*, XVI, 321–24.

12 Ibn Qudāma, *Kāfī*, IV, 300.

13 Qarāfī, *Furūq*, III, 5, where he argues that any income from the Public Treasury does not constitute salary (what he calls *ajr*, i.e., wage) since such pay exposes the judge to the charge of bias (*la-dakhalat al-tuhma*).

14 Nawawī, *Rawḍa*, VIII, 127; Ibn 'Ābidīn, *Ḥāshiya*, V, 362–63, but also 372–73.

15 This appears to be the unanimous position of all Sunnite schools. The Twelver-Shī'ites, however, permitted a *qāḍī* to adjudicate disputes involving his own descendants and ascendants. See Ṭūsī, *Khilāf*, II, 603–04.

16 Nawawī, *Rawḍa*, VIII, 124–26; Ḥaṭṭāb, *Mawāhib*, VI, 117; Māwardī, *Ḥāwī*, XVI, 47–50; al-Ḥusām al-Shahīd, *Sharḥ*, 59. See also chapter 4, section 3, above.

17 Ṭūsī, *Khilāf*, II, 590–91.

18 Nawawī, *Rawḍa*, VIII, 112–14; Ibn Qudāma, *Mughnī*, XI, 403–05; Mawāq, *Tāj*, VI, 135; Ḥaṭṭāb, *Mawāhib*, VI, 135–37; Ṭūsī, *Khilāf*, II, 591.

Anyone enjoying sanity and discretion can bring a lawsuit (*daʿwā*) against another,[19] although certain other conditions must be met before the process of adjudication can begin. Fulfillment of these conditions renders the suit sound (*ṣaḥīḥa*), which gives the plaintiff the right to demand the judge to summon the defendant to appear before the court, and, failing that, to render judgment in the case. A defective suit (*nāqiṣa*) is one that has fulfilled all essential requisites but lacks a requirement or requirements that, once met, can rectify the suit (such as the initial failure to specify with reasonable precision the object of dispute).[20] Such rectification, once made, renders the suit sound. But if rectification proves impossible because the deficiency is incurable, then the suit is deemed null and void (*bāṭila*; *fāsida*). Some causes invalidating a suit include a claim governed by a statute of limitations (*taqādum al-zamān*),[21] or one in which the plaintiff has no standing (*fuḍūlī*), acting with neither entitlement nor legal authorization.[22]

To be "sound," a *daʿwā* thus must issue from a concerned party who cannot be inconsistent or contradictory in the claims he or she makes; these must be certain in their language and must state with a high degree of specificity, *mutatis mutandis*, the nature, characteristics, size, value and location of the matter or object under dispute.[23] If the object is real property, its location must be described in relation to surrounding property, and if it is a movable property, its characteristics, size, shape, color, value, etc. must, as appropriate, be specified.[24] Any lack of specificity in describing the disputed object also renders testimonial evidence ineffective, if not inadmissible, since the testimony must correspond to the object being disputed.[25]

The *fiqh* distinguishes between individual and collective rights, the latter arising from legal acts and instruments involving a class of persons, not an individual or a number of specific persons (e.g., partners or inheriting members of a family). A common example of an act giving rise to a collective right is a *waqf* dedicated to the poor and the needy or to

19 Kāsānī, *Badāʾiʿ*, VIII, 411; [Miṣrī, *Reliance*, 632–35; Ibn Rushd, *Distinguished Jurist's Primer*, II, 555–56, 567–68].

20 Ḥaṭṭāb, *Mawāhib*, VI, 124–25.

21 Although, as a rule, rights are inextinguishable, the political sovereign can impose certain time limits on hearing particular suits. A well-known case in point is the Ottoman limitation of fifteen years on most claims, except for inheritance and *waqf*. Bāz, *Sharḥ*, II, 983–90; Ibn ʿĀbidīn, *Ḥāshiya*, V, 419 ff.; Ḥaṭṭāb, *Mawāhib*, VI, 128–29. Some jurists argued that in matters of *ḥudūd*, *qiṣāṣ* and *liʿān*, no statute of limitations whatsoever is applicable. See Ibn Nujaym, *Ashbāh*, 222.

22 See chapter 7, sections 1, ii and 8, above.

23 Ibn Abī al-Damm, *Adab*, 143–47.

24 Ḥalabī, *Multaqā*, II, 108–09.

25 Ibn Abī al-Damm, *Adab*, 143; Ibn Qudāma, *Kāfī*, IV, 315.

the Muslim community at large, such as hospitals, soup kitchens, public drinking fountains (including reservoirs for water supply), bridges, mosques, public baths and cemeteries. Except for *qadhf*,[26] all *ḥudūd* offenses belong to this collective category of rights, as these are "public" offenses. A collective *daʿwā* may be brought by any person or persons, since the *muddaʿī*, the claimant or plaintiff, stands as a representative of the class of beneficiaries or of the community at large. This is known as *daʿwā al-ḥisba*, and is cognate to the institution of *muḥtasib* and the practice of *iḥtisāb*.[27] In matters of "public" interest (including Quranic *ḥudūd* offenses), and in the absence of intrusive state mechanisms, it was historically the *qāḍī* and the *muḥtasib* who fulfilled some of the functions associated in modern law with public prosecution.[28]

In dealing with any valid, sound suit, the *qāḍī*'s first task is to determine who the plaintiff is,[29] since that determination has the consequence of allocating a certain type of proof to him or her, whereas the defendant must submit to a different evidential procedure. The plaintiff's burden of proof is deemed "graver," since by bringing a suit he seeks to change the status quo, the presumption of continuity and, in fact, the presumption of the defendant's innocence. Yet, no school or jurist defines the plaintiff exclusively on the grounds of bringing the suit before the court. The Mālikites and Shāfiʿites hold the plaintiff to be the party whose claim to change the status quo or any such presumption is weaker than that of the other party.[30] The presumption of innocence (*barāʾa*), for instance, dictates that X's claim against Y with regard to an outstanding debt be supported by X with evidence (*bayyina*) if Y denies the debt (*inkār*, *nukūl*). But if X does not produce satisfactory evidence, Y, in order to establish innocence, is required to do no more than swear an oath (*yamīn*) of non-indebtedness to X. Confession (*iqrār*), on the other hand, does not require further proof.[31] Presumption of continuity also dictates that a "natural state of affairs" is assumed to exist until the contrary is proven. Thus a triply divorced woman who claims that her ex-husband divorced her during his death-illness must prove that the divorce occurred during his death-illness, if the other relatives deny this having been the case. By the same token, an assumption of innocence as well as presumption of continuous benign relations holds true until shown otherwise, for any claim involving malicious conduct requires proof. Such presumptions

[26] See chapter 10, section 2, ii, above. [27] Ibn Mufliḥ, *Furūʿ*, VI, 524.
[28] Māwardī, *Aḥkām*, 207–23. See also chapter 5, sections 2–3, above.
[29] See Qarāfī, *Furūq*, IV, 160–65, where he observes that this issue has been highly controversial among jurists.
[30] Ḥaṭṭāb, *Mawāhib*, VI, 124.
[31] Buhūtī, *Rawḍ*, 604–05; [Ibn Rushd, *Distinguished Jurist's Primer*, II, 567].

also dictate that prolonged, unhindered and undisputed possession of property signals ownership, and any claim to the contrary must be supported by evidence. Hence, the Shāfiʿite Nawawī defines the matter thus: "The plaintiff is he who claims a hidden matter (*amran khafiyyan*) that diverges from what is apparent (*ẓāhir*); whereas the defendant is he who agrees with that which is apparent. [Or else], the plaintiff is one who is left alone and is required to do nothing if he were to adopt silence [i.e., to abandon the suit], whereas the defendant [once he is sued] cannot be left alone, and cannot abandon [the suit if he wishes to do so]."[32]

The Ḥanafites and Ḥanbalites approach the distinction differently. The former take the position that the plaintiff is the party who, if he/she chooses to abandon making the claim, cannot be compelled to persist in it, whereas the defendant has no choice of forgoing this option.[33] The Ḥanbalites adopt this definition and add to it the element of initiative. Thus, the plaintiff must also be the one who brings the suit whereas the defendant is the one who is the target of the suit.[34]

In disputes in which no presumption can be made in favor of a defendant, or when a presumption of possession cannot be established, both parties are regarded at one and the same time as plaintiffs and defendants. In a case where a person claims to have rented a house to another for a certain amount, whereas the latter claims that the amount covers the rent of the surrounding land, both are required to adduce evidence (*bayyina*), a fact which puts both in the position of being plaintiffs. Disputes between and among joint owners or disputes over consideration (*thaman*) in sales and dowers also entail placing the two parties in the position of plaintiffs and defendants simultaneously.[35]

The majority of jurists espouse the view that it is the plaintiff who determines jurisdiction, but the Ḥanafites confer the right of determining this on the defendant since he is assumed to be innocent of any charge until proven otherwise. Some Mālikites, among other non-Mālikites, distinguished the object in dispute, arguing that the suit should be brought in the same jurisdiction where the disputed property is located. But the authoritative Mālikite position holds that the jurisdiction should be where the defendant resides. Those jurists who admit the method of communication between *qāḍīs* (*kitāb al-qāḍī ilā al-qāḍī*)[36] generally allow the plaintiff to bring the suit before any *qāḍī* of her choice. The Twelver-Shīʿites

[32] Nawawī, *Rawḍa*, VIII, 287; Ibn Abī al-Damm, *Adab*, 131–35.
[33] Ḥalabī, *Multaqā*, II, 108. [34] Buhūtī, *Kashshāf*, VI, 409.
[35] Shāfiʿī, *Umm*, VI, 323–24.
[36] Mawāq, *Tāj*, VI, 142; Nawawī, *Rawḍa*, VIII, 162–63. On *kitāb al-qāḍī ilā al-qāḍī*, see Hallaq, "*Qāḍīs* Communicating."

appear to have rejected this type of communication categorically, espousing the view that no court decision can be made on the basis of testimonies garnered through such doubtful means.[37]

A person making a claim against another is expected to request the latter to appear with him before the court. Agreement to this request comes highly recommended by no less than the Quran itself.[38] However, should the defendant refuse to do so, the plaintiff's request is not automatically implemented by the *qāḍī* if the defendant's presence involves for him or her any hardship due to illness or long-distance travel to the location of the court. The jurists disagree over the measure of hardship when distance is involved, some opining that three days of travel constitutes such hardship, while others limit it to anything longer than a day.[39] The Mālikites, Shāfiʿites and Ḥanbalites do not insist on the appearance of the defendant before the presiding *qāḍī*, allowing the latter to communicate in writing, through *kitāb al-qāḍī ilā al-qāḍī*, with the judge presiding in the locale where the defendant resides.[40]

Should the defendant live within reasonable proximity of the court before which a suit is brought, he must appear before the court if and when the *qāḍī* requests him to do so (typically done when a *daʿwā* has been certified by the *qāḍī* as "sound"). Non-appearance or refusal to appear would be deemed a moral-cum-legal violation, since the enjoinment to appear before justice is a command issuing from both the Quran and the sovereign, represented by his *qāḍī*s. Upon refusal, the *qāḍī* has the prerogative of sending his assistants (*aʿwān*) to bring the defendant to court. Should they fail to accomplish this task, and depending on the severity of the charge, the *qāḍī* may seek the assistance of the police (*shuraṭ*, *shurṭa*) or the governor's soldiers, who may use coercion to bring the defendant to court.

Finally, the disputing parties may also turn to arbitration (*taḥkīm*) to resolve their disagreement.[41] Once the arbiter (*ḥakam*) reaches a decision, no party may retract, and the decision is binding. Jurists universally agree that between appointment of the arbiter and the moment in which he begins to arbitrate any party may withdraw, but they disagree over whether they can do so during the proceedings. They likewise disagree over the validity of arbitration in several areas of the law, the Ḥanafites precluding *ḥudūd* and retaliation, and the Ḥanbalites and Shāfiʿites adding to this

[37] Ṭūsī, *Khilāf*, II, 595. [38] Quran, 24:48–51.
[39] Nawawī, *Rawḍa*, VIII, 245; Ṭūsī, *Khilāf*, II, 599–600.
[40] Ibn Qudāma, *Kāfī*, IV, 302; Ibn Qudāma, *Mughnī*, XI, 458–66; *al-Fatāwā al-Hindiyya*, III, 381.
[41] See chapter 4, above.

exclusion family law as well.[42] The *qāḍī* must enforce the arbiter's decision if it is legally sound and if it agrees with his own school's doctrine; otherwise, he has the competence to revoke the arbitrative judgment.[43]

2. Testimony

In theory and practice, the Sharīʿa accords primary importance to oral testimony (*shahāda*), regarding it as the most evincive of all forms of evidence (*bayyina*).[44] The strong association of *shahāda* with *bayyina* has rendered these two terms nearly interchangeable, although *bayyina* includes other types of evidence, such as the oath (*yamīn*), confession/acknowledgment (*iqrār*) and circumstantial indicants (*qarāʾin al-aḥwāl*).[45] *Shahāda* is defined as attestation with regard to a right of a second party against a third, in contradistinction, for instance, to *iqrār*, defined as a right owed to a second party by the attesting party.[46] It must involve the certain knowledge (*ʿilm al-yaqīn*) of having seen and heard a particular event or occurrence, all testimony based on probability and conjecture being inadmissible. The *qāḍī* not only conducts cross-examination of the witnesses but also employs individuals whose task it is to check, in the community, on the witnesses' character.[47] Abū Ḥanīfa and the Twelver-Shīʿites, among others, opined that the judge should not examine the character of witnesses (in non-*ḥudūd* and non-*qiṣāṣ* suits) unless the defendant objects to their probity.[48] Giving testimony is a religious obligation whenever one is capable of fulfilling it (*farḍ kifāya*),[49] and if (a) harm may come to someone due to the refusal to testify, and (b) there are no other witnesses, then it becomes an obligatory duty (*farḍ ʿayn*). Being morally and legally obligated, witnesses – according to some jurists – must not charge fees for their testimonies, unless their livelihood has been adversely affected, in which case the party for whom they are testifying may recompense them for the loss. The Ḥanbalites and Shāfiʿites permit

42 Ibn Qudāma, *Kāfī*, IV, 280–81; Ḥalabī, *Multaqā*, II, 78; Nawawī, *Rawḍa*, VIII, 105.
43 Ḥalabī, *Multaqā*, II, 77; Mawāq, *Tāj*, VI, 112; Ibn Abī al-Damm, *Adab*, 121–23.
44 [Miṣrī, *Reliance*, 635–38; Ibn Rushd, *Distinguished Jurist's Primer*, II, 556–60.] For a useful discussion of oral and written evidence in actual commercial litigation, see Messick, "Commercial Litigation," 203–12.
45 More on *qarāʾin*, see Hallaq, "Notes on the Term *Qarīna*."
46 See chapter 7, section 13, above.
47 Ramlī, *Nihāya*, VIII, 251–54; Ibn Qudāma, *Kāfī*, IV, 290.
48 Examination of witnesses' character in *ḥudūd* and *qiṣāṣ* is deemed to be essential in the doctrines of all schools and scholars, the reason being that in these suits, there is no room for "a shade of doubt" insofar as evidence is concerned. See chapter 10, above; Ibn Māza, *Muḥīṭ*, XII, 280; Ṭūsī, *Khilāf*, II, 591–92.
49 Ibn Mufliḥ, *Furūʿ*, VI, 548; Buhūtī, *Kashshāf*, VI, 433.

witnesses to collect fees for their work, deeming the activity a contract of hire (*ijāra*).[50]

The jurists distinguish between charging (*taḥammul*) and discharging (*adāʾ*) testimony. The *taḥammul* comes into being by the act of "taking in" the information and data of the testimony, that is, of recording it in the witness's mind as a matter of fact. The *adāʾ* in effect represents the giving or releasing of that information before a magistrate. Almost any person can engage in *taḥammul* (including slaves, non-Muslims, minors and even the temporarily insane). However, the conditions for *adāʾ* are much more stringent, requiring, at the time of discharging the testimony, that a slave has been freed (according to some jurists),[51] that a minor reach the age of majority, and that a non-Muslim convert to Islam.[52] The Ḥanafites reject a blind person's charging and discharging of testimony, but the Mālikites, Ḥanbalites and Twelver-Shīʿites permit his testimony in matters that involve, and completely depend upon, hearing.[53] The "discharging" witness must also be: (a) capable of speech, although Mālik permitted him to convey his testimony through signs, and some Ḥanbalites through writing; (b) capable of accurate reporting (*ḍabṭ*) and not be absent-minded, careless or stupid;[54] (c) trustworthy and possessed of personal rectitude (*ʿadl*), the latter being defined as someone who has not committed a grave sin and who does not persist in committing minor sins. Abandoning the pillars of religion constitutes a grave sin, and so does habitual engagement in deeply immoral acts (*fisq*) or practicing unseemly professions (e.g., dancers, singers and clowns);[55] (d) male, if testifying in matters involving *ḥudūd* punishments;[56] (e) free of any involvement in *qadhf*; and (f) not subject to the proven charge of conflict of interest (*tuhma*), that is, a testimony in favor of a relative[57] or in a matter that may accrue benefit to the witness himself. In the same vein, testimony against a long-standing enemy, a rival tribe, etc., is invalid and must be dismissed by the judge.[58]

[50] Ibn Mufliḥ, *Furūʿ*, VI, 550; Ibn Qudāma, *Mughnī*, XI, 376–77.

[51] The Ḥanafites and some Shāfiʿites rejected the testimony of slaves. However, most jurists, including the Twelver-Shīʿites, admitted the validity of a slave's testimony in favor of, and against, anyone except their own masters. Ṭūsī, *Khilāf*, II, 613.

[52] See *al-Fatāwā al-Hindiyya*, III, 450; Ibn Qudāma, *Mughnī*, XII, 84; Ṭūsī, *Khilāf*, II, 613. *Dhimmī*s can testify to a Muslim's bequest in the absence of qualified Muslim witnesses. Most jurists admit non-Muslims' testimony against their co-religionists, but not against Muslims. The Twelver-Shīʿites do not admit the testimony of a person who does not believe in the Twelvers' doctrine of the Imamate. Ṭūsī, *Khilāf*, II, 613–14, 624. Practice, at least in eighteenth- and nineteenth-century Damascus, appears to have been less strict than doctrine. See al-Qattan, "*Dhimmī*s in the Muslim Court," 437 f.

[53] Ṭūsī, *Khilāf*, II, 612. [54] Ibn Qudāma, *Kāfī*, IV, 338. [55] *Ibid.*, IV, 338–40.

[56] See chapter 10, section 2, i, above. [57] Ibn ʿAbd al-Rafīʿ, *Muʿīn*, II, 647–49.

[58] Buhūtī, *Sharḥ*, III, 554–55.

The importance of certainty in attesting to the factuality of an alleged occurrence means that written testimony cannot be accepted at face value, without witnesses recalling that someone had in fact written the record in question. In Shāfiʿite doctrine, and according to a Ḥanafite opinion, a *qāḍī* cannot act on the basis of a record (e.g., of a witness's testimony or otherwise) he had at one point written but he no longer remembers.[59] Many jurists also held the view that a witness's testimony is invalid if it is based on his own writing, and if he does not remember having written it down. (The general principle by which written records, unaccompanied by oral testimony, are rejected as having no evidentiary value ultimately rests on the assumption that in documentary evidence there is no moral accountability. In the nature of it, oral testimony does not allow for avoidance of this accountability.)

The number of witnesses required varies according to the nature of the transaction, infraction or dispute in question. We saw that four male witnesses are required to prove the charge of fornication/adultery (*zinā*).[60] Theft, highway brigandage and drinking alcohol require two male witnesses. The majority of jurists permit the testimony of women in most areas of the law, with the exception of *ḥudūd* and *qiṣāṣ*; a man and two women in marriage, divorce, guardianship, agency and other similar contracts; and one male witness and an oath for most pecuniary contracts.[61] It is a universal doctrine that one woman's testimony is both admissible and sufficient in matters related to midwifery, forensic examination of the female body, nursing and other areas of testimony where women are knowledgeable and men cannot intrude.[62] In the same vein, most jurists admit a solitary witness in matters of expertise, such as a doctor's testimony as to the extent of bodily injury or a master-builder's testimony as to the soundness of a structure. In the opinion of the great majority of jurists, producing a number of witnesses greater than the law requires (*niṣāb*) does not strengthen a party's case, except for some Mālikite jurists who thought the added testimonies lend further corroboration.[63]

The testimony of a witness who ceases to meet the necessary qualifications of witnessing must be dismissed if the *qāḍī* has not yet rendered

[59] Nawawī, *Rawḍa*, VIII, 142. [60] See chapter 10, section 2, i, above.

[61] Nawawī, *Rawḍa*, VIII, 252. However, attesting to commercial and pecuniary transactions is not deemed of the essence. Shaʿrānī, *Mīzān*, 271 (cf. lines 2–3, 22–23).

[62] The Twelver-Shīʿites also adopt this doctrine to the exception of nursing infants (*riḍāʿ*). Ṭūsī, *Khilāf*, II, 608–09. See also Shaham, "Women as Expert Witnesses," 44 ff.

[63] Nawawī, *Rawḍa*, VIII, 335; Marghīnānī, *Hidāya*, III, 173; Ibn Qudāma, *Mughnī*, XII, 176. In certain cases, the Twelver-Shīʿites give weight to additional witnesses. Ṭūsī, *Khilāf*, II, 636–37.

judgment; but if he has, the judgment will not be revoked. However, its implementation will be suspended in matters where the slightest suspicion dictates the lifting of prescribed penalties, such as in matters of *ḥudūd* and *qiṣāṣ*. Otherwise, the judgment will be implemented, and the witness must pay damages to the party that has incurred loss due to his or her testimony. The party that has won the case due to the invalid testimony incurs no liability. If the witness deliberately lies in order to inflict harm on a party, then the witness is punished accordingly. False testimony leading to capital punishment is grounds for condemning the false witness to the same punishment according to all schools except the Ḥanafites. They hold the opinion that death resulting from false testimony is an indirect act of homicide, which entails the payment of blood-money. If one of two witnesses retracts his testimony after implementation of the judgment, he is liable to compensate the victim half of his or her loss. If one or two witnesses, out of four, retract their testimony in a case that requires only two witnesses, then they are not culpable and the judgment remains in effect. If three of them retract, then all three share equally in the payment of half the damages to the party adversely affected by their testimony. If one out of four witnesses in a *zinā* suit retracts or contradicts any of the other three with regard to the details of the sexual act, he, along with the other witnesses, is charged with slander (*qadhf*), and penalized accordingly.[64] In nearly all other cases, a false witness (*shāhid zūr*) is deemed to have committed a serious offense, punishable by a humiliating display (*tashhīr*) in the marketplace after the Friday prayer, when people tend to gather. Beating, imprisonment and, during *tashhīr*, painting the face black are also prescribed.[65] Furthermore, a false witness will never be able to testify again.[66]

Testimony to the effect that a plaintiff owns a certain object or property is deemed, if not supported by any further evidence, to be weaker than the fact of possession (*thubūt yad*) by the defendant. Possession is generally a preponderant factor in favor of the party that proves (or enjoys) it,[67] for the claims of both sides (in the absence of further evidence) have equal value and thus are useless in any determination of ownership.[68] If a third party has possession of the disputed property, but without having proof of ownership, and if the two parties produce evidence of their ownership that is deemed to be equivalent in weight, then the third

[64] On *qadhf*, see chapter 10, section 2, ii, above.
[65] Nawawī, *Rawḍa*, VIII, 129; Māwardī, *Ḥāwī*, XVI, 320–21. Further on this, see chapter 10, section 4, above.
[66] Māwardī, *Ḥāwī*, XVI, 319–21. [67] Qarāfī, *Furūq*, IV, 171.
[68] Ṭūsī, *Khilāf*, II, 635–36.

party retains ownership according to most schools (in keeping with the preponderating principle of *thubūt yad*), but the Ḥanafites divide the value among the two.[69]

When a witness cannot attend court – due to illness, for instance – two other witnesses may testify on his or her behalf by conveying the content of the testimony to the *qāḍī*. The two witnesses become secondary (*shuhūd far*ʿ; sing., *shāhid far*ʿ) whereas the original witness is regarded as the principal (*shāhid aṣl*). This testimonial conveyance – known as *al-shahāda ʿalā al-shahāda* (lit. attesting to testimony) – is generally admitted in non-punitive spheres of the law, such as pecuniary contracts, marriage, divorce, manumission, etc. The Ḥanafites reject it in matters that do not tolerate the slightest of doubt, such as *ḥudūd* and *qiṣāṣ*. The *qāḍī* himself may also appear as a secondary witness before another court. The secondary witness must meet the same qualifications required of witnesses in general, and must, in addition, engage in *istirʿāʾ*, namely, the act of the primary witness dictating to the secondary witnesses the content of the testimony. However, *istirʿāʾ* is not required should the secondary witnesses have already heard the primary witness give his testimony before another *qāḍī*. The Shāfiʿites and Ḥanbalites require for the validity of the secondary testimony that the reason of the primary witness's unavailability continue to hold until the *qāḍī* passes his verdict. If not, the primary witness must herself appear before the court and, in this case, *al-shahāda ʿalā al-shahāda* ceases to be admissible.[70]

3. Oaths

A plaintiff bringing suit without basing himself on a *bayyina* may request that the defendant take an oath, essentially swearing on the name of God that he is telling the truth about having or not having done or said something. Oaths can be intensified (*taghlīẓ*) in non-pecuniary litigation,[71] by accentuating in the language of the oath the reference to God, e.g., by referring to a list of God's attributes or, for the oath-taker, by facing the Kaʿba while taking the oath.[72] The defendant is normatively the oath-taker, although in certain cases oaths may be made by plaintiffs. In such cases they are requested by the *qāḍī* himself, especially in matters involving women seeking spousal support from their absent husbands or a lender

69 On the various positions with regard to *yad*, see Shaʿrānī, *Mīzān*, 274–75.

70 Ibn Abī al-Damm, *Adab*, 295 ff.; Maqdisī, *ʿUdda*, 633–36.

71 Including homicide, marriage, *ṭalāq*, manumission, agency, guardianship, etc. Nawawī, *Rawḍa*, VIII, 310; Ṭūsī, *Khilāf*, II, 618–19.

72 Nawawī, *Rawḍa*, VIII, 309–11; Ibn Abī al-Damm, *Adab*, 185–89.

seeking repayment of debt from a borrower who died. In certain circumstances, both parties are asked to take (mutual) oaths (*taḥāluf*), particularly in disputes over the price, value, measure or characteristics of an object of sale (in which case, the contract will be cancelled once the oaths have been taken).[73] Oaths are deemed to be evidence because they represent and constitute a means to counter a claim,[74] usually made by the plaintiff. The Ḥanafites take the position that if the defendant refuses to take the oath (*nukūl*), the judge is bound to find in favor of the plaintiff. Thus, taking the oath represents evidence that has the force of rebutting a charge.

Since oaths come into play when the plaintiff cannot produce *bayyina*, they are said to have the power to terminate disputes once and for all, at least according to the Mālikites, since, once taken, they have the power to cancel out the plaintiff's allegation. The majority of jurists, however, permit the plaintiff to return with new evidence, and to launch a new suit altogether. But the Mālikites do not terminate a case with the refusal of the defendant to take the oath. Instead, they, together with the Shāfiʿites and some Ḥanbalites, espouse the position that the duty to take the oath reverts back to the plaintiff (a procedure known as *radd al-yamīn*).[75] The plaintiff will have a court decision in his favor if he takes the oath, but the decision will be against him should he not do so, the reasoning here being that the refusal of the defendant amounts to the plaintiff's producing a witness, for according to these jurists/schools, the plaintiff would normally win his case based on one witness and a single oath (in pecuniary contracts, that is). So the refusal of the defendant to take the oath, coupled with the plaintiff's own oath, produce the same weight as the required witness-plus-an-oath.

73 Ibn Abī al-Damm, *Adab*, 180–82.
74 Kāsānī, *Badāʾiʿ*, VIII, 418; [Miṣrī, *Reliance*, 620–24; Ibn Rushd, *Distinguished Jurist's Primer*, I, 488–515; II, 560–66].
75 Nawawī, *Rawḍa*, VIII, 322–23; Ibn Abī al-Damm, *Adab*, 161–62.

Part III

The sweep of modernity

13 The conceptual framework: an introduction

> From the eighteenth century onward, European states increasingly made their power visible not only through ritual performance and dramatic display, but through the gradual extension of "officializing" procedures that established and extended their capacity in many areas. They took control by defining and classifying space, making separation between public and private spheres; by recording transactions such as the sale of property; by counting and classifying their populations, replacing religious institutions as the registrar of births, marriages and deaths; and by standardizing languages and scripts. The state licensed some activities as legitimate and suppressed others as immoral or unlawful. With the growth of public education and its rituals, it fostered official beliefs in how things are and how they ought to be. The schools became the crucial civilizing institutions and sought to produce moral and productive citizens. Finally, nation-states came to be seen as the natural embodiments of history, territory and society.
>
> The establishment and maintenance of these nation-states depended upon determining, codifying, controlling, and representing the past. The documentation that was involved created and normalized a vast amount of information that formed the basis of their capacity to govern. The reports and investigations of commissions, the compilation, storage, and publication of statistical data on finance, trade, health, demography, crime, education, transportation, agriculture, and industry – these created data requiring as much exegetical and hermeneutical skill to interpret as an arcane Sanskrit text.[1]

For reasons yet to be satisfactorily explained, so-called early modern Europe[2] developed unprecedented forms of military and economic power[3] that enabled it to encroach on the Muslim domains, first along

[1] Cohn, *Colonialism and its Forms of Knowledge*, 3. For an expanded discussion, see Thomas, *Colonialism's Culture*, 33–45.

[2] "So-called" because arrogating to this usage an unqualified meaning vitiates the immensely important political geography that gave rise to the name in the first place. On this problem, see Hodgson, *Rethinking World History*, 3–34.

[3] Mainstream scholarship on the "causes" giving rise to early modern and modern Europe has not yet provided answers to what I call genealogical or primary questions, such as the latent causes eliciting the secondary causes of an "agricultural revolution," a "military revolution" or an "industrial revolution." From this perspective, Europe's history of the

the north-western coast of Africa, and then in the East Indies and elsewhere. By the end of the nineteenth century, Europe had subjugated some nine-tenths of the globe's territories,[4] leaving a number of minuscule and, at that time, insignificant and peripheral Muslim lands outside its hegemony. Although the sixteenth-century conquests were, like their Crusading predecessors, launched in the name of religion, the true, underlying motives had more to do with plundering the wealth of the vanquished domains.[5] As material profit was the prime motive, it was natural that direct and indirect colonization should concern itself, in the first instance, with the means by which the laws of dominated lands could be transformed so as to render them subservient to colonial economic and commercial imperatives.[6] This is the first crucial issue to be borne in mind when approaching the legal history of all colonized lands, including those that had been for centuries under the rule of Islam. In due course we shall observe that some of the first Western legal insertions into the native legal structures were commercial codes that were instrumental in opening up colonized markets to economic exchange on European terms.

Simultaneous with commercial intrusions, or following immediately upon their heels, was the establishment of European penal codes, evidently needed to instate a situation of "law and order" commensurate with the new realities dictated by European economics and political hegemony. I say political, because, as we shall see in some detail, the economic and commercial agenda were systematically and aggressively pursued through political means, especially in the case of indirect colonialism. The penal innovations were, in the final analysis, no different. The European penal system, whether in its domestic environment or as a product exported to the colonies and quasi-colonies (e.g., the Ottoman Empire), can be viewed no longer merely "as an apparatus of prohibition and repression of one class by another, nor as an alibi for the lawless violence of the ruling class" but rather as "a mode of political and economic management which exploits the difference between legality and illegalities."[7]

It was not long after the colonization process began that it became obvious to all the hegemonic powers that a constant grip on the wealth

last five or six centuries has yet to be written. For background, see Glete, *Warfare at Sea*, 73–111; Tallett, *War and Society*, 9–13, 39–44, 65, 168–88; Parker, *Military Revolution*; Levenson, *European Expansion*, 43, 52–58.

4 Headrick, *Tools of Empire*, 3–4. 5 See sources cited in n. 3, above.

6 Roberts and Mann, "Law in Colonial Africa," 3 f., and *passim*. Compare, for instance, with the tortuous arguments of J. Fisch on the vindication of colonialist law as an end in itself rather than as an expedient means. Fisch, "Law as a Means," 15–16.

7 Foucault, *Power/Knowledge*, 141.

of a country could not be maintained without securing the political and cultural spheres, both being essential to relieving the colonies of their wealth. Culture and politics stood – in European eyes at least – entwined with the legal. Bureaucracy and administration of the European variety were – as part of empire's political structure – called upon to regulate both the commercial and penal fields. But regulation along Western lines could hardly be separated from the soil from which it sprang, a soil cultivated in Europe for half a millennium, and now called the nation-state – the paramount institution in the modern project.[8] In other words, there was no escaping the fact that the essential desideratum for establishing an effective system for commercial gain was doomed to failure without the critical support of the bureaucratic and administrative infrastructure, and these in turn could in no way be introduced to the colonies and protectorates without the system that produced, regulated and enveloped them. That system, which harnessed modern technology most efficiently,[9] was the nation-state. Thus, it soon became obvious that to install a long-term and efficient mechanism for the economic exploitation of the colonies, the nation-state system, with all its legal arsenal, had to be exported as an essential first act.

Furthermore, what made this exportation more easily achievable was that, with the generally violent break-up of the native social and political systems (resulting from either destructive wars or economic devastation, or both), the local elites, supported by the colonialists themselves, were all too willing and ready to step into the void in order to seize hold of power; and it must be said that a power suddenly gained is an absolute power, in that it has not had time to develop the "ecological" checks and balances characteristic of long-lived traditional societies. Hence the relatively sudden appearance of the overwhelming majority of dictatorships, as well as the unprecedented forms of patriarchy that pervade the so-called Third World countries.[10] The most pervasive problem in the legal history of the modern Muslim world has therefore been the introduction of the nation-state and its encounter with the Sharīʿa.[11] It would be no exaggeration to

[8] Tilly, *Coercion, Capital and European States*, 14–15.

[9] In fact, modern technology – from all-important means of communication to medical science – grew in tandem with the development of the state and its colonialist ambitions. Therefore, to argue that the state harnessed modern technology implies that the former predated the latter – a clear case of logical fallacy. Rather, inasmuch as the "state made war and war made the state," the state was as instrumental in the development of technology as technology was instrumental in making the state. See sources cited in n. 3, above, and Mann, *States, War and Capitalism*, 75 and *passim*.

[10] In good part the topic of chapter 16, below.

[11] To say that the structure and function of the modern state (generally, and in the Muslim world particularly) are severely under-researched and misunderstood by many legal

state that there is virtually no problem or issue in this history that does not hark back to the conceptual, structural and institutional discord that exists between the thoroughly indigenous Islamic/customary laws, and the European-grown imports that were the inevitable concomitant of the nation-state and its modern legal system.[12]

A conceptual analysis of the disharmony between Islamic law and the nation-state (mainly after the middle of the nineteenth century) is foundational, in that all chronological accounts of legal permutations – the concern of the following chapters – presuppose and rest upon the analytical difference between the preexisting *system* (largely defined by the Sharīʿa) and that *system* which came to replace it (the modern nation-state). Before we proceed, however, a caveat is in order. Henceforth, all references to the state must not be understood as reductive, taking the state to be a unified, unidimensional and cohesive body. It is a fundamental feature of the state, as the site of power relations, to encompass competing and conflicting agendas and institutions. For as a site of power relations – which we have analyzed in a different context in the first part of the Introduction to this book – it is bound to encompass such oppositional tendencies that we have characterized as "force fields."[13] It is true that the state is not one thing, but a conglomerate of oppositional forces, departments, staffs, agencies and individuals, each and all of whom conceive and articulate their functions within the state in individualistic terms and in accord with a perspectivist logic. They work in opposition to each other no doubt, but also simultaneously work together, and efficiently at that.

For purposes of anthropological and other social analysis, the distinctions in the "force field" of the state are eminently useful,[14] but such distinctions are not essential in terms of the differences in the overall legal and juridical operation of the state as compared to another, qualitatively different system. However forceful and numerous the competing agencies of the state may be, the state is a species whose members behave in a particular way, cover distance and time in a particular way, and, like all other organisms, feed on their prey in a particular way. Surely, every state

historians in the field of Islamic studies is to state the obvious. The effects of this problem can be seen not only in the study of modern legal history but also, to the same degree, in interpreting the pre-modern period.

12 There is a great merit to the argument that one of the chief problems with the recently fashionable project of "nation-building" is the fact that the nation-state exported to Muslim countries required at least five centuries of history to develop in Europe; non-Western countries, however, are nowadays expected to be fully integrated nation-states within a few decades, if not a few years (the cases of Afghanistan and, to some extent, Iraq being notable examples).

13 See Introduction, section 2, above.

14 Starr, "When Empires Meet," 231 f.

is different, just as every snake or hawk is a unique creature. But snakes and hawks, by their nature, live and perform certain functions that are particular to them, however much their individual members differ in strength, shape or aggressivity. And the state is a particular modern creature that fulfills fairly well-defined functions of governance and dominance (including welfare and a host of charitable works), no matter how much its agencies and institutions may conflict, and no matter how much one individual state may differ from another. A state is a state, just as a hawk is a hawk, and not, say, a sparrow. And that is where an analytical and functional comparison between the state, as a legal organism, and Islamic law may be apt.

The first and starkest feature that renders these two entities incompatible is that both belong more or less to the same genus in that they are – in their own, markedly different, ways – machines of governance. Both are designed to organize society and to resolve disputes that threaten to disrupt their respective orders – however different these orders may be, and however different the reasons for, and ways of, engaging these orders.

Second, and more specifically, both are legally productive mechanisms or, put simply, lawgivers. But couldn't they, as organisms having the same specialization, coexist? The short answer must be in the negative. Judged by historical experience (a venue that perforce renders complex any definition), Islamic law could and did accommodate a measure of legal intervention by the political sovereign, but to an extent that did not exceed the peripheral or the marginal, especially in terms of determining the substance of the law.[15] (This relative jural self-sustenance is not to be confused with the proposition that the formation of Islamic law was to some degree affected by the institutions of political governance, a proposition that renders the Sharīʿa's marked independence even more remarkable). While it is a given that Islamic law under the Ottomans – the most state-like dynasty of Islam[16] – was administered significantly by means of state apparatus, the *corpus juris* applied was overwhelmingly of *sharʿī* pedigree. Thus, while Islamic law is tolerant of administrative competition, it is only thinly tolerant of substantive juristic intervention. The nation-state, on the other hand – also judged by the very fact of its historical evolution[17] – had developed even less tolerance to legislative,

15 See chapter 5, above.

16 It is eminently arguable that the Ottoman Empire during the late fifteenth century and all of the sixteenth had developed as efficient a bureaucracy and administration as Atlantic Europe did during the same period. See Abou-El-Haj, *Formation of the Modern State.*

17 For excellent, but varying, accounts of the rise of the modern state, see Mann, *States, War and Capitalism*; van Creveld, *Rise and Decline*; Tilly, *Coercion, Capital and European States*; and especially, in the context of Britain, Corrigan and Sayer, *Great Arch.* I am indebted to Nicholas Dirks for referring me to this last work.

administrative and bureaucratic competition. Its staunchly centralized nature largely precluded any palpable tolerance of other systems.[18]

Third, in theory as well as in practice, both systems claim ultimate legal sovereignty. At least in juristic political theory, government (*siyāsa*) – the incomplete, and certainly "stunted," equivalent of the modern nation-state – stood subservient to the Sharīʿa. The *raison d'être* of *siyāsa* (whose invocation must *always* presuppose and announce the presence of the civil population) is to serve the interests of the law, not the other way round. Needless to say, the ruler constantly attempted to manipulate this *siyāsa* in his own favor, but the rules of the game – on which rested the much coveted prize of legitimacy – remained defined by the Sharīʿa. That legal sovereignty should remain, in both theory and practice, within the realm of the Sharīʿa is a fact that, on the other hand, hardly squares with the modern nation-state's totalistic appropriation of this paramount form of sovereignty. A nation-state without jural sovereignty is no state at all.

Fourth, Islamic law and the nation-state operated in two opposing directions, the latter compelling and pushing toward an exclusive and ultimate center, the former demonstrably centrifugal. In a way typical of Islamic structures (evident in social organization, urban and rural economic organization, mosque architecture and pre-modern dynastic bureaucracies),[19] law operated horizontally, so to speak. Aside from judicial appointments which were nominally, if not symbolically, hierarchical, the administration of justice was largely limited to the self-structured legal profession. If there was a hierarchy it was within the profession itself, and was in nature epistemic rather than political or social. Yet, the hierarchy within Islamic law was largely[20] universal and self-sufficient, unlike the hierarchy existing in the judicial system of the nation-state, a hierarchy that ultimately reports to the higher political orders. The referential authorities of the *qāḍī* are other *qāḍī*s and *muftī*s. Hard cases were decided with the juristic assistance of the *muftī*, and appeals did not usually travel upward in a hierarchy, but were heard by

[18] This is not to say that such intolerance has eradicated "legal pluralism," but it is to assert the *systemic and exclusive* legal dominance of the state, especially in modern Islamic countries. On legal pluralism, see Merry, "Legal Pluralism," 869–79. Evidence of this dominance is the very focus of the scholarly field of legal pluralism. Merry states (874): "The concern [of the field] is to document other forms of social regulation that draw on the symbols of the law, to a greater or lesser extent, but that operate in its shadows; its parking lots, and even down the street in mediation offices."

[19] With the partial exception of the Ottomans. See chapter 15, below.

[20] This is to allow for the occasional but informal complaints that were made to the ruler or provincial governor, a practice falling under the rubric of *maẓālim*. See chapter 5, sections 3–4, above.

the succeeding judge.[21] And even when some complaints were made to the highest offices of the "state" (as happened in the Ottoman Empire), they were made directly and given – with explicit intention – the personal attention of the ruler. This was a personal form of justice, not corporate. By contrast, the nation-state's jural system is perforce hierarchical from within, and answers to an external state hierarchy that both sustains and envelops it.

Fifth, the modern state represents itself, and is represented in discourse about it, as an abstract legal entity, this being a fundamental feature of its ideological make-up. The function of this ideological constitution "is to misrepresent political and economic domination in ways that legitimate subjection," which is to say that it "is the distinctive collective misrepresentation of capitalist societies" whose prop is that "ideological project," that "exercise in legitimation."[22] The state, at least according to Marxist analysis, hides the domination of one class over others,[23] the act of "hiding" here being one of its quintessential features. Its self-representation as

[21] Powers, "Judicial Review." The successor review system was made tenable by virtue of the fact that judges served for relatively short periods of time, usually between six months and two years.

[22] Abrams, "Notes on the Difficulty of Studying the State," 75, 76. Abrams avers (76–77) that the state:

> is first and foremost an exercise in legitimation – and what is being legitimated is, we may assume, something which if seen directly and as itself would be illegitimate, an unacceptable domination. Why else all the legitimation-work? The state, in sum, is a bid to elicit support for or tolerance of the insupportable and intolerable by presenting them as something other than themselves, namely, legitimate, disinterested domination. The study of the state, seen thus, would begin with the cardinal activity involved in the serious presentation of the state: the legitimating of the illegitimate. The immediately present institutions of the state system – and in particular their coercive functions – are the principal object of that task. The crux of the task is to over-accredit them as an integrated expression of common interest cleanly dissociated from all sectional interests and the structures – class, church, race and so forth – associated with them. The agencies in question, especially administrative and judicial and educational agencies, are made into state agencies as part of some quite historically specific process of subjection; and made precisely as an alternative reading of and cover for that process ... The state is, then, in every sense of the term a triumph of concealment.

See also Mitchell, "Limits of the State," 91. Mitchell's argument – that there exists a gray zone in which society conduces to the "definition" and constitution of the state – does not undermine the position (underlying my own views here) that this very zone is an integral part of the practice and *modus vivendi* of the state. I suspect that Mitchell's argument has been taken for granted in Althusser's distinction between Repressive State Apparatus and Ideological State Apparatus. See the latter's *Essays on Ideology*, 16–18, 27–30 and *passim*. (The unawareness of this "triumph of concealment" in Islamic legal studies remains staggering, as evidenced, for example, in Arjomand, "Islamic Constitutionalism," 116–37, esp. 124–25. See also the Introduction to this book, section 1, n. 15, above.)

[23] Althusser, *Essays on Ideology*, 13–14.

the "first ideological power over man"[24] masks its agenda for which social engineering becomes one of the tools for the fulfillment of this agenda. The Sharīʿa, by the constitution of its *fiqh* (as well as by its actual socio-economic history), neither promoted economic classes nor encouraged capitalistic or class dominance. But more importantly, the Sharīʿa, lacking this agenda and serving no class in particular, did not develop the need to hide itself behind an impenetrable ideology, one that, in the case of the modern state, has befuddled scholars and continues to defy palpable analysis.[25] (It may well be argued that this "absence" in the Sharīʿa might explain, at least in good part, the "failure of Islam" to develop into a modern economy, and therefore into a "modern society.")

Sixth, and stemming from the preceding two considerations, is the central fact that Islamic law is a grass-roots system that takes form and operates within the social universe; it travels upward with diminishing velocity to affect, in varying degrees and forms, the *modus operandi* of the "state." The jurists themselves emanate from the very society and societal culture that they serve; and the law as ideology and doctrine required that they be so.[26] It is one of the most striking features of Islamic law, as a doctrinal and jural system, that it is generated at the very social level on which it is applied. In sharp contradistinction, the law of the nation-state (however democratically representative of the "people's will") is superimposed from a central height in a downwards direction, first originating in the mighty powers of the state apparatus and thereafter deployed – in a highly structured but deliberately descending movement – to the individuals constituting the social order, those individuals who are harnessed as national citizens (fathers and mothers in the nation's families; economically productive agents; tax-payers, soldiers, etc.). A society subject to Islamic law is one that is largely self-governing, in which law, and the morality intertwined with it, largely operates in the interest of that society. By contrast, a society subject to the nation-state is one that is ruled from above. If men (and now women) run the modern bureaucracy and make law on behalf of the corporate entity that is the nation-state, then the latter, as M. Weber and S. Quṭb have both aptly observed, is little more than the rule of man over man,[27] albeit a rule that is corporate in nature. This is not to suggest that the modern nation-state developed and exercised its powers in disregard of the subjects it ruled, but it is to argue that through

[24] Abrams, "Notes on the Difficulty of Studying the State," 64, drawing on Friedrich Engels.
[25] Mitchell, "Limits of the State"; Abrams, "Notes on the Difficulty of Studying the State."
[26] See chapters 1, 3, 4 and 5, above.
[27] For Weber, see Lassman, "Rule of Man," 83–98; for Sayyid Quṭb, *Milestones*, 94–95 and *passim*.

its sophisticated systemic structures the state integrated its national citizens, shaped them in new ideological forms and coerced them into submission to "a set of very specific patterns."[28]

Seventh, and finally, while Islamic law and the nation-state shared the general goal of organizing society and adjudicating disputes, they did so to significantly different effects. Intrinsic to its behavior, the nation-state is systemically and systematically geared toward the homogenization of both the social order and the national citizen. To accomplish these goals, it engages in systemic surveillance, disciplining and punishment. Its educational and cultural institutions are designed to manufacture the "good citizen" who is respectful of the law, submissive to notions of order and discipline, industrious and economically productive. Discipline-cum-punishment is integral to, and a unique feature of, the modern nation-state. The resultant "good citizen" is one who can *efficiently* serve the state, the father – and much less frequently the mother – of all. Obedience to the law, which presupposes submission and – more importantly – discipline, is then the prop upon which the state stands. Without the law and its tools of surveillance and punishment, no state apparatus can exist. Ergo the centrality, in the definition and concept of the state, of the element of violence, and of the exclusive right to threaten with its use. The modern state, insofar as I am aware, is the only entity in human history that has arrogated to itself this exclusive right. That the citizen has accepted – or has been conditioned into accepting – this right of the state (which has considerable legal, economic, political, ideological and cultural ramifications)[29] is perhaps the most salient measure of the success of its project. Islamic law, by contrast, has never concerned itself with creating the national citizen, nor any other kind of citizen, and to this extent it shares none of the features of the state in this regard. It did not arrogate to itself monopoly over violence, nor did it – as compared with the modern state – attempt to subordinate society and the individual to the systemic control of a higher political order.

With its trenchant pluralistic bent and variegated attitudes to almost every aspect of life, not to mention its nearly infinite forms of practice and regional/geographical variations, the Sharīʿa could hardly be expected to produce homogeneity. Aside from the higher transcendental aims, Islamic law had little interest in the social order other than resolving

[28] Dreyfus and Rabinow, *Michel Foucault: Beyond Structuralism*, 214. On the power of ideology in the formation of the state's national citizen and in his/her production through the law, see Althusser, *Essays on Ideology*, 1–60; Abrams, "Notes on the Difficulty of Studying the State," 64–69, and *passim*.

[29] Ramifications even for the manner of studying the state. See Abrams, "Notes on the Difficulty of Studying the State."

disputes in a manner least disruptive to the social order, social harmony being paramount in the eyes of both the legists and the ruling dynasties. The latter no doubt attempted to exploit the entrenched Sharīʿa system for the purpose of advancing their own interests, but lacking the constitutive features of the modern state (technology, bureaucracy, extensive administration, efficient tools of communication, etc.), they remained throughout subservient to the paradigmatic imperatives of the Sharīʿa's rule of law. The Sharīʿa, as we saw,[30] was suspicious of the ruler's executive power, and insisted on an economic and social system that served the interests of the communities of believers, not those of the ruler (or ruling class). That the general goal of Islamic law has always and everywhere been to maintain individuals – to the greatest extent possible – in their social positions, remains one of the most valid generalizations about this legal system. (This remains true even of those fragments of it that have survived into modernity, as the works of Rosen and Starr have aptly shown.) Put differently, unlike the punitive nature of the state, which created the citizen by subduing him along with society at large, Islamic law mediated conflicts and arbitrated disputes in a constant effort to mend ruptures in the social fabric.

It was in the interest of Islamic law to reinforce the community and its structures, for – in its operation, functioning, and indeed survival as a legal system – it depended on the community. Its prescribed harsh punishments, whenever they were applied (and mostly they were not), were conceived of as exemplary, intended to deter the forces of corruption which almost always translated into social disharmony (and, of course, rebellion against political authority). But it seems also true that because Islamic law never constituted part of a machinery of coercive justice, its prescribed penalties represented the furthest extent to which the law was prepared to go. This did not mean that punishment was applied wherever an infraction took place (which explains why, for instance, every large Middle Eastern city boasted, among other "unseemly" features, a healthy population of prostitutes), but the limit was designed as a possible invocation against excesses whenever social pressures demanded the strict application of penalties. (This perhaps explains, as we shall see in due course, why the British colonialists, among others, thought of Islamic criminal law as unduly lenient, lacking in punishments, inefficient, and conducive neither to the propagation of discipline nor to the imposition of "law and order.")[31]

[30] See chapters 4 and 5 and Part II, above.

[31] Singha, *Despotism of Law*, 2, 49–75; Dirks, *Scandal*, 221. See also chapter 14, section 1, below.

If both Islamic law and the nation-state were constituted as governing organs that by necessity were lawgivers, they fundamentally differed in the articulation of their *modus operandi* and ultimate objectives. As universal lawgivers, they were mutually exclusive. And since their aims and their cultural and social *Weltanschauungen* were so different, such coexistence was precluded *a priori*. It was this teleological difference that pitted the state against Islamic law. In this competition, the latter had no chance of withstanding the assault, much less winning the jural war, against the material, bureaucratic and military powers of the state. The victory of the nation-state was not only one of displacing Islamic law, but also one which entailed the reordering of Muslim economic, political and social structures. The Muslim believer, through this project of reordering, was converted into the "good national citizen." The rest would be politics.[32]

On a more specific analytical level, the nation-state confronted Islamic law as a purely legislative entity, our second point above. The nation-state's jural *modus vivendi* was codification, a method that entails a conscious harnessing of a particular tool of governance. It is, put differently, a deliberate choice to exercise legal and political power, a choice that at once accomplishes a multitude of tasks. The most essential feature of the code is the *production* of order, clarity, concision and authority.[33] Modern codes, the legal experts agree, have come to replace "all previous inconsistent customs, mores, and law."[34] This replacement is also totalistic, since codes must also fulfill the requirement of completeness and exclusivity. They must comprehensively cover the area they claim to regulate, an act that perforce precludes both the substantive application and – equally significant – the authority of any competing law. Were an exception to be made permitting the coexistence of other forms of (preexisting) law, this too would be allowed only by virtue of the code's permission.[35] In other words, modern codes invariably claim exclusive and superior authority, over and above all previous law.

[32] A rich field of inquiry is the emergence in the modern Muslim world of a discourse of politics that was virtually absent from the world that lived under the governance of Sharīʿa and dynastic rule. The change, in other words, represented a shift from a culture of legality to one that revolved around the political practices of the modern state, generating an unprecedented political discourse that we now take for granted. This in part explains why current debates surrounding the Sharīʿa are imbued with politics and political markers of identity, not law. For a general elaboration on this theme, see Hallaq, "What is Sharīʿa?"

[33] This is the essential point made, for instance, by Stone, "Primer," 303–10, esp. at 303–04, although he also acknowledges that codification is the state's (and its reformers') tool for effecting a "new economic and social order."

[34] Bayitch, "Codification," 161–91, esp. at 164.

[35] Obviously, the common law is an exception, but then the vast majority of Islamic states did not adopt this system, Egypt being a prime example of a British protectorate opting for French-inspired law.

Nor is this all. Codes must be systematic and clear, arranged rationally and logically, and rendered easily accessible to lawyers and judges.[36] By their very nature, they are not only declaratory and enunciative of their own authority, but also universal in the statement of rules; hence their concision. They pay direct attention neither to the particular case nor to the human individual. As an enhancement of this feature, they are always abstract, "to the point," and deliberately preclusive of the concrete. It was considered a virtue that the "French and German Civil Codes could be held within the boards of a volume while the common law required a full library" to house it.[37] Considerations of economy, as always, are paramount. But the primary attribute of the code is its capacity to create uniformity, an attribute in keeping with the homogenizing ethic of universal modernity. This also explains why it was to the civil codes of western Europe – and not to the English common law – that, as a rule, the Afro-Asian reformers turned. Thus, codes must achieve uniformity not only within themselves but also in their application. The sway of the code's authority therefore extends beyond its own definition and encroaches upon the administration and implementation of justice.[38]

Islamic law, on the other hand, runs counter to the great majority of the code's attributes. First, Islamic law *depended*, in both theory and practice, on the cooperation of customary (*ʿāda*, *ʿurf*) and royal law (*siyāsa sharʿīyya*).[39] Nowhere did Islamic law operate exclusively, and everywhere customary law was entwined with it in the realm of practice. Nor, in this connection, was Islamic law self-declaratory, in that it did not pronounce itself – at least in practice and largely in theory – as the bearer of exclusive authority that had come to replace others in the field. By its hermeneutic and highly individualistic nature, Islamic law was not systematic according to the European perception of the world, although an expert in it may view the matter entirely otherwise. Similarly, from a modern perspective, Islamic law may be described as obscure and complex, unlike the "clear and accessible" code. While the code is by any standard more accessible than most *fiqh* treatises, the argument of clarity is no more than a relative one. An adept expert in *fiqh* may find it as clear as the modern lawyer finds the code. Admittedly, however, Islamic law cannot be said to have internal uniformity, since plurality of opinion – the so-called *ijtihād*ic pluralism – is its defining feature *par excellence*. It was on the diversity of its own character that, interestingly, it thrived (and insisted), and it was *in* this diversity that it found the flexibility to

[36] This, according to Stone ("Primer," 303–04), being the *raison d'être* of the code.
[37] Stone, "Primer," 306. [38] See Bayitch, "Codification," 162–67.
[39] See chapters 4 and 5, above, as well as Hallaq, "Prelude to Ottoman Reform."

accommodate, through variant legal norms, different situations that would otherwise have come under the same codified rule. Plurality of opinion answered not only the multiplicity of particular and special situations but also the exigencies of legal change.[40] Its plurality ran counter to the spirit of uniformity, since homogenization was largely absent from its agenda. And since its interest lay in the individual as a singular worshiper of God, there was no need for an abstract and universalizing language. Most importantly, however, it was the declaratory nature of the code as well as its uniformity of substance and legal effect that betrayed a will-to-power which emanated from the higher offices of the nation-state; by contrast, in Islamic law such a will-to-power could not exist except at the level of the abstract and theoretical, that is, the metaphysical and the theological.

That codes must be systematic, clear and accessible is also a function of the difference in the roles played by the *faqīh*, on the one hand, and the modern lawyer-judge, on the other. The modern lawyer-judge is the representative and agent of the nation-state, an extension of its agency, and one who studies and applies the code as a technocrat. But he or she does not produce the law of the code through an agency independent of the heavy administrative machinery of the state (reflecting, instead, the almost exclusive interests of the civil population), a fact leading to far-reaching effects. The nation-state apparatus of control and surveillance produced the subordinate lawyer-judge – subordinate, that is, to the commanding powers of the state and its systemic structures. Being a technocrat and a specialist in the province of law, the lawyer-judge has become confined to the technical study of law, which is the nation-state's tool to accomplish, among other things, control and order for the sake of efficient management of an economically productive citizenry. (For while the individual enters into several relationships with the state, that of taxation is the most intimate of all.)[41] The *faqīh*, on the other hand, served a different imperative, mostly transcending the limitations of technocracy. Among the *faqīh*s, the *qāḍī*s tended to serve as technocrats, but never all of them and not for the entirety of their professional careers. For *qāḍī*s often "wore other hats," so to speak, such as those of *muftī* and author-jurist[42] (which involved them in a particular moral relationship with the society that they served and represented). Thus a significant number, if not a

[40] Hallaq, *Authority*, 121–235.
[41] This is certainly accurate in the case of Euro-American states, and is gradually becoming the paradigm of state-building in even poor Muslim nations, as the recent national debate in Egypt amply demonstrates.
[42] Hallaq, *Authority*, 166–74.

majority, of the major (and commanding) *faqīh*s were intellectuals who routinely engaged in specialized studies of other disciplines, from history, theology and literature, to philosophy, logic, medicine and astronomy. Their prime objective was the discovery and articulation of the law, and they marshaled their interdisciplinary knowledge toward the accomplishment of that goal. They produced the law, and they accumulated the highest forms of authority, namely, the epistemic and the moral. They, the *mujtahid*s and the leading *muftī*s, were thus the public intellectuals who spoke truth to power, social and religious morality being their guide. They lived and functioned within an independent system, which they themselves, with their own societies, had fashioned. This, generally speaking, cannot be claimed as an attribute of the modern lawyer-judge, and for good reason: the truth of the latter is *ipso facto* the one produced by the *very system* which he/she serves and through which he/she was produced; and this system is almost entirely controlled by the all-powerful state. The separation between and among the legislative, judicial and executive powers – in any case, not very effective in the vast majority of today's Muslim countries – remains ultimately subservient to the *systemic structures* and the "episteme" of the state itself, be it in the Muslim East or in the Western world.

14 The jural colonization of India and South-East Asia

1. British India

During the first century and a half of British presence in India, the colonial ambition was by necessity limited to commercial exploitation, and dependent for most of this period on special privileges extended to the East India Company (EIC) by its host, the Mughal emperor. From the end of Akbar's reign (in 1605), down to Aurangzeb's rule (1658–1707) and beyond, the EIC was perforce the ally of the Mughals. Thus, until the early 1750s, the EIC could not interfere in, and in fact depended upon, native law and customs in resolving any disputes that involved native persons or native institutions.

The primary, if not the sole, goal of the EIC was commercial profit,[1] which explains why its interests demanded as much "law and order" as was necessary to conduct trade in a regular and "orderly" fashion.[2] These relatively modest ambitions permitted the EIC to act the role of guest in the lands of the Mughals, a role exhibiting an amicability that was to diminish not only with the decline of the latter's power during the wars of the successor states, but also with the concomitant militarization and increasing aggressiveness of the Company. For the EIC had over time acquired many of the features of a modern state, and acted with an increasing sense of sovereignty that entailed warring, raising taxes and administering justice to its employees and – in time – to Indians as well.[3]

By 1757, and after a military confrontation with the Nawab of Bengal in the so-called Battle of Plassey, the EIC asserted its dominance, henceforth embarking upon the massive project of colonizing India, both economically and juridically. In the eyes of the British, economic and commercial desiderata were intimately connected with the particular vision of a legal system structured and geared in such a manner as to accommodate an

[1] Cohn, *Colonialism and its Forms of Knowledge*, 61; Dutt, "Exploitation of India," 41–52.
[2] Kugle, "Framed, Blamed and Renamed," 260.
[3] Cohn, *Colonialism and its Forms of Knowledge*, 58.

"open" economic market. The legal system was, and continued to be, the template that determined and set the tone of economic domination. But most importantly for the British, the avid desire to reduce the economic costs of controlling the country by force and violence – entirely consistent with, and subsidiary to, their materialist desideratum – stood in direct correlation with the maximization of the role of law. Law was simply more financially rewarding than brute power.[4]

And so it was not until the appointment of Warren Hastings as Governor of Bengal in 1772 that a new stage in the British legal designs for India began.[5] The appointment ushered in the so-called Hastings Plan, to be implemented first in Bengal. The Plan conceived a multi-tiered system that required exclusively British administrators at the top, seconded by a tier of British judges who would consult with local *qāḍī*s and *muftī*s (*mulavi*s) with regard to issues governed by Islamic law. At the lowest rung of judicial administration stood the run-of-the-mill Muslim judges who administered law in the civil courts of Bengal, Madras and Bombay. The Plan also rested on the assumption that local customs and norms could be incorporated into a British institutional structure of justice that was regulated by "universal" (read: British) jural ideals.

Hastings' tax-collectors also doubled as chief justices of two types of court: the Diwani and Faujdari. The former, applying Islamic law to Muslims and Hindu law to Hindus, was a civil tribunal but also charged with the task of levying tax. The latter court, endowed with criminal jurisdiction, applied Islamic law in the way these justices, after consulting their *pandit*s and *mulavi*s, understood that law.[6] These British magistrates-cum-collectors are said to have been struck by both the staggering variety of opinion and the pliability of Islamic (and Hindu) law – features that led the British to phase out these indigenous experts whose loyalty was considered suspect.[7]

It is debatable whether or not the British found the atomized nature of Islamic (and Hindu) law as problematic as it was made to appear in twentieth-century Western scholarship, for the common law system was not, after all, of a dramatically different nature. Islamic law certainly

[4] By the same materialist logic, and despite the fact that the "legal option" was much less expensive to maintain, the colonizing powers almost everywhere sought to reduce even the costs of the judicial administration itself. See Benton, "Colonial Law and Cultural Difference," 564.

[5] Menski, *Hindu Law*, 164 ff.

[6] Singha, *Despotism*, 1–35; Cohn, *Colonialism and its Forms of Knowledge*, 62; Anderson, "Legal Scholarship," 67.

[7] On Sir William Jones' own suspicions, see Strawson, "Islamic Law and English Texts," 36–37.

resembled the common law tradition far more than it did the continental legal systems that fundamentally depended on codification.[8] Yet, to deal with what was seen as an uncontrollable and corrupted mass of individual juristic opinion, the Oxford classicist and foremost Orientalist Sir William Jones (1746–94) proposed to Hastings the creation of codes or what he termed a "complete digest of Hindu and Mussulman law."[9] The justification for the creation of such an alien system within Islamic (and Hindu)[10] law was articulated in a language that problematized this law by casting it as unsystematic, inconsistent and mostly arbitrary – attributes that were to be much later elaborated in a virtuoso sociological typology by no less than Max Weber himself.[11] (It was probably Jones' idea of an undisciplined and uncontrollable legal interpretation of the Mussulmans' magistrates and *mulavis* that gave Weber – and the entire field of Orientalism before Weber – his burlesque notions of *Kadijustiz*.)[12] The challenge thus represented itself in the question of how to understand and legally manage native society in an economically efficient manner, which in part shaped Jones' ambition of constructing a system that offered "a complete check on the native interpreters of the several codes."[13]

It is highly debatable as to whether Jones in particular and the British in general genuinely misunderstood the nature of Islamic (and Hindu) law or whether they feigned such a misunderstanding in their bid to facilitate their total control over the judicial system. It is instructive that Jones, as one of the architects of Anglo-Muhammadan law, was thoroughly aware, as he himself put it, of the "wonderful analogy between the works of the Arabian and English lawyers."[14] But such analogies, while legally apt, lost their force once the cultural habits of natives entered the equation. Cohn's insightful analysis of Jones' attitude toward Hindu law and its Indian subjects applies fully, if not *a fortiori*, to Islamic law and Indian Muslims:

8 For a conceptual comparison between codified law and Islamic law, see the previous chapter.

9 Cited in Cohn, *Colonialism and its Forms of Knowledge*, 69.

10 On Hindu law under the British and on the emergence of Anglo-Hindu law, see Menski, *Hindu Law*, 156–85.

11 Rheinstein, *Max Weber on Law*, 206–13 (and n. 48). For a critique of Weber's writings on Islamic law, see Gerber, *State, Society*, 25–57. For a general but useful critique of his typology of legal orders, see Berman and Reid, "Max Weber as Legal Historian," 225–37.

12 The expression, it must be said, was originally that of R. Schmidt, not Weber's. See Gerth and Mills, *From Max Weber*, 216–21, as well as sources cited in the previous note.

13 Cited in Cohn, *Colonialism and its Forms of Knowledge*, 69; Anderson, "Legal Scholarship," 74.

14 As cited in Strawson, "Islamic Law and English Texts," 36 (from Jones' introduction to his own translation of the *Sirājiyya*).

There was an inversion and contradiction in Jones's efforts to fix and translate what he believed to be the crucial aspects of Hindu law. Jones was trained in English common law, which although it embodied principles, legislation, ideas of natural law, and the concept of equity and justice, was essentially seen as case law. Case law was a historically derived law based on the finding of precedent. It was flexible and above all subject to multiple interpretations by judges and lawyers. Jones and other jurisprudes of his time saw the English common law as responsive to historical change. Because the manners of a nation of people – or today we might say their culture – could change, legislation would be ineffective "unless it was congenial to the disposition, the habits, religious prejudices, and approved immemorial usages of the people for whom it was enacted." But it appears that Jones believed that even though manners, habits, dispositions, and prejudices were not fixed or immutable, the Hindus of India had usages that were fixed from time immemorial. Unlike the British with their case law, in which a lawyer could trace changes both in manners and in customs as well as in the law, the Hindus therefore lived a timeless existence, which in turn meant that differences and interpretations offered by pandits must have arisen from ignorance or venality.[15]

Hastings appears to have been as impressed by Jones' proposal as by the cultural and legal assumptions on which it was based. For it was not long before he commissioned the translation of Marghīnānī's *Hidāya* into Persian, a version that Charles Hamilton in turn used for his own translation (1791) into English.[16] A year later, Jones himself translated *al-Sirājiyya*, this time directly from the Arabic.[17] This treatise on inheritance was adopted in translation to compensate for the silence of the *Hidāya* on this important branch of the law.[18] The immediate purpose of these translations was to make Islamic law directly accessible to British judges who deeply mistrusted the native *mulavi*s advising them on points of law.[19]

The choice of the *Hidāya* was not fortuitous. The text was authored by one of the most esteemed jurists in the Ḥanafite school, to which adhered the great majority of India's Sunnite Muslims. To cite it, the British thought, was to reduce the likelihood of juristic disagreement, the source of the much detested legal pluralism. Furthermore, it was concise enough to qualify as a code. In fact, it was the briefest authoritative manual

15 Cohn, *Colonialism and its Forms of Knowledge*, 71. Hastings himself also held that the Hindus "had been in possession of laws which continued unchanged, from remotest antiquity." Cited in *ibid.*, 66.

16 Recently retranslated into English by Nyazee. See Bibliography, below.

17 *Al-Sirajiyah or the Mahomedan Law of Inheritance.* Two more translations on inheritance appeared in subsequent years: W. H. Macnaghten, *Principles and Precedents of Moohumudan Law*, and F. Elberling, *A Treatise on Inheritance, Gift, Will, Sale, and Marriage.*

18 The *Hidāya* does deal with bequests, however. See Marghīnānī, *Hidāya*, IV, 231 ff. On omissions from the translated text and on its later uses in colonial education, see Strawson, "Islamic Law and English Texts," 27–28.

19 Anderson, "Legal Scholarship," 74; Kolff, "Indian and British Law Machines," 213–14.

of Ḥanafite law that could serve in such a manner. And it was precisely here where the usefulness of this text lay. Its brevity reflected the authoritative doctrine of the Ḥanafite school as Marghīnānī, the distinguished Transoxianan author-jurist, saw it. It did not, however, sum up the general doctrine of the school, much less its range, especially in South Asia; as all such authoritative texts do, it stated only what Marghīnānī considered, in his *own age and region* (twelfth-century Farghāna and, more widely, Transoxiana), to be the commonly practiced and accepted doctrines of the school (common acceptance and practice of a doctrine being constitutive of epistemic and juristic authority).[20]

The importance of the *Hidāya* in the Ḥanafite school lay not in its own, intrinsic virtues, but rather in the fact that it afforded an authoritative basis and a convenient platform on which to compile the numerous commentaries that emerged throughout the centuries to come. It constituted not the law, but the interpretive basis on which the law might be founded in a particular time and place. For insofar as application of the law was concerned, it was the commentary, rather than the *Hidāya* itself, that was the practical judicial desideratum. The *Hidāya* was and remained important as a commentarial substrate as well as a *madrasa* textbook – although even in this latter function it also required the professor's commentary. In and by itself, it was therefore far less important than the British appeared to assume, for their formal use of it qualitatively differed from its nativist, heuristic use as a peg for commentarial and practice-based jurisprudence.

The translation of the *Hidāya* amounted in effect to its codification, for by severing it from its Arabicate interpretive and commentarial tradition, it ceased to function in the way it had done until then. Thus, the "codification" of the *Hidāya* (and through it, of the Islamic law of personal status broadly speaking) served at least two purposes. First, it accomplished what the British had attempted for so long, namely, to curb the judicial "discretion" of the *qāḍī* and, more specifically, the *mulavi*s and *muftī*s who assisted the courts. It is also instructive to see in this policy of curbing *Kadijustiz* – which the British viewed as judicial discretion *par excellence* – a systemic attempt at transforming Islamic law into a state law, where the legal, judicial and jural independence of the socially grounded legal profession would be displaced by the corporate and ultra-social agency of the state. Thus, by making the text of the law available to the British judges, these Muslim legists were eliminated as jural middle men, leaving the British with the sole power and prerogative to adjudicate in the name of Islamic law. And second – a further step toward totalistic

[20] Hallaq, *Authority*, 155–64.

control – the act of translation-cum-codification represented a replacement of the native system's interpretive mechanisms by those of English law. Thus, the seemingly innocuous adoption of the translation amounted in effect to what might be termed a policy of "demolish and replace."

There was yet a third, somewhat oblique, purpose that was served by casting Arabic-Islamic juristic texts in a fixed form, namely, an English rendering that, by the very fact of its linguistic transmutation, ceased to be related organically to the Arabicate juristic and hermeneutical tradition of Islam. This purpose was the shutting out of customary law, which not only was multifarious but without which Islamic law could not function. The adoption of the *Hidāya* as both a summary and a code of personal status represented for the British the equivalent of a nation-state's legal decree that was to apply by virtue of that state's will-to-power. By definition unwritten, customary law did not enjoy the same status as written law, and was consistently described as "primitive," "tribal," "traditional" or "native,"[21] terms that carried highly pejorative and condescending connotations.[22] This silencing, if not stamping out, of custom from "official" law was intended, first, to streamline (or homogenize) the otherwise complex and complicated jural forms with which the British had to deal, and second, to deprive Islamic law of one of its mainstays: the communal and customary laws that were entwined with the Sharīʿa on the level of application. Thus the *very act* of translation uprooted Islamic law from its interpretive–juristic soil, and, at one and the same time, from the native social matrix in which it was embedded and on which its successful operation depended.

The impact of the translations on the administration of justice was not to be fully realized until the beginning of the next century. But they served an immediate epistemological function in the colonialist articulation of Islam, for as Michael Anderson has insightfully averred, the translations not only engendered the notion of an "essentialist, static Islam incapable of change from within," but also created and promoted the fundamental discursive practice of all classical Orientalism, namely, that a proper

[21] See Merry, "Legal Pluralism," 875 ff.; Hooker, *Legal Pluralism*, 119 ff.; Glenn, *Legal Traditions of the World*, 56–57; Fisch, "Law as a Means," 15.

[22] The British attitude to unwritten law represented a microcosm of the general European attitudes toward colonized cultures. The matter was perhaps best framed by Arnold J. Toynbee (*A Study of History*, I, 36) who averred that "[w]hen we Westerners call people 'natives' we implicitly take the cultural colour out of our perception of them. We see them as wild animals infesting the country in which we happen to come across them, as part of the local flora and fauna and not as men of like passion with ourselves. So long as we think of them as 'natives' we may exterminate them or, as is more likely to-day, domesticate them and honestly (perhaps not altogether mistakenly) believe that we are improving the breed, but we do not begin to understand them."

understanding of India and the Orient "could not be had without a detailed study of the classical legal texts."[23]

As was to happen later in the Ottoman Empire, the transference of authoritative Arabicate legal texts into another language reflected both the nationalization-cum-colonization of juridical institutions and a concomitant dialectic of cause and effect relative to the weakening of the Arabicate epistemology and hermeneutics of the holy law. By the early years of the nineteenth century, the courts of India had begun to depend heavily on these translations, which not only made less sense when shorn of their sociological and native hermeneutical contexts, but also were replete with inaccuracies and plain juristic-linguistic errors. In 1865, Neil Baillie added to this repertoire of translated texts an English rendering of an abbreviated version of *al-Fatāwā al-Hindiyya*, but nothing in his endeavor would change the face of the jural project of colonial policies. If anything, it enhanced the evolution of colonial law. The so-called Anglo-Muhammadan law could not have emerged in the form and content that it did without these Anglicized texts and their British interpreters.

Anglo-Muhammadan law therefore was the law that the British created, or caused to be created, in their Indian colony. The designation refers less to the fact that it was the British who determined a particular application of the law in an Islamic judicial and juristic context, and much more to the fact that it was a heavily distorted English legal perspective on Islamic law that was administered to Muslim individuals. It may even be argued that Anglo-Muhammadan law at times involved the forceful application of English law as Islamic law[24]– exemplified only in part by *Abul Fata v. Russomoy Dhur Chowdhury* (1894), wherein the Privy Council deliberately ignored Ameer Ali's opinion regarding the law of *waqf*, and instead decided the matter on the basis of the English law of trust. (It was not until two decades later that this ruling was reversed in the 1913 Mussalman Waqf Validating Act.) Yet, no systematic importation of raw English regulations was involved in the creation of this hybridity; rather, what was mostly implicated was the imposition of English jural principles grounded in the colonizers' highly subjective notions of "justice, equity and good conscience" – notions that were bound to alter the shape of Islamic *fiqh* itself.

Furthermore, the Anglo-Muhammadan law was no less affected by the British perceptions of governance, themselves heavily derived from the intractable connections between law and the modern state. For instance,

[23] Anderson, "Legal Scholarship," 74; also see Kugle, "Framed, Blamed and Renamed," 258–59; Strawson, "Islamic Law and English Texts," 26.
[24] Hooker, *Legal Pluralism*, 96.

governors Hastings and Cornwallis (1786–93) both rejected, as did their British counterparts elsewhere,[25] the entire tenor of the Sharīʿa law of homicide (*dimāʾ*) on the grounds that this law granted private, extrajudicial privileges to the next of kin, who are empowered to mete or not mete out punishment (ranging from retaliation, to payment of blood-money, to pardon) as they saw fit. This right, they held, was the exclusive preserve of the state which, by definition, had the "legitimate" right to exercise violence.[26] Reflecting an entrenched state-culture of monopoly over violence, Cornwallis further argued that too often criminals escaped punishment under the rule of Islamic law, a situation that would not be allowed to obtain under what he must have seen as an efficient state discipline.[27] His voice echoed Hastings' complaint that Islamic law was irregular, lacking in efficacy and "founded on the most lenient principles and on an abhorrence of bloodshed."[28] (Ironically, these colonial perceptions of Islamic law have been diametrically reversed during the last three or four decades.)

Already integral to colonial policy, these views became legal reality between 1790 and 1861, when Islamic criminal law was gradually replaced by its British counterpart: homicide became an entirely public offense, and the relatives of the victim were deprived of the right to retaliate or levy blood-money. Retaliation became the state's prerogative, and the loss otherwise incurred by the victim's family was vitiated by the modern conception that the citizen is, within the boundaries of the law, the property of the state. Unintentional homicide and homicide without fault commanded no compensation whatever, and penalties incurring amputation (which in the economic calculations of the British made no sense) were abolished altogether. By 1861, no trace of Islamic criminal law was to survive.[29] As Nicholas Dirks has perceptively noted, "British justice [in India] turned out to be far more draconian – in practice as well as in principle – than Islamic justice had been, resorting much more frequently to capital punishment, and much less often to community-based methods of enforcement and reconciliation . . . [The Company] was far more concerned with public order, and with the specific use of the law to protect its own trade and commerce as well as authority, than was the old regime."[30]

The translation and codification of Islamic law must thus be seen as causally linked not only to the production of the so-called Anglo-Muhammadan law, but also to the very colonialist notion that to govern

[25] See, e.g., Alon, "Tribal System." [26] van Creveld, *Rise and Decline*, 155–70.
[27] Singha, *Despotism*, 2, 49–75. [28] Dirks, *Scandal*, 221.
[29] Peters, *Crime*, 109–19. [30] Dirks, *Scandal*, 221.

India (or any other possession) automatically entailed changing its jural *modus operandi*. And to do so, it was ineluctable not only that the native agency had to be suppressed at any cost, but that new and "improved" *local* (but not necessarily native) agencies had to be cultivated. As Thomas Macaulay, a member of the EIC's ruling council, declared, the aim of the British was to foster a group of educated men, "Indian in blood and color, English in taste, in opinions, in morals and in intellect."[31] This group, consisting mostly of lawyers trained in Britain, co-produced Anglo-Muhammadan law, although the British unquestionably were its ultimate architects. Among these were such distinguished and relatively influential "natives" as Sir Syed Mahmood,[32] who, perhaps unwittingly, participated in the production of this legal hybridity. The colonialist project (and discursive practice) that cast the Sharīʿa in a rigidly codified form placed this local legal elite in a paradox. In their struggle to resist the British domination of their country's life, they had to vindicate and rationalize their resistance by the logic of the very Anglo-Muhammadan law that they were attempting to curb.[33] This condition represented one of the most typical ironies of colonized peoples: what they deemed to be the unjust law of occupation was the only available and legitimate means by which they could bargain against their occupiers. That they were not passive agents hardly needs stating, yet in their bid for agency they were systematically and systemically bound by the colonizer's higher will-to-power and, specifically, by the terms that this power dictated. Native agency could claim a certain domain of activity, but it was obviously far from free.[34]

To say that native agency was systemically constrained is in effect to argue that the system by which the colonized peoples lived and ordered their lives was a system that worked against them by virtue of the fact that it was, first of all, superimposed on them, and second, *inherently* structured so as to serve the interests of the colonizer. The gradual – but ultimately final – displacement of the native legal culture thus meant that while the use of the colonizer's system may have at certain points permitted the colonized natives to argue for (and at much fewer points, receive) some

[31] Macaulay, "Minute on Indian Education," 249.

[32] On Syed Mahmood's legal career and life, see Guenther, "Syed Mahmood and the Transformation of Muslim Law."

[33] A point incisively made by Kugle, "Framed, Blamed and Renamed," 359. Cf. the exaggerated claims for native agency made by Benton, *Law and Colonial Cultures*, as well as Brown, *Rule of Law*, 5 ff. For a brief theoretical response, see Introduction, section 2, above.

[34] See, again, Benton, *Law and Colonial Cultures*, who seems to build a paradoxical case for a native agency that, under colonial rule, has the semblance of free will.

of the colonizer's own rights and benefits, the natives were doing so not only by the rules and terms of the hegemonic order but, consequently, by the new social, economic, political, legal and other realities brought about by the new rulers. The native lawyers may indeed have been "quick to perceive opportunity in th[e] legal scape,"[35] but the opportunity was British-dictated, not their own, and it was British-constricted, not free. This is, after all, one of the fundamental and defining meanings of colonialism.

Yet, British colonialism did afford the landed class an opportunity to fill the cracks in the power structures created by the gradual demolition of the native legal institutions and the legal system as a whole.[36] The emerging Anglicized legal system was structurally (and thus inherently) geared to enhancing the capitalistic and landed-gentry interests of the *zamindars*, a fact which contributed to bolstering and enriching these interests against those of the agrarian countryside. But this was not all. Prior to colonization, and in almost all Muslim lands, entitlement to land took the form of usufruct, but the English law of property created a new notion of wealth whereby ownership *qua* ownership of land became a desideratum. Against this newly emerging legal backdrop, the powerful families would resort to the seemingly new phenomenon of establishing family endowments in order to prevent the fragmentation of their estates when inherited according to Quranic rules.[37] The Mussalman Waqf Validating Act (1913), a product of the Muslim community's political resistance against British courts and colonialist policy, was one of the fruits of agency, although a by-product of this agency was the creation of an ever wider gap between economic classes. That colonial law was engaged in the formation of socio-economic, political and other forms of power hardly needs demonstration; that it engaged those who came into contact with it at all levels in the social and political hierarchy needs even less argument; but to say that colonial law, the product of a distinct and highly structured political and capitalistic hierarchy, could afford agency to the overwhelming majority of the (impoverished) Indian population is to ignore the structures as well as the operations and effects of power.[38]

Furthermore, and as we will see again later,[39] the "opportunity" opened to the Indians by their British masters was one that permitted an easy coalescing of a new and strengthened patriarchy that significantly chipped

35 Benton, "Colonial Law and Cultural Difference," 586.

36 On shoring up the powers of the landed class, see Saiyid, *Muslim Women of the British Punjab*, 13–19.

37 Powers, "Orientalism, Colonialism and Legal History," 554–63.

38 See Introduction, section 2, above.

39 See chapter 16, section 2 and *passim*, below.

away at women's rights and privileges.[40] Whether judged as a gain or a loss in the struggle against the British colonizer, and irrespective of what the Indians made of the opportunities they perceived or with which they were provided, they worked with a system whose terms, substantive possibilities and directions were not of their own choosing.

Another salient systemic change effected by the creation of Anglo-Muhammadan law was the rigidification of Islamic law, a symptom of the attempt to remold Islamic law in the image of the concision, clarity, accessibility and blind-justice tendency of European jural conceptions. We had occasion to discuss the construction, out of Islamic juristic treatises, of code-like texts which resulted in one sort of rigidification. Yet another rigidifying process was the conversion of the Sharīʿa court into a body that operated on the doctrine of *Stare Decisis*, the obligation of courts to follow the uncontroversial previous judicial decisions of higher courts.[41]

This system could have evolved in Islam, but for a good reason did not. The Sharīʿa assigned legal expertise and, more importantly, epistemic authority to the *muftī* and author-jurist,[42] not to the *qāḍī* who, while possessing more or less the same amount of legal knowledge as did his British counterpart, was deemed – *qua qāḍī*[43] – insufficiently qualified to "make" law. *Ijtihād*ic hermeneutics was the very feature that distinguished Islamic law from modern codified legal systems, a feature that permitted this law to reign supreme in, and accommodate, as varied and diverse cultures, sub-cultures, local moralities and customary practices as those which flourished in Java, Malabar, Khurāsān, Madagascar, Syria and Morocco. But insofar as judicial practice was concerned, the bindingness of a ruling according to the specifically British doctrine of precedent deprived the *qāḍī* of the formerly wider array of opinions to choose from in light of the facts presented in the case. Once a determination of law in a specific case was made binding, as would happen in a British court, the otherwise unceasing hermeneutical activities of the Muslim *muftī*-cum-author-jurist would have no place in judicial life; indeed, he would

40 Only as late as 1832 the Great Reform Act "increased the electorate by 280,814 men in England and Wales. In 1833 one in five men in England and Wales, one in eight men in Scotland, and one in twenty men in Ireland could vote. In 1886 the total electorate for England, Wales and Scotland was 1,902,270 men out of a total population (in 1891) of around 33 million, some 17 million of whom were female. Full franchise democracy (one adult person one vote) arrives only in 1950." Corrigan and Sayer, *Great Arch*, 17.

41 Further on *Stare Decisis*, see chapter 4, section 4, above.

42 Two juristic roles discussed in detail in Hallaq, *Authority*, 166–235.

43 On the epistemic authority of the *qāḍī qua qāḍī*, see *ibid.*, 168–74.

subsequently disappear from the legal as well as the intellectual life of the jural community.

Enshrining in Anglo-Muhammadan law a doctrine of *Stare Decisis* in effect transformed the sources of legal authority altogether. Instead of calling upon the school (*madhhab*ic) principles and the juristic authorities whose props were the dialectics of textual sources and context-specific social and moral exigencies, the Anglo-Muhammadan lawyer and judge were forced to look to the higher courts, and the higher courts in turn to the Privy Council which sat in London, not Delhi or Bombay. It is remarkable that the Privy Council was not constituted as a law court but functioned as an advisory body on legal matters to the king or queen. Its members, who also heard appeals from the colony, were both judges and politicians, although after 1876 they were drawn mainly from the Law Lords.[44] More importantly, the Council was remote not only geographically – given its stupendous distance from the real concerns of the colonized natives and their deployed colonizers – but also, and from a distinctly jural perspective, epistemically. This epistemic replacement of Islamic legal authority by its British counterpart encouraged the gradual desiccation of Islamic law in its Anglo-Muhammadan version. It had the effect of transforming Islamic law in India into an impotent hybrid that, on the one hand, fell short of the "civilized" legal standards of the colonizer and, on the other, miserably failed to defend the interests of the very tradition and society that it was supposed to serve.

The doctrine of *Stare Decisis* also stimulated far-reaching changes in the way the courts worked. The product of an intensive "book-keeping" culture,[45] the logic of *Stare Decisis* required the maintenance of a systematic recording of law reports, an activity which began in some parts of India during the early decades of the nineteenth century and which was systematized for the whole colony in the Indian Law Reports Act of 1875. A by-product of this process – one of whose attributes was an unwavering emphasis upon the physical act of recording data – was a fundamental change in the Islamic law of evidence where oral testimony based on integrity, morality and rectitude was paradigmatic. Long before the 1875 Act, the British began the practice of recording testimony which, once

[44] Anderson, "Legal Scholarship," 75–76.

[45] On the debate about book-keeping as a fundamental feature of modern capitalism, see Yamey, "Accounting and the Rise of Capitalism." See also Goody, *East in the West*, 49–81. Goody's arguments in refutation of the thesis that it was European rationality which gave rise to double-entry book-keeping are compelling. Arguably, however, the intensity with which these methods of book-keeping were practiced (and which gave them a life of their own) is related to the rise of new forms of capitalism in Europe.

committed to the court record, acquired too a fixed form. But this was an interim development, for the British introduced further reforms in 1861 and 1872, whereby the English law of procedure fully supplanted both its Islamic and its Anglo-Muhammadan counterparts.

Anglo-Muhammadan law, in its individual constituents as well as its integral whole, appears to have been an interim colonialist solution that mediated the British domination of India for over a century. The embryonic notions of imbuing Indian legal traditions with Anglicizing elements began as early as 1772 when a new doctrine propounded by Hastings declared that wherever native laws were deemed silent on a matter, British principles of "justice, equity and good conscience" would apply. But it was not until nearly a century later that a major displacement of Anglo-Muhammadan law was to be effected, especially after the transforming effects of the 1857 Rebellion. The 1860s and 1870s witnessed the abolition of slavery, as well as the Islamic laws of procedure, criminal law and evidence. All these were superseded by British laws enacted by statute. By the end of the century, and with the exception of family law and certain elements of property transactions, all indigenous laws had been supplanted by British law. But all this was introduced piecemeal, answering, in an *ad hoc* and generally incremental manner, the growing anxiety of the British to exercise control over their Indian subjects, especially after the events of 1857 and in a world where London ruled directly, rather than through the EIC (dissolved that year). In this picture, Anglo-Muhammadan law represented no more than the middle stage which permitted firming up the colonialist hold over economic, political and legal power.

Yet, no success can be imputed to jural colonization – or any colonization for that matter – without an essential correlative process which operated both conjointly and subliminally. As Nicholas Dirks poignantly observes, it was the channeling out to the non-European world of a mass of "cultural technologies" that sustained and strengthened British – and other – jural colonialism. For without these technologies neither Anglo-Muhammadan law nor its successors could have been possible. "The cultural effects of colonialism have too often been ignored or displaced into the inevitable logic of modernization and world capitalism; but more than this, it has not been sufficiently recognized that colonialism was itself a cultural project of control. Colonial knowledge both enabled conquest and was produced by it."[46]

[46] See Nicholas Dirks' introduction to Cohn's *Colonialism and its Forms of Knowledge*, ix.

2. British Malaya

In most regions of the Malay Peninsula (and Java), the jural forms of Islam had not succeeded in penetrating until the later decades of the nineteenth century.[47] In the Straits Settlements – comprising Penang, Singapore and Malacca – Islamic law was only one of a number of local legal practices.[48] The textual culture of Islamic law, as well as its "state"-connected judiciary, was unable to establish itself until this late date. It was only around this time that reference to the authoritative *fiqh* texts began to be made[49] and that the study of *ḥadīth* established itself in the *pesantren* curriculum. In the Federated and Unfederated States – comprising Selangor, Perak, Pahang and Negri Sembilan for the former, and Johor, Trengganu, Kelantan and Kedah for the latter – Islamic law was somewhat more established, but its modes of judicial operation in relation to the local rajas and sultans differed from its Indian and Middle Eastern counterparts.

Until the nineteenth century, the normative code of conduct and adjudication largely rested with the customary laws that governed the entirety of the Malayan and Indonesian worlds. Especially in the Straits Settlements, but also elsewhere, elements of Hindu, Siamese and Chinese laws were also present. But *adat*, generally meaning right conduct,[50] dominated. In Peninsular Malaya, *adat* consisted, generally speaking, of two types, the *adat temenggong* and the *adat perpateh*.[51] The former, evolving under Hindu "law" and overlaid with Islamic influence, were in part and in select regions committed to writing as early as the seventeenth century (if not earlier) and pertained to the rights of the ruler, very much in the vein of *siyāsa sharʿiyya*.[52] The ruler could make war on infidels, and punish adulterers, thieves and other public offenses, including the harboring of fugitive slaves; he

[47] Peletz, *Islamic Modern*, 25–59. Islam, represented largely in the persons of traders and missionaries, began to find its way to the Malay Peninsula in the fourteenth century, Malacca and its rulers having been an important base for the spread of the religion throughout the Malay States. See also Federspiel, *Sultans*, 18–21, who argues that the slow spread of Islam is attributable to the fact that the "Muslim traders were not missionaries but people devoted to economic enterprises."

[48] Federspiel, *Sultans*, 50–51. [49] Hooker, *Islamic Law in South-East Asia*, 84.

[50] Minattur, "Nature of Malay Customary Law," 327. Speaking of Sumatra a century and a half ago, William Marsden observed that "there is no word in the language of the island which properly and strictly signifies law; nor is there any person or class of persons among the *Rejangs* regularly invested with legislative powers. They are governed in their various disputes by a set of long-established customs (*adat*) handed down to them from their ancestors, the authority of which is founded on usage and general consent. The Chiefs, in pronouncing their decisions, are not heard to say, 'so the law directs,' but 'such is the custom'." Cited in *ibid.*, 328.

[51] Hooker, *Adat Laws in Modern Malaya*, 71 ff., 209 ff.

[52] Minattur, "Nature of Malay Customary Law," 329.

was the default owner of abandoned rice fields, and had the exclusive right to levy taxes. In outline, these specifications were common to all the law-books of the *adat temenggong*, propounded in the vast territories of the Malay world. But in their detail, especially relating to penalties, they differed from one locale to the next. In some areas, for instance, adultery commanded a pecuniary fine or public shaming, while in others one hundred lashes were required. In matrilineal Minangkabau of West Sumatra, the two adulterers had to be married to each other. For theft, the penalty ranged from cutting off the hand, to payment in camels, to death (in Malacca).

Adat temenggong represented an admixture of, or a compromise between, pre-Islamic forms of Malay customary law – most probably unwritten in its pre-Islamic versions – and provisions of the Sharīʿa. Their varied forms and the extent to which each accommodated *sharʿī* values also reflect the varying degrees to which these values had penetrated, and were absorbed by, the different Malay societies.[53] But Islamic law also consciously accommodated *adat*, upholding as always the universal principle that customary usages must always be taken into account in administering justice.[54]

Adat perpateh, on the other hand, represented a group of customary practices largely related to land ownership and its devolution along matrilineal lines of descent.[55] These matrilineal and matriarchal customs were summed up in verse and proverbial forms (*perbilangan adat*) and transmitted orally from one generation to the next. Unlike *adat temenggong*, *adat perpateh* were not conceived as, or intended to be, a site of coercive application, the will of a higher political power, but were rather viewed as a code of ethics and good behavior, the violator of which had mostly to reckon with the moral sanctions of his or her community. Petty crime and minor disputes that could not be successfully mediated by the family heads (*mamak*) were resolved by the heads of the clans, known as *buapa*s. More important infractions and conflicts were adjudged by the tribal chiefs, the *lembaga*s, whereas capital offenses belonged to the jurisdiction of the *undang*, the effective "provincial" rulers.[56]

Yet, the greatest bulk of the *adat perpateh* operated at the local level and was managed by the immediate community. Much like the customary social practices that Islamic law assumed in Central and West Asia, in *adat* the extended family was held responsible for its individual members; the cause of social harmony in these units could be served neither by mutilation nor by imprisonment. While moral punishment was an effective

[53] Hooker, *Legal Pluralism*, 143–45, 150. [54] Hooker, *Concise Legal History*, 150.

[55] A detailed account of matrilineal *adat* is provided by Hooker, *Adat Laws in Modern Malaya*, 14–21. See also Minattur's useful article, "Nature of Malay Customary Law."

[56] Minattur, "Nature of Malay Customary Law," 333–37.

means to control infractions, the more serious concern lay in compensating the victim in such a way as to restore him – wherever possible – together with his social unit, to the position in which they stood before the conflict. Indeed, the creation of harmony and peace was the *raison d'être* of *adat*, expressed in the maxim "Adat sentosa di-dalam negeri."[57]

The *adat* also offered more than a guide to social and legal practices. The *perbilangan* (a verse from which these *adat* are decoded) "explains the nature of the real world, the nature of man and his relationship with that world, and provides detailed rules of conduct and ... a coherent normative system."[58] The British colonists regarded these *adat perpateh* as representing a "democratic" system, whereas the *adat temenggong* were seen as both aristocratic (emanating from the ruler) and autocratic (affirming his punitive prerogatives).[59] This may in part explain why *adat perpateh* were eventually integrated into the state legislation, at least in Negri Sembilan.[60] But this form of *adat* existed in relatively few regions and was not, strictly speaking, entirely matrilineal, since only the real estate of the deceased – notably lands, houses and their contents – devolved upon the daughters. Although the sons usually inherited all remaining property (cash, jewelry, tools, fishing boats, etc.), real property remained the residue of power and prestige, and only women could own it. Yet, although the matrilineal privilege was by no means nominal, and although these *adat* diverged in many respects from Islamic law, the two systems were not seen as incompatible. Indeed, in rural societies, the majority of the population hardly made any distinction between the two.

Gradually, over the course of the second half of the nineteenth century, the British extended their domination[61] through jural forms. By the 1880s, they were ordering their magistrates – who often were not trained in law – to apply the "law prevalent in Mahomedan States supplemented when necessary by the laws of Great Britain . . . Native laws and customs should be allowed due rights, but as no body of native law is in the hands of Magistrates for enforcement, reference should be made to head-quarters in cases of difficulty turning entirely on native custom."[62] Although these instructions applied to Perak (in 1882), Selangor (in 1890) and Sungai

[57] *Ibid.* 349–50, and *passim.* [58] Hooker, *Islamic Law in South-East Asia*, 162.

[59] Hooker, *Legal Pluralism*, 146.

[60] *Ibid.*, 151; Hooker, *Islamic Law in South-East Asia*, 162.

[61] The British took Georgetown in 1786 and established Singapore as a British colony in 1819. In 1824, an agreement between the Netherlands and Britain divided the region between them, with the former taking what is now Indonesia and the latter acquiring the Malay Peninsula as a protectorate, later (in 1895) officially designated as the "Protected States."

[62] Cited in Peletz, *Islamic Modern*, 48.

Ujung (in 1894), the general pattern of British involvement elsewhere (including India and Africa)[63] was similar. Criminal justice was mostly in British hands and, apart from the application of family law and pre-trial arbitration-cum-mediation, the native Malays were largely precluded from participating in the judicial process. This preclusion was particularly evident in criminal jurisdiction, partly because of the rarity of offenses committed by Malays,[64] but mainly because penal law was deemed central to maintaining "law and order" in the colonies. As we saw, this was the case not only in India, but also in British tropical Africa (where Sharīʿa courts were allowed to adjudicate criminal cases but where at the same time British administrative officers could at will transfer these cases to the British magistrates).[65]

By 1868, a series of British courts had been established, including a Supreme Court of the Straits Settlements. In 1873, the Supreme Court was divided up into four courts, and the Court of Quarter Sessions was established as a criminal court. In the same year, British commercial law was introduced to the Settlements. With the creation of a Court of Appeal, the judicial system acquired features that were to survive into modern Malaysia. (So, incidentally, did the commercial provisions which were reenacted in the Civil Law Act in 1956, and later amended in 1972.) But the overall effect of subjecting *adat* to the *Stare Decisis* doctrine – not to mention to the British acts, charters and regulations – was transformative, in that the flexible *adat* were rendered rigid by virtue, first, of giving them unified interpretations and, second, of committing them to writing. As had happened to Islamic law elsewhere, the jural command in most areas of the Malay States moved from the local/family/community level to that of the state, where the final coercive authority was henceforth to reside. As in the Ottoman Empire[66] and India, this new centralizing order brought with it a system of bureaucratization that – through forms, writing and recorded procedure – further imposed the will of a higher power over the lives of individuals.

Yet, with the growth of colonial law in the Malayan Peninsula, Islamic law was also taking a similar turn. By the end of the nineteenth century, and as a direct reaction to British control, Islamic norms and institutions began to infiltrate, like never before, most societies in the Peninsula. Not only did the practice of Islamic rituals grow sharply, but the involvement of the *qāḍī* in the management of social and communal

[63] Anderson, "Colonial Law in Tropical Africa," 435.
[64] The great majority of the convicted being Chinese and, in relatively fewer cases, Indians. Peletz, *Islamic Modern*, 49 and 293, n. 44.
[65] Anderson, "Colonial Law in Tropical Africa," 441. [66] See next chapter.

life intensified.[67] These changes were in part instigated by Sumatran and other Muslim reformers whose activities in Malacca, Singapore and elsewhere in the Peninsula encouraged stricter adherence to Islamic norms. Yet, no less important a factor was the reaction of the native Malayan elites to British colonialist policies which increasingly militated to reduce the effective political and jural power of native rulers. These constrictions seem to have propelled the indigenous ruling elite to pursue other traditional venues of legitimacy, primary among which was an emphasis on, and the implementation of, Islamic law.[68] Strict enforcement of dietary laws, fasting, mosque attendance and prohibition of alcohol consumption were joined with an explicit ban on, and narrow definition of, sexuality and incestuous conduct. This increase in the powers of the *qāḍī* was not only worrisome to the local village and clan leaders – whose traditional authority was partly undermined by the infiltration of Islamic norms and practices – but proved also problematic in that it disturbed the indigenous regulations on property devolution, especially in local cultures that were structured along matrilineal lines. The conflict of laws in the sphere of devolution of property upon death and divorce would continue to be one of the major issues facing lawyers, judges and reformers in what was to become modern Malaysia and Indonesia. It is instructive that the invocation and vehement stress on Islamic law at the end of the nineteenth century in Malaya was to be replicated a century later, not only in modern Malaysia and Indonesia but also, and even more pronouncedly, in multiple corners of the Muslim world.

3. The *Nederlandsch-Indië*

When Dutch ships arrived in Java in 1596, they encountered the Mataram Kingdom, which was in the process of displacing the Hindu-Javanese Kingdom of Majapahit. As in the Malay and Ottoman lands, the administration of justice under the Majapahit was of dual nature. *Pradata* law represented the sovereign's jurisdiction and was based on royal Indian codes that had been adapted over time to the Javanese environment. As the highest judge of the *pradata* tribunals, the King presided over cases of murder, rebellion, treason, arson and robbery. As the province of the ruling powers, *pradata* justice did not penetrate local culture, leaving a wide sphere within society open to the application of distinct, indigenous

[67] Such reactions, it is noteworthy, were common to other colonies. For the Moroccan example (including a dramatic increase in religious sentiments and astounding spread of *madrasas* under the French), see Bidwell, *Morocco under Colonial Rule*, 55 f.

[68] Peletz, *Islamic Modern*, 52–53.

and unwritten customary *adat* laws, known as the *padu*. The Mataram Kingdom maintained this dual form of judicial administration, but considerable changes were forthcoming, especially with the accession of Sultan Agung (r. 1613–45). Agung was the first Mataram ruler to introduce to the Kingdom significant elements of Sharīʿa justice, replacing much of the Indian-Javanese judiciary with Islamic legal experts (who later came to be known as the *penghulus*).[69] Thus, a marked Islamization of Javanese law was begun only after the arrival of the Dutch and, receiving only lukewarm support from some sultans, did not gain general acceptance until much later.

Due to the fact that they could not bring all or the majority of the Indonesian Islands under their control until the second decade of the twentieth century,[70] and partly because their interests were largely focused on commercial profit, the Dutch did not interfere in native legal affairs until about the middle of the nineteenth century.[71] As D. Lev has aptly put it, the Dutch East India Company from the outset "resolved to respect local law – another way of saying that, by and large, they could not have cared less – except where commercial interests were at stake."[72] A partial exception occurred in 1811 or thereabouts, when the British, having displaced the Dutch in the course of the Napoleonic wars, appointed Raffles as governor, who in turn undertook a series of reforms in the legal domain. Raffles declared all land to be state property, a principle that the Dutch happily adopted after they retrieved the colony in 1814.[73]

By the middle of the century, the dissonance between the Dutch concept of rule – a product of deeply rooted but evolving processes of European centralization – and the practices of a pluralistic and localized legal culture increasingly came to the fore. The *rechtsstaat* in Holland began first with its own colonial settlers. Beginning in 1848, a number of codes were promulgated, all of which, except for rules relating to civil (*Burgelijk Rechtsvordering*) and criminal procedure (*Strafvordering*) in native courts, pertained to the European settlers. Although in many respects these were identical to the Dutch codes at home, they were "simplified" so as to make arrest, detention and conviction of an Indonesian commoner easier than it was to do the same to a Dutchman in Holland.[74] "Commoner" is appropriate here because the law, in its intended plurality, did not treat all natives as equals. The Javanese aristocracy, senior

[69] Ball, *Indonesian Legal History*, 37–47.
[70] On Dutch rule of Indonesia in general, see Federspiel, *Sultans*, 96 ff.
[71] Hooker, *Legal Pluralism*, 252; Fasseur, "Colonial Dilemma," 240–42.
[72] Lev, "Colonial Law," 58. [73] Hooker, *Concise Legal History*, 188.
[74] Lev, "Colonial Law," 61.

officials, bureaucrats and military officers were granted a privileged status in Dutch courts, thus empowering them as collaborators and, after independence, as a politically powerful class that filled the power cleavages left by colonialism. Aside from a Japanese minority living in the archipelago, who were treated in the manner of Javanese aristocracy, the other commercially active minorities – Arabs, Indians and especially Chinese – were treated as Indonesians under criminal law, but as Europeans under commercial law.[75]

On the other hand, attempts to impose a civil code on the colonized population were quickly – if not easily – frustrated.[76] Yet, it must be clear that the absence of noticeable judicial and legislative interference in civil matters was not the mark of benevolence – or mere indifference – toward the natives, but rather the result of a reluctant, even confused policy severely lacking in knowledge of the various local customs and widely diverse legal sub-cultures of the natives. It is doubtful that by the middle of the nineteenth century (and after more than two centuries of colonizing Java) the Dutch possessed either the cultural or the legal knowledge to administer their colony effectively, and in this respect they differed much from the British from whom they stood to learn.

As "law and order" constituted the conceptual and material backbone of colonialist administration, the Dutch, after some failed efforts, finally succeeded in promulgating a penal code for natives in 1873. This was a near-identical copy of the Dutch national code, which was in turn modeled after the French penal code. It was not until 1886 that Holland finally drafted and adopted its own penal code, but attempts to draft a cognate code for the archipelago remained ink on paper. Nonetheless, the administration of criminal justice on the ground remained for the greater part in Dutch, not native, hands. Since the native district and regent courts, as well as the Sharīʿa and *adat* courts, handled minor and non-monetary cases, all criminal cases and major offenses were tried at the next level, namely, at the *Landraden* courts, which also handled important civil cases pertaining to the natives. For example, all matters of *waqf* and the all-important area of inheritance fell within the jurisdiction of these courts. Until the 1920s, the chairmen of the latter – who could overrule their native colleagues on the bench – were exclusively Dutch. But ultimate authority did not lie even in the hands of these chairmen, for appeals were heard at the *Raden van Justitie*, the high Dutch courts (numbering six in total), whose jurisdiction was presumably confined to the Dutch colonial settlers alone.[77]

[75] *Ibid.*, 62. [76] Hooker, *Concise Legal History*, 191. [77] Lev, "Colonial Law," 59.

The Sharīʿa courts were connected with the *Landraden* in two ways: on the one hand, the *qāḍīs* served as advisors to the *Landraden* magistrates, but on the other, the Sharīʿa court decisions, to be enforced, needed the validation of the Dutch courts. (This judicial dependency continued to obtain in Indonesia until very recently.)[78] In 1882, the Dutch reorganized the Islamic courts (now called "priest-courts," *priesterraden*), creating a collegial system whereby the Sharīʿa bench would consist of three magistrates (at times more). The reorganization was intended to expunge the influence of the Javanese aristocracy, which exercised much power over the appointment and dismissal of Sharīʿa officials. Yet, the new courts were not adequately integrated into the judicial system, nor were they provided with powers of enforcement. No system of appointing judges was established, and no budget was created to pay their salaries. Serious criticism of these reforms forced the Dutch to create, in the 1930s, the Islamic High Court to hear appeals from all the religious courts of Java. A parallel system was established also in Madura and Kalimantan.

But if the Dutch formally recognized a dual system of justice, one for natives and the other for their own, then what about those natives who converted to Christianity and whose (mostly, if not wholly, invented) plight as a minority persecuted by the dominant native culture commanded the attention of the powerful Christian groups at home? This portrayal of native Christians as victims of their savage brothers was largely the work of L. W. C. van den Berg, another Dutch Orientalist who penned on this subject an inflammatory discourse.[79] (The end result of the debate over these native Christians was no more than a law of marriage that provided a new basis for the converts' matrimonial regimes.) Nor did van den Berg limit himself to solving problems that he alone had diagnosed; he also "improved" colonialist knowledge in other ways. In 1882, he published, at the instigation of the government of the Netherland Indies, a translation of Nawawī's *Minhāj al-Ṭālibīn*, with the declared purpose of using it to facilitate colonial administration.[80] His choice of this book not only reflected the importance of Nawawī in the Archipelago's Shāfiʿite tradition, but also strongly implied his own enthusiastic support of the position that the Sharīʿa, not *adat*, was the paradigmatic law of these islands.

We have no good reason to doubt that *adat* law had originally existed in oral form, and that despite the fact that it was in part recorded – probably during the Islamic period and mainly in the Malay Peninsula – this orality

[78] See chapter 16, section 4 (E), below. [79] Fasseur, "Colonial Dilemma," 247.

[80] An English translation of van den Berg's version was made by E. C. Howard, again to be used by the British in the territories of Aden, later to become South Yemen.

remained one of its hallmarks. But orality had and still has – even in "simple" societies of the present – a function. Orality requires communal participation in, and understanding of, customary law. Knowledge in this environment ceases to lie with a specialized class of people, such as *faqīh*s or modern lawyers. Instead, it is knowledge of common behavior, perceived as such in relative terms by those upon whom it is incumbent to conduct themselves in a particular way. All in all, legal knowledge of this sort does not reside with an elite as much as it is diffused in the community, although some, especially the elders, may know it better than others.[81] If no writing is required, then no commentaries are needed; thus, no commentators or jurists can become the locus of either legal or epistemic authority. The preclusion of writing therefore entails the exclusion of codification, an essential tool of a centralized state authority. The structure and constitution – or more categorically, the nature – of the *adat* depend on the crucial fact of their being in a state of orality, a state of fluidity. In their original form, then, the *adat* as a whole constitute a state of affairs, a practice, a state of mind, a moral code and a cosmology, but they can scarcely be reduced to our modern notions of law, operating as the legal organ of a coercive state or even as that of a loving God.

Like Islamic law, *adat* were not intended to apply in letter, but represented a guide to proper conduct or a maximal limit to what can be tolerated by a particular, local community. The writing down of *adat* practices did not considerably affect their fluidity, for the record remained both partial and unofficial, in that – as we have noted – only a fraction of *adat* was committed to writing and whatever was recorded was not perceived as constituting a law or a code in any modern sense of the term. They could not have, at any rate, represented more of an official law than any *fiqh* book. And so under Dutch colonization, *adat* begin to metamorphose, acquiring in the process different and unprecedented characteristics. Chief among these was an elision into rigidity.[82] Yet, it is not difficult to understand why the Dutch insisted on capturing *adat* in written form. Coming from the continental legal tradition, the Dutch could not conceive of any unwritten law as law properly speaking, and if *adat* were to have any force they would have to be endorsed by the written law. Thus, to be so sanctioned, *adat* law had first to be identified and set down in writing.[83]

[81] Ironically, this was well understood by the distinguished Orientalist and advisor to the Dutch governor of Indonesia Snouck Hurgronje, *Achehnese*, I, 10–12. On the retention of custom among the Malay, see Peletz, *Islamic Modern*, 34.

[82] Hooker, *Concise Legal History*, 192–93. [83] Fasseur, "Colonial Dilemma," 248.

While India had its Sir William Jones, Indonesia boasted Cornelius van Vollenhoven, an influential Dutch Orientalist specializing in *adat* – or what was by his time called *adatrecht*, as coined by the other stellar Dutch Orientalist Christian Snouck Hurgronje. This field of study confirmed the legal duality that had been "discovered" by the Dutch. There is no real indication that this duality was construed by the Malay peoples in oppositional terms; nor was the relationship between one and the other problematized. Rather, before the end of the nineteenth century, *adat* and Sharīʿa appear to have been viewed as complementary and intertwined.[84] But Snouck's "discovery"[85] of *adat*, and van Vollenhoven's elevation of the study of this discovery into a "science"[86] in effect opened a Pandora's box within the political and legal life of Indonesia that has not been closed to this day.

Hailing from a pedigree of Dutch scholars who viewed Islam as a threat (very much in the same vein as the French saw this religion and its law in Algeria),[87] van Vollenhoven vehemently espoused the position that *adat*, not the Sharīʿa, should be held to govern the pluralistic societies of the Netherlands Indies. Criticizing the proponents of Sharīʿa,[88] he argued that *adat* exercised such a wide sway over the Archipelago's population that Islamic law stood in comparison as both thin on the ground and virtually irrelevant.[89] (Remarkably, all this knowledge he managed to garner from two, rather brief, visits to the colony.) He also espoused the view that any attempt at weakening *adat* was nothing less than an invitation to open the floodgates to Islam,[90] a religion seen by van Vollenhoven and many of his compatriots not only as a native political tool of unification, but as the very religion that had threatened Christendom for centuries. Furthermore, to side with *adat* was to promote secularism, the new religion of Europe.[91] Among other initiatives, he compiled an extensive work in which he committed to writing the otherwise oral *adat*,[92] identifying eighteen versions of it, when in fact the Archipelago consisted of over a thousand islands, each with its own version (or versions) of *adat*.

[84] This much is admitted by Snouck Hurgronje himself. See his *Achehnese*, I, 13–14.

[85] "The Discovery of Adat Law" was the title of one of van Vollenhoven's articles. See Fasseur, "Colonial Dilemma," 239.

[86] Holleman, *Van Vollenhoven on Indonesian Adat Law*, L; Fasseur, "Colonial Dilemma," 240.

[87] See next chapter, section 6.

[88] Van Vollenhoven poured his wrath mainly upon van den Berg, who stated, as noted earlier, that Islamic law as well as other religious laws is as "binding" as *adatrecht*. Snouck Hurgronje fiercely criticized van den Berg, citing similar reasons. See his *Achehnese*, I, 12–15.

[89] Holleman, *Van Vollenhoven on Indonesian Adat Law*, 7–8, 11.

[90] *Ibid.*, 122 (last sentence); see also Lev, "Colonial Law," 66.

[91] Lev, *Islamic Courts*, 9–10. [92] I.e., *Het Adatrecht van Nederlansch-Indië*.

But van Vollenhoven's work was not the first to do so, for he had, in his early career, instigated the Minister of the Colonies to order J. H. Alting (the president of the native courts) to compile a large work on Minahasa's *adat*.[93] Thus, all of this cumulative scholarship had a perduring effect, not only in articulating a particular, yet unprecedented, distinction and separation between *adat* and Sharīʿa, but in qualitatively remolding *adat* into an unrecognizable form. Once written, the *adat* "violated a primary principle of *adat* law theory, that the *adat* lived in local tradition. Now, written, it lived in books, which Dutch judges, and Indonesian judges half a century later, used as if they were codes."[94]

This scholarly accomplishment was the first step in defining, shaping and implementing a colonialist policy that had long wavered between *adat* and Sharīʿa as the official law of the colony. As had occurred in British India, the participation of Orientalism was at the center of determining the form and substance of the law to be administered to the natives. Thus, under the direct impact of van Vollenhoven's scholarly engagement, and the influence of a powerful group of his students,[95] the Dutch government declared, in 1927, that *adat*, and not the Sharīʿa, was the normative law. Once this determined approach became official policy, institutional changes began to take effect, and further scholarship aimed at systematizing *adat* (specially by Bernard Ter Haar) came to bolster that policy with renewed vigor. Henceforth, Dutch scholars and their native students – who hailed mainly from the *prijaji* Javanese aristocracy – as well as colonialist advisors and administrators were officially trained in *adatrecht* as the paradigmatic law. The confluence of the Dutch and native elites' interests ensured the relegation of the Sharīʿa to a largely secondary status, where it would be accepted only insofar as it was provisionally allowed to modify *adat* in a particular locale (this having been termed "reception theory").[96]

Concurrent with these later judicial and legal developments was the gradual introduction to Java and Madura of the Dutch educational system that proved itself – here as in the Ottoman Empire and elsewhere[97] – instrumental not only in facilitating the legal transformation but also in accelerating the latter's dissemination and extending its cultural roots deeper in the new Muslim soil. Put differently, the introduction of Western-style schools, wittingly or not, tended to produce a number of effects besides the obvious Westernization of education in Muslim lands. In the Ottoman Empire, it facilitated the ousting of Sharīʿa legists by the

93 Fasseur, "Colonial Dilemma," 247. 94 Lev, "Colonial Law," 66.
95 Lev, *Islamic Courts*, 19–20. 96 Lev, "Colonial Law," 64–65; Lev, *Islamic Courts*, 19–20.
97 See next chapter.

ready supply of a new Westernized elite whose interest it was to promote the Western institutions upon which it depended. But more importantly, Western education was both the prerequisite to, and the means of, naturalizing the new cultural technology without which no hegemony would be viable. In Indonesia no system of *madrasa*s could be established on any scale similar to that which had existed in the Ottoman Empire, and thus the Dutch schools (which numbered more than a thousand by 1910, and which were quickly imitated by the natives)[98] did not have the same effect. Their primary effect lay in affording to the native population an opportunity to rise in the Western system, which was the locus of government and power. It gave the Javanese and other elites the means of education that prepared them to pursue their legal studies in Western institutions, whether these were located in Batavia or Leiden. And it was from amongst this elite that students of the *adatrecht*, many of whom advocated the reception theory, emerged.

On the other hand, and as happened in Malaya earlier, the Islamic impulse grew as colonial power consolidated its grip over the colony. Just as the legal transformations in the Ottoman Empire and Egypt informed each other, so too were the religious movements of South-East Asia influenced by the Hejazi–Egyptian world of Muslim legal scholarship and religious thought. By the early decades of the twentieth century, the European steamship became the dominant mode of transportation in the Indian Ocean, a phenomenon that promptly brought with it a tremendous increase in the number of Javanese scholars studying in the Hejaz and Cairo's al-Azhar University, the latter of which had, significantly, been undergoing reform at the instigation of Muḥammad ʿAbduh (and later Shaltūt).[99] The modernization of Muslim education at al-Azhar, together with the theologically inclined Najdite jurisprudence, were to be appropriated into a Javanese context, all this constituting a considerable influence on the conception of religious education – and therefore religious law – in the Archipelago, especially in Java and Madura (not to mention North Sumatra, Aceh and Malacca). The overall result was an increase in Islamic consciousness, both as a marker of cultural identity and as a prop for a counter-movement that generated resistance not only to the secularized national elite but to the centuries-old and venerable *adat* as well.

[98] Shiraishi, *Age in Motion*, 28–29.

[99] On these returning students, see Feener, *Muslim Legal Thought*, 13–18. On some of Muḥammad ʿAbduh's ideas, see chapter 17, section 1, below. On Shaltūt, see *The Oxford Encyclopedia of the Modern Islamic World*, III, 44–45.

15 Hegemonic modernity: the Middle East and North Africa during the nineteenth and early twentieth centuries

1. The background

By the end of the sixteenth century, three Muslim empires ruled large and prosperous territories throughout Asia, Europe and Africa. To the east stood the Mughal Empire, to the west, the powerful Ottoman Empire, and at the center, stretching over the Iranian plateau, the Ṣafavids. Between 1709 and 1739, the Ottomans engaged in four relatively successful wars that seemed to prove their military competence against Russia and the central European states. The peace that prevailed during the next three decades also seemed to convince the Ottomans of the superiority of their military power, even as Europe during this very period was embarking on one of the most rapid advances in military technology, military discipline and organization. However, the ensuing three wars with Russia, ending in 1774, 1792 and 1812, resulted in crushing Ottoman defeats, as well as the loss of the northern shores of the Black Sea and Crimea. By the last of these wars, Arabia and Egypt had defected, the former taken by the Wahhābites and the latter by Muḥammad ʿAlī. The Empire appeared on the verge of crumbling.

The stunning military defeats starting during the last third of the eighteenth century spurred a new wave of Ottoman concessions (*imtiyāzāt*) that were to continue, and build upon, the benevolent capitulations granted to a number of European states during the preceding centuries. But it was in the wake of the 1774 Russian–Ottoman war, and the signing in that year of the Küçük Kaynarca Treaty, that a long series of concessions in favor of Russia and western European states were made. All these states managed to secure for their subjects who traded and resided in the Empire, as well as for the non-Muslim Ottomans, a set of rights and privileges far superior to those enjoyed even by Muslim Ottoman subjects themselves.[1] These capitulations, which increased and intensified with

[1] For a detailed account of the capitulations, see *Encyclopaedia of Islam*, s.v., "Imtiyāzāt," III, 1178–95; van den Boogert, *Capitulations and the Ottoman Legal System*, 19–52, and *passim*.

time, were not without corresponding Ottoman resentment and a profound perception that these concessions seriously impinged on the Empire's sovereignty.

The rise during the eighteenth century of European and Russian military power meant dramatic and in effect unprecedented corollary increases in military expenditure for the Ottomans.[2] The financial resources needed to remedy the military weakness of the Ottoman center lay in the provinces which, in order to produce the necessary income, in turn needed central military control. That a strong army was needed to raise money, and that money could not be raised efficiently without a strong army, constituted the most fundamental dilemma for the Ottomans (as well as for many Asian rulers) during the second half of the eighteenth century. This circle had always existed, and was, as a rule, managed relatively successfully. But during that century, the almost incalculable rise of European military technology was too extensive and too rapid for the Ottomans – as well as for all Afro-Asian dynasties – to be able to adjust to the swiftly changing realities. Add to this a high level of inflation which brought with it not only higher prices but countless popular riots. Just when the demand on financial and material resources was at its highest, not to mention unprecedented, provincial income was on the decline. The consequences were devastating.

With the weakening of central power and authority, provincial governors, the Janissaries and tax-collectors (let alone the *aʿyān* families)[3] lacked the restraints and the checks and balances that had been characteristic of the sixteenth and seventeenth centuries. The provincial officials, whose fear of central *siyāsa* punishment had constituted a deterrent against their abuses, now acted with a free hand, not only against the local populations but also in defiance of the courts and law of the land. Extortion, harsh taxation and violent punishment of civilians began to occur with increasing frequency and without the option of recourse to higher courts of justice. Toward the end of the eighteenth century, governors, who were not trained judges, began to adjudicate civil cases, hitherto the distinct purview of the Sharīʿa court. This hijacking of the *qāḍī*'s functions appears to have been motivated by the lure of hefty fines that these governors could extort from the increasingly powerless population and from those who happened to be caught in the web of executive surveillance. Punishments were at times corporal, going beyond the Sharīʿa prescriptions, but they were almost always sure to include a pecuniary penalty, constituting another

2 On European military advances, see Mann, *States, War and Capitalism*; Glete, *Warfare at Sea*; Tallett, *War and Society*; Parker, *Military Revolution*; Levenson, *European Expansion*.
3 On this class, see McGowan, "The Age of the Ayans," 658–77.

source of income for the ruling provincial elite. The level of intimidation dramatically increased, and on-the-spot punishments without trial became ever more frequent. Yet the governor was not the only one who set himself up as an extra-*sharʿī* magistrate. The commander of the Janissaries as well as tax-farmers established their own tribunals and prisons, and held themselves to be judges of sorts.[4] The Janissaries in particular tyrannized neighborhoods, looted shops, and extorted large sums of money from residents and guild members.[5] The presence in the provinces of the authority of central government was hardly noticeable. The rate of crime rose and the public order that had prevailed during the past centuries became no more than a memory, which itself could not have lasted long.[6]

With the Empire in near disarray and its armies defeated by the Russians and Europeans, the Sublime Porte realized that reform of the military system had become imperative. But due to the stubborn resistance of the Janissaries and their allies, Selim III's attempts at reform ended in failure as well as in his own execution in 1808. His successor, Mahmud II (r. 1808–39), was aware of the balance of power in the Palace, and had to calculate his steps slowly and carefully before he abolished the Janissary corps once and for all in 1826. Because of this, as well as for other reasons to be discussed later, the year 1826 or thereabouts must mark not only the first step of real and far-reaching changes in the law, but a significant turning point in the process of modernization.

With the abolishment of the Janissaries in the capital, and consequently the weakening of the Janissaries in the provinces, the central government was now free to strengthen its hold on political and military power. But there was also an important economic side to this military reform. As the Janissaries were also guildsmen who engaged in crafts and the manufacture of goods as much as they participated in military campaigns, they constituted a formidable force promoting economic protectionism, a fixture of the Ottoman guild system and thus of the Ottoman economy at large.[7] The elimination of the Janissaries, the most powerful advocates of protectionism, thus opened the door to economic liberalism, a development that fulfilled the long-standing demands and pressures of the capitalist European powers.

[4] One could add to the list of extra-judicial tribunals the rights granted to European consuls who by then had enjoyed capitulatory rights in Muslim lands for centuries. See Leibesny, "Development of Western Judicial Privileges," 312 ff.

[5] Marcus, *Middle East*, 73, 108, 114–15.

[6] The near-chaos at the end of the eighteenth century may explain the construction of the reign of Suleyman the Lawgiver as idealistic, or at any rate more ideal than it really was. See İnalcık, "Suleiman the Lawgiver," 105–06.

[7] Quataert, "Age of Reform," 764.

A dozen years after the extinction of the Janissaries, the ground had been adequately prepared to impose on the Empire a "reform" program that would open its population and markets to European exploitation. The 1838 Treaty of Balta Limanı between the Sublime Porte and the British not only confirmed all previous capitulatory privileges but now ensured the final removal of any form of monopoly that could protect Ottoman manufacturers against European competition. In effect, it abolished all restrictions on foreigners' movement within the Empire, thereby exposing the hitherto protected and surviving Ottoman economic sectors to the annihilating competition of the European market. Thus, the famous reformist 1839 Gülhane Decree came to confirm and sanction trends that had begun earlier, but it also formalized a state of affairs that was now to be taken for granted when further reforms were to be imposed in the future. This Decree, in effect an Ottoman payment to the superpowers (Britain, Austria, Prussia and Russia) for their aid against the separatist Egyptian Muḥammad ʿAlī, rejected traditional economic forms and declared material wealth a desideratum. All indigenous impediments to economic development were to be removed, and the model of change would become European culture, science and capital.[8]

While the decline of the Ottoman economy was among the major factors in precipitating the so-called reforms, the latter in turn managed to impoverish the economy and as a result wreak havoc with old social and economic structures. In earlier periods, protectionism meant that the suppliers of raw materials, whether local peasants and farmers or foreign suppliers, were bound to sell to the guilds at controlled prices, usually determined by the government and sanctioned by the *qāḍī*. The gradual elimination of protectionism, coupled with a sharp rise in the price of raw materials, left most, if not all, the guilds during the first half of the nineteenth century virtually bankrupt, a fact that led to their extinction soon afterwards. For example, the important and sizeable guild of silk cloth-makers, which supplied Ottoman officialdom with their uniforms, faced such a fate due to its inability to secure affordable raw materials.[9] The elimination of this centuries-old guild forced a change in official dress that was not only Western in style, but also manufactured in Britain with cotton that was cheaply secured from colonized India.[10] The ramifications of this process, initiated and encouraged by the

[8] See Mardin, "Development of the Sharīʿa," 284. For the full text of the Decree, see Hertslet, *Map of Europe*, II, 1002–05.

[9] Quataert, "Age of Reform," 890–91.

[10] See Issawi, "De-industrialization and Re-industrialization," 470, where he states that, in the 1820s and 1830s, factories "in Europe were pouring out cheap goods, and peace and increased security in the Mediterranean made it possible to land them in the Middle East

reforms, were graver than the limited phenomenon of guild decline and extinction. With their disappearance as a market force, the Ottoman economy was transformed into a mere supplier of raw materials, the monetary and market value of which was, like Indian cotton, determined by European manufacturers.[11] Yet another devastating effect resulting from the collapse of guilds was the vacuum left in a sphere in which they played a crucial role, namely, judicial organization and the administration of urban populations (discussed in chapters 4 and 5, above). Their vanished administrative functions thus left a gap that the rising modern state, with its apparatus of surveillance, was only too willing to take over.

Opening Ottoman markets to European capitalism was only a part of what the Gülhane Decree was intended, both directly and obliquely, to accomplish, though it was perhaps the most important goal. Another, better-known, aspect of the Decree – not entirely separate from this goal – was to grant equality to all subjects of the Empire, irrespective of their religion. The new distributive freedoms had of course little to do with any intrinsic democratic interest that Europe had in the religious minorities of the Ottoman Empire, and much more with increasing European interests among segments of Ottoman populations that might act as middlemen, in both the economic and political spheres. Having secured the Ottoman economic market as a source of raw materials and having ensured the political cooperation of the sultanate, the European powers found it unnecessary to break up the Empire, now the so-called "sick man of Europe." Keeping the sick man alive was also dictated by the rival interests of Russia, Britain and France, whose potential disagreement over how the Empire might be divided amongst them kept such a division a remote possibility, at least until the middle of World War I. That the Empire was "sick" became, by virtue of European military and economic superiority, a self-evident reality; that it had been "of Europe," being all but directly colonized by it, was an undeniable truth.

at low cost ... To this should be added the effects of several treaties concluded between Middle Eastern and European governments, treatises that froze import duties at very low levels and opened up the Middle Eastern market ... *As a result, in Turkey and Iran internal duties paid by native producers were much higher than import and other duties paid by foreigners* ... [T]he impact was confined to the ports and coastal area, but with the development of railways and improvements of road transport in the latter decades of the nineteenth century it gradually spread inland. The effect of the textile trade was catastrophic ... [In Iran, Iraq and Tunisia] a similar process was under way" (emphasis mine).

11 On these developments in Greater Syria, see the work of Chevallier, "Western Development and Eastern Crisis," 205–22; Turgay, "British–German Trade Rivalry," 168–87, esp. at 168–73.

Similar developments occurred on the Iranian front under the Qājārs (1779–1924). Within four decades of their coming to power, the Qājārs had suffered crushing military defeats at the hands of the Russians and, just as in the Ottoman Empire, by 1828 Iran lost much of its territory in the Caucasus as well as all rights to navigate the Caspian Sea. The 1828 Treaty of Turcomanchay, and the Persian–British treaty of 1836, placed foreign subjects and their property outside Persian jurisdiction, and created special tribunals to adjudicate cases involving foreigners and Persians. As happened in the Ottoman Empire, no judicial decision of these courts could be deemed valid or binding without the final approval, not of Persian courts, but of the consul or ambassador. In addition to this political subjugation, wars with Russia and the Ottomans had a devastating effect on Iran's economy and reduced the populations of its major cities to half their usual size. Identical effects began to show themselves in the independent Muslim principalities in Transoxiana, Afghanistan and North Africa. The Khanate of Khīva and the Mangits lost their continental trade and were reduced to no more than local, small-time merchants. The usurpation by the Europeans of the sea trade and the unprecedented efficiency of European navigation significantly detracted from the importance of land routes, the backbone of Irano-Transoxianan commerce. By the middle of the nineteenth century, it was a rare Muslim country that had escaped surrendering its political and juridical powers in favor of foreign nationals and, particularly, in favor of European states.

2. The reconstitution of the Ottoman legal system

Inasmuch as the Gülhane Decree of 1839 ushered new ideas into Ottoman conceptual and political life, it also formally acknowledged and sanctioned foundational transformations that had been underway for some time.[12] The previous year had, for instance, seen the promulgation of a new penal code pertaining to Sharīʿa judges and *Ḳazaskers* (Ar. *Qāḍī-ʿaskars*), together with administrative and organizational reforms that had already begun during the preceding decade under the direction of Mahmud II. A year earlier, in 1837, an imperial committee had been convened to prepare a series of proposals for judicial and administrative reforms, to draft codes and administer their implementation. But all this had roughly been on the minds of reformers since 1826, if not sometime before. For it was in this year, and for the first time in Islamic history, that

[12] Cf. Abu Manneh, "The Islamic Roots of the Gülhane Rescript."

the *vakıfs* (Ar. *waqfs*) supervised by the Dārüssade Ağa, the Şeyhülislam (Ar. Shaykh al-Islām), the grand vizier and a number of important others were placed under the control of Mahmud II's new Imperial Ministry of Endowments, thus depriving these particular statesmen of an independent economic base. Shortly thereafter, the incomes of more substantial *vakıfs* were claimed by the Ministry, "until the major *evkaf* of all the chief dignitaries of state had been taken away from them."[13] Within less than a decade, the well-nigh absolute powers of the Ministry[14] had enabled it to seize the incomes of all major *vakıfs* in the Empire, in the process creating salaried posts for local notables who would administer the endowments on behalf of Istanbul.

The Ministry further seized the Water Works Administration, since public fountains and the public water supply were largely constituted as *vakıf* endowments. But the most striking fact about these expropriations was the volume of property involved. At the beginning of the nineteenth century, it is estimated, more than half of real property in the Empire was consecrated as *vakıf*.[15] The government's economic and political gains were thus enormous: economically, it had become the "middleman" who secured considerable profits in the process of collecting the revenues of the endowments and then paying out salaries for the minimal upkeep and operation of the *vakıf*-foundations. In part due to the government's diverting of funds to military and other projects, and in part due to corruption within the ranks of the Ministry,[16] this pay-back of salaries to the educational and other public endowments progressively declined, reaching zero point by the middle of the century. The central *vakıf* administration was charged with financing and supervising, at its own expense and obviously from endowment money, military and public projects, such as the building of tramways in Istanbul and of yarn factories for the production of military uniforms[17] – all of which were intended to, and did indeed, strengthen the emerging modern state, but at the expense of the traditional recipients of the *vakıf* revenues.

[13] Barnes, *Introduction*, 74: "It was Mahmud's intention that the majority of landed property and roofed property revenue … should return to its original condition as property belonging to the state. This was not an idle claim, for the majority of evkaf in the Ottoman dominions was arāzī-i emiriye-i mevkufe, mīrī (state) lands that were made vekif; more specifically, the taxes to mīrī lands had been made vakıf … The principle applied was that property which originally belonged to the state remained with the state. And in this respect all evkaf was evkaf-ı hümayūn (royal *waqfs*)" (85–86). See also Çizakça, *History*, 84–85; Deguilhem, "Government Centralization of Waqf," 224–26.

[14] Çizakça, *History*, 81–82. [15] Barnes, *Introduction*, 83. [16] Çizakça, *History*, 82–83.

[17] Barnes, *Introduction*, 127; Çizakça, *History*, 85; Öztürk, "Batılılaşma Döneminde Vakıfların Çözülmesine," 301–02. I owe this reference to Selim Argun.

The mosques, and the *medresses* (Ar. *madrasas*) along with them, appeared to many observers to stand at the brink of total collapse.[18] These "middleman" profits – shared in part by the presumably salaried notables – thus correspondingly dulled, albeit momentarily and to a limited extent, the severity of the financial crises of the Empire. Politically, the absorption of the *vakıfs* into the central imperial administration weakened the allies of the now vanished Janissaries, i.e., the ulama and the *softas* (law students) who had shown some resistance to the early reforms.[19] Thus, the reorganization of *vakıf* administration, which reflected the rise of an aggressive new form of bureaucratization, delivered, together with the abolition of the Janissaries, the first major blow to the strong position of the traditional legal profession in the Empire. (The Iranian experience also attests to an overarching systemic transformation that led to an *étatist* administration of *waqf*. In 1854, the Ministry of Pensions and Awqāf was created, and a decade later it became mandatory for every *waqf* foundation and administrator to register with the Ministry all assets under their control.)

The salarization of *vakıf* administration constituted the first step toward the salarization of the entire legal profession, which was to take effect in the wake of the 1839 Decree. During this period, there was a series of minor, but important, judicial reforms that aimed at instituting new policies for judicial appointments, including entry exams, and the replacement of court fees as funding for the judiciary – a hallmark of Ottoman practice – by salaries.[20] Like all other civil servants, the *qāḍīs* were now prohibited from collecting dues on inheritance division or for issuing deeds or court documents.[21] Their monthly salary was to be paid directly by a salaried imperial comptroller (*muhassıl*; Ar. *muḥaṣṣil*) who had now himself been charged with collecting all court revenues.[22] Furthermore, in an effort to create a clear distinction between the judicial

[18] Barnes, *Introduction*, 118–20, invoking the commentary of Charles McFarlane, Bishop Southgate, and the British consul to the island of Rhodes. The latter wrote that "[e]ducation morally and physically is set aside. Notwithstanding ... a soup kitchen at Rhodes from which soup is distributed thrice a week to the indigent musulmans, no other pious or benevolent institutions exist on the island. There is no hospital, no infirmary, no asylum; the lame, the blind, the mad, and the old are all left to their fate." In the same vein, McFarlane, exceptional in comparison with his compatriots, severely criticized the reformers who "have laid their greedy hands on nearly all the vakoufs [= *waqfs*] of the empire ... Hence, with very few exceptions, we see the heads of the mosques and the medressehs in abject poverty, the rabble of [religious] students in rags, the most beautiful of the temples and minarets shamefully neglected and hurrying into decay ... It is notorious that since the vakoufs have been administered by the government nothing has been done to maintain the works of public utility."

[19] Heyd, "Ottoman Ulema," 35.

[20] Hertslet, *Map of Europe*, II, 1005.

[21] See chapter 5, section 4, above.

[22] İnalcık, "Application of the Tanzimat," 100.

and executive spheres, the provincial governors as well as the grand vizier were deprived of their tribunals,[23] thus becoming an integral part of the steadily centralized court system.

These fundamental changes were made to be concomitant with institutional restructuring. Already in 1838, Mahmud II created the so-called Supreme Council of Judicial Ordinances, a body that not only prepared the grounds for the later Niẓāmiyye (Ar. Niẓāmiyya) courts but also signaled the removal of the judiciary from the Sharīʿa domain to that of the state. The Supreme Council set itself up as the highest court in the land, controlling and supervising the activities of all courts as well as all quasi-judicial assemblies of provincial governors.

In 1840, and in the spirit of the 1839 Decree, a modern-style penal code that was yet grounded in Islamic criminal precepts was promulgated. Closely following the *maẓālim* conception of governance, this code was duly concerned with the misconduct of public officials. Furthermore, new local councils began to be formed of civil notables, a *qāḍī*, a *muftī*, and representatives of the local communities, including non-Muslims. These councils were, much as before the reform, responsible for civil, judicial and financial matters, but their new organization and formal constitution were intended to mark a departure from the traditional, *qāḍī*-centered administration. Whereas the *qāḍī* had been the leading judicial and administrative officer in the pre-reform councils, he was now relegated to a secondary position, or at least as one among many others of equal importance.[24] The new leaders were the government employees, the administrators and those who were soon to become the bureaucrats. It was these persons, together with the notables representing segments of the community, who were in charge of hearing the major suits brought before the *qāḍī*'s court. Whereas before the reform the "court assembly" assisting the *qāḍī* in *legal matters* consisted of the learned scholars (*ahl al-ʿilm*), now they were non-Sharʿī figures who represented the interests of the community in an official, state-determined capacity. These officials emerged, as before, from within the community, but it was now the central government, not the social ecology[25] and the local consensual and communitarian perception of leadership, that decided how, when and under what conditions they should serve. This shuffling of powers, as H. İnalcik has rightly noted, "was aimed at bringing provincial administration under more stringent control by the central government by freeing it somewhat from the power of the local *ulemā* and notables."[26]

[23] Heyd, "Ottoman Ulema," 51.
[24] İnalcık, "Application of the Tanzimat," 108.
[25] See chapter 4, section 3, above.
[26] İnalcık, "Application of the Tanzimat," 108.

However, aside from installing a modern system aimed at improving the method of tax collection,[27] the most serious change that came in the wake of the Gülhane Decree was the gradual rise of the Niẓāmiyye courts, named after the so-called New Order (Niẓām-i Cedīd; Ar. Niẓām Jadīd; hence Tanẓīmāt). This Order, which produced new courts, new laws, a new judicial process and – by the end of the century – a new legal culture, operated at the nominal instigation of the sultan who, for the first time in the history of the Empire (and of Islam as a whole), placed himself as well as his bureaucratic legislative council above the Sharīʿa. His power to legislate the *ḳānūn*s (Ar. *qānūn*s), which had complemented and supplemented but had never overridden the Sharīʿa and its *fiqh*, now became overarching and universal.

This process of course did not happen overnight, and took a few decades after the Gülhane Decree to accomplish, but the structural and substantive transformations in the sultan's legal power began to occur before the first half of the nineteenth century had come to a close. To argue, therefore, that the Sultan's New Order promulgations constituted and represented a natural extension of his *siyāsa sharʿiyya* powers (which generated the *ḳānūn*s) amounts not only to missing the obvious qualitative differences in the introduction of this Order but also to ignoring the colossal external forces that were shaping and determining the way the Empire was to run its business.[28] These forces, however, depended on the indigenous support of Istanbul's Westernized bureaucrats, who stood firmly behind the sultan's moves, if they didn't actually pull the strings. It was Rashīd Pasha, the Ottoman ambassador to London and Paris, who, during the 1830s, was Istanbul's prime mover in the direction of reform *à la française*. The sultans after Mahmud II were somewhat less interested. But the push for modernization nonetheless intensified when the influential Rashīd Pasha – having assumed the office of grand vizier several times, and served twice as foreign minister – began promoting and grooming reform-minded men who would inherit his ambition to refashion the Ottoman Empire "in the image of Europe."[29] The story of reform between the 1840s and late 1860s was very much the creation of Rashīd and his two successors and "disciples": Ali Pasha (1815–71) and Fuat Pasha (1815–69).

The sultan's powers – largely representing the will-to-power of these three men, and reflecting the enormous European and Russian pressures on the Empire – at first began to encroach on the religious law from the

27 A point constantly argued by İnalcık, *ibid.*, 102–16, and *passim*.
28 Cf. Abu Manneh, "The Islamic Roots of the Gülhane Rescript."
29 Cleveland, *History*, 82.

outside, namely from areas which the Sharīʿa did not directly regulate and where it required the sovereign to enact supplementary laws as part of his *siyāsa sharʿiyya* duties. A commercial Niẓāmiyye court was first established in Istanbul with a jurisdiction pertaining to disputes between and among Ottoman subjects and European nationals. A criminal court, with the same jurisdiction between various nationals, was created in 1847. In addition to the pluralistic constitution of magistracy presiding over the bench, these courts introduced a new procedural principle whereby the weight of testimony was not determined by religious status; thus Christians and Jews, Ottoman or not, could testify against their Muslim fellow subjects. Yet, what was striking about the powers of these new courts, especially the latter, was the fact that foreign consuls and consular representatives of European states enjoyed the right to veto the decisions of the court against their respective nationals, thus in effect holding powers that entitled them to entirely neutralize court verdicts at will.

Under clear French influence, the first Westernized code of commerce was promulgated in 1850. A second penal code was introduced the next year, defining, with more specific details, the jurisdictional boundaries between the Sharīʿa courts and the new criminal courts. In 1854, the Supreme Council was transformed into the Supreme Council of the Tanẓīmāt, making one of its first acts the promulgation of a new criminal code (1854) that showed the greatest dependence yet, this time on the French penal code of 1810. The new name of the Supreme Council epitomized the worldview of the Ottoman modernizers who saw in their reforms a means to accomplish "order," "regularity" and "law," all of which stood in diametrical opposition to the steadily diminishing Sharīʿa culture that was perceived as lacking on these counts. In their totality, "*niẓām*," "*niẓāmiyye*" and "*tanẓīmāt*" constituted a regimenting discursive practice, and reflected Foucauldian notions of discipline, law, inspection and incarceration. Indeed, these notions found expression not only in the evolving judicial structures and codes (as well as reporting,[30] statistics,[31] centralized supervision and surveillance), but also in

[30] It suffices to mention here the *Ceride-i Mehakim*, a legal digest that was – thanks to the modern technology of mass print and communication – centrally produced and intended to homogenize judicial practices throughout the Empire. It provided a register of hard cases that could be, and were, used as a basis for the uniform application of law. Arguably, the *Ceride* promoted a notion of *Stare Decisis* which we have discussed in the context of the Anglo-Muhammadan Law in India (see previous chapter). On the *Ceride* and its use as a source for writing Ottoman legal history, see Rubin, "Ottoman Modernity." On the role of print technology in the reform, see Opwis, "Changes in Modern Islamic Legal Theory," 33–36, and sources cited therein.

[31] Müge Göçek and Hanioğlu, "Western Knowledge, Imperial Control."

the significant fact that the Niẓāmiyye legal order generated – along with a distinctive legal culture of its own – an unprecedented and colossal prison system that was part of this culture and that could accommodate inmates for up to twenty years. Contrast this with the fact that such prison terms and prison systems were entirely unknown to the Sharīʿa.

With the conclusion of the Crimean wars of 1853–56, the Ottomans incurred further debts to France and Britain, both politically (for their military support against the Russians) and financially (for the major loans the British made to Istanbul).[32] These debts translated into further, intense hegemonic pressures on the Porte, resulting in another series of concessions embodied in the Humāyūn Decree of 1856. Unlike its 1839 predecessor, which was compiled by Ottoman senior statesmen, the 1856 Decree was drafted with intensive consultation of the French, British and Austrian ambassadors. It moved further away from the Islamic principles of governance, not mentioning the Quran or the Sharīʿa once, for instance.[33] It emphasized European-style representative government, and further gave non-Muslim minorities formal rights (again, defined by Western conceptions of governance) equal to those enjoyed by the Muslim subjects of the Empire. This was not only a European imposition, but an Ottoman strategy that aimed at appeasing and absorbing the nationalist sentiments that were making themselves known in the provinces. The constitution of the new Niẓāmiyye courts reflected this new reality no less than did the structural changes in the laws of evidence and procedure.

Commercial, penal and even civil courts were to be created with justices of mixed nationalities, a fact that gave these courts the epithet of "mixed courts." Already in 1846, the reformist Ahmet Çevdet Pasha – certainly not a secularist – was chosen to chair the Committee of Justice which had begun to codify various laws, an effort that culminated in the promulgation of the Penal Code of 1858 and the Land Law of the same year. Likewise, a series of French-inspired commercial codes, including a maritime commercial code, were promulgated for the benefit of the new courts. Each of these codes was introduced in the midst of a constellation of circumstances that were governed by a powerful agenda, namely, to strengthen the central government and increase its revenues. Under the increasing pressure of growing debts to European lenders, the criminal and commercial codes were introduced with a view to regulating the social and economic orders in the provinces, which had grown too powerful for Istanbul.

[32] See, e.g., Hertslet, *Map of Europe*, II, 1234–36, and *passim*. [33] *Ibid.*, II, 1243–49.

Similarly, the Land Law of 1858 required the cultivators of state land (*mīrī*) to register their lots under their names, a step intended to secure direct payment of taxes to the central government, thus eliminating the intermediaries who traditionally claimed a percentage of the revenue. In Egypt, the process had started earlier, but in all cases the land code, in both of its varieties, was also designed to implement a policy aimed at tying the peasants to the land.[34] Although it was purported that these modernizing codes were conceived as a contribution to the emergence of private property,[35] their effects on peasants (a large segment of the population) were disastrous in more than one way. Fearing conscription and excessive taxes, they registered the lands they cultivated in the name of deceased family members, city magnates or rural notables. The end result was the conversion of their position from controllers of land to tenants who could be evicted at will. Another result in some regions was a sudden dispossession of land, since the absentee landlords could, and did, sell large lots without consideration of any rights the peasants might have (the same situation that obtained in Palestine where Zionist agencies purchased much of the land from notables who lived outside of the country).[36]

The new land code (in both the Ottoman Empire and Egypt) had the remarkable effect of producing, toward the end of the century, a landed class that rivaled the religious elite in terms of political and material power. The families who profited from the changes brought about by the new land and other codes, and by the emerging bureaucratic and administrative structures, were secular in orientation. Yet, some religious families also held large tracts of land, continued to hold on to their positions of power, and managed to partake in the advantages these land codes had created for members of the upper social strata. And in order to compete in the market of new economic realities, they inserted themselves in the secular bureaucracies of the state, gradually changing their "specialization" and identity as members of a privileged religious establishment.[37] By the end of the century, the children of these families, both

[34] A declared goal of the Ministry of Agriculture, established for the first time in 1846, was to settle Bedouins, and force them to cultivate land and pay taxes. See Karpat, "Land Regime," 86.

[35] Yet another function of the code. See, in this context, chapter 13, above. For an insightful analysis of notions of private property in Islamic and Western law, see Akarlı, "Gedik," 168–69.

[36] See Khoury, *Urban Notables*, 26–28; Karpat, "Land Regime," 69–90. For Egypt, see Mitchell, *Rule of Experts*, 54–79. On the Palestine land purchase, see Shafir, *Land, Labor and the Origins of the Israeli–Palestinian Conflict*, 22–36 and *passim*. I owe the latter reference to Gabi Piterberg.

[37] Khoury, *Urban Notables*, 28.

secular and originally religious, were largely integrated into the state bureaucratic machinery and politics at the district, provincial and national levels. This social transformation of the religious elite explains, at least in good measure, why the upper ulama class did not mount any serious resistance to the major changes that took place, *inter alia*, in the legal system.[38]

In the midst of these foundational and structural changes, European pressures on Istanbul continued to increase dramatically. Deeply in debt after the Crimean wars, the Ottomans secured, in 1860, substantial loans from Britain, but not without the latter attaching to the loan-agreement certain political and economic strings. As if the capitulations and concessions in favor of foreign nationals were not enough, the British demanded and secured further allowances pertaining to the purchase of real property in the Empire. The introduction of the land codes, which had essentially privatized real property, was one step in this direction. But in order to maximize the opportunity for profit, they also demanded, and received the promise, that the *vaḳıf* system – which barred much real property from entering the open market – would be abolished.[39]

Over the next two decades, the pressure was renewed with added vigor by both the British and the French, whose scholars – doubling as colonialist officers – were already propounding the idea that *vaḳıf*s not only reflected a primitive mode of existence and belonged to the decadent history of the now maligned "church," but also impeded economic development and thus the much desired "progress."[40] These pressures, coupled with Istanbul's conviction of the superiority of Western culture, created a mood among the reformist bureaucrats that translated into a massive ideological campaign portraying *vaḳıf* as a cause of cultural malaise and material decline. In 1909 the reformers moved aggressively against the *vaḳıf*, thus initiating a process which led eventually to its abolition in the Turkish Republic and elsewhere. But the ideological preparation for this move had been underway since as early as the middle of the preceding century.

In 1864, with the Law of Provincial Administration, there came a significant, but short-lived, attempt at reorganizing and restructuring the judiciary at the provincial level, where a two-tiered set of courts (called in fact "councils") was created, one of first instance and the other of

[38] Further on this theme, see section 4, below. On the correspondence of this transformation to conscious colonial knowledge, see Massignon, "Résultats sociaux," 565.

[39] Çizakça, *History*, 80; Öztürk, *Türk Yenileşme Tarihi Çerçevesinde Vakıf Müessesesi*, 192. I owe the latter reference to Selim Argun.

[40] See section 6, below.

appeal. The latter, a second-instance court, was composed of three Muslim magistrates and three non-Muslims (all of whom were Ottoman). On the bench of the former there presided, in equal numbers, Sharīʿa judges as well as elected members of the civil service, signaling a yet further step in formalizing the process by which civil officers and technocrats had now come to share the judicial powers of the *qāḍī*s. Conversely, installing Sharīʿa judges in the new courts[41] suggests that there was a confluence between the traditional and new legal professions, one that barred the drawing of neat lines of separation between the two systems. This concourse was further augmented by the fact that the Sharīʿa courts themselves also underwent a modernizing administrative and procedural reorganization, although their jurisdiction was becoming increasingly limited to the spheres of personal status and *vaḳıf*. The *nāʾib*s (provincial *qāḍī*s) were classified into five ranks, and their tenure was limited to two years in any one place that was not the home of the *nāʾib* himself.[42] The old principle of rotation (mostly an Ottoman practice anyway) was greatly reinforced, leaving the villages and towns of the provinces in the hands of judges who were not always familiar with the distinctive local customs (a process that ultimately contributed to the homogenization of regional differences and to the creation of the streamlined citizen of the state).

This centralizing policy was combined with another: now, all levels and ranks of the Sharīʿa – and Niẓāmiyye – judiciary were appointed by Istanbul, and the age-long principle of judicial delegation ceased for good. This administrative act, together with the payment of salaries directly from Istanbul, further consolidated centralized control, and transformed the Sharīʿa court into the direct hand of the state. Judicial centralization was manifested in the creation, as part of the Niẓāmiyye courts, of the Court of Cassation (Mahkeme-i Temyīz), whose seat was in Istanbul, comprising both civil and criminal sections. And for the benefit of supervision by the Istanbul Ministry of Justice, all courts were ordered to report the cases they adjudicated once every three months.[43]

The increasing intervention of the state gained further momentum in 1868 when the Supreme Council of Judicial Ordinances was for the first time split into two bodies, one intended to be legislative and the other judicial. The former acquired the name "Council of State," a clear French

[41] Including the integration of the essentially Ḥanafite *Mecelle* (Ar. *Majalla*) into their fields of application, as we shall shortly see.

[42] Agmon, "Social Biography," 88.

[43] In practice, however, the courts did not fully abide by this order, especially in the beginning. See Rubin, "Ottoman Modernity," 56. On keeping detailed *maḥḍar*s in Sharīʿa courts, see also further below.

influence, while the latter became known as the High Court of Justice. Thus, the law, which was earlier made and applied by the jurists themselves, was now made to originate from within state organs that were deemed not only judicial but also exclusively legislative, which is another way of saying that the state began to arrogate to itself the right not only to apply the law but to decide what it was.

The transposition of Islamic law from the fairly independent and informal terrain of the jurists to that of the highly formalized and centralized agency of the state found manifestation in the compendium entitled *Mecelle-i Ahkām-ı Adliye* (Ar. *Majallat al-Aḥkām al-ʿAdliyya*),[44] produced by a committee headed by the Sharīʿa jurist Ahmet Çevdet Pasha who, on this score at least, won the debate against the powerful Westernizer Ali Pasha. The latter had called for the adoption of the French *Code Civil* of 1804 (known as the *Code Napoléon*),[45] but Ahmet Çevdet Pasha insisted that the law had to be faithful to the cultural constitution of the Empire. Between 1870 and 1877, the sixteen books making up the *Mecelle* (containing 1,851 articles in the Turkish language) were published, all dealing with civil law and procedure to the exclusion of marriage and divorce. One of the aims of the *Mecelle* was to provide, in the manner of a code,[46] a clear and systematic statement of the law for the benefit of *both* the Sharīʿa and Niẓāmiyye courts, a statement that was geared to a professional elite that had lost touch with Arabicate juristic hermeneutics. Yet, the source of this codification was the *corpus juris* of the Ḥanafite school, especially those opinions within it that seemed to the drafters to offer – especially in their reconstituted form – a modernized version of Islamic law, which Ahmet Çevdet Pasha himself thought to "suit the present conditions."[47] The opinions chosen did not necessarily reflect the authoritative doctrines in the Ḥanafite school, nor were they, strictly speaking, all exclusively Ḥanafite, for some of them were imported from the other schools after being generally approved by the later Ḥanafites.[48]

The *Mecelle* was to be implemented in the Niẓāmiyye courts, whose staff were increasingly being trained in non-*fiqh* law. But since no juristic opinion was truly binding on any judge without the sovereign's intervention, the *Mecelle*, after its complete publication, was promulgated as a sultanic code (a momentous act sanctioning, once and for all, the supreme authority of the state, and depressing that of the Sharīʿa). Yet, while in

[44] Later the object of many commentaries. See, e.g., Bāz, *Sharḥ*; Ḥaydar, *Durar al-Ḥukkām*; and Kāshif al-Ghiṭāʾ, *Taḥrīr al-Majalla*.

[45] See chapter 16, section 2, on the role of this *Code* in the development of a new patriarchy.

[46] See chapter 13, above. [47] Onar, "Majalla," 295.

[48] Anderson, "Law Reform in Egypt," 217.

structure and appearance the *Mecelle* was code-like, it did not really function as codes do, enjoying unrivaled, exclusive authority.[49] In practice, it continued to coexist with the books of the jurists, or whatever was left of them on the benches of the slowly vanishing *qāḍīs*. And it was soon to have a fierce rival in the 1880 Code of Civil Procedure, modeled, again, after the French example. Toward the close of the century, procedure was steadily and rapidly gaining greater importance, it being increasingly seen, in the manner of all modern legal systems, as the backbone of the law. The highly formalized and complex procedural processes represented a large domain in which the Sharīʿa was almost totally replaced.

It was obvious to the reformers and even to their opponents that the venture of the *Mecelle* was a last-ditch effort to salvage the Sharīʿa as a law in force, but it was also an attempted remedy applied to a problem that had originated as a remedy. The systematic substitution of Turkish for Arabic as the language of instruction in new schools[50] was in part a phenomenon integral to the intentional spreading of nationalist feelings that were harnessed as a tool to keep the Empire from disintegrating into various ethnic groupings. The Sharīʿa faced the challenge of adapting not only to the rapidly changing economic and material conditions brought about by modernity, but also to a linguistic de-centering whereby the new institutions and the legal personnel that staffed them literally communicated in a language that was not the language of the traditional law.[51]

Thus, the Sharīʿa's rival was not only the modern state, but the nationalism that the state had so efficiently harnessed.[52] The *Mecelle* was thus as much an attempted linguistic (i.e., nationalist) remedy as it was a legal one (although its production also created another dialectic by which, on the one hand, knowledge of the Arabicate tradition – central to the law – was weakened, and on the other, the chances of success in closing the gap between any *Mecelle*-like effort and the demands of the economic and political orders were greatly reduced). Ultimately, however, the *Mecelle* was less about such linguistic–nationalist matters than it was about a discreet political assertion of *legal* power. It said once and for all that, like the now centralized Sharīʿa courts themselves, the *fiqh* from now on was not the province of the jurists but rather that of the state. If the reforms were to work, then there could be no distinction between administration, laws and codes: everything had to be centralized. And if European

[49] See chapter 13, above. [50] Further on these new schools, see below.
[51] On the global movement of using language as a means of constructing nationalism, see the insightful analysis in Anderson, *Imagined Communities*, especially 67–82.
[52] On nationalism as the secularized religion of the state, see Asad, *Formations of the Secular*, 187–94.

governments achieved success by commanding the law and its judicial system, the senior Ottoman bureaucrats thought, so must we.

As the nineteenth century progressed, Ottoman central power grew ever stronger. True, the political example that Europe provided, and which it itself followed, was an important factor. But it was also the readiness of the European powers to expend whatever it took to build in Istanbul a strong centralized government, as they no doubt preferred to secure privileges from a strong center rather than from a multiplicity of provincial governments. Banks (1856), railroads (1854) and the telegraph were successively introduced to the sultans, but the latter were not always as aggressive in installing these modern techniques in their realm. The Morse Telegraph, for instance, was first shown to ʿAbd al-Majīd in 1847, but was not adopted until much later.

Yet, on the whole, the European model of a centralized state was steadily being realized due to the gradual loss of Ottoman territory, which permitted the bureaucrats, with the help of modern technology, to tighten their grip over a less expansive Empire. At the same time, the size of the bureaucratic machine grew, like its European counterpart, to colossal proportions, needing half a million civil servants to operate it before the century came to a close.[53] Bureaucratic centralization manifested itself in the appropriation of what had before always lain in the non-governmental sphere. Between 1847 and 1869, for example, a significant wave of change in the realm of education was effected.[54] During the former year, a Ministry of Public Education was established, and in 1851 the Academy of Arts and Sciences was created for the purpose, *inter alia*, of drafting textbooks for public schools. More than a decade and a half later, in 1869, the Regulation of Public Education Act – prepared under the guidance of the French Minister of Education[55] – brought the different schools in the Empire under a single comprehensive system, and declared natural sciences superior to all other fields of knowledge (including jurisprudence, deemed in Islamic cultures as the queen of all sciences).[56] For the first time, every school was to report to the Ministry in Istanbul, where educational methods and subject-matter were centrally determined and, thereby, removed as far as possible from the religious realm. This policy represented a near-universal tendency, insightfully described by Benedict Anderson in the context of inventing nationalism:

[53] Quataert, "Age of Reforms," 765. Also see Heyd, "Ottoman Ulema," 47. On the importance of bureaucracy in the construction of the modern nation-state, see Gerth and Mills, *From Max Weber*, 196–244; van Creveld, *Rise and Decline*, 128–43.

[54] On reengineering the educational system, see Fortna, *Imperial Classroom.*

[55] Somel, *Modernization of Public Education*, 4, 86; Fortna, *Imperial Classroom*, 15, 27, 113.

[56] Although theology competed for this title. See Hallaq, "Logic, Formal Arguments," 333.

> [O]ne has to remember that in complete contrast to traditional, indigenous schools, which were always local and personal enterprises (even if, in good Muslim fashion, there was plenty of horizontal movement of students from one particularly well-reputed ulama-teacher to another), the government schools formed a colossal, highly rationalized, tightly centralized hierarchy, structurally analogous to the state bureaucracy itself. Uniform textbooks, standardized diplomas and teaching certificates, a strictly regulated gradation of age-groups, classes and instructional materials, in themselves created a self-contained, coherent universe of experience. But no less important was the hierarchy's geography. Standardized elementary schools came to be scattered about in villages and small townships ... junior and senior middle-schools in larger towns and provincial centers; while tertiary education (the pyramid's apex) was confined to the colonial capital ... [The students] knew that from wherever they had come they still had read the same books and done the same sums. They also knew ... that all these journeyings derived their "sense" from the capital, in effect explaining why "we" are "here" together.[57]

These legal and educational changes were implemented *mutatis mutandis* in the capital and the various provinces. Iraq, to some extent, constituted an exception, in that it was taken from the Qājārs as late as 1843 when the reforms had already long begun. The Ottomans granted no exceptions to the local Shīʿite population and its *mujtahid*s. The occupation began with the imposition of Sunnite forms of worship in Shīʿite mosques and the takeover of the shrines of Karbala and Najaf. This policy was in good measure motivated by financial considerations, and expressed through such means as the imposition of the *waqf* reforms – already implemented in Ottoman lands in 1826 – on the shrine cities and their large endowments. Most importantly, the Ottomans introduced Ḥanafite courts in place of their Shīʿite counterparts, declaring invalid all rulings emanating from the latter (to my knowledge, an unprecedented imposition in Islamic history).[58] This change not only signified the dominance and sovereignty of the new masters – whose smallest administrative unit had for long been the Ḥanafite law court – but also weakened the Shīʿite religious hierarchy by depriving it of the financial benefits that accrued to it from court fees (not to mention *waqf* revenues and the alms-tax), while simultaneously propping up and enriching the Ottoman provincial treasury.

Yet, the effects of the reforms were not seriously felt in Iraq until the appointment of Midhat Pasha as governor in 1869, when he embarked on

[57] Anderson, *Imagined Communities*, 121–22.

[58] Even the Ṣafavids (907–1145/1501–1732), who converted Iran from a dominantly Ḥanafite to a Shīʿite jurisprudence, accomplished the task by a gradual process, not by an oppressive jural colonization as the modernizing Ottomans were to do later in Iraq. For an excellent account of this Ṣafavid project, see Abisaab, *Converting Persia*.

the introduction of several modernizing measures ranging from settling tribes and creating city councils (as had already happened elsewhere in the Empire) to building secular schools in Sunnite Iraq. The educational reforms did not affect the Shīʿite population in any significant way. Rather, it was the conscription of the Shīʿite *madrasa* students which caused massive migrations out of Iraq, and which resulted in the registration of major *mujtahid* families as Iranian nationals. The alienation of the Shīʿites created a major rift that could never permit their accommodation, and therefore the province of Iraq itself, within the Empire.[59]

The final series of major acts aimed at consolidating the Ottoman state's legal powers began in 1879 and lasted until the Young Turks era. A Ministry of Justice, which was to bring under its wings the Sharīʿa and Niẓāmiyye courts, was established in 1879, thus unifying a hitherto fairly heterogeneous system. Several codes pertaining to the competence of tribunals, judicial salaries, public prosecution, and civil and criminal procedure came into existence. Until 1879, there was still one Court of Cassation in Istanbul, and the lines of demarcation between the jurisdictions of the courts of first instance and those of appeal were not always clear. Thus, a three-tiered court system was supposed to be established, including a series of arbitration courts in the villages, but these were not actually created until much later, and then only in a gradual manner. The provincial capitals were each allocated an appeals court which was to hear both criminal and civil cases directed to them from courts of first instance. Unlike Sharīʿa courts, all new courts functioned using a panel of judges whose number varied from one court, or level of court, to the next. But the provincial Sharīʿa judges continued, until 1908, to function in the new courts, especially the provincial Sharīʿa Chief Justice who also presided over the civil section of the provincial court of appeal. Even more significant was the establishment in this period of new law schools to train judges and lawyers who would staff the new Niẓāmiyye courts.[60]

A decade later, in 1888, a new system of examinations and rules for the appointment of judges was established. In the new system, judges were assigned by the Ministry of Justice, abrogating the policy of their election instituted earlier. Another act of 1888 required the Ministry to maintain – in perfect keeping with the modern state – systematic records on every official working in the judicial system. The Sharīʿa courts themselves were also instructed to expand their documentary range, recording not only the

59 Litvak, *Shiʿi Scholars*, 150–64.

60 The first such school offered a one-year program with the aim of providing legal training in the *Mecelle*, the land code, the penal code, maritime law and procedural law. See Rubin, "Ottoman Modernity," 65.

traditional *maḥḍar* (minutes) of the case, but a detailed account of every case, its legal proceedings, and all state and official documents adduced in the process of adjudication. This keeping of records was, in line with Western court procedure, occasioned by the establishment of appeal courts where a full review of the appealed case depended upon the submission of extensive documentary evidence. By this point, oral testimony and the traditional procedural laws that were predicated on it became largely obsolete. No less important, however, was the critical need for the state to exercise surveillance over the *qāḍī*s' performance and their *modus operandi.*[61]

It is true that the modernizing elite in Istanbul was intent on building a highly centralized system, a tool of efficient governance that might one day rid the Empire of European hegemony. Yet the pressures to which Istanbul was subjected were not proportionate to its drive or desire for modernization, these pressures having reached all intrusive levels short of direct conquest and colonization. The gap between direct colonization and hegemony equipped them with an agency that allowed for some resistance. We will have occasion to note that Istanbul was not categorical in its desire to dismantle the Sharīʿa court system since this jurisdiction reflected a jural domain that was unfavorable to the excessive privileges of European powers. Thus, the highly gradual process by which these courts were marginalized may be explained as part of this resistance and as a defense of sovereignty.

The Ottomans also passed several laws that were fashioned with the specific goal of reducing the encroachments of the capitulations. In 1865, a press law was promulgated, permitting foreigners to publish in the Empire only if they conformed to its laws. Two years later, a land law also predicated foreigners' rights to buy land in the Empire upon their conformity to Ottoman law and payment of Ottoman taxes. These laws struck not only at the excessive privileges the European powers and their nationals held, but at the prerogatives these had secured for their protected allies within the Empire, namely, the religious minorities. The 1869 law of nationality and naturalization defined the subjects of the Empire in national – not religious – terms, and forbade Ottoman citizens from possessing another nationality. This act struck at the heart of the Russian and western European practices of granting cooperative non-Muslim Ottomans citizenship in their respective countries. But the final blow came in 1914, when, with the Empire's termination of the capitulations once and for all, the entire structure of special Niẓāmiyye courts originally

[61] Agmon, "Social Biography," 88–89.

erected for adjudicating disputes between foreign nationals and Ottomans were dissolved.

The processes of modernization, bureaucratization and secularization introduced by the so-called reforms created neither a clear nor a decisive reaction from the Ottoman religious establishment. It is remarkable that the offices of the Şeyhülislam (Bab-ı meşihat) as well as the two *Ḳazasker*s (of Rumelia and Anatolia) were strengthened by Selim III and, especially, the aggressive reformer Mahmud II. The latter made these three offices, especially that of the Şeyhülislam, full partners in his campaign to reform the law and government,[62] since their approval was at the time still essential for implementing any serious change. The Şeyhülislam, the most powerful of the three, acquired a permanent seat in Mahmud II's new cabinet, a double-edged move which, on the one hand, coopted this prestigious office more than ever, while on the other hand allowing it to continue to represent its constituent interests in the Empire. In any case, its absorption into the cabinet signaled the beginning of the end of that office. Yet, the significance of this temporary augmentation of power in the hands of the Şeyhülislam does not appear to have been fully comprehended by the office's occupants at the time. It seems certain that the legal elite of Istanbul did not perceive the rise of their political prestige as a tactical move that permitted the sultan and his modernist bureaucrats to use the Şeyhülislam in a campaign that ultimately was to lead to the eradication of the Sharīʿa institutions, together with their personnel. An index of this process of eradication was the rapid loss of powers in the office of Şeyhülislam. In 1917, its role became confined to issuing *fatwā*s which could now be ignored by the state at will, and a few years later the office was abolished altogether along with the caliphate itself.

Nor do the provincial legists seem to have understood the processes which were to affect them in the long run in profound and crucial ways, mainly due to the gradual nature by which reform was introduced. In part, it was also due to the fact that the men of the Sharīʿa largely continued to serve in the same or similar functions as before, and their ousting appeared to be more a case of a professional generation dying out than the dismissal of a whole profession from office. The creation of secular schools began to attract the next generation, who found in these schools greater opportunity – and potentially superior pay – than in the increasingly depleted institutions teaching the Sharīʿa. Thus, ulama families, often in positions of power, would direct their children to study in the new schools in preparation for careers in the newly created secular courts

[62] Heyd, "Ottoman Ulema," 83–86; Kushner, "Place of the Ulema," 55.

and bureaucracy, for after all, their educational backgrounds equipped them to pursue such careers better than others. While it is true that centralization policies weakened these ulama families, the chipping effects of these policies were felt in the long run, not suddenly, and certainly not within the span of a single career or a single generation.

It is difficult to say to what extent the Sublime Porte's policy deliberately planned this gradual and generational ousting, for it was the inescapable reality of the Ottoman regime that it would have, at any rate, been unable to rapidly replace the *ʿilmiyye* (Ar. *ʿilmiyya*) class with secular bureaucrats and lawyers due to mere shortage in supply. We recall that Sharīʿa-trained *qāḍīs* continued to serve even on the benches of the civil sections in Niẓāmiyye courts. But the fact that they were needed by the Sublime Porte and that they were so hard to replace did not mean that the Porte could have allowed them to continue to operate on their own terms.

The gradual phasing out of the *sharʿī* professional elite cannot perhaps be better illustrated than in the career of the Nāʾib's College that was founded about midway through the nineteenth-century reform process. Spanning seven decades, its history represents not only the decline of the religious establishment but also the manner by which the new centralized state, through imposing discipline and surveillance, managed to change and finally eradicate the religious establishment while pushing forward with secular replacements.

The establishment in 1854–55 of the Nāʾib's College for the training of judges signifies not only the institutional legal changes that were taking place but also the increasing tendency to effect a nationalist and surveillance culture within the court in particular and the judiciary at large. Established at the instigation of the reformist Şeyhülislam Mehmet Arif Effendi, it was a college located in a secular building, not a mosque. It was distinctly geared toward legal practice enacted at the court, and far less interested in the academic study of juristic manuals.[63] Unlike the *medrese*, which revolved around the study of "closed" texts on the authority of prominent jurists, the Nāʾib's College consisted of three graded classes, each requiring about ten months to complete. It issued diplomas in the name of the College as a corporate entity, and teachers – instead of issuing the *ijāza* as independent pedagogical authorities – were now relegated to the rank of institutional functionaries, thus becoming contained by, and absorbed into, this corporate personality on behalf of an increasingly centralizing state. An attendance register was kept and absenteeism was

[63] For an excellent account of the rise and career of this college, see Akiba, "New School for Qadis," 125–63, esp. at 134.

punished. As in the Egyptian "reforms," discipline and surveillance were incorporated as integral features of the College.[64]

With the 1874 Law of the Sharīʿa Judiciary, the modernizing movement further emphasized the Turkish character of the College while, at the same time, de-emphasizing the role of Arabicate sciences and texts. This de-emphasis, as much a juristic move as it was a nationalist one, was concomitant with another significant juridico-political policy, namely, the establishment in 1876 of the first modern and full-fledged law school and the introduction of the codified *Mecelle* into the curriculum of the College. The new school was intended to produce lawyers and judges to staff the new Niẓāmiyye courts, while the codified *Mecelle* was intended for the use of these courts. The production of modern lawyers also precipitated the promulgation in the same year of the Law of Attorneyship, which applied to Istanbul and which regulated this profession as an integral part of the Ministry of Justice. In 1880, this law was made to apply to all provinces as well, and stipulated the requirement of an entry exam.[65] Yet another feature enhancing this transformation was the promotion of Turkish writing as a method of retaining knowledge and recording fact and evidence, a new idea and practice that ran in diametrical opposition to the method of memorization that characterized the *medrese* education and the entire culture that produced it. By the late 1870s therefore, and as reflected in the modest phenomenon of the Nāʾib's College, the embryo of a nationalist state was already formed, an embryo that was to develop into a full-fledged state power that commandeered the law through codification and controlled its subject-citizen through the surveillance of the written record.

The *Mecelle* and the new – and now all-important – laws of procedure and evidence appear to have been among the chief subjects taught at the College during the 1880s. The College's graduates were destined to serve in both the Sharīʿa and the Niẓāmiyye courts, although a candidate's entry into the latter required the direct approval of the Ministry of Justice.[66] However, it was becoming increasingly obvious that the training of these judges was not commensurate with the sort of skills needed to operate the Niẓāmiyye courts. In 1908, therefore, the curriculum of the Imperial Law School in Istanbul, mostly non-*sharʿī* in nature, was added to the College's program of study. It included courses on land law, civil and criminal procedure, commercial law, maritime law and international law.[67] But the retention in it of Sharīʿa subjects further marginalized the College within the growing current of a secularized law. Despite new

[64] Mitchell, *Colonizing Egypt*, 68–79. [65] Rubin, "Ottoman Modernity," 65–66.
[66] Akiba, "New School for Qadis," 146. [67] *Ibid.*, 150.

decrees that aimed to reform and presumably improve its curriculum and functioning, the number of its graduates fell from about one hundred in 1914 to twelve two years later. The decline of its appeal could well be attributed to the much more promising career opportunities afforded by the new law schools. In 1924, unsurprisingly, the Nā'ib's College was completely abolished by the new Republic as part of a general purge of the Sharī'a.

3. Modernizing Egyptian law

The intertwined and complex relationships between the Ottoman Empire and its autonomous Egyptian province perhaps explain the general similarities in their checkered legal careers as indirect colonies of the European powers (Egypt, in any case, for most of the nineteenth century). The efforts of Selim III and Mahmud II may be said to have largely been combined in the project of Muḥammad 'Alī, the first modernizing ruler of Egypt. Like them, Muḥammad 'Alī's most serious challenge was to solve the riddle of European military and naval supremacy. Although the Napoleonic "expedition" had failed, the threat of European domination was vigorously renewed, especially by Britain. A way out of falling prey to such conquests was to modernize, which meant for Muḥammad 'Alī building a strong army and navy for defense, and a merchant marine for exports that were to be produced by local agriculture and industry.[68] One of the first projects he undertook was the physical elimination of the Mamlūk elite in 1811, as well as the systemic dismantling of the old tax-farming system. An integral part of his agricultural reform was to confiscate land that was frequently, if not mostly, under the regime of *waqf* (although the policy of land confiscation was to be partly reversed later). Thus, long before Istanbul decided to commandeer the *waqfs*, Muḥammad 'Alī had already done so, promising the *waqf* dependants an income via the agency of the state.[69] Several other administrative reforms were carried out, but these appeared to have neither a clear direction nor a unified sense of purpose. A Supreme Council (al-Dīwān al-'Ālī), headed by Chief Justices from the four legal schools, was established in order to deal with, among many other matters, mercantile disputes involving foreigners. This Council appears to have been instituted with the dual purpose of: (a) accommodating extrajudicial commercial litigation arising from the extensive economic hegemony that the Europeans exercised in Egypt;

[68] For a useful account of Muḥammad 'Alī's policies, see Marsot, *Short History*, 54–66.
[69] Baer, "Waqf Reform," 61–76.

and (b) inserting centralizing elements into the judiciary. Very little else changed on the level of the lower courts, however.

Although Muḥammad ʿAlī acted as the *de facto* ruler of Egypt, he remained during the 1830s bound by the spirit, if not the letter, of the Sublime Porte's reformist agenda, represented in the latter's policies leading up to the 1839 Decree.[70] Such demands, however, were not difficult to oblige, as interest in modernization was equally intense in Egypt. But local considerations gave it a particular form and process. In 1836 or thereabouts, French experts, at the invitation of Muḥammad ʿAlī, submitted to him a report with a number of recommendations pertaining to improvements in the military and economic spheres. The crux of the recommendations was the forging of a centralized administration, which could regulate nearly every aspect of life in Egypt, from the army and guilds, to public traffic and water supply. These regulations, permeating spheres of life that had never before been subjected to such high-level scrutiny, became the hallmark of Muḥammad ʿAlī's regime as much as it became that of the Ottomans and every other modernizing regime.

Following the French experts' recommendations, Muḥammad ʿAlī issued in 1837 the so-called *siyāsatnāme*, a reform plan that, much like the new administrative and judicial measures of the day, consciously took Europe and the European practice of government as a model to be emulated.[71] The *siyāsatnāme* laid down the general foundations for the changes that were to be carried out during the next few decades.[72] By the time the Ottoman Decree of 1839 was sent to him from Istanbul for implementation, he could confirm that he had already done most of what was required. This was a reference to replacing, among other things, the Sharīʿa law of offenses by a largely non-*sharʿī* codification of his own.[73] Already in 1837, and following the dictates of the *siyāsatnāme*, seven councils (*dīwān*s) were created with the explicit goal of centralizing the administration of the country and its provinces (with the exception of Syria, which had in the interval gained its autonomy). But, as with the Ottoman Decree of 1839, the administrative, executive and judicial spheres within these Councils were not clearly distinguished. For example, the Justice Council of 1842, which represented a specialized function of the Sublime Council of 1837, was responsible for the administration of military and naval tribunals and the disciplinary conduct of state employees. In other words, this was no more than a reorganization of

70 Anderson, "Law Reform in Egypt," 209. 71 Ziadeh, *Lawyers*, 18–19.

72 For a useful description of the contents of the *siyāsatnāme*, see Hamed, "Siyasatname."

73 Anderson, "Law Reform in Egypt," 210; see also Baer, "Tanzimat in Egypt," 29–31.

the traditional *maẓālim* justice system, where distinctions between various legal and political powers had not yet been clearly conceived.

In step with, and parallel to, these reforms, Muḥammad ʿAlī had already sent in 1828 the first group of students to Paris, to study, among other things, law. After a three-year course, they returned to Egypt and were immediately engaged to translate French codes and law manuals under the direction of the Azharite Shaykh Ṭahṭāwī. Together with Ṭahṭāwī, these students were to produce, during the late 1860s, an Arabic translation of the French codes, both civil and commercial. Other codes of criminal and civil procedure were translated soon thereafter.

A major move toward reform occurred in 1845, with the establishment in Cairo and Alexandria of merchant councils over which local and European judges presided. The law regulating these councils also introduced the practice of legal representation, a step that planted the seed for the rise of a modern lawyering profession in Egypt.[74] Yet, these councils were not invested with any serious measure of sovereignty. Penal issues involving Europeans, including criminal offenses committed by them against Egyptians, were removed from local jurisdiction and regulated and adjudicated by the respective European powers present in the country.[75] In 1853, Khedive Saʿīd adopted the 1850 Ottoman Commercial Code – largely of French origin – which was the law followed by these merchant councils. But the dramatic expansion of European trade in Egypt – an expansion intimately connected with the financial crises of, and colossal debts incurred by, the government – called for another reform in 1861. At this time, the so-called Cairo Commission was established to deal with matters involving foreigners in all legal spheres except land, which was left to the jurisdiction of the Sharīʿa courts. Again, this Commission applied the French-modeled laws already adopted by Istanbul's bureaucrats. Its bench was composed of Egyptian and European judges, and included in addition an Armenian, a European, a Greek and a Jew.

In the meantime, the Sharīʿa courts in theory continued to have general jurisdiction, but with the increasing influence and scope of the new courts, their range was steadily being narrowed down. They were already limited to land and real property in general, matters of personal status, and criminal cases involving blood-money.[76] Then in the early 1880s their power was curtailed even more drastically, due in large measure to the corresponding development of the new courts.

The importance of the 1861 Commission lay in the fact that it gave birth, in 1876, to the Mixed Courts.[77] Their "mixed" constitution reflected

[74] Ziadeh, *Lawyers*, 14. [75] Anderson, "Law Reform in Egypt," 211.
[76] Ziadeh, *Lawyers*, 16. [77] Hill, "Courts and Administration," 100.

the increased interference of France and Britain, among others, in the affairs of Egypt. The Europeans further extended their influence via these courts not only to the affairs of foreigners but also to the whole gamut of the country's commercial life.[78] They also introduced the notion of jurisdictional hierarchy, where courts of first instance were established in Cairo, Manṣūra and Alexandria, with a single court of appeal in the latter. One year before the establishment of these courts, a series of laws – based mostly on French law[79] – was passed in anticipation, namely, the Civil Code, the Penal Code, the Commercial Code, the Code of Maritime Commerce, the Code of Civil and Commercial Procedure, and the Code of Criminal Procedure.

Regulated by French codes and presided over by a majority of European judges nominated by their respective countries, the Mixed Courts in effect constituted a juridico-economic regime by which Egypt's financial and, indeed, political life was controlled. Producing "some forty thousand written opinions," and rendering the "Egyptian government ... subject to their jurisdiction and their judgments," there was "practically no litigation of any large or general importance which [was] not attracted to their jurisdiction."[80] And as if to increase the alienation of the native Sharīʿa courts and their users, the Mixed Courts, which quickly appropriated most of the spheres of law, began to require advocacy as a prerequisite for filing suits before them. In 1877, when the Mixed Bar Association held its first meeting, it boasted seventy-nine members, none of whom was an Egyptian.[81] On the other hand, the 1880 Code of Procedure came to confine the Sharīʿa courts' jurisdiction to matters of personal status, inheritance, *waqf*, gifts and crime.[82] By 1896, the latter jurisdiction had been removed from their competence, further limiting their sphere of action to family law, broadly so defined. Furthermore, the Sharīʿa courts were ordered to report all their transactions pertaining to real property to the Mixed Courts of first instance, although the latter were not obliged to reciprocate.[83]

Aside from the increasingly limited jurisdiction of the Sharīʿa courts, the Mixed Courts extended their sway, and managed to unify the legal

[78] On the Mixed Courts, see Brinton, *Mixed Courts of Egypt*, 11–39 and *passim*; Hoyle, *Mixed Courts of Egypt*, 1–21, 31 ff.

[79] These French-based codes included minuscule sections from the Sharīʿa pertaining to death-illness, to unjustified enrichment in real property, in the lease of *waqf* and in the distribution of an estate, and to some matters related to preemption (*shufʿa*). See Anderson, "Law Reform in Egypt," 217; Anderson, "Sharīʿa and Civil Law," 29–46.

[80] Brinton, *Mixed Courts of Egypt*, xxiii–xxiv.

[81] Ziadeh, *Lawyers*, 29.

[82] On Egyptian criminal law during the later years of the nineteenth century, see Peters, "Islamic and Secular Criminal Law," especially 76 ff.

[83] To which Muḥammad ʿAbduh objected. See his *Taqrīr fī Iṣlāḥ al-Maḥākim*, 24–25.

system like never before. This fierce tendency to centralize was in the interests of both the Khedive and the foreign powers. Ironically, the machinery and tools of the modern nation-state were called upon by both the colonizers and the colonized, for through these modern governing instruments the colonizers aimed to colonize, whereas the colonized wanted, at most, to decolonize and, at least, escape colonization unscathed. Yet, strengthening the Mixed Courts was distinctly more in the interests of the Powers than in those of the Khedive. Their growing exclusivity as judicial organs, plus the powers conferred upon their magistrates in terms of spectacular salaries and life-appointments,[84] were all designed to render them efficaciously conducive to serving European economic interests. With a majority of European judges applying free-market oriented codes, the harnessing of Egypt as an open market became less difficult to accomplish.

As with many colonial projects, the Mixed Courts became a bone of contention among the competing European powers. Until 1882, Britain refused to expand its jurisdiction or any aspect of its influence lest its colonialist competitors seize such an opportunity to shift the balance of power. But once Britain occupied Egypt after crushing the ʿUrābī Revolt of 1882, it felt secure enough to permit the Egyptian government to create the so-called national courts. When the Council of Ministers began deliberating the creation of these courts, it was thought that, by accepting some European presence on the benches of these new courts, it would be possible to bring a quicker end to the nationally abhorred Mixed Courts. And so it was determined that the national courts would include one foreign judge at each court of first instance and two foreign judges in each court of appeal. The new court system began work in March 1884, with only one court of appeal in Cairo (not to be reinforced until 1925, when a sister court was created in Asyūṭ). And to eliminate diversity – inconsistent with the aims and *modus operandi* of the modern state system – the Court of Cassation (Maḥkamat al-Tamyīz) was abolished, thereby limiting the new system to two tiers or levels, a constitution also consistent with the Mixed Courts' structure, on which the national courts were modeled.[85] Yet, the new courts also adopted the substantive laws that were applied in the Mixed Courts (and reissued in 1883), save for the code of preliminary enquiry and the penal code, which were to be drafted in accordance with the demands of local conditions.[86] Other Sharīʿa elements retained in the 1883 wave of codification were the laws of preemption (*shufʿa*), transfer of debts (*ḥawāla*), the right to cancellation of

[84] Brinton, *Mixed Courts of Egypt*, 45, 89. [85] Ziadeh, *Lawyers*, 34.
[86] Anderson, "Law Reform in Egypt," 218–19.

contract (*khiyār al-sharṭ*), and the contract of delayed delivery (*salam*).[87] With these exceptions, the various codes, including a new commercial code, were compiled by European lawyers who wrote them first in the French language, whence they were translated into Arabic.[88]

On the other hand, the Sharīʿa and its courts were progressively marginalized, not through changing Islamic law itself, but rather by means of procedural amendments which deprived it of application. For example, in a series of procedural restrictions starting in the 1870s and culminating in 1911,[89] the courts were expressly precluded from hearing litigation in the absence of written evidence. The systematic ousting of oral testimony, the cornerstone of the Sharīʿa courts' operation, was followed by a reconstituted law of procedure that reflected a written – in contradistinction to oral – tradition that served the state's purpose of counting, accounting, surveillance and control. The marginalization of the Sharīʿa was thus itself an act not only of dismantling but at once one of building a system of courts and law that functioned to serve the state. Writing, as an instrument of keeping records on the individual citizen, was an essential ingredient of order, and order had become the *raison d'être* of the law. But for control to be efficacious, it had to be enshrined in the system upon which the courts and the law depended. Following the lead of the new educational system introduced by the Ottomans, including the new curriculum and structure of Istanbul's Nāʾibs' College, Egypt also introduced a system of schools and law colleges that was intended to invent a new concept of the individual whose body and mind were subjected to and fashioned by discipline and surveillance,[90] two techniques that were for the first time incorporated as integral features of both the judicial and educational systems.

4. Non-reaction

To be sure, the Ottoman and Egyptian Tanẓīmāt and post-Tanẓīmāt reforms did provoke occasional resistance on the part of the lower-ranking Sharīʿa legists,[91] but the receptivity to the reforms shown by their

[87] On these *fiqhī* laws, see chapter 7, sections 2, 3 and 7, above.
[88] Ziadeh, *Lawyers*, 35.
[89] That is, the 1910 Amendment (Number 31) to the 1897 Law of the Organization and Procedure of Sharīʿa Courts – an amendment that was to be implemented a year later, in 1911.
[90] Mitchell, *Colonizing Egypt*, 81–85, 101–04.
[91] For opposition to the reforms by the lower-ranking ulama (as well as by *āghā*s and provincial others), see İnalcık, "Application of the Tanzimat," 111. For other demonstrations and the 1909 counter-revolution, see Heyd, "Ottoman Ulema," 35–36; Kushner, "Place of the Ulema," 72–73; and Ahmad, *Young Turks*, 14–46.

higher-ranking counterparts has for long invited explanation. Why, in other words, did the reforms not precipitate active or consequential resistance on the part of the ulama?

First, as chapters 3 and 5 have shown in some detail, the Ottoman policy of governance was to absorb, to the highest degree possible, the legal elite into its bureaucratic and administrative ranks. The establishment of imperial *medreses*, centered in Istanbul, created a highly stratified legal/religious profession, where a few families in the capital monopolized the more lucrative and influential positions, leaving thousands of *softas*, the law students, competing for a very limited number of posts, none of which was at the highest level. These high-ranking posts were reserved for the sons of the elite *ʿilmiyye* families, the so-called legal aristocracy. Furthermore, if the low-ranking legists and *softas* in the capital were marginalized in terms of opportunity and power, then the ulama of the provinces, especially of the Arab peripheries, were doubly deprived of the opportunity to fill any powerful positions. This situation, by definition, reflected the divisions among the ulama within the capital and between the capital and the provinces, a fact that explains, on the one hand, the constant resentment exhibited by the legists in the Arab provinces during the eighteenth and nineteenth centuries, and the revolts, riots and militant resistance of the *softas* and lower-ranking legists in Istanbul.[92]

But there was more to the Ottoman policy of enlisting the ulama in the administration: it has been abundantly documented that the Sublime Porte also managed to enlist its legists and legal aristocracy in the diplomatic service, to serve as anything from ambassadors to treaty negotiators to peace conference delegates.[93] In other words, by the middle of the eighteenth century, and well before the reforms were started, the elite ulama families were incorporated, if not coopted, into the emerging state-machinery in a fashion not markedly different from that of other civil servants. For instance, the political elite, the State Council, whose task was the deliberation of important governmental and political matters, was, significantly, often convened in the Palace of the Şeyhülislam. Other members of this Council were the two *Ḳazaskers*, the Kadı (Ar. Qāḍī) of Istanbul, the Head Professors of imperial mosque-*medreses*, and "many other ʿulemā," whose inclusion was "considered necessary in order to make them share the responsibility for grave and unpopular decisions and to prevent them from subsequently criticizing the government's policy either openly or secretly."[94] (A closely similar process of coopting obtained also in Morocco under the French, where the latter, in order

[92] Heyd, "Ottoman Ulema," 35–36. [93] *Ibid.*, 45–47. [94] *Ibid.*, 44.

to preempt opposition, guaranteed the ulama a privileged status in their society.)[95]

That this legal elite, as an integral part of the powerful governing machinery, had a stake in the well-being of the Empire emerges as a crystal-clear fact. So does the fact that the protection of their interests compelled this elite not only to participate in, but also to encourage and justify the entire program of the pioneering (but, because of this, crucial and risky) reform that paved the way (and trained minds for) the later reengineering of law. When the sultans and later bureaucrats began to chip away at the powers of this legal aristocracy, the latter had no real popular backing, such as their predecessors had enjoyed in Baghdad, Cairo, Samarqand and Bukhāra. Together with moral capital, they had lost the support of the grass-roots, the rank-and-file legists of the Empire who had developed an irreparable resentment of this aristocracy. Having become "the men of the Sultan," these latter had, in the spirit of the age-old practice of *muṣādara*,[96] rendered themselves dispensable at royal will. Just as they had bartered the law – which was their *raison d'être* – for political gain, the Porte bartered them for its own purposes.

Second, and closely connected with this legal aristocracy, the reforms during the early – and, again, crucial – period were not presented to the subjects of the Empire as innovations or as a set of imitative moves on the model of the West, but rather as necessary steps to guard Islam and the Empire. "Standing up to the unbelievers" was declared a religious duty aimed at the preservation and protection of Islam. Whatever steps were needed to accomplish these tasks were justified in the name of *ḍarūra*, an otherwise minor legal principle that renders permissible what is, under certain circumstances, prohibited.[97] The subject population, including secondary tiers of government officials, had no good reason to suspect that the legal authorities who had been the conscience of the community and its guardians for over a millennium would collaborate with a secular government – Māwardī's sultanic power (*shawka*) – ready to compromise and finally bring to an end the very religion that gave rise to the Empire and its civilization in the first place.

Third, and as this chapter has shown, the general approach to reform in the Ottoman and Egyptian contexts was to adopt a Western-minded and Western-structured legal system side-by-side with that of the Sharīʿa. The new courts and codes, fully controlled by the new nation-state, did not, at least initially, have the declared ambition of uprooting the traditional Sharīʿa structures, but only that of operating symbiotically along parallel

[95] Eickelman, *Knowledge and Power*, 165–66. [96] See chapter 5, section 3, above.
[97] On the uses of this concept in modern legal thought, see chapter 17, below.

lines. In fact, during the nineteenth century, there was a sustained defense of the Sharīʿa and its courts, if for no other reason than the sense that the Niẓāmiyye courts, virtually imposed on them by the European powers, were conducive to the capitulations which in turn had undermined Ottoman sovereignty.[98] The Sharīʿa courts represented a bastion of resistance, however weakened they were becoming, for they did not play by the economic or legal rules of Europe. In due time, however, and through the medium of the new legal system and reforms, the state embarked on a gradual process by which it renegotiated the spheres of influence between the two legal systems, first by strengthening the new Niẓāmiyye system, financially and otherwise, and second by enlarging its jurisdiction and areas of application.

The highly gradual nature of the reform was further combined with a structural transformation in the function of *sharʿī* institutions. First, the substantive religious law was reduced in scope but not entirely phased out, the *Mecelle* being an interim experiment of sorts. These slow transformations represented an insidious yet effective means of change. Family law, of immediate relevance to all individuals in society, was maintained, at least nominally; although by casting it in a codified form it ceased to be part of the Sharīʿa as a "process," as one scholar has aptly put it.[99] It also changed masters, the state taking over in this role. But the effect of maintaining the Sharīʿa, albeit in a codified form, seemed less dramatic and drastic than its total abolition would have signified. Second, while the contents of the law and legal theory (*uṣūl al-fiqh*) were slowly narrowed down and marginalized, what was left was recast in modern terms and continued to be taught as academic disciplines at the newly created Sharīʿa colleges and modern universities, and even as part of the curricula taught at the new Western-style law faculties. The major traditional *madrasa*s, such as the Egyptian al-Azhar and the Shīʿite *ḥawza*s of Najaf and Qum, were maintained intact, but their relevance ceased to be judicial and was limited to an educational role. Al-Azhar, for instance, has since become the burden of the Ministries of Education and Waqf, not its counterpart, the Ministry of Justice.

Yet, while these transformations were taking place, very few Sharīʿa scholars and judges lost their careers, for they continued, on the one hand, to preside over areas of family law (including in the civil sections of Niẓāmiyye courts), while on the other serving to fill the rapidly expanding

98 Rubin, "Ottoman Modernity," 103–11, and *passim*, for a discussion of the role the European powers played in promoting the Niẓāmiyye courts to the detriment of the Sharīʿa courts.

99 Brown, "Shariʿa and State," 363–65.

bureaucratic positions that had opened up with the expanding of the power of the state. Since they constituted the majority of the Empire's administrators and "civil servants," they stood, initially at least, to gain from prominent opportunities for employment in this ever-expanding bureaucracy. In the course of time, as already intimated, the early Tanẓīmāt generation was to groom the next generation – mostly their children, who would have grown up to study Sharīʿa, but did not – as bureaucratic servants, thus easing much of the traditional legal profession into a modified form of non-Sharīʿa, state service. We have no empirical data, but the half million officials who operated the colossal bureaucratic machine toward the end of the century[100] also included many ulama.[101] Furthermore, law as content then was transposed from the realm of discursive and judicial practice to that of education. Studying Sharīʿa became an academic curiosity and a theoretical discipline. But in one form or another, it still managed, though not by any feat of its own, to remain afloat. Sharīʿa, in the early phase of reform, was thus slowly and steadily marginalized, then later more substantively and institutionally neutralized, and still later structurally and systemically ousted from the mainstream of legal life – being left to stand, in tatters, on the periphery.

5. The Qājārs' attempted reforms

As Turkomans, the Qājārs lacked the religious authority that their Ṣafavid predecessors enjoyed, an authority that rested on claims of descent from the Prophet's family. Partly in compensation for this lack of religio-political legitimacy, the Qājārs invested heavily in the religious institution, dedicating much property in the way of *waqf*.[102] This gesture, however, failed to coopt the ulama into the power structures of the ruling dynasty, leaving their relationship no closer – and certainly less trusting – than it was between their Sunnite counterparts and the ruler prior to the tenth/sixteenth century. By the time they established their rule, not only had Twelver-Shīʿism come to reassert itself with renewed vigor (after Nādir Shah [r. 1736–47] had attempted to reinstall Sunnism),[103] but Uṣūlism had, once and for all, won the day against Akhbārism.[104] Thus, by the time of European encroachment, the religious institution and its personnel (recipients of major endowments and religious taxes)[105] stood in

[100] Quataert, "Age of Reforms," 765. On the importance of bureaucracy in the construction of the modern nation-state, see sources cited in n. 53, above.
[101] Kushner, "Place of the Ulema," 66–69.
[102] On this in general, see Halm, *Shiʿa Islam*, 115 f.
[103] Cole, *Sacred Space*, 69.
[104] See chapter 2, section 9, above.
[105] On income from these taxes, see Halm, *Shiʿa Islam*, 91 ff., 108–09.

a more powerful position *vis-à-vis* the political establishment than had their pre-sixteenth-century Sunnite predecessors, and most certainly their Ottoman counterparts (whose power was manifestly dependent on the political sovereign).

Persia's political and military troubles began at roughly the same time as those of the Ottoman Empire and Egypt, and they were directly related, as elsewhere, to the superiority of Russo-European military technology. The key events were two major military defeats at the hands of the Russians between the 1790s and 1820s, culminating in the Turkmanchay Treaty of 1828. Under this treaty, the Russians were to receive capitulatory treatment in conducting business in Persia, and any disputes arising between them and Qājār subjects on Persian territory were to be adjudicated by a mixed tribunal applying Russian law.[106] Numerous other privileges were granted over the century, primarily to both the Russians and the British.[107] Almost immediately thereafter, the special privileges allotted to Russian traders were extended to all foreigners – this marking a break from earlier practices where all commercial disputes involving foreigners were adjudicated by a Sharīʿa court. Furthermore, and as happened in the Ottoman Empire, Russia, among others, attempted to secure special rights for the *dhimmī*s of Persia, but these attempts did not meet with the success enjoyed by their counterparts in the Ottoman Balkans.

"Reforms" intended to remedy these "maladies" were started early on, even before the defeats leading to the 1828 treaty. As with Muḥammad ʿAlī in Egypt and Sultan Selim III in the Ottoman Empire, military reforms were attempted in Persia during and after 1809, with the assistance of Britain. But these reforms never materialized on any large scale. Instead, changes were piecemeal, initially reflected in such acts as sending, around 1828, students to Europe in order to follow courses in a variety of new disciplines. Western education was accompanied by a stress on translating European works into Farsi. Between 1851 and 1853, under the initiative of Prime Minister Amīr Kabīr, an educational reform resulted in the founding of a new, European-style school that came to be known as Dār al-Funūn. With the full backing of Kabīr, Nāṣir al-Dīn Shah (r. 1848–96) also attempted to centralize the legal system by subsuming all courts under the jurisdiction of a *dīvānkhāneh*, but his attempts, seen as too ambitious, were quickly thwarted. The *dīvānkhāneh* in theory retained the right to choose the venue of litigation as well as to ratify Sharīʿa courts' decisions. Furthermore, this higher court also reserved for itself the right

[106] Floor, "Change and Development," 133–34. [107] *Ibid.*, 119, 133–36.

to review and reverse all decisions of the Sharīʿa courts that involved litigation between Muslims and non-Muslim subjects of the Empire.

However, little of these reforms took real effect, just as the 1851 proposal – modeled after the 1839 Ottoman Gülhane Decree and submitted by Chief Justice Mīrzā Nūrī – was categorically rejected. Failure also attended the series of reforms begun in 1858, when the newly established Council of Ministers set up provincial departments of justice that were aimed at centralizing the judiciary. Under the initiative of Mīrzā Mushīr al-Dawla, who had spent more than a decade as the Qājār envoy to Istanbul, a plan of legal reform was submitted to the Shah, but this too met the same fate.

Another serious plan was drafted in 1871 by Mīrzā Mushīr in his new capacity as Ṣadr-i Aʿzam. Receiving the Shah's stamp of approval, this plan suggested, among other things, the creation of a system of Western-style, hierarchical courts with special codes to be applied in them. Not only these, but all other attempts at reform failed during the long reigns of Nāṣir al-Dīn Shah and his successor, and there was little, if anything, accomplished by 1906.[108] Even the National Consultative Assembly, established during that same year, could produce no more than a Basic Law that affirmed the supremacy of the Sharīʿa, and, for the purpose of ensuring this supremacy, a five-*mulla* committee was formed. Nonetheless, the Basic Law introduced the idea of the separation of powers, and granted judges life tenure in an effort to enhance the concept of the rule of law. The reform-minded intellectuals who flourished around the turn of the century viewed these developments as contributing "too little, too late" in light of the crises facing Iran, and in light of the stern calls voiced much earlier by the likes of Mīrzā Mālkom Khān, ʿAbd al-Raḥīm Talebov and Mīrzā Yūsuf Khān.[109]

To be sure, the Qājār legal reforms – if they can be called that at all – were slow to come. Compared with the Egyptian and Ottoman reforms, they cannot be said to have started in earnest until the reign of Reza Shah (1925–42), a phenomenon that invites explanation. In sum, the main impediment was Iran's incompatibility with centralization. Between the collapse of the Ṣafavids in 1732 and the consolidation of the Qājārs in 1794, the country had enough time to fall prey to multiple competing tribal chieftains who aspired for general control. The Qājārs arrived in the midst of this scene, and were too weak to bring the chieftains under their command. Their fiscal system also adopted the abhorrent practice of

[108] Ringer, "Negotiating Modernity," 41.
[109] For a general context in light of the constitutional debate, see Sohrabi, "Revolution and State Culture."

selling tax-farming offices to the highest bidder who, to recuperate the high fees, had to extort taxes at the price of depleting local resources. Peasants and all tax-paying subjects developed a great deal of resentment and distrust of the ruler.

The problem of decentralization and severe lack of government control was further aggravated by the rise, not only of chieftains, but of the powerful Shīʿite *mujtahid*s who stepped in to fill the vacuum.[110] For beginning with Ismāʿīl (r. 1501–24), the Ṣafavid shahs, as I already intimated, had proclaimed themselves representatives of the hidden Imams, thus investing themselves with attributes of infallibility and divine authority that embraced both the political and the legal realms. Neither the Qājārs nor any of their ephemeral competitors made such religious or legal claims, thereby creating a void. Replacing the religious powers of the Ṣafavid shahs, the Uṣūlist *mujtahid*s stepped in and proclaimed their own divine representation on behalf of the Imams, thus complementing the exclusively temporal competence of the Qājārs. After the decline of the Ṣafavids, but certainly by the rise of the Qājārs, Twelver-Shīʿism became a grass-roots movement, standing apart from the ruler and his government. The *fatwā*s of the great *mujtahid*s could therefore pronounce any imperial decree invalid with impunity, and for such acts it was easy for the *mujtahid*s to garner massive support from their followers, namely, the majority of the population that had been overly burdened by excessive taxation and maltreatment.[111]

The ulama thus continued largely unperturbed in their control over the judiciary and education, and the new Dār al-Funūn – unlike the new Ottoman and Egyptian schools – was ineffective in producing a Westernized elite that formed a cadre pushing for reform.[112] Whereas hundreds of thousands of new bureaucratic positions opened in the course of applying Ottoman and Egyptian centralization policies (thus permitting the formation of new reform-minded generations), the Qājār bureaucracy – which barely reached the outskirts of the capital – was too small to accommodate even the relatively few graduates of Dār al-Funūn. Real reform had thus to await the end of the first quarter of the twentieth century.

6. *Droit musulman-algérien*

In July 1830, a French naval expedition took Algiers, beginning an extraordinarily brutal occupation that was to last for no less than a century and

110 On Uṣūlism in Twelver-Shīʿism, see chapter 2, section 9, above.

111 Keddie, *Qajar Iran*, 17; Cleveland, *History*, 111–12.

112 On the ulama's reaction to the founding of Dār al-Funūn, see Ringer, "Negotiating Modernity," 42–45.

a quarter. It was not until a decade after this conquest that the occupation forces were able to extend their power beyond the littoral and into the interior of what is today known as Algeria. But the French were very quick to use the law as a tool of conquest, and the Algerian experience provides a supreme model of the use of raw legal power to accomplish colonialist objectives. What make the Algerian case an especially intense colonial experiment are such crucial facts as: (1) the French perceived themselves as replacing the Ottomans as masters of a colony that had never enjoyed a sovereign status;[113] in effect, what had belonged to the Ottomans now belonged to them; (2) a large, and in time powerful, French population settled in this colony as permanent residents, claiming it as their land;[114] (3) France, in time, began to harbor the design to claim the country, not as a colony, but as an integral part of France;[115] and (4) the French settlers continued for decades to exercise tremendous pressure on their Paris government to facilitate their commercial ambitions by granting them land or by permitting them to purchase real property from the natives on a large scale.

Thus, while the colonial interest in the Ottoman Empire was to penetrate the local consumer markets, in Algeria the French interest was direct appropriation and exploitation of the agricultural and mineral resources of the country. The problem, as the French saw it, was that too many Muslims lived in the country and, what is more, that these natives somehow possessed all the lands coveted for commercial exploitation. As genocide involving a population of over 2 million natives was – at least at the time – not a practical option for the colonial authorities,[116] freeing the land from the grip of the natives by other means dominated all considerations, in the legal field no less than in the political.

The coveted land happened to be under various types of ownership, all regulated by Islamic law. In addition to freehold title (*milk*) and state land (*mīrī* or *beylik* lands), there was the all-important *waqf* land (North African *habous*) which alone constituted no less than one-half of arable land.[117] The latter, as elsewhere in the Muslim world, had also formed a

[113] Christelow, *Muslim Law Courts*, 12.

[114] According to the statistics of 1901, there were 364,000 French settlers in Algeria. See Abun-Nasr, *History*, 256. The *colon* population accumulated tremendous political wealth as a result of the material wealth they garnered at the expense of plundering lands owned by native Muslims. See Christelow, *Muslim Law Courts*, 15.

[115] In the 1848 French Constitution, Algeria was declared a French territory. Abun-Nasr, *History*, 249–50. See also Massignon, "Résultats sociaux," 559–68.

[116] Although hundreds of thousands of Algerians (by some estimates close to a million) had died as a result of the French occupation by the time France pulled out of this colony. On genocide as a modern phenomenon, see Bauman, *Modernity and the Holocaust*.

[117] Powers, "Orientalism, Colonialism and Legal History," 537.

substantial part of non-landed real property, especially religious and educational institutions, as well as residential buildings. By hook or by crook, the French settlers managed to amass a good deal of property coming from the *waqf* domain, and, as a result, it became common practice for many natives – who were beneficiaries of the endowments – to sue for restoration of the sequestered property to its original *waqf* state.

During the first year of conquest, France had already declared the entire colony, including *habous* or *waqf* lands, to belong to the public domain. In 1844, the *habous* were confiscated and the administration was charged with the task of funding the religious and educational endowments and their employees.[118] (This centralizing act – simultaneously depleting the income of these endowments – was nearly identical to the *waqf* centralization policy of the Ottoman Mahmud II in 1826 and thereafter.) Furthermore, disputes over illegally seized *waqf* property had been resolved in 1840, when a decree retroactively declared all property in the hands of the *colon*s, whether acquired lawfully or not, to be lawfully owned by its colonial usurpers. Deprived of their *waqf* income and support, the legitimate Muslim beneficiaries were left to fend for themselves. By 1844, all aspects of property law in the Sharīʿa were replaced by French law, which by design was made to facilitate the commercial ambitions of the settlers. Further steps toward this goal – and specifically toward forcing the *waqf* properties onto the open market – were taken when, against every principle in Islamic law, all *waqf* property was deemed to be, legally speaking, alienable. Nevertheless, the Muslim natives generally refused to sell or buy *waqf* property, rendering this policy somewhat ineffective.

The legal fray that accompanied the *habous* appropriation, as well as the attendant political and military policies that undergirded that fray, was not the domain of politicians alone. French lawyers, jurists and academicians who knew anything useful about North Africa (and some who knew very little) began to discourse on matters legal and otherwise. Many of them were *colon*s who were mostly both scholars and civil servants, and who often became involved in the colonialist administration of justice. After the middle of the century, they began to produce what became a massive bulk of legal literature about Islamic law in its North African context, especially about the theory and practice of the dominant Mālikite school. (This literature, it is worth noting, was to become an integral part of Western scholarship on, and therefore Western knowledge of, Islam.)[119]

118 Christelow, *Muslim Law Courts*, 23.

119 For example, Sautayra and Cherbonneau, *Droit musulman du statut personnel;* Mercier, *Le habous ou ouakof.* From the Italian perspective, see Santillana, *Instituzioni di diritto musulmano.*

Certain of these writings acquired an academic guise but some were in the nature of legislation, exemplified in the so-called *Code Morand*. This juridical and legislative body of discourse came to be known as the *droit musulman-algérien*, somewhat cognate to, but larger in scope and academic interest than, the British colonialist notion of Anglo-Muhammadan Law.

Like their British and Dutch counterparts, French Orientalists – co-founders of the field of Islamic legal studies[120] – proved to be quite helpful in the implementation of the government's and settlers' policies.[121] As far as *habous* was concerned, for instance, the French administration attempted to control the religious endowments through a series of legislative enactments, aided along the way by the French Orientalists who "campaigned to discredit the institution among the Algerians themselves."[122] This campaign, if not struggle, to "conquer the minds" was as essential a project for the colonists as any material conquest. And much of this project revolved around the production of cultural and academic discourse. There ensued a flood of argument to the effect that there exists a fundamental distinction between family and public *waqf*s – a notion that had never acquired the same meaning in Muslim cultures. Since French scholars by then understood the importance of the founding revelation in Islam and the epistemic centrality of its early carriers and transmitters, they began to argue that family *waqf* was a development that occurred subsequent to this formative and foundational phase, distinctly implying that it was an inauthentic accretion, a *bidʿa* (innovation), so to speak. They next insinuated a link of causality, namely, that the belated invention of family endowments was aimed at circumventing the fragmenting effects of the Quranic law of inheritance which operates by the principle of shares.[123] Accordingly, family *habous* and Quranic inheritance were declared – on behalf of Muslims – mutually exclusive; and since the *raison d'être* of the former was the skirting of the dictates of the latter, family endowments were deemed both immoral and illegal. This argument was offered in parallel to another: that family endowments inherently tied down property and prevented it from "efficient" exploitation, a fact that ineluctably led to economic stagnation. From here, it was a short and easy step to link this stagnation with cultural malaise and, indeed, a stunted civilizational progress.

[120] See Introduction, sections 1 and 2, above.
[121] In the context of North Africa, see Buskens, "Islamic Commentaries," 66–67, 71, 76–77; Powers, "Orientalism, Colonialism and Legal History," *passim*. See also the colonizing counsel of the illustrious Orientalist Massignon, "Résultats sociaux."
[122] Powers, "Orientalism, Colonialism and Legal History," 536.
[123] See chapter 8, section 6, above.

The singling out of family endowments as reprobate appeared in the 1850s as a move concomitant with an unusually liberal call by the *colon*s and their government to the effect that Islamic law must be centralized in an effort to build an Algerian religious unity. The condemnation of the family endowments, while underscoring the Quran's integrity – which was part of a call to maintain the "true" form of Islam – constituted a two-in-one strike aimed at opening the gates to the application of Quranic rules of inheritance which would, perforce, break up property held in joint ownership. This material ambition combined with the fear that, if Islamic law were to be completely dismantled and assimilation were to run its full course, the Algerian Muslims would demand full political rights.[124] The contradictions between the need to absorb and control the law and its native subjects, on the one hand, and keeping these colonized subjects at bay and away from the exercise of political power, on the other, underlined much of the colonial policy of the French. But it still served several ends at one and the same time. The Islamic legal system was asserted but centralized and bureaucratized, thereby imposing on it a form of European rationality alien to it. And maintaining it not only served enormous economic interests but provided an example to the Ottomans to afford their subjects the *liberté et égalité* of the French Revolution.

Having discursively established the dispensability of family endowments, the *colon*s and the supporting Orientalists moved to the next stage of argument, a stage that had been generated by a new reality. Toward the end of the century, enormous areas of cultivable land had already fallen into the hands of the *colon* entrepreneurs, with the result that the need to maintain the argument for the Quran's integrity had by then largely vanished. Thus, having already accepted the premise that the Quranic law of inheritance was fragmentary (which in the first place had caused Muslims themselves to circumvent it), the Orientalists now set out to reform the Islamic law of succession, at least by discoursing on it in the form of scholarly treatises. But in their bid to "conquer the minds," they further enlisted the efforts of their Middle Eastern students who had come from various Arab regions to study with them. For example, Professor M. Morand, President of the Faculté de Droit d'Alger, supervised doctoral works by such students who called for reforming the Quranic law of inheritance or setting it aside altogether. (It must be emphasized that the discourse of this campaign – against *waqf* in particular but also against the Sharīʿa in general – was inseparable from the Ottoman discourse which imbibed its inspiration from French cultural models.)

[124] Christelow, *Muslim Law Courts*, 20, 131.

On another front, French penal law was promulgated in 1859, while in 1873 the so-called *Loi Warnier* decreed that all land in Algeria was to be regulated by French law and, what is more, that the Muslim courts would henceforth be confined to adjudging cases pertaining to personal status, including inheritance. The systematic displacement of the penal system reached a high point in 1881 with the promulgation of the repressive *Code de l'Indigénat* which empowered civil administrators to mete out harsh punishments, without due process, against Muslim subjects charged with any one of forty-one specified offenses. These punishments included detention without trial, collective punishment and discretionary confiscation of property. The Code continued in force until 1927.

The French, however, did not limit their attention to criminal and commercial matters. As promulgators of a "civilizing" mission, they saw themselves as advocates of causes that went beyond efficient exploitation of natural resources and labor. Whereas in most other parts of the Muslim world no government, whether local or foreign, risked the introduction at the time of any changes in civil law, the French repeatedly attempted to implement a civil law that would alter what were seen as unprogressive, if not uncivilized, rules. From the middle of the nineteenth century and for many decades thereafter, they promulgated and retracted many codes and decrees, including the famous *Code Morand* of 1916, which was never applied. Like several other decrees, this *Code* attempted to effect a number of fundamental changes to matters of personal status. As M. B. Hooker aptly noted, a salient characteristic of these codes and decrees was their fundamental misunderstanding of the role of custom in the variations of applying the law.[125] Local uniqueness and variety, entirely understood and accommodated in Islamic law, were nearly non-existent concepts in the French outlook on law, which took as its point of departure the assumption that subject citizens were equal and therefore should stand before the law indistinguishably.

By 1871, the Algerian ulama class was in disarray, in part because certain of their numbers lost moral authority by cooperating with the French. This coopting was the inevitable by-product of the French reordering of local political organization, a reordering reminiscent of the Ottoman reconstructive introduction of the municipal councils. While many of the ulama serving on these councils represented the interests of their fellow Muslims, there were others – together with notables and landed aristocracy – who cooperated, or appeared to cooperate, with the French beyond what were seen as appropriate bounds.[126] But the more

[125] Hooker, *Legal Pluralism*, 209–10. [126] Christelow, *Muslim Law Courts*, 14–15, 20.

significant reason for the decline of their status and power had to do with the depletion of the resources that had been at their disposal and that now largely vanished into the hands of the French after the centralization and large-scale confiscation of *waqfs*. These transformations in the *habous* system affected not only their economic status but their command of the field of education, on both the elementary and law-college levels. Like the Ottomans before them, the French created an educational monopoly on the production of Muslim legists and *qāḍīs*. The *madrasas* of Algiers, Tlemcen and Constantine became the official colleges from which future *qāḍīs* were to be recruited. But the poor (now centralized) funding of these *madrasas*, among other factors, contributed to a dramatic lowering of the standards of legal education, and consequently of the quality of *qāḍīs* and law professors (a phenomenon that would persist in the great majority of today's Muslim countries). Simultaneously, the streamlining of education permitted the French to inject a pro-colonialist reading into the legal training of these men,[127] another phase in the project of "conquering the mind." The French judges also began to displace *qāḍīs* and religious courts, and all litigation pertaining to real property and crime, even when the parties to the litigation were all Muslim, was removed from the purview of Sharīʿa jurisdiction. The effect of the overall tendency to encroach on the domain of the Sharīʿa led to a dramatic reduction in the number of Muslim courts in the country, from an already reduced 184 in 1870 to 61 in 1890.[128]

7. Morocco: the emergence of a nation-state's law

Colonized by the French as a protectorate in 1912, Morocco was not subject to direct conquest, as was Algeria. Instead, the French exercised control by means of the native structures and native elites who were willing to cooperate. In a manner typical of other cases of colonialism, the French avoided interfering in native domains that did not affect their interests and hegemony, a fact that created a dual system of political and social governance: on the one hand, there emerged a newly created French system that monopolized public administration, commercial life and the sphere of penal law – that sphere through which "law and order"[129] could be imposed as prerequisites for general control. (Islamic criminal law, whose enforcement was the domain of the Sharīfian dynasty, was substituted by French penal law, an act on which the nationalists capitalized

[127] *Ibid.*, 23; Christelow, "Transformation of the Muslim Court," 224.
[128] Abun-Nasr, *History*, 258. [129] Hoisington, "Cities in Revolt," 445.

as one of usurping the divine *ḥudūd* law.)[130] Family law, on the other hand, was not of direct interest to the French, and so they left it alone, at least initially.[131] As happened in Algeria, the French government deployed the skills of French Orientalists who, drawing on their predecessors' accomplishments in Algeria, started their Moroccan "project" in earnest in 1930.

The promulgation of the 1930 *Dahir berbère* (which, among other things, abolished tribal customary law and created different schools for Berbers and Arabs) led to vehement protests because it was seen not only as a confirmation of setting aside the Sharīʿa, but also – and far more importantly – as a blatant attempt on the part of the French to divide Arabs and Berbers by further sharpening national and cultural differences between them.[132] That the thrust of the opposition was directed against the political device of "divide and rule" is attested by the well-acknowledged fact that the *Dahir berbère* ushered in the Moroccan national movement for independence.

Upon gaining independence in 1956, the new national government began its legal work by abolishing the *Dahir berbère* along with the Berber courts. Muhammad V (r. 1927–53 and 1957–61) and his government also began work on the codification of family law, a reform the French had already considered since 1953. That the national government embarked on codification of the law of personal status – originally a colonialist project – is perhaps the clearest evidence of the rootedness of the structures representing the nation-state (and no less evidence of the non-immunity of the Sharīʿa law of personal status). The reasons for this reform were presented in terms of discarding the accretions of the "sterile" past, and a restoration of the "real" Islam of the pristine age.[133] But it was also a measure against diversity and the interpretive freedoms exercised by *muftī*s and jurists. As the colonial French government had done, the law had to be opened up to the inspection and, thus, control and surveillance of the state, while the entire legal profession had to submit to the higher wisdom and knowledge of that state. This is perhaps the most powerful political and legal tradition that colonialism has bestowed on the colonies and their inhabitants.

130 On *ḥudūd*, see chapter 10, section 2, above.

131 For a profile of the legal history of modern Morocco, see An-Na'im, *Islamic Family Law*, 178–79; Bidwell, *Morocco under Colonial Rule*, 262–81.

132 Bidwell, *Morocco under Colonial Rule*, 57; Hoisington, "Cities in Revolt," 434–36; Landau, *Moroccan Drama*, 144–45.

133 Buskens, "Islamic Commentaries," 88.

It is instructive that one of the declared aims of codifying family law was to produce "unity and clarity,"[134] where the codified law of the Sharīʿa would be accessible to the new Moroccan lawyers trained in the French legal system. Like their Ottoman and Egyptian counterparts, the Western-trained lawyers of North Africa ceased to have interpretive access to the *fiqh* works. The Sharīʿa had become estranged to such a degree that a Western mechanism (= codification) was now required to intercede between these lawyers and their own history and legal culture. The *fiqh* works, now seen as the antithesis of this "unity and clarity," are obscure, complicated, disorderly and inaccessible. The native legal tradition has thus been relegated to the exotic and the foreign, part of a distant and inaccessible past that needs to be translated into the modern language of order, clarity and control. That which is clear is by definition intellectually accessible; that which is so accessible is understood; and that which is understood can be controlled and managed. In the case of modern Islamic countries, therefore, codification serves a double-tiered purpose. First, as in the Europe of the nation-state, the code was a universal tool of control exercised by the state over the legal profession and its interpretive freedoms. As an essential tool of centralization, the code was readily and quickly adopted by the post-colonial state, even when the colonizer's legal tradition was one of common law (e.g., British India and Malaysia). Second, and on a lower level in the interplay of power, the code served the legal representatives of the new nation-state not only in their bid to displace the Sharīʿa system, but also to create for themselves a new niche of power in the emerging nation-state structures. As the political native elites of the colonies immediately leapt into the gaps of power left by what Massad called the "colonial effects,"[135] the Western-trained native lawyers did the same, in their specific case displacing what was once a powerful class of legal professionals.

Yet, the modern realities of the nation-state could not be categorically severed from the past, if only because the realities of the past were seen as the sources of legitimacy, whereas the present reality was overshadowed by colonialism and its devastating effects. The new Moroccan code was thus significantly titled *Mudawwanat al-Aḥwāl al-Shakhṣiyya*, reflecting a curious duality that evokes at once the new legislative powers of the nation-state and the tradition of *sharʿī* Mālikism. The term *mudawwana* (lit. register, written document) acquired notoriety in North African Mālikism due to the fact that it was the title of one of

[134] According to the speech of the then Crown Prince, Hasan II. Cited in Buskens, *ibid.*
[135] Massad, *Colonial Effects*.

the most authoritative compendia recording the accepted opinions of the school's eponym.[136] The compound designation "*al-aḥwāl al-shakhṣiyya*," on the other hand, is a neologism introduced into the Arabic language from the European "personal status" or, more accurately, "*statut personnel.*"

The title, in so many ways, reflects the hybridity of the code itself. The great majority of rules inscribed in the code are Mālikite, but with a significant twist. While classical Mālikism followed the *madhhab* doctrine that was deemed authoritative,[137] the Moroccan legislators at times opted for those opinions that may have been considered weak or "less correct" by the standards of the classical school. Yet, these opinions did serve modern exigencies; favoring the betterment of women's position in the modern world, they were harvested for codification, thus becoming law when once they had been relegated to near doctrinal obscurity.

Thus the tradition was opened widely to appropriation, for the legitimacy derived therefrom was so powerful that the controversial parts of it were preferable to pronouncements or decrees issued in the name of the state. Whereas the 500-year history of the European nation-state has allowed it to cultivate a good deal of legitimacy, and thus pronounce on matters legal, economic and social, the recently born (or imported) Muslim state has nowhere managed to cultivate a degree of legitimacy that can compete with even the weakest, oldest and most controversial parts of the Sharīʿa. Want of legitimacy (as well as considerations of social custom, no doubt) dictated the retention of the Mālikite tradition, but the codified form spoke of the appropriation of law by the modern agency that is the nation-state. More specifically, the latter appropriated not only the law as a category, and not only Islamic law in every variety of it, but also, by implication and extension, the very history that produced that law. The exclusive jural hegemony of the nation-state becomes all the more striking in light of the identity of the code's drafters. After all, it was ʿAllāl al-Fāsī, the foremost nationalist leader, who contributed so much to the creation of this code. A Salafī and a *fiqh* specialist, and hardly a Francophone, he expressed – as far as I know – no qualms whatsoever about the "code" as a form of juristic expression. On the contrary, in fact, he and his colleagues, royal and otherwise, deemed the code a sign and a tool of national unity against the divisiveness of the French and their *Dahir berbère*.[138] The absence of qualms was not

[136] See Saḥnūn, *Mudawwana*.
[137] For the criteria of authoritativeness, see Hallaq, *Authority*, 133–52.
[138] Johnston, "ʿAllāl al-Fāsī," 84 ff.; Maddy-Weitzman, "Women, Islam," 399.

only the function of a utilitarian approach but also the result of the new yet normalized realities of governance. Under French influence and with French interventions, the Sharīfian dynasty adopted both the conceptions and the tools of centralized states. Al-Fāsī and his compatriots, in Morocco, Tunisia, Iran and elsewhere, saw no reason to question, much less problematize, the nation-state.

16 Modernizing the law in the age of nation-states

1. Introduction

It should by now be clear that, between the early years of the nineteenth century and the second decade of the twentieth, the Sharīʿa – which had dominated the legal scene for over a millennium in the central lands of Islam, and for centuries in other regions – was largely reduced in scope of application to the area of personal status, including child custody, inheritance, gifts and, to some extent, *waqf*. In the Malay States and the Indonesian Archipelago, its sphere was even narrower, partly due to the *adat* which had long prevailed in some of these domains, and partly due to the metamorphosis of some Sharīʿa laws into English law (as happened in the law of *waqf*). The present chapter follows the fortunes (indeed misfortunes) of Islamic law in the subsequent period, roughly from the end of the Second World War until the dawn of the twenty-first century.

It goes without saying that it is impossible here to provide an account of every new code and statute promulgated in Muslim countries, much less to offer a meaningful analysis of their details. I shall instead describe and analyze trends, movements and themes that can be identified as having played central roles in twentieth-century legal history, and the way they anticipated or paved the grounds for the emerging Muslim will to (re-) instate what is perceived to be Islamic law. But with this general approach in mind, we would do well to describe first the methods that the emerging nation-states used to restrict the scope and influence of Islamic law while strengthening their bureaucratic and legal powers. We would also do well to remember that since the history of the period in question was largely determined by the proto-nationalist and nationalist political elites, and since these elites generally continued the same patterns of systemic governance as the colonialist powers that they replaced,[1] the narrowing down of the Sharīʿa by both regimes must be seen more as an inherent part of the power dynamics of the evolving modern state rather than as a teleological

[1] Pollard, "Learning Gendered Modernity," 249–51, 261 ff.

effort to progress toward a more "sophisticated"[2] legal culture or to its "inevitable" form, "modern civilization." We would do even better to keep constantly in mind the fact that the latter "civilizing" discourses were the very ideological props deployed by colonialism, colonialist modernity and the post-colonial nationalist regimes in an effort to concentrate power in the hands of the state.[3] For although these discourses represented a powerful tool in the "cultural technology" of hegemonic modernity – and thus of hegemonic nationalism – they can hardly be said to constitute the real causes for this legal restructuring.

An archetype of this technology is the very term "reform,"[4] used extensively by Euro-American scholars to describe legal changes in the Muslim world over the past century (and longer in India). Its accurate equivalent in Arabic is "*iṣlāḥ*," the conceptual basis of equivalent terms used in other Islamic languages; "reform" and "*iṣlāḥ*" possess a nearly identical meaning: "to change into an improved form" and "to improve by change." In the English language it has the added nuance of "[putting] an end to an evil by enforcing or introducing another method."[5] The ideological baggage inherent in the widespread terms "reform" and "*iṣlāḥ*" is thus an integral part of the myth of improvement through progress, itself a major component of cultural technology. What we need to address, therefore, are the changes that permitted the transformation from a distinctly and characteristically Islamic order to that of the modern. To call this transformation "reform" is to engage, obliquely and often unconsciously, in political discourses that find their origins in colonialist ideology and cultural technology.

We of course do no better in adopting the term "modern" and its variants "modernity," "modernization" and "modernism." But unlike the problems latent in the language of "Islamic reform," which have thus far largely escaped scholarly critical comment, "modernity" and the "modern" have been systematically critiqued, no less by Eastern analysts (especially by the Subaltern School)[6] than by Western intelligentsia. It is within

[2] See, for example, Peters, "Administrators and Magistrates," 379.

[3] On the "cultural revolution" associated with the rise of the state, see Corrigan and Sayer, *Great Arch*. On the role of law in articulating national identity, see Massad, *Colonial Effects*, esp. 18–49.

[4] On the conceptual problems of this term, see the general Introduction to this work, section 1, above.

[5] *Merriam-Webster Eleventh Collegiate Dictionary*. This is to be sharply contrasted with the centuries-old conception of *tajdīd* (renewal), seen to be integral to the Islamic system of belief and practice. See Hallaq, "On the Existence of Mujtahids."

[6] On this school and its critics, see Lal, "Subaltern Studies," 135–48; Young, *White Mythologies*, 199–216 and *passim*.

the understanding brought out by this multifaceted critique that any favorable use of the term "modern" must be tempered.

Yet, the ultimate cultural prop of "reform" in general, and of "reform" of family law in particular, forms an integral part of the much larger hegemony of cultural knowledge that constructed a historical narrative of Islamic law in which "reform" constituted the only logical solution. Islamic law was said to be, by definition, religious and idealistic, removed from the concerns of the individual as well as from the society it was supposed to serve. "Criminal law" and "public law" – as if such designations ever existed in the vocabulary of Islam – were *ab initio* irrelevant. They did not attend to the exigencies of the real world, where the "state" – an Orientalist back projection of the modern nation-state – was conceived on behalf of Islamic law as unrealistically marginal, and where the criminals were let loose by a legal system that had miserably failed to fulfill its mission in the "effective" manner of European law (where a premium was placed on punishment).[7]

Law was thus divorced from state and society in all its branches save for religious rituals and personal status. But this "divorce" between Islamic law, on the one hand, and "society and state," on the other, was, in this largely paradigmatic narrative, the result of another fundamental feature "inherent" in Islamic law, namely, its inability to change. This stultifying stagnation was branded with the catch-all epithet "The Closure of the Gate of *Ijtihād*," a phrase designed to sum up Islamic legal history since the tenth century. That there was an extensive causal relation between, on the one hand, a colonial will to manage and rule the native populations and, on the other, the claim that Islamic "public law" had lost touch with reality was a matter noted only during the last half century, when direct colonial exploitation had exhausted both itself and the colonies – or appeared to have done so. Roughly the same time-frame can be assigned to the discovery that the closure of the famous Gate was nothing more than a myth, and a central one at that.[8] The effects of this cultural knowledge were not only heavily present in colonial and neo-colonial policies and politics but, infinitely more important, in the shaping of native knowledge. When European colonists did not accord Islamic laws of personal status any strategic importance (since these laws did not interfere with the processes of systemic (re)ordering for the purposes, *inter alia*, of material exploitation), their scholars promoted the idea that these governments had refrained from instigating "reform" out of

[7] See, e.g., the discussion in chapter 14, section 1, above.
[8] For a reevaluation, see Hallaq, "Was the Gate of Ijtihad Closed?"

respect for the sanctified regard in which Muslims held their laws of personal status.

This sensibility, of course, demonstrates the relevance and centrality of this law to the individual Muslim, when the rest of the law, save for that of rituals, had no place in the real modern world. This relatively new construction of Islamic law, like modern law itself, appeared as a displacement of a qualitatively different native legal system and an equally different native historical narrative. The legal changes themselves, the "reforms," have been offered as evidence of the validity of the superimposed modern narrative and of the inefficiency of the ulama, their "corruption" and their utter lack of desire for "improvement" and "progress." Thus, the very narrative that constituted the justification-cum-rationalization for demolishing the legal structures of Islam became, perforce, the knowledge that Muslims acquired of their own history in general and their legal history in particular (the latter being itself a new invention). I say "perforce" because this knowledge was an indispensable logical subject, a prerequisite for the legal transmutations to take place. This cultural knowledge in effect amounted to the conquest of the mind, and this particular conquest, the colonial powers well understood, was more crucial than the conquest of the body: for whereas the latter enabled a partial control, the former yielded a totalistic dominance.[9]

Muslims' *modern* knowledge of their own (legal) history, and thus of their historical selves, is a field in which dominant discourses determined the shape of present and future law. The sacredness and sensitivity of the laws of personal status, once marked as such, were taken as the point of reference for the modern politics of identity. If family law emerged as "the preferential symbol of Islamic identity,"[10] it did so not only because it was built into Muslim knowledge as an area about which they should display sensitivity, but also because it represented what was taken to be the last fortress of the Sharīʿa to survive the ravages of modernization.

What was left for the Sharīʿa to regulate was personal status, now seen to include, in addition to marriage and divorce, such areas as inheritance, child custody and gifts. While the popular Muslim imagination, even today, appears to hold these remnants of the Sharīʿa to be an authentic and genuine expression of the *fiqhī* family law, the fact of the matter is that even this sphere of law underwent structural and foundational changes that ultimately resulted in its being severed from both the substance of classical *fiqh* and the methodology by which *fiqh* had operated. For to maintain this methodology would have amounted to maintaining not

[9] In this context, see Yeğenoğlu, *Colonial Fantasies*, 95–120.
[10] Hélie-Lucas, "Preferential Symbol," 391–407; Moors, "Debating," 150.

only the Arabicate hermeneutics but also, by extension, the human and institutional bearers of this complex epistemic tradition. This, in other words, would have required the maintenance of the very system that produced the entire sociology of legal knowledge, including the institutions of *waqf* and *madrasa*. But we have seen that these otherwise independent institutions stood in the way of the emerging state, which is to say that they represented an impediment to centralization, be it fiscal, legal or otherwise. Thus, it was both essential to and an inevitable consequence of the ways of the nation-state that personal status had to be severed from its own, indigenous jural *system*, its own ecological environment.

This severance was effected through various devices that included both administrative and interpretive techniques. Attributed to nebulous origins in Islamic tradition and history, these devices were cultivated and augmented to yield results that had never been entertained before. The first of these devices was a concept that has come to be used, often implicitly, to justify any and all change in the law. In pre-modern *fiqh*, one was permitted to avoid harm to oneself even if this entailed a violation of the law, e.g., consuming ritually impure food if one is threatened with starvation. This substantive legal principle, the concept of "necessity" (*ḍarūra*),[11] was fundamentally transformed by modern legists in two ways: first, it was transposed from the domain of substantive law (where it regulated relatively few cases) to the realm of legal theory that in turn came to regulate the construction and operation of positive law generally. Second – and partly derivative of the first – the scope of the principle was widened beyond recognition, so that instead of delimiting the boundaries of "necessity" within those of the law, the law in its entirety was (re)defined within utilitarian principles of necessity. The legal principle was thus turned on its head, from being subordinate to the larger imperative of the law to being the dominating and all-encompassing principle.

The second device was procedural,[12] which is to say that without changing certain parts of Islamic positive law, it was possible through this device to exclude particular claims from judicial enforcement, thus in effect leaving *fiqhī* law mere ink on dusty paper. For instance, in deference to religious sentiments, child marriage was not explicitly outlawed, but to cancel the effects of this *fiqhī* law, the office of the registrar – which now effectively possesses the authority to declare what is legal and

[11] For more on this in the context of legal theory, see the next chapter.
[12] The following four devices were identified by Norman Anderson, but my account with regard to the stipulation of contractual terms differs from his. See his *Law Reform*, 42–82. A summary of Anderson's discussion is to be found in H. Liebesny, *Law of the Near and Middle East*, 136–39. See also Anderson's "Eclipse of the Patriarchal Family," 224–25.

what is not – was instructed to register only those contracts the parties to which have attained the age of majority. A similar change was effected in the area of oral testimony and oral evidence, where the courts were instructed not to hear claims lacking documentary and written evidence. Again, the traditional competence of the ruler's *siyāsa sharʿiyya* had been expanded beyond recognition, giving the modern state an unqualified prerogative to control the law of procedure and legal administration, just as it controlled substantive law.

The third device, one of the most effective methods by which new positive law was created from the virtual dispersal-cum-restructuring of *fiqh*, consisted of an eclectic approach that operated on two levels: *takhayyur* and *talfīq* (lit. "selection" and "amalgamation"). The former involved the incorporation not only of "weak" and discredited opinions from the school, but also of opinions held by other schools. The options opened up by this device seemed boundless, since it was not only Twelver-Shīʿite opinions that could be absorbed by the codes of Sunnite countries, but so also could those of the long defunct Ẓāhirite school. *Talfīq* involved an even more daring technique. While *takhayyur* required the harvesting of opinions, for a single code, from various schools, *talfīq* amounted to combining elements of one opinion from various quarters within and without the school. The product thereof was entirely new, because the opinions now combined had originally belonged to altogether different and perhaps incongruent premises.[13] Both devices, it may be noted, had been forbidden in Islamic law, for both the jurists and "state authorities." In pre-modern Sharīʿa, the individual Muslim had the freedom to choose among the schools, in whole or in part, but he or she was bound to whichever school chosen for a transaction (until the entire effects of that transaction have been exhausted, e.g., a Shāfiʿite marriage can no more be dissolved by Mālikite law than a dispute over a Ḥanbalite partnership adjudged according to Ḥanafite law). Examples of this double-tiered device were the severe restrictions placed on the effects of formulas of *ṭalāq* uttered by Muslim husbands, and on conditional repudiation arising from taking oaths or making threat-pronouncements. In some countries, notably Egypt and Iraq, this device was used to produce radical changes even in inheritance law, e.g., making lawful a bequest in favor of an heir, with the proviso that the total bulk of the bequeathed property not exceed one-third of the estate. The consent of the other heirs was furthermore no longer required.[14]

[13] See Liebesny, *Law of the Near and Middle East*, 138; Hallaq, *History*, 210, 261.
[14] Cf. chapter 8, section 6, above.

The fourth device is the so-called neo-*ijtihād*, an interpretive approach that is largely free of what we have here called Arabicate hermeneutics. In a sense, the device of *takhayyur* and *talfīq* rests on this general approach, since the act of combining different, if not divergent, elements of one opinion entails a measure of interpretive freedom. But there are other examples of a new kind of interpretation, such as limiting the period of pregnancy to one year, a period which some authoritative classical jurists, working hard to keep conceptions out of wedlock within family bounds, had extended at times to up to four years. Another example is the 1956 Tunisian Code of Personal Status which prohibits polygamy on the grounds that the Quran explicitly predicated the permission to marry up to four wives on the man's ability to treat them with complete fairness and justice, a requirement that was interpreted by the law-makers as essentially idealistic and impossible to achieve.[15]

The fifth and final device, much like the first, represents a new application of the old but restricted principle that any law that does not contradict the Sharīʿa may be deemed lawful. Prohibition of child marriage and unilateral divorce by the husband are seen as belonging to this category of law.

In their entirety, these devices, directly as well as obliquely, did the bidding of the state in absorbing the Islamic legal tradition into its well-defined structures of codification. But the most substantive of these devices were the third and the fourth, with the former literally supplying much of the law, remolding it with a view to producing particular, intended effects. We will discuss the most important of these effects in the next section, but for now we must note the most salient by-product of this structural difference, namely, the difference between the discursive unraveling of law in the Sharīʿa and in codified systems. In Part I of this book, it was shown that, despite the systemic hermeneutical tendency to determine an authoritative opinion in each school, *ijtihād*ic plurality could not be curbed. And it was this plurality that was in part responsible not only for legal change, but also for flexibility in the application of the law.[16] Women, for example, could resort to any school, and the *qāḍī* in actual practice could apply any opinion from within that school to accommodate a particular situation. Codification, on the other hand, eliminates almost all such juristic and hermeneutical possibilities, leaving both the litigants

[15] In the Explanatory Memorandum of this Code, the state still invokes religious authority of the ulama, whose "opinion" on the matter is presumably based on the Quranic verse 4:129: "You shall never be able to deal equally between your wives, however much you wanted to."

[16] This is one of the main findings in Hallaq, *Authority*.

and the judge with a single formulation and, in all likelihood, a single mode of judicial application. For it is eminently arguable that unifying and homogenizing the law – and all that which constitutes the world of the Subject – is one of the primary concerns of the modern state.

2. The law of personal status and the new patriarchy

The engineering of these devices and their orchestration to produce particular effects was the work of the modern state, the appropriator and possessor of the law. That this state was the most central and commanding modern institution ever to enter the world of Islam is nothing short of a truism. As the primary and leading institution of European modernity, it constantly defined, redefined and influenced nearly every entity with which it came into contact. Whether incorporated into the Muslim world by imposition or by mimesis, its defining, constitutive and fundamental features were nearly identical everywhere. It incorporated within its boundaries the exclusive right to wage war outside and, with the same exclusivity, to exercise violence within its own domains; it declared itself sovereign while developing systemic mechanisms of surveillance and discipline; it lived on nationalism as the body lives on circulated blood; it appropriated the exclusive right to make and enforce law; and in all of this it was the "big father" of the citizen. As a man was head of the family, the state was the head of society. The nation-state thus combined among its attributes the power to rule and subdue, and the right and duty to defend, promote and claim possession of the nation, nationhood, nationality and their subject – the citizen.

Nationalism has always been a masculine conception that subordinates the feminine. It is, at the same time, a distinctly racial conception that stems from a certain assumption, if not a "scientific" premise, of purity of blood. The conception would vanish into absurdity if the French nation were to be seen to have been formed with the assistance of Italian, Arab or Chinese sperm. For sperm is central to this conception. In nineteenth-century Europe, the blood of a nation was not only a matter of symbolism and semiotics, but a scientific project. Galton, Spencer, Darwin and Gardner, among others, asserted that every part of the human body and every attribute of personality contribute, through the blood, to the formation of the sperm.[17] And it was this biological and evolutionary operation that maintained the uniqueness of nations. From this logic followed the conception that it was the man, not the woman, who determined

[17] Barker-Benfield, "Spermatic Economy," 65.

national attributes, which is another way of saying that man – through his sperm – defined and literally constituted the nation as the subject of the state. As an archetypal figure, he likewise constituted it as an object of sovereignty. In this design, women became instruments of reproduction, while the modern state appropriated the right to determine "the uses of women's reproductive skills."[18]

The nation-state that the Muslims encountered was – and continues to be – a masculine entity and, in its nineteenth- and early twentieth-century form, a thoroughgoing patriarchal order.[19] As we saw in the earlier chapters in this Part, it was the French model that dominated the colonialist scene in the Middle Eastern (and African) countries. Even Egypt, an otherwise British protectorate, opted for that model.[20] And it is not difficult to see why this should have been the case. One of the most salient features of the nation-state was its totalistic appropriation of the domain of law, an appropriation that presupposed centralization and bureaucratization of the legal system. There was no room for judges' law-making, otherwise a defining attribute of the British case law system. Case law is a diffused phenomenon, lacking in concentricity, a clear voice of authority, and a textual homogeneity that can pronounce the laws of the state in an authoritatively clear and unmistakable fashion. A strong colonialist regime (and later nationalist governance) thus required the code, the statute and the act as tools of total control. Even the British engaged in this form of legislation in their jural reconstruction of the colonies.

It was no coincidence that the code, the very tool that represented and embodied the agendas of the nation-state,[21] was also the chief method by which the jural modalities of the Orient were reengineered. And the French model not only supplied the political form of the nation-state's hegemony; it also – and importantly – furnished the legal content and substance that bolstered this hegemony. If sperm was seen to constitute the nation, so was the state's law. But for it to make the nation, shape it and represent it, the law had to be equally national, the very embodiment of the nation's will, aspirations and worldview. In the final analysis, the law is and must be the quintessential expression of the state's will.

Inasmuch as the law is a manifestation of the state and its will to power, the family, as a prototype of the nation, is the reconstituted invention of the state, whether in Europe or the Muslim world. The ideal family, consisting of a two-parent household, lacked the complex social networks that otherwise engendered loyalty among and between the many members

18 Hatem, "Professionalization of Health," 67.
19 For a general background analysis, see Sharabi, *Neopatriarchy*.
20 Ghaṣūb, "al-Qawānīn al-Waḍʿiyya," 20–24. 21 See chapter 13, above.

of the extended family and clan. The nuclear family, constituted by national ideology and a capitalist mode of production (both inherent to the structures of European and most other states),[22] was thus the object of the social project of engineering; it was, in fact, a quintessential of the imagining of the state and its ideological and political practices. And having been assigned to fulfill this role, the family is shaped by the state's law through regulation of marriage, divorce and inheritance, as well as an array of practices that define and dictate those relationships producing the family.[23] Yet, the family itself arguably stands with the state as mutually constitutive: the state's power to authorize and dissolve marriage manifests itself as a set of practices from which it derives its own sovereignty, while the family has thus contributed to shaping the modern state, though on terms that suit the state and its systematic and systemic programs to reengineer (or sanction preexisting parts of) the social order, among others.[24]

During the colonial period, when the nation-state was being imported into the Muslim world from Europe, the agenda of the colonial powers did not include the reengineering of the Muslim family, for the construction of states *qua* states in the lands of Islam was not originally what the colonists aimed to accomplish. Material exploitation, the quintessential project of colonialism, did not require this reengineering, a situation that allowed (as we saw earlier) colonial apologists to make a virtue of non-necessity. As we will see in due course, many Islamic countries indirectly embarked on modifying family law as early as the second decade of the twentieth century, but the project of reengineering the family via legal mechanisms did not begin in earnest until the colonies acquired, *mutatis mutandis*, autonomy or independence. Nevertheless, as we saw in earlier chapters, the colonial powers did, directly and obliquely, cause the dismantling of the *waqf* institution, which was undoubtedly linked in numerous structural ways with family life and the laws that regulated that life. Furthermore, when France developed the unique colonial idea of absorbing Algeria into the French nation, it repeatedly attempted to alter the personal laws of the Sharīʿa and replace them with what was seen as more progressive and civilized rules. From the middle of the nineteenth century onward, they attempted to enforce many codes and decrees, most

[22] Further on this theme, see the paragraphs toward the end of this section.

[23] On how this formation developed first in England, see the work of Corrigan and Sayer, *Great Arch*.

[24] Joseph, "Kin Contract and Citizenship," 151–53; Joseph, "Public/Private," 83–88; Yilmaz, "Secular Law," 119. For England, see Corrigan and Sayer, *Great Arch*, 12, 36–37, 95–96, and *passim*.

notably the *Code Morand*,[25] a code that was devised, *inter alia*, to redesign the Muslim family on lines conceived by the *état suprême* of post-Revolutionary France. In the end it was due to the determined resistance of the Algerians that such attempts resulted in failure, and surely not to the lack of French effort.

As the nationalist elites slowly began to displace the colonists, the project of governance could no longer be limited to the unidimensional aim of material exploitation. The basic structures of the state apparatus were already in place, and the goal would now become total rule, a desideratum that all nineteenth-century European states had already attained at home. This type of rule, together with what the French had attempted to do in Algeria, would become one of the primary objectives of the new nationalist elites. The recently independent states in the Islamic world would continue a project of governance that the colonists had little motive to pursue in the colonies, for the project, in its full manifestation, did not serve colonialist goals. But once political independence was secured, the nationalist leadership pursued state-building in earnest. Tellingly, what this leadership had resisted under colonial rule, it would insist upon after independence. For instance, under the French, the Tunisian and Algerian nationalists vehemently opposed any change in the law of personal status, but as soon as the French were made to leave, and as soon as the former assumed power, they almost immediately embarked on a program of "reform" in this presumably sensitive legal sphere.

The early, half-hearted Ottoman codification of personal status, as well as the later nationalist codification projects, found its inspiration in the only available model of governance: the European nation-state in general, and the French version of it in particular. The French Civil Codes (from 1804 until the middle of the twentieth century), to which the Ottoman Empire, the post-colonial nation-states and so much of Africa owed a debt, did not hesitate to declare the man to be the predominant figure in the home. In the 1804 Civil Code, and thereafter until its 1938 successor, it is unambiguously stated that the "husband owes protection to his wife, the wife obedience to her husband."[26] Even as late as 1970, in French law the husband still stood as "the head of the family." (Similarly, until 1949, the West German Civil Code granted the husband the right to "decide all matters of matrimonial rights" while the so-called Equality Law of 1957 [art. 1356.I] opens with the statement that "The wife's responsibility is to run the household.") Therefore it was this legal culture, directly arising

[25] See chapter 15, section 4, above.
[26] This and the next two sentences draw on Glendon, "Power and Authority," 6–9.

from the nation and its state, that defined the parameters of post-colonial nationalism. Partha Chatterjee's apt description of the Indian context equally applies to others: nationalism, Chatterjee observed, "conferred upon women the honor of a new social responsibility and by associating the task of female emancipation with the historical goal of sovereign nationhood, bound them to a narrow, and yet entirely legitimate, subordination."[27]

This subordination finds ample manifestation in the provisions of the Ottoman Law of Family Rights of 1917, a law that represented in the Ottoman domains the first state-sponsored codification of the Islamic law of personal status. The significance of this Law lay not only in the fact that it was the first attempt of this kind, but, more importantly, in its spacio-temporal propagation. For whereas Turkey seceded from the entire edifice of Islamic law in 1926, the Law of 1917 remains in effect as the Muslim denominational law of Lebanon and Israel to this day, and continued to be the official law of Syria until 1949 and Jordan until 1951. What adds to the significance of this Law is not only the fact that it is the major survival of the Sharīʿa in the post-Ottoman era, but that it purportedly set out to improve the lot of Muslim women. But did it?

The Family Law of 1917 generally did not depart from the provisions of the Sharīʿa, but it did codify them, and thus subjected them to the rigidity of a single linear language devoid of the plurality and multiple juristic nuances and variations that the *fiqh* had afforded. The hallmark of this codifying transmutation was, as we have repeatedly noted, the appropriation of the law by the nation-state, a transmutation that announced the clear message that, even when the law was both substantively and substantially that of the Sharīʿa, it was ultimately the state that determined this fact and what part – or what combination thereof – was or was not law. This precisely is the meaning of sovereignty, and sovereignty is no one else's business but the state's.

Yet, in the very process of reenacting Islamic law into a codified body of rules, linguistic presentation, focus, brevity, detail and attention, all played a significant part in recasting and remolding the law, all of which factors entered into the calculation of what effects the law was supposed to produce. Thus, while *fiqh* provides a staggering body of discourse respecting the wife's right to various types of support from her husband,[28] the 1917 Law reduces this discourse to two articles whose brevity deprives the modern court of the full view of these rights. (In pre-modern Ḥanafite law, by contrast, the wife's rights to support are discussed at great length, often

[27] Chatterjee, "Colonialism," 629–32. [28] See chapter 8, section 5, above.

spanning dozens of pages.)[29] All that emerges from the multiplicity of pre-modern rights[30] is a "legal house" (*maskin sharʿī*),[31] language that might be interpreted by modern judges in light of customary practice (thus maintaining a measure of continuity), but a practice that was constantly shifting in favor of new realities that tended, with time, to supersede the earlier ones, if not remove them from judicial memory. "Legal house," together with the provision (art. 72) stressing the wife's right to refuse living with the family of her husband,[32] seems to be a recognition of the rising importance of privacy and companionate marriage, but it simultaneously takes away, again through silence, the pre-modern set of rights that "constructed the wife as a social being with needs for companionship that must be accommodated by the presence of relatives, neighbors, or even hired companions."[33]

Yet, the legal reduction of matrimonial relationship (formerly predicated upon complex social relations within an extended family structure) to companionate marriage simultaneously constituted a step toward constructing the wife as a housewife in a family unit headed by the husband (*rabb al-ʿāʾila*; lit. master or head of the family), a notion that is entirely absent from the *fiqh*. Indeed, article 73 of the 1917 law requires the husband to treat his wife kindly, but imposes on her the obligation of obedience.[34] The latter, in *fiqh* heritage narrowly defined in terms of sexual availability, is now dissociated from an intricate system of obligations to which the husband too was bound. "Obedience" has undergone abstraction and expansion, and has furthermore been merged into the highly unrestricted French civil notion of wifely obedience marshaled to produce an effective means of subordination. Little of this changed even much later. A recent study of the 1957 Moroccan family law convincingly argues that the so-called reforms in that country have indeed produced a consolidated patriarchal hold within a reinterpreted field of the Sharīʿa, while simultaneously undermining the intricate guarantees and

[29] For instance, in the Ḥanafite work of Ibn al-Humām, the exposition of law pertaining to wifely *nafaqa* required over 17,000 words. See his *Sharḥ*, IV, 378–409. Similarly, in the magisterial Shāfiʿite work of Nawawī, the same discussion occupied almost 10,000 words. See his *Rawḍa*, VI, 449–89. These space allocations are common in all the schools. See also Appendix A, Book no. 43.

[30] See sources cited in previous note, as well as chapter 8, section 5, above.

[31] Article 70. The Law is found in *Majmūʿat al-Qawānīn*, 353–77.

[32] This right was fully recognized by pre-modern jurists. See Marghīnānī, *Hidāya*, II, 43.

[33] Tucker, "Revisiting Reform," 11.

[34] Article 1105 of the Civil Code of Iran (1934) states: "In relation between spouses, the headship of the family is a privilege of the husband." Likewise, Article 105 of the Indonesian Civil Code (*Kitab Undang-Undang Hukum Perdata*) stipulates that "Every husband shall become the head of the family."

multi-layered safety nets that the Sharīʿa had provided in practice before the dawn of modernity and its nation-state.[35]

A further index of women's subordination relates to the post-colonial promotion of the man/husband as head of the family, to be obeyed and even revered. We recall that the pre-modern Muslim jurists regarded the inability of the husband to fulfill his marital duties as constituting *nushūz* (disobedience), in which case he was required to grant his wife a *khulʿ* without remuneration to him.[36] Husbands, in other words, were as much subject to the charge of *nushūz* as wives, although their liabilities were assumed to take different forms. In modern national codes, *nushūz* becomes exclusively a woman's liability, the result of failure to perform a variety of functions assigned to her by the law. Thus, in the Algerian code, the wife can be accused of *nushūz* simply for failure to accord the husband respect as head of the family; in Libya and Yemen, *nushūz* arises for failing to attend to the needs and affairs of the matrimonial home; in Morocco, it arises for failure to show respect to the husband's parents.[37]

These grounds for *nushūz* were clearly not so expansive in pre-modern *fiqh*, having been mainly limited to sexual inaccessibility. In *fiqh*, the family was constituted as a social group based on kinship, a group whose members had rights and duties, but where no one was *legally* designated as head. Materially and economically (a wide scope of social existence), women were legally independent, having the same rights as men. Husbands could not legally control their wives' property. Nor was the woman required to respect her husband's parents any more than he was required to respect hers.[38] Nor, moreover, was she required by law to attend to the affairs and daily needs of the matrimonial home, it being explicitly stipulated as the husband's duty. But this is not all. A host of rights that women enjoyed in *fiqh* were entirely lost in modern legislation, not the least of which was the husband's responsibility to pay for suckling his own children, for the cleaning and cooking expenses of the matrimonial household, and for servants to attend to his wife's personal needs.[39]

These privative, and distinctly gender-based, transformations were made possible by several factors that combined to produce multiple effects

[35] Mir-Hosseini, *Marriage*, 191–98; Sonbol, "*Ṭāʿa* and Modern Legal Reform."

[36] See chapter 8, section 3, above; ʿAynī, *Bināya*, V, 510–11.

[37] Compare this with pre-modern Mālikite doctrine, which was largely abandoned even in traditionally Mālikite countries. Welchman, *Beyond the Code*, 283–92, and *passim*. On *nushūz* as a tool of exchanging one patriarchal regime for another in the Israeli context, see Abou-Ramadan, "Islamic Legal Reform," 29–69, especially at 63–66.

[38] To the best of my knowledge, this point was never raised in the *fiqh* works.

[39] Ḥiṣnī, *Kifāya*, II, 146; Ibn al-Humām, *Sharḥ*, IV, 378–79; Māwardī, *Ḥāwī*, XI, 427, 431–32; Ibn Qudāma, *Kāfī*, III, 251.

in different sites, effects that invariably served to increase the subordination of women. One of the crucial factors was the collapse during the nineteenth-century of local markets in most countries of the Muslim world, a far-reaching phenomenon causally linked to the European domination of the newly created open markets in these countries. Integral to this economic transformation, which led to the rise of alternative modes of economic production, was the disappearance of the home economy (involving, *inter alia*, weaving and spinning), in which women not only had played a crucial role, but also, through their economic performance, had benefited from the financial independence that this afforded.[40]

A second factor was the rise of new political, legal, economic and bureaucratic elites that were either essential to building the new state system or subordinated to its structures. Taking as their model late nineteenth-century Europe – which had barely begun to grant its women the right to full personhood (be it in terms of suffrage or owning property in marriage) – the new Muslim elites (almost exclusively male) filled the gaps in the changing structures of power through mimesis.[41]

Third, and arising from the second factor, was the importation by the new national elite of European systems and philosophies of education which assigned to women the role of raising the national citizen of the future. Women, important and sublime though their role was in manufacturing the successful and productive nation, were nonetheless expected to stay at home, with their children.[42] Yet another factor was the very creation of gaps due to the changing structures of power, which were, in the first place, a logical – though not always temporal – prerequisite for the rise of the factors we have just outlined. For the rise of the machinery of the nation-state was an act of displacement, and aside from the economic transformation, the displacement affected the jural structures, their Arabicate hermeneutics and the entire system of legal checks and balances that had hitherto been engraved onto the social order and its practices. The language of the 1917 Law was an exact reflection not only of the loss of these checks and balances but also of the interplay between these different factors.

Yet another factor enhancing this prejudicial transformation was the gradual rise of a new and anomic psycho-social order, one that grew

[40] Quataert, *Ottoman Manufacturing*, chapters 2–3; Tucker, *Women in Nineteenth Century Egypt*, chapter 3.

[41] Mimesis that is anchored, nonetheless, in European technological, material and cultural hegemony. In this context, but from the European perspective, see Fuchs, *Mimesis and Empire*. For a literary narrative about the problematic reception of modern bureaucratic procedure in a non-urban Muslim society, see al-Hakim, *Maze of Justice*.

[42] On this theme in general, see Abu-Lughod, *Remaking Women*.

concomitantly with the continual reduction of the extended family and the simultaneous increase in the prominence of the nuclear family.[43] That this socio-familial transformation – to which we shall return later – was due to the changing modes of economic production is clear, but what has not been sufficiently taken into account is the dialectical relationship between these social and economic transformations and the new notion of individualism. While the incomes of extended family members largely belonged to an indistinguishable fiscal pool that was often perceived as group-owned and that consisted of goods and commodities along with cash, in the emerging nuclear family, and because of the rise of a massive bureaucratic elite, the man's salaried income was an individualized act of remuneration, an income earned through a narrowly defined job in which no other family member took part. An increasing sense of individualism, combined with a male-oriented national state, a new male-oriented economy and bureaucracy, and a wholesale collapse of the domestic economies that had been the exclusive domain of women, all combined to produce legal codes and legal cultures that, under the banner of modernity, tended to subordinate women rather than liberate them.

Equally important in the 1917 Law, and analyzable in the same fashion, is its haunting brevity in dealing with the modes of marital dissolution afforded to the wife. The Law quietly affirmed the husband's absolute right to effect divorce by *ṭalāq*[44] when, at the same time, it severely abridged the discourse about *khulʿ*,[45] formerly a common recourse available to women who wished to rid themselves of a bad marriage.[46] Article 116 makes mention of it in passing, without describing any of the substantive or procedural legalities associated with it. As one scholar has perceptively noted, "[o]nly the closest reader of the Law would notice that such a divorce had legal standing."[47] By contrast, as we recall, the *fiqh* consecrated pages upon pages to discussing this form of marital repudiation.[48] Furthermore, while the *fiqh* had in practice permitted a woman to sue for marital annulment only after one year of her husband's failure to provide support[49] (due, *inter alia*, to insolvency, desertion or disappearance), the

43 This argument does not require the premise that the nuclear family is an exclusively modern creation, which it is not.
44 For the woman's contractual right to protect herself against polygamy (a right that long pre-dates the 1917 Law), see the discussion in this chapter about polygamy, below.
45 See chapter 8, sections 2–3, above.
46 Tucker, "Revisiting Reform," 11–12; Zilfi, "We Don't Get Along," 272; Rapoport, *Marriage*, 4; Jennings, "Women," 82–87.
47 Tucker, "Revisiting Reform," 12.
48 See chapter 8, section 3, above.
49 According to some jurists, a woman can sue for annulment if her husband was not sexually available to her after six months. See Najdī, *Ḥāshiya*, VI, 437–38. For the Syrian and Palestinian practice based on a one-year duration, see Tucker, "Revisiting Reform," 16.

1917 Law expanded this period to four years (art. 127), thus exacerbating the wife's plight. On the whole, the 1917 Law reduced the multiple and multi-layered *fiqh* rights of women instead of expanding them. Yet, while maintaining many of the male legal prerogatives versus the female, the new law restricted male rights in other respects, all in favor of closer state control and surveillance over family life.[50] But the overall end result was one that intercalated women into a regimented domestic sphere, and all this on the ruins of what had once been a largely open social public space that allowed extraordinarily free latitude of economic transaction in both the private and public domains.[51]

But mimesis had to continue, as it had from the beginning of European hegemony, as an integral feature of modernity. In fact, modernity reinvented mimesis, and deployed it as a part of its arsenal. The rise of proto-feminist movements in Euro-America during the first half of the twentieth century redefined the discourses of colonial cultural technology, with the result that promoting the feminist agenda immediately resounded in the Muslim world at large. Whereas the "segregated Muslim woman" had, in the nineteenth century, been the focus of European and American commentary and criticism, in the twentieth century she had become in this critical commentary the victim of a merciless patriarchy, from which she had to be rescued. Yet there was little, if any, recognition that the new forms of patriarchy were directly caused by the displacements/transformations just outlined. As part of the cultural technology of domination, the critique chimed with the agenda of the ruling elites of the Muslim states, and was reflected in the changes that these states made to the substance of the law. Women had become a priority in fashioning the new nation, and redesigning the law was yet one more means of achieving this end.

3. Engineering family law

Integral to the project of social engineering was a specific effort to increase the contractual options of the wife. Through the methods of *takhayyur* and *talfīq*, most states reconstituted the marriage contract along the lines of Ḥanbalite doctrine, which permitted the inclusion of as many terms as the parties might wish to stipulate, as long as no term was contrary to the aims of the contract.[52] By implication, this reconstitution also meant that the terms and conditions could not violate the established principles of the law or the parties' interests as ensured by the contract itself. This widely

[50] Asad, "Conscripts of Western Civilization," 341–42.
[51] See chapter 4, section 5, above. [52] Buhūtī, *Kashshāf*, III, 216–26.

adopted contractual doctrine permitted women to include stipulations that served to protect their own interests within marriage, such as the right to work outside the marital home; to divorce her husband; to forbid him from taking a second wife; or, on penalty of divorce, to prohibit him from moving the marital home to another locale without her consent.

As we recall,[53] these terms, excluding the first, had been frequently included in marriage contracts, even when these were concluded according to the Ḥanafite and Mālikite schools. With our evidence coming mainly from Egypt, we may speculate that the extent of such inclusions varied in time and place. What the twentieth-century state accomplished in this respect was to systematize the right to these inclusions, thereby raising the scale minima of women's rights. Yet, Muslim women have not leapt to take advantage of the newly available contractual options.[54] In an effort to increase this proportion, the state began actively to encourage the use of such options by women. In 1995, for instance, the Egyptian Ministry of Justice prepared a draft marriage contract that could be used by couples as a model and be modified in accordance with their wishes and needs – this contract's purpose was to make the entire range of legal possibilities known to the average citizen.[55] Furthermore, by setting the terms and conditions in a ubiquitously available and standard document, the conditions would acquire a routine-like character, thereby making them in effect an integral part of the law rather than an addendum that women would have to negotiate or for which they would have to bargain. A similar, standard contract was drafted in 1975 in Iran and reformulated under the Islamic Republic in 1982. The new model contract, reflecting changes in positive law, contained several standard conditions, including the wife's right to take half of her husband's assets that he had accumulated during marriage, provided that he divorced her for no fault of hers. (The 1982 Law also gave the woman the right to the value of all her labor during the marriage, if she were determined by the court not to be at fault in the breakdown of the marriage.) By the terms of the model contract, she would also be entitled to divorce him should he abandon or mistreat her, marry another, or default on maintenance. This standard(ized) contract had something of a *sharʿī* appearance, since the husband, by accepting these conditions – which he now had to – could be said to have delegated to his wife the powers to divorce herself from him should he default on any of the stipulated conditions.[56] (Incidentally, these powers of delegated divorce [*ṭalāq al-tafwīḍ*] were fully recognized and intricately elaborated

53 Chapter 4, section 5, and chapter 8, above.
54 See, e.g., Welchman, "Special Stipulations"; Welchman, *Beyond the Code*, 163–82.
55 Moors, "Debating," 161. 56 Mir-Hosseini, *Marriage*, 55–58.

in *fiqh*, but never integrated into any standard contract, an unknown practice in the first place.)[57]

As we said earlier, the insertion of these conditions was nothing new, and the traditional Sharīʿa courts of virtually all schools have in practice accepted the inclusion of such conditions. But this inclusion had been the exclusive prerogative of the wife, a piece of ammunition with which she was supplied as a matter of protection. Nevertheless, in many modern "reforms," partly out of a preoccupation to equalize the rights of men and women, this prerogative of inserting conditions has now been bestowed on men in several Muslim countries, thereby enhancing the subordination of women in the name of equality.

Financially, marriage in the nation-state was to be reengineered supposedly in order to strengthen the position of women. Now integrated into the legal institution of marriage are guarantees for the maintenance to which wives are entitled by operation of the law, i.e., even if the guarantees were not stipulated as part of any agreement. This is classical doctrine reenacted. As we noted earlier, maintenance consisted of the provisions of clothing, shelter and food. The reforms have made it, as *fiqh* had done for centuries, an inextinguishable obligation on the part of the husband to provide for his wife, holding any part of his estate liable for seizure by the court to defray the costs of maintenance. Likewise, a wife was contractually entitled to a dower. This remained both a legal requirement and a social and customary practice. Although in India and Pakistan the extravagant stipulations of dower caused legislation to counter abuses in this domain (forcing the parties to stipulate reasonable amounts of dower), most states, especially in the Arab world, continued to enhance this feature of the marriage contract. In Egypt, for instance, dower not only continued to be an essential feature in the validity of the marriage contract, arising by operation of the law, but the wife also retained priority of claim over all other claims of debt against the husband's estate. Her right to dower is inextinguishable, and the husband's failure to pay it can land him in prison. And in order to enhance the husband's ability to surrender the amount of the dower to his wife, he is required to provide a guarantor, who will be equally culpable upon failure to pay. (It is remarkable that these rights continue to be stated according to a logic and language that is highly gendered. In a world where an increasing number of Muslim women nowadays hold more lucrative jobs than their husbands, who may be unemployed, the law has not yet managed to neutralize its language to

[57] On the various forms of *ṭalāq al-tafwīḍ*, see Ibn ʿĀbidīn, *Ḥāshiya*, III, 314 ff., 325 ff., 331 ff.; Nawawī, *Rawḍa*, VI, 44–50; Ibn Qudāma, *Mughnī*, VIII, 298 ff.

reflect the rights of the husband in cases where women are the breadwinners.)[58]

In the great majority of Muslim states, especially those traditionally of Mālikite affiliation, several restrictions were placed on the powers of the marriage guardian who, as we saw in chapter 8, was normatively defined as a male relative who had significant powers in determining who his ward should or would marry. Some of these male prerogatives were maintained until about the middle of the twentieth century, but they have increasingly come under attack since. Under pressure from feminist groups, the Moroccan government, for instance, came to change some of the assumptions about guardianship by proclaiming it "the woman's right," a change that actually reflects a reversal of rights. In the *fiqh* corpus, the guardianship of the senior male agnate amounted to a representational right whereby the interests of the family and the group would be considered together with the marital interests of the ward. The Moroccan legislature aimed to guarantee this right by stipulating that marriage could not be concluded "without her consent," but they also found it impossible to ignore the fact that Moroccan society, like nearly every other Muslim society, places a premium on the family as well as on inter-familial relations. Article 12 of the Code of Personal Status thus offers a guarantee for the family, as represented by the guardian, to the effect that the social network within which the marriage is embedded must play a role in the contractual process. While her consent is indispensable, the guardian, this article stipulates, "concludes the marriage on her behalf." But guarantees were also installed in favor of a woman whose guardian might refuse to conclude a marriage that she desired. Several states thus permit women of marrying age to petition the courts to obtain permission to marry against the objections of relatives, including male guardians. On the other hand, in the laws of Pakistan and India, a minor girl married by her father or grandfather must wait until the age of eighteen before she can seek judicial dissolution of her marriage.

The Moroccan case exemplifies what may be called the transitional problematics of modernizing societies, where traditional communal norms coexist alongside, yet simultaneously oppose, modern notions of individualism. Expanding the freedom of the individual within the interests of the enveloping group – however modified these interests may be – appears to represent a new stage in the transition toward more individualism and less communalism. It may be a matter of time before the law moves on to the sphere of exclusive individualism, where the extended family and

[58] Husseini, "UNIFEM Launches 'Progress of Arab Women 2004'"; Halpern, "Jordan's New Female Workforce."

community can be declared, for legal purposes at least, defunct. It is always worth remembering that while the institution of guardianship represented – even in practice – a certain power of patriarchy, it was not only about that power, as modern scholarship often makes it to be. The guardian, we recall, also represented the voice of the nuclear and extended family, and even the immediate community.[59] For marriage in Muslim societies, past and present, has never been an affair relevant only to the couple.

Together with changing notions of community and individualism came another transformation in the social values that define adulthood, a transformation that has largely been due to major shifts in economic structures and modes of production. Early in the twentieth century, most Muslim states raised the age of marriage, and some have criminalized the marriage of minors. The 1929 Indian Child Marriage Restraint Act prescribed penalties for any marriage where the bridegroom had not reached eighteen and the bride fifteen. The latter was raised to sixteen in Pakistan's 1961 Muslim Family Laws Ordinance. In other countries, such as Egypt, no code (yet)[60] explicitly prohibits marriage of minors, but by installing strict registration requirements (see the previous section), severe restrictions were placed on such practices. All countries in the Middle East now prescribe the age of eighteen for bridegrooms, but the age has varied in the case of brides: Iraq requires eighteen, Jordan and Syria seventeen, Algeria sixteen, and Tunisia and Morocco fifteen.

None of these areas of the law was so politically charged as that of polygamy, however. The first step taken in further limiting[61] the scope of this practice was the Ottoman Law of 1917 which provided that, in her marriage contract, a wife may stipulate that, should her husband take a co-wife, she has the right to claim a judicial divorce. This device, centuries old, became commonplace in subsequent legislation throughout the Muslim world, but was often combined with other means – also centuries-old – to empower wives to sue for dissolution should certain unfavorable conditions arise in their marriage. These means consisted of (a) predicating (*taʿlīq*) *ṭalāq* upon the occurrence of certain conditions, and (b) delegating the husband's power (*tafwīḍ*) of *ṭalāq* to a third party or to the wife herself, which power was to be exercised upon the occurrence of particular

59 See chapter 8, section 2, above.

60 This may soon change, as a proposed law raising the age to 18 years for both sexes may pass. On the current law of marriage, see Guindy, "Family Status Issues."

61 This practice does not appear to be common among Muslims, past or present. See Tucker, "Marriage and Family," 165–79; Zilfi, "We Don't Get Along," 269, and sources cited in n. 15 therein; Yilmaz, "Secular Law," 124; Gerber, "Social and Economic Position," 232; Jennings, *Christians and Muslims*, 29, 36, 385.

conditions construed by the wife as disadvantageous to her, including her husband taking a co-wife.

Yet another approach to curbing polygamy was taken in a number of Egyptian legislative proposals during the 1920s, but these were not to become actual law until the 1950s and 1960s, and in such countries as Syria and Tunisia before Egypt itself. The device was administrative in nature, requiring any man desiring to take a co-wife to petition the court for permission. The 1961 Muslim Family Law Ordinance of Pakistan made the consent of the wife a further requirement alongside the court's permission. The court, however, could still refuse his request independently of the wishes of the wife, and this on either of two grounds: his financial inability to support two wives, or his inability to treat them in an equally just manner. These considerations, especially the latter, were based on the Quranic verse 4:3 which enjoins a husband to treat his wives justly. Some countries, such as Syria, opted for financial considerations as the chief grounds for a decision, while other countries deemed the notion of justice (which does not, in its widest interpretation, preclude financial considerations) as paradigmatic. The most drastic position taken on the issue of justice was that of Tunisia. In the 1956 Law of Personal Status, polygamy was declared a criminal infraction, categorically prohibited on the grounds that it is impossible for any man to be just, as the Quran requires, in the same manner to two wives.

Equally fundamental changes to the law were effected in the sphere of paternity. In the interest of preserving social harmony and the integrity of the family, the Sharīʿa stretched the limits of conception and pregnancy with a view to ascribing children, as much as possible, to the "marriage bed." The basic and primary legal assumption (*al-barāʾa al-aṣliyya*) was that "children belong to the marriage bed" (*al-walad lil-firāsh*). The *fiqh* schools differed with regard to the minimal period in which, after the marriage begins, the child may be deemed legitimate, as well as in regard to the maximum period after the marriage is dissolved or the mother widowed. The former period, in minimalistic doctrine, was fixed at six months, while the latter extended between two and five years, depending on the particular school. The Twelver-Shīʿites constituted an exception in fixing it at ten months, although they were a numerical and doctrinal minority. In general, therefore, the Sharīʿa promoted the integration of children into family units, discouraging any tendency to single out children as illegitimate. To prove a child illegitimate, evidence had to be beyond any doubt, "reasonable doubt" being insufficient. In other words, there could not exist even a semblance of doubt (*shubha*). Furthermore, mere acknowledgment (*iqrār*) by the father that the child was his was deemed conclusive, even if the physical union of the parents may have been impossible for any period prior to six months before the birth.

Much of this has been changed in favor of, first, limiting the scope of legitimacy, and, second, de-privatizing of paternity claims and declarations. In India and Pakistan, following English law, the father's acknowledgment is inadmissible if physical union between him and the mother was impossible before the marriage took place, and if the child is not born within 280 days of that marriage. The Arab states have preserved some elements of the *fiqh* doctrine, while at the same time rejecting the highly tolerant limits that it stipulated and that must have significantly conduced to resolving disputes that might otherwise have arisen. Thus, the Egyptian law of 1929 places a one-year limit on the determination of legitimacy after divorce or after the death of the husband, declaring the period of gestation to be no longer than one year.

Although prior to the nineteenth century *ṭalāq* was not the most common form of dissolving marriage, the cultural industry of modernity has made it a morally repugnant instrument, associated with male domination, capriciousness and downright oppression. Associated and combined with the exclusive male right to polygamy (another highly infrequent practice),[62] *ṭalāq* came to symbolize, on the one hand, the tyranny of the Eastern male and, on the other, the wretched existence of the Muslim female. The male's absolute right to divorce was to be therefore curbed, in whole, and, if this proved impossible, at least in part. Foremost of these reforms was the declaration as invalid of any pronouncement of divorce made as an oath, under duress, in a fit of anger, while intoxicated, or – in some countries – during the menstruation period of the wife. Only statements made with the intent to dissolve a problematic marriage were now deemed valid, although they might not necessarily lead to dissolution. Also abolished in most Muslim countries was the so-called "triple divorce," a formula that abridges into a single statement the three pronouncements of *ṭalāq*, each of which should be made during a period when the wife is free from menstruation.

In most Muslim countries, the mere declaration of *ṭalāq* has been held ineffective without registering it in court. In Morocco, for instance, a husband need not petition the court for *ṭalāq*, nor, therefore, does he need to vindicate it on any grounds, but he must register it. In most Muslim countries, on the other hand, women who seek a judicial divorce must explain to the court the reasons for their petition. But the court has been made indispensable, for it has appropriated the exclusive right to

[62] See chapter 4, section 5, above.

execute *ṭalāq*, making it no longer the right of the husband, with or without registration. In some countries, the husband may apply for *ṭalāq* without having to state any grounds, while in other countries both parties are equally obliged to state the grounds for their request. In Iranian law under the Shah (1967), while both parties faced the same procedural obligation, women's scope for these grounds was expanded beyond that available for husbands. Under the Islamic Republic of Iran, the 1967 Law was struck down, but several elements of it survived in the Special Civil Courts Act. A wife's consent to *ṭalāq* continues to be a requirement, although the husband no longer needs to provide grounds for his wish to divorce when petitioning the court. In the great majority of Muslim countries, wives are now said to be able to file for marital dissolution on two additional grounds, namely, the husband's failure to provide spousal or family support, or his taking another wife. This does not mean, however, that such rights were not available to women before the twentieth century, for, as we saw earlier,[63] it was in fact the common practice of both the courts and society in the case of the first grounds (i.e., failure to maintain) and a contractual option available to women in the case of the second (i.e., taking on another wife) that guaranteed such rights. The difference now is that the law is declared, made explicit and sanctioned by the state, and its procedure has been bureaucratized and formalized. Most importantly, perhaps, it allows state officials to wrap themselves in the robes of reform, but the substance has surely not changed to any notable extent.

In the same vein, much of the Sharīʿa's law of marital dissolution was integrated into the civil codes of Muslim states in the name of reform, but a reform deprived of the complex system of checks and balances that the *fiqh* had extensively supplied. In addition to the two grounds for judicial divorce listed in the previous paragraph, the legislators included the following: defect in body or in mind that makes married life intolerable or dangerous; impotence that renders normal sexual relations impossible; cruelty and maltreatment, which included – depending on the definition of the particular state – anything from physical abuse to taking on another wife; absence for a prolonged period of time; and, finally, marital discord. In some Muslim countries, while a woman can sue for, and obtain, divorce on any of these grounds, she is obligated to pay the husband a consideration decided upon by the court. Again, none of these grounds is new to the law as it was known before Europe encroached on the Muslim world. As we recall, a woman could petition the *qāḍī* for dissolution of her

[63] See chapter 4, section 5 and chapter 8, section 5, above.

marriage for almost any reason, including all of the above, as well as for such reasons as "disliking her husband due to his ugly appearance or as a result of discord between the two."[64] The Egyptian Law of 1929 stipulates that "if a wife claims that her husband is causing her harm in such a way as to make it impossible for people of her social class to continue the marital relationship, she may petition the judge to dissolve the marriage, whereupon he shall grant her a single, irrevocable divorce, provided that the abuse is proven and he has failed in reconciling them. If, however, the judge denies her petition and she subsequently reiterates the allegation but cannot prove the abuse, the judge shall appoint two arbitrators."[65] Thus, in the modern system, the procedural requirement of proving maltreatment must obtain before a wife is liberated from a bad marriage. The *fiqh*, by contrast, acknowledged the woman's inability to cohabit as intrinsic grounds for dissolution, although arbitration and reconciliation before a final verdict remained, in effect, a mandatory requirement.[66]

Modern Muslim codes continue to affirm the importance of the *fiqh* norm of mediation (*taḥkīm* or *ṣulḥ*) between husband and wife, a necessary step before the dissolution of a marriage is effected.[67] In twentieth-century codes, it has become formalized and homogenized in almost every country, and it has become an official requirement to be fulfilled before effecting any type of divorce, including – perhaps especially – *ṭalāq*. Needless to say, the necessity for mediation in pre-modern law was normative, both in the sphere of the *qāḍī* and in the social site in which the marital conflict occurred. We simply do not know whether mediation was involved in the social context of *ṭalāq*, although in all probability *ṭalāq* did not reach the *qāḍī* in his official capacity of judge, and thus it would be difficult to see how the latter's official mediation (directly or by proxy) was involved.[68] In today's civil codes, on the other hand, mediation appears as a ubiquitous stipulation, formalized in specific procedural requirements.[69]

The method of *takhayyur* was also deployed to effect changes in the law pertaining to the mother's right to child custody, which extended, according to the Ḥanafites, to seven years for boys and nine for girls. Traditionally Ḥanafite countries have raised this bar to some extent. For example, the 1929 Egyptian law stipulated ten years for boys and twelve

64 Shīrāzī, *Muhadhdhab*, IV, 253–54. Similarly, see the Ḥanafite ʿAynī, *Bināya*, V, 506. See also chapter 8, section 3, above.
65 See Article 6, Law of 1929, cited in Naveh, "Tort of Injury," 22, note 16.
66 Ibn al-Ḥājib, *Jāmiʿ*, 287 f. 67 Welchman, *Beyond the Code*, 283 ff.
68 "Official mediation" is intended to allow for the "private" engagement of the *qāḍī* as an influential social figure.
69 On the changing nature of mediation in modernized law (in the case of Israel) and its contribution to facilitating divorce, see Abou Ramadan, "Divorce Reform," 255–74.

years for girls, and the 2005 law (No. 4) has further raised the age to fifteen years for both.[70] But these countries could have adopted a more significant change, as the Mālikite school did grant the mother the right to custody of boys until puberty and girls until marriage. While most of North Africa and the Sudan have adopted this Mālikite law, Tunisia, a traditionally Mālikite country, has opted for a policy more in line with the Ḥanafite doctrine.[71] In the Iranian Civil Code of 1382 H (2003), the age was raised to seven for both boys and girls, this being based on a minority view in Twelver-Shīʿite *fiqh*.[72] At the same time, many other Muslim countries left to the *qāḍī*'s discretion decisions on custody according to the best interests of the child. Yet, irrespective of where the children live, the father remains responsible for their maintenance, and in several countries, for their education. In this respect, there was little to no change from the rules of *fiqh*.

The sphere of inheritance, on the other hand, was subjected to significant changes. The Sunnite system of succession in effect arose from a modified tribal system that served the interests of the extended, agnatic relations, i.e., those who guaranteed the survival of the group and whose entitlement to the estate of the deceased was repayment for the security they extended to the propositus and to his/her immediate relatives while he or she was alive. The Quran incorporated into this system much to serve the interests of mothers, daughters, wives, sisters and sons' daughters. But the system remained, in a particular way, largely patriarchal, and the emphasis remained focused on agnatic relations that guaranteed the group's security. The concatenation formed by these relations translated into an extended family that permeated the Bedouin as well as urban environment. The extended family, in other words, was the relevant unit of social and economic support within both the clan and the town's or city's neighborhood (*ḥāra*).[73]

The introduction of modern forms of capitalism and the attendant fundamental changes in modes of production have, *inter alia*, led to the collapse not only of the earlier modes of production but also to the transformation of the social map: a society whose typical family structure was of the extended type has become characterized by the widespread and growing phenomenon of the nuclear family. Loyalties are no longer to fathers, uncles and the other "patriarchs" of the family who once formed a

[70] Kosheri *et al.*, "Egypt," 247. [71] An-Na'im, *Islamic Family Law*, 182–83.
[72] Ansari-Pour, "Iran" (2003–04), 270. Before 2003, the mother had the right to be custodian for the first two years in the case of daughters, and seven years in the case of sons. An-Na'im, *Islamic Family Law*, 110.
[73] See chapters 4 and 5, above.

veritable safety net for the needy of the family, the ill and the infirm, and the orphans and divorcees. Each family unit was henceforth "on its own," the unit having become the parents, their children and grandchildren, and their fathers and mothers, whenever all these coexisted. It is this unit that reflects the "model family" promoted by the modern state, not only because this is the predominant European model – the exporter of this state – but also because the new "Islamic" nation-state could easily secure the loyalty of such a nuclear family as the defined and articulated site of the good citizen. The loyalties within clans and tribes, being quasi-political, can hardly be divided. Thus, the modern nation-state, which also was fundamentally engaged in, and intertwined with, the new forms of capitalism and new economic modes of production, had a profound interest in refashioning the modern family into a family that is distinctly nuclear.

In reengineering the law of inheritance, the legislators of the modern state leaned heavily on the method of *takhayyur*, combining elements from various schools to produce effects that were inconceivable under the *fiqh* system. An important material source on which the legislators drew was Twelver-Shīʿite law, regarded for centuries as unorthodox and even antithetical to Sunnite doctrine and practice. The Twelver-Shīʿite system of succession drastically departs from agnatic arrangements as conceived by Sunnite *fiqh*. It just so happens that the Shīʿite system of succession – which represents the site of the greatest difference between Sunnite and Twelver-Shīʿite legal conceptions – has become more suitable to the realities and demands of the modern nuclear family than any configuration that its Sunnite counterpart can produce. Accordingly, many of its elements were introduced in several Sunnite countries, and in Iraq it was made the law of the entire population, including Sunnites and Kurds. As we saw earlier,[74] Twelver-Shīʿite law favors a nuclear conception of the family and pays special attention to the females in it. Thus, in the case of a daughter who survives her father together with an uncle, the father's estate in Sunnite *fiqh* will be divided into two equal shares between the two heirs. In Twelver-Shīʿite law, on the other hand, the daughter inherits the entire estate, a modern way of devolving family property.

Some legislators, such as those of Tunisia, opted to modify and augment the Mālikite system of succession while drawing on principles of other Sunnite legal schools. By way of incorporating the principle of *radd* (lit. return)[75] – hitherto unknown in the Mālikite school – they made

[74] See chapter 8, section 6, above.

[75] On *radd*, see Mūṣilī, *Ikhtiyār*, V, 99–100; Nawawī, *Rawḍa*, V, 45 ff.; Liebesny, *Law of the Near and Middle East*, 181. See also chapter 8, section 6, above.

provisions for the spouse relict and provided that a daughter and a son's daughter "shall take the residue of the estate by *radd* even in the presence of an agnate in his own right, such as a brother or uncle."[76] The result was virtually identical to the effects produced in the Twelver-Shīʿite system, in that daughters were given precedence over agnates. Also of Twelver-Shīʿite inspiration was the unrestricted principle – adopted in Egypt, Iraq and the Sudan – that while the bequest cannot exceed one-third of the testator's total inheritable wealth, the latter can choose an heir whose normal share will then be augmented with the additional one-third.

The modern permissibility of "bequeathing to an heir" has also afforded a solution to the problem of the son of a predeceased son who, according to the *fiqh* rules, was entirely excluded from his grandfather's inheritance. The nature of the support dynamics within the extended family was such that an orphaned grandson was usually taken care of by his grandparents, uncles and aunts, which explains why the *fiqh* did not see good reason to allot the deceased father's share to his surviving son by representation. Orphans were routinely, and as a matter of course, absorbed by the family unit in which their parents had lived, which also explains why the relatives continued, over the centuries, to be the recipients of the deceased's share. With the emergence in modernity of the nuclear family as an archetype, and with the exponential rise in mobility, such orphans needed protection, as the extended family which used to take care of them has suffered a major decline (in many areas disappearing entirely). No solution from within the *fiqh* was forthcoming, since inserting the orphaned grandson into the equation of Islamic inheritance would wreak havoc with the entire system.[77] The solution was instead pioneered by Egyptian legislators and consisted in the statutory decree that any grandfather who has orphaned grandsons must make a will that allots them what their father would have inherited had he been alive, with the proviso that such an allotment not exceed one-third of the grandfather's total estate. In the event that the latter did not make such a bequest, or that his bequest did not observe the decreed rule, the court had to rectify the will accordingly.

By the year 2000 no fewer than eight countries in the Middle East had made the estate of the grandparent liable for an obligatory bequest in favor of the orphaned grandchild.[78] This solution was not welcomed

[76] Anderson, *Law Reform*, 151 (I have slightly altered Anderson's translation).
[77] As Anderson has shown. See his *Law Reform*, 154.
[78] Carroll, "Pakistan Federal Shariat Court," 75. On this burning issue in Pakistan, see also Carroll, "Orphaned Grandchildren in Islamic Law," 409–47.

in all Muslim states, however, Pakistan voicing a strong opposition on the grounds that such a legislation makes compulsory what the Quran intended to be a freely chosen act.[79]

The laws of succession and bequests were closely tied in with reengineering the law of *waqf*, especially in the Middle East and North Africa. In the previous chapter, we saw that *waqf* was a prime target of attack in the modernizing project initiated by both the colonialist powers and the native nationalist elites. The discourse generated by the French Orientalists during the 1840s filtered through to the Ottoman territories and, later, to the successor states. This discourse – aided by both the nationalist elite and native scholars who had studied at the feet of the European Orientalists – manufactured a distinction between family and public *waqfs*, a distinction that Muslim cultures had not made.[80] It further injected into the nationalist ideology the notion that family *waqf* was a development in Islamic history from after the formative period, and therefore without legitimacy, since it was based neither on Prophetic tradition nor on that of the Companions (*salaf*); the implication here being that later developments, modern ones included, were as good as any other, especially if the "modern" developments excelled earlier ones in "civilizational sophistication." Even more remarkable was the creation in this discourse of a causal link between the "invention" of family endowments and an attempt by Muslim societies over the centuries to circumvent the stipulations of the Quranic law of inheritance, which operates by the principle of shares and which, therefore, leads to the fragmentation of property. What is noteworthy about this discourse in the context of mid-twentieth-century nation-states is that the *waqf*'s "betrayal" of the Quranic spirit was one that – ironically – contradicted an invented spirit designed to promote the nuclear family and, unwittingly, to conform to Shīʿite law.

As if this did not furnish them with enough ammunition for the attack on *waqfs*, the French colonists, the Ottoman ruling elite and the counterparts of the latter in the successor nation-states furthermore blamed economic malaise on the *waqf* since, it was argued, family endowments inherently tie up property in perpetuity and prevent it from efficient development in a free market economy. And since the economy is indispensable to modern development, then impeding material progress amounts to halting the march toward civilization. Thus *waqf*, the main prop of civil society in

[79] Carroll, "Pakistan Federal Shariat Court," 76. The national debate on this possibility continues, however.

[80] See, e.g., typical juristic discussions: Shīrāzī, *Muhadhdhab*, III, 671–702; Shaʿrānī, *Mīzān*, II, 136–37; Ibn al-Ḥājib, *Jāmiʿ*, 448–50.

Islamic civilization for over a millennium, and a chief instrument of its social welfare and safety-net,[81] became synonymous with civilizational retardation and regress. In Kemalist Turkey, the entire institution of family *waqf* was abolished in 1926, while charitable non-family *waqfs* were nationalized as public welfare institutions.

The process of eradicating *waqf* was nowhere as sudden as it was in Turkey, however. Before the elimination of family *waqfs* altogether in a number of other Muslim countries, the nationalist governments attempted to restrict the scope of the Sharīʿa laws of *waqf* by aligning them with their policies of refashioning the "model (nuclear) family." But in order to accomplish this, the *waqf* administration was not allowed to continue in accordance with its former independent practices, where private administrators acted independently of the "state" although they were generally supervised and occasionally inspected, or audited, by the *qāḍīs*. With their centralization within the framework of government ministries, the *waqfs* were subjected to unprecedented rules, foremost among which was the requirement of registration for any act pertaining to the creation, revocation, renovation or alteration in the income distribution of any *waqf*. Egypt led the way in the Middle East region. It declared in 1946 that religious *waqfs*, especially mosques, would be henceforth designated as perpetual, as had been the case under the Sharīʿa; but not so private or family *waqfs*, which were now limited to sixty years (as in Lebanon) or to the lifetimes of two series of beneficiaries. Upon the dissolution of the *waqf*, the property would have to revert either to the beneficiaries or to the founders' heirs, depending on the particular conditions the law set for each circumstance. But there was, in both Egypt and Lebanon, another major limitation on the freedom of *waqf* founders to establish a foundation whose value was larger than one-third of their inheritable estate. In the event that the *waqf* did exceed the one-third limitation, then the excess on the one-third had to be divided among his heirs according to their shares in the inheritance of that property. This limitation soon became common legislation, having been passed as recently as 1992 in the Yemen.

In 1949, Syria went even further, centralizing the administration of all public *waqfs* in a government ministry, and abolishing all *waqfs* whose beneficiaries were in whole or in part members of a family. The same drastic measure was enacted in Egypt in 1954, and in 1957 all agricultural

[81] The family and immediate community having been as important. Furthermore, if rulers invested in social welfare (hospitals, soup kitchens, public drinking fountains, public baths, etc.) it was almost always through the acts of founding *waqfs*. More on the latter, see van Leeuwen, *Waqfs and Urban Structures*, 9 ff., 86 ff., and *passim*; and chapters 3 and 4, above.

lands that had been established as *waqf* were confiscated as part of Nasser's nationalization program. A similar program of nationalizing land was undertaken in Algeria in 1971. A number of other countries also followed suit in abolishing family *waqfs*, some of the last being Libya, in 1973, and the United Arab Emirates, in 1980.

Yet another method devised to reduce the family *waqfs* was the lifting of several restrictions that ensured perpetuity under the *fiqh* rules. The 1991 Algerian law stipulated (in addition to abolishing family *waqfs*) that a founder may revoke his own *waqf* deed or change any of its terms. The 1992 Yemeni law went so far as to bestow on the beneficiaries of a family *waqf* the right to revoke the deed and to distribute the property according to their shares in the inheritance.

In South-East Asia, there were fewer changes in the *waqf* law, since by the dawn of the twentieth century the fundamentals of that law had already changed in the region, as they had in the Indian subcontinent. In the Malay States and the Straits Settlements, much of the *waqf* had been transformed into what were in effect English trusts, a fact that significantly reduced the interest of donors, which in turn drastically diminished the size of family and even public endowments. In Indonesia, the basic law that regulated *waqf* was promulgated in 1937 under Dutch colonial rule, but its effects on the *waqf* and its administration have been purely procedural, regulating the modalities of founding and registering *waqfs*. Generally speaking, the economic role of *waqf* in South-East Asia does not seem to have been as central as it was throughout Central Asia, the Middle East and North Africa; which explains why colonialist pressures to abolish so much of the *waqf* did not arise in South-East Asia as they did in other parts of the Muslim world.

4. The state, the ulama and the Islamists

A. Definitions: state, ulama, secularists and Islamists

The periodization of history produces a neat narrative and an orderly account of events, and it is precisely for this reason that it should be resisted, however tempting. The shorter the period concerned, the more periodization should be resisted, and this is eminently the case of the modern period, especially after the First World War. In this chapter, we have discussed the processes by which the law was modernized, as well as the cultural and other forces that underlay these transformations. Notable Westernizing trends began in India at the end of the eighteenth century, and in the Middle East at the beginning of the nineteenth, culminating in the 1940s and 1950s. The changes, as we saw, were massive, involving the structural dismantling of the Sharīʿa legal system, and leaving behind a distorted and gradually diminishing veneer of Islamic law of personal status. At one point, it seemed that Islam as a religious force, as a *nomos*, was out of favor, having once and for all lost to the modernists and their new states. But the 1970s and early 1980s saw powerful events that appeared to stop the collapse of this religious force. The questions that lie before us then are: what are the sources of the re-Islamicization trends that appeared during and after the 1970s? In light of our caveat regarding periodization, how far back do the origins of these sources extend? Are they a reenactment of pre-modern Islamic tendencies or are they modernist, *sensu stricto*? What have they managed to accomplish in terms of metamorphosing the secularist legal changes, the engineered law, into an Islamicized jural narrative? What methods and means have they pursued in order to accomplish this end, and where and when?

To produce a manageable account of jural developments since the 1970s, a number of assumptions have been made about the "actors" involved. I take it as a reasonably valid proposition that there are four major actors on the legal scene who are not always neatly distinguished from one another, namely, the state, the "secular" modernists, the ulama and the Islamists. Throughout Part III, we have pointed out several features that have necessarily made the nation-state in the Islamic world a *modern* entity. That is to say that governance in Islamic lands had to acquire modernist structures by force of necessity in order for the nationalist elite not only to challenge direct and indirect Western colonialism but also, while attempting to accomplish this task, to rule their own populations efficiently. But this trajectory involved an absurdity: to resist Western political and military hegemony, the state had to adopt modern technology, modern culture and modern institutions – in short, modernity in as mature and complete a form as could be imported or assimilated, according to need. Yet, the modernization process, forced to depend for all its major features on a capitalist economy and/or technology, led to economic and other forms of dependency on one Western country or another (and in the 1950s and 1960s on the Soviet Union as well). Thus, to free themselves of the clutches of colonialism (a quintessential phenomenon in, and inherent to, modernity), the Muslim states adopted modern institutions and cultures that led them to new colonialist trappings.

The second actor is the camp commonly described as secularist-modernist, a significant camp during the 1940s and 1950s, though it slowly declined over the next three decades, becoming a relative minority after the early 1990s. Whatever strength it could garner since then appears to have stemmed from its association with the state, whose tendencies, generally speaking, have all along been secular (with the obvious exception of such countries as Saudi Arabia and, later, Iran).

Marginally stronger than the secularists (at least until recently) are the ulama who, as a rule, survive as pockets in various Muslim countries, but by no means in all of them. South-East Asia, Pakistan, Iran and Egypt represent more prominent sites of ulama strength, Iran especially, where they have been commanding the state since 1979. In Saudi Arabia they constitute a powerful actor in domestic politics and especially in the legal system. Yet, thus far, in no Sunnite country has the Iranian experiment of exclusive ulama rule been replicated. In Egypt and Pakistan, as we shall see momentarily, the ulama play a not inconsiderable role versus the state, at times standing in tension with it, at others, in accommodation.

The latest but by far the most significant actor is the Islamist camp, distinguishing itself from the ulama in two critical ways, among others of lesser significance: the first is that the ulama, strictly speaking, continue to uphold their "traditional" hermeneutic or a semblance thereof, which is to say that they continue to espouse the authority of their legal sources, treatises, *madhhab*ic schools, leading jurists and ways of instruction (although none of these spheres is an exact replica of actual historical practice). A second important difference is professional loyalty to their area of specialization: they have continued to dedicate themselves to religious knowledge, either by acquiring it as students or by imparting it as teachers, professors, *muftī*s or preachers. Although their functions are now nearly exclusively educational (i.e., not legal in the sense that obtained before the nineteenth century), they remain largely dissociated from other technical professions. (But this is not to say that such religious universities as al-Azhar do not offer programs of study in the sciences.)

Since the 1970s, the Islamists have come to represent an influential and pervasive camp, stretching across the entire Muslim world, and spanning the whole gamut of the social order and economic classes. Generally speaking, they are not trained in traditional disciplines, nor (in part as a consequence) do they read the classical sources with the same perspective as the ulama. They are trained in a wide variety of modern technical disciplines, ranging from engineering and medicine to accounting, business and teaching in "secular" schools. Those of the Islamists who discourse on matters religious and legal seem willing to employ any modern hermeneutical amalgam. Their hermeneutic – which is everything they say, and how and why they say it – is one of complex hybridity. They are not bound by an established or a given reading of the Quran and the Prophetic Sunna, as the ulama generally are. As we shall see, their interpretive techniques of these sources can invoke a wide range of principles from the social or natural sciences.[82] In other words, having shed the mantle of traditional juristic and hermeneutical authority, the Islamists do not feel bound by the cultural and epistemic systems developed throughout Islamic intellectual and legal history. The recent proliferation of *fatwās* on the Internet, in print media and in video-recordings attests to a multifarious production of "religious knowledge" that has consistently lacked any axis of authority. Aside from Pakistan's Mawdūdī and Egypt's Sayyid Quṭb, whose writings have attracted significant numbers of Muslim readers around the world, and apart from a few other secondary writers, the Islamists, in terms of religious-legal authority, have thus far not unified their ranks under any clearly identified banner or ideology, which is to say that their camp – if the term is at all apt – is highly diverse.

But this diffusion of authority is also endemic, though to a lesser extent, among the ulama as well as to the so-called secular modernists. The latter cannot be classified in any uniform terms, for they may range from atheists (who are relatively few) to believers in God who do not wish to see religion play any role in the state, its politics or the public sphere. On the other hand, some ulama have in effect, though not formally, joined the Islamist camp, as is the case with certain members of the lower echelons of Egypt's famous al-Azhar. Their Islamist affiliation is attested not only by the political positions they adopt, but also by their hybridized interpretive mechanisms that are no longer loyal to the Azharite juristic hermeneutic. Arguably, the reverse is also true, namely, that the Islamists have penetrated Azhar's lower ranks, and continue to do so. The boundaries are never neat, not even on the level of state involvement.

In the remainder of this chapter, I discuss the main contours of juridico-political developments in a number of key Muslim countries, where trends have been set and where tensions and accommodations between and among these four camps have had noticeable but varied effects. As noted in the opening paragraph of this chapter, it is impossible here – or even in a thicker tome – to cover with any reasonable detail all fifty or so Muslim countries, since our concern lies with movements and determinative currents. I shall therefore limit my discussion to a few Muslim countries, while briefly remarking on a few others by way of comparison.

B. *Egypt*

We begin with Egypt, as it offers, after British India (whose relevance for us is now limited to Pakistan), the longest experiment in jural modernization

[82] A prominent example being Muḥammad Shaḥrūr, discussed in the next chapter, section 9.

and, simultaneously, perhaps one of the fiercest tendencies to contest jural secularization in the name of one Islamic ideology or another. Since Muḥammad ʿAlī, Egypt has enjoyed a relatively strong state, and from the middle of the nineteenth century it began to develop upper social classes imbued with vehemently secularist tendencies. But at no point was Egypt devoid of influential Islamic groups. The Azhar and its ulama were still forces to be reckoned with even after the exhausting effects of the nineteenth-century "reforms." In fact, despite the chipping effects of Nasser's institutional and administrative engineering around the middle of the twentieth century, Azhar grew phenomenally in size, increasing the number of its institutes from 212 in 1963 to 3,161 in 1993. Its student population increased from about 65,000 to almost a million during the same period.[83] But even more phenomenal growth occurred in another religious movement that was to become far more popular and pervasive. In 1928, Egypt witnessed the birth of the Muslim Brothers, an association created by the Arabic language teacher Ḥasan al-Bannā (1906–49). Spreading in the 1950s to Jordan, Syria, Sudan, Iran, Pakistan, Malaysia and Indonesia, the movement gained momentous strength, in Egypt as well as outside it, by virtue of having acquired an influential ideologue in the figure of Sayyid Quṭb, later considered a martyr after being executed by Nasser's regime in 1966.

These two Islamic camps, represented by Azhar and the Brotherhood, advocated different visions of the Sharīʿa, but viewed its implementation in the social order, as a matter of principle, a desideratum. Regarding themselves as custodians of the *fiqh* hermeneutic and the *sharʿī* tradition, the Azharites, generally speaking, advocated a conventional version of the Sharīʿa, largely derived from the *fiqh* of the schools.

The Muslim Brothers, on the other hand, had a wider view of juridical possibilities, allowing for an Islamic law that could be modified to reflect the changing realities of the world, in ways comparatively far more open to interpretive possibilities. But the change was not to be of the sort dictated by the Western colonizer, for that form of change was precisely what had to be resisted and overcome. The colonizer's change was as detrimental to Muslim spiritual and social life as the conservatism of the Azhar ulama whom the Muslim Brothers vehemently opposed. Modernity, which in the Brothers' discourse appeared distinct from Westernization,[84] did not

[83] Zeghal, "Religion and Politics," 379.

[84] See, e.g., Sayyid Quṭb who saw Western mores and social values as noxious but welcomed with open arms the luminous Western achievements in technology and science, as if the two had been historically distinct and organically separate from each other. See his *Milestones*, 8–9.

pose any particular problem, that is, if it is assumed that modernity *qua* modernity consciously posed itself as an intellectual subject in the thought of – at least – Bannā and Quṭb. But this perhaps is too much to assume, for it seems that the effects of science, technology and industry were not, in the thought of these two men, appreciated in the social and moral realms. Although the Muslim Brothers, including Bannā and Quṭb, never explained exactly what form of Sharī'a might be adopted in the new, avant-garde Muslim society, it is clear that religious morality was expected to lie at the center of the social order. Morality represents, *par excellence*, the basis of any project of rebuilding a new Muslim society, and as such the Sharī'a to be implemented would have to rest on a moral social order. Living a moral life appears even as a predicate to the introduction of any *shar'ī* order and explains at least in part the formation, in the 1980s, of local grass-roots Islamist communities throughout Egypt. Somewhat similar to the pre-modern *ḥāra*s we described in chapter 4, these mostly urban, lower middle-class communities fashioned themselves into cohesive neighborhoods with their own systems that encompassed schools, hospitals, mosques, preachers, "banking" operations for mutual financial support, and other social-communal services. (Similar phenomena have also emerged in Gaza and southern Lebanon, Ḥamās' and Ḥizbullāh's networks being, respectively, prime examples.) Most of these Egyptian neighborhoods are populated by Islamists (who are by no means political activists in the majority of cases), although lower-rank, techno-Azharites[85] have also come to share these habitats.[86] Thus, the growth of the religious movement would ultimately bring unprecedented pressure upon the government to take seriously the popular request to implement the Sharī'a. But how did the state finally succumb to these pressures?

The fundamentals of the politics of law that we discussed in chapter 5 continued to be, in their bare essentials, largely operative on the Egyptian scene during the twentieth century. The regime needed Azhar to legitimize its nationalist and socialist projects, which were intended, as elsewhere, to reengineer the social order in the image of the ideal nation which is materially and culturally productive, just, successful and, most importantly, independent and free. On the other hand, Azhar, having become subordinated more than ever to the state and its apparatus, could not but oblige. Nasser's regime brought Azhar to heel, first by nationalizing much of the *waqf* property in 1952, then by excluding its personnel from

[85] This term refers to those Azharites who study the sciences, who have no considerable knowledge of the interpretive *fiqh* tradition, and who often ally themselves with the Islamists, politically and professionally. See discussion below.
[86] See generally Zaman, *Ulama*, 148.

the national courts in 1955. But it was the 1961 "reform" that had the most drastic effect on Azhar, in both more and less predictable ways. The first major change was the introduction of scientific subjects into the curriculum, such as engineering and medicine, which, on the one hand, predictably liberalized Azhar but, on the other, created a class of techno-Azharites who – unpredictably – came in the 1970s to share and indeed strengthen the ranks of the Islamists.[87] Nasser also subjected Azhar's entire administration to the state, and made the appointment and dismissal of its head (Shaykh al-Azhar) a direct responsibility of the President's office. Having mercilessly suppressed the Muslim Brothers and outlawed their political formations, and having systemically and systematically subordinated the Azhar to the state, Nasser and his regime could easily afford to ignore all religious sentiments that voiced a concern about the implementation of the Sharīʿa.

These concerns might have continued to fall on deaf ears had the Arab regimes been more successful in their projects, including their conflicts with Israel. The crushing defeat of 1967 ultimately brought Nasser himself to his knees, and the Muslim Brothers sprang back – from imprisonment, torture and deprivation – with a great deal of resentment. Azhar dramatically transformed its discourse, now invoking notions of repentance (*tawba*), and casting the so-called Setback (*Nakba*) as a lesson from God and exhorting Muslims to reconsider their erroneous ways, not least of these being Nasser's socialism. Even Nasser himself spoke of the Setback as a divine intimation, a call for purification.[88]

It was Sadat's liberalizing policies that ushered in a new stage in the rise of the Islamist movement. Alleviating the oppression against the Muslim Brothers and releasing the group's members from prisons, Sadat began his rule with a policy of appeasement, promising, furthermore, to consider ways to implement the Sharīʿa. Article 2 of the 1971 Constitution referred to the Sharīʿa as "a principal source" of legislation. (In 1969, a Supreme Court had been created and in 1971 it was renamed as the Supreme Constitutional Court [SCC], whose function was to curb infringements by the legislative and executive branches.)[89] Although a legislative parliamentary committee was to prepare laws in line with Article 2, and although Azhar was supposed to, and did, provide direction and assistance in drafting these laws, nothing came of what was, with the benefit of hindsight, little more than an act of lip service on the part of the

87 A point insightfully made by Zeghal, "Religion and Politics." 88 *Ibid.*, 381–82.

89 Brown, *Rule of Law*, 102. On the SCC, see Sherif, "Rule of Law," 1–34; for the Court's reporter, see *al-Maḥkama al-Dustūriyya al-ʿUlyā*. For a critique of the 1969 judicial events, see Bishrī, *al-Qaḍāʾ al-Miṣrī*, 18–25.

regime.[90] With a judiciary and a Parliament staffed by a liberal and secularized majority, Article 2 was pushed aside as a descriptive (even rhetorical) rather than a prescriptive proposition.[91]

In the meantime, the Islamist movement gained strength, and the ruling elite needed Azhar more than ever to combat the increasing pressure coming from the Islamists. The more Azhar was needed and the more it offered its support to the regime, the more assertive it became, and the more it called for the implementation of the Sharīʿa. And to avert the political sting of the Islamists, the regime was willing to make concessions on the less innocuous legal front, concessions that happened to favor its ally, Azhar. And so in 1980, the Constitution was amended, and Article 2 changed to stipulate that the Sharīʿa "is the principal source of legislation" (*al-maṣdar al-raʾīsī lil-tashrīʿ*).

But not much happened. No Islamic laws were passed, and no new cases were to constitute any step in that direction. Frustrated by the government's lack of legislative action, the Islamists mounted challenges to the SCC, bringing cases regarding laws they alleged (often rightly so) to be in contradiction to the Sharīʿa, and requesting that the SCC declare them, by virtue of Article 2, unconstitutional. This challenge also included Law No. 44 of 1979, the so-called Jihān's Law (which extended the duration of child custody for divorced mothers, and, even more importantly here, made a husband's marriage to a second wife an element automatically constituting harm to the first wife and therefore giving rise to divorce by operation of the law). But this Law, as well as the other cases reviewed, was dismissed without reference to their (in)compatibility with Article 2, which was one way for the SCC to avoid defining, once and for all (it was thought), what is exactly meant by the term "Sharīʿa" mentioned in Article 2. Jihān's Law was struck down on the grounds that it was passed through unconstitutional means,[92] and the cases were dismissed on grounds of non-retroactivity. The Sharīʿa of Article 2 was left undefined.

It took over two decades for the SCC to deliver a definition of what the Sharīʿa, in its opinion, meant. In 1993, and under overwhelming pressure from the Islamists, it pronounced that the Sharīʿa in effect amounts to the broad legal principles laid down in the Quran, as defined

[90] Between 1969 and 1976, for instance, the Shaykh of Azhar, ʿAbd al-Ḥalīm Maḥmūd, was instrumental in drafting several texts, including a law of *ḥudūd* and an Islamic constitution. See Zeghal, "Religion and Politics," 382; Zaman, *Ulama*, 146.

[91] Lombardi, "Islamic Law," 85.

[92] This Law was replaced by the 1985 Law No. 100, requiring a wife whose husband married another woman to show that the second marriage was injurious to her. See Naveh, "Tort of Injury," 16–41.

by the consensus of jurists over the centuries. These were defined as fundamental principles, not specific rules, and as general and universal principles they are applicable to any society in any age. A case in point is the principle that law should not be harmful to Muslims. Accordingly, any law that does not violate any of these principles is one that does not stand in contradiction with the Sharīʿa. But who is to make a determination of these general principles, and how? How is the actual power, or mere potential, of laws to harm or to benefit to be determined?

In answer to these questions, the SCC took the bold position that any judge presiding in the national courts can be a valid interpreter of these general Sharīʿa principles; which, in effect, amounted to the proposition that these principles are so general that any person having basic knowledge of "Islamic *fiqh*" – but who is sufficiently trained in modern law – can derive such principles from the Quran and the consensual practices of the jurists over the preceding twelve or thirteen centuries. The SCC's answer became the new bone of contention between the state and the Islamists. The challenge put forth by the latter was as much legal as political. Echoing Shāfiʿī's critique of the Ḥanafites from twelve centuries ago, the Islamists still insisted – as their ideologue Quṭb had done half a century earlier – that such exercises in hermeneutic are nothing short of human legislation producing a system where men rule over each other.[93] The secular training of the national-court judges equipped them, even with the best of intentions, to extract nothing more than the most general of principles. Their well-nigh ignorance of *fiqh*, of Quranic exegesis, of *ḥadīth* (which the SCC largely ignored as a valid legal source),[94] and even of basic skills in classical legal Arabic, largely barred them from any genuine understanding of what Sharīʿa's *fiqh* signified or even technically meant. It is common knowledge – for anyone familiar with the modern Arab legal profession – that this profession as a rule considers the *fiqh* to be culturally remote, juristically complex and a judicially obscure system of rules, and for those members who have little sympathy for the Islamists, *fiqh* is downright primeval, ultraconservative and anti-modern. The Islamists pushing the SCC to adopt a more sensitive position toward a "genuine" Sharīʿa have insisted – and rightly so – that deriving such inordinately broad principles not only leads the court to indulge in utilitarian reasoning about law and society, but also lodges it in an arbitrary world where judges who know next to nothing about the religious and legal texts will be able to pronounce on God's law. Indeed, a close analysis

93 Quṭb, *Milestones*, 46–47, 94–95, 130, and *passim*. For Max Weber's similar position, see Lassman, "Rule of Man," 83–98.

94 Lombardi, *State Law*, 262.

of some of the cases that the SCC has decided shows this much.[95] Thus far, in the Egyptian experiment at least, a definition of Sharīʿa that can garner popular and majoritarian legitimacy continues to be elusive.

C. *Pakistan*

Another country witnessing a significant push toward Islamization of laws, Pakistan emerged from the ruins of British India with a distinct Islamic identity, articulated by the anti-colonial nationalists as justification for their independence. It was emphasized that its *raison d'être* was neither geographical nor ethnic, but rather religious in nature. God was declared in the March 1949 Objectives Resolution as the sole sovereign of the Universe, a sovereign whose authority was "delegated to the State of Pakistan." This assertion, from the dawn of independence, betrayed the tension between the sovereignty of God and that of the state, for the jural history of Pakistan has been characterized by a potent tension implicit in the claims of "delegated" sovereignty. The political ruling elite, including Muhammad Ali Jinnah, was modernist and Westernizing, promoting the political, administrative and bureaucratic interests of what, in every way, was a nation-state. Yet, the Objectives Resolution, while insisting on purely Western concepts of governance, promised that "Muslims shall be enabled to order their lives … according to the teachings and requirements of Islam as set out in the Holy Quran and the sunna."[96]

The 1949 Objectives Resolution was regarded as a Preamble to the constitution, which was not to be promulgated until 1956. In the interim, the ulama maintained an organized and sustained pressure on the government toward implementing the promises made in the Resolution. One of the specific proposals on which they insisted was that the government should review Pakistani legislation with a view to expunging any law that stood in contravention of the Sharīʿa. The prevalent idea appears to have been that the Sharīʿa is constituted of the traditional set of rules adopted by the historical schools, not the sort of general principles later advocated by the Egyptian SCC. When the Constitution was finally promulgated in 1956, Article 198 stipulated that "no law shall be enacted that is repugnant to the Injunctions of Islam as laid down in the Holy Quran and the Sunna."[97] However, the potential effects of this Article were *ab initio* depleted by the restricting provisions of clauses 2 and 3. In their aggregate, these two clauses required that a temporary advisory committee submit a

[95] See, for example, Lombardi's analysis in *State Law*, 218–53, especially at 234, 239, 251.
[96] Collins, "Islamization of Pakistani Law," 550; Zaman, *Ulama*, 88.
[97] An-Na'im, *Islamic Family Law*, 230.

proposal to the National Assembly seeking to rectify any law contrary to the Sharīʿa, but they effectively precluded the courts from hearing any cases that bore on Article 198.

The 1958 crisis that led to the abolition of the Constitution prevented the appointment of any committee and thus the National Assembly never carried out the provisions of Article 198. By the end of that year, Ayyub Khan had seized power and embarked on implementing a policy of modernization. One such far-reaching legislation was the Muslim Family Laws Ordinance of 1961, a law that was at the time typical in the Middle East but that ran against the wishes of a relatively strong Pakistani ulama constituency. One indicator of the legal tensions in Pakistan was the inheritance problem we have already discussed with regard to the children of a predeceased son.[98] The 1961 Ordinance, acknowledging the principle of representation, decreed that the child of a predeceased child had the right to inherit what his or her parent would have inherited had he or she been alive. The next year saw the enactment of a new Constitution that was modernist in tenor, omitting not only any mention of Pakistan as an "Islamic Republic" (as in the 1956 Constitution) but also the entirety of the repugnancy clause. However, public discontent and pressure forced Ayyub Khan to restore both provisions, although these alterations remained superficial and were no more than a form of appeasement.

The repugnancy provision was in effect left dormant, and the law of Pakistan continued to preserve, until the late 1970s, its Anglo-Muhammadan form, whereby the courts continued to apply the law according to the common law case method. The civil war of 1971, the political changes occurring as a result and the new 1973 Constitution brought no change, although the repugnancy clause was included, again to no effect, in this Constitution.

But the Middle East and the Islamic world had changed by the 1970s. As mentioned earlier, the 1967 Arab defeat had caused a major self-reassessment, accompanied by a rediscovery of Islam as a political force. A gradual yet potent increase in Islamic consciousness spilled over beyond the Arab world, augmenting the local and nation-specific problems of each country. The 1979 Iranian Revolution was not the spark that ignited this consciousness, but rather a powerful symptom of the currents sweeping the region, as well as the Islamic world at large, since 1967. The 1970s may well be called the decade of Islamic incubation. In 1979, Zia al-Haqq seized power and it was clear that his growing religious constituency could no longer be ignored or silenced through legislative lip service. As in

[98] Other changes introduced have been discussed in section 3, above.

Sadat's Egypt, the political legitimacy of the regime rested squarely on satisfying this constituency. Zia al-Haqq immediately made it clear that his regime would pursue a program of Islamicization, and he followed up on his promise by enacting Islamic laws on religious tax (*zakāt*), usury (*ribā*) and *ḥudūd*, most of which laws follow the *fiqh* regime very faithfully.

The Objectives Resolution of 1949, having up to this point received no concrete constitutional status, was formally incorporated as the Preamble to the Constitution, and the statutory language pertaining to repugnancy issues was strengthened.[99] Furthermore, each High Court was supposed to have a Shariat Bench, but this was streamlined into a single Federal Shariat Court (FSC) in 1980. The latter was to decide on which laws contravened the Sharīʿa, and once a law was found by it to be repugnant, it would cease to have any effect. Yet, the FSC's power was constrained by structural and other limitations. First, appeals to the Supreme Court could reverse the FSC's decisions. Second, the FSC could not adjudicate the full range of the law: the Constitution, fiscal law, procedural law and law of personal status were entirely excluded from its jurisdictional purview. Third, in its early period, the five judges who staffed the FSC all came from the national courts, which is to say that none of them was a member of the ulama class.[100] It was not surprising then that the FSC's decisions were not always consistent with the Shariat ordinances promulgated by General Zia, nor were they in conformity with the traditional *fiqh* rules.

In due course, however, the FSC's bench began to be populated by members of the ulama class, and General Zia renewed his commitment to Islam as part of his bargain for political legitimacy. The price of the bargain was the 1988 Enforcement of Shariat Ordinance which decreed that the Sharīʿa was the "supreme source of the law in Pakistan and the Grundnorm for guidance of policy-making by the state." But the earlier substantive exclusions from the purview of this court as well as appeals of its decisions to the Supreme Court remained in place, showing, at the end of the day, where true legal power lay.[101]

The aforementioned exclusions were challenged in 1981 by the Peshawar Shariat Bench which interpreted the exclusions as bearing on the Sharīʿa itself, not the state's legislative pronouncements on personal status. Accordingly, it ruled that the inheritance rights prescribed by section 4 of the 1961 Muslim Family Law Ordinance were repugnant to Sharīʿa and that the orphaned grandchild was not entitled to his or her parent's share had he or she been alive. The decision was appealed by

[99] Carroll, "Orphaned Grandchildren in Islamic Law," 437–38.
[100] Collins, "Islamization of Pakistani Law," 569–70. [101] Zaman, *Ulama*, 89.

the Government, and the higher court overturned it on jurisdictional grounds, stating that the Peshawar Bench was not empowered to make such a determination, and that this matter fell to the competence of the legislature alone (including its advisory Council of Islamic Ideology).

The persistence of the 1961 Ordinance[102] is a marker of the modest extent to which substantive Islamicization took place in Pakistan. No less is it a marker of the political uses the founding fathers and subsequent politicians made of the Sharīʿa.[103] But the few changes that have occurred in this sphere during the last several years are indicative of a larger trend, as we shall see shortly. The FSC declared that as of March 2000, section 4 allowing orphaned grandchildren to be represented in inheritance would no longer have effect, and delegated to the legislature the task of finding a solution for those grandchildren who, with this decision, were left to fend for themselves.[104] The Court agreed with the proposal of the Council of Islamic Ideology that a requirement be placed upon the aunts and uncles of the orphaned children, to provide and care for them as members of their own families. But the social and moral conditions, the Court agreed, were not yet ready for such an obligation to be imposed. Although a moral community does not require external interference (one form of which is a legislative enactment), there must exist at least an elementary form of this community for such an enactment, first, to be accepted, and second, to have a constructive effect on the emergence and full formation of the moral community. In its decision, the Court wrote: "If the piety which is a prerequisite of an Islamic Social Order had been prevalent, it [viz., imposition of obligation upon uncles and aunts] could well have been a good solution but in the situation in which we are placed, we are of the view that the better solution would be the making of a Mandatory will in favor of the orphaned grandchildren."[105]

Why a mandatory will, unknown to Sharīʿa, and not the imposition of a duty of care upon the relatives, something practice and custom have always known? Perhaps it is because the rule of one-third bequest is an available Islamic legal instrument that can, with little tweaking, serve the purpose. But it may also be that behind the reluctance to impose an obligation upon relatives – thus in effect leaving the Court with one option – is the conviction that with the modernizing changes in society and

[102] Lau, "Pakistan" (2002–03), 375. [103] Ali, "Sigh of the Oppressed?," 109, 121.

[104] Carroll, "Pakistan Federal Shariat Court," 80; An-Na'im, *Islamic Family Law*, 234.

[105] Carroll, "Pakistan Federal Shariat Court," 75 f. In the mandatory scheme, the bequest must apportion to them according to what their deceased parent would have inherited had he or she been alive, with the proviso that such apportion does not exceed one-third of the grandfather's total estate. Should the latter not make such a bequest, the court must assume that the grandparent did do so. See section 3, above.

the virtual non-existence of a moral community, the imposition not only will end in failure, but will meet with stiff popular resistance. In Quṭbian terms, then, the social order must first develop its moral character before it is ready for the implementation of Sharīʿa. Whether or not the Court articulated the moral–jural ramifications of the case in these terms, its decision certainly demonstrated that at least it arrived at an intuitive understanding of the functional and organic interdependence between and among the moral, communal and legal spheres *within* the Sharīʿa. But the tenacity of the 1961 Ordinance and the entanglement of Pakistan's ruling elite in "modernizing" policies – in good part dictated by international hegemonic powers – have carried the day, effectively leaving the Court, the Islamists and the ulama, however differently they articulate Islam, in a minority position.[106]

D. Iran

As noted earlier, significant changes to the Sharīʿa did not come until the Pahlavi dynasty assumed power in 1925 under Reza Shah, who ruled until 1941. The hallmark of his rule was a fierce concern with centralization, a method of governance effective in subduing competition to the main ruler. But centralization needed technology which, in the case of Pahlavi Iran, the British were more than willing to provide. Not only were tribal chiefs (who nearly incapacitated the Qājārs) subdued, but the Shah embarked on a project of eliminating the ulama and their institutions, and at least succeeded in weakening them dramatically. He confiscated their *waqf*s and placed their administration in the hands of the Ministry of Education. Any ulama retained as administrative or educational personnel were now paid by the government, depriving them of their traditional independence. This was a state victory that lagged behind its Ottoman counterpart by about three-quarters of a century.

Also very much in line with changes the Ottomans had long since effected, the Pahlavi regime immediately introduced two new and important enactments: the Code of Judicial Organization and the Principles of Civil Procedure (both in 1927). A new state system of courts was thus established, with judges and prosecutors as civil servants. In 1931, the Act of Marriage was promulgated, implementing changes that reflected, as we saw earlier, the increased interest of the state in the reengineering of

[106] This being also attested by their inability to bring about enactments in most fields to their satisfaction. See Lau, "Pakistan" (2001–02), 325–26. On the inability of the provincial government to go beyond the Federal legislation, see Ali, "Sigh of the Oppressed?"

family life.[107] This Act was the result of preparatory work conducted by a commission composed of ulama and European-trained lawyers. The rest of the legislation on family law, including inheritance and gifts, was enacted in 1935. The years 1967 and 1975 witnessed two further waves of changes to family law, the latter year having introduced the Family Protection Act, the hallmark of which was the abolishing of the husband's right to unilateral divorce (*ṭalāq*). Needless to say, the sphere of family law was the only reserve of the Sharīʿa, however thin it had become. For all intents and purposes, the rest of the law and legal system were of entirely Western inspiration, the French influence manifestly dominating.[108]

The monumental Iranian revolution of 1979 produced colossal political and conceptual ruptures, within Iran and outside it no less. Yet, interestingly, the sphere of law, the supposed hallmark of the Islamic Republic, experienced a relatively small, indeed nominal, measure of Islamization for years after the Revolution took place.

Originating, as we saw, in the Uṣūlist school,[109] the concept of Wilāyat al-Faqīh (Pers.: Vilāyat-i Faqīh) became the theoretical foundation of governance in the new Islamic Republic. In line with over three centuries worth of Twelver Uṣūlist doctrine, but simultaneously charged with intense anti-colonialism,[110] Khomeini (the charismatic leader and theorist of the Revolution) argued that as long as the Imam remains in hiding (*ghayba*), the Chief Jurist, the Marjaʿ al-Taqlīd, must fulfill the role of political and religious ruler, representing the Imam's functions in all worldly and spiritual affairs. In fact, this doctrine was formally enshrined in the 1979 Constitution of the new Republic, where Article 5 states that a jurist or a group of jurists who each have fulfilled the qualifications of *ijtihād*[111] are entitled to exercise leadership, provided the Imam continues to be absent.[112] The extension of the Faqīh's powers to the political, military and other secular realms was justified, in Khomeini's discourse, by reasoning to the effect that, for an Islamic state to be run in genuine compliance with the Sharīʿa, it must be supervised and administered by the ultimate expert in the law, the Marjaʿ al-Taqlīd.[113]

[107] See sections 2–3, above.

[108] A useful general survey of the history of Iranian family law may be found in Yassari, "Iranian Family Law in Theory and Practice," 43–64.

[109] See the last section of chapter 3, above, on the Uṣūlist/Akhbārist controversy.

[110] See, for example, his introductory pages to *al-Ḥukūma al-Islāmiyya*, 7–22.

[111] See point 8, chapter 2, section 9, above. [112] Schirazi, *Constitution of Iran*, 13.

[113] Khomeini, *al-Ḥukūma al-Islāmiyya*, 45–52, 76; Khomeini, *Islam and Revolution*, 59–60; see also generally Halm, *Shiʿa Islam*, 139 f.

This position, it must be noted, represented an expansion on the doctrine he elaborated during the decade or so before the Revolution. In that earlier version, the Marjaʿiyya plays a supervisory role – very much like that prescribed by the 1906 Constitution – whereby the Jurist or Jurists evaluate(s) all legislation in order to ensure that laws stand in conformity with the rules of the Sharīʿa.[114] As we just saw, this position was revised shortly before 1979 so that governance, including the supreme exercise of political power, might rest exclusively in the hands of the Marjaʿiyya. In both versions of the doctrine, the Marjaʿiyya is responsible for exercising *ijtihād* in those unprecedented cases that may befall the Community and its State, but otherwise the Marjaʿ is to regard and treat the established law of the Sharīʿa, at least in its broad outlines and foundational principles, as unchangeable.[115] This permanency of the law as structure and principles constituted the essence of the Islamic rule of law,[116] a feature that continues to be advocated and cherished by the majority of Islamists today.

Toward the end of his life, however, Khomeini modified his doctrine for the second time. Now he maintained that the Islamic Faqīh-Ruler is neither bound nor defined by the Sharīʿa and its laws, and can make his own determination of what the law is. The Jurist(s) can abrogate even the essential pillars of Islam – such as pilgrimage – and demolish mosques, among other things, if "the interests of the Islamic country" are threatened.[117] Very much in the spirit of the modern state which sees itself – and acts – as a system whose function is to create and impose discipline with a view to correcting any deviation from the self-established norm, Khomeini fully absorbed this modernist perception of the law's function. He adopted the view, unknown – in its modernist political connotations – to pre-modern Islamic jurists of any strand, that "Islam regards law as a tool, not as an end in itself. Law is a tool and an instrument for the establishment of justice in society, a means for man's intellectual and moral reform and his purification."[118] Qasim Zaman has argued that this doctrine, which granted the Faqīh-Ruler absolute authority over and above the law, was precisely what the Sunnite ulama feared most. For "in the guise of upholding Islam the state might make it subservient to its own goals and ultimately absorb it within itself."[119] It is this "guise," representing no more than a thin veneer, that marks the superficial difference between a self-declared secular state and a self-declared Islamic

114 Arjomand, "Islamic Constitutionalism," 118.
115 Khomeini, *Islam and Revolution*, 79. 116 See Hallaq, *Origins*, chapter 8.
117 For this argument, see Zaman, *Ulama*, 105–06. Cf. Khomeini, *al-Ḥukūma al-Islāmiyya*, 41–44.
118 Khomeini, *Islam and Revolution*, 80. 119 Zaman, *Ulama*, 107.

state. The ulama as well as the Islamists – Sunnite and Shīʿite – have yet to discover that, in the final analysis, a state is a state.[120]

Be that as it may, very little in Khomeini's doctrine was implemented immediately, for even the Jurist-Ruler himself, the Supreme Leader, could not overhaul the Shah's state with the speed he hoped for, and in fact he died before much of his legal ideology was implemented. Part of the reason may lie in the paradox of his conception that Islamic governance grounded in the Sharīʿa's rule of law was gradually fading away in favor of a modernist perception of governance (a change that can be explained by the weight of his experience as a political leader of a modern state which, under the Shah, had cultivated a sophisticated system of surveillance and bureaucracy). Yet Khomeini's paradox was that of the Islamic Republic as well, for the tension between the Islamic ideal, even in its modernized form, and the reality of the modern state was and remains dominating.

This tension is exemplified in several features of the Republic. Consider, for instance, the limitations in the 1979 Islamic Constitution. Article 4 requires that "All civil, penal, financial, economic, administrative, cultural, military, political laws and other laws or regulations must be based on Islamic principles ... absolutely and generally."[121] Yet, the mechanism created to implement Islamicization of laws was not programmed in absolute Islamic terms. The Constitution provides for a supervisory council of six Sharīʿa jurists and another six Western-trained lawyer-jurists whose task it is to ensure that all bills presented to the Parliament stand in conformity with Islamic law. The juristic qualifications of the latter six members might well be questioned, at least on grounds of lack of familiarity with the *fiqh* and its hermeneutical underpinnings. Furthermore, according to Article 167, the court judges are supposed to adjudicate each case on the basis of codified law, and in the absence of such a law their decisions must conform to a *fatwā* issued by a learned Sharīʿa jurist.[122] This Article effectively preserves much of the Pahlavi legal system, since it was understood by all parties concerned that the transformation aspired to in the various Articles that require comprehensive, systemic and systematic Islamicization cannot obtain except through a piecemeal process. And this is in fact what happened. As late as two decades later, in 2000, the Procedure of General and Revolutionary

120 Further on this theme, see the useful analysis of Zubaida, *Islam, the People and the State*, chapter 6, especially pp. 172–81.

121 Rezaei, "Iranian Criminal Justice," 57; Schirazi, *Constitution of Iran*, 10; Fatemi, "Autonomy and Equal Rights," 287.

122 Rezaei, "Iranian Criminal Justice," 58. The Iranian Constitution of 1979 is available at www.iranchamber.com/government/laws/constitution.

Courts (PGRCC) replicated most of these stipulations, stating that if any law is inadequate or unclear, or does not exist in regard to a case at issue, the court must make recourse to a *fatwā* based in Islamic legal principles or the *qāḍī* must himself perform *ijtihād*. However, should the law be found by the judge to contradict the state's enacted law, the case must be sent to another court for adjudication.[123] The state, as we shall see further below, must reign supreme, a situation that hardly squares with Khomeini's own assertion that "[Islamic] law alone ... rules over society. Even the limited powers given to the Most Noble Messenger and those exercising rule after him have been conferred upon them by God ... in obedience to divine law."[124]

In the first months of the Revolution, the symbols that captured the sensitive images of the Sharīʿa received the first attention. For this was the testing ground. How can an Islamic state, an Islamic Revolution, continue to uphold the idolatrous laws of the sacrilegious Shah? So night clubs, alcohol shops, music (including videos and cassettes), dance and sale of pork were immediately outlawed. The Constitution shortly thereafter came to prohibit usury, mentioning it by name (Article 43). And within four months of the new Republic's birth, the Islamic law of offenses, including the *ḥudūd*, *qiṣāṣ* and *taʿzīr*,[125] was instated in lieu of the Shah's criminal code, which was based on the 1816 French Penal Code. However, even this instatement of penal law was tenuous, requiring additional enactments in 1982, 1988, 1989, 1992 and 1996 to give it a concrete and more complete form. And in the process of installing the *taʿzīr* within a modern state system, the government felt compelled to fix the penalties for various offenses,[126] in effect taking away the most characteristic property of what makes *taʿzīr* what it is, namely, the judge's social, moral and legal evaluation of a particular and unique situation which every case represented. It is the *ad hoc* balance that the *qāḍī* struck among these three and other considerations which gave *taʿzīr* its features and distinguished it from *ḥudūd*. Failure to recognize that the conceptual foundations of *taʿzīr* have always assumed that each case presents unique moral conditions was a reflection not only of the moral community's undoing but also of the modern state's inherent role in metamorphosing the otherwise independent Sharīʿa into a form of state law. The reasoning behind creating this uniformity – that resists the idea and practice of applying different penalties for the same crimes – bespeaks the inevitable

[123] Ansari-Pour, "Iran" (2000–01), 355–56; Ansari-Pour, "Iran," (2005–06), 421.
[124] Algar, *Islam and Revolution*, 56–57.
[125] On the *fiqh* of these offenses, see chapter 10, sections 3–4, above.
[126] Schirazi, *Constitution of Iran*, 223–26.

discomfort that the modern state displays in the face of heterogeneity: the Subject must always be uniform.

The supremacy of the state was not merely a conceptual residue of modernist influences on Islamic modes of governance, but rather a conscious choice of how the Islamic Iranian experience, or at least the influential Khomeini and other Ayatullahs surrounding him,[127] articulated its own concept of political modernity. In Khomeini's view, Islamic law is not merely a tool by means of which certain social and moral goals can be accomplished, but a tool that is derivative of the state, the cardinal ordinance of God. "The state is the most important of God's ordinances and has precedence over all other derived ordinances of God."[128] The state does not operate within the framework of the law; rather, it is the law that operates within the state. "If the powers of the state were [only] operational within the framework of God's ordinances, the extent of God's sovereignty and the absolute trusteeship given to the Prophet would be a meaningless phenomenon devoid of content."[129]

This vision of the state entirely comports with Khomeini's other pronouncements that, in the name of the state, the Faqīh-Ruler could suspend with impunity Sharīʿa rules, major and minor, if the "country's" interest required doing so.[130] In this vision, institutionalized checks and balances, both Western and Islamic, are absent. Weber's bureaucratic rationality, which gives the state its juristic and corporate personality, has been abdicated by the Jurist-Ruler and perhaps the Council of Guardians, who in theory and in practice have the final say as to what is Islamic, i.e., what is lawful and what is not. They appear to be the only ones who decide what the "country's interest" is. At the same time, these powers of determining the law in the name of the state in no way reflect the tradition of the Sharīʿa, wherein the conjoined effects of the stability of the law and its supremacy guarantee, as they in fact did, that the "state" always operates under the rule of law.

In the meantime, little in the way of Islamization was accomplished. This was clear from the frustrations Khomeini himself expressed in a 1982 speech.[131] After that speech, the Parliament began to push toward Islamic legislation in earnest, declaring that all laws in the Republic deemed by the government institution applying them to be un-Islamic must be submitted

[127] Such as Āyatullāh Āzārī Qummī. See Schirazi, *Constitution of Iran*, 230, 240.

[128] It would, therefore, be missing a crucial point to argue – as Arjomand does – that in Khomeini's Iran the Sharīʿa "came back with vengeance and swallowed the modernized state and its constitution." See his "Islamic Constitutionalism," 125.

[129] Khomeini's speech (1988), cited in Schirazi, *Constitution of Iran*, 230.

[130] Zaman, *Ulama*, 105–06. Cf. Khomeini, *al-Ḥukūma al-Islāmiyya*, 41–44.

[131] Schirazi, *Constitution of Iran*, 163–64.

to the Council of Guardians for review. But the Council immediately countered by affirming that, as long as a law was not officially declared un-Islamic, it should be applied provisionally until further notice, which would be presumably after the Council of Guardians had reviewed its substance. As it turned out, this position of 1982 expressed the Republic's gradual approach to Islamization over the next two and a half decades. It was an approach that adopted a pragmatic policy, where the accommodation of the jural facts on the ground took precedence over any consideration of Islamization that might cause paralyzing or harmful ruptures to the political system.

The first manifestation of this pragmatic policy was the relegalization of music on radio and television, trade in videos and cassettes, chess and other forms of entertainment.[132] The reasoning, embodied in a *fatwā* that Khomeini issued, resorted to the juristic distinction between harmful and beneficial forms of entertainment, and what was restored, it was said, was entertainment of the latter form. But the reality behind relegalization of "permissible" entertainment was the ineffectiveness of the 1979 prohibition, which brought to the fore the inability of the government to ban popular practices. Although this was presented to the public not as a retreat but as a policy operating in favor of public interest (*maṣlaḥa*), to the religious leadership it was, as their *fatwā*s suggest, a mitigated concession in favor of modernity's pernicious effects, for such legislation would at least allow Islamic television programs and classical Iranian music to compete with their Western counterparts. It was an act of opting for the lesser evil. Prohibition on all forms of music would have meant that only black market and thus Western music was being consumed.

This retreat had a parallel in the law of *taʿzīr* whose penalties, as we noted, were fixed by the state. Faced with criticism by some of the Ayatullahs themselves (on the ground that the discretionary nature of *taʿzīr* is of the essence), the government could neither abrogate them nor restore their discretionary features. So the law had perforce to stay but – in order to vitiate the criticism of the mullahs – it was given the designation "state regulations," a nomenclature that amounts to a declaration of withdrawing these penalties from the sphere of Sharīʿa. Like all *sharʿī* elements that have come to symbolize and capture the *modern* essence of "Islamic law," penal law was pursued with particular vigor, but like much else, several modernizing adjustments to the traditional system had to be made. Other modern institutions within the judiciary had to be accommodated and given a *sharʿī* veneer. For instance, the

[132] *Ibid.*, 241–42.

jury, required in trials of "political and press offenses,"[133] was claimed to have a *sharʿī* pedigree, represented in the habitual attendance of *ahl al-ʿilm* in pre-modern courts of law,[134] an attendance whose intent and purpose was to ensure "due process" and fair trials, but not to pass judgments. (Apparently, the immeasurable gap between the jury's legal knowledge and training and that of the *ahl al-ʿilm* was also not deemed a relevant factor in the analogy.) Similar adaptations were made to rationalize and justify the legal profession, lawyerly practices and related matters – all of which had been introduced to Iran from the West. In the final analysis, the great majority of laws adopted before and *after* the Revolution were Western in inspiration and content, and they remain so. International laws, international conventions and treaties continue to be ratified every year,[135] the traditional law of *jihād* notwithstanding.[136]

E. Indonesia

The vigorous Dutch push on behalf of *adat* since the end of the nineteenth century – which presupposed the articulation of a divide between these *adat* and the Sharīʿa and which was made at the expense of the latter – generated massive resentment, not least because the Dutch were seen to be tampering with legitimate authority in both legal spheres.[137] What exacerbated the matter further was their decision to eliminate the Islamic courts during the last few years before their final departure in 1950. All in all, it can be safely said that Dutch policies since 1882, and until they left, did nothing but strengthen the Indonesian popular resolve to persist in their commitment to their religion and its juridical institutions. On the other hand, the structures of political and legal power bequeathed by the Dutch to the largely secular native elite continued business as usual, notwithstanding this elite's opposition to colonial rule. Generally speaking, after independence the colonial judicial structures were maintained, together with their deliberate policies of dividing the population on lines of economic and political power.[138] All commercial laws and laws of industrial property and patents were maintained, as were all *adat* laws applicable to Indonesians. The Sharīʿa in its restricted family spheres

[133] Ansari-Pour, "Iran" (2003–04), 267–68.
[134] On these court attendees, see chapter 4, section 3, above.
[135] On some of the latest of such ratifications, see the Bibliography's entries of Ansari-Pour, under "Iran" (2000–01), 362–63; (2002–03), 347; (2003–04), 274; and (2004–05), 330–31.
[136] See chapter 10, above.
[137] Lev, *Islamic Courts*, 28. For a general context, see chapter 14, section 3, above.
[138] Lev, "Colonial Law."

was initially kept as before, and Indonesian Christians continued to be governed by their own Marriage Law. The laws that the Dutch had applied to the Europeans were now applied to the Chinese, though certain parts of these laws were generalized to all Indonesian nationals. The near absence of legal change in the Republic was given official sanction in Article 2 of the 1945 Constitution which stipulated that "All existing institutions and regulations of the state shall continue to function so long as new ones have not been set up in conformity with the Constitution."[139]

One result of the political compromise the Dutch had to make before their departure was the establishment in 1946, after the defeat of the Japanese occupation, of a Ministry of Religion. In part, this was also a competitive measure, calculated to match the efforts expended by the Japanese to promote Islam as a means of controlling the population. Many Islamic institutions were subsumed under the administration of this Ministry. The Directorate of Religious Justice became the Ministry's division responsible for the administration of Muslim courts. In the long run, this Ministry came to play a significant role in the promotion of Islamic law, both in terms of spreading its courts and judicial practices, and in creating an educational system that was conducive to the development of an Indonesian religio-legal identity. This Ministry tended, then as now, to be staffed by persons who did not hail from the upper Westernized elite that the Dutch had bequeathed to the country, an important fact in light of the power dynamics that were to determine the extent to which the Sharīʿa was to be accommodated.

Together with support from Islamist parties, the Ministry of Religion (later Ministry of Religious Affairs) pressed for the creation of Islamic courts on various Indonesian islands, this in defiance of the influential Ministry of Interior that was backed by the largely anti-Islamic, secularist nationalist elite. By 1957, Sharīʿa courts (Mahkamah Syariah) were convened in Sumatra and Java, and appellate religious courts for the other islands were established in Java. But in all of these developments the Dutch colonial legacy was considerable, for not only did these courts amount to very little in terms of their jurisdiction, but the scope of this jurisdiction was at times very different from one place to the next. The Dutch judicial policies established for Java and Madura (and later Kalimantan) between 1882 and 1937 reduced the Sharīʿa courts in these islands to the adjudication of cases pertaining to marriage,[140] but more specifically to divorce; on the other hand, the newer courts of Sumatra and

[139] Cited in Lukito, "Law and Politics," 17. [140] Hooker, "State and Shariʿa," 35.

elsewhere adjudicated spheres as varied as *waqf*, public funds (including *zakāt*), gifts, bequests and inheritance. The unification of the judicial system thus posed a great challenge to the independent state, as the Javanese courts wished to acquire wider jurisdiction, especially over inheritance,[141] while the other courts, especially in Sumatra, resisted giving up what they had already gained at high cost.

During the first years after formal independence, the Sharī'a courts were affected by a number of factors. Internal administrative and procedural inconsistencies, coupled with inadequate funding for both administration of the courts and training of their officers and magistrates, remained something of a debilitating problem for years. More importantly, however, these courts were only a part of a wider ethnic, religious, legal and cultural diversity which the state was assiduously trying to homogenize. The elite's knowledge that law is a powerful mechanism of social engineering led to the promulgation of the 1947 Law No. 7, which positioned the Supreme Court and Chief Public Prosecutor at the pinnacle of authority in the legal system. Law No. 23 of the same year abolished the customary courts of Java and Sumatra, areas that had locally governed themselves under the Dutch. The evolving hegemony of the nation-state, which resembled that of the Dutch in Holland, but less so that of the Indonesian colony, was not to pass without notice. It is significant that this law asserted, in defensive terms, the sovereignty of the new Republic, stating that the Republic was not "merely the successor of the Netherlands-Indies Administration."[142] The process of unification continued unabated. A year later, in 1948, Law No. 19 introduced a three-tiered court system (first instance, appeal and supreme court) but did not account in these provisions for the *adat* and Sharī'a courts. The Sharī'a and *adat* courts were amalgamated into these courts.[143]

An attempt at organizing the religious courts came in 1957, when the central government defined the functions of these courts and the procedures for appointing their officers. No principles or laws of the Sharī'a were stated, and the courts, modeled after their civil counterparts, were collegiate – another Dutch legacy. The laws of evidence were those used in civil courts, not those of the *fiqh*, and so were the description and reporting of court cases. Following the Dutch policy, the new nation-state adopted the principle that the Sharī'a courts should not deal with property and financial matters, which were, as noted earlier, deputed to the civil courts.

[141] On the "inheritance problem," see Lev, *Islamic Courts*, 187–205, where he also remarks that the Javanese Sharī'a courts did not in practice relinquish all adjudication over inheritance matters.

[142] Lev, "Judicial Unification," 20. [143] Lukito, "Law and Politics," 21, 25.

Needless to say, such a dichotomization of divorce and property jurisdiction is artificial, and proved to be problematic, since in land-owning rural communities the two spheres were inseparable.

The national debate during the 1950s was redolent of the discourse over the places of *adat* and Sharīʿa in the country's legal system. The pluralism of *adat* ran against the wishes of the secular nationalists whose strategy was to depict the *adat* as backward and anti-modern. Likewise, the weaker voices in this secularist-nationalist camp made the same arguments against the Sharīʿa. The proponents of *adat*, though, were powerful enough to gain some concessions in the 1960s, when the Basic Law of Agrarian Affairs declared that the *adat* law provides a source of law in the Republic, taking the place of colonial law. But this concession was sharply limited by the introduction of conditions to the effect that any use of such customary laws should not impede the construction of a just and prosperous society. Substantively, in the meantime, the colonial law persisted quietly under a nationalistic guise.[144]

On the other hand, the Sharīʿa courts survived this debate more successfully, partly due to the aura of legitimacy which Islam generated, and partly because the legal "code" by which they were regulated (mainly of Shāfiʿite pedigree) was, unlike the pluralist *adat*, consistent with aims of the national unification project. It is also very likely that the government realized the relevance of these courts to the daily lives of the rural population. Whereas no secular courts could play the role of a mediator, the Sharīʿa courts – also in Malaysia and elsewhere – fulfilled a major role in arbitrating and mediating disputes *before* reaching the level of formal adjudication.[145] Thus, Law No. 14 of 1970 affirmed the judicial powers of Sharīʿa courts, thereby appeasing a majority of citizens to whom the legislation was not just a legal act, but also a symbolic and political one. On the one hand, the law in effect was curbed through the concomitant affirmation of the "silent" colonial principle that *sharʿī* decisions, to be effective, required the ratification of the secular courts. The religious Marriage Law of 1974 was, in application, subject to these very limitations.

In time, however, these limitations were removed. Under the increasing pressures of Islamicization and of the Islamists of Indonesia, as well as the emergence of strong civil Islamic movements,[146] and despite the stiff

[144] *Ibid.*, 23–24.

[145] See Peletz, *Islamic Modern*, 30; Hanna, "Administration of Courts," 54; Raymond, "Role of the Communities," 39–40; Starr, "Pre-Law Stage," 120; Marcus, *Middle East*, 109. See also chapter 4, above.

[146] A succinct and useful analysis is to be found in Hefner, "Varieties of Muslim Politics," 136–51.

opposition of the "secularist" and non-Muslim groups, Law No. 7 (1989) was passed, unifying the Sharīʿa courts throughout the islands and, significantly, reversing the principle of ratification, the so-called *executoire verklaring*. Henceforth, the Sharīʿa courts' decisions were self-validating, needing no sanction from the secular courts. As of 1991, these courts began to base their decisions on the new Compilation of Islamic Law in Indonesia, which reflected a modernized version of Islamic law that was also intended to create more consistency and uniformity within the country. In this Compilation polygamy remained legal under certain conditions and inter-faith marriage continued to be banned.

After the collapse of the Suharto regime in 1998, the process of decentralization (known as Otonomi Daerah) took on a new dynamic that resulted in a number of developments, often contradictory, on both the federal and district levels. Laws no. 10 and 32 of 2004 recognized the relative autonomy of Indonesia's districts, giving the federal government exclusive powers over national and international policies, but leaving the domestic affairs of the districts to be decided largely by the districts themselves. Sixteen districts have since signed on to the Sharia District Regulation (Peraturan Daerah Sharia; abr. Perda Sharia), including Aceh, Padang, Banten, Cianjur, Tangerang, Jombang, Bulukumba and Sumbawa. The main content of the Regulation is the application of Sharīʿa teachings, understood and expressed variably by different districts. Some have passed laws requiring the donning of Muslim dress, whereas others limited it to civil servants; other districts also criminalized prostitution, and the sale and consumption of alcohol, and regulated the collection of *zakat*.[147] On the other hand, in 2004, and under pressure from international and local human rights groups, the Ministry of Religious Affairs proposed a draft law to replace the 1991 Compilation. The proposed law – in which polygamy was to be strictly outlawed, and inter-faith marriage unconditionally legalized – led to a major national debate and, for obvious reasons, drew the fierce opposition of Islamists and influential ulama.[148] The debate continues.

F. Turkey

The case of Turkey represents a unique example of a society that has clung to Islamic jural values despite the structural, even radical, dismantling of the Sharīʿa legal system over nearly a century. By 1926, exactly

[147] The various laws are listed in Candraningrum, "Perda Sharia."
[148] Harisumarto, "Indonesia Draft Sharia Law."

one hundred years after the first state act against the *waqf*s and law colleges,[149] the adamantly secular Kemalist regime completely scrapped Islamic law, replacing it with a host of European codes, the most notable being the Swiss Civil Code, the German Commercial Code and the Italian Criminal Code. The intention was not only to distance Turkey from the perceived "backwardness" of the Muslim world and its cultural and other problems, but also to engender in it a new cultural ethic that was "rational," "scientific" and ultimately modern. The transformation, in other words, was to be legal, cultural and "civilizational." No less drastically than in other Islamic countries, the Turkish Republic attempted to reengineer and refashion the family and the mosaic of national life. No rules of the Sharīʿa were to continue to exist, including such of its features as polygamy and the religious ceremony surrounding marriage. Religion, if it were to remain at all, was to be kept to the private sphere.

Yet, Islamic practices at the local level survived despite all attempts of the state to secularize society.[150] Islamic values and practices remain pervasive in Turkish society, suggesting the failure of the Republican elite to make religion a private belief.[151] As an indicator of this pervasiveness, the ceremonial Islamic *nikah* is still a preferred form of marriage among many Turks, in both rural and urban areas. During the 1970s, half a century after the drastic Westernization of the law was effected, one-half of all marriages in Turkey were concluded according to both civil state law and through a religious ceremony, and no less than 15 percent were concluded according to religious tradition and thus had no status according to state law. In the 1990s, at least 82 percent of marriages in urban societies, and 87 percent in rural societies, were performed according to both civil law and religious ritual. In popular perception, legitimacy of marriage rested solely in the *sharʿī nikah*, and children born within civil marriages were normatively regarded as "bastards." Nor was polygamy eliminated, despite the fact that it has been criminalized since 1926. Again, in both rural and urban areas it is being practiced, as it was before the ban. While during the last quarter of the nineteenth century it hovered in Istanbul at around 2.5 percent of all marriages (reflecting sporadic traditional practice), in the 1970s it continued at a slightly lower rate of 2 percent at the national level, and in the rural areas during the last few years at no less than 4.4 percent, in some locales reaching 10 percent. In other spheres of life as well, such as business, banking, finance and insurance, "Muslim law is referred to and obeyed by many people despite

[149] See chapter 15, especially section 2, above. [150] Dumont, "Power of Islam," 88–94.
[151] Yilmaz, "Secular Law," 120. This paragraph draws on this useful article, esp. at 122–28.

the non-recognition of the state." As in Egypt, Indonesia and several modernizing Muslim countries, local communities are reconstituting their lives according to what they perceive to be Islamic religious and legal moralities. Their moral communities are attempting to provide antidotes to the intrusive powers of the overarching state.[152]

[152] This theme was repeatedly raised by many Azharites whom this author interviewed in early 2008.

17 In search of a legal methodology

1. Introduction

Arguably, by the middle of the twentieth century the Sharīʿa had been reduced to a fragment of itself at best and, at worst, structurally speaking, to a nonentity. The chipping away by the modern state of the Sharīʿa resulted in: first, the collapse of the financial and *waqf* foundations that sustained the legal profession and its reproductive mechanisms; second, the gradual displacement of this profession by a class of modern lawyers and judges who came from a newly rising bourgeoisie and/or transformed ulama families; third, the replacement of institutional legal structures by modern law faculties and modern hierarchical courts of law; and fourth, the introduction of a massive bulk of commercial, criminal, civil and other laws that either replaced the *fiqh* or were imported in order to accommodate the new legal needs that arose as a result of exposure to the new and open international markets (whose props were industrialization and constantly evolving technologies, not the mercantile and agricultural substrates which largely defined the pre-modern Muslim economies). The totality of these effects, I have argued elsewhere, amounted to the effective structural demise of the Sharīʿa,[1] notwithstanding the continuing viability of the law of personal status, which finds its roots in the *fiqh* but has become transformed in function and modality to a state law.[2] The manner of Sharīʿa's functioning as well as the moral community that permitted and nourished its operation no longer exist.

Together with the Sharīʿa, a number of major institutions and practices met their demise, including artisanal professions, societies and guilds, kinship structures, household crafts, and entire ways of life. None, however, was so lamented by a majority of Muslims as was the Sharīʿa, which alone became, among all the forms that have vanished, an integral marker of modern identity. In the view of an increasing majority, Islam is not

[1] Hallaq, "Can the Sharīʿa Be Restored?"
[2] This having been the theme of the previous chapter.

Islam without its Sharīʿa (or at least a *sharīʿa*), and the passage of time has made the call to restore it ever more intense. If the call has acquired a renewed urgency, it has done so as a response to modernity – to its secularism, excessive rationalism, materialism, economic deprivations, militarism, colonialism, oppressive nation-states, and virtual lack of moral community. From these perspectives, the massive call to implement Sharīʿa – currently so powerful especially among Muslim youth nearly everywhere – is readily analyzable as a movement toward postmodernity.[3] That this call is as much a political grievance as it is a legal one is shown, among other things, by the concomitant demand to restore the caliphate, a particular political/religious regime that represents an "Islamic" alternative mode of governance versus the intrusive and all-dominating modern state.

Integral to any conception of Sharīʿa is a theoretical, methodological and, perhaps, hermeneutical system that is expected by modern Muslim intellectuals to underlie the means by which legal norms and rules are to be derived. In other words, a new *uṣūl al-fiqh* is expected to arise out of the ashes of the old system, an *uṣūl* theory that is suitable to the ever-changing conditions of modernity. That a call for the emergence of a (neo-)*uṣūl al-fiqh* persists appears to be a function of both necessity and historical legacy. First, in any complex culture,[4] law is self-conscious and necessarily must be anchored in a theoretical discourse that rationalizes and justifies law's prescriptions, its methods, precepts and rationales. And second, in terms of historicity, the call to restore a form of Sharīʿa necessarily invokes that of which it was an integral part for a millennium. And there is no more immediate and direct link than that which stood between the *fiqh* and *uṣūl al-fiqh*. Yet, whereas pre-modern *uṣūl al-fiqh* emerged out of a constellation of legal communities that shared a particular vision of the universe and a highly integrated legal episteme,[5] any conception of a modern *uṣūl* theory faces the challenge of division along lines that are local, regional, ethnic, national and etatist – all of which stand in opposition to the meaning of Muslim community, at least that community which survives in the modern Muslim imagination.

Be this as it may, if modern thinkers continue to speak of the need for a modern *uṣūl*ist theory of law, and if they insist on calling whatever theory they cared to propose "*uṣūl al-fiqh*," it is – as we intimated earlier – the force of tradition that has dictated this nomenclature, not necessarily the

[3] On this important theme, see the excellent work of Euben, *Enemy in the Mirror*.
[4] I.e., that does not, anthropologically speaking, qualify as a "simple society."
[5] I borrow the term as well as its connotations from Foucault. See Introduction, sections 1 and 3, above.

content of their theories. That the nomenclature is so hard to dispose of is testimony to the formidable weight of *uṣūl al-fiqh*. It is necessary, furthermore, not only as a rationalizing discourse and, according to many, a juristic hermeneutic, but as a matter of religious and political legitimacy. Consciousness of its historical dominance as a powerful legal and intellectual field is matched only by its power as the receptacle of the methods whose use necessarily implicates the Quran and the Sunna, and how these texts are to be used as a guide to the good life. In other words, any conception of the law, however ultimately defined, must rest on and presuppose a consciously formulated legal methodology.

Central to any new theory there remains the centuries-old question regarding the balance between the roles of reason and revelation in any juristic formation.[6] The formative epoch of Islam, spanning the first four centuries or so, produced a wide range of movements and intellectual currents featuring a varied mixture of reason and revelation, ranging from those who assigned reason a paramount position to those who denied it even the most marginal of roles. Ashʿarite legal theology, considerably dominating the Sunnite scene, and sustaining therein most pre-modern legal theories of *uṣūl*, held human intellect to be largely incapable of any determination of the rationale behind God's revelation. God's ultimate wisdom was, in this theology, simply incomprehensible. Thus, the rationale for legal rules and guidance was to be sought in intimations and indications within the structures of the revealed texts, a phenomenon that readily explains the paramount status of the texts. So beyond these textual indications, nothing was to be attributed to God's rationale and intention. Accordingly, the negation of man's rational supremacy – itself one of the grand signs of surrendering to the intellectual powers of a higher order – rendered *uṣūl al-fiqh* dependent on a conception of law and morality that must be sought in the world of texts, revealed (= Quran) and semi-revealed (= Sunna). And to make out the *jural* meaning of these texts, an Arabicate system of interpretation, grammar and syntax became essential, occupying a good third of space in any work of legal theory. Humble and devoid of intellectual (as well as other) arrogance, the human race – in both legal theory and theology – was to understand that it does not dominate the world, that it must live within the rules of nature, this latter being the most obvious sign and proof (*āya*) of God's own existence.[7] The determination of how humans should live, how they should regulate and judge their affairs, could not be a human decision, despite the fact that God with all His wisdom Himself created the human mind

[6] Further on this, see Hallaq, *History*, 255 ff.
[7] See, e.g., Hallaq, "Ibn Taymiyya on the Existence of God," 58 ff.

and endowed it with the highest intellectual aptitude. At best, then, the human mind is a tool that deciphers textual meanings within social contexts, but does not independently produce meanings of its own. Hobbes would have no place in such a system. Law, therefore, is a synthesis between reason and revelation, but a synthesis that does not allow the revealed texts to be dominated by the caprice of the human mind.

Enter modernity, with its pronounced – some would even say capricious – rationality. The marginalization of religion and the concomitant triumph of secularism in the West produced a form of rationalism that has played a powerful role in the colonialist project, one that Muslims had to contend with, in a patently conscious manner, as early as the second half of the nineteenth century. Humanism was little more than a euphemism for man's dominance over the world, including the natural one. In the name of God's creation of the human mind – even in the theistic Hobbesian tradition – man becomes a sort of viceroy, disposing of the affairs of the world at will. The theoretical predicament of Muslims thus consisted, and continues to consist, of the need to accommodate modernity's rationality within the parameters of their tradition, its texts, culture and, no less, the tradition's perceived legacy in the constitution of present political and ideological identity. (For to say that the predicament is as much political and ideological as it is legal is surely to state the obvious.)

The search for a solution to this predicament began toward the last quarter of the nineteenth century, with the activist writings of the Egyptian intellectual Muḥammad ʿAbduh (d. 1905). ʿAbduh's contribution lay not in proposing a new legal theory, but rather in crafting a theology that instigated a relative break from the pre-modern Ashʿarite conception of causality and rationality. A chief postulate of this theology, considerably influenced by Muʿtazilite thought (and no doubt reflecting an indirect Kantian influence), was that sound human reason is, on its own, capable of distinguishing between right and wrong. If there appears to be a contradiction between reason and revelation concerning any particular issue, it is because one or the other has been misunderstood. This doctrine (otherwise known as *darʾ taʿāruḍ al-ʿaql wal-naql*)[8] received full support in mainstream theological and juristic circles, but ʿAbduh gave it a heavier Muʿtazilite twist in maintaining that reason is not simply a partner of revelation but can in effect displace it as a guide to human action. Yet, while the determination of the value of an act is the province of reason, the penalty or reward that results from the commission or omission of the

[8] See, for instance, a major expounder of this tenet: Ibn Taymiyya, *Darʾ Taʿāruḍ al-ʿAql wal-Naql*.

act is the jurisdiction of revelation. Thus, the use of reason is maximized, yet the religious tenor is not set aside. But the balance stands clearly in favor of an unprecedentedly favorable approach to materialism, whereby Muslims are called upon not to concern themselves overly with the hereafter to the detriment of their worldly life, since the best way to live as a Muslim is to pursue material progress.[9]

With this theology, ʿAbduh provided a break with pre-modern theological and juristic conceptions, paving the way for the subsequent emergence of a wide variety of theories that came to express positions ranging from the religious to the secular.[10] In what follows, and without any intention of being exhaustive, I will deal with some of the more important and influential writers on modern conceptions of legal theory.

2. Muḥammad Rashīd Riḍā: toward a theory of natural law

ʿAbduh's new theology provided his student, Riḍā, with the necessary tools to appropriate from traditional legal theory certain concepts that the latter would use to rationalize the materialist exigencies of modernity. The cornerstone of his thesis, and the theses of many after him, rested on the notion of *maṣlaḥa*, an important but controversial concept among pre-modern legal theoreticians.[11] Riḍā faced the challenge of having to recast the concept in such a way as to render it palatable to his contemporaries and simultaneously divest it of the fetters of the traditional theoretical discourse, since the theory of *maṣlaḥa* – as we saw in chapter 2 – was intricately connected and interwoven with legal causation (*taʿlīl*). What was required for Riḍā's theory was no less than to extract *maṣlaḥa* from its larger theoretical context, and to amplify it in such a way as to make it stand on its own feet.

Thus, Riḍā's first step was to insist on what he characterized as the pure form of Islam, embodied in nothing more than the Quran, the Sunna and the Companions' consensus. This form was said by Riḍā to have been what the Companions knew; once it was abandoned, the Muslim community split into schools and sects, falling ever since into a perennial state

[9] Kerr, *Islamic Reform*, 103–86.

[10] This is not to arrogate to ʿAbduh, by way of causality, the role of a "founder" of a new ideology that constituted an epistemic break with preceding mainstream theologies. Rather, he is to be seen as having articulated *one* representation of a widely emerging movement whose varied expressions and voices needed a historically grounded justification and rationalization, both of which he happened to provide.

[11] Hallaq, *History*, 112–13.

of disunity.[12] All legal subject-matter elaborated by the pre-modern jurists was therefore to be set aside. The common Muslim individual, he argued, stands helpless before the formidable and intricate doctrines elaborated by these jurists, for their "hair-splitting" discourses resulted in a highly technical law that is difficult to comprehend and even more difficult to implement. The contemporary wholesale importation of Western codes into Muslim countries is but one consequence of this inherited complexity. Thus blaming the over-use of reasoning in Sharīʿa and its resultant complexities for causing jural colonization of the Muslim world, he goes on to argue that another part of the problem is the Sharīʿa's penchant for finding answers to every real and imaginary problem, a feature that led to its becoming increasingly immoderate and intolerant. He argues that the Quran has enjoined Muslims not to inquire into any issue that the Prophet did not touch upon, for this can only lead to the swelling of the body of legal obligations, making adherence to the law arduous if not impossible.[13]

Islam, as the title of his work indicates, is a religion of ease and leniency, not hardship.[14] In expounding on this theme, he adduces a number of "premises," the first of which is the well-known tenet that Islam came to perfect earlier religions. Second, the Quran is the foundation of Islam. Third, whereas the Prophetic narrative concerning matters of worship (*ʿibādāt*) are infallible, those narratives pertaining to the social and economic transactions of everyday life (*muʿāmalāt*) are not. None other than the Prophet himself, as admitted by the very Prophetic narrative, erred in some of these matters. Fourth, God perfected all matters related to *ʿibādāt*, since these do not change in time or place. But because the worldly affairs, the *muʿāmalāt*, do change from time to time, and from place to place, God laid down only broad and general principles according to which these matters should be treated. Riḍā's implication here seems to be that because of this level of generality, plus the falsifiability of the Prophetic narrative, the determination of what the *muʿāmalāt* mean in different times and places remains within the boundaries of man's discretion, not God's. Fifth is the general principle that, all things being equal and religion being lenient, *muʿāmalāt* are assumed to be permissible, unless proven to be otherwise. Sixth, the forefathers abhorred not only unwarranted queries about legal matters, but also excessive reasoning and undue indulgence in rational thought, Riḍā's point being to warn against those secular–rationalist "reformers" who call for the total abolition of the Sharīʿa, as indeed happened in Kemalist Turkey. Seventh, after

[12] Opwis, "*Maṣlaḥa*," 200–01. [13] Riḍā, *Yusr*, 12–23.
[14] *Yusr al-Islām* may be translated as "leniency of Islam."

the generation of the Companions, the community experienced strife and division, and this, in Riḍā's opinion, was due to misuse of the legal methods of inference. Communal disharmony prevented the occurrence of consensus, leaving Muslims with the consensus of the Companions as the only credible *ijmāʿ* that can constitute a source of law.[15]

In setting forth these premises, Riḍā appears to prepare the grounds to steer a middle course between the ulama camp advocating the traditional status and function of Sharīʿa and those secularists who wish to abolish it and replace it with state law. By, on the one hand, criticizing the traditional ulama's indulgence in what he saw as trivial minutiae of hypothetical and speculative legal reasoning and, on the other, distancing himself from free thought and excessive rationality, he was distinguishing himself as a member of the so-called "middle community," characterized by its "moderates who affirm the possibility of reviving Islam and of renewing its true identity by following the Book, the sound Sunna, and the guidance of the pious ancestors" (*salaf*).[16]

Qiyās here is missing, not because Riḍā denies it the status of a source (which he probably was on the verge of doing), but by virtue of the fact that he views *qiyās* as problematic, a euphemism for his view of it as restrictive.[17] Yet, whatever aspects of *qiyās* he curtailed, he made up for these exclusions by expounding his own, enlarged concept of *maṣlaḥa*. Far from being a simple exchange of juristic technique, this compensation turns out to be a potent one, as it allows Riḍā to jettison the centuries-old and highly principled methodology of doing law.

Riḍā has already noted that the Quran and the Sunna perfected the doctrinal prescriptions of religious works and ritual laws, the clearly pronounced and segregated category of *ʿibādāt*. But this is not true of the *muʿāmalāt*, the "worldly interests," which tend to change with time and place and at every turn require re-elaboration.[18] However, careful in his bid to garner legitimacy for his discourse, he attempts to place himself within the mainstream doctrine pertaining to *maṣlaḥa* in *uṣūl al-fiqh*. He argues that it is a common misconception that the majority of traditional *uṣūl* theorists regarded *maṣlaḥa* as a questionable legal source; in fact, he affirms, it was a method integral to the processes of determining the *ʿilla* by means of suitability (*munāsaba*) and relevance (*mulāʾama*).[19]

In *uṣūl al-fiqh*, a suitable *ʿilla* is one that the jurist derives rationally. If the *ʿilla* finds support in the revealed texts, it is regarded as valid; but if

[15] Riḍā, *Yusr*, 24–28. [16] *Ibid.*, 7. [17] *Ibid.*, 44–46.
[18] On the significance of this modern separation between *ʿibādāt* and *muʿāmalāt*, see Hallaq, "Fashioning the Moral Subject."
[19] See chapter 2, section 7, above, and Hallaq, *History*, 88 ff.

it happens to contradict the tenor of the texts, it must be rejected. Also recognized is a third type of *ʿilla*, one that neither contradicts nor agrees with a specific passage in the texts, but is inductively and overwhelmingly corroborated by the general spirit and intention of the law, what Ghazālī and Shāṭibī, among others, have called *maqāṣid al-sharīʿa*.[20] This reasoning, Riḍā vigorously asserts, perfectly accords with that type of *maṣlaḥa* which met the universal approval of the Muslim jurists throughout the centuries. Here he cites a number of these jurists who pronounced on the universal admissibility of this type of *maṣlaḥa*, and further implies that *fiqh* derived through *qiyās* in the formative period represented a roundabout way of arriving at the same conclusions through *maṣlaḥa*.[21]

With the changing realities of Islam in the twentieth century, Riḍā asserts, the *muʿāmalāt*, be they political, judicial or civil in nature, should be determined by one of five different types of evidence. The first is the revealed language that enjoys certainty in both signification and transmission, and which therefore yields rulings and legal values that are likewise certain. No other evidence may override such language unless it is a more weighty revealed text (*arjaḥ*; *murajjaḥ*), which meets the same conditions of linguistic clarity and sound transmission, but whose strength, on one or another count, happens to be superior (e.g., the "weightier" text being *mutawātir lafẓī*, whereas the "less weighty" text is *mutawātir maʿnawī*).[22] Curiously, Riḍā also argues that such clear and soundly transmitted language may be superseded by a principle derived from a general survey of the Sharīʿa, which Shāṭibī had called "inductive corroboration."[23] One such principle is that of necessity (*ḍarūra*), which also, at any rate in Riḍā's view, overrides any other consideration in the absence of relevant revealed texts. Needless to say, by elevating the concept of necessity to an inductively drawn principle, the Quran and the Sunna would be subordinated to the *maṣlaḥa* principles inferred from *maqāṣid al-sharīʿa*. Whereas Ghazālī's and Shāṭibī's *maqāṣid* are inductively inferred from the existing body of *fiqh*, Riḍā's *maqāṣid* would be progressively reduced to an induction whose subject-matter is the state's *tashrīʿ*, a word that Riḍā understood as belonging to the realm of positive legislation.

The second type of evidence, equally binding, consists of unambiguous texts on the validity of which the Companions reached consensus. But Riḍā's language strongly implies that this evidence is also subject to

[20] For a detailed account of *maqāṣid*, see Hallaq, *History*, 112–13, 168–74, 180 ff.
[21] Riḍā, *Yusr*, 70–74; Kerr, *Islamic Reform*, 194–95. [22] See chapter 2, section 5, above.
[23] Hallaq, *History*, 162–206, esp. 180–89; and more generally, Hallaq, "On Inductive Corroboration," 6–31.

the exceptions of necessity and inductive *maṣlaḥa* stated in the first type. The third type is textual evidence that does not meet the standards set for the first two types. Yet, after investigation and analysis, these texts might be found authentic and amenable as the foundation of law. But in all cases, they are likewise subject to the overriding principles of necessity and *maṣlaḥa*. The fourth type dictates that other texts pertaining to the customary practices of Muslims are binding unless necessity and/or public interest dictate setting them aside. The fifth and final type of evidence requires that all matters finding no textual support in the revealed sources must be left up to human discretion and decided by the two overriding principles. Following ʿAbduh, Riḍā asserts that whatever rules are created on the basis of these principles would be valid, since such rational considerations do not contradict revelation.[24]

Riḍā's anchoring of all law (i.e., of *muʿāmalāt*, defined by Western legal standards as law proper)[25] in the otherwise limited concept of necessity, which in turn is validated by the principle of *maṣlaḥa*, amounts, in the final analysis, to a total negation of traditional legal theory. In effect he draws extensively on a minor concept, of highly limited application, in order to suppress the rest of it. He also heavily draws on the theories of Ṭūfī and Shāṭibī, who can scarcely be said to represent the mainstream of pre-modern jurists, appropriating their discourses for his own needs – which is to say that he takes their theses out of their historical contexts. Be that as it may, aside from matters of worship and religious ritual, which he insists are to remain within the parameters of revelation, Riḍā upholds a legal theory strictly anchored in natural law, where considerations of human need, interest and necessity would reign supreme in elaborating a legal corpus. Any revealed text, notwithstanding its epistemological strength, could be set aside if it were to contravene these considerations. His, then, is a theory that constitutes a radical shift from the traditional Sharīʿa, which had a long history of accommodating itself to changing social needs without allowing itself to abandon its hermeneutical ties to revelation.

3. ʿAbd al-Wahhāb Khallāf: caught in the middle

Acting as a Sharīʿa judge and, later, as a professor of law at Cairo University, ʿAbd al-Wahhāb Khallāf (d. 1956) lived the hybridity of Islamic and Western law in Egypt's legal experiment.[26] In his widely read work *Maṣādir al-Tashrīʿ al-Islāmī fi-mā lā Naṣṣa fīh* (*The Sources of Islamic*

[24] Riḍā, *Yusr*, 76–78.
[25] On this modern distinction, see Hallaq, "Fashioning the Moral Subject."
[26] See chapter 15, section 3, above.

Legislation in Matters Not Covered by the Revealed Texts), he attempts to pave the way for a new *uṣūl al-fiqh*, one that comports with the changing conditions of the present age (with him as with Riḍā and the majority of recent thinkers on the subject, modernity as a condition is never problematized).

If correctly understood, Khallāf argues, the sources of the law "are flexible, rich and fit for responding to the interests of human beings and to developing conditions."[27] As the title indicates, however, cases covered by clear texts are not subject to legal reasoning, nor are those cases that have been subject to the consensus of earlier generations of jurists. Accordingly, the laws of inheritance, being Quranic and mostly unequivocally clear and specific, are not subject to modern *ijtihād*. Everything else, however, is subject to the operations of *ijtihād*, which, Khallāf is right to point out, constitute in effect the great bulk of the legal corpus. Just as the latter was formulated in light of the requirements and conditions of the past, succeeding generations need to reconsider them in light of their own needs and conditions. Therefore, provided that no clear text or consensus exists, a former *ijtihād* with regard to textually unregulated cases may be supplanted by a fresh *ijtihād* based upon newly arising circumstances. Moreover, the Sharīʿa is known to promote the welfare and good of the community, and since these are subjective values, they are mutable under changing conditions.[28]

One of Khallāf's fundamental premises is that since the overall purpose of the Sharīʿa is to promote the welfare of human kind, the difference between *qiyās* and *maṣlaḥa* consists in the former being based on specific revealed texts and the latter not. Nonetheless, apparently following Riḍā, he deems *maṣlaḥa* to be superior to *qiyās* in that it is a more flexible method that can accommodate change.[29] The force of *maṣlaḥa* becomes evident when custom (*ʿurf*, *ʿāda*) is considered. Khallāf first appears to argue that any custom contravening the revealed texts must be deemed invalid, this argument comporting with the position that he established earlier concerning the finality of the certain and clear revealed texts (*nuṣūṣ*). But when he begins to elaborate on the pliability of *maṣlaḥa*, it transpires that custom, even when it contradicts such texts, may be deemed legal. For instance, if an illicit form of contract, such as life insurance, happens to become widespread in a particular society, then need and necessity – elements of *maṣlaḥa* – will have to outweigh the imperatives of the revealed texts.[30]

[27] Khallāf, *Maṣādir*, 5. [28] *Ibid.*, 8–11. [29] *Ibid.*, 40–42, 70 ff.
[30] *Ibid.*, 70–80, 124–25. See also Opwis, "*Maṣlaḥa*," 211–13.

Toward the end of his work, Khallāf introduces a chapter that he titles "The Sources of Islamic Legislation Are Flexible and Take Cognizance of People's Interests and their Progress."[31] Noteworthy here is not only Khallāf's use of the word "legislation" (*tashrīʿ*) – which acknowledges the dominating role of the state in making law – but also his systematic attempt to restrict the purview of the revealed sources. Invoking the by now all too familiar polarity between *ʿibādāt* and *muʿāmalāt*, he asserts that the Quran intentionally provided only general guidance to Muslims concerning the *muʿāmalāt*, the point being that God meant to leave specifics of the law unregulated so that legislation might take changing realities into account (this carries the unprecedented theological implication that God not only anticipated the modern nation-state, but also willed it). Furthermore, the Quran was not meant to be understood strictly according to its letter, but rather according to its spirit. But Khallāf does not go beyond this terse proposal, giving no clue – much less an articulate vision – as to how this spirit may be deduced with a view to producing specific legislation. Nor does he explain, in the least, how the Quranic rules which he had accepted as binding (e.g., inheritance) should be interpreted to accommodate social change.

The same problems also arise in his discussions of Prophetic Sunna. Its most authenticated and binding part, textually as formidable a hermeneutical authority as the Quran, is given an even more ambiguous solution than that accorded the latter. On the one hand, Khallāf appears to argue that this Sunna must continue to be binding at all times and in all places (the traditional position), but on the other hand, he strongly implies that bindingness is contingent on the concomitance of the Prophetic rules with considerations of *maṣlaḥa*; namely, when *maṣlaḥa* is not served, these rules do not apply.[32]

Thus Khallāf's writings, like Riḍā's, leave us with an almost exclusive reliance on the concepts of necessity and *maṣlaḥa*, without articulating a methodology in respect of how these principles should work interpretively in light of (a) the demands of revelation and how such demands might be methodologically *and* methodically explained away, for after all neither Riḍā nor Khallāf could simply declare the revealed sources to be immaterial, and both did claim to be speaking about a law that is Islamic;[33] and (b) the philosophical, moral and hermeneutical controls, among others, with which any policy of public interest should be fitted.

[31] Khallāf, *Maṣādir*, 131 ff. [32] *Ibid.*, 139.
[33] As attested in their works discussed here, and their titles.

4. Muḥammad Sa'īd al-Būṭī: the limits of *maṣlaḥa*

In 1965, the Syrian Būṭī (b. 1929)[34] received his doctorate in Sharī'a from al-Azhar University, having submitted as his dissertation what he later published under the title *Ḍawābiṭ al-Maṣlaḥa fī al-Sharī'a al-Islāmiyya*, a widely read book. Later he became the Dean of the Sharī'a Faculty at the University of Damascus, where he also taught the subject for years. His *Ḍawābiṭ* represents a rearticulation of the role of rationality in traditional legal reasoning, particularly in reaction to what he saw as the excesses committed by twentieth-century so-called *maṣlaḥawī*[35] thinkers and their utilitarian forerunners in Europe.

The notion of *shar'ī maṣlaḥa*, Būṭī argued, rests on a number of fundamental assumptions, all of which contradict Western utilitarian principles which, at the beginning of his work, Būṭī briefly expounds through a critique of such figures as Jeremy Bentham and J. S. Mill. The first of such assumptions is grounded in a transcendental conception of legal morality, where *maṣlaḥa* and its antonym, *mafsada* (lit. harm), cannot be restricted to this life alone but must take account of the hereafter as well. The second is that *maṣlaḥa* cannot be shortsightedly limited to the material aspects of the world and certainly cannot be reduced to hedonism, but must be equally based on corporal and spiritual human needs. Finally, the third assumption is that *maṣlaḥa* dictated by religion constitutes the foundation of worldly based *maṣlaḥa*s, with the consequence that the former has precedence over, and controls, the latter. All that may be found in worldly *maṣlaḥa*s to contradict the religiously dictated *maṣlaḥa* must be relinquished, for the integrity of religious *maṣlaḥa* is supreme.[36] Here, Būṭī again levels an attack on Western materialist and utilitarian thinkers, accusing them of severe metaphysical myopia. In fact Būṭī's attack is extraordinarily perceptive in that, while his concern lies with the Muslim *maṣlaḥawī* thinkers, he is fully aware of the Western genealogy of their "myopic" theories. He accurately captures the essence of the 'Abduh–Riḍā project that had spread throughout the Muslim world, criticizing its advocates as "those who thought *maṣlaḥa* to be a second, self-sufficient and independent religion that abrogates whatever of the first [true] religion it sees fit, and declares invalid anything it wants."[37]

The Sharī'a not only pays attention to *maṣlaḥa*, but is suffused by it. It is a law of human nature, he argues, that inasmuch as people subordinate the

[34] For a short biography, see Christmann, "Islamic Scholar," 58–60.
[35] A relatively recent usage referring to those thinkers who ground their theories in an expanded concept of *maṣlaḥa*.
[36] Būṭī, *Ḍawābiṭ*, 45, 54, 58. [37] *Ibid.*, 59.

less important to that which is more important and elevated in status, they utilize certain *maṣlaḥa*s for the sake of accomplishing greater objectives. It is a fundamental principle of *maṣlaḥa* itself to sacrifice a minor and a lesser good for gaining greater *maṣlaḥa*s. And these latter are all ever-present in the Sharīʿa, taking the form of five universals that are summed up under the rubrics of religion, life, mind, family and property.[38] Going beyond any of these would be to go above all of them, and consequently render meaningless the meaning and function of the law. Here, he quotes Shāṭibī who has "attained the pinnacle of precision" in describing the matter:

> If reason is permitted to transcend the source of revelation, it would then be permissible to invalidate Sharīʿa by means of reason – an inconceivable possibility. The very meaning of Sharīʿa is to ordain for the subjects certain limits pertaining to their acts, pronouncements and beliefs. Those are Sharīʿa's contents. If reason is permitted to overstep one of these limits, then it can overstep all others, for what is good for one thing is good for that which is analogous to it (*li-mithlihi*).[39]

Therefore, within the purview of the five universals and the particular rules derived therefrom, the Sharīʿa invariably heeds *maṣlaḥa* and alleviates hardship, as evident in many of its rules. It also acknowledges and accommodates customary practices, as long as these practices do not impinge on its rules and precepts, for it is not true that all customs are good and beneficial.

Būṭī adroitly rejects the distinction between ritualistic and transactional laws (*ʿibādāt/muʿāmalāt*), a distinction whose function is to create a line of separation between the religious and the secular, and, in effect, to divide the world into a duality (which has become a cardinal practice in Christian Europe). Būṭī does not elaborate a moral philosophy to sustain this rejection, but it is clear that he appreciates the effects of religious morality on willing submission to the law. "All that the Sharīʿa includes, in terms of tenets, ritual laws and mundane legal transactions (*ʿaqāʾid, ʿibādāt and muʿāmalāt*) guarantees the realization of the believers' *maṣlaḥa*, in both of its divisions, the worldly and the eschatological," for these tenets and laws do not accept division and in effect constitute various "rings making up one chain."[40] The totality of these, in their immediate and other-worldly concerns, leads to one set of works (*ʿamalan wāḥidan*) in the individual's life. The tenets of religion confer on the individual the certainty of God's existence, of His final authority as lawgiver, and of a meaningful existence. The creed of Islam, in other words, is the moral foundation of the law, without which there would be no conviction, much less certainty, of the necessity to abide by the law as a divinely ordained message. There is thus

[38] See chapter 2, section 8, above. [39] Būṭī, *Ḍawābiṭ*, 64–65.
[40] *Ibid.*, 85. See also Hallaq, "Fashioning the Moral Subject."

no meaning or purpose for these tenets without the obligation to abide by the so-called ritualistic and transactional laws. Būṭī here makes the compelling argument that the only meaningful law – in a meaningful human existence – is one that is grounded in a religious morality that does not waver along shifting utilitarian notions of good. It is eminently worthy of note that, of all Muslim thinkers on the subject, Būṭī displays the acutest awareness of the existential value of religious morality as the foundation of law as well as of living. His concern with this foundation, albeit indirect, appears to echo Sayyid Quṭb's preoccupation with the moral vacuum created by the modern condition.[41]

The rejection of utilitarian principles inevitably leads to a distrust of human rationality as the basis of legal construction. The intellect simply cannot independently decide particular legal rulings. Any contradiction between "real *maṣlaḥa*" (*ḥaqīqiyya*) and the dictates of the revealed texts is an imaginary one (*mawhūma*), resulting from a deficiency in the contemplator's thinking. It might be thought, for instance, that *maṣlaḥa* requires that *ribā* (usury/interest) be permissible, but this is no more, Būṭī argues, than fanciful thinking contradicting God's word. The same might be thought about *maṣlaḥa*'s insistence on monogamy. But permitting *ribā* and forbidding polygamy run against the Quran's decrees, which have a purpose and wisdom that go beyond the immediate desires of modern society.[42]

Būṭī allocates more than two-thirds of his work to demonstrating that *maṣlaḥa* is bounded by various methodological considerations, all of which derive from the traditional theory of *uṣūl al-fiqh*. He invokes in detail the Ghazālian–Shāṭibian discourse on the five universals, in which all considerations of *maṣlaḥa* are grounded. However, he views *maṣlaḥa* to be of two types, one grounded in the Quran, the Sunna and consensus and the other anchored in *qiyās* and other *ijtihād*ic methods of inference. The former is permanent and unalterable, whereas the latter is adaptable, within the boundaries of the law, to the changing conditions of society.[43] The scale of such changes, however, is qualitatively set within a premodern context, where the law allows for graded transitions rather than exponential leaps. Such leaps, as in notions of good contradicting the dictates of the Quran and the Sunna, cannot be accommodated as law, for the law cannot and must not change at the pleasure of changing human predilections and constantly shifting notions of pleasure and good (*pace* J. S. Mill). "Had the changing [condition of] times enjoyed any authority over legal rulings and had they possessed the ability to alter them, the

[41] Quṭb, *Milestones*, 7, 141–60, and *passim*. [42] Būṭī, *Ḍawābiṭ*, 117.
[43] *Ibid.*, 276–77.

landmarks of Sharīʿa would have been erased long ago."[44] Būṭī concludes by affirming the moral responsibility set on the shoulders of those whose business it is to exercise *ijtihād*. He who sets himself up as a *mujtahid* must understand the correct forms of *maṣlaḥa* – those which are Sharīʿa-based – and must "distinguish them from notions of good that the masters of modern civilization and material culture have propounded ... Many of the maladies with which we have been afflicted seep into our lives under the labels of such values and notions of good."[45]

5. Hasbi and Hazairin: Indonesian jurisprudence and legal essence

The central quandary of Hasbi Ash-Shiddieqy's (d. 1975) thought – as indeed that of the great majority of Indonesian thinkers during the second half of the twentieth century – is how to reconceptualize the relationship between the modern conditions in (what has emerged as) Indonesia, on the one hand, and the legal and ritual imperatives seen to have been emitted by the Quran and the Sunna, on the other. The success of Islam as a vital normative force would thus depend on the success of this project of readjustment, a project which involved "opening the gate of interpretation" fully, as called for by earlier influential thinkers, most notably Ahmad Hassan (d. 1958).[46]

Essential in Hasbi's thought was the widespread distinction between *ʿibādāt* and *muʿāmalāt*, a distinction whose function for him was the separation between that which is commanded by the higher Law and that which is left to the realm of human affairs. Like Riḍā, he asserts that whatever was enacted throughout Islamic history under *muʿāmalāt* is an accretion, the work of humans whose lives and circumstances differed from those of modern Indonesian Muslims. These are in particular Arab accretions, or "Arab *fiqh*"[47] which has been handed down as generic *fiqh*, claiming applicability to Muslims worldwide. The distance between Arab *fiqh* and the Indonesian reality is therefore binary: in addition to the historical difference that underlies the contradictions between pre-modern Arab culture and Western-based modernity, there lies the crucial difference of national identity, where the distinct cultural, social, customary and other values of Indonesian societies must come to the fore and not

[44] *Ibid.*, 412.
[45] *Ibid.*, 413. See also Opwis, "*Maṣlaḥa*," 213 ff., esp. 220; Christmann, "Islamic Scholar," 68–70.
[46] Noer, *Modernist Muslim Movement*, 85–88; Hassan, "Question and Answer," 360–64.
[47] Feener, "Indonesian Movements," 101.

be subordinated to a dominating foreign culture. Accepting this domination was a constitutive feature of Indonesian *taqlīd*, from the very beginning, when Indonesia turned Muslim.

A correct understanding of history then becomes indispensable not only to distinguishing the predecessors' and Arabs' accretions from that which is eternally decreed, but also places in a correct perspective the modern Indonesian conditions versus the divine imperative. This stance, fundamental to the form and content of Hasbi's theory, owes much to Middle Eastern reformist thought whose media – in the case of Hasbi and a number of Indonesian others – were Muḥammad Muṣṭafā al-Marāghī (d. 1945) and particularly Maḥmūd Shaltūt (d. 1963).[48] Influenced in turn by the Indian Shāh Walī Allāh (d. 1762), Shaltūt, like many others, emphasized the distinction between binding and non-binding Prophetic Sunna, a distinction that lay at the core of Hasbi's thought. On the other hand, from Marāghī (who was a disciple of ʿAbduh), Hasbi seems to have borrowed the idea of renewed and historically unconstrained *ijtihād* which requires modern Muslims to transcend the boundaries of the *madhhab*ic legal schools. A "correct" understanding of the Quran and the Sunna thus not only leads to shedding the shackles of the past, but also constitutes a proper guide to appropriating – in the manner of *talfīq*[49] – any legal element from any historical school of law.

Hasbi seems to have believed that in the Quran and the Sunna there lies a kernel of objective truth that can be culled by the Muslim reader/interpreter, irrespective of the latter's ethnic or national background, and regardless of any geopolitical or cultural difference. The task of the reformer is thus defined, first, by the recovery of this objective kernel, and second, by reconciling this divine truth with the particular conditions and practices of the reformer's society. This formula perhaps best sums up Hasbi's blueprint for the creation of an Indonesian *madhhab*, one that answers the exigencies of the country better than the traditional schools have ever done, including the all-influential Shāfiʿism. The latter, like its counterparts, was as much responsible for *taqlīd* and its resultant distortions of what should have emerged as a unique and efficiently modern Indonesian *fiqh*.

Hasbi, it must be said, did not delve in any great detail into the hermeneutical mechanics of unearthing the divine will. His ideas come close to the Double Movement Theory that F. Rahman was to espouse in some detail three or four decades later.[50] All current problems – for which

[48] On Shaltūt, generally, see Zebiri, *Maḥmūd Shaltūt and Islamic Modernism*; on Marāghī, see *Oxford Encyclopedia of the Modern Islamic World*, III, 44–45.
[49] On *talfīq*, see previous chapter, section 1. [50] See section 8, below.

solutions need to be found – are transferred back to the Quranic/Prophetic message with a view to teasing out the latter's full implications with regard to these problems; subsequently, the deduced Quranic/Prophetic norms are transposed onto the respective problems of the day. However, Hasbi does not appear to go beyond these generalities, suspending further commentary on the precise hermeneutical structure and interpretive system by which such implications are to be inferred. Be that as it may, whatever interpretive skills are required, they would be provided by those trained at the State Institutes of Islamic Studies (IAIN), who would perform a collective form of *ijtihād*. The collectivism comfortably places the new Indonesian *fiqh* in a modern consultative body politic, a modernized version of the classical and venerable institution of *shūrā*.[51]

Hasbi's thought shares much in common with that of another influential Indonesian legal thinker. Unlike the *ʿālim*-oriented Hasbi, Hazairin (d. 1975) grew up under the secularist intellectual influence of Ter Haar, a professor of *adatrecht* at the University of Indonesia and a senior advisor to the Dutch East Indies (DEI).[52] Like his teacher, Hazairin was an expert on *adat*, the chosen law of the DEI after 1927. And in contrast to the Achehnese Hasbi, who initially even refused to learn the Latin alphabet, Hazairin was quick to learn Dutch and graduate, in 1936, with a doctorate in *adatrecht*. Yet, despite the absence of any marked religious education during his youth, and despite his expertise in *adatrecht* and his Westernized leanings, Hazairin increasingly turned to Islam and religious law which, by all indications, he understood to be a fundamental source for political and legal legitimacy in Indonesia. Instead of making *adatrecht* the standard by which *fiqh* is to be judged – the essence of the Dutch Reception Theory – Hazairin forcefully turned the Theory on its head, making *adat* wholly subsidiary to Islamic law in its new Indonesian garb. (Indonesian lawyers after independence generally turned against *adat*, mostly in favor of a unifying national law of Western inspiration and, to a lesser extent, to the Sharīʿa, since *adat* was viewed by both advocates as having failed to contribute to national unity and was therefore regarded as fractious and divisive in nature.)[53]

In his bid to contribute to the formation of an Indonesian jurisprudence – a matter almost invariably cast in terms of accommodating Islamic law to the distinct conditions and demands of that country – he had first to dismantle the cumulative and still authoritative tradition of the ulama who, by erecting the classical *fiqh* edifice (which he also saw as "Arab" in essence), had managed to deprive their successors (which

[51] Feener, *Muslim Legal Thought*, 59–69. [52] See chapter 14, section 3, above.
[53] Lev, "Colonial Law," 69.

we here take to be modern Indonesians) of the juristic freedom to confront – through *ijtihād* – the revealed texts directly. In his view, it is this edifice which constituted not only the barrier to legal renewal but also the cause of Sharīʿa's inability to deal successfully with the exigencies of the modern age. Yet, Hazairin's – and Hasbi's – success in problematizing the Arab jural hegemony was not matched by awareness of the problems of modernity and its conditions. The desired leap into legal modernity was conceived as liberation from the clutches of the past, but not, by the very act of liberation, as substituting one set of shackles for another.

Hazairin generally shies away from offering a complete blueprint aiming to reconstitute a methodology of law, a neo-*uṣūl al-fiqh* that forms the foundations of a new Indonesian jurisprudence and law;[54] instead, he leaves this task to a future generation of legal specialists who would design and produce a specific type of Indonesian *ijtihād*. Like Hasbi and many other Indonesian intellectuals, he espoused a collective form of *ijtihād* that would reflect the Archipelago's immense diversity and that would be organized under the aegis of semi-official and state councils. A Fatwa Council whose membership consisted of these emerging legal specialists could advise both the populace and the government on religious issues of the day and participate as an integral organ of the modern state apparatus. But in all cases, the new Indonesian *fiqh* was to be an entirely new context-specific creation (an exclusively Indonesian product, as it were) that would not admit of the *talfīq* that Hasbi accepted and in fact advocated. And herein lies an important difference between the two thinkers, a difference that has had profound implications for renewal movements in the Muslim world ever since: entailed in the acceptance of *talfīq* is the adoption of expediency as a ready tool of change. The principles of the law are thereby subordinated to the dictates of change, in whatever direction change might lead. Here, local agency is depleted of all will, of any determination as to destination, and reduced to finding the means that can carry it in that direction. While the rejection of *talfīq*, on the other hand, is no guarantee of the avoidance of such subordination, it is a first step in transcending expediency as a means of constructing a substantive legal doctrine. Indeed, rejection of *talfīq* in the context of a hermeneutic – like the one Hazairin appears to wish for – strongly implies a rejection of expediency as an independent way of doing law. Major and minor principles, derived from religious texts, nativist social morality and nativist custom, as well as modern exigencies, tend to affirm agency and various

54 Cammack, "Islam and Nationalism in Indonesia," 177 ff.

sorts of independence. This rejection thus has, at a minimum, the potential for reflecting indigenous will in the processes of making law.

Yet, despite his great reluctance to engage in a systematic exposition of a new hermeneutic, Hazairin did attempt to forge a certain beginning for a new methodology, a project that may be considered one of his most impressive accomplishments. In his search to articulate an Indonesian jurisprudence, he argued the need to create a fundamental distinction between Sharīʿa strictly-so-defined and Arab intrusions upon it, since Arab customs and social structures had intensely commingled with it such that for many centuries it was thought that the two were one and the same. This myopia, he thought, represented a major form of the deleterious "blind *taqlīd*" of the "ways of the traditional *ʿulama'* and the Arab social practices of a thousand years ago."[55] Thus, the isolation of these practices from the "true" Sharīʿa leads, for instance, to a new understanding of the all-important law of inheritance, which Hazairin attempts to offer.

In reinterpreting the key Quranic verses pertaining to the devolution of property upon death, he formulated the so-called Bilateral Theory, which ran against the traditional Sunnite law of inheritance.[56] He rejected this Sunnite *fiqh*'s categorization of heirs, and replaced it with another, namely: (a) heirs entitled to a fixed Quranic share; (b) heirs who stand in a particular "relationship" with the propositus; and (c) representatives of predeceased heirs (the latter not recognized as heirs by Sunnite *fiqh*). The innovativeness of his theory lay in extracting two principles that are, severally and aggregately, new to Sunnite *fiqh* (but not entirely to that of the Twelver-Shīʿite variety): that the Quran fully embodies and sanctions the principle of representation, and that there is a system of priority among classes of relatives. The synthesis between these two principles, on the one hand, and the configuration of Quranic sharers, on the other, yielded a new inheritance theory that bestowed equal rights of property devolution upon male and female heirs. This Hazairin achieves through a fresh linguistic and interpretive examination of the relevant Quranic verses,[57] where words are not only given new meanings and connotations but also set in new relationships *vis-à-vis* each other.

Hazairin's reinterpretation is grounded in neither sociological nor anthropological hermeneutic, although the ultimate driving motive was the particular constitution of the Indonesian social order. But because its linguistic *modus vivendi* dominates, the question that remains is how the

[55] Cited in Feener, "Indonesian Movements," 111. [56] See chapter 8, section 6, above.

[57] For a reasonably detailed account of Hazairin's theory, see the useful article of Cammack, "Islamic Inheritance," esp. 298–304.

Indonesian social order dictates a specific methodology of interpretation that organically and structurally reflects the unique and context-specific hermeneutical connections between the text of revelation and Indonesian jural realities. In other words, since the new doctrine of inheritance is the only specific application Hazairin provided for his general theory of "Indonesian *fiqh*," and since the doctrine appears to be based on a generic – rather than a specifically "Indonesia-grounded" – hermeneutic, the modalities of recreating this *fiqh* continue to await articulation.

Be that as it may, despite the different, if not opposing, backgrounds from which Hasbi and Hazairin hailed, and despite the differences in their intellectual and juristic make-up and approaches, they both operated wholly within a nationalist, post-colonial context, sharing much in common. Their projects, as seen in their opposition to the Arab juristic and hegemonic influence, amounted in the final analysis to advocacy of a national Indonesian jurisprudence that exceeded even the homogenizing tendencies of Dutch rule. For instance, while the Dutch still recognized as valid numerous forms of regional *adat*, Hasbi, and particularly the *adatrecht*-specialist Hazairin, called for the unification of this plurality into one body of law (guided by a renewed Sharīʿa) aimed at bringing about the unification of what they saw as the great Indonesian *umma*. And despite their anti-colonialist program, they, like Muslim reformers elsewhere, succumbed to the modernizing/colonialist imperative in advocating a law that not only was homogenizing but also could never escape the grip of the modern nation-state.

6. Abdulkarim Soroush: caught in modernity

An arch-modernist who remains, thus far, captivated by the imperatives of the modern project without questioning its foundational premises, Soroush (b. 1945)[58] largely dismisses *uṣūl al-fiqh* and *fiqh* as inherently incapable of accommodating themselves to the contingencies of the modern world. It must be stated at the outset that Soroush offers no alternative theory substituting for that which his "deconstructionist" project sets out to demolish. His reformation purports to go to the theoretical and methodological foundations of the law, rooting out the "old" system and replacing it with a "truly" modern philosophy and law, the shape and form of which are apparently to be determined at a future date.

Viewing the Sharīʿa as intrinsically archaic, he argues that its function, language and logic are irrelevant to modernity. It is "my conviction," he

58 For brief biographical accounts, see Cooper, "Limits of the Sacred," 39–44; Jahanbakhsh, "Islam, Democracy," 242–46; Soroush, *al-Qabḍ wal-Basṭ*, 15–17.

states, that "our *fiqh* is precisely equivalent to the natural sources of the past that have been emptied of their reserves."[59] Why this is so, and how modernity has contributed to this state of affairs, is a question that, to my knowledge, he never tries to answer. What he does try instead is to articulate the reasons why the Sharīʿa is obsolete, restating the familiar thesis that the Sharīʿa is divisible into essential and accidental attributes, a typology that is distinctly Aristotelian. The essence of the Sharīʿa, however, is a particular legal form appropriate for all times and places.[60] In Soroush's project, this form must be rationally conceived in accordance with European social and natural sciences. The rest, the accidentals, linguistic and cultural, are the Arabic accretions to the Sharīʿa, including the "propositions," "theories" and "concepts" used in the construction of the system; the historical events and narratives that made their way into the interpretation of the revealed texts; the *fatwā*s and legal writings of the jurists; and, finally, the "forgeries, attitudes and alterations that the disbelievers have formulated regarding religion."[61] The distinction, in other words, is the familiar one between religion and religious knowledge, the former being divine, perfect and immutable, the latter profane, mutable, time-bound and relative. And it is this distinction that constitutes and represents his Theory of Contraction and Expansion.[62] Thus, once the Sharīʿa is reduced to an essence, one that is devoid of any sociological, anthropological or historical content (the very antithesis of his own insistence on the centrality of the social sciences in any such analysis), it is no challenge to remap it in accordance with Soroush's intellectual ideal: a positive law that is modern and that finds its inspiration in scientific rationalism.

Trained in chemistry, pharmacology, Western philosophy and the history of science, as well as in the Islamic legal sciences (which by all indications he seems to approach as a severely constrained philologist), he vehemently argues for the need to construct law in an entirely new way, one that derives its inspiration from Western social science and "rational" philosophy. Yet, his proposal for reform hardly exceeds two main theses, namely, the irrelevance of Islamic law to modernity and the need to ground the new law in secular rational philosophy. This is not to say that Soroush negates the importance of religion or the Sharīʿa, for he no

[59] As translated by Dahlén, *Islamic Law, Epistemology and Modernity*, 236. See also the implications of his statements in Soroush, *Reason, Freedom, and Democracy*, 78–79.

[60] Mir-Hosseini, "Construction of Gender," 23–24.

[61] As translated by Dahlén, *Islamic Law, Epistemology and Modernity*, 214.

[62] The subject of his *Qabḍ wa-Basṭ-i Tiʾūrīk-i Sharīʿat*, translated into Arabic as *al-Qabḍ wal-Basṭ fī al-Sharīʿa*, esp. at 29–48, 75–78, 97–99, 119–25, 157 ff.; Jahanbakhsh, "Islam, Democracy," 247–51; Cooper, "Limits of the Sacred," 43.

doubt regards them as the essential right of any society that chooses to adopt them. After all, he is a champion of democracy. But he conceives of religious truth to be an integral part of general knowledge, thus subsuming religion under rational philosophical enquiry. The *fiqh*, on the other hand, he sees as an externality, dichotomous with but not identical to faith. Whereas faith is an inner state, *fiqh* is a matter of practice, the domain of works. A state based on *fiqh* is an authoritarian state, emphasizing the ritualistic and technical sides of the law.[63] In order to escape this fate, law must therefore be based on faith. Soroush, however, does not question the fundamental assumption he makes that *fiqh* stands separate from faith, whereas the entire range of the Islamic tradition, past and present, Sunnite and Shīʿite, never separated the two.[64] Faith (*īmān*) was the constant basis of *fiqh*, which constituted the moral praxis that engendered faith in fundamentally physical, psychological and spiritual ways.

It turns out that Soroush regards *fiqh* as no more and no less than a legal code, applied through human agency in the same manner as man-made laws are enforced in modern states.[65] By reducing the notion of *fiqh* to positive law, Soroush in effect empties *fiqh* of its moral content (not to mention its eschatological force), a fact that explains why he views *fiqh* as an external tool that is distinct from faith and why "morality strides ahead of the law."[66] But his replication of the disjunction between law and morality comes as no surprise, as it is inescapable in a system where religion is largely relegated to the private sphere, and where the limits of what counts as law are drawn by a hegemonic state whose determinative preoccupation is the public sphere.[67] The equation of *fiqh* with positive law also betrays Soroush's understanding of the latter, an understanding that is heavily colored both by modern processes of entexting "Islamic law"[68] and, equally, by the conceptual transformation of this law at the hands of the state.[69] Missing from this conception, therefore, is not only the moral imperative but also the communal function of the Sharīʿa as a system antithetical to the all-or-nothing solutions[70] that modern law, on the whole, insists on and that Soroush seems to accept so readily.

But this is by no means the only Orientalized understanding detectable in Soroush's thought. It is a recurrent theme in his writings that Islamic

[63] Jahanbakhsh, "Islam, Democracy," 258. [64] Hallaq, "Fashioning the Moral Subject."

[65] Dahlén, *Islamic Law, Epistemology and Modernity*, 227–28, and 234, where the author discusses Soroush's argument that religion (and by implication Islamic law) must concern itself with the hereafter, leaving all matters relative to this world to the state's management.

[66] Soroush, "Ideal Islamic State," 2; Soroush, *Reason, Freedom, and Democracy*, 146–47.

[67] Zubaida, *Law and Power*, 216. [68] Hallaq, "What is Sharīʿa?"

[69] *Ibid.*, and chapters 13 and 16, above. [70] See chapter 4, section 2, above.

law is based on *taqlīd*, a concept and practice that lacks the feature of *taḥqīq* (critical, rational investigation),[71] which, he claims, is a characteristic feature of Ṣūfī and (Western) philosophical investigations. As such, Islamic law is lacking in rationality and rationalist foundations.[72] Instead of viewing *taqlīd* as law's quintessential requirement of juristic and judicial continuity, predictability and conformity to normative jural values (without which law, any law, ceases to count as law),[73] he takes it to be, as a non-jurist might, the opposite side of intellectual creativity, i.e., a thought-based concept that is bereft of jural practice and devoid of a commanding ontology.[74] He goes so far as to argue that *fiqh* must be anchored within the paradigmatic assumptions and investigative frameworks of the modern sciences, including anthropology, sociology and even the natural sciences.[75] Justice, therefore, is not, and cannot be, grounded in religion or religious epistemology;[76] on the contrary, religion must be grounded in a notion of justice that is defined by, and anchored in, humanism. Thus justice, as a social tool, must be grounded in the same terrain as *fiqh*, with which it must integrally mesh. In short, law, even if it were to be religious, is, like religion itself, socially determined and socially constructed, which is to say that it mutates and undergoes changes indefinitely. *Ijtihād* must therefore be the natural product of the rationality prevailing in any particular era, and our era is modernity.[77] Soroush appears content to provide this general solution, shying away from any precise proposal for a legal methodology by which Muslims – at least in a particular country – should construct their law. This may be not a failing but rather a conscious position that affirms the constant need for reinterpretation, obviously of the texts, but also of the very principles of interpretation.

7. Muḥammad Saʿīd ʿAshmāwī: contextual implications

Like Būṭī, Ashmāwī's (d. 1932) distinguished career spanned the academic and legal professions, but his involvement in the legal profession was less within a Sharīʿa context than within Westernized legal practice. In addition to service on the Egyptian Court of Appeal, he worked as a

[71] For a detailed analysis of *taqlīd* and its functions, see Hallaq, *Authority*, 86–120.
[72] Dahlén, *Islamic Law, Epistemology and Modernity*, 223–24. This curious characterization of *taqlīd* might strike one as a ramified distortion of Weber's contorted view of what he called *Kadijustiz*. See also chapter 14, section 1, above.
[73] See Hallaq, *Authority*, ix, 57–120. [74] Cooper, "Limits of the Sacred," 48.
[75] Dahlén, *Islamic Law, Epistemology and Modernity*, 228.
[76] Jahanbakhsh, "Islam, Democracy," 268.
[77] Dahlén, *Islamic Law, Epistemology and Modernity*, 294, 352.

member of the State Commission for Legislation, as a Chief Justice of the Criminal Court, and as a professor of Islamic and comparative law at Cairo University.

Like Soroush and Hazairin, ʿAshmāwī distinguishes between law as a pure idea, a sort of essence, and law as a social construction or elaboration of that idea. The former represents the meaning of law as found in the mind of God, whereas the latter is embodied in the historical constructions and accretions of legal systems that are society's attempt to give practical and concrete meaning to God's pure idea. Accordingly, the former is infallible whereas the latter, being a human product, is susceptible to error; the former is endowed with objectivity and thus unaffected by change or permutation, whereas the latter involves the human weakness of subjectivity and thus cannot be dissociated from a particular social reality and a particular history; the former's validity, in sum, is eternal, whereas the latter is valid only for a particular place and time.[78]

The challenge of deciphering the differences between the pure law and the social, cumulative legal construction lies in identifying the founding principles of the religious law, what ʿAshmāwī calls the "general principles of Sharīʿa."[79] Remarkably, his first principle echoes Quṭbian discourse, and seems to appreciate anthropological insights into the workings of Islamic law in pre-modern societies: the paramount principle is that the Sharīʿa is a state of mind. It presumes the existence of a generous and loving spirit that pervades society and its members. Without this spirit, the law cannot command willing obedience, which expresses a genuine desire to conform to both the letter and the lofty aspirations of the divine command. Society must thus be permeated by this spirit for Sharīʿa to find a meaningful and genuine application.[80]

Second, there exists a dialectical relationship between the divine texts and the human reality for and in which the text was revealed. A proper understanding of this relationship is crucial, for the Book is nothing less than a "living creature" which dynamically interacted with the mundane experiences and the social fabric of the first Muslim generation. This, ʿAshmāwī argues, is where the pre-modern jurists went terribly wrong, where they interpreted the texts in isolation from the particular human reality in and for which they were revealed. A key example is the interpretation of Q. 5:3 ("This day I [God] perfected for you your religion"), which was taken to mean that the Quran contains all that which the Muslim individual needs in order to live as a good Muslim; that Islam, in other words, has become perfect. More importantly, it was universally

[78] ʿAshmāwī, *Uṣūl*, 52–53. [79] *Ibid.*, 55–56. [80] *Ibid.*, 56–60.

understood as a categorical statement applicable to all situations and times. But, ʿAshmāwī argues, a careful examination of the historical context shows that this verse was revealed in connection with a particular event, making its applicability limited. When the Prophet and his Companions entered Mecca and performed pilgrimage, the Quran meant only that with this performance all the ritual practices required for the perfection of Islam as a religion had at last come to completion.[81] The perfection was one of ritual practice, nothing more.

Third, and related to the foregoing principle, the Quran and the Sunna must be understood in the context of their intimate links with the norms, practices and values of the society in and for which they were ordained. Just as Islam came into existence on the heels of other monotheistic religions, it also emerged out of a particular society with which it had a certain relationship, and from which it derived some of its norms, e.g., the pre-Islamic penalty of cutting off a thief's hand. What ʿAshmāwī seems to be arguing here is that the Sharīʿa must be closely linked to, and ought to reflect the values and norms of, the societies it regulates, including the modern one.

Fourth, the Sharīʿa, being closely connected with the reality it regulates, has the ability to change according to changing conditions and circumstances. Drawing on Quranic evidence pertaining, *inter alia*, to the gradual prohibition imposed on the consumption of wine, ʿAshmāwī argues that revelation itself was modified along the demands reality imposed, for wine was initially permitted, then declared repugnant, and finally categorically prohibited, a process that reflected the increasing problems its consumption caused in the midst of the Prophet's social environment. He notes that some Muslim jurists of centuries ago understood this phenomenon, affirming that the rules of Sharīʿa have undergone modification and change in consonance with changes in social and other customs.

Finally, the fifth principle – carrying further the implications of the second, third and fourth – states that perfecting the Sharīʿa can be attained only by systematically bringing it to bear upon the social and human exigencies that are in a continuous state of flux. The divine act of bestowing different systems of law on different societies (attested in Q. 5:48) has no meaning other than the will to give each society a law that corresponds to its particular character and needs. And if God has taken into account the needs of each society *at the time of revelation*, then each society ought to follow this divine decree by attending to its own law in relation to its own

[81] *Ibid.*, 59, 70.

changing needs and circumstances. From all this ʿAshmāwī concludes that the Sharīʿa is compatible with progress.

In illustration of how these principles should be applied toward producing specific legal rulings, ʿAshmāwī first turns to the law of *jihād*. Recalling the general principles he has stated, he stresses that the revelation, as it has ineluctably intertwined with the concrete realities of early Muslim societies, must be understood properly. When the Quran enjoined fighting against non-believers, it was directly related to belligerence against the Prophet, and nowhere does it recommend violence against non-Muslims unless these first attack the Prophet. Nor, still, does the Quran command Muslims to launch war against non-Muslims with a view to converting them to Islam, for if God's plan had been to make all people adopt Islam, He (as attested in a number of verses)[82] would have created them all Muslims in the first place. The true Sharīʿa, then, commands fighting only when Muslims come under attack. The law calls for such drastic measures solely in self-defense. If anything, ʿAshmāwī affirms, the Sharīʿa unambiguously urges peace: "If they incline to peace, you should also incline to it" (Q. 8:61).[83]

Using a similar contextual interpretation of the revealed texts, ʿAshmāwī takes up usurious interest (*ribā*). The Quranic provisions relative to *ribā* were revealed to a society in which the normative practice was to charge debtors excessively high rates of interest, whose cumulative size would exceed the principal within a relatively short period of time. Thus, in the Arabian society that the Quran addressed, usurious transactions amounted to a flagrant exploitation of the debtor. God intended to put an end to this inhumane practice, not to commercial and profitable transactions, at which the civilization of Islam excelled. Now, since the function of interest in a modern economy is not the unjustified enrichment of lenders but rather the protection of the money's value, interest is necessary, for if lenders are not protected, there will be no lending, leading to even more hardship for the needy. Furthermore, the main bulk of lending in modern economies occurs at the corporate level, and the reason behind it is not need but rather the desire to invest and increase corporate profits. Interest in such an economy, ʿAshmāwī thinks, can hardly be characterized as exploitative. Yet, all this does not address the most important type of borrowing in Islamic legal morality, namely, borrowing by the poor, the needy and the wretched of the earth, who are amply recognized by the

[82] E.g., Quran 6:35; 2:256; 2:62; 5:96.

[83] For a more detailed account of ʿAshmāwī's theory of *jihād*, see chapter 11, section 3, above.

Quran. ʿAshmāwī replies that it is difficult nowadays to determine who has a genuine need for financial assistance and who has not. Setting a reasonable rate of interest on non-commercial loans would be as justified as, for example, setting a minimum age for marriage. But realizing the severity of poverty in Egypt, he also proposes that the state might consider establishing a system of lending according to need, granting interest-free loans for certain essential needs, such as covering funeral expenses. ʿAshmāwī's cardinal point in this context is that a sound historical-textual analysis leads to the conclusion that in the particular circumstances of early Muslim society usury was understandably prohibited because it was mercilessly exploitative, but today's borrowing is not, and therefore interest must be legally permitted.[84]

It does not seem to occur to ʿAshmāwī to view the Quranic prohibition as a principled moral-philosophical *Weltanschauung* that runs in diametrical opposition to the exploitative logic of modern capitalism as much as it was designed to oppose the Qurayshi economic aristocracy. Such an approach might well alter the conclusions of the very principles he expounded at the outset, since it can also be argued, quite convincingly, that a contextual interpretation of the revealed texts results precisely in the affirmation that the Quranic prohibition on exploitation is relevant as much, if not more, to the laissez-faire, entrenched modern capitalism as it is to the comparatively paltry transgressions of seventh-century Arabia's rich and powerful. Thus, according to the very principles ʿAshmāwī himself lays down, the prohibition on interest, or at least severe restrictions on it, may represent the true intention of divine wisdom and, furthermore, constitute a moral (even post-modern) solution to a major worldwide problem, i.e., that the poor are becoming poorer and inordinately more numerous and the rich richer and numerically far fewer. But then, to be fair to ʿAshmāwī, he wrote at a time when such post-modern criticism was still emerging.

The application of ʿAshmāwī's principles appears even less convincing when he deals with the case of intoxicants, the *sharʿī* prohibition on their consumption, and penalties involved therein. To begin with, he is not clear as to whether they must be strictly prohibited or merely avoided, that is, whether the injunction is a moral or legal prohibition. Furthermore, his definition of the Quranic term *khamr* is artificially restrictive, for he argues (citing a minority opinion) that the term means fermented grape-juice, and the Quranic prohibition applies only to this beverage, not to other alcoholic beverages. This literalism is inconsistent with ʿAshmāwī's

[84] ʿAshmāwī, *Uṣūl*, 110–16.

own principles, which call for contextual analysis: for understanding the relationship between society's norms and values, on the one hand, and the intention of revealed texts, on the other. On the whole,[85] ʿAshmāwī's methodology at times is overly restrictive and, at others, may be deemed – by a large Islamist majority – to lack moral and other boundaries. ʿAshmāwī's ideas were vehemently opposed during the 1980s, and do not seem to be faring better at present.

8. Fazlur Rahman: the primacy of divine intention

Fazlur Rahman (d. 1988)[86] opposed both the traditional literal approach to revelation and what he deemed to be a subjective determination of the law on the basis of necessity and *maṣlaḥa*.[87] The former, the product of a bygone era, is rigid and incapable of accommodating modernity, whereas the latter is highly relativistic, based as it is on concepts lacking a methodology that controls and carefully articulates the premises, the conclusions and the lines of reasoning. Rahman takes strong exception to traditional legal theory and its authors, blaming them for a fragmented view of the revealed texts. Both the legal theorists and the exegetes treated the Quran and the Sunna atomistically, approaching verses and individual *ḥadīth*s as independent units of analysis. The lack of an integrated view of the sources was thus responsible for the absence of a worldview "that is cohesive and meaningful for life as a whole."[88] For a correct understanding of the Quranic and Sunnaic message as a whole, it is of the essence to analyze these texts against a background of sixth- and seventh-century Arabian society, in its economic, political, social and tribal institutions. This approach is the only guarantee for a proper evaluation of what Rahman calls the import of revelation, what Soroush called the essence of the law, and what ʿAshmāwī dubbed as God's pure Sharīʿa. It is this import, this essence, which should be extracted for the purpose of transference to the modern context.

But how is this context to be uncovered? Rahman offers the example of wine, declared prohibited by *fiqh* on the basis of Q. 5:90-91. Earlier, however, in 16:66-69, the Quran declares wine among the blessings of God, along with milk and honey. Between these two verses, two more

[85] For a detailed analysis of these and other cases with which he deals, see Hallaq, *History*, 236–41.

[86] Rahman was a Pakistani intellectual and a prolific scholar of Islam who taught mostly in North American universities. For biographical information, see Sonn, "Fazlur Rahman," III, 408.

[87] Rahman, "Toward Reformulating," 223. [88] Rahman, "Interpreting the Qur'an," 45.

came to state an intermediate position,[89] leading to the final prohibition in 5:90-91. Muslim jurists concluded from all this that the Quran sought to wean Muslims from certain ingrained habits in a gradual fashion, and without resorting to a sudden and abrupt ban, calling this the Law of Graduation. But this Law, Rahman argues, is insufficient to explain the overall context, especially the significance of the seeming contradiction among the various verses. As he sees it, in the Meccan period, the Muslims were a minority, constituting a small, controllable community in which alcohol consumption did not raise a problem. But when the Meccans converted to Islam at a later stage, there were many amongst them who were in the habit of drinking. The evolution of this minority into a community and then into a sort of body politic in Medina coincided with the growing problem of alcohol consumption, leading to the final Quranic prohibition. Thus, the Law of Graduation must be viewed in conjunction with the events surrounding the legal value being decreed, bringing together Quranic verses and Prophetic reports that appear fragmentary in nature. It is only the totality of these considerations that can permit a proper understanding of the context and which, in turn, makes possible the extraction of a general principle embodying the rationale behind that legal value or ruling.

The failure of the traditional jurists to seek, and thus comprehend, a unifying principle out of what appears to be disjointed divine discourse has led, Rahman insists, to chaos. To illustrate this chaos, Rahman takes the sensitive matter of polygamy. In 4:2, the Quran complains of guardians' abuse and unlawful appropriation of the property of orphaned children with which they were entrusted. In 4:126, the Quran enjoins these guardians to marry their female wards when they come of age. Accordingly, in 4:2-3, the Quran says that if guardians cannot return the property they misappropriated, and if they marry their wards, they may marry up to four, provided they treat them justly; otherwise, they should marry only one. On the other hand, in 4:127, the Quran declares that it is impossible to do justice among a plurality of wives, thus involving itself in a semblance of contradiction, as was the case with wine. But it must not be forgotten, Rahman asserts, that the whole Quranic discussion on this matter occurred within the limited context of orphaned women. The traditional jurists failed to see this limitation, with the direct consequence that marriage to four wives became universally permissible, relegating the command to do justice to a mere recommendation. In doing so, the traditional jurists turned the issue of polygamy right on its head, taking a

[89] Quran 2:219 and 4:43.

specific verse to be binding, and the general principles to represent a recommendation. It is the general principle that should govern, not the specific ruling. The latter, Rahman insists, should be subsumed under the former.[90] The precedence that should be accorded to the justice verse is dictated not only by the context of the divine discourse on polygamy but also by the powerful Quranic theme on the need for justice.

More important still is that the derivation of general principles from specific rulings must be undertaken with full consideration of the *sociological forces that produced* these rulings. Since the Quran gives, or at least intimates, the reason for certain rulings, an understanding of these reasons becomes essential for drawing general principles. The multi-faceted elements making up the revealed texts, along with the context and background of revelation, must therefore "be brought together to yield a unified and comprehensive socio-moral theory squarely based upon the Quran and its *sunna* counterparts."[91]

The process of eliciting general principles represents what Rahman terms the First Movement, the first step in his methodology that he dubbed the Double Movement Theory. The trajectory of the First Movement proceeds from the particular to the general (eliciting the general principles), whereas the Second Movement proceeds from the general to the particular, that is, the general principles elicited from the revealed sources are brought to bear upon the present conditions in Muslim societies. This presupposes a thorough understanding of these conditions, equal in magnitude to that required to understand the revealed texts with their background. But since the present condition can obviously never be identical to the Prophetic past, and since it could differ from it "in certain important respects," it is required that "we apply these general principles ... to the current situation espousing that which is worthy of espousing and rejecting that which must be rejected."[92] Just what the criteria are for rejecting certain "important respects" and not others is a crucial question that Rahman does not seem to answer decisively. For if these respects are important and may nevertheless be neutralized, then there is no guarantee that essential Quranic and Sunnaic elements or even principles will not be set aside. A weak point in Rahman's theorizing therefore lies in the not altogether clear mechanics of the Second Movement, that is, the application of the systematic principles derived from the revealed texts and their contexts to a given situation in the present.

[90] Rahman, "Interpreting the Qur'an," 49. [91] Rahman, "Toward Reformulating," 221.
[92] Rahman, "Interpreting the Qur'an," 49.

Furthermore, the cases he proffers in illustration of his theory are few in number and do not represent the full gamut of legal problematics. What of those cases in which only a textual statement is to be found, with no contextual information? How do modern Muslims address fundamental problems facing their societies when no textual statement is to be found? What if the morality of the law as advocated by the texts of revelation should oppose or contravene modern morality and modern legal precepts? What guarantees exist – in a faithful implementation of the First Movement of generating principles – that the revealed texts are not read subjectively in light of modern dictates and desiderata? As is the case with ʿAshmāwī, Rahman does not make it his concern to delve into larger philosophical and moral questions plaguing the modern project, questions that need to be asked and answered before the contents of the Double Movement can be determined. In the projects of all the thinkers we have thus far discussed, except perhaps for that of Būṭī, modernity is represented as a Muslim problem, but is not problematized in and of itself.

9. Muḥammad Shaḥrūr: a theoretical paradigm shift

In a controversial work published in 1992,[93] the Syrian intellectual Shaḥrūr advances an innovative and unique hermeneutic that derives its inspiration from his training as an engineer, as well as from his readings in mathematics and physics. Whereas Soroush subordinates the Islamic subject-matter to the control of rationalism and science, Shaḥrūr employs the techniques of the natural sciences in order to make the revealed texts come to life, to speak a language unheard before.[94]

He begins with the basic argument that the Quran, being eternal, is as much a guide for later generations as it was for the first generations of Muslims.[95] The relationship that exists between the text and its readers in any given age renders these readers best qualified to understand the meaning of revelation for their own lives and concerns. In other words, since each era has a hermeneutic of its own, the exegetical tradition of the earlier centuries can no longer claim a monopoly over interpretation, and modern Muslims must find their own way to the meanings of revelation.

[93] Shaḥrūr, *al-Kitāb wal-Qurʾān*. For a critique of Shaḥrūr, see Muftāḥ, *Ḥadāthiyyūn*, 88–95, 103–06, 126–29, 249–60, and *passim*.

[94] On Shaḥrūr in the context of interpretation and authority, see Eickelman, "Islamic Religious Commentary," 124–28, 140–46.

[95] For a useful discussion of the place of the Quran in Shaḥrūr's thought, see Browers, "Islam and Political *Sinn*," 57–72.

In fact, he goes further, arguing that modern Muslims are better equipped to understand the Quran than their predecessors since they enjoy a more "sophisticated" culture. Here, he invokes the Quranic verse (9:97) that speaks of Bedouins as staunch disbelievers, his assumed reason being that they lacked "culture." Since modern Muslims enjoy a higher level of both culture and scientific knowledge than their predecessors ever possessed, they are better equipped to understand revelation than any of these predecessors were.[96]

A key distinction in Shaḥrūr's theory pertains to Muhammad's functions as a Prophet and as a Messenger. As a Prophet, Muhammad received a body of information having to do with religion and belief, whereas as a Messenger he was, in addition, the recipient of a corpus of legal instructions. The Prophetic role, then, was a religious-spiritual function, whereas the Messenger's role was a legal one. Shaḥrūr's distinction within the body of Sunna parallels another, related to the Text of Revelation: the Text can be seen as either the Quran or "the Book," depending on the function intended. Prophetic information – deemed textually ambiguous and capable of varying interpretations– is the Quran. In "the Book," on the other hand, the legal subject-matter is univocal, but nevertheless capable of being subjected to *ijtihād*. But Shaḥrūr's *ijtihād* is not the familiar one, for there is a clear difference between *ijtihād* and interpretation. Interpretation involves the ability to see two or more meanings in certain types of (ambiguous) speech, whereas *ijtihād* does not involve interpretation in the conventional sense but rather refers to a process whereby legal language is taken to yield a certain legal effect suitable to a particular place or time. The change of the place or time will thus alter the results of *ijtihād*.

The Book, the embodiment of the legal message, is characterized by two contradictory, diametrically opposing yet complementary attributes; namely, "straightness" and "curvature." Both attributes are integral to the Message, coexisting in a symbiotic relationship. Curvature, being integral to the natural order, is intrinsic to human nature and exists in the material, objective world. Things in the universe, from galaxies to electrons, do not move in a linear fashion, but in curves. The world of law constitutes an essential part of the natural world, where curvature may be represented by social customs, habits and traditions that exist in harmony with a particular society, but which change from one society to another, and within a given society diachronically. However, these forces of curvature come up against other opposing forces that work to temper the extent of curvature,

96 Shaḥrūr, *al-Kitāb wal-Qur'ān*, 44–45, 472.

namely, straightness. The legal order is the result of the dialectic between these two forces.

Whereas curvature is a natural force, straightness is God's conscious design. In Shaḥrūr's thought, then, Deism has no place. Curvature always stands in need of straightness, but not the other way round. Being the natural state of affairs, human beings need not seek curvature, for it is *ab initio* ingrained in their nature.[97] This dialectic, in which the constants and permutations are intertwined, betrays the law's adaptability at all times and places. But what is the nature of the balance in this dialectic between curvature and straightness? The answer to this question constitutes the bulk of Shaḥrūr's Theory of Limits, a theory which sets a Lower and an Upper Limit on all human actions. Whereas the Lower Limit represents the minimum required by the law in a particular case, the Upper Limit sets the maximum. Just as nothing short of the minimum is legally allowable, so nothing above the maximum may be deemed lawful. Infractions occur when these Limits are transcended, with penalties imposed accordingly.

The two Limits can and do function separately in this theory, but they may combine in one fashion or another to produce a total of six Limits.[98] First, there is the Lower Limit standing independently. The Quranic prohibition on marrying blood relatives – mother, sisters, daughters, etc. – constitutes an exclusion from the rest, i.e., those who can lawfully be married. The exclusion is the Lower Limit. Second, there is the Upper Limit standing independently, as in the case of cutting off the hand as punishment for theft (*sariqa*).[99] The penalty, representing the Upper Limit, cannot be exceeded, but can, under extenuating circumstances, be mitigated. Third, there is the case where the two Limits stand conjoined. In 4:11, for example, the Quran stipulates that the share of the male in inheritance is equivalent to that of two females. Here, there is a determination of the Upper Limit for men and the Lower Limit for women, irrespective of whether the woman is an income earner. The woman's share cannot be less than one-third of the estate; the man's can be no more than two-thirds. If the woman receives two-fifths of the estate and the man three-fifths, then neither the Upper nor the Lower Limit is violated. The proportion allotted to each is determined by the particular conditions prevailing in a given time and place. Be this as it may, the example amply demonstrates the movement of curvature within the Limits that represent straightness, as well as the will of the law as perceived to be suitable to a given society and its needs. Law must therefore not be reduced to the straightforward application of centuries-old religious texts

[97] *Ibid.*, 449–50. [98] *Ibid.*, 453–66.
[99] For an account of the law, see chapter 10, section 2, iv, above.

to modern conditions, for that would amount to eliminating from the law the essential attribute of curvature.

Fourth, there is the instance of two Limits meeting at one point, namely, when the punishment cannot be mitigated, it being the case that maximum and minimum punishments are one and the same. The Quranic insistence on inflicting on the adulterer, male or female, a hundred lashes "without pity" (24:2) is a case in point. The fifth instance is when the curvature moves between the two Limits but reaches neither. Sexual contact between men and women exemplifies this type. Beginning from a point above the Lower Limit, where the sexes are not to touch each other, the curvature moves upward in the direction of the Upper Limit where persons come close to committing adultery but do not. Finally, in the sixth type, the curvature moves between a positive Upper Limit and a negative Lower Limit. The Upper Limit can be represented by loans on which interest is charged, the Lower Limit by payment of alms-tax. Since these Limits are positive and negative – one involving receiving, the other giving out money – there lies in between a point equivalent to zero, where, for instance, an interest-free loan may be located.

The example given in the sixth type elicits from Shaḥrūr a detailed discussion of interest (*ribā*). Having analyzed a number of Quranic verses, he reaches the conclusion that the prohibition on interest in Islam is neither conclusive nor categorical.[100] The Quranic allocation of alms-tax to the needy (9:60) is taken by Shaḥrūr as an indication of their inability to pay back loans, much less the interest these loans generate. It is precisely for this impoverished segment of society that "God blighted usury and made alms-giving fruitful."[101] And it is this segment that society at large must support, without expecting anything in return. However, there is another segment in society that can repay debts, but not the interest accumulating on them. In this case, people must pay back only the sum borrowed, this being the midpoint between the positive Upper Limit and the negative Lower Limit. The remaining sections of society, the more prosperous majority, do not qualify for these exceptions, for no harm will come to them if they satisfy their loans plus whatever interest they owe. But in no case should the interest exceed the principal, since this overcharge will become usury (*ribā*), which the Quran defines and severely prohibits.[102]

As part of the application of the Theory of Limits, Shaḥrūr addresses another thorny issue: polygamy. Accusing the traditional jurists of

[100] Shaḥrūr, *al-Kitāb wal-Qur'ān*, 464–68. [101] Quran 2:276.

[102] Quran 3:130: "O you who believe: Devour not usury, doubling and quadrupling [the principal]."

misunderstanding revelation on this score (which he acknowledges to be due to their particular perspective), he argues, like ʿAshmāwī, that these jurists thought religion to have reached perfection by the time of the Prophet's death. Islam did bring about serious reforms in the status of women, but Shaḥrūr argues that these were only first steps that were intended to continue after the first/seventh century. In other words, the new religion was introducing gradual changes in order to avoid ruptures in social, economic and other structures. The jurists' construction perceived this reform not as an ongoing process but rather as a complete model, one frozen in time. It is precisely here, Shaḥrūr maintains, that the Theory of Limits acquires significance, for it transforms polygamy into a noble practice.

The Limits set for polygamy are defined by Quran 4:2-3, earlier discussed in connection with Rahman's methodology, with which Shaḥrūr has much in common and which he sharpens to greater effect.[103] Clearly, the Lower Limit is monogamy, whereas the Upper Limit is marriage to four wives. The problem with the traditional jurists, Shaḥrūr argues, is that they took the permission to marry "women" to refer to the whole class of women, when in fact the text of the verse in no way allows for this generalization. Marriage to more than one wife is clearly and inextricably linked to widowed women with children, not any women. That God did allow a second, a third and a fourth wife, and that He did not mention the first, suggests that the first belonged to a different category, excluded from this permission. Thus, the first wife may be any woman, but not so the second, third and fourth wives, who must have been widowed, and must be coming to the marriage with young children. On the other hand, the husband's entry into a polygamous marriage is justified only by the obligation of care he is expected to provide. Otherwise, Shaḥrūr insists, there is no point to the Quranic approval of polygamy. The Book enjoins men not to marry more than one wife if they cannot treat with complete equality and impartiality the young orphans who come to the marriage with their widowed mothers. The crux of the Book's discourse on polygamy is not about the men and women entering into this marital relationship, but rather about the orphans who are the focus of much Prophetic and Quranic discourse.[104]

Although the archetype of Shaḥrūr's theory is the Book, the Sunna is equally important. Like the Book, but unlike the traditional methodology of *uṣūl al-fiqh*, it is not intended to provide solutions for specific and

103 This issue draws further commentary from Shaḥrūr in his later work *Naḥw Uṣūl Jadīda*, 301–11.

104 Shaḥrūr, *al-Kitāb wal-Qurʾān*, 598–600.

concrete cases, but rather to furnish the methodological path (*minhāj*) for constructing a system of law, a path defined through the Theory of Limits. And once this theory is elaborated, there would be no need for other legal sources. Thus *qiyās* has no place in this theory, for it not only deals with particular cases (an approach unsuitable within the Theory of Limits) but is, in Shaḥrūr's opinion, downright oppressive. Likewise, the Theory of Limits renders superfluous the notion of consensus because this Theory rests on an epistemology that does not, by definition, require certainty; indeed, as long as the Lower and Upper Limits are respected, law is ever changing.

10. Būṭī (again) versus Marzūqī: the demonstrability of crisis

While certain trends in fashioning new legal thought can be detected, especially around the themes of *maṣlaḥa*, *maqāṣid* and necessity, the foregoing discussions show a wider multiplicity of orientations that can scarcely agree on a unified set of principles, and much less on a coherent theory that fills the vacuum resulting from the collapse of pre-modern *uṣūl al-fiqh*. The disparity between and among the various approaches finds an eloquent manifestation in a dialogue between Būṭī and Muḥammad Ḥabīb al-Marzūqī (b. 1947), a Tunisian, French-trained philosopher who goes by the nickname Abū Yaʿrub. The most salient characteristic of this dialogue is the utter absence of common grounds of recognition, where the very fact of crisis in *uṣūl al-fiqh* is contested most vehemently. The dialogue appeared in print in 2006, bearing the title *Ishkāliyyat Tajdīd Uṣūl al-Fiqh* (*Problematic of the Renewal of Legal Theory*). The publisher, the Lebanese-Syrian Dār al-Fikr, declares the volume part of a wider effort to promote understanding of "important current issues" through engaging major writers in dialogues with each other. Marzūqī initiates the discussion, Būṭī replies, and then they respond to each other in a second round. The disparity of their respective positions illustrates not only the existence of this crisis but also its ramified meaning. The two thinkers stand at opposite ends of the spectrum of current Islamic and Islamist legal thought, this diametrical opposition being emblematic of the absence of a trajectory and of the persistent presence of erratic discourses that have yet to find their moorings. If there was an epistemic breakdown in the systems of Sharīʿa sometime during the nineteenth century, and there surely was, then this dialogue demonstrates the persistent paralysis created by that breakdown.

As modern Europe took shape, there was general agreement about the European past, about the abuses of the church, of feudalism, landed gentry, aristocracy and much else that was to be relegated to the bygone "dark ages" and to the pre-Enlightenment. But that situation has not obtained in the Muslim world, for reasons that are not (important as they are) of interest to us here.[105] What is rather of immediate significance in this context is the crucial fact that the fundamental disagreement among Muslim intellectuals on this matter effected differing worldviews, and consequently disparate attitudes toward history's jural legacies and the latter's role in the formation of a legal theory that can resolve the problems that the epistemic break occasioned in the wake of modernization. Like Soroush, 'Ashmāwī and many others, Marzūqī levels vehement attacks against the ulama, the legal schools and their eponymic imams. In his view, the schools and their imams, together with Muslim rulers, usurped the legislative powers that should have belonged to the Umma, in his discourse a term that appears ambiguous (if not anachronistic), wavering between the traditional conceptions of the religious community and the modern nation. These schools have succeeded in nothing more than "legislating popular legend," thus unlawfully inserting themselves between God and his Umma.[106] Būṭī, like many others, fails to see any justification for these attacks, regarding the schools' heritage as the foundation upon which any attempt at "renewing" *uṣūl al-fiqh* must rest. Later we will return to this concept of "renewal" and the meaning he assigns to it.

Marzūqī writes in a mostly post-modern, abstract style, which he brings to bear on a long legal history that he approaches from a distinctly philosophical perspective. He vehemently attacks the theories of *qiyās*, *maṣlaḥa* and *maqāṣid*, charging their proponents with deviation from, and circumvention of, both the true meaning of revealed texts and the consensus of the Umma, a deviation through which the authority of legislation has illegitimately been usurped. Deviation and circumvention, immoral at best, are also represented by methods of linguistic analysis (*taḥlīl lisānī*) that do no more than justify prevalent historical conventions, thereby subordinating the revealed texts to the dictates of these conventions.[107] Liability does not stop here, however. The theory of *maqāṣid* is said to be grounded in a teleological philosophy that denies knowledge of this world, knowledge that is in turn subordinated to transcendental explanations that incapacitate knowledge in the first place.[108] The end result of this usurpation has been the total loss of the Umma's reason (*fiqdān al-rushd*),

[105] Although this subject of enquiry – still awaiting the attention of both Islamists and Muslim historians – has much to commend it.
[106] Marzūqī and Būṭī, *Ishkāliyyat*, 39, 45–47.
[107] *Ibid.*, 50, 88, 93. [108] *Ibid.*, 95–100.

a loss that has rendered its behavior more akin to that of herds (*quṭʿān*) than humans.[109] What is now needed, Marzūqī argues, is an effort by which the mediating authority of the jurists (*al-sulṭa al-wasīṭa*) can be eliminated.[110]

The effort to which Marzūqī refers had already been made, he claims, by Ibn Taymiyya and Ibn Khaldūn, who "accomplished a revolution" in both epistemology and ontology. Ibn Taymiyya's "revolution" was conducted against the philosophy and speculative theology on which law was founded.[111] Ibn Khaldūn's "revolution," on the other hand, was both "scientific" and historical, leading to innovation in philosophical and practical knowledge (*falsafa tārīkhiyya wa-ʿamaliyya*). These revolutions ultimately led to a reconsideration of the methods and tools deployed by the four Sunnite legal schools, in an attempt to dispense with their authority and replace them with direct access to the "source of legislation" (*nabʿ al-tashrīʿ*).[112]

The essence of this legislation is the duty, incumbent upon every Muslim individual (*farḍ ʿayn*), to command good and forbid evil. Marzūqī's insistence on this individual duty is intended to eliminate the mediatory role of the ulama who "usurped the Umma's will."[113] The total sum of this individual engagement constitutes a collective, communal morality and ethics (*akhlāq al-jamāʿa*) that provides legitimacy for the law and the fountain from which the spirit of legality flows.[114] Legislation, however, may be either direct or mediated through representative bodies that operate by established rules. First and foremost among these institutions is the caliphate, the head of legislative authority, which is empowered to lay down laws even in the absence of guidance from the revealed texts.[115] Nowhere, however, does Marzūqī define the boundaries between individual duty and the institutional/caliphal powers in making or "finding" the law. Which of the legal and moral laws should the individuals within the Umma generate? And which are those that must remain as the preserve of the caliph and "other" legislative institutions? What are those "other" institutions? What is their mandate? How should they interact with the responsible individual, the object of the *farḍ ʿayn*? How are they to be regulated and modulated versus the agency of the caliphate? What methods of interpretation should any and all of those agencies, empowered to engage in legislation, exercise in their encounter with the modern

109 *Ibid.*, 90. 110 *Ibid.*, 64–65.

111 Marzūqī refers to the *Muqaddima* of Ibn Khaldūn and the refutative works of Ibn Taymiyya. For the former, see Rosenthal's translation of the *Muqaddima*, and for the latter, Hallaq's *Ibn Taymiyya Against the Greek Logicians*.

112 Marzūqī and Būṭī, *Ishkāliyyat*, 53–54.

113 *Ibid.*, 190. 114 *Ibid.*, 118. 115 *Ibid.*, 64.

condition and the revealed sources? And when no revealed source can afford guidance on a given issue, what assumptions and methods of legal reasoning should be adopted? On all of this, Marzūqī is nearly silent, and he admits that he does not have comprehensive answers to the fundamental questions raised by his own proposal. Yet, he asks: How should an Umma lay down laws as it sees fit, and how can it

> change them according to its continually developing *ijtihād*? … For this is the true meaning of sacred positive law, because it is laid down by the Umma which is alone the legislator that has the right to the claim of infallibility after revelation ceased to be forthcoming and after mediation [presumably between the revealed texts and the masses] has been suspended.[116]

The Umma, being infallible, may then legislate, on the basis of revealed texts, but also in their absence or silence. In Marzūqī's conception, the Umma, whose membership consists of moral individuals, embodies the will and power to legislate. Yet, Marzūqī does not care to expound, even in outline, on the means by which the law should be formulated by the Umma and its representatives (apparently the caliph), when the texts are present and when they are silent. Rather, he appears intensely concerned with the moral and aesthetic constitution of the future Umma, although his language and exposition – typical of the great majority of modern Muslim writers on legal theory – never transcend generalities that are at best ambiguous and vague. The "legislator," the discoverer of the law, must enjoy qualities that are necessarily divested of the spiritual and temporal tyranny through which both the legists and the rulers had usurped the jural and other rights of the Umma. These constructive qualities must be enjoyed by both the *mujtahid* and the *mujāhid*. The *mujtahid*, the "Advocate of Truth," is the theoretician who contributes to the formation of the structures of the law as well as to the formulation of the legal rules in all their details. The *mujāhid*, on the other hand, is the "Advocate of Patience," by which Marzūqī means the consummate art of worldly practice in concert with the knowledge arrived at through *ijtihād*. The realization of these two qualities in the Umma, the sum total of its members, is tantamount to the accomplishment of the Taymiyyan and Khaldūnian "revolutions," which were respectively responsible for generating these qualities.

Marzūqī certainly cannot be accused of elitism. The qualities of the *mujtahid/mujāhid* must be shared by every member of the Umma, and because the foundation of the law is the desideratum of "commanding good and forbidding evil," the implementation of this desideratum

[116] *Ibid.*, 125.

becomes a *farḍ ʿayn* to be conducted in conformity with these two summative attributes. As may be expected, these fine attributes are to be cultivated through a system of education that is specially designed to accomplish such ends. Once the *mujtahid/mujāhid* is produced, and once he or she takes up the task along with the other members of the Umma, civil society will, by necessity, emerge. And since it is produced by the system, this society will in turn become indispensable for the reproduction of the system. We are not told, however, how the desirable individual, who is produced by the culture of civil society, is to partake in the production of that society which is in turn assumed to produce that individual. Needless to say, the process envisioned is circular in nature.

This society is produced by, and is in turn productive of, those values which "create the human being who conserves the [true] meanings of humanity."[117] We are made to think – again, not without apprehensions of circularity – that underlying the attributes of the *mujtahid/mujāhid* there lies a set of values that Marzūqī deems foundational, defining the system he prescribes much as the five legal norms of traditional *uṣūl al-fiqh* had defined and reflected the *fiqh* system. These values, consisting of five types, are: (a) taste – pertaining to the arts and, apparently, to the aesthetic aspects of life; (b) living – related to the economy and the material world of profit and prosperity; (c) intellectual reflection, including science and knowledge; (d) practice, i.e., of government, politics and ethics; and (e) existence, relating to philosophy, religion, spirituality and religious belief. We are left with little, if any, indication as to how these values are to be tapped, through which mechanisms or hermeneutic – or other – procedures, and by which human agency or agencies within the body of the Umma. It is clear, however, that whoever bears the responsibility of legislation must be faithful to the true "Islamic values and ethics," and the ulama must not be permitted to play any role beyond their possible function as technical counselors (*mustashārūn fanniyyūn*), "just like any other councilors" who are experts in their own fields (e.g., engineers, physicians, etc.).[118]

It is quite indicative of the unbridgeable gap separating Marzūqī from Būṭī that, in a book intended to bring them into a debate with each other, the latter neither addresses the former personally nor attempts to rebut his ideas directly. Marzūqī is not even mentioned by name. Būṭī's concern is rather with the central issue revolving around the meaning of "renewal" (*tajdīd*) and how such notions of "renewal" bear on *uṣūl al-fiqh*. Būṭī appears to assume, and with good reason, that his unnamed interlocutor

[117] *Ibid.*, 129. [118] *Ibid.*, 191.

means by "renewal" a total displacement of *uṣūl al-fiqh*, displacement that he rejects vehemently. The hermeneutical and other rules by which the law is derived are said by Būṭī to be objective, having emerged from the "semiotic rules of the Arabic language." Once one believes in God, one is bound to accept these rules of language as well as the essential methods of exegesis because all of these are dictated by the very sources given to Muslims by the God in whom they believe. One is no more permitted to change these rules than to tinker with the sources and inferential methods of the Sharīʿa, "these latter having ultimately been derived or deduced from the Book of God."[119] Whims, desires and wants are insufficient justification for changing the rules of, or replacing, the Sharīʿa, for rule is God's alone (*al-ḥākimiyya hiya lil-Lāh waḥdah*).[120] Substantive Sharīʿa law is the "fruit" of God's discourse (*khiṭāb*), which the latter sent to his worshipers. Būṭī further argues that those who espouse such drastic "renewal" (= displacement) are under the obligation to justify a methodology (*manhaj*) that aims to accomplish both the canceling out of the Sharīʿa and the construction of a new law. The justification must in turn be justified, until, that is, the final justification is assuredly established on an unshakable, apodictic foundation, akin, if not identical, to the certainty of untainted belief in divine will and power. Refusal to offer such a justification indicates nothing less than "absolute aimlessness," behind which there is concealed a language and culture of desires, lascivious instincts and, in short, hedonism.

In his response to Būṭī, Marzūqī rightly finds no shared grounds on which the debate can progress meaningfully. He expresses astonishment at Būṭī's total denial of "crises," averring that such claims are readily contradicted by an undeniable reality in which "*fiqh* has nowadays become marginal in the life of Muslims," representing no more than a "nominal" and "remote justification" of secularist and positivist legislation. The refusal to acknowledge this stark reality suggests to Marzūqī the existence of a double crisis, namely, the very crisis of Sharīʿa's marginalized presence and that of the failure to recognize that such a crisis exists in the first place.[121] Yet, Marzūqī's position generates its own aporias. If the Taymiyyan and Khaldūnian revolutions were indeed "accomplished" – as he claims – and if they led to a reconsideration of the reasoning methods of the four schools, then why speak of the ulama's historical "usurpation" of the Umma's legislative powers (which we cannot but assume to have been restored by these revolutions) and not of the state's usurpation that resulted in the secularist and positivist legislation? In Marzūqī's discourse,

[119] *Ibid.*, 162–63, 170. [120] *Ibid.*, 163. [121] *Ibid.*, 192, 194, 198, 222.

neither of these aporias is even detected, much less addressed. Despite the two revolutions, the ulama remain culpable, and the state taken for granted.

Emblematic of Būṭī's denial of crisis, Marzūqī argues, is his insistence on the traditional "mechanics of the Arabic language," which are said to be productive of the signifiers that generate the law. For Marzūqī, legislation can hardly be reduced to hermeneutics and linguistic analysis, for law, in effect, is a sociological process mediated by the knowledge of "experts" who strive (*yajtahidūn*) to offer solutions to the problems of their society and age. Insinuated here is the view that the production of law cannot significantly depend on linguistic operations or on any such reasoning methods organically tied to these operations. Yet, dispensing with Būṭī's Arabicate hermeneutics demands a substitute, a method by which the law is formulated. But no method is proposed, not even in outline.

In the final segment of the debate, Būṭī complains that he understands very little of Marzūqī's argument. This confession, to be sure, is in no way intended as self-deprecation, it being rather a subtle attack on Marzūqī's abstract indulgences and vagueness as to alternatives for those elements of the Sharīʿa he rejects. Furthermore, the Taymiyyan and Khaldūnian "revolutions" are dismissed by him as figments of Marzūqī's wild imagination, for only he sees revolution in their writings. (The possibility of such an accusation had been predicted much earlier in the book by Marzūqī himself.)[122] Having repeatedly criticized Marzūqī for his silence on the alternatives to the traditional Sharīʿa that Marzūqī wishes to displace, Būṭī goes on to restate his theory of law, much in the same vein as he outlined it in his *Ḍawābiṭ* (discussed in section 4, above).

To say that the two writers start from entirely different assumptions is to understate the matter. To say that this disparity in outlook is highly indicative of a larger problem within the disintegrated Muslim legal culture is to understate the matter even further. For one thing, Marzūqī and Būṭī belong to two different, yet not altogether distinguishable, camps: Marzūqī may be typified as belonging to the Islamist camp, one of whose defining features is rejection of the juristic and hermeneutical authority of the past; Būṭī represents the ulama camp, but with an Islamist twist, for he shares with the Islamist camp a critique of modernity on distinctly moral grounds. With the ulama, he shares a hermeneutic. Marzūqī, on the other hand, alludes to the need for an Islamically grounded morality, but fails to articulate the difference between this morality and modernity's counter-morality. This failure, or rather near silence, suggests a lack of

[122] *Ibid.*, 145.

concern with one of the foremost components in the socio-religious and political platform of Islamism. In this respect, Būṭī comes across more as an Islamist, specifically of the Quṭbian type. But unlike Quṭb, who denies the ulama any privileged status, Būṭī insists on the continuing relevance to the modern world of traditional *uṣūl al-fiqh*, *fiqh* and their proponents. Yet, even Būṭī, the most ardent critic of modernity's hedonism and materialism, does not deny the necessity of making some adjustments to the historical and traditional Sharīʿa, adjustments dictated by modern exigencies. But though such adjustments may be in order, they cannot be made on Western modernity's terms; rather, they must accord with Sharīʿa's unchanging fundamental principles. That Būṭī cannot be neatly located in a single camp, and that he simultaneously, though partially, treads Islamist ideological terrains, are testimony to the dangers of classification.

Yet, despite its dangers, classification remains, paradoxically, useful. Among all the writers we have discussed here, we take no risk in making the categorical but obvious statement that Būṭī and Soroush stand at the extreme ends of the spectrum, with Khallāf and Riḍa (in this order) located next to Būṭī, and Marzūqī and Shaḥrūr (in this order) located next to Soroush. In the middle of the spectrum, we can place Rahman, Hazairin, Hasbi and ʿAshmāwī. The differences as well as the intersecting similarities between and among all these thinkers not only defy neat classification but at once also affirm their failure to provide indigenous solutions to the epistemic havoc wrought by modernity.

18 Repercussions: concluding notes

It cannot be overstated that, for over a millennium, the Sharīʿa represented a complex set of social, economic, moral and cultural relations that permeated the epistemic structures of the social and political orders. It was a discursive practice in which these relations intersected with each other, acted upon each other and affected one another in multiple ways. Involving institutions, groups and processes that resisted, enhanced and dialectically affected each other, this discursive practice manifested itself as much in the judicial process as in writing, studying, teaching and documenting. It involved a political representation in the name of Sharīʿa values, and strategies of resistance against political and other abuses, as well as a cultural rendering of law in practice, where cultural categories meshed into *fiqh*, legal procedure, moral codes and much else. It involved a deeply moral community which law, in its operation, took as granted, for it is a truism that the Sharīʿa itself was constructed on the assumption that its audiences and consumers were, all along, moral communities and morally grounded individuals. It involved a complex and sophisticated intellectual system in which the jurists and the members of the legal profession were educators and thinkers who, on the one hand, were historians, mystics, theologians, logicians, men of letters and poets, and, on the other, contributed to the forging of a complex set of relations that at times created political truth and ideology while at other times it confronted power with its own truth. It involved the regulation of agricultural and mercantile economies that constituted the vehicle for the maintenance of material and cultural lives that spanned the entire gamut of "classes" and social strata. It involved a theological substrate that colored and directed much of the worldview of the population whose inner spiritual lives and relationships were in daily touch with the law. Indeed, this theological substrate encompassed the mundanely mystical, the esoterically pantheistic and the rationally philosophical, thereby creating complex relations between the Sharīʿa and the larger spiritual and intellectual orders in which, and alongside which, it lived and functioned. The Sharīʿa then was not only a judicial system and a legal doctrine whose function was to regulate social relations and resolve and mediate disputes, but also a discursive practice that structurally and organically tied itself to the world around it in ways that were vertical and horizontal, structural and linear, economic and social, moral and ethical, intellectual and spiritual, epistemic and cultural, and textual and poetic, among much else.

Yet, while constituting the total sum of these relations, the Sharīʿa (as we saw in chapters 4 and 5) was distinctive in that it cultivated itself within, and derived its ethical and moral foundations from, the very social order which it came to serve in the first place. While in its textual and technical exposition it was, by necessity, of an elitist tenor, very little else in it was elitist. Its personnel hailed from across all social strata (especially the middle and the lower classes), and operated and functioned within communal and popular spaces. The locus of the *qāḍī*'s court, the professor's classroom and the *muftī*'s assembly was the yard of the mosque, and when this was not the case it was the marketplace or a private residence. That these sites served, as they did, a multiplicity of other social and religious–communal functions strongly suggests that the intersection of the legal with the communal was a marker of the law's populism and communitarianism. The same can be said of legal knowledge, which, as we saw, could scarcely have been more widespread across the entire range of society. The Sharīʿa defined, in good part (and together with Ṣūfism), paradigmatic cultural knowledge. Enmeshed with local customs, moral values and social practices, it was a way of life.

Legal doctrine (*fiqh*) gave direction and method to, but generally did not coercively superimpose itself upon, social morality. Because the *qāḍī* was an immediate product of his own social and moral universe, he was constituted – by the very nature of his function – as the agency through which the *fiqh* was mediated and made to serve the imperatives of social harmony. Procedurally, too, the work of the court appealed to pre-capitalist and non-bureaucratic social constructions of moral probity that sprang directly from the local site of social practice. The institution of witnessing would have been meaningless without local knowledge of moral values, custom and social ties. Without such knowledge, the credibility of testimony itself – the lynchpin of the legal process – would have been neither testable nor demonstrable. Rectitude and trustworthiness, themselves the foundations of testimony, constituted the personal moral investment in social ties. To fail their test was to lose social standing and the privileges associated with it. Thus, the communal values of honor, shame, integrity and socio-religious virtue entered the judicial arena as part of a dialectic with the prescriptive assumptions of *fiqh*.

Furthermore, *fiqh*'s pluralism (*ikhtilāf*) constituted in effect one of Sharīʿa's socio-political dimensions. Pluralism not only was a marker of a strong sense of judicial relativism but also stood in stark contrast with the spirit of codification, another modern means of homogenizing the law and, consequently, the subject population. Nor was *fiqh* limited to being a hermeneutical manifestation of divine will. It was also a socially embedded system, a mechanism and a process, all of which were created for the social order by the order itself. From this perspective, then, the *fiqh* operated in a dual capacity: first, it provided an intellectual superstructure that culturally positioned the law within the larger tradition that conceptually defined Islam, thereby constituting it as a theoretical link between metaphysics and theology, on the one hand, and the social and physical world on the other; and second, it aimed discreetly at the infusion of legal norms within a given social and moral order, an infusion whose method of realization was largely mediation rather than imposition. The Muslim adjudicatory process, with its *fiqh*, was therefore never remote from the social world of the disputants, advocating a moral logic of distributive justice rather than a logic of winner-takes-all. Restoring parties to the social roles they enjoyed prior to the legal process called for moral compromise, where each party was permitted to retain a partial gain. Preserving social order presupposed both a court and a malleable *fiqh* that was acutely attuned to the system of social and economic cleavages. For despite the fact that cleavages – including class and other prerogatives – constantly asserted themselves, morality was the lot, and indeed the right, of everyone.

Moreover, in the world of practice, the *fiqh* did not constitute a totalizing statement of the "law," nor was it engaged in transforming reality or managing or controlling society. Attributing to *fiqh* roles of control and management (resembling a Foucauldian conception) would be a distinctly modern misconception, a back-projection of our notions of law as an etatist instrument of social engineering. This misconceived attribution perhaps explains why legal Orientalism has insisted on the "divorce" between "Islamic law" and social and political realities since the early third/ninth century, saving only for the areas of family law and, obviously, ritual. What Orientalism took to be a divorce was really a modulated state of affairs in which the legal system allowed for the mediation of the agency of custom and social morality. It would be a mistake then to equate *fiqh* with law in the distinctively modern sense.

Fiqh was a process of explicating doctrine, an intellectual engagement to understand all the possible ways of reasoning and interpretation pertaining to a particular case. It was not the case that was of primary importance, nor its multiple solutions. Rather, it was the principle illustrated by a group of cases which constituted an illustration of how the principle is to be defined, delimited, refined, articulated, restricted and, very importantly, distinguished from another cognate principle yielding a different set of cases. It was thus the principle of the *fiqh* that mattered, not the individual cases and opinions, which were, on balance, more illustrative than prescriptive. Individual opinions, strictly speaking, did not constitute law in the same sense in which we now understand the modern code, regulation or "case law," nor was it the "legal effect" of stating the will of a sovereign that the Muslim jurists intended to accomplish in any way. Their law was an interpretive and heuristic project, not "a body of rules of action or conduct prescribed by [a] controlling authority."[1] It was not a "solemn expression of the will of the supreme power of the state,"[2] for there was no *state* in the first place. The *fiqh* was the intellectual and hermeneutical work of private individuals, jurists whose claim to authority was primarily epistemic, but also religious and moral. It was not political in the modern sense of the word, and it did not involve coercive or state power. Nor was it subject to the fluctuations of legislation, reflecting the interests of a dominant class. In its stability, but without rigidity, it represented an unassailable fortress within which the rule of law compared favorably to its much-vaunted modern counterpart.

Furthermore, the *fiqh* was not an abstraction, nor did it apply equally to "all," for individuals were not seen as indistinguishable members of a generic species, standing in perfect parity before a blind lady of justice. Each individual and circumstance was deemed unique, requiring *ijtihād* that was context-specific. This explains why Islam never accepted the notion of blind justice, which also explains why there was no point in *stating* the law in the way that it is recorded in today's legal codes. Rather, the law was an *ijtihād*ic process, a continuously renewed exercise in hermeneutic. It was an effort at mustering principles as located in specific life-situations, requiring the legists to do what was right at a particular moment of human existence. The *fiqh*, even in its most detailed and comprehensive accounts, was no more than a juristic guide that directed the judge and all legal personnel on the ground to resolve a situation in due consideration of the unique facts involved therein. The *fiqh* as a *sharʿī* manifestation, as a fully realizable and realized worldly "law," was not fully revealed unto society until the jural principles meshed with social reality and until the dialectic of countless social, moral, material and other types of human relations involved in a particular case was made to come full circle.

The foregoing characterization of the Sharīʿa and its *fiqh*, partial as it may be, bespeaks a complex reality that has largely disappeared. Over the past two centuries or so, the Sharīʿa has been transformed from a worldly

[1] A standard definition of (Western) law. See *Black's Law Dictionary*, 795. [2] *Ibid.*

institution and culture to a textuality that not only represents the subtracted differential between the pre-modern organic structure and its entexted version, but also engages the very characteristic of being entexted in a politics that the pre-modern counterpart did not know. Which is to say that even the surviving residue, the entexted form, functions in such uniquely modern ways that the very residue is rendered foreign, in substance and function, to any possible genealogical counterpart.

Profoundly epistemic and structural, this transformation was the outcome of the confrontation between the Sharīʿa and the most significant and weighty institution that emerged out of, and at once defined, modernity, i.e., the state. Conceptually, institutionally and historically, the state came into sustained conflict with the Sharīʿa, initially coexisting with it in a condition of contradiction, but soon succeeding in displacing it once and for all. Among the specific effects of this contest for mastery over the law was the desiccation and final dismantling of the Sharīʿa's institutional structures, including its financially independent colleges and universities, and the jural environment that afforded Muslim legists the opportunity to operate and flourish as a "professional" group. This dismantling (with the benefit of hindsight, inevitable and expected) finally led to the extinction of this group as a species, to the emergence of a new conception of law, and, in short, to the rise of a new legal and cultural "episteme." Sharīʿa's subject-matter became no more than positive law, emanating from the state's will to power. The transformation was embodied in, and represented by, a complex process that operated at nearly every level in the uneven relationship between colonialist modern Europe – the creator and exporter of the modern state – and Muslim (and other) societies around the world. The forces behind the transformation were, among many others, centralization, codification (in the widest sense of the word), bureaucratization, jural homogenization and – to ensure totalistic compliance – ubiquitous militarization, all of which are in fact the props of the modern state project. And, systemically speaking, all these forces operated in tandem against indigenous constituents, be they legal or otherwise. That these forces often competed among themselves in no way undermined or contradicted their systemic trajectory.[3]

As we have seen, it was in British India that the "entexting" of *fiqh* first occurred – where, that is, the *fiqh* was *fixed* into texts as a conceptual act of codification. British India, subjected to direct forms of colonialism, displayed the processes and effects of crude power and hegemonic discourse more clearly than, say, the Ottoman Empire, although the latter was

[3] For the theoretical articulation of this point, see Introduction, section 2, above.

no less affected by hegemonic modernity, in all its aspects, than any other directly colonized subject. The Indian experiment (and no less the Ottoman) served an immediate epistemological function in the colonialist articulation of Islam. What amounted to a large-scale operation by which Islamic jural practices were reduced to fixed texts created a new way of understanding India and the rest of the Muslim world. Integral to this understanding was the pervasive idea that to study Islam and its history was to study texts, and not its societies, social practices or social orders. Entexting the Sharīʿa therefore had the effect of severing nearly all its ties with the anthropological and sociological legal past, much like the consignment of events to the "dark ages" or medieval period in the European historical imagination. Once the anthropological past was trampled under by an entexted Sharīʿa, the very meaning of *fiqh* was severely curtailed, if not transformed, having been emptied of the content and expertise necessary for a genuine evaluation of Sharīʿa-on-the-ground, and of its operation within an "ecological" system of checks and balances. It was also, as a consequence, stripped of much of its previous relevance. The new nationalist elites, endowed with the legacy of colonial state structures, aggressively pursued this severance of Sharīʿa from its anthropological past. Entexting served the nation-state's project of social engineering very well.[4]

This severance, I have already intimated, engages the entexted Sharīʿa in a new world of politics, a world that its pre-modern counterpart did not know. The act of severance, in other words, was almost perfectly correlated with the process by which the surviving residue of *fiqh*, the entexted body, was transplanted into a new environment. The transformation was then two-pronged, engendering juristic/jural rigidity through entexting, and politicization through transplantation. Whereas the pre-modern Sharīʿa and its *fiqh* operated largely outside dynastic rule, the entexted and transplanted *fiqh* had now come to be lodged *within* the structures of the state. To say that this transformation subjected the *fiqh* and Sharīʿa to a profound process of politicization is merely to state the obvious. The Sharīʿa, however conceived by its modern followers, stands today as the centerpiece of political contention.

The road to politicization began at the moment when the so-called reforms allowed the state to appropriate the law as a legislative tool,

[4] With the obvious exception of such countries as Saudi Arabia, whose continuing application of the Sharīʿa renders this severance largely unnecessary. Yet, this is not to say that the modern Saudi state structures did not transform the Sharīʿa in other, fundamental ways. On the place of Sharīʿa in the Kingdom of Saudi Arabia, see Vogel, *Islamic Law and Legal System*.

changing dramatically a thousand-year-old situation in which the typical Islamic proto-state administered a law neither of its own making nor subject to the ruler's will to power. "In the modern state," as Talal Asad poignantly observes, "law is an element in political strategies – especially strategies for destroying old options and creating new ones."[5] Values centering on the family as a discrete social unit, on property, crime, punishment, a particular sexuality, a particular conception of gender, of rights, of morality and of much else, have all been created and recreated through the law. Yet, the intractable presence of the state – the virtually all-powerful agent exercising the option of reengineering the social order – has preempted any vision of governance outside its parameters. To practice law in the modern era is to be an agent of the state. There is no law proper without the state, and there is no state without its own, exclusive law. "Legal pluralism" can no doubt exist, but only with the approval of the state and its law.[6] State sovereignty without a state-manufactured law is no sovereignty at all.

If the way to the law is through the state, then neither Sharīʿa nor *fiqh* can ever be restored, reenacted, or refashioned (by Islamists or ulama of any type or brand) without the agency of the state. More importantly, none of these restorative options can be realized without the contaminating influence of the state, rendering extinct the distinctiveness of pre-modern Sharīʿa as a non-state, community-based, bottom-up jural system. This distinctiveness would be impossible to replicate. In the modern state, politics and state policy mesh with law, creating a powerful ideological and cultural technology as well as producing other potent instruments that are wielded in the service of the state in (re-)fashioning the social order, whose habitus is precisely that machinery which produces the citizen.

And so when the Sharīʿa (however imagined) is reasserted in any Muslim country, as happened, for instance, in Iran in 1979 and thereafter, the entexted conception combines with another conception of state-appropriated law to produce an aberrancy, one whose domestic advocates (seeking legitimacy) and external foes (seeking condemnation of Islamic revolutionary regimes) are equally happy, though for entirely different reasons, to call what ensues "Sharīʿa." Given the absence of epistemic access to the Sharīʿa's anthropological past, both its advocates and its foes are left wandering in the dark. Inasmuch as the Shah's state, like all states in the West and the East, virtually destroyed and then refashioned its social order and reconstituted (without much success) its moral fabric,

[5] Asad, "Conscripts of Western Civilization," 335; Zubaida, *Law and Power*, 153–56.
[6] See chapter 13, n. 18, above.

the new Islamic Republic, inheriting an utterly inescapable state apparatus, attempted to reinstate the Sharīʿa and fill the perceived moral void through the now familiar tools of state engineering. The Sharīʿa became the state's tool, for only to the state could it have been subordinated. Theft, homosexuality, extra-marital sex, music, American cultural icons and much else became the focus, if not the rhetoric, of the new reengineering in the name of the Sharīʿa. Yet, this reengineering was the work of a moralizing state, and was by no means dictated by the mechanisms associated with Sharīʿa's traditional ways of functioning. At the end of the day, the Sharīʿa has ceased to be even an approximate reincarnation of its historical self. That it would be impossible to recreate it along with the kind of social order it presupposed and by which it was sustained is self-evident. To claim, however, that its modern expression can be altogether dispensed with is unrealistic. The Sharīʿa has become a marker of modern identity, engulfed by modern notions of culture and politics (but, ironically, much less by law). To assert that this marker will persist for some time to come would be to understate the case.

Appendix A: Contents of substantive legal works

Treatises on legal doctrine (*fiqh*) tend to differ from each other in terms of the organization of their subject-matter, although the chapters on rituals always occupy in these works first place and follow a fixed order (i.e., ablution, prayer, alms-tax, fasting and pilgrimage). The differences in the order of treatment of other legal spheres, at times great, can be attributed to the various ways the legal schools conceived of the logical and juristic connections between one area of *fiqh* and another, which is to say that the most significant organizational variations between and among *fiqh* works can be attributed to school affiliation and the particular commentarial and interpretive tradition in each of them. Organizational variation can also be easily detected in the diachronic developments within one and the same school. It must be said that the synchronic and diachronic variations in the organization of these works within and across the schools both remain a fertile subject of enquiry.

What follows is a schematic account of *fiqh* subject-matter as presented in the relatively later work *al-Mīzān al-Kubrā* by ʿAbd al-Wahhāb al-Shaʿrānī (d. 973/1565), an Egyptian Shāfiʿite jurist who attempted to show that, despite the seemingly great differences among the major jurists of the four Sunnite schools, they all derived their doctrines legitimately from one and the same "font of Sharīʿa" (I, 7–8, 11, 47, 54).

Generally, Muslim jurists gave the main topics of *fiqh* the title *kitāb* ("book"), e.g., *Kitāb al-Wakāla* (the Book of Agency), which, in our modern organizational scheme, we recognize as chapter. A sub-chapter was termed "*bāb*." Shaʿrānī adopts this terminology as well. In longer and detailed works, a further division is adopted. The *bāb* would be broken into a number of *faṣl*s (sections), and these would in turn be divided into *mas'ala*s (questions, issues), and further into *far*ʿs (specific cases). Some author-jurists of long treatises divide the *kitāb* into *faṣl*s, dispensing with the designation *bāb*.

Like many jurists, Shaʿrānī conceives of the *fiqh* as falling into four major fields, which he calls "the four quarters" (II, 80), i.e., "rituals, sales, marriage and injuries." Each of these terms, used in this context by him as well as by many of his colleagues metaphorically, stands for a staggering variety of subjects that belong to a single quarter. Thus, the "quarter of sales" would encompass, among many other subjects, partnerships, guaranty, gifts and bequests, while that of "marriage" would cover as varied a field as dissolution of matrimony, foster relationships, custody, and wifely and family support (*nafaqāt*). In the same vein, the "quarter of injuries" includes homicide, the Quranic *ḥudūd* punishments and *jihād*, among other topics. Works of *fiqh*, as does Shaʿrānī's *Mīzān*, often end with what we term procedural law,[1] supplemented by coverage of slave manumission. Many Ḥanafite and Mālikite works end instead with inheritance and bequests.

In addition to Shaʿrānī's account of the organization of subject-matter, I will offer a brief commentary on the differing placement of topics in certain schools. It will also be noticed that the main "book" topics are followed by two percentages. The first represents the percentage of space Shaʿrānī allocated to the discussion of the topic in his work, calculated after having excluded the introductory pages (5–127) that do not directly bear on the exposition of legal doctrine. The second percentage refers to the space that Manṣūr al-Buhūtī (d. 1051/1641) allocated to these topics in his standard Ḥanbalite work *Sharḥ Muntahā al-Irādāt* (3 vols., consisting of a total of about 1,750 pages; by contrast, the conventional legal topics in Shaʿrānī's *Mīzān* occupy about 440 pages). Because Shaʿrānī's work is specifically concerned with disagreements among the schools, it does not accurately reflect the weight of topics within the overall genre of *fiqh*, since a relatively minor topic could generate more controversy (and therefore occupy more space) than a larger one on which disagreements are less intense.[2] Therefore, in order to give a more representative account in terms of space allocation, I have chosen to present the proportions of the material in Buhūtī's work, which – at least in the edition I use – does not contain editorial footnotes and commentary, as these would have distorted the calculations when pages were counted. This exercise is intended to give a *general* idea of the discursive attention each topic received in *fiqh*, but the reader should keep in mind that the percentages given here are approximate and have often been rounded.[3] The point is

[1] Discussed under Books 51–53, below.

[2] Illustrative of this imbalance are *ṣalāt* (Book 2) and Quranic shares of inheritance (Book 30). The former receives 23.4%, close to a quarter of all *fiqh* subject-matter, but the important Quranic inheritance receives a meager 0.6%, since the relative clarity of the Quran on this matter precluded much juristic disagreement.

[3] It will also be clear that the total of percentages does not come to a hundred, since certain marginal topics, classified independently under "sections" (*abwāb*), have not been included here.

that when Buhūtī allocates, for instance, 13.8% to prayer and only 1.1% to agency, he can be said to have given a general representation of the relative weight of these topics in the overall discursive juristic tradition.

A. The First Quarter:
   1. Book of Purity (*Ṭahāra*; 8.6%, 6.1%)
   2. Book of Prayer (*Ṣalāt*; 23.4%, 13.8%)
   3. Book of Alms-Tax (*Zakāt*; 4.3%, 4.2%)
   4. Book of Fasting (*Ṣawm*; 3.4%, 2%)
   5. Book of Pilgrimage (*Ḥajj*; 6.8%, 5.4%)
   6. Book of Food and Drink (*Aṭʿima*; 1%, 0.8%) [many jurists discuss this and the following Book toward the end of the Third Quarter]
   7. Book of Hunting and Slaughtering Animals (*al-Ṣayd wal-Dhabāʾiḥ*; 0.7%, 0.5%)

B. The Second Quarter
   [The Mālikites and Ḥanafites usually treat these topics in the Third Quarter, with the exception of inheritance and bequests, which are generally delayed to the very end of their works.]
   8. Book of Sales (*Buyūʿ*; 3.5%, 4.9%)
   9. Book of Pledge (*Rahn*; 0.6%, 1%)
   10. Book of Insolvency and Interdiction (*al-Taflīs wal-Ḥajr*; 0.7%, 1.5%)
   11. Book of Amicable Settlement (*Ṣulḥ*; 0.35%, 0.5%)
   12. Book of Transfer (*Ḥawāla*; 0.2%, 0.2%)
   13. Book of Guaranty (*Ḍamān, Kafāla*; 0.4%, 0.6%)
   14. Book of Partnership (*Sharika*; 0.3%, 0.4%)
   15. Book of Agency (*Wakāla*; 0.6%, 1.1%)
   16. Book of Acknowledgments (*Iqrār*; 0.5%, 1.8%)
   17. Book of Deposit (*Wadīʿa*; 0.2%, 0.5%)
   18. Book of Loans (*ʿĀriya*; 0.2%, 0.5%)
   19. Book of Unlawful Appropriation (*Ghaṣb*; 0.8%, 2%)
   20. Book of Pre-emption (*Shufʿa*; 0.5%, 0.9%)
   21. Book of Sleeping Partnership (*Qirāḍ, Muḍāraba*; 0.4%, 0.8%)
   22. Book of Agricultural Lease (*Musāqāt*; 0.35%, 0.4%)
   23. Book of Rent and Hire (*Ijāra*; 0.8%, 2%)
   24. Book Cultivating Waste Land (*Iḥyāʾ al-Mawāt*; 0.37%, 0.6%)
   25. Book of Charitable Trusts (*Waqf*; 0.34%, 1.6%)
   26. Book of Gifts (*Hiba*; 0.34%, 1.2%)
   27. Book of Found Property (*Luqṭa*; 0.34%, 0.6%)
   28. Book of Foundling (*Laqīṭ*; 0.1%, 0.5%)
   29. Book of Rewards for Returning Escaped Slaves (*Jiʿāla*; 0.2%, 0.2%)
   30. Book of Quranic Shares (in inheritance; *Farāʾiḍ*; 0.6%, 4%)
   31. Book of Bequests (*Waṣāyā*; 0.9%, 2.5%)

C. The Third Quarter
  [The Mālikites and Ḥanafites usually treat these topics in the Second Quarter.]
  32. Book of Marriage (*Nikāḥ*; 2.3%, 3.4%)
  33. Book of Dower (*Ṣadāq*, *Mahr*; 0.8%, 1.3%)
  34. Book of Contractual Dissolution of Marriage (*Khul*ʿ; 0.34%, 0.7%)
  35. Book of Unilateral Dissolution of Marriage by Husband (*Ṭalāq*; 1.1%, 3.7%)
  36. Book of Re-marriage by the Same Couple (*Rijʿa*; 0.3%, 0.4%)
  37. Book of Husband's Oath not to have Sexual Intercourse with his Wife (*Īlāʾ*; 0.22%, 0.4%)
  38. Book of Husband's Oath not to have Sexual Intercourse with his Wife (*Ẓihār*; 0.36%, 0.6%)
  39. Book of Husband's Accusing his Wife of being Unfaithful (*Liʿān*; 0.56%, 0.52%)
  40. Book of Oaths (*Aymān*; 2%, 1.7%)
  41. Book of Waiting Periods (*ʿIdad*; 0.6%, 1.2%)
  42. Book of Foster Relationships (*Riḍāʿ*; 0.2%, 0.5%)
  43. Book of Family Support (*Nafaqāt*; 0.57%, 1.2%)
  44. Book of Custody (*Ḥaḍāna*; 0.2%, 0.2%)

D. The Fourth Quarter
  45. Book of Torts (*Jināyāt*; 0.85%, 1.8%)
  46. Book of Blood-Money (*Diyāt*; 2%, 1.8%)
  47. Book of Quranically Regulated Infractions (*Ḥudūd*; 5.9%, 3.3%)
    a. Sub-chapter on Apostasy (*Ridda*)
    b. Sub-chapter on Rebels (*Bughāt*)
    c. Sub-chapter on Illicit Sexual Acts (*Zinā*)
    d. Sub-chapter on Accusing Someone of Illicit Sexual Act (*Qadhf*)
    e. Sub-chapter on Theft (*Sariqa*)
    f. Sub-chapter on Highway Robbers (*Quṭṭāʿ al-Ṭarīq*)
    g. Sub-chapter on Drinking Intoxicants (*Shurb al-Muskir*)
  48. [Book][4] of Discretionary Punishments (*Taʿzīr*; 0.8%, 0.1%)
  49. Book of *Jihād* (*Siyar*; 0.8%, 2%) [the Mālikites, some Ḥanbalites and the Twelver-Shīʿites usually place this Book at the end of the First Quarter]
  50. Book of Division of Booty (*al-Fayʾ wal-Ghanīma*; 1.9%, 0.6%)
  51. Book of Judges and Judgeship (*Aqḍiya*; 1.8%, 3.4%)
  52. Book of Suits and Evidence (*al-Daʿāwā wal-Bayyināt*; 0.8%, 0.9%)

[4] Shaʿrānī classifies this as a *bāb*, not as a *kitāb*.

53. Book of Testimonies (*Shahādāt*; 1.5%, 2%)
54. Book of Manumission (*ʿItq*; 0.5%, 0.8%)
55. Book of Manumission after Master's Death (*Tadbīr*; 0.2%, 0.2%)
56. Book of Manumission for Payment (*Kitāba*; 0.35%, 0.9%)
57. Book of Female Slaves who had Children with their Master (*Ummahāt al-Awlād*; 0.35%, 0.15%)

Appendix B: Chronology

This chronology, in Gregorian dates, is intended to aid beginners in identifying landmarks and important dates in the history of the Sharīʿa. In the case of movements and historical processes (e.g., personal schools, the Great Rationalist–Traditionalist Synthesis, the decline of Akhbārism, etc.), the dates should be taken as rough estimates of their beginning and/or end. In other words, this chronology merely represents a general guide and cannot replace the nuanced and more complex descriptions offered throughout this book.

610	Prophet Muhammad receives the first revelation.
622	Muhammad migrates to Medina.
632	Death of Muhammad.
632–80s	Rise of the Prophet's *sīra* (biography) and Sunna.
632–34	Caliphate of Abū Bakr.
634–44	Caliphate of ʿUmar [I] b. al-Khaṭṭāb.
635	Conquest of Damascus.
639	Conquest of Byzantine Egypt.
640	Conquest of Sasanid Persia.
644–56	Caliphate of ʿUthmān b. ʿAffān.
656–61	Caliphate of ʿAlī.
661–749	The Umayyad dynasty.
680s–	Scholars and early judges begin to study and specialize in Prophetic Sunna.
680s–90s	Shurayḥ active in adjudication.
690s–730s	Rise of the class of private legal specialists and study circles (*ḥalaqa*s).
711–13	Conquest of Sind and Transoxiana.
717–20	Reign of Caliph ʿUmar (II) b. ʿAbd al-ʿAzīz.
740	Date by which most functions in the Muslim court had been set in place.
740–	Rise of personal legal schools.
749–1258	The ʿAbbāsid dynasty.

750–1031	The Umayyad dynasty in Spain.
750–	The beginning of systematic exposition of *fiqh* (legal doctrine).
762	The founding of Baghdad.
765	Death of Ibn Abī Laylā, a distinguished Kūfan jurist and judge.
767	Death of Abū Ḥanīfa, the eponym and main leader of the Ḥanafite school.
773	Death of Awzāʿī, a leading Syrian jurist around whom a personal legal school had evolved.
777	Death of Sufyān al-Thawrī, a leading Kūfan jurist around whom a personal legal school had evolved.
795	Death of Mālik b. Anas, a leading Medinese jurist and the eponym of the Mālikite school.
798	Death of Yaʿqūb Abū Yūsuf, a leading Kūfan jurist, first chief justice in Islam and "co-founder" of the Ḥanafite school.
800	Legal doctrine acquires its full-fledged form.
804	Death of Muḥammad b. Ḥasan al-Shaybānī, a leading Kūfan jurist and "co-founder" of the Ḥanafite school.
800–950	Evolution of the Great Rationalist–Traditionalist Synthesis.
820	Death of Ibn Idrīs al-Shāfiʿī, the eponym and doctrinal leader of the Shāfiʿite school.
820–900	Compilation of Prophetic *ḥadīth*.
833–48	The Miḥna.
854	Death of Ibrāhīm b. Khālid Abū Thawr, a leading Iraqian jurist around whom a personal legal school had evolved.
855	Death of Aḥmad Ibn Ḥanbal, a distinguished traditionist and eponym of the doctrinal Ḥanbalite school.
860–900	Compilation of Prophetic *ḥadīth* in canonical collections.
860–950	The formation of legal schools (*madhhab*s) as doctrinal entities.
868–905	The Ṭūlūnids rule Egypt.
880	Death of Muḥammad b. Shujāʿ al-Thaljī, a leading Iraqian Ḥanafite jurist.
909–1171	The Fāṭimid dynasty.
918	Death of the outstanding Shāfiʿite jurist and theologian Ibn Surayj.
920–70	The first major expounders of a full-fledged theory of law (*uṣūl al-fiqh*).
920–1000	Peak activity of the *mukharrijūn* (see chapter 1, section 7, above).

923	Death of Abū Bakr al-Khallāl, instrumental in the formation of a doctrinal Ḥanbalite school.
935–69	The Ikhshīds rule Egypt.
939	Death of Muḥammad b. Yaʿqūb al-Kulaynī, a major compiler of Shīʿite *ḥadīth*.
939	The beginning of the Greater Occultation in Twelver-Shīʿism.
945–1055	The Būyids rule Baghdad.
945	Death of ʿUmar b. Ḥusayn al-Khiraqī, instrumental in the formation of a doctrinal Ḥanbalite school.
969	The Fāṭimids conquer Egypt and found Cairo.
977–1186	The Ghaznawids rule Transoxiana and Afghanistan.
991	Death of Ibn Bābawayh al-Qummī, a major Shīʿite traditionist.
1000–	The introduction of the *madrasa* institution to Iraq.
1012–55	The Būyids extend their rule over all of Iraq.
1030–1120	The production, by several jurists, of foundational treatises on legal theory (*uṣūl al-fiqh*).
1055–1157	The Saljūqs rule Iraq.
1065–	The Saljūqs, through their vizier Niẓām al-Mulk, establish great *madrasa*s in Baghdad.
1067	Death of Shaykh al-Ṭāʾifa al-Ṭūsī, a major Twelver-Shīʿite jurist and traditionist, and one of the first expounders of a Shīʿite legal theory (*uṣūl al-fiqh*).
1077–1307	The Saljūq state of Rūm.
1092	Death of the Saljūq vizier Niẓām al-Mulk.
1169–1252	The Ayyūbids rule Egypt (and Syria until 1260).
1206–1526	The Delhi sultanate.
1250–1517	The Mamlūks rule Egypt.
1347–61	Reign of the Mamlūk Sultan al-Nāṣir Ḥasan, interrupted between 1351 and 1354.
1389–1922	The Ottoman Empire.
1453	The Ottomans capture Constantinople.
1501–1732	The Ṣafavids rule Iran.
1515–1872	The Khanate of Khīva in Transoxiana.
1526–	Beginning of the Moghal Empire in India.
1600	The British East India Company is chartered.
1600–	The beginning of the confrontation between the Twelver-Shīʿite Uṣūlists and the Akhbārists.
1602	The Dutch East India Company is chartered.
1757	The Battle of Plassey and acquisition of Bengal by the East India Company.

1772	Warren Hastings becomes Governor-General of India.
1779–1924	The Qājār dynasty in Iran, consolidating its rule in 1794.
1786	Charles Cornwallis becomes Governor-General of India.
1791	Charles Hamilton publishes his translation of Marghīnānī's *Hidāya* into English.
1800	The final decline of the Akhbārist school.
1804	The promulgation in France of the *Code civil* (*Code Napoléon*), later influential in several Muslim countries.
1805–11	Muḥammad ʿAlī consolidates his grip over Egypt, eliminating the Mamlūks and preparing for significant reforms.
1808–39	The reign of the reformist Ottoman Sultan Mahmud II.
1826	The abolition of the Janissary corps by Mahmud II.
1826	*Waqf*s are placed under the control of the Imperial Ministry of Endowments, Istanbul.
1826	The Straits Settlements come under the rule of the East India Company.
1828	Muḥammad ʿAlī sends the first group of Egyptian (law) students to Paris. At, or around, this time the Ottomans and the Qājārs do the same.
1830	The French conquer Algiers.
1830–80	Drastic weakening of the ulama class in the Ottoman Empire, Egypt and French Algeria.
1837	The proclamation of the *siyāsatnāme* by Muḥammad ʿAlī in Egypt.
1839	The proclamation of the Ottoman Gülhane Decree.
1839–76	The age of Ottoman Tanẓīmāt.
1845	The establishment in Cairo and Alexandria of merchant councils.
1847–69	First major wave of educational reforms in the Ottoman Empire.
1850	A commercial, French-based, code promulgated in the Ottoman Empire.
1853–56	The Crimean Wars and Ottoman defeat.
1854–55	The establishment of the Nāʾib's College in Istanbul.
1856	The proclamation of the Humāyūn Decree.
1857	The Indian Rebellion.
1858	Promulgation in the Ottoman Empire of the Penal Code and Land Law.
1859	French penal code enacted in Algeria.
1860s	Egyptian legal experts begin translating French civil, commercial, penal and procedural codes into Arabic.

1860–80	Gradual restriction of Sharīʿa's application to personal status in the Ottoman Empire and Egypt.
1864	Promulgation in the Ottoman Empire of the Law of Provincial Administration.
1867	The Straits Settlements become a Crown colony.
1869	Death of Fuat Pasha (b. 1815), a leading Ottoman reformist.
1870–77	The publication of the Ottoman *Mecelle-i Ahkām-ı Adliye* (Ar. *Majallat al-Aḥkām al-ʿAdliyya*).
1871	Death of Ali Pasha (b. 1815), a leading Ottoman reformist.
1873	*Loi Warnier* pertaining to land promulgated in French Algeria.
1874	The promulgation, in the Ottoman Empire, of the Law of the Sharīʿa Judiciary.
1874–75	The promulgation in Egypt of the Civil Code, the Penal Code, the Commercial Code, the Code of Maritime Commerce, the Code of Civil and Commercial Procedure, and the Code of Criminal Procedure (all of which greatly influenced by French law).
1875	The promulgation of the Indian Law Reports Act.
1875	The establishment of the Mixed Courts in Egypt.
1876	The establishment in Istanbul of the first modern law school.
1880	Code of Civil Procedure enacted in the Ottoman Empire.
1880–1937	Sharīʿa in Indonesia is restricted by the Dutch to family law, with the exception of *waqf* in Sumatra.
1881	The French occupy Tunisia.
1881	*Code de l'indigénat* enacted in French Algeria, and applied until 1927.
1890–	The emergence of the myth of closing the gate of *ijtihād*.
1905	Death of Muḥammad ʿAbduh, the Grand Mufti of Egypt and a major reforming intellectual.
1906	Adoption of a new constitution in Iran.
1912	Morocco declared a French protectorate.
1916	*Code Morand* promulgated in French Algeria.
1917	Ottoman Law of Family Rights enacted.
1920	Family Law Act No. 25 promulgated in Egypt.
1923	Turkey declares itself a republic.
1924	Atatürk abolishes the caliphate.
1925–42	Rule of Reza Shah Pahlavi in Iran and the beginning of a major wave of legal reforms.
1926	Last purge of the Sharīʿa in Kemalist Turkey.

1927	The Code of Civil Procedure and the Code of Judicial Organization promulgated in Iran.
1928	The birth of the Muslim Brothers movement in Egypt.
1929	Indian Child Marriage Restraint Act promulgated.
1929	Family Law Act No. 25 promulgated in Egypt.
1930	The French proclaim the *Dahir berbère* in Morocco.
1931	The Act of Marriage promulgated in Iran.
1935	A new civil code in Iran.
1937	The Dutch enact new laws to regulate *waqf*s in Indonesia.
1945	Adoption of a constitution in Indonesia.
1946	Laws No. 48 (on *waqf*) and No. 71 (on legacies) enacted in Egypt.
1947	Pakistan declares its independence.
1948	Law No. 19 (judicial organization) enacted in Indonesia.
1949	Mixed courts abolished in Egypt.
1949	Adoption of the Objectives Resolution in Pakistan.
1949	A new civil code in Syria.
1949	Death of Ḥasan al-Bannā, the founder of the Muslim Brothers.
1950–	The Muslim Brothers spread their influence to Jordan, Syria, Sudan, Iran, Malaysia and elsewhere in the Muslim world.
1951	A new civil code in Iraq.
1951	Law of Family Rights enacted in Jordan.
1952	Law No. 180 (abolishing family *waqf*s) enacted in Egypt.
1953	A new civil code in Lybia.
1953	The Syrian Law of Personal Status enacted.
1955	Law No. 462 enacted, abolishing Sharīʿa courts in Egypt.
1956	The Code of Personal Status promulgated in Tunisia.
1956	The promulgation of the Constitution in Pakistan.
1957–58	The promulgation of the Law of Personal Status (*Mudawwana*) in Morocco.
1959	The Code of Personal Status promulgated in Iraq.
1959	Law Regulating the Judiciary enacted in Kuwait.
1961	Muslim Family Laws Ordinance promulgated in Pakistan.
1963–93	Al-Azhar expands dramatically.
1964	Adoption of a new constitution in Algeria.
1966	Sayyid Quṭb, ideologue of the Muslim Brothers, executed by the Nasser regime.
1967	Family Protection Act promulgated in Iran.
1969	The Supreme Court in Egypt renamed the Supreme Constitutional Court.

1973	The adoption of a new constitution in Pakistan.
1973	A constitution adopted in Syria.
1974	A marriage law enacted in Indonesia.
1975	The Family Protection Act amended in Iran.
1975	The Syrian Law of Personal Status amended.
1979	The Islamic Revolution in Iran; the adoption of a new constitution.
1979	Law No. 44 (Jihān's Law) promulgated in Egypt.
1980–96	A number of changes introduced to the criminal code in Iran.
1980	The Civil Code enacted in Kuwait.
1984	The Kuwait Code of Personal Status enacted.
1984	Family Code enacted in Algeria.
1985	Law No. 100, replacing Jihān's Law of 1979.
1989	Law No. 7 enacted in Indonesia (for the unification of Sharīʿa courts).
1989	The Iranian Constitution amended, expanding presidential powers.
1991	A constitution adopted in the Republic of Yemen.
1991	Enactment of the Compilation of Islamic Law in Indonesia (Kompilasi Hukum Islam di Indonesia).
1992	Law of Personal Status (No. 20) promulgated in Yemen.
1996	A new constitution adopted in Algeria, repealing its 1976 predecessor.
2000	The Procedure of General and Revolutionary Courts promulgated in Iran.
2003	Iranian Civil Code promulgated.
2003–07	A major wave of legislative enactments in occupied Iraq.

Bibliography

In classifying entries, no account is taken of the letter *ʿayn*, the *hamza* and the Arabic definite article *al-*.

1. SOURCES IN ARABIC

ʿAbduh, Muḥammad, *Taqrīr fī Iṣlāḥ al-Maḥākim al-Sharʿiyya* (Cairo: Maṭbaʿat al-Manār, 1317/1900).

Aḥmadnagarī, ʿAbd al-Nabī b. Aḥmad, *Jāmiʿ al-ʿUlūm fī Iṣṭilāḥāt al-Funūn, al-Mulaqqab bi-Dustūr al-ʿUlamāʾ*, 4 vols. (repr.; Beirut: Muʾassasat al-Aʿlamī lil-Maṭbūʿāt, 1975).

ʿAlamī, ʿĪsā b. ʿAlī, *Kitāb al-Nawāzil*, 3 vols. (Rabat: Wizārat al-Awqāf wal-Shuʾūn al-Islāmiyya, 1983).

ʿAlī, Jawād, *al-Mufaṣṣal fī Tārīkh al-ʿArab qabl al-Islām*, 10 vols. (Beirut: Dār al-ʿIlm lil-Malāyīn, 1970–76).

ʿĀmilī, Muḥammad b. Ḥasan al-Ḥurr, *Wasāʾil al-Shīʿa ilā Taḥṣīl Masāʾil al-Sharīʿa*, 20 vols. (Beirut: Muʾassasat al-Aʿlamī lil-Maṭbūʿāt, 1427/2007).

ʿAshmāwī, Muḥammad Saʿīd, *Uṣūl al-Sharīʿa* (Beirut: Dār Iqraʾ, 1983).

ʿAsqalānī, Ibn Ḥajar, *Bulūgh al-Marām min Adillat al-Aḥkām*, ed. Muḥammad Amīn Kutubī (Beirut: Dār al-Rāʾid al-ʿArabī, 1407/1987).

Rafʿ al-Iṣr ʿan Quḍāt Miṣr, printed with Kindī, *Akhbār Quḍāt Miṣr*, ed. R. Guest (Cairo: Muʾassasat Qurṭuba, n.d.); French trans., Mathieu Tillier, *Vies des Cadis de Miṣr* (Cairo: Institut Français d'Archéologie Orientale, 2002).

Astarābādī, Muḥammad Amīn, *al-Fawāʾid al-Madaniyya* (n.p.: Dār al-Nashr li-Ahl al-Bayt, 1984).

ʿAynī, Abū Muḥammad Maḥmūd b. Aḥmad, *al-Bināya fī Sharḥ al-Hidāya*, ed. Muḥammad ʿUmar, 12 vols. (Beirut: Dār al-Fikr, 1990).

Azharī, Abū Manṣūr, *al-Zāhir fī Gharīb Alfāẓ al-Shāfiʿī*, published as vol. I of Māwardī's *al-Ḥāwī al-Kabīr* (Beirut: Dār al-Kutub al-ʿIlmiyya, 1414/1994).

Bāʿalawī, ʿAbd al-Raḥmān b. Muḥammad, *Bughyat al-Mustarshidīn fī Talkhīṣ Fatāwā baʿḍ al-Aʾimma min al-ʿUlamāʾ al-Mutaʾakhkhirīn* (Cairo: Muṣṭafā Bābī al-Ḥalabī, 1952).

Baghdādī, Ibn Ghānim b. Muḥammad, *Majmaʿ al-Ḍamānāt* (Cairo: al-Maṭbaʿa al-Khayriyya, 1308/1890).

Baghdādī, al-Khaṭīb, *Tārīkh Baghdād*, 14 vols. (Cairo: Maṭbaʿat al-Saʿāda, 1931).

Bājī, Abū al-Walīd, *Iḥkām al-Fuṣūl fī Aḥkām al-Uṣūl*, ed. ʿAbd al-Majīd Turkī (Beirut: Dār al-Gharb al-Islāmī, 1986).

Baṣrī, Abū al-Ḥusayn, *al-Muʿtamad fī Uṣūl al-Fiqh*, ed. Muhammad Hamidullah *et al.*, 2 vols. (Damascus: Institut Français, 1964–65).

Bāz, Salīm Rustum, *Sharḥ al-Majalla*, 2 vols. (repr.; Beirut: Dār al-Kutub al-ʿIlmiyya, 1305/1887).

Bishrī, Ṭāriq, *al-Qaḍāʾ al-Miṣrī bayn al-Istiqlāl wal-Iḥtiwāʾ* (Cairo: Maktabat al-Shurūq al-Duwaliyya, 1427/2006).

al-Waḍʿ al-Qānūnī al-Muʿāṣir bayna al-Sharīʿa al-Islāmiyya wal-Qānūn al-Waḍʿī (Cairo: Dār al-Shurūq, 1417/1996).

Buhūtī, Manṣūr b. Yūnus b. Idrīs, *Kashshāf al-Qināʿ ʿan Matn al-Iqnāʿ*, ed. Muḥammad ʿAdnān Darwīsh, 6 vols. (Beirut: Dār Iḥyāʾ al-Turāth al-ʿArabī, 1999–2000).

al-Rawḍ al-Murbiʿ bi-Sharḥ Zād al-Mustaqniʿ (Beirut: Dār al-Jīl, 1997).

Sharḥ Muntahā al-Irādāt, al-Musammā Daqāʾiq Ūlī al-Nuhā li-Sharḥ al-Muntahā, 3 vols. (Cairo?: n.p., n.d.).

Būṭī, Muḥammad Saʿīd Ramaḍān, *Ḍawābiṭ al-Maṣlaḥa fī al-Sharīʿa al-Islāmiyya* (Damascus: al-Maktaba al-Umawiyya, 1966–67).

see also under Marzūqī.

Dhahabī, Shams al-Dīn, *Siyar Aʿlām al-Nubalāʾ*, ed. B. Maʿrūf and M. H. Sarḥān, 23 vols. (Beirut: Muʾassasat al-Risāla, 1986).

Dimashqī, Abū Zurʿa, *Tārīkh Abī Zurʿa al-Dimashqī*, ed. Shukr Allāh b. Niʿmat Allāh al-Qawjānī (n.p., 1970).

Faraj, Muḥammad ʿAbd al-Salām, *al-Farīḍa al-Ghāʾiba*, trans. in part by J. G. Jansen, *The Neglected Duty: The Creed of Sadat's Assassins and Islamic Resurgence in the Middle East* (New York: Macmillan, 1986).

al-Jihād: al-Farīḍa al-Ghāʾiba (n.p., n.d.).

al-Fatāwā al-Hindiyya, compiled by al-Shaykh al-Niẓām *et al.*, 6 vols. (repr.; Beirut: Dār Iḥyāʾ al-Turāth al-ʿArabī, 1400/1980).

Ghaṣūb, ʿAbduh Jamīl, "al-Qawānīn al-Waḍʿiyya al-Faransiyya wal-Sharīʿa al-Islāmiyya: Taqārub wa-Tabāʿud," in *Māʾatay ʿĀm ʿalā Iṣdār al-Taqnīn al-Madanī al-Faransī, 1804–2004* (Beirut: Manshūrāt al-Ḥalabī al-Ḥuqūqiyya, 2005): 17–48.

Ghazālī, Abū Ḥāmid Muḥammad b. Muḥammad, *Iḥyāʾ ʿUlūm al-Dīn*, 5 vols. (Aleppo: Dār al-Waʿy, 1425/2004).

al-Mankhūl min Taʿlīqāt al-Uṣūl, ed. Muḥammad Ḥasan Haytū (Damascus: Dār al-Fikr, 1980).

Mukhtaṣar Iḥyāʾ ʿUlūm al-Dīn, al-Musammā Lubāb al-Iḥyāʾ, ed. Maḥmūd Bayrūtī (Damascus: Dār al-Bayrūtī, 1428/2007).

al-Mustaṣfā fī ʿIlm al-Uṣūl, ed. al-Shaykh Muḥibb Allāh b. ʿAbd al-Shakūr (Būlāq: al-Maṭbaʿa al-Amīriyya, 1322/1904).

al-Wasīṭ fī al-Madhhab, ed. Abū ʿAmr al-Ḥusaynī, 4 vols. (Beirut: Dār al-Kutub al-ʿIlmiyya, 1422/2001).

Ḥalabī, Ibrāhīm b. Muḥammad, *Multaqā al-Abḥūr*, ed. Wahbī al-Albānī, 2 vols. (Beirut: Muʾassasat al-Risāla, 1409/1989).

Ḥasanī, ʿAbd al-Ḥayy, *Tahdhīb al-Akhlāq*, ed. ʿAbd al-Mājid al-Ghawrī (Damascus: Dār al-Fārābī, 1423/2002).

Ḥaṭṭāb, Muḥammad b. Muḥammad, *Mawāhib al-Jalīl li-Sharḥ Mukhtaṣar Khalīl*, 6 vols. (repr.; Beirut?: Dār al-Fikr, 1412/1992).

Ḥaydar, ʿAlī, *Durar al-Ḥukkām: Sharḥ Majallat al-Aḥkām*, 3 vols., 16 parts (repr.; Beirut: Dār al-Kutub al-ʿIlmiyya, 1991).

Ḥillī, al-Muḥaqqiq Najm al-Dīn Jaʿfar b. Ḥasan, *Maʿārij al-Uṣūl*, ed. M. Raḍawī (Qum: Maṭbaʿat Sayyid al-Shuhadāʾ, 1403/1982).

Sharāʾiʿ al-Islām fī Masāʾil al-Ḥalāl wal-Ḥarām, 4 vols. (Beirut: Dār al-Qāriʾ, 1425/2004).

Ḥiṣnī, Taqī al-Dīn Muḥammad, *Kifāyat al-Akhyār fī Ḥall Ghāyat al-Ikhtiṣār*, 2 vols. (Surabaya: Maṭbaʿat al-Hidāya, n.d.).

al-Ḥurr al-ʿĀmilī, *see* ʿĀmilī, Muḥammad b. Ḥasan.

al-Ḥusām al-Shahīd, Ibn Māza ʿUmar b. ʿAbd al-ʿAzīz, *Sharḥ Adab al-Qāḍī*, ed. Abū al-Wafā al-Afghānī (Beirut: Dār al-Kutub al-ʿIlmiyya, 1994).

Ibn ʿAbd al-Barr, Abū ʿUmar Yūsuf, *Jāmiʿ Bayān al-ʿIlm wa-Faḍlihi* (Beirut: Dār al-Kutub al-ʿIlmiyya, n.d.).

Ibn ʿAbd Rabbih, Aḥmad b. Muḥammad, *al-ʿIqd al-Farīd*, ed. Muḥammad al-ʿAryān, 8 vols. (Cairo: Maṭbaʿat al-Istiqāma, 1953).

Ibn ʿAbd al-Rafīʿ, Abū Isḥāq Ibrāhīm, *Muʿīn al-Ḥukkām ʿalā al-Qaḍāyā wal-Aḥkām*, ed. Muḥammad b. Qāsim b. ʿAbbād, 2 vols. (Beirut: Dār al-Gharb al-Islāmī, 1989).

Ibn Abī al-Damm, Ibrāhīm b. ʿAbd Allāh, *Adab al-Qaḍāʾ aw al-Durar al-Manẓūmāt fī al-Aqḍiya wal-Ḥukūmāt*, ed. Muḥammad ʿAṭāʾ (Beirut: Dār al-Kutub al-ʿIlmiyya, 1987).

Ibn ʿĀbidīn, Muḥammad Amīn, *Ḥāshiyat Radd al-Muḥtār ʿalā al-Durr al-Mukhtār Sharḥ Tanwīr al-Abṣār*, 8 vols. (Beirut: Dār al-Fikr, 1399/1979).

al-ʿUqūd al-Durriyya fī Tanqīḥ al-Fatāwā al-Ḥāmidiyya, 2 vols. (Cairo: al-Maṭbaʿa al-Maymūniyya, 1893).

Ibn Abī Shayba, Abū Bakr ʿAbd Allāh b. Muḥammad b. Ibrāhīm, *al-Muṣannaf*, 9 vols. (Beirut: Dār al-Kutub al-ʿIlmiyya, 1416/1995).

Ibn Aʿtham, Abū Muḥammad Aḥmad, *al-Futūḥ*, 8 vols. (Beirut: Dār al-Kutub al-ʿIlmiyya, 1986).

Ibn Bābawayh, Muḥammad b. ʿAlī al-Qummī, *Man lā Yaḥḍuruhu al-Faqīh*, 4 vols. (Beirut: Dār al-Aḍwāʾ, 1985).

Ibn Barhān, Aḥmad b. ʿAlī, *al-Wuṣūl ilā ʿIlm al-Uṣūl*, ed. ʿAbd al-Ḥamīd Abū Zunayd, 2 vols. (Riyad: Maktabat al-Maʿārif, 1984).

Ibn al-Farrāʾ, Muḥammad b. Abī Yaʿlā, *Ṭabaqāt al-Ḥanābila*, ed. Muḥammad al-Fiqī, 2 vols. (Cairo: Maṭbaʿat al-Sunna al-Muḥammadiyya, 1952).

Ibn Ḥajar al-Haytamī, *al-Fatāwā al-Kubrā al-Fiqhiyya*, 4 vols. (Cairo: ʿAbd al-Ḥamīd Aḥmad al-Ḥanafī, 1938).

Ibn al-Ḥājib, Jamāl al-Dīn b. ʿUmar, *Jāmiʿ al-Ummahāt*, ed. Abū ʿAbd al-Raḥmān al-Akhḍarī (Damascus and Beirut: al-Yamāma lil-Ṭibāʿa wal-Nashr, 1421/2000).

Ibn Ḥazm, ʿAlī b. Aḥmad, *Marātib al-Ijmāʿ fī al-ʿIbādāt wal-Muʿāmalāt wal-Muʿtaqadāt* (Beirut: Dār al-Āfāq al-Jadīda, 1978).

Muʿjam al-Fiqh, 2 vols. (Damascus: Maṭbaʿat Jāmiʿat Dimashq, 1966).

Ibn Ḥibbān, Muḥammad, *Kitāb al-Thiqāt* (Hyderabad: ʿAbd al-Khāliq al-Afghānī, 1388/1968).

Mashāhīr ʿUlamāʾ al-Amṣār, ed. M. Fleischhammer (Cairo: Maṭbaʿat Lajnat al-Taʾlīf wal-Tarjama wal-Nashr, 1379/1959).

Ibn al-Humām, Kamāl al-Dīn, *Sharḥ Fatḥ al-Qadīr*, 10 vols. (repr.; Beirut: Dār al-Fikr, 1990).

Ibn Kathīr, Abū al-Fidā', *Tafsīr al-Qur'ān al-'Aẓīm*, ed. Ḥusayn Zahrān, 4 vols. (Beirut: Dār al-Kutub al-'Ilmiyya, n.d.).

Ibn Khaldūn, 'Abd al-Raḥmān, *al-Muqaddima: Kitāb al-'Ibar wa-Dīwān al-Mubtada' wal-Khabar fī Ayyām al-'Arab wal-'Ajam wal-Barbar wa-man 'Āṣarahum min dhawī al-Sulṭān al-Akbar* (Beirut: Dār al-Kutub al-'Ilmiyya, n.d.); trans. Franz Rosenthal, *The Muqaddimah: An Introduction to History*, 3 vols. (London: Routledge and Kegan Paul, 1958).

Ibn Khallikān, Shams al-Dīn Aḥmad, *Wafayāt al-A'yān*, 4 vols. (Beirut: Dār Iḥyā' al-Turāth al-'Arabī, 1417/1997).

Ibn al-Laḥḥām, 'Alī b. 'Abbās al-Ba'lī, *al-Qawā'id wal-Fawā'id al-Uṣūliyya*, ed. Muḥammad al-Fiqī (Beirut: Dār al-Kutub al-'Ilmiyya, 1403/1983).

Ibn Manẓūr, Jamāl al-Dīn Muḥammad, *Lisān al-'Arab*, 15 vols. (Beirut: Dār Ṣādir, 1972).

Ibn Māza, Burhān al-Dīn Ṣadr al-Sharī'a al-Bukhārī, *al-Muḥīṭ al-Burhānī li-Masā'il al-Mabsūṭ wal-Jāmi'ayn wal-Siyar wal-Ziyādāt wal-Nawādir wal-Fatāwā wal-Wāqi'āt, Mudallala bi-Dalā'il al-Mutaqaddimīn*, ed. Na'īm Aḥmad, 25 vols. (Karachi: Idārat al-Qur'ān wal-'Ulūm al-Islāmiyya, 1424/2004).

Ibn Māza, 'Umar, *see* al-Ḥusām al-Shahīd.

Ibn Mufliḥ, Shams al-Dīn Muḥammad, *al-Ādāb al-Shar'iyya*, ed. Shu'ayb al-Arna'ūṭ and 'Umar al-Qayyām, 4 vols. (Beirut: Mu'assasat al-Risāla, 1418/1977).

Kitāb al-Furū', 6 vols. (Beirut: 'Ālam al-Kutub, 1985).

Ibn Muftāḥ, 'Abd Allāh, *al-Muntaza' al-Mukhtār min al-Ghayth al-Midrār, al-Ma'rūf bi- Sharḥ al-Azhār*, 10 vols. (Ṣa'da, Yemen: Maktabat al-Turāth al-Islāmī, 1424/2003).

Ibn al-Munāṣif, Muḥammad b. 'Īsā, *Tanbīh al-Ḥukkām 'alā Ma'ākhidh al-Aḥkām* (Tunis: Dār al-Turkī lil-Nashr, 1988).

Ibn al-Mundhir, Muḥammad b. Ibrāhīm al-Nīsābūrī, *al-Iqnā'*, ed. Muḥammad Ḥasan Ismā'īl (Beirut: Dār al-Kutub al-'Ilmiyya, 1418/1997).

Ibn al-Nadīm, *al-Fihrist* (Beirut: Dār al-Ma'rifa lil-Ṭibā'a wal-Nashr, 1398/1978). Trans. B. Dodge, *The Fihrist of al-Nadim: A Tenth-Century Survey of Muslim Culture* (New York: Columbia University Press, 1970).

Ibn al-Najjār, Taqī al-Dīn, *Muntahā al-Irādāt*, ed. 'Abd al-Mughnī 'Abd al-Khāliq, 2 vols. (Cairo: Maktabat Dār al-'Urūba, 1381/1962).

Ibn Naqīb, *see* Miṣrī.

Ibn Nujaym, Zayn al-Dīn b. Ibrāhīm, *al-Ashbāh wal-Naẓā'ir* (Beirut: Dār al-Kutub al-'Ilmiyya, 1413/1993).

Ibn Qāḍī Shuhba, Taqī al-Dīn, *Ṭabaqāt al-Shāfi'iyya*, ed. 'Abd al-'Alīm Khān, 4 vols. (Hyderabad: Maṭba'at Majlis Dā'irat al-Ma'ārif al-'Uthmāniyya, 1398/1978).

Ibn al-Qāṣṣ, Aḥmad b. Muḥammad, *Adab al-Qāḍī*, ed. Ḥusayn Jabbūrī, 2 vols. (Ṭā'if: Maktabat al-Ṣiddīq, 1409/1989).

Ibn Qudāma, Muwaffaq al-Dīn, *al-Kāfī fī Fiqh al-Imām Aḥmad Ibn Ḥanbal*, ed. Ṣidqī Jamīl and Salīm Yūsuf, 4 vols. (Beirut: Dār al-Fikr, 1992–94).

al-Mughnī, 14 vols. (Beirut: Dār al-Kutub al-ʿIlmiyya, n.d.).

Taḥrīm al-Naẓar fī Kutub Ahl al-Kalām, ed. and trans. George Makdisi, *Censure of Speculative Theology* (London: Luzca & Co., 1962).

Ibn Qudāma, Shams al-Dīn Abū al-Faraj ʿAbd al-Raḥmān, *al-Sharḥ al-Kabīr ʿalā Matn al-Muqniʿ*, printed with Muwaffaq al-Dīn Ibn Qudāma's *Mughnī*.

Ibn Rajab, ʿAbd al-Raḥmān, *al-Qawāʿid fī al-fiqh al-Islāmī*, ed. Ṭāha Saʿd (Beirut: Dār al-Jīl, 1408/1988).

Ibn Rushd al-Ḥafīd, *see under same entry, section 2 of this Bibliography*.

Ibn Rushd, Muḥammad b. Aḥmad (al-Jadd), *Fatāwā Ibn Rushd*, ed. al-Mukhtār b. Ṭāhir al-Talīlī, 3 vols. (Beirut: Dār al-Gharb al-Islāmī, 1978).

Ibn Saʿd, Muḥammad, *al-Ṭabaqāt al-Kubrā*, 8 vols. (Beirut: Dār Bayrūt lil-Ṭibāʿa wal-Nashr, 1958).

Ibn Taymīyya, Taqī al-Dīn, *Darʾ Taʿāruḍ al-ʿAql wal-Naql*, ed. ʿAbd al-Laṭīf ʿAbd al-Raḥmān, 5 vols. (Beirut: Dār al-Kutub al-ʿIlmiyya, 1997).

Mukhtaṣar al-Fatāwā al-Miṣriyya (Cairo: n.p., 1949).

Naqd Marātib al-Ijmāʿ, printed with Ibn Ḥazm, *Marātib al-Ijmāʿ*.

"*Risāla fil-Istiḥsān*," *see under* Makdisi, "Ibn Taymīya's Autograph Manuscript on *Istiḥsān*."

Jammāʿīlī, ʿAbd al-Ghanī b. ʿAbd al-Wāḥid, *al-ʿUmda fī al-Aḥkām*, ed. Muṣṭafā ʿAṭāʾ (Beirut: Dār al-Kutub al-ʿIlmiyya, 1986).

Jawzī, ʿAbd al-Raḥmān ʿAlī, *Aḥkām al-Nisāʾ*, ed. ʿAbd al-Qādir ʿAbd al-Qādir (Damascus: Dār al-Wathāʾiq, 1427/2006).

Jazīrī, ʿAbd al-Raḥmān, *al-Fiqh ʿalā al-Madhāhib al-Arbaʿa*, ed., ʿAbd al-Laṭīf Baytiyya, 5 vols. (Beirut: Dār Iḥyāʾ al-Turāth al-ʿArabī, n.d.).

Juwaynī, Imām al-Ḥaramayn, *al-Burhān fī Uṣūl al-Fiqh*, ed. ʿAbd al-ʿAẓīm Dīb, 2 vols. (Cairo: Dār al-Anṣār, 1400/1980).

Kāsānī, ʿAlāʾ al-Dīn b. Masʿūd, *Badāʾiʿ al-Ṣanāʾiʿ fī Tartīb al-Sharāʾiʿ*, ed. ʿAlī ʿĀdil and Muʿawwaḍ ʿAbd al-Mawjūd, 9 vols. (Beirut: Dār al-Kutub al-ʿIlmiyya, 1997).

Kāshif al-Ghiṭāʾ, Muḥammad Ḥusayn, *Taḥrīr al-Majalla*, 3 vols. (Qum: al-Majmaʿ al-ʿĀlamī lil-Taqrīb bayna al-Madhāhib al-Islāmiyya, 1422/2001).

Khallāf, ʿAbd al-Wahhāb, *Maṣādir al-Tashrīʿ al-Islāmī fī-mā lā Naṣṣa fīh* (Cairo: Dār al-Kitāb al-ʿArabī, 1955).

Khumaynī (Khomeini), Āyatullāh, *al-Ḥukūma al-Islāmiyya*, ed. Ḥasan Ḥanafī (Cairo: n.p., 1979).

al-Istiṣḥāb ([Iran]: Muʾassasat al-ʿUrūj, 1417/1996).

Khurashī, Muḥammad b. ʿAbd Allāh, *Ḥāshiyat al-Khurashī ʿalā Mukhtaṣar Sīdī Khalīl*, 8 vols. (Beirut: Dār al-Kutub al-ʿIlmiyya, 1417/1997).

Khushanī, Abū ʿAbd Allāh Muḥammad b. Ḥārith, *Uṣūl al-Futyā fī al-Fiqh*, ed. Muḥammad Majdūb (Beirut: al-Muʾassasa al-Waṭaniyya lil-Kitāb, 1985).

Kindī, Muḥammad b. Yūsuf, *Akhbār Quḍāt Miṣr*, ed. R. Guest (Cairo: Muʾassasat Qurṭuba, n.d.).

Kulaynī, Muḥammad b. Yaʿqūb, *al-Kāfī*, ed. Muḥammad Jaʿfarī, 10 vols. (Tehran: Group of Muslim Brothers, 1978).

Kurdarī, Muḥammad b. Shihāb Ibn Bazzāz, *al-Fatāwā al-Bazzāziyya al-Mussamātu bil-Jāmiʿ al-Wajīz*, printed on the margins of *al-Fatāwā al-Hindiyya*, IV and V (repr.; Beirut: Dār Iḥyāʾ al-Turāth al-ʿArabī, 1980).

Laknawī, ʿAbd al-Ḥayy, *al-Fawāʾid al-Bahiyya fī Tarājim al-Ḥanafiyya* (Benares: Maktabat Nadwat al-Maʿārif, 1967).

Al-Maḥkama al-Dustūriyya al-ʿUlyā: al-Aḥkām allatī Aṣdarathā al-Maḥkama, 5 vols. (Qalyūb: Maṭābiʿ al-Ahrām al-Tijāriyya, n.d.).

Majallat al-Aḥkām al-ʿAdliyya, *see* Bāz, Salīm Rustum.

Majlisī, Muḥammad Bāqir, *Biḥār al-Anwār al-Jāmiʿa li-Durar Akhbār al-Aʾimma al-Aṭhār*, 111 vols. (Beirut: Muʾassasat al-Wafāʾ, 1983).

Majmūʿat al-Qawānīn, *see* Ramaḍān.

Mālik b. Anas, *al-Muwaṭṭaʾ* (Beirut: Dār al-Jīl, 1414/1993).

Maqdisī, ʿAbd al-Raḥmān b. Ibrāhīm, *al-ʿUdda: Sharḥ al-ʿUmda fī Fiqh Imām al-Sunna Aḥmad Ibn Ḥanbal al-Shaybānī*, ed. Khālid Muḥammad Muḥarram (Sidon, Beirut: al-Maktaba al-ʿAṣriyya, 1416/1995).

Marghīnānī, Burhān al-Dīn ʿAlī b. Abī Bakr, *al-Hidāya: Sharḥ Bidāyat al-Mubtadī*, 4 vols. (Cairo: Muṣṭafā Bābī al-Ḥalabī, n.d.); trans. I. Khan Nyazee, *Al-Hidāya: The Guidance*, I (Bristol: Amal Press, 2006). Also *see* Hamilton, Charles.

Marzūqī, Abū Yaʿrub and Muḥammad Saʿīd al-Būṭī, *Ishkāliyyat Tajdīd Uṣūl al-Fiqh* (Beirut and Damascus: Dār al-Fikr, 2006).

Mawāq, Muḥammad b. Yūsuf, *al-Tāj wal-Iklīl fī Sharḥ Mukhtaṣar Khalīl*, printed on the margins of Ḥaṭṭāb, *Mawāhib al-Jalīl*.

Māwardī, ʿAlī Muḥammad b. Ḥabīb, *al-Aḥkām al-Sulṭāniyya wal-Wilāyāt al-Dīniyya* (Cairo: Dār al-Fikr, 1983).

al-Ḥāwī al-Kabīr, ed. ʿAlī Muʿawwaḍ and ʿĀdil ʿAbd al-Mawjūd, 18 vols. (Beirut: Dār al-Kutub al-ʿIlmiyya, 1994).

al-Mawsūʿa al-Fiqhiyya, 45 vols. (Kuwait: Dār al-Ṣafwa lil-Ṭibāʿa wal-Nashr, 1990–).

Miṣrī, Ibn Naqīb, *ʿUmdat al-Sālik*, ed. and trans. N. H. M. Keller, *The Reliance of the Traveller* (Evanston, IL: Sunna Books, 1991).

Muftāḥ, Jīlānī, *al-Ḥadāthiyyūn al-ʿArab fī al-ʿUqūd al-Thalātha al-Akhīra wal-Qurʾān al-Karīm* (Damascus: Dār al-Nahḍa, 1427/2006).

Muṣaylihī, Sāmiya ʿAlī, "al-Bighāʾ fī Miṣr fī al-ʿAṣr al-Mamlūkī, 648–923 H/1250–1517AD," *Ḥawliyyāt Ādāb ʿAyn Shams*, 33 (2005): 108–63.

Mūṣilī, ʿAbd Allāh Maḥmūd b. Mawdūd, *al-Ikhtiyār li Taʿlīl al-Mukhtār*, 5 vols. (Cairo: Muṣṭafā Bābī al-Ḥalabī, 1951).

Najdī, ʿAbd-al-Raḥmān b. Muḥammad b. Qāṣim al-ʿĀṣimī, *Ḥāshiyat al-Rawḍ al-Murbiʿ Sharḥ Zād al-Mustaqniʿ*, 7 vols. (Beirut: n.p., 1419/1998–99).

Nasāʾī, Aḥmad b. Shuʿayb, *Kitāb ʿIshrat al-Nisāʾ*, ed. ʿAmr ʿAlī ʿUmar (Beirut: Dār al-Jīl, 1412/1992).

Nawawī, Muḥyī al-Dīn Yaḥyā b. Sharaf, *al-Majmūʿ: Sharḥ al-Muhadhdhab*, 12 vols. (Cairo: Maṭbaʿat al-Taḍāmun, 1344/1925).

Rawḍat al-Ṭālibīn, ed. ʿĀdil ʿAbd al-Mawjūd and ʿAlī Muʿawwaḍ, 8 vols. (Beirut: Dār al-Kutub al-ʿIlmiyya, n.d.).

Niẓām, Shaykh, *see al-Fatāwā al-Hindiyya.*

Qāḍīkhān, Fakhr al-Dīn Ḥasan b. Manṣūr al-Ūzajandī, *Fatāwā Qāḍīkhān*, printed on the margins of *al-Fatāwa al-Hindiyya*, I–III.

Qāḍīzādeh, Shams al-Dīn Aḥmad, *Natāʾij al-Afkār fī Kashf al-Rumūz wal-Asrār*, printed as vols. VIII–X of Ibn al-Humām, *Sharḥ Fatḥ al-Qadīr.*

Qaffāl, Abū Bakr Muḥammad, *see* Shāshī.
Qalqashandī, Aḥmad b. ʿAlī, *Ṣubḥ al-Aʿshā fī Ṣināʿat al-Inshā*, ed. Muḥammad Ḥusayn Shams al-Dīn, 14 vols. (Beirut: Dār al-Kutub al-ʿIlmiyya, 1987).
Qarāfī, Abū al-ʿAbbās Aḥmad b. Idrīs, *al-Furūq, aw Anwār al-Burūq fī Anwāʾ al-Furūq*, ed. Khalīl al-Manṣūr, 4 vols. (Beirut: Dār al-Kutub al-ʿIlmiyya, 1418/1998).
Qārī, Aḥmad b. ʿAbd Allāh, *Majallat al-Aḥkām al-Sharʿiyya ʿalā Madhhab al-Imām Aḥmad Ibn Ḥanbal* (Jeddah: Maṭbūʿāt Tihāma, 1981).
Quṭb, Sayyid, *Maʿālim fī al-Ṭarīq*, trans. as *Milestones* (Cedar Rapids, IA: The Mother Mosque Foundation, 2003).
Ramaḍān, ʿĀrif Afandī, *Majmūʿat al-Qawānīn: Taḥtawī ʿalā Jamīʿ al-Qawānīn al-Maʿmūl bi-Mūjabihā fī Jamīʿ al-Bilād al-ʿArabiyya al-Munsalikha ʿan al-Ḥukūma al-ʿUthmāniyya* (Beirut: al-Maṭbaʿa al-ʿIlmiyya, 1927).
Ramlī, Khayr al-Dīn, *al-Fatāwā al-Khayriyya*, printed on the margins of Ibn ʿĀbidīn, *al-ʿUqūd al-Durriyya*.
Ramlī, Muḥammad Shams al-Dīn b. Shihāb al-Dīn, *Nihāyat al-Muḥtāj ilā Sharḥ al-Minhāj*, 8 vols. (Cairo: Muṣṭafā Bābī al-Ḥalabī, 1357/1938; repr. Beirut: Dār Iḥyāʾ al-Turāth al-ʿArabī, 1939).
Rāzī, Fakhr al-Dīn Muḥammad b. ʿUmar, *al-Maḥṣūl fī ʿIlm al-Uṣūl*, 2 vols. (Beirut: Dār al-Kutub al-ʿIlmiyya, 1408/1988).
Riḍā, Rashīd, *Yusr al-Islām wa-Uṣūl al-Tashrīʿ al-ʿĀmm* (Cairo: Maṭbaʿat Nahḍat Miṣr, 1956).
Saḥnūn b. Saʿīd al-Tanūkhī, *al-Mudawwana al-Kubrā*, ed. Aḥmad ʿAbd al-Salām, 5 vols. (Beirut: Dār al-Kutub al-ʿIlmiyya, 1415/1994).
Sajāwandī, Sirāj-al-Dīn Muḥammad b. Muḥammad, *Al-Sirajiyah or the Mahomedan Law of Inheritance* (Calcutta: The Sanskrit Press, 1861).
Sālim, al-Sayyid ʿAbd al-ʿAzīz, *Tārīkh al-ʿArab fī ʿAṣr al-Jāhiliyya* (Alexandria: Muʾassasat Shabāb al-Jāmiʿa, 1990).
Samarqandī, Abū al-Layth, *Fatāwā al-Nawāzil* (Hyderabad: Maṭbaʿat Shams al-Islām, 1355/1936).
Samarqandī, Abū Naṣr, *Rusūm al-Quḍāt*, ed. M. Jāsim al-Ḥadīthī (Baghdad: Dār al-Ḥurriyya lil-Ṭibāʿa, 1985).
Ṣanʿānī, Abū Bakr ʿAbd al-Razzāq, *al-Muṣannaf*, ed. Ayman Azharī, 12 vols. (Beirut: Dār al-Kutub al-ʿIlmiyya, 2000).
Ṣanʿānī, Aḥmad b. Qāsim al-Yamānī, *al-Tāj al-Mudhahhab li-Aḥkām al-Madhhab*, 4 vols. (Ṣanʿāʾ: Dār al-Ḥikma al-Yamāniyya, 1414/1993).
Sarakhsī, Muḥammad b. Aḥmad Shams al-Dīn, *al-Mabsūṭ*, 31 vols. (Beirut: Dār al-Kutub al-ʿIlmiyya, 1993–94).
al-Uṣūl, ed. Abū al-Wafā al-Afghānī, 2 vols. (Cairo: Dār al-Maʿrifa, 1393/1973).
Shāfiʿī, Muḥammad b. Idrīs, *al-Risāla*, ed. Muḥammad Kīlānī (Cairo: Muṣṭafā Bābī al-Ḥalabī, 1969).
al-Umm, ed. Maḥmūd Maṭarjī, 9 vols. (Beirut: Dār al-Kutub al-ʿIlmiyya, 1413/1993).
Shahīd al-Thānī, Ḥasan b. Zayn al-Dīn, *Maʿālim al-Dīn wa-Malādh al-Mujtahidīn*, ed. Mahdī Muḥaqqiq (Tehran: Shirkat-i Intishārāt ʿIlmī va Farhangī, 1985).
Shaḥrūr, Muḥammad, *al-Kitāb wal-Qurʾān: Qirāʾa Muʿāṣira* (Cairo and Damascus: Sīnā lil-Nashr, 1992).

Naḥwa Uṣūl Jadīda lil-Fiqh al-Islāmī: Fiqh al-Mar'a (Damascus: al-Ahālī lil-Ṭibā'a wal-Nashr wal-Tawzī', 2000).

Shaltūt, "The Koran and Fighting," *see under* Shaltūt, *section 2, below.*

Sha'rānī, 'Abd al-Wahhāb b. Aḥmad b. 'Alī, *al-Mīzān al-Kubrā al-Sha'rāniyya*, ed. 'Abd al-Wārith 'Alī, 2 vols. (Beirut: Dār al-Kutub al-'Ilmiyya, 1418/1998).

Shāshī, Abū 'Alī Aḥmad b. Muḥammad, *Uṣūl al-Shāshī* (Beirut: Dār al-Kitāb al-'Arabī, 1402/1982).

Shāshī, Sayf al-Dīn Abū Bakr Muḥammad al-Qaffāl, *Ḥilyat al-'Ulamā' fī Ma'rifat Madhāhib al-Fuqahā'*, ed. Yāsīn Aḥmad Ibrāhīm Darārka, 8 vols. (Amman: Dār al-Bāz, 1988).

Shāṭibī, Abū Isḥāq Ibrāhīm, *al-Muwāfaqāt fī Uṣūl al-Aḥkām*, ed. Muḥyī al-Dīn 'Abd al-Ḥamīd, 4 vols. (Cairo: Maṭba'at 'Alī Ṣubayḥ, 1970).

Shawkānī, Muḥammad b. 'Alī, *Irshād al-Fuḥūl ilā Taḥqīq al-Ḥaqq min 'Ilm al-Uṣūl* (Surabaya: Sharikat Maktabat Aḥmad b. Nabhān, n.d.).

al-Sayl al-Jarrār al-Mutadaffiq 'alā Ḥadā'iq al-Azhār, ed. Maḥmūd Ibrāhīm Zāyid, 3 vols. (Damascus and Beirut: Dār Ibn Kathīr, 2000).

Shaybānī, Muḥammad b. al-Ḥasan, *al-Aṣl*, 5 vols. (Beirut: 'Ālam al-Kutub, 1990).

al-Shaykh al-Niẓām, *see al-Fatāwā al-Hindiyya.*

Shīrāzī, Abū Isḥāq Ibrāhīm, *al-Luma' fī Uṣūl al-Fiqh*, ed. M. al-Na'sānī (Cairo: Maṭba'at al-Sa'āda, 1326/1908); trans. Eric Chaumont, *Kitab al-Luma' fi Usul al-Fiqh (Le livre des rais illuminant les fondaments de la compréhension de la loi): théorie légale musulmane* (Berkeley, CA: Robbins Collection, 1999).

al-Muhadhdhab fī Fiqh al-Imām al Shāfi'ī wa bi-Dhayl Ṣaḥā'ifihi al-Naẓm al-Musta'dhab fī Sharḥ Gharīb al-Muhadhdhab, ed. Zakariyyā 'Umayrāt, 6 vols. (Beirut: Dār al-Kutub al-'Ilmiyya, 1995).

Sharḥ al-Luma', ed. 'Abd al-Majīd Turkī, 2 vols. (Beirut: Dār al-Gharb al-Islāmī, 1988).

Ṭabaqāt al-Fuqahā', ed. Iḥsān 'Abbās (Beirut: Dār al-Rā'id al-'Arabī, 1970).

Soroush, Abdolkarim, *al-Qabḍ wal-Basṭ fī al-Sharī'a* (Beirut: Dār al-Jadīd, 2002).

Subkī, Tāj al-Dīn, *Ṭabaqāt al-Shāfi'iyya al-Kubrā*, 6 vols. (Cairo: al-Maktaba al-Ḥusayniyya, 1906).

Subkī, Taqī al-Dīn, *Fatāwā al-Subkī*, 2 vols. (repr.; Beirut: Dār al-Ma'rifa, n.d.).

Ṭabarī, Ibn Jarīr, *Tafsīr al-Ṭabarī al-Musammā Jāmi' al-Bayān fī Ta'wīl al-Qur'ān*, 13 vols. (Beirut: Dār al-Kutub al-'Ilmiyya, 1426/2005).

Ṭūfī, Najm al-Dīn Sulaymān, *Sharḥ Mukhtaṣar al-Rawḍa*, ed. 'Abd Allāh al-Turkī, 3 vols. (Beirut: Mu'assasat al-Risāla, 1407/1987).

Ṭūsī, Muḥammad b. al-Ḥasan Shaykh al-Ṭā'ifa, *al-Istibṣār fī-mā Ikhtalafa min al-Akhbār*, 3 vols. (Najaf: Dār al-Kutub al-Islāmiyya, 1376/1957).

al-Khilāf fī al-Fiqh, 2 vols. (Tehran: Maṭba'at Rangīn, 1377 H).

Tahdhīb al-Aḥkām, 10 vols. (Najaf: Dār al-Kutub al-Islāmiyya, 1959–62).

'Uddat al-Uṣūl fī Uṣūl al-Fiqh, ed. 'Alī al-Khurāsānī, 2 vols. (Bombay: Maṭba'at Dat Parsād, 1312–18/1894–1900).

Wakī', Muḥammad b. Khalaf, *Akhbār al-Quḍāt*, 3 vols. (Beirut: 'Ālam al-Kutub, n.d.).

Wansharīsī, Aḥmad b. Yaḥyā, *al-Mi'yār al-Mu'rib wal Jāmi' al-Mughrib 'an Fatāwī 'Ulamā' Ifrīqiyya wal-Andalus wal-Maghrib*, 13 vols. (Beirut: Dār al-Gharb al-Islāmī, 1401/1981).

Wathā'iq al-Maḥākim al-Shar'iyya al-Miṣriyya 'an al-Jāliya al-Maghāribiyya ibāna al-'Aṣr al-'Uthmānī, ed. Abdal Rehim Abdal Rehim, *Documents of the Egyptian Courts Related to the Maghariba*, 3 vols. (Zaghouan: Centre d'Études et de Recherches Ottomanes, Morisques, de Documentation et d'Information, 1994).

Zarkashī, Shams al-Dīn Muḥammad b. 'Abd Allāh al-Miṣrī, *Sharḥ al-Zarkashī 'alā Mukhtaṣar al-Khiraqī*, ed. 'Abd Allāh b. 'Abd al-Raḥmān al-Jabrīn, 7 vols. (Riyadh: Maktabat al-'Ubaykān, 1413/1993).

Zarqā, Muṣṭafā Aḥmad, *al-Madkhal al-Fiqhī al-'Āmm*, 2 vols. (Damascus: Dār al-Qalam, 1998).

Zayla'ī, 'Uthmān b.'Alī, *Tabyīn al-Ḥaqā'iq: Sharḥ Kanz al-Daqā'iq*, 6 vols. (Būlāq: al-Maṭba'a al-Kubrā al-Amīriyya, 1313/1895).

2. SOURCES IN OTHER LANGUAGES

Aaron, Richard Ithamar, *A Theory of Universals*, 2nd edn (Oxford: Clarendon Press, 1967).

Abdal Rehim, Abdal Rehim, *see under Wathā'iq al-Maḥākim al-Shar'iyya, above.*

Abisaab, Rula Jurdi, *Converting Persia: Religion and Power in the Safavid Empire* (London: I. B. Tauris, 2004).

"The Ulama of Jabal 'Amil in Ṣafavid Iran, 1501–1736: Marginality, Migration and Social Change," *Iranian Studies*, 27 (1994): 103–22.

Abou El Fadl, Khaled, *Rebellion and Violence in Islamic Law* (Cambridge: Cambridge University Press, 2001).

Abou-El-Haj, Rifa'at, *Formation of the Modern State* (Albany: State University of New York Press, 1991).

Abou Ramadan, Moussa, "Divorce Reform in the Sharī'a Court of Appeals in Israel (1992–2003)," *Islamic Law and Society*, 13, 2 (2006): 242–74.

"Islamic Legal Reform: Sharī'a Court of Appeals and Maintenance for Muslim Wives in Israel," *Hawwa*, 4, 1 (2006): 29–75.

Abrams, Philip, "Notes on the Difficulty of Studying the State," *Journal of Historical Sociology*, 1, 1 (1988): 58–89.

Abu-Lughod, Janet L., *Cairo: 1001 Years of the City Victorious* (Princeton, NJ: Princeton University Press, 1971).

Abu-Lughod, Lila, ed., *Remaking Women: Feminism and Modernity in the Middle East* (Princeton, NJ: Princeton University Press, 1998).

"The Romance of Resistance: Tracing Transformations of Power through Bedouin Women," *American Ethnologist*, 17 (1990): 41–55.

Veiled Sentiments: Honor and Poetry in a Bedouin Society (Berkeley: University of California Press, 1986).

Abu-Manneh, Butrus, "The Islamic Roots of the Gülhane Rescript," *Die Welt des Islams*, 34 (1994): 173–203.

Abun-Nasr, Jamil M., *A History of the Maghrib* (Cambridge and New York: Cambridge University Press, 1975).

Adams, Charles, "Mawdudi and the Islamic State," in John L. Esposito, ed., *Voices of Resurgent Islam* (New York: Oxford University Press, 1983), 99–133.

Agmon, Iris, "Social Biography of a Late Ottoman Shari'a Judge," *New Perspectives on Turkey*, 30 (2004): 83–113.

Ahmad, Ahmad Atif, *Structural Interrelations of Theory and Practice in Islamic Law: A Study of Six Works of Medieval Islamic Jurisprudence* (Leiden: Brill, 2006).

Ahmad, Feroz, *The Young Turks: The Committee of Union and Progress in Turkish Politics, 1908–1914* (Oxford: Clarendon Press, 1969).

Aijmer, G. and J. Abbink, eds., *Meanings of Violence: A Cross Cultural Perspective* (Oxford: Berg, 2000).

Akarlı, Engin Deniz, "Gedik: A Bundle of Rights and Obligations for Istanbul Artisans and Traders, 1750–1840," in Alain Pottage and Martha Mundy, eds., *Law, Anthropology, and the Constitution of the Social: Making Persons and Things* (Cambridge: Cambridge University Press, 2004), 166–200.

"Law in the Marketplace: Istanbul, 1730–1840," in M. Masud *et al.*, eds., *Dispensing Justice in Islam: Qadis and their Judgments* (Leiden: Brill, 2006), 245–70.

Akiba, Jun, "From Kadı to Naib: Reorganization of the Ottoman Sharia Judiciary in the Tanzimat Period," in Colin Imber and K. Kiyotaki, eds., *Frontiers of Ottoman Studies: State, Province, and the West*, I (London: I. B. Tauris, 2005), 43–60.

"A New School for Qadis: Education of the Shari'a Judges in the Late Ottoman Empire," *Turcica*, 35 (2003): 125–63.

Ali, Shaheen Sardar, "Sigh of the Oppressed? 'Islamisation' of Laws in Pakistan under Muttahida Majlis-e-Amal: The Case of the North West Frontier Province," *Yearbook of Islamic and Middle Eastern Law 2003–04*, vol. X (Leiden: Brill, 2006): 107–24.

Alon, Y., "The Tribal System in the Face of the State-Formation Process: Mandatory Transjordan, 1921–46," *International Journal of Middle East Studies*, 37 (2005): 213–40.

Althusser, Louis, *Essays on Ideology* (London: Verso, 1984).

Anderson, Benedict, *Imagined Communities: Reflections on the Origin and Spread of Nationalism*, 2nd edn (London and New York: Verso, 2006).

Anderson, J. N. D., "Colonial Law in Tropical Africa: The Conflict between English, Islamic and Customary Law," *Indiana Law Journal*, 35, 4 (1960): 433–42.

"Eclipse of the Patriarchal Family in Contemporary Islamic Law," in J. N. D. Anderson, ed., *Family Law in Asia and Africa* (London: George Allen and Unwin, 1968), 221–34.

"Law Reform in Egypt: 1850–1950," in P. M. Holt, ed., *Political and Social Change in Modern Egypt* (London: Oxford University Press, 1968), 209–30.

Law Reform in the Muslim World (London: Athelone Press, 1976).

"The Sharī'a and Civil Law: The Debt Owed by the New Civil Codes of Egypt and Syria to the Sharī'a," *The Islamic Quarterly*, 1 (1954): 29–46.

Anderson, Michael R., "Legal Scholarship and the Politics of Islam in British India," in R. S. Khare, ed., *Perspectives on Islamic Law, Justice, and Society* (Lanham, MD: Rowman & Littlefield, 1999), 65–91.

An-Na'im, Abdullahi, *Islamic Family Law in a Changing World* (London: Zed Books, 2002).

Ansari, Zafar Ishaq, "Islamic Juristic Terminology before Šāfiʿī," *Arabica*, 19 (1972): 255–300.

Ansari-Pour, M. A., "Iran," *Yearbook of Islamic and Middle Eastern Law 2000–01*, VII (The Hague: Kluwer Law International, 2002): 349–63.

"Iran," *Yearbook of Islamic and Middle Eastern Law 2002–03*, IX (Leiden: Brill, 2004): 341–49.

"Iran," *Yearbook of Islamic and Middle Eastern Law 2003–04*, X (Leiden: Brill, 2006): 267–75.

"Iran," *Yearbook of Islamic and Middle Eastern Law 2004–05*, XI (Leiden: Brill, 2007): 321–31.

"Iran," *Yearbook of Islamic and Middle Eastern Law 2005–06*, XII (Leiden: Brill, 2008): 415–29.

Antoun, Richard T., "Fundamentalism, Bureaucracy, and the State's Co-optation of Religion: A Jordanian Case Study," *International Journal of Middle East Studies*, 38 (2006): 369–93.

"The Islamic Court, the Islamic Judge, and the Accommodation of Traditions: A Jordanian Case Study," *International Journal of Middle East Studies*, 12 (1980): 455–67.

Arjomand, S. A., "Islamic Constitutionalism," *Annual Review of Law and Social Science*, 3 (2007): 115–40.

Asad, Talal, "Conscripts of Western Civilization," in Christine W. Gailey, ed., *Civilization in Crisis: Anthropological Perspectives* (Gainsville: University Press of Florida, 1992), 333–51.

Formations of the Secular: Christianity, Islam, Modernity (Stanford, CA: Stanford University Press, 2003).

Ayalon, David, "The Great Yāsa of Chingiz Khan," in David Ayalon, *Outsiders in the Lands of Islam: Mamluks, Mongols, and Eunuchs* (London: Variorum Reprints, 1988): ch. IV.

Baer, Gabriel, "The Administrative, Economic and Social Functions of Turkish Guilds," *International Journal of Middle East Studies*, 1, 1 (1970): 28–50.

"Guilds in Middle Eastern History," in M. A. Cook, ed., *Studies in the Economic History of the Middle East* (London: Oxford University Press, 1979), 11–30.

"Tanzimat in Egypt: The Penal Code," *Bulletin of the School of Oriental and African Studies*, 26, 1 (1963): 29–49.

"Waqf Reform in Egypt," *St. Anthony's Papers: Middle Eastern Affairs* (London: Chatto & Windus, 1958): 61–76.

Ball, John, *Indonesian Legal History, 1602–1848* (Sydney: Oughtershaw Press, 1982).

Ball, Warwick, *Rome in the East: The Transformation of an Empire* (London and New York: Routledge, 2000).

Barker-Benfield, B., "The Spermatic Economy," in M. Gordon, ed., *The American Family in Social-Historical Perspective* (New York: St. Martin's Press, 1973), 377–78.

Barnes, J. R., *An Introduction to the Religious Foundations in the Ottoman Empire* (Leiden: E. J. Brill, 1986).

Bassiouni, Cherif, "Evolving Approaches to Jihad: From Self-Defense to Revolutionary and Regime-Change Political Violence," *Chicago Journal of International Law*, 8, 1 (2007): 119–46.

Bauman, Zygmunt, *Liquid Modernity* (Cambridge: Polity Press, 2000).
Modernity and the Holocaust (Ithaca, NY: Cornell University Press, 1989).
Society under Siege (Cambridge: Polity Press, 2002).
Bayitch, S. A., "Codification in Modern Times," in A. N. Yiannopoulos, ed., *Civil Law in the Modern World* (Kingsport: Louisiana State University Press, 1965), 161–91.
Beeston, A. F. L., "The Religions of Pre-Islamic Yemen," in J. Chelhod, ed., *L'Arabie du Sud et Civilisation*, 3 vols. (Paris: Editions G.–P. Maisonneuve et Larose, 1984), I, 259–69.
Benton, Lauren A., "Colonial Law and Cultural Difference: Jurisdictional Politics and the Formation of the Colonial State," *Comparative Studies in Society and History*, 41 (2000): 563–88.
Law and Colonial Cultures: Legal Regimes in World History, 1400–1900 (Cambridge: Cambridge University Press, 2002).
Berkey, Jonathan Porter, *The Transmission of Knowledge in Medieval Cairo: A Social History of Islamic Education* (Princeton, NJ: Princeton University Press, 1992).
Berman, Harold and Charles Reid, "Max Weber as Legal Historian," in Stephen Turner, ed., *The Cambridge Companion to Weber* (New York: Cambridge University Press, 2000), 223–39.
Bidwell, Robin, *Morocco under Colonial Rule: French Administration of Tribal Areas 1912–56* (London: Frank Cass, 1973).
Black's Law Dictionary, 5th edn (St Paul, MN: West Publishing Co., 1979).
Bourdieu, Pierre, "Rethinking the State: Genesis and Structure of the Bureaucratic Field," in George Steinmetz, ed., *State/Culture: State Formation after the Cultural Turn* (Ithaca, NY: Cornell University Press, 1999), 53–75.
Bowen, J. "Qurʾān, Justice, Gender: Internal Debates in Indonesian Islamic Jurisprudence," *History of Religion*, 38, 1 (1998): 52–78.
Bravmann, M. M., *The Spiritual Background of Early Islam* (Leiden: E. J. Brill, 1972).
Brinton, Jasper Yeates, *The Mixed Courts of Egypt* (New Haven: Yale University Press, 1930).
Brock, S. P., "Syriac Views of Emergent Islam," in G. H. A. Juynboll, ed., *Studies on the First Century of Islamic Society* (Carbondale: Southern Illinois University Press, 1982), 9–21.
Browers, M., "Islam and Political *Sinn*: The Hermeneutics of Contemporary Islamic Reformists," in M. Browers and Charles Kurzman, eds., *An Islamic Reformation?* (Lanham, MD: Lexington Books, 2004), 54–78.
Brown, Nathan J., *Rule of Law in the Arab World: Courts in Egypt and the Gulf* (Cambridge: Cambridge University Press, 1997).
"Shariʿa and State in the Modern Muslim Middle East," *International Journal of Middle East Studies*, 29 (1997): 359–76.
Bulliet, Richard W., "The Shaikh al-Islam and the Evolution of Islamic Society," *Studia Islamica*, 35 (1972): 53–67.
Buskens, L., "Islamic Commentaries and French Codes: The Confrontation and Accommodation of Two Forms of Textualization of Family Law in Morocco," in H. Driessen, ed., *The Politics of Ethnographic Reading and*

Writing: Confrontations of Western and Indigenous Views (Saarbrücken: Breitenbach, 1993), 65–100.

Calder, Norman, "Doubt and Prerogative," *Studia Islamica*, 70 (1989): 57–78.

"Law," in Seyyed Hossein Nasr and O. Leaman, eds., *History of Islamic Philosophy*, vol. I (London and New York: Routledge, 1996), 979–98.

"Legitimacy and Accommodation in Safavid Iran: The Juristic Theory of Muḥammad Bāqir al-Sabzavārī (d.1090/1679)," *Iran*, 25 (1987): 91–105.

Cammack, Mark, "Islam and Nationalism in Indonesia: Forging an Indonesian Madhhab," in Peri Bearman *et al.*, eds., *The Islamic School of Law* (Cambridge, MA: Islamic Legal Studies Program, 2005), 175–90.

"Islamic Inheritance Law in Indonesia: The Influence of Hazairin's Theory of Bilateral Inheritance," *Australian Journal of Asian Law*, 4, 1 (2002): 295–315.

Candraningrum, Dewi, "Perda Sharia and the Indonesian Women's Critical Perspective," available at www.asienhaus.de/public/archiv/Paper PERDASHARIA.pdf.

Carroll, Lucy, "Orphaned Grandchildren in Islamic Law of Succession: Reform and Islamization in Pakistan," *Islamic Law and Society*, 5, 3 (1998): 409–47.

"The Pakistan Federal Shariat Court, Section 4 of the Muslim Family Laws Ordinance, and the Orphaned Grandchild," *Islamic Law and Society*, 9, 1 (2002): 70–82.

Chamberlain, Michael, *Knowledge and Social Practice in Medieval Damascus, 1190–1350* (Cambridge: Cambridge University Press, 1994).

Chardin, Jean, *Voyages de Monsieur le Chevalier Chardin en Perse*, III (Amsterdam: Jean Louis de Lorme, 1709).

Chatterjee, Partha, "Colonialism, Nationalism, and Colonized Women: The Contest in India," *American Ethnologist*, 16, 4 (1989): 622–33.

The Nation and its Fragments (Princeton, NY: Princeton University Press, 1993).

Chevallier, Dominique, "Western Development and Eastern Crisis in the Mid-Nineteenth Century: Syria Confronted with the European Economy," in William Polk and R. Chambers, eds., *Beginnings of Modernization in the Middle East* (Chicago: University of Chicago Press, 1960), 205–22.

Christelow, Allan, *Muslim Law Courts and the French Colonial State in Algeria* (Princeton, NJ: Princeton University Press, 1985).

"The Transformation of the Muslim Court System in Colonial Algeria: Reflections on the Concept of Autonomy," in A. Al-Azmeh, ed., *Islamic Law: Social and Historical Contexts* (London and New York: Routledge, 1988), 215–30.

Christmann, A., "Islamic Scholar and Religious Leader: Shaikh Muhammad Sa'id Ramadan al-Buti," in John Cooper *et al.*, eds., *Islam and Modernity: Muslim Intellectuals Respond* (London: I. B. Tauris, 2000), 57–81.

The Civil Code of Iran, trans. M. A. R. Taleghany (Littletom, CO: Rothman and Co., 1995).

Çizakça, Murat, *History of Philanthropic Foundations: The History of the Islamic World from the Seventh Century to the Present* (Istanbul: Bogaziçi University Press, 2000).

Cleveland, William L., *A History of the Modern Middle East* (Boulder, CO: Westview Press, 2004).

Cohen, Amnon, *A World Within: Jewish Life as Reflected in Muslim Court Documents from the Sijill of Jerusalem (XVIth Century)*, 2 vols. (Philadelphia: University of Pennsylvania Press, 1994).

Cohen H. J., "The Economic Background and Secular Occupations of Muslim Jurisprudents and Traditionists in the Classical Period of Islam (Until the Middle of the Eleventh Century)," *Journal of the Economic and Social History of the Orient* (January 1970): 16–61.

Cohn, Bernard, *Colonialism and its Forms of Knowledge: The British in India* (Princeton, NJ: Princeton University Press, 1996).

Cole, Juan Ricardo, *Sacred Space and Holy War: The Politics, Culture, and History of Shi'ite Islam* (London: I. B. Tauris, 2002).

Collins, Daniel P., "Islamization of Pakistani Law: A Historical Perspective," *Stanford Journal of International Law*, 24 (1987–88): 511–84.

Cooper, John, "The Limits of the Sacred: The Epistemology of 'Abd al-Karim Soroush," in John Cooper *et al.*, eds., *Islam and Modernity: Muslim Intellectuals Respond* (London: I. B. Tauris, 2000), 38–56.

Corrigan, Philip and Derek Sayer, *The Great Arch: English State Formation as Cultural Revolution* (Oxford: Basil Blackwell, 1985).

Coss, Peter, *The Moral World of the Law* (Cambridge: Cambridge University Press, 2000).

Coulson, Noel James, *A History of Islamic Law* (Edinburgh: Edinburgh University Press, 1964).

Succession in the Muslim Family (Cambridge: Cambridge University Press, 1971).

Crecelius, Daniel, "Incidences of Waqf Cases in Three Cairo Courts: 1640–1802," *Journal of the Economic and Social History of the Orient*, 29 (1986): 176–89.

Crone, P., *Pre-Industrial Societies* (Oxford: Blackwell, 1989).

Crone, Patricia and M. Cook, *Hagarism: The Making of the Muslim World* (Cambridge: Cambridge University Press, 1977).

Crone, Patricia and M. Hinds, *God's Caliph: Religious Authority in the First Centuries of Islam* (Cambridge: Cambridge University Press, 1986).

Dahlén, Ashk P., *Islamic Law, Epistemology and Modernity* (New York and London: Routledge, 2003).

Davies, Wendy, "Local Participation and Legal Ritual in Early Medieval Law Courts," in Peter Coss, ed., *The Moral World of the Law* (Cambridge: Cambridge University Press, 2000), 48–61.

Deguilhem, Randi, "Consciousness of Self: The Muslim Woman as Creator and Manager of *Waqf* Foundations in Late Ottoman Damascus," in Amira Sonbol, ed., *Beyond the Exotic: Women's Histories in Islamic Societies* (Syracuse, NY: Syracuse University Press, 2005), 102–15.

"Government Centralization of Waqf Administration and its Opposition: The Syrian Example," *British Society for Middle East Studies (BRISMES)* (July 1991): 223–30.

Dirks, Nicholas B., *The Scandal of Empire: India and the Creation of Imperial Britain* (Cambridge, MA: Belknap Press, 2006).

Donaldson, Laura E. and Pui-lan Kwok, *Postcolonialism, Feminism, and Religious Discourse* (New York and London: Routledge, 2002).

Donner, Fred, "The Role of Nomads in the Near East in Late Antiquity (400–800 C.E.)," in F. M. Clover and R. S. Humphreys, eds., *Tradition and Innovation in Late Antiquity* (Madison: University of Wisconsin Press, 1989), 73–88.

Dreyfus, Hubert and Paul Rabinow, *Michel Foucault: Beyond Structuralism and Hermeneutics* (Chicago: University of Chicago Press, 1983).

Driessen, Henk, *The Politics of Ethnographic Reading and Writing* (Saarbrüken and Fort Lauderdale: Verlag Breitenbach Publishers, 1993).

Dumont, Paul, "The Power of Islam in Turkey," in Olivier Carré, ed., *Islam and the State in the World Today* (New Delhi: Manohar, 1987), 76–94.

During Caspers, Elisabeth C. L., "Further Evidence for 'Central Asian' Materials from the Arabian Gulf," *Journal of the Economic and Social History of the Orient*, 37 (1994): 33–53.

Dussaud, René, *La Pénétration des Arabes en Syrie avant l'Islam* (Paris: Paul Geuthner, 1955).

Dutt, Palme R., "The Exploitation of India: A Marxist View," in M. D. Lewis, ed., *The British in India: Imperialism or Trusteeship?* (Boston: D. C. Heath and Co., 1962), 41–52.

Edens, C. and Garth Bawden, "History of Taymāʾ and Hejazi Trade during the First Millennium B.C.," *Journal of the Economic and Social History of the Orient*, 32 (1989): 48–97.

Eickelman, Dale F., "Islamic Liberalism Strikes Back," *Middle East Studies Association Bulletin*, 27 (1993): 163–68.

"Islamic Religious Commentary and Lesson Circles: Is There a Copernican Revolution," in Glenn W. Most, ed., *Commentaries – Kommentare*, Aporemata: Kritische Studien zur Philologiegeschechte 4 (Göttingen: Vandenhoeck and Ruprecht, 1999), 121–46.

Knowledge and Power in Morocco: The Education of a Twentieth-Century Notable (Princeton, NJ: Princeton University Press, 1985).

Elberling, F., *A Treatise on Inheritance, Gift, Will, Sale, and Marriage* (Serampore: Serampore Press, 1844).

Eliash, Joseph, "The Ithnā ʿAsharī-Shīʿī Juristic Theory of Political and Legal Authority," *Studia Islamica*, 29 (1969): 17–30.

Encyclopaedia of Islam, 12 vols., 2nd edn (Leiden: E. J. Brill, 1960–2004).

Ephrat, Daphna, *Learned Society in a Period of Transition: The Sunni Ulama of Eleventh-Century Baghdad* (Albany: State University of New York Press, 2000).

Euben, Roxanne L., *Enemy in the Mirror: Islamic Fundamentalism and the Limits of Modern Rationality* (Princeton, NJ: Princeton University Press, 1999).

Fadel, Mohammad, "The Social Logic of *Taqlīd* and the Rise of the *Mukhtaṣar*," *Islamic Law and Society*, 3, 2 (1996): 193–233.

"Two Women, One Man: Knowledge, Power, and Gender in Medieval Sunni Legal Thought," *International Journal of Middle East Studies*, 29, 2 (1997): 185–204.

Fahmy, Khalid, "The Police and the People in Nineteenth-Century Egypt," *Die Welt des Islams*, 39 (1999): 1–38.

Fasseur, C., "Colonial Dilemma: Van Vollenhoven and the Struggle between Adat Law and Western Law in Indonesia," in W. J. Mommsen and J. A. De

Moor, eds., *European Expansion and Law: The Encounter of European and Indigenous Law in 19th- and 20th-Century Africa and Asia* (Oxford: Berg, 1992), 240–42.

Fatemi, S., "Autonomy and Equal Rights to Divorce with Specific Reference to Shii Fiqh and the Iranian Legal System," *Islam and Christian–Muslim Relations*, 17, 3 (July 2006): 281–94.

Fay, Mary Ann, "Women and Waqf: Toward a Reconsideration of Women's Place in the Mamluk Household," *International Journal of Middle East Studies*, 29, 1 (1997): 33–51.

Federspiel, Howard, *Sultans, Shamans, and Saints: Islam and Muslims in Southeast Asia* (Honolulu: University of Hawai'i Press, 2007).

Feener, Michael, "Indonesian Movements for the Creation of a 'National Madhhab'," *Islamic Law and Society*, 9, 1 (2002): 83–115.

Muslim Legal Thought in Modern Indonesia (Cambridge: Cambridge University Press, 2007).

Fierro, Maribel, "Ill-Treated Women Seeking Divorce: The Qur'ānic Two Arbiters and Judicial Practice among the Malikis in Al-Andalus and North Africa," in M. Masud *et al.*, eds., *Dispensing Justice in Islam: Qadis and their Judgments* (Leiden: Brill, 2006), 323–47.

Firestone, R., *Jihād: The Origins of Holy War in Islam* (New York: Oxford University Press, 1999).

Fisch, Jorg, "Law as a Means and as an End: Some Remarks on the Function of European and Non-European Law in the Process of European Expansion," in W. J. Mommsen and J. A. De Moor, eds., *European Expansion and Law: The Encounter of European and Indigenous Law in 19th- and 20th-Century Africa and Asia* (Oxford: Berg, 1992), 15–38.

Floor, Willem M., "Change and Development in the Judicial System of Qajar Iran (1800–1925)," in Edmond Bosworth and Carole Hillenbrand, eds., *Qajar Iran: Political, Social, and Cultural Change 1800–1925* (Costa Mesa, CA: Mazda, 1983), 113–47.

Flynn, Thomas, "Foucault's Mapping of History," in G. Gutting, ed., *The Cambridge Companion to Foucault* (Cambridge: Cambridge University Press, 1994), 28–46.

Fortna, Benjamin C., *Imperial Classroom: Islam, the State, and Education in the Late Ottoman Empire* (Oxford: Oxford University Press, 2002).

Foucault, Michel, *The Archaeology of Knowledge*, trans. A. M. Sheridan Smith (London: Routledge, 1969).

Discipline and Punish: The Birth of the Prison, trans. Alan Sheridan, 2nd edn (New York: Vintage, 1995).

Ethics, Subjectivity and Truth, ed. P. Rabinow, trans. Robert Hurley *et al.* (New York: The New Press, 1994).

The Foucault Reader, ed. Paul Rabinow (New York: Pantheon Books, 1984).

The History of Sexuality, I, trans. Robert Hurley (London and New York: Pantheon Books, 1978).

Les mots et les choses ([Paris]: Gallimard, 1966).

Power: Essential Works of Foucault, 1954–1984, ed. James Faubion, trans. Robert Hurley *et al.* (New York: The New Press, 1973).

Power/Knowledge: Selected Interviews and Other Writings, 1972–1977, ed. Colin Gordon, trans. Colin Gordon *et al.* (New York: Pantheon Books, 1980).

"*Society Must Be Defended*" (New York: Picador, 1997).

"Truth and Juridical Forms," in Foucault, *Power: Essential Works of Foucault*, 1–89.

Fuchs, Barbara, *Mimesis and Empire: The New World, Islam, and European Identity* (Cambridge: Cambridge University Press, 2001).

Gerber, Haim, "Social and Economic Position of Women in an Ottoman City, Bursa, 1600–1700," *International Journal of Middle East Studies*, 12 (1980): 231–44.

State, Society, and Law in Islam: Ottoman Law in Comparative Perspective (Albany: State University of New York Press, 1994).

Gerth, H. H. and C. W. Mills, ed. and trans., *From Max Weber: Essays in Sociology* (New York: Oxford University Press, 1958).

Ghazaleh, Pascale, "The Guilds: Between Tradition and Modernity," in N. Hanna, ed., *The State and its Servants: Administration of Egypt from Ottoman Times to the Present* (Cairo: The American University in Cairo Press, 1995), 60–74.

Giddens, Anthony, *The Consequences of Modernity* (Stanford, CA: Stanford University Press, 1990).

Gleave, Robert, *Akhbārī Shīʿī Uṣūl al-Fiqh and the Juristic Theory of Yūsuf b. Aḥmad al-Baḥrānī* (London: I. B. Tauris, 1997).

Inevitable Doubt: Two Theories of Shīʿī Jurisprudence (Boston: Brill, 2000).

Glendon, Mary Ann, "Power and Authority in the Family: New Legal Patterns as Reflections of Changing Ideologies," *American Journal of Comparative Law*, 23, 1 (1975): 1–33.

Glenn, Patrick H., *Legal Traditions of the World: Sustainable Diversity in Law* (Oxford: Oxford University Press, 2000).

Glete, Jan, *Warfare at Sea, 1500–1650* (London: Routledge, 2000).

Göçek, Fatma and M. D. Baer, "Social Boundaries of Ottoman Women's Experience in Eighteenth-Century Galata Court Records," in M. C. Zilfi, ed., *Women in the Ottoman Empire: Middle Eastern Modern Women in the Early Modern Era* (Leiden and New York: Brill, 1997), 48–65.

Göçek, Fatma and M. Hanioglu, "Western Knowledge, Imperial Control, and the Use of Statistics in the Ottoman Empire," *Center for Research on Social Organization Working Paper Series* (1993): 105–16.

Goitein, S. D., "The Birth-Hour of Muslim Law," *Muslim World*, 50, 1 (1960): 23–29.

A Mediterranean Society: The Jewish Communities of the Arab World as Portrayed in the Documents of the Cairo Geniza, 3 vols. (Berkeley: University of California Press, 1978).

Studies in Islamic History and Institutions (Leiden: E. J. Brill, 1966).

"A Turning Point in the History of the Islamic State," *Islamic Culture*, 23 (1949): 120–35.

Goody, Jack, *The East in the West* (Cambridge: Cambridge University Press, 1996).

Gradeva, Rissitsa, "On Judicial Hierarchy in the Ottoman Empire: The Case of Sofia from the Seventeenth to the Beginning of the Eighteenth Century," in

M. Masud *et al.*, eds., *Dispensing Justice in Islam: Qadis and their Judgments* (Leiden: Brill, 2006), 271–98.

Guenther, Allan M., "Syed Mahmood and the Transformation of Muslim Law in British India" (PhD dissertation: McGill University, 2004).

Guindy, Adel, "Family Status Issues among Egypt's Copts: A Brief Overview," *Middle East Review of International Affairs*, 11, 3 (2007). Available at http://meria.idc.ac.il/journal/2007/issue3/jv11no3a1.html. Accessed November 15, 2007.

Gulliver, P. H., "Dispute Settlement without Courts: The Ndendeuli of Southern Tanzania," in Laura Nader, ed., *Law in Culture and Society* (Chicago: Aldine, 1969), 24–68.

"Process and Decision," in P. H. Gulliver, ed., *Cross-Examinations: Essays in Memory of Max Gluckman* (Leiden: E. J. Brill, 1978), 29–52.

Gutting, Gary, "Foucault and the History of Madness," in G. Gutting, ed., *The Cambridge Companion to Foucault* (Cambridge: Cambridge University Press, 1994), 47–70.

Haeri, Shahla, *Law of Desire: Temporary Marriage in Shi'i Iran* (Syracuse, NY: Syracuse University Press, 1989).

Hakim, Tawfik, *Maze of Justice: Diary of a Country Prosecutor*, trans. A. Eban (Austin: University of Texas Press, 1989).

Hallaq, Wael, "The Authenticity of Prophetic Ḥadīth: A Pseudo-Problem," *Studia Islamica*, 89 (1999): 75–90.

Authority, Continuity and Change in Islamic Law (Cambridge: Cambridge University Press, 2001).

"Can the Shari'a Be Restored?" in Yvonne Y. Haddad and Barbara F. Stowasser, eds., *Islamic Law and the Challenges of Modernity* (Walnut Creek, CA: Altamira Press, 2004), 21–53.

"Fashioning the Moral Subject: Sharī'a's Technologies of the Self" (Ms.), 35 pages.

"From *Fatwās* to *Furū'*: Growth and Change in Islamic Substantive Law," *Islamic Law and Society*, 1, 1 (1994): 29–65.

A History of Islamic Legal Theories (Cambridge: Cambridge University Press, 1997).

Ibn Taymiyya against the Greek Logicians (Oxford: Clarendon Press, 1993).

"Ibn Taymiyya on the Existence of God," *Acta Orientalia*, 52 (1991): 49–69.

"*Ifta'* and *Ijtihad* in Sunni Legal Theory: A Developmental Account," in Muhammad Khalid Masud *et al.*, eds., *Islamic Legal Interpretation: Muftis and their Fatwas* (Cambridge, MA: Harvard University Press, 1996), 33–43.

"Logic, Formal Arguments and Formalization of Arguments in Sunnī Jurisprudence," *Arabica*, 37 (1990): 315–58. Reproduced in Hallaq, *Law and Legal Theory in Classical and Medieval Islam* (Aldershot: Variorum, 1995), ch. III.

"Model *Shurūṭ* Works and the Dialectic of Doctrine and Practice," *Islamic Law and Society*, 2, 2 (1995): 109–34.

"Non-Analogical Arguments in Sunni Juridical *Qiyās*," *Arabica*, 36, 3 (1989): 286–306. Reproduced in Hallaq, *Law and Legal Theory in Classical and Medieval Islam* (Aldershot: Variorum, 1995), ch. II.

"Notes on the Term *Qarīna* in Islamic Legal Discourse," *Journal of the American Oriental Society*, 108, 3 (1988): 475–80. Reproduced in Hallaq, *Law and Legal Theory in Classical and Medieval Islam* (Aldershot: Variorum, 1995), ch. X.

"On the Authoritativeness of Sunni Consensus," *International Journal of Middle East Studies*, 18 (1986): 427–54. Reproduced in Hallaq, *Law and Legal Theory in Classical and Medieval Islam* (Aldershot: Variorum, 1995), ch. VIII.

"On the Origins of the Controversy about the Existence of Mujtahids and the Gate of Ijtihad," *Studia Islamica*, 63 (1986): 129–41. Reproduced in Hallaq, *Law and Legal Theory in Classical and Medieval Islam* (Aldershot: Variorum, 1995), ch. VI.

"On Inductive Corroboration, Probability and Certainty in Sunnī Legal Thought," in N. Heer, ed., *Islamic Law and Jurisprudence* (Seattle: University of Washington Press, 1990), 3–31. Reproduced in Hallaq, *Law and Legal Theory in Classical and Medieval Islam* (Aldershot: Variorum, 1995), ch. IV.

The Origins and Evolution of Islamic Law, in W. Hallaq, series ed., Themes in Islamic Law, no. 1 (Cambridge: Cambridge University Press, 2004).

"A Prelude to Ottoman Reform: Ibn ʿĀbidīn on Custom and Legal Change," in I. Gershoni *et al.*, eds., *Histories of the Modern Middle East: New Directions* (Boulder, CO: Lynne Rienner, 2002), 37–61.

"Qāḍīs Communicating: Legal Change and the Law of Documentary Evidence," *al-Qanṭara*, 20 (1999): 437–66.

"The *Qāḍī*'s *Dīwān* (*Sijill*) before the Ottomans," *Bulletin of the School of Oriental and African Studies*, 61, 3 (1998): 415–36.

"The Quest for Origins or Doctrine? Islamic Legal Studies as Colonialist Discourse," *UCLA Journal of Islamic and Near Eastern Law*, 2, 1 (2002): 1–31.

Review of *The Search for God's Law: Islamic Jurisprudence in the Writings of Sayf al-Din al-Amidi*, by Bernard Weiss, in *International Journal of Middle East Studies*, 26, 1 (1994): 152–54.

"A Tenth–Eleventh Century Treatise on Juridical Dialectic," *Muslim World*, 77, 2–3 (1987): 198–227.

"*Uṣūl al-Fiqh*: Beyond Tradition," *Journal of Islamic Studies*, 3 (1992): 172–202. Reproduced in Hallaq, *Law and Legal Theory in Classical and Medieval Islam* (Aldershot: Variorum, 1995), ch. XII.

"Was the Gate of Ijtihad Closed?" *International Journal of Middle East Studies*, 16 (1984): 3–41. Reproduced in Hallaq, *Law and Legal Theory in Classical and Medieval Islam* (Aldershot: Variorum, 1995), ch. V.

"Was al-Shafiʿi the Master Architect of Islamic Jurisprudence?" *International Journal of Middle East Studies*, 25 (1993): 587–605.

"What is Sharīʿa?" in *Yearbook of Islamic and Middle Eastern Law, 2005–2006*, XII (Leiden: Brill, 2007), 151–80.

Halm, Heinz, *Shiʿa Islam: From Religion to Revolution*, trans. Allison Brown (Princeton, NJ: Markus Wiener, 1997).

Halpern, Orly, "Jordan's New Female Workforce," *Christian Science Monitor*, December 17, 2004, available at: www.csmonitor.com/2004/1217/ p07s01-wome.html. Last accessed November 21, 2007.

Hamed, Raouf Abbas, "The *Siyasatname* and the Institutionalization of Central Administration under Muhammad ʿAli," in Nelly Hanna, ed., *The State and its Servants: Administration in Egypt from Ottoman Times to the Present* (Cairo: The American University in Cairo Press, 1995), 75–86.

Hamilton, Charles, *Hedaya or Guide: A Commentary on the Mussulman Laws* (Lahore: New Books Company, 1957).

Hanna, Nelly, "The Administration of Courts in Ottoman Cairo," in Nelly Hanna, ed., *The State and its Servants: Administration of Egypt from Ottoman Times to the Present* (Cairo: The American University in Cairo Press, 1995), 44–59.

Construction Work in Ottoman Cairo (1517–1798) (Cairo: Institut Français d'Archéologie Orientale, 1984).

Making Big Money in 1600: The Life and Times of Isma'il Abu Taqiyya, Egyptian Merchant (Syracuse, NY: Syracuse University Press, 1998).

Hardisty, James, "Reflections on Stare Decisis," *Indiana Law Journal*, 55, 1 (1979–80): 41–69.

Harisumarto, Sukino, "Indonesia Draft Sharia Law Triggers Controversy," *United Press International*, October 23, 2004.

Hassan, Ahmad, "Question and Answer," in Charles Kurzman, ed., *Modernist Islam, 1840–1940* (Oxford: Oxford University Press, 2002), 360–64.

Hassan, Hussein, "The Promissory Theory of Contracts in Islamic Law," *Yearbook of Islamic and Middle Eastern Law 2001–02*, VIII (The Hague: Kluwer Law International, 2003): 45–72.

Hatem, Mervat F., "The Professionalization of Health and the Control of Women's Bodies as Modern Governmentalities in Nineteenth Century Egypt," in M. Zilfi, ed., *Women in the Ottoman Empire* (Leiden: Brill, 1997), 66–79.

Haviland, William A., *Cultural Anthropology* (New York and Montreal: Holt, Rinehart and Winston, 1975).

Headrick, Daniel R., *The Tools of Empire: Technology and European Imperialism in the Nineteenth Century* (New York: Oxford University Press, 1981).

Hefner, Robert, "Varieties of Muslim Politics: Civil versus Statist Islam," in Fuad Jabali and Jamhari, eds., *Islam in Indonesia: Islamic Studies and Social Transformation* (Montreal and Jakarta: Indonesia–Canada Islamic Higher Education Project, 2002), 136–51.

Hejailan, Hussam Salah, "Saudi Arabia," *Yearbook of Islamic and Middle Eastern Law 2000–2001*, VII (The Hague: Kluwer Law International, 2002): 271–81.

Hélie-Lucas, Marie-Aimée, "The Preferential Symbol for Islamic Identity: Women in Muslim Personal Laws," in Valentine M. Moghadam, ed., *Identity Politics and Women: Cultural Reassertions and Feminisms in International Perspective* (Boulder, CO: Westview Press, 1994), 188–96.

Hertslet, Edward, *The Map of Europe by Treaty: Showing the Various Political and Territorial Changes Which Have Taken Place since the General Peace of 1814*, 4 vols. (London: Butterworths, 1875).

Heyd, Uriel, "The Ottoman Ulema and Westernization in the Time of Selim II and Mahmud II," in Albert Hourani, Philip S. Khoury and Mary C. Wilson, eds., *The Modern Middle East: A Reader* (London: I. B. Tauris, 1993), 29–59.

"Some Aspects of the Ottoman Fetva," *Bulletin of the School of Oriental and African Studies*, 32, 1 (1969): 35–56.

Studies in Old Ottoman Criminal Law, ed. V. L. Ménage (Oxford: Clarendon Press, 1973).

Hill, Enid, "Courts and Administration of Justice in the Modern Era," in N. Hanna, ed., *The State and its Servants: Administration in Egypt from Ottoman Times to the Present* (Cairo: The American University in Cairo Press, 1995), 98–116.

Hirsch, Susan F., "Kadhi's Courts as Complex Sites of Resistance: The State, Islam, and Gender in Postcolonial Kenya," in S. Hirsch and M. Lazarus-Black, eds., *Contested States: Law, Hegemony and Resistance* (New York: Routledge, 1994), 207–30.

Hodgson, Marshall G. S., *Rethinking World History: Essays on Europe, Islam, and World History* (Cambridge: Cambridge University Press, 1993).

The Venture of Islam, 3 vols. (Chicago: University of Chicago Press, 1974).

Hoisington, William, "Cities in Revolt: The Berber Dahir (1930) and France's Urban Strategy in Morocco," *Journal of Contemporary History*, 13, 3 (1978): 433–48.

Holleman, J. F., ed., *Van Vollenhoven on Indonesian Adat Law: Selections from Het Adatrecht van Nederlandsch-Indië* (The Hague: Martinus Nijhoff, 1981).

Hooker, M. B., *Adat Laws in Modern Malaya: Land Tenure, Traditional Government, and Religion* (Kuala Lumpur: Oxford University Press, 1972).

A Concise Legal History of South-East Asia (Oxford: Clarendon Press, 1978).

Islamic Law in South-East Asia (Singapore: Oxford University Press, 1984).

Legal Pluralism: An Introduction to Colonial and Neo-Colonial Laws (Oxford: Clarendon Press, 1975).

"The State and Shariʿa in Indonesia," in A. Salim and A. Azra, eds., *Shariʿa and Politics in Modern Indonesia* (Singapore: Institute of Southeast Asian Studies, 2003), 33–47.

Hoyland, R. G., *Seeing Islam as Others Saw It: A Survey and Evaluation of Christian, Jewish and Zoroastrian Writings on Early Islam* (Princeton, NJ: The Darwin Press, 1997).

Hoyle, Mark S. W., *The Mixed Courts of Egypt* (London: Graham & Trotman, 1991).

Hurvitz, N., "Biographies and Mild Asceticism: A Study of Islamic Moral Imagination," *Studia Islamica*, 85 (1997): 41–65.

"The *Mukhatṣar* of al-Khiraqī and its Place in the Formation of Hanbali Legal Doctrine," in R. Shaham, ed., *Law, Custom, and Statute in the Muslim World* (Leiden: Brill, 2007), 1–16.

Husseini, R., "UNIFEM Launches 'Progress of Arab Women 2004' Report," July 19, 2004. Available at www.jordanembassyus.org/07192004004.htm. Last accessed November 21, 2007.

Ibn Rushd, Muḥammad b. Aḥmad (al-Ḥafīd), *The Distinguished Jurist's Primer*, trans. I. Khan Nyazee, 2 vols. (Reading: Garnet Publishing, 1994–96).

Imber, Colin, *Studies in Ottoman History and Law* (Istanbul: Isis Press, 1996).

İnalcık, Halil, "Application of the Tanzimat and its Social Effects," *Archivum Ottomanicum*, 5 (1973): 97–127.

"Suleiman the Lawgiver and Ottoman Law," *Archivum Ottomanicum*, 1 (1969): 105–38.

Indonesian Civil Code, trans. Rany Mangunsong (Jakarta: PT Gramecdia, 2004).

Issawi, Charles, "De-industrialization and Re-industrialization in the Middle East since 1800," *International Journal of Middle East Studies*, 12, 4 (December 1980): 469–79.

Ivanova, Sveltana, "The Divorce between Zubaida Hatun and Esseid Osman Ağa: Women in the Eighteenth-Century Shariʿa Court of Rumelia," in Amira el-Azhary Sonbol, ed., *Women, the Family, and Divorce Laws in Islamic History* (Syracuse, NY: Syracuse University Press, 1996), 112–25.

Jacques, R. Kevin, *Authority, Conflict, and the Transmission of Diversity in Medieval Islamic Law* (Leiden: Brill, 2006).

Jahanbakhsh, Forough, "Islam, Democracy and Religious Modernism in Iran (1953–1997): From Bazargan to Soroush" (PhD dissertation: McGill University, 1997).

Jennings, Ronald C., *Christians and Muslims in Ottoman Cyprus and the Mediterranean World, 1571–1640* (New York and London: New York University Press, 1993).

"Divorce in the Ottoman *Sharia* Court of Cyprus, 1580–1640," *Studia Islamica*, 78 (1993): 155–67.

"Kadi, Court and Legal Procedure in 17th C. Ottoman Kayseri: The Kadi and the Legal System," *Studia Islamica*, 48 (1978): 133–72.

"Limitations of the Judicial Powers of the Kadi in 17th C. Ottoman Kayseri," *Studia Islamica*, 50 (1979): 151–84.

Studies on Ottoman Social History in the Sixteenth and Seventeenth Centuries: Women, Zimmis and Sharia Courts in Kayseri, Cyprus, and Trabzon (Istanbul: Isis Press, 1999).

"Women in Early 17th Century Ottoman Judicial Records: The *Sharia* Court of Anatolian Kayseri," *Journal of the Economic and Social History of the Orient*, 18 (1975): 53–114.

Johansen, Baber, "Casuistry: Between Legal Concept and Social Praxis," *Islamic Law and Society*, 2, 2 (1995): 135–56.

The Islamic Law on Land Tax and Rent: The Peasants' Loss of Property Rights as Interpreted in the Hanafite Legal Literature of the Mamluk and Ottoman Periods (London and New York: Croom Helm, 1988).

"Legal Literature and the Problem of Change: The Case of the Land Rent," in Chibli Mallat, ed., *Islam and Public Law: Classical and Contemporary Studies* (London and Boston: Graham and Trotman, 1993), 29–47.

Johnston, David, "ʿAllāl al-Fāsī: Sharīʿa as Blueprint for Righteous Global Citizenship," in Abbas Amanat and Frank Griffel, eds., *Sharīʿa: Islamic Law in the Contemporary Context* (Stanford: Stanford University Press, 2007), 83–103.

Jones, William, *Al-Sirajiyah or the Mahomedan Law of Inheritance* (Calcutta: The Sanskrit Press, 1861).

Joseph, Suad, "The Kin Contract and Citizenship in the Middle East," in Marilyn Friedman, ed., *Women and Citizenship* (Oxford: Oxford University Press, 2005), 149–69.

"The Public/Private – The Imagined Boundary in the Imagined Nation/State/ Community: The Lebanese Case," *Feminist Review*, 57 (1997): 73–92.

Kamali, Hashim, *Principles of Islamic Jurisprudence* (Selangor: Pelanduk Publications, 1989).

Karpat, Kemal H., "The Land Regime, Social Structure, and Modernization in the Ottoman Empire," in William Polk and Richard Chambers, eds., *Beginnings of Modernization in the Middle East: The Nineteenth Century* (Chicago: University of Chicago Press, 1968), 69–90.

Katz, Marion H., *Body of Text: The Emergence of the Sunnī Law of Ritual Purity* (Albany: State University of New York Press, 2002).

Keddie, Nikki R., *Qajar Iran and the Rise of Reza Khan* (Costa Mesa, CA: Mazda, 1999).

Kelsay, John, *Arguing the Just War in Islam* (Cambridge, MA: Harvard University Press, 2007).

Kerr, Malcolm, *Islamic Reform: The Political and Legal Theories of Muḥammad ʿAbduh and Rashīd Riḍā* (Berkeley: University of California Press, 1966).

Khan, Hamid, *Islamic Law of Inheritance* (Karachi: Pakistan Law House, 1999).

Khomeini, Ruhollah, *Islam and Revolution: Writings and Declarations*, trans. Hamid Algar (Berkeley, CA: Mizan Press, 1981).

Khoury, Philip, *Urban Notables and Arab Nationalism* (Cambridge: Cambridge University Press, 1983).

Kimber, Richard, "The Qurʾanic Law of Inheritance," *Islamic Law and Society*, 5, 3 (1998): 291–325.

King, G. R. D., "Settlement in Western and Central Arabia and the Gulf in the Sixth–Eighth Centuries A.D.," in G. R. D. King and A. Cameron, eds., *The Byzantine and Early Islamic Near East*, 3 vols. (Princeton, NJ: The Darwin Press, 1994), II, 181–212.

Knost, Stefan, "The *Waqf* in Court: Lawsuits over Religious Endowments in Ottoman Aleppo," in M. Masud *et al.*, eds., *Dispensing Justice in Islam: Qadis and their Judgments* (Leiden: Brill, 2006), 427–50.

Kolff, D. H. A., "The Indian and the British Law Machines: Some Remarks on Law and Society in British India," in W. J. Mommsen and J. A. De Moor, eds., *European Expansion and Law: The Encounter of European and Indigenous Law in 19th- and 20th-Century Africa and Asia* (Oxford: Berg, 1992), 201–35.

Kosheri, Rashed, *et al.*, "Egypt," *Yearbook of Islamic and Middle Eastern Law 2004–05*, XI (Leiden: Brill, 2007): 241–47.

Kozlowski, Gregory C., "Imperial Authority, Benefactions and Endowments (Awqaf) in Mughal India," *Journal of the Economic and Social History of the Orient*, 38, 3 (1995): 355–70.

Kugle, Scott A., "Framed, Blamed and Renamed: The Recasting of Islamic Jurisprudence in Colonial South Asia," *Modern Asian Studies*, 35, 2 (2001): 257–313.

Kuhn, Thomas S., *The Structure of Scientific Revolutions* (Chicago: University of Chicago Press, 1970).

Kuran, Timur, "Islamic Influences on the Ottoman Guilds," in Kemal Çiçek, ed., *The Great Ottoman-Turkish Civilization* (Ankara: Yeni Türkiye, 2000), II, 43–59.

Kushner, David, "The Place of the Ulema in the Ottoman Empire during the Age of Reform (1839–1918)," *Turcica*, 19 (1987): 51–74.

Lal, Vinay, "Subaltern Studies and its Critics: Debates over Indian History," *History and Theory*, 40, 1 (2001): 135–48.

Landau, Rom, *Moroccan Drama, 1900–1955* (San Francisco: American Academy of Asian Studies, 1956).

Lapidus, Ira M., "The Arab Conquests and the Formation of Islamic Society," in G. H. A. Juynboll, ed., *Studies on the First Century of Islamic Society* (Carbondale: Southern Illinois University Press, 1982), 49–72.

A History of Islamic Societies (Cambridge: Cambridge University Press, 1988).

Lassman, Peter, "The Rule of Man over Man: Power, Politics, and Legitimation," in Stephen Turner, ed., *The Cambridge Companion to Weber* (New York: Cambridge University Press, 2000), 83–98.

Lau, Martin, "Pakistan," *Yearbook of Islamic and Middle Eastern Law 2001–02*, VIII (The Hague: Kluwer Law International, 2003): 312–28.

"Pakistan," *Yearbook of Islamic and Middle Eastern Law 2002–03*, vol. IX (Leiden: Brill, 2004): 372–78.

Leaman, Oliver, *An Introduction to Medieval Islamic Philosophy* (Cambridge: Cambridge University Press, 1985).

Lecker, Michael, "On the Markets of Medina (Yathrib) in Pre-Islamic and Early Islamic Times," in M. Lecker, *Jews and Arabs in Pre- and Early Islamic Arabia* (Aldershot: Variorum, 1998), 133–46.

Leiser, Gary, "Notes on the Madrasa in Medieval Islamic Society," *Muslim World*, 76, 1 (1986): 16–23.

Leonard, Jerry, "Foucault and (the Ideology of) Genealogical Legal Theory," in J. Leonard, ed., *Legal Studies as Cultural Studies* (Albany: State University of New York Press, 1995), 133–51.

Lev, Daniel S., "Colonial Law and the Genesis of the Indonesian State," *Indonesia*, 40 (October 1985): 57–74.

Islamic Courts in Indonesia: A Study in the Political Bases of Legal Institutions (Berkeley: University of California Press, 1972).

"Judicial Unification in Post-Colonial Indonesia," *Indonesia*, 16 (October 1973): 1–37.

Levenson, J., *European Expansion and the Counter-Example of Asia, 1300–1600* (Englewood Cliffs, NJ: Prentice Hall, 1967).

Levi, Giovanni, "On Microhistory," in Peter Burke, ed., *New Perspectives on Historical Writing* (Cambridge: Polity Press, 2001), 97–119.

Liebesny, H., "The Development of Western Judicial Privileges," in M. Khadduri and H. J. Liebesny, eds., *Law in the Middle East* (Washington, DC: Middle East Institute, 1955), 312–27.

Law of the Near and Middle East (Albany, NY: SUNY Press, 1975).

Litvak, Meir, *Shiʿi Scholars of Nineteenth-Century Iraq: The Ulama of Najaf and Karbala* (New York: Cambridge University Press, 1998).

Lombardi, Clark B., "Islamic Law as a Source of Constitutional Law in Egypt: The Constitutionalization of the Sharia in a Modern Arab State," *Columbia Journal of Transnational Law*, 37, 1 (1998): 81–123.

State Law as Islamic Law: The Incorporation of the Sharīʿa into Egyptian Constitutional Law (Leiden: Brill, 2006).

Lowry, Joseph, "Does Shāfiʿī have a Theory of Four Sources of Law?" in Bernard Weiss, ed., *Studies in Islamic Legal Theory* (Leiden: Brill, 2002), 23–50.

"Legal-Theoretical Content of the *Risāla* of Muḥammad b. Idrīs al-Shāfiʿī" (PhD dissertation, University of Pennsylvania, 1999).

Lukito, Ratno, "Law and Politics in Post-Independence Indonesia: A Case Study of Religious and Adat Courts," in A. Salim and A. Azra, eds., *Sharīʿa and Politics in Modern Indonesia* (Singapore: Institute of Southeast Asian Studies, 2003), 17–32.

Lutfi, Huda, "A Study of Six Fourteenth Century Iqrārs from al-Quds Relating to Muslim Women," *Journal of the Economic and Social History of the Orient*, 26 (1983): 246–94.

Macaulay, Thomas Babington, "Minute on Indian Education," in John Clive and Thomas Pinney, eds., *Selected Writings* (Chicago: University of Chicago Press, 1972), 237–51.

Macnaghten, W. H., *Principles and Precedents of Moohumudan Law* (Madras: Higginbotham, 1890).

Maddy-Weitzman, Bruce, "Women, Islam, and the Moroccan State: The Struggle over the Personal Status Law," *Middle East Journal*, 59, 3 (2005): 393–410.

Madelung, Wilferd, "The Early Murjiʾa in Khurāsān and Transoxania and the Spread of Ḥanafism," *Der Islam*, 59, 1 (1982): 32–39.

Maghen, Ze'ev, *Virtues of the Flesh: Passion and Purity in Early Islamic Jurisprudence* (Leiden: Brill, 2005).

Mahmood, Saba, *Politics of Piety: Islamic Revival and the Feminist Subject* (Princeton, NJ: Princeton University Press, 2005).

Makdisi, George, "Ashʿarī and the Ashʿarites in Islamic Religious History," *Studia Islamica*, 17 (1962): 37–80.

Censure of Speculative Theology: An Edition and Translation of Ibn Qudāma's Taḥrīm an-Naẓar fī Kutub ahl al-Kalām, with Introduction and Notes: A Contribution to the Study of Islamic Religious History (London: Luzac, 1962).

"Ibn Taymīya's Autograph Manuscript on *Istiḥsān*: Materials for the Study of Islamic Legal Thought," in G. Makdisi, ed., *Arabic and Islamic Studies in Honor of A. R. Gibb* (Cambridge, MA: Harvard University Press, 1965), 446–79.

The Rise of the Colleges: Institutions of Learning in Islam and the West (Edinburgh: Edinburgh University Press, 1981).

"The Significance of the Schools of Law in Islamic Religious History," *International Journal of Middle East Studies*, 10 (1979): 1–8.

Makdisi, John, "Legal Logic and Equity in Islamic law," *American Journal of Comparative Law*, 33, 1 (1985): 63–92.

Mandaville, Jon, "The Muslim Judiciary of Damascus in the Late Mamluk Period" (PhD dissertation, Princeton University, 1969).

Mann, Michael, *States, War and Capitalism* (Oxford: Basil Blackwell, 1988).

Marcus, Abraham, "Men, Women and Property: Dealers in Real Estate in Eighteenth-Century Aleppo," *Journal of the Economic and Social History of the Orient*, 26 (1983): 137–63.

The Middle East on the Eve of Modernity: Aleppo in the Eighteenth Century (New York: Columbia University Press, 1989).

Mardin, Ebül'ula, "Development of the Sharīʿa under the Ottoman Empire," in M. Khadduri and H. J. Liebesny, eds., *Law in the Middle East* (Washington, DC: Middle East Institute, 1955), 279–91.

Mardin, Serif, "The Just and the Unjust," *Daedalus*, 120, 3 (1991): 113–29.

Marmura, Michael, "Some Aspects of Avicenna's Theory of God's Knowledge of Particulars," *Journal of the American Oriental Society*, 82 (1962): 299–312.

Marsot, Afaf Lutfi Al-Sayyid, *A Short History of Modern Egypt* (Cambridge: Cambridge University Press, 1985).

Massad, Joseph, *Colonial Effects: The Making of National Identity in Jordan* (New York: Columbia University Press, 2001).

Massignon, Louis, "Les résultats sociaux de notre politique indigène en Algérie," in *Opera Minora*, ed. Y. Moubarac, III (Liban: Dar al-Maaref, 1963), 559–68.

Masud, Muhammad Khalid, Brinkley Messick and David S. Powers, *Islamic Legal Interpretation: Muftis and Their Fatwas* (Cambridge, MA: Harvard University Press, 1996).

McGowan, B., "The Age of the Ayans, 1699–1812," in Halil İnalcık and Donald Quataert, eds., *An Economic and Social History of the Ottoman Empire 1300–1914* (Cambridge: Cambridge University Press, 1994), 637–758.

Melchert, Christopher, *The Formation of the Sunni Schools of Law* (Leiden: E. J. Brill, 1997).

Menski, Werner, *Hindu Law: Beyond Tradition and Modernity* (Oxford: Oxford University Press, 2003).

Mercier, Ernest, *Le habous ou ouakof* (Alger: A. Jourdan, 1895).

Meriwether, Margaret L., "The Rights of Children and the Responsibilities of Women: Women as *Wasi*s in Ottoman Aleppo, 1770–1840," in A. Sonbol, ed., *Women, the Family and Divorce Laws in Islamic History* (Syracuse, NY: Syracuse University Press, 1996), 219–35.

"Women and Waqf Revisited: The Case of Aleppo, 1770–1840," in Madeline C. Zilfi, ed., *Women in the Ottoman Empire: Middle Eastern Women* (Leiden: E. J. Brill, 1997), 128–52.

Merry, Sally Engle, "Legal Pluralism," *Law and Society Review*, 22, 5 (1988): 869–96.

Messick, Brinkley, *The Calligraphic State: Textual Domination and History in a Muslim Society* (Berkeley: University of California Press, 1993).

"Commercial Litigation in a Sharīʿa Court," in M. Masud *et al.*, eds., *Dispensing Justice in Islam: Qadis and their Judgments* (Leiden: Brill, 2006), 195–218.

"Indexing the Self: Intent and Expression in Islamic Legal Acts," *Islamic Law and Society*, 8, 2 (2001): 151–78.

Miller, Larry Benjamin, "Islamic Disputation Theory: A Study of the Development of Dialectic in Islam from the Tenth through Fourteenth Centuries" (PhD dissertation, Princeton University, 1984).

Miller, William Ian, *Eye for an Eye* (Cambridge: Cambridge University Press, 2006).

Minattur, J., "The Nature of Malay Customary Law," *Malaya Law Review*, 6, 2 (1964): 327–52.

Mir-Hosseini, Ziba, "The Construction of Gender in Islamic Legal Thought and Strategies for Reform," *Hawwa*, 1, 1 (2003): 1–28.

Marriage on Trial: A Study of Islamic Family law: Iran and Morocco Compared (London and New York: I. B. Tauris, 1993).

Miṣrī, *The Reliance of the Traveller, see under* Miṣrī, *above.*

Mitchell, Ruth, "Family Law in Algeria before and after the 1404/1984 Family Code," in R. Gleave and E. Kermeli, eds., *Islamic Law: Theory and Practice* (London: I. B. Taurus, 1997), 194–204.

Mitchell, Timothy, *Colonising Egypt* (Cambridge: Cambridge University Press, 1988).

"Limits of the State: Beyond Statist Approaches and their Critics," *American Political Science Review*, 85, 1 (1991): 77–96.

Rule of Experts: Egypt, Techno-Politics, Modernity (Berkeley: University of California Press, 2002).

Modarressi, Hossein, "Rationalism and Traditionalism in Shi'i Jurisprudence: A Preliminary Survey," *Studia Islamica*, 59 (1984): 141–58.

Mohanty, Chandra T., Ann Russo and Lourdes Torres, *Third World Women and the Politics of Feminism* (Bloomington: Indiana University Press, 1991).

Moors, Annelies, "Debating Islamic Family Law: Legal Texts and Social Practices," in M. L. Meriwether and Judith E. Tucker, eds., *Social History of Women and Gender in the Modern Middle East* (Boulder, CO: Westview Press, 1999), 141–75.

"Gender Relations and Inheritance: Person, Power and Property in Palestine," in Deniz Kandiyoti, ed., *Gendering the Middle East* (Syracuse, NY: Syracuse University Press, 1996), 69–84.

Mottahedeh, Roy, *Loyalty and Leadership in an Early Islamic Society* (Princeton, NJ: Princeton University Press, 1980).

Motzki, Harald, *The Origins of Islamic Jurisprudence: Meccan Fiqh before the Classical Schools*, trans. Marion H. Katz (Leiden: Brill, 2002).

"The Role of Non-Arab Converts in the Development of Early Islamic Law," *Islamic Law and Society*, 6, 3 (1999): 293–317.

Mundy, Martha, "Ownership or Office: A Debate in Islamic Hanafite Jurisprudence over the Nature of the Military 'Fief,' from the Mamluks to the Ottomans," in Alain Pottage and Martha Mundy, eds., *Law, Anthropology, and the Constitution of the Social: Making Persons and Things* (Cambridge: Cambridge University Press, 2004), 142–65.

el-Nahal, Galal H., *The Judicial Administration of Ottoman Egypt in the Seventeenth Century* (Chicago and Minneapolis: Bibliotheca Islamica, 1979).

Narayan, Uma, "The Project of Feminist Epistemology: Perspectives from a Nonwestern Feminist," in Sandra Harding, ed., *The Feminist Standpoint Theory Reader: Intellectual and Political Controversies* (New York: Routledge, 2004), 213–24.

Naveh, Immanuel, "The Tort of Injury and Dissolution of Marriage at the Wife's Initiative in Egyptian *Maḥkamat al-Naqḍ* Rulings," *Islamic Law and Society*, 9, 1 (2002): 16–41.

Needham, Joseph, *Science and Civilization in China*, 7 vols. (Cambridge: Cambridge University Press, 1954–).

Newman, A., "The Nature of the Akhbārī/Uṣūlī Dispute in Late Ṣafawid Iran. Part 1: ʿAbdallāh al-Samāhijī's 'Munyat al-Mumārisīn'," *Bulletin of the School of Oriental and African Studies*, 55, 1 (1992): 24–38.

"The Nature of the Akhbārī/Uṣūlī Dispute in Late Ṣafawid Iran, Part 2: The Conflict Reassessed," *Bulletin of the School of Oriental and African Studies*, 55, 2 (1992): 250–61.

Nietzsche, Friedrich, *Human, All Too Human*, trans. R. J. Hollingdale (Cambridge: Cambridge University Press, 1996).

"On Truth and Lies in a Nonmoral Sense," in Daniel Breazeale, ed. and trans., *Philosophy and Truth: Selections from Nietzsche's Notebooks of the Early 1870's* (Atlantic Highlands, NJ: Humanities Press, 1979), 80–86.

Noer, Deliar, *The Modernist Muslim Movement in Indonesia, 1900–1942* (Singapore and Kuala Lumpur: Oxford University Press, 1973).

Omar, Farouk, "Guilds in the Islamic City during the Abbasid Period (749–1258 A.D.)," in *The Proceedings of International Conference on Urbanism in Islam (ICUIT)*, vol. II (Tokyo: The Middle East Cultural Center, 1989), 198–217.

Onar, S. S., "The Majalla," in M. Khadduri and H. J. Liebesny, eds., *Law in the Middle East* (Washington, DC: Middle East Institute, 1955), 292–308.

Opwis, Felicitas, "Changes in Modern Islamic Legal Theory: Reform or Reformation?" in M. Browers and Charles Kurzman, eds., *An Islamic Reformation*? (Lanham, MD: Lexington Books, 2004), 28–53.

"*Maṣlaḥa* in Contemporary Islamic Legal Theory," *Islamic Law and Society*, 12, 2 (2005): 182–223.

Ortaylı, İlber, *Studies on Ottoman Transformation* (Istanbul: Isis Press, 1994).

Oxford Encyclopedia of the Modern Islamic World, vol. III (New York: Oxford University Press, 1995).

Öztürk, Nazif, "Batılılaşma Döneminde Vakıfların Çözülmesine Yol Açan Uygulamalar," *Vakıflar Dergisi*, 23 (1994): 297–309.

Türk Yenileşme Tarihi Çerçevesinde Vakif Müessesesi (Ankara: Türkiye Diyanet Vakfi, 1995).

Palme-Dutt, R. "The Exploitation of India: A Marxist View," in M. D. Lewis, ed., *The British in India: Imperialism or Trusteeship?* (Boston: D. C. Heath and Co., 1962), 41–52.

Parker, Geoffrey, *The Military Revolution: Military Innovation and the Rise of the West, 1500–1800* (Cambridge: Cambridge University Press, 1988).

Pearl, David and Werner Menski, *Muslim Family Law* (London: Sweet & Maxwell, 1998).

Pedersen, Johannes, *The Arabic Book*, trans. Geoffrey French (Princeton, NJ: Princeton University Press, 1984).

Peirce, Leslie, *Morality Tales: Law and Gender in the Ottoman Court of Aintab* (Berkeley: University of California Press, 2003).

"'She Is Trouble ... and I Will Divorce Her': Orality, Honor, and Misrepresentation in the Ottoman Court of ʿAintab," in Gavin Hambly, ed., *Women in the Medieval Islamic World: Power, Patronage, and Piety* (New York: St. Martin's Press, 1998), 269–300.

Peletz, Micheal G., *Islamic Modern: Religious Courts and Cultural Politics in Malaysia* (Princeton, NJ: Princeton University Press, 2002).

Peters, Rudolph, "Administrators and Magistrates: The Development of a Secular Judiciary in Egypt, 1842–1871," *Die Welt des Islams*, 39, 3 (1999): 378–97.

Crime and Punishment in Islamic Law: Theory and Practice from the Sixteenth to the Twenty-First Century, in Wael Hallaq, series ed., Themes in Islamic Law, no. 2 (Cambridge: Cambridge University Press, 2005).

Islam and Colonialism (The Hague: Mouton, 1979).

"Islamic and Secular Criminal Law in Nineteenth Century Egypt: The Role and Function of the Qadi," *Islamic Law and Society*, 4, 1 (1997): 70–90.

Petry, Carl F., "Class Solidarity versus Gender Gain: Women as Custodians of Property in Later Medieval Egypt," in N. Keddie and B. Baron, eds., *Women in Middle Eastern History: Shifting Boundaries in Sex and Gender* (New Haven, CT: Yale University Press, 1991), 122–42.

"Conjugal Rights versus Class Prerogatives: A Divorce Case in Mamlūk Cairo," in Gavin Humbly, ed., *Women in the Medieval Islamic World: Power, Patronage, and Piety* (New York: St. Martin's Press, 1998), 227–40.

Piotrovsky, Mikhail B., "Late Ancient and Early Medieval Yemen: Settlement, Traditions and Innovations," in G. R. D. King and Avril Cameron, eds., *The Byzantine and Early Islamic Near East*, 3 vols. (Princeton, NJ: The Darwin Press, 1994), II, 213–20.

Pollard, Lisa, "Learning Gendered Modernity: The Home, the Family, and the Schoolroom in the Construction of Egyptian National Identity (1885–1919)," in Amira Sonbol, ed., *Beyond the Exotic: Women's Histories in Islamic Societies* (Syracuse, NY: Syracuse University Press, 2005), 249–69.

Potts, D. T., *The Arabian Gulf in Antiquity*, 2 vols. (Oxford: Clarendon Press, 1990).

Powers, David S., "Four Cases Relating to Women and Divorce in al-Andalus and the Maghrib, 1100–1500," in M. Masud *et al.*, eds., *Dispensing Justice in Islam: Qadis and their Judgments* (Leiden: Brill, 2006), 383–409.

Law, Society, and Culture in the Maghrib, 1300–1500 (Cambridge: Cambridge University Press, 2002).

"Legal Consultation (futyā) in Medieval Spain and North Africa," in Chibli Mallat, ed., *Islam and Public Law: Classical and Contemporary Studies* (London and Boston: Graham & Trotman, 1993), 85–106.

"On Judicial Review in Islamic Law," *Law and Society Review*, 26 (1992): 315–41.

"Orientalism, Colonialism and Legal History: The Attack on Muslim Family Endowments in Algeria and India," *Comparative Studies in Society and History*, 31, 3 (July 1989): 535–71.

Studies in Qur'an and Hadith: The Formation of the Islamic Law of Inheritance (Berkeley: University of California Press, 1986).

Powers, Paul R., *Intent in Islamic Law: Motive and Meaning in Medieval Sunnī Fiqh* (Leiden: Brill, 2006).

al-Qattan, Najwa, "Dhimmis in the Muslim Court: Documenting Justice in Ottoman Damascus, 1775–1860" (PhD dissertation, Harvard University, 1996).

"*Dhimmīs* in the Muslim Court: Legal Autonomy and Religious Discrimination," *International Journal of Middle East Studies*, 31, 3 (1999): 429–44.

"Litigants and Neighbors: The Communal Topography of Ottoman Damascus," *Comparative Study in Society and History*, 44, 3 (2002): 511–33.

Quataert, Donald, "The Age of Reforms, 1812–1914," in Halil İnalcık and Donald Quataert, eds., *An Economic and Social History of the Ottoman Empire 1300–1914* (Cambridge: Cambridge University Press, 1994), 759–943.

Ottoman Manufacturing in the Age of the Industrial Revolution (Cambridge: Cambridge University Press, 1993).

Rafeq, Abdul-Karim, "The Application of Islamic Law in the Ottoman Courts in Damascus: The Case of the Rental of *Waqf* Land," M. Masud *et al.*, eds., *Dispensing Justice in Islam: Qadis and their Judgments* (Leiden: Brill, 2006), 411–25.

Rahman, Fazlur, "Interpreting the Qur'an," *Inquiry*, 3 (May 1986): 45–49.

"Towards Reformulating the Methodology of Islamic Law: Sheikh Yamani on 'Public Interest' in Islamic Law," *New York University Journal of International Law and Politics*, 12 (1979): 219–24.

Rapoport, Yossef, *Marriage, Money and Divorce in Medieval Islamic Society* (Cambridge: Cambridge University Press, 2005).

Raymond, A., "The Role of the Communities (Tawa'if) in the Administration of Cairo in the Ottoman Period," in Nelly Hanna, ed., *The State and its Servants: Administration of Egypt from Ottoman Times to the Present* (Cairo: The American University in Cairo Press, 1995), 32–43.

Rayner, S. E., *The Theory of Contracts in Islamic Law* (London: Graham & Trotman, 1991).

Repp, Richard Cooper, *The Müfti of Istanbul: A Study on the Development of Ottoman Learned Hierarchy* (London and Atlantic Highlands, NJ: Ithaca Press, 1986).

Rezaei, Hassan, "The Iranian Criminal Justice under the Islamization Project," *European Journal of Crime*, 10, 1 (January 2002): 54–69.

Rheinstein, Max, ed., *see* Weber.

Ringer, Monica, "Negotiating Modernity: Ulama and the Discourse of Modernity in Nineteenth-Century Iran," in R. Jahanbegloo, ed., *Iran between Tradition and Modernity* (Lanham, MD: Lexington Books, 2004), 39–50.

Roberts, Richard and Kristin Mann, "Law in Colonial Africa," in Kristin Mann and Richard Roberts, eds., *Law in Colonial Africa* (Portsmouth, NH: Heinemann, 1991), 3–58.

Rosen, Lawrence, *The Anthropology of Justice: Law as Culture in Islamic Society* (Cambridge: Cambridge University Press, 1989).

"Justice in Islamic Culture and Law," in R. S. Khare, ed., *Perspectives on Islamic Law, Justice, and Society* (Lanham, MD: Rowman & Littlefield, 1999), 33–52.

The Justice of Islam: Comparative Perspectives on Islamic Law and Society (Oxford: Oxford University Press, 2000).

Rosenthal, Franz, *see* Ibn Khaldūn.

Rubin, Avi, "Ottoman Modernity: The Nizamiye Courts in the Late Nineteenth Century" (PhD dissertation, Harvard University, 2006).

Rubin, Uri, "Ḥanīfiyya and Kaʿba: An Inquiry into the Arabian Pre-Islamic Background of Dīn Ibrāhīm," *Jerusalem Studies in Arabic and Islam*, 13 (1990): 85–112.

Sabahi, Hatim M., *Darb Zubayda: The Pilgrim Road from Kufa to Mecca* (Riyadh: Riyadh University Libraries, 1980).
Sadka, Emily, *The Protected Malay States, 1875–1895* (Kuala Lumpur: University of Malaya Press, 1968).
Sagiv, David, *Fundamentalism and Intellectuals in Egypt, 1973–1993* (London: Frank Cass, 1995).
Said, Edward W., *Culture and Imperialism* (New York: Knopf, 1993).
Orientalism (New York: Vintage Books, 1979).
Saiyid, Dushka, *Muslim Women of the British Punjab: From Seclusion to Politics* (New York: St. Martin's Press, 1998).
Santillana, David, *Istituzioni di diritto musulmano Malichita*, 2 vols. (Rome: Pubblicazioni dell'Istituto per l'Oriente, 1925).
Sautayra, Edouard and Eugene Cherbonneau, *Droit musulman du statut personnel et des successions*, 2 vols. (Paris: Maisonneuve et Cie, 1873–74).
Schacht, Joseph, "From Babylonian to Islamic Law," *Yearbook of Islamic and Middle Eastern Law 1994*, I (London: Kluwer Law International, 1995): 29–33.
An Introduction to Islamic Law (Oxford: Clarendon Press, 1964).
The Origins of Muhammadan Jurisprudence (Oxford: Clarendon Press, 1950).
Schirazi, Asghar, *The Constitution of Iran: Politics and the State in the Islamic Republic*, trans. John O'Kane (London and New York: I. B. Tauris, 1997).
Seng, Yvonne J., "Invisible Women: Residents of Early Sixteenth-Century Istanbul," in Gavin Hambly, ed., *Women in the Medieval Islamic World: Power, Patronage, and Piety* (New York: St. Martin's Press, 1998), 241–68.
"Standing at the Gates of Justice: Women in the Law Courts of Early Sixteenth-Century Isküdar, Istanbul," in Susan Hirsch and M. Lazarus-Black, eds., *Contested States: Law, Hegemony and Resistance* (New York: Routledge, 1994), 184–206.
Serjeant, R. B., "The Constitution of Medina," *Islamic Quarterly*, 8 (1964): 3–16.
Serrano, Delfina, "Twelve Court Cases on the Application of Penal Law under the Almoravids," in M. Masud *et al.*, eds., *Dispensing Justice in Islam: Qadis and their Judgments* (Leiden: Brill, 2006), 473–92.
Shafir, Gershon, *Land, Labor and the Origins of the Israeli–Palestinian Conflict 1882–1914* (Cambridge: Cambridge University Press, 1989).
Shaham, Ron, "Women as Expert Witnesses in Pre-Modern Islamic Courts," in R. Shaham, ed., *Law, Custom, and Statute in the Muslim World* (Leiden: Brill, 2007), 41–65.
Shaltūt, Maḥmūd, "The Koran and Fighting," trans. in R. Peters, *Jihad in Classical and Modern Islam: A Reader* (Princeton, NJ: Markus Wiener, 1996), 60–101.
Sharabi, Hisham, *Neopatriarchy: A Theory of Distorted Change in Arab Society* (New York: Oxford University Press, 1988).
Shatzmiller, Maya, *The Berbers and the Islamic State* (Princeton, NJ: Markus Wiener, 2000).
Sherif, Adel O., "The Rule of Law in Egypt from a Judicial Perspective: A Digest of the Landmark Decisions of the Supreme Constitutional Court of Egypt," in E. Cotran and M. Yamani, eds., *The Rule of Law in the Middle East and the*

Islamic World: Human Rights and the Judicial Process (London: I. B. Tauris, 2000), 1–34.

Shiraishi, Takashi, *An Age in Motion: Popular Radicalism in Java, 1912–1926* (Ithaca, NY: Cornell University Press, 1990).

Siddiqi, Muhammad Zameeruddin, "The Institution of the Qazi under the Mughals," *Medieval India*, 1 (1969): 240–59.

"The Muhtasib under Aurangzeb," *Medieval India Quarterly*, 5 (1963): 113–19.

Singha, Radhika, *A Despotism of Law: Crime and Justice in Early Colonial India* (Delhi: Oxford University Press, 1998).

Slemon, Stephen, "The Scramble for Post-colonialism," in Bill Ashcroft *et al.*, eds., *The Post-colonial Studies Reader* (London: Routledge, 1995), 45–52.

Snouck Hurgronje, C., *The Achehnese*, trans. A. W. S. O'Sullivan, 2 vols. (Leiden: E. J. Brill, 1906).

Sohrabi, Nader, "Revolution and State Culture: The Circle of Justice and Constitutionalism in 1906 Iran," in George Steinmetz, ed., *State/Culture: State Formation after the Cultural Turn* (Ithaca, NY: Cornell University Press, 1999), 253–88.

Somel, Selcuk Akin, *The Modernization of Public Education in the Ottoman Empire, 1839–1908: Islamization, Autocracy, and Discipline* (Leiden: Brill, 2001).

Sonbol, Amira El-Azhary, "*Ṭāʿa* and Modern Legal Reform: A Reading," *Islam and Christian–Muslim Relations*, 9, 3 (1998): 285–94.

Sonn, Tamara. "Fazlur Rahman," in John L. Esposito, ed., *The Oxford Encyclopedia of the Modern Islamic World*, 4 vols. (New York: Oxford University Press, 1995), III, 408.

Soroush, Abdolkarim, "The Ideal Islamic State: An Unattainable Quest," 2. Available at www.drsoroush.com/English/News_Archive/E-NWS-20060108-TheIdealIslamicState-AnUnattainableQuest.html. Last accessed May 9, 2007.

al-Qabḍ wal-Basṭ, see section 1 of this Bibliography, above.

Reason, Freedom and Democracy in Islam (Oxford: Oxford University Press, 2000).

Spectorsky, Susan, "*Sunnah* in the Responses of Isḥāq B. Rāhawayh," in Bernard Weiss, ed., *Studies in Islamic Legal Theory* (Leiden: Brill, 2002), 51–74.

Spivak, Gayatri Chakravorty, "Can the Subaltern Speak?" in P. Williams and L. Chrisman, eds., *Colonial Discourse and Post-Colonial Theory: A Reader* (New York: Harvester Wheatsheaf, 1993), 66–111.

Starr, June, "A Pre-Law Stage in Rural Turkish Disputes Negotiations," in P. H. Gulliver, ed., *Cross-Examinations: Essays in Memory of Max Gluckman* (Leiden: E. J. Brill, 1978), 110–32.

"When Empires Meet: European Trade and Ottoman Law," in Susan Hirsch and M. Lazarus-Black, eds., *Contested States: Law, Hegemony and Resistance* (New York: Routledge, 1994), 231–52.

Strawson, John, "Islamic Law and English Texts," *Law and Critique*, 6, 1 (1995): 21–38.

Stol, M., "Women in Mesopotamia," *Journal of the Economic and Social History of the Orient*, 38, 2 (1995): 123–44.

Stone, Ferdinand F., "A Primer on Codification," *Tulane Law Review*, 29 (1954–55): 303–10.

Tallett, Frank, *War and Society in Early Modern Europe, 1495–1715* (London and New York: Routledge, 1992).
Thomas, Nicholas, *Colonialism's Culture: Anthropology, Travel and Government* (Princeton, NJ: Princeton University Press, 1994).
Thung, Michael, "Written Obligations from the 2nd/8th to the 4th Century," *Islamic Law and Society*, 3, 1 (1996): 1–12.
Tibawi, A. L., "Origin and Character of al-Madrasah," *Bulletin of the School of Oriental and African Studies*, 25 (1962): 225–38.
Tilly, Charles, *Coercion, Capital and European States: AD 990–1990* (Cambridge, MA: Blackwell, 1990).
Toulmin, Stephen, *Cosmopolis: The Hidden Agenda of Modernity* (Chicago: University of Chicago Press, 1992).
Toynbee, Arnold J., *A Study of History*, abridgement by D. C. Somervell, 2 vols. (New York: Oxford University Press, 1947).
Tsafrir, Nurit, *The History of an Islamic School of Law: The Early Spread of Hanafism* (Cambridge, MA: Islamic Legal Studies Program, 2004).
Tucker, Judith E., *In the House of the Law: Gender and Islamic Law in Ottoman Syria and Palestine* (Berkeley: University of California Press, 1998).
"Marriage and Family in Nablus, 1720–1856: Toward a History of Arab Marriage," *Journal of Family History*, 13, 1 (1988): 165–79.
"Revisiting Reform: Women and the Ottoman Law of Family Rights, 1917," *Arab Studies Journal*, 4, 2 (1996): 4–17.
Women in Nineteenth Century Egypt (Cambridge: Cambridge University Press, 1985).
Turgay, Üner A., "The British–German Trade Rivalry in the Ottoman Empire, 1880–1914: Discord in Imperialism," in J. L. Warner, ed., *Cultural Horizons* (Syracuse, NY: Syracuse University Press, 2001), 168–87.
Tyan, Émile, "Le notariat et le régime de la preuve par écrit dans la pratique du droit musulman," *Annales de l'École Française de Droit de Beyrouth*, 2 (1945): 1–99.
Udovitch, Abraham L., *Partnership and Profit in Medieval Islam* (Princeton, NJ: Princeton University Press, 1970).
Van Bruinessen Martin, "Tarekat and Tarekat Teachers in Madurese Society," in H. de Jonge *et al.*, eds., *Across Madura Strait* (Leiden: KITLV Press, 1995), 91–117.
van Creveld, Martin L., *The Rise and Decline of the State* (Cambridge: Cambridge University Press, 1999).
van den Boogert, Maurits H., *The Capitulations and the Ottoman Legal System* (Leiden: Brill, 2005).
van Leeuwen, Richard, *Waqfs and Urban Structures: The Case of Ottoman Damascus* (Leiden: Brill, 1999).
van Vollenhoven, Cornelius, *Het Adatrecht van Nederlansch-Indië*, 3 vols. (Leiden: E. J. Brill, 1918).
VerSteeg, Russ, *Early Mesopotamian Law* (Durham, NC: Carolina Academic Press, 2000).
Vikør, Knut S., *Between God and the Sultan: A History of Islamic Law* (Oxford: Oxford University Press, 2005).

Vogel, Frank, *Islamic Law and Legal System: Studies of Saudi Arabia* (Leiden: Brill, 2000).

Wakin, Jeanette A., *The Function of Documents in Islamic Law: The Chapters on Sales from Ṭaḥāwī's Kitāb al-Shurūṭ al-Kabīr* (Albany: State University of New York Press, 1972).

"Interpretation of the Divine Command in the Jurisprudence of Muwaffaq al-Dīn Ibn Qudāmah," in N. Heer, ed., *Islamic Law and Jurisprudence: Studies in Honor of Farhat J. Ziadeh* (Seattle: University of Washington Press, 1990), 33–53.

Wallerstein, Immanuel Maurice, *Uncertainties of Knowledge* (Philadelphia: Temple University Press, 2004).

Weber, Max, *Max Weber on Law in Economy and Society*, ed. Max Rheinstein (Cambridge, MA: Harvard University Press, 1966).

From Max Weber, see Gerth, H. H. and C. W. Mills.

Weiss, Bernard G., "Knowledge of the Past: The Theory of *Tawātur* according to Ghazālī," *Studia Islamica*, 61 (1985): 81–105.

"Language and Tradition in Medieval Islam: The Question of al-Ṭarīq Ilā Maʿrifat al-Lugha," *Der Islam: Zeitschrift fur Geschichte und Kultur des Islamischen Orients*, 61, 1 (1984): 92–99.

The Search for God's Law: Islamic Jurisprudence in the Writings of Sayf al-Din al-Amidi (Salt Lake City: University of Utah Press, 1992).

The Spirit of Islamic Law (Athens: University of Georgia Press, 1998).

ed., *Studies in Islamic Legal Theory* (Leiden: Brill, 2002).

Welchman, Lynn, *Beyond the Code: Muslim Family Law and the Sharʿi Judiciary in the Palestinian West Bank* (The Hague: Kluwer Law International, 2000).

"Special Stipulations in the Contract of Marriage: Law and Practice in the Occupied West Bank," *Recht van de Islam*, 11 (1994): 55–77.

Wichard, Johannes Christian, *Zwischen Markt und Moschee* (Paderborn: F. Schöningh, 1995).

Wikan, Unni, *Behind the Veil in Arabia: Women in Oman* (Chicago: University of Chicago Press, 1991).

Würth, A., "A Sanaʿa Court: The Family and the Ability to Negotiate," *Islamic Law and Society*, 2, 3 (1995): 320–40.

Yamey, Basil S., "Accounting and the Rise of Capitalism: Further Notes on a Theme by Sombart," *Journal of Accounting Research*, 2, 2 (1964): 117–36.

Yanagihashi, Hiroyuki, *A History of the Early Islamic Law of Property* (Leiden: Brill, 2004).

Yassari, Nadjma, "Iranian Family Law in Theory and Practice," *Yearbook of Islamic and Middle Eastern Law 2002–3*, IX (Leiden: Brill, 2004): 43–64.

Yeğenoğlu, Meyda, *Colonial Fantasies: Towards a Feminist Reading of Orientalism* (Cambridge: Cambridge University Press, 1998).

Yilmaz, Ihsan, "Secular Law and the Emergence of Unofficial Turkish Law," *Middle East Journal*, 56, 1 (2002): 113–31.

Young, Robert J. C., "Foucault on Race and Colonialism," *New Formations*, 25 (Summer 1995): 57–65.

White Mythologies (London and New York: Routledge, 1990).

Young, Walter, "Defining Casuistry in Islamic Law" (Unpublished paper; presented at the 41st Annual Meeting of the Middle East Studies Association, November 2007, Montreal), 107 pages.

Zaman, Muhammad Qasim, *Religion and Politics under the Early ʿAbbāsids* (Leiden: Brill, 1997).

The Ulama in Contemporary Islam: Custodians of Change (Princeton, NJ: Princeton University Press, 2002).

Zantout, Mida R., "*Khulʿ* Between Past and Present" (MA thesis, McGill University, 2006).

Zarinebaf-Shahr, Fariba, "Women, Law, and Imperial Justice in Ottoman Istanbul in the Late Seventeenth Century," in Amira el-Azhary Sonbol, ed., *Women, the Family, and Divorce Laws in Islamic History* (Syracuse, NY: Syracuse University Press, 1996), 81–96.

Zebiri, Kate, *Maḥmūd Shaltūt and Islamic Modernism* (New York: Oxford University Press, 1993).

Zeghal, Malika, "Religion and Politics in Egypt: The Ulema of al-Azhar, Radical Islam, and the State (1952–94)," *International Journal of Middle East Studies*, 31, 3 (1999): 371–99.

Ziadeh, Farhat Jacob, "Equality (Kafāʾah) in the Muslim Law of Marriage," *American Journal of Comparative Law*, 6 (1957): 503–17.

Lawyers, the Rule of Law and Liberalism in Modern Egypt (Stanford, CA: Hoover Institute, 1968).

Zilfi, Madeline C., *The Politics of Piety: The Ottoman Ulema in the Postclassical Age (1600–1800)* (Minneapolis: Bibliotheca Islamica, 1988).

"We Don't Get Along: Women and Hul Divorce in the Eighteenth Century," in M. C. Zilfi, ed., *Women in the Ottoman Empire: Middle Eastern Modern Women in the Early Modern Era* (Leiden and New York: Brill, 1997), 264–96.

Zubaida, Sami, *Islam, the People and the State: Essays on Political Ideas and Movements in the Middle East* (London and New York: Routlege, 1989).

Law and Power in the Islamic World (London and New York: I. B. Tauris, 2003).

Index

a fortiori argument, 49, 50, 103, 105–06
a maiore ad minus, 50, 105
a minore ad maius, 50, 105
'Abbāsids, 131, 149, 198
'Abd al-Majīd, Sultan, 413
'Abduh, M., 395, 503–04, 508, 511, 515
ablution, 108, 120, 121, 551
abode of Islam, *see dār al-Islām*
abode of war, *see dār al-ḥarb*
Abraham, 31, 319
abrogation, *see naskh*
absentees, 53, 54
Abū Bakr, 35, 36, 38, 41, 43, 131
Abū Ḥanīfa, 63–67, 69, 179, 252 n. 68, 277, 291, 302, 305, 306, 320, 321, 330, 342 n. 3, 348
Abū Ja'far al-Manṣūr, 134
Abū Yūsuf, 64–65, 132, 179, 277, 302, 305, 321
acceptance, in contracts, *see qabūl*
Aceh, 136, 497
acknowledgment, *see iqrār*
acquittance, *see ibrā'*
'āda, *see 'urf*, customary law and *adat*
adab al-qāḍī, 325, 342
'adāla, 137; *see also 'adl*
'adāletnāme, 215 n. 69
adat, 384–86, 387, 389, 390, 391, 392–94, 443, 493, 495, 496, 516, 517, 519, 544; *perbilangan*, 385, 386; *perpateh*, 384–86, 392–94; *temenggong*, 384–86; *see also* customary law
adatrecht, 393, 394, 395, 516, 519
'adl, 95, 144, 170, 267, 277, 313, 349; *see also 'adāla*
Afghanistan, 401
Africa, 358, 387, 396, 451, 453
agency, *see wakāla* and *wakīl*
agricultural leases, 245
Agung, Sultan, 389
āḥād, 94, 95, 97, 99, 100
ahl al-ḥadīth, 47, 55–60
ahl al-'ilm, 170, 177, 404, 493
ahl al-kitāb, 278, 328, 331, 332, 338; *see also dhimmī*; Christians; Jews
ahl al-ra'y, 57
ahliyya, 226; *ahliyyat al-adā'*, 227; *ahliyyat al-wujūb*, 227
Ahmad Hassan, 514
Ahmad Khan, *see* Sayyid Ahmad Khan
Ahmet Çevdet Pasha, *see* Çevdet Pasha
ajīr khāṣṣ, 257 n. 92, 257
ajīr mushtarak, 257 n. 92, 257
ajnabī, 287 n. 101, 287, 306
Akbar, Sultan, 152, 323, 371
akhbār, 118; *see also ḥadīth*
Akhbārist school, 116–24, 429
'alā al-fawr, 237, 307
'alāniya, *see jahr*
alcohol, 32, 36, 207, 281, 297, 298, 307 n. 60, 310, 312 n. 14, 315–16, 319, 350, 388, 524, 526, 527, 528
Aleppo, 175, 192, 193, 194, 195, 279 n. 57
Alexandria, 141, 422
Algeria, 21, 393, 432–38, 439, 452, 453, 456, 473
Algiers, 438
'Alī b. Abī Ṭālib, 43
Ali Pasha, 405, 411
alimony, *see nafaqa*
alms-tax, *see zakāt*
Alting, J. H., 394
amān, 332–33, 334
amāna, 251, 252, 255, 262, 264, 265, 266, 267, 302
Ameer Ali, 377
amicable settlement, *see* mediation
'āmil, in *muḍāraba*, 254–56
Amīr Kabīr, 430
Amman, 340
amr, 90–92
analogy, 49, 50, 101, 105; *see also qiyās*
Anatolia, 186, 191
'Anbarī, 132